# The Use of Psychological Testing for Treatment Planning and Outcomes Assessment

*Third Edition*

Volume 1   General Considerations

# The Use of Psychological Testing for Treatment Planning and Outcomes Assessment

*Third Edition*

## Volume 1   General Considerations

Edited by

## Mark E. Maruish
*Southcross Consulting*

**LEA**
**2004**

LAWRENCE ERLBAUM ASSOCIATES, PUBLISHERS
Mahwah, New Jersey                                      London

Senior Consulting Editor:          Susan Milmoe
Editorial Assistant:               Kristen Depken
Cover Design:                      Kathryn Houghtaling Lacey
Textbook Production Manager:       Paul Smolenski
Full-Service Compositor:           TechBooks
Text and Cover Printer:            Hamilton Printing Company

This book was typeset in 10/12 pt. Palatino, Italic, Bold, and Bold Italic.
The heads were typeset in Palatino and Berling, Bold, Italics, and Bold
Italics.

Lawrence Erlbaum Associates, Inc., Publishers
10 Industrial Avenue
Mahwah, New Jersey 07430
www.erlbaum.com

**Library of Congress Cataloging-in-Publication Data**

The use of psychological testing for treatment planning and outcomes
    assessment / edited by Mark E. Maruish.—3rd ed.
      p.   cm.
    Includes bibliographical references and index.
    Volume 1: ISBN 0-8058-4329-9 (casebound : alk. paper) – Volume 2: ISBN 0-8058-4330-2
    (casebound : alk. paper) – Volume 3: ISBN 0-8058-4331-0 (casebound : alk. paper)
    1. Psychological tests.   2. Mental illness—Diagnosis.   3. Mental
    illness—Treatment—Evaluation.   4. Psychiatric rating scales.
    5. Outcome assessment (Medical care)   I. Maruish, Mark E. (Mark Edward)

  RC473.P79U83   2004
  616.89′075–dc22                                              2003025432

Printed in the United States of America
10  9  8  7  6  5  4  3  2  1

*For my family*

# Contents

# *Preface*

Like other medical and behavioral health care services, the practice of test-based psychological assessment has not entered the era of managed care unscathed. Limitations placed on total moneys allotted for psychological services have had an impact on the practice of psychological testing. However, for those skilled in its use, psychological testing's ability to help quickly identify psychological problems, plan and monitor treatment, and document treatment effectiveness presents many potentially rewarding opportunities during a time when health care organizations must (a) provide problem-focused, time-limited treatment; (b) demonstrate the effectiveness of treatment to payers and patients; and (c) implement quality improvement initiatives.

With the opportunity at hand, it is now up to those with skill and training in psychological assessment to make the most of this opportunity to contribute to (and benefit from) efforts to control health care costs. However, this may not be as simple a task as it would appear. Many trained professionals are likely to have only limited knowledge of how to use test results for planning, monitoring, and assessing the outcomes of psychological interventions. Consequently, although the basic skills are there, many well-trained clinicians—and graduate students as well—need to develop or expand their testing knowledge and skills so as to be better able to apply them for such purposes. This need served as the impetus for the development of the first two editions of this book, and the development of this third edition of the work attests to its continued presence.

In developing the contents of this and the previous editions of this work, it was decided that the most informative and useful approach would be one in which aspects of broad topical areas are addressed separately. The first area has to do with general issues and recommendations to be considered in the use of psychological testing for treatment planning and outcomes assessment in today's behavioral health care environment. The second and third areas address issues related to the use of specific psychological tests and scales for these same purposes, one dealing with child and adolescent instruments, the other dealing with adult instruments. The fourth area concerns the future of psychological testing, including future developments in this area. For the current edition, issues related to future developments have been incorporated into the general considerations section. Because of increased content and a desire to better meet the needs of individual practitioners, each of the three sections is now printed in a separate volume.

Volume 1 of this third edition represents an update and extension of the first and fourth parts of the second edition. It is devoted to general considerations that pertain to the need for and use of psychological testing for treatment planning and outcomes assessment. The introductory chapter provides an overview of the status of the health care delivery system today and the ways in which testing can contribute to making the system more cost-effective. Three chapters are devoted to issues related to treatment planning, whereas five chapters focus on issues related to outcomes assessment. The first of the planning chapters deals with the use of psychological tests for screening purposes in various clinical settings. Screening can serve as the first step in the treatment planning process; for this reason, it is a topic that warrants the reader's attention. The second of these chapters presents a discussion of the research suggesting how testing may be used as a predictor of differential response to treatment and its outcome. Each of these chapters represents updated versions of the original work. The next chapter deals with treatment planning within Prochaska's Transtheoretical Model—a widely accepted and researched approach that takes the patient's stage of readiness to change into consideration in developing and revising treatment plans.

The five chapters on the use of testing for outcomes assessment are complementary. The first provides an overview of the use of testing for outcomes assessment purposes, discussing some of the history of outcomes assessment, its current status, its measures and methods, individualizing outcome assessment, the distinction between clinically and statistically significant differences in outcomes assessment, and some outcomes-related issues that merit further research. The next four chapters expand on the groundwork laid in this chapter. The first of these four presents an updated discussion of a set of specific guidelines that can be valuable to clinicians in their selection of psychological measures for assessing treatment outcomes. These same criteria also are generally applicable to the selection of instruments for treatment planning purposes. Two chapters provide a discussion of statistical procedures and research design issues related to the measurement of treatment progress and outcomes with psychological tests. One chapter specifically addresses the analysis of individual patient data; the other deals with the analysis of group data. As noted in the previous editions of this work, knowledge and skills in these areas are particularly important and needed by clinicians wishing to establish and maintain an effective treatment evaluation process within their particular setting. The other outcomes-related chapter presents a discussion of considerations relevant to the design, implementation, and maintenance of outcomes management programs in behavioral health care settings.

Volume 1 also includes a chapter addressing a frequently neglected topic in discussions of outcomes assessment, that is, ethical considerations related to outcomes assessment. The volume concludes with a future-oriented chapter, written to discuss predictions and recommendations related to the use of psychological assessment for treatment planning and outcomes assessment.

Volumes 2 and 3 address the use of specific psychological instruments for treatment planning and outcome assessment purposes. Volume 2 deals with child and adolescent instruments, with one chapter devoted to a review of the research related to the conceptualization of quality of life (QOL) as is applies to children and how it has evolved over the years. The purpose of this chapter is to present a foundation for the future development of useful measures of child QOL—something that currently appears to be in short supply. Volume 3 focuses on instruments that are exclusively or primarily intended for use with adult populations.

Instruments considered as potential chapter topics for Volumes 2 and 3 were evaluated against several selection criteria, including the popularity of the instrument among clinicians; recognition of its psychometric integrity in professional publications; in the case of recently released instruments, the potential for the instrument to become widely accepted and used; the perceived usefulness of the instrument for treatment planning and outcomes assessment purposes; and the availability of a recognized expert on the instrument (preferably its author) to contribute a chapter to this book. In the end, the instrument-specific chapters selected for inclusion were those judged most likely to be of the greatest interest and utility to the majority of the book's intended audience.

Each of the chapters in the second edition had previously met these selection criteria; thus, Volumes 2 and 3 consist of updated or completely revised versions of the instrumentation chapters that appeared in the first edition. Both volumes also contain several new chapters discussing instruments that were not included in the second edition for one reason or another (e.g., was not developed at the time, has only recently gained wide acceptance for outcomes assessment purposes). Indeed, recognition of the potential utility of each of these instruments for treatment planning or evaluation served as one impetus for revising the second edition of this work.

A decision regarding the specific content of each of the chapters in Volumes 2 and 3 was not easy to arrive at. However, in the end, the contributors were asked to address those issues and questions that are of the greatest concern or relevancy for practicing clinicians. Generally, these fall into three important areas: (1) What the instrument does and how it was developed; (2) how one should use this instrument for treatment planning and monitoring; and (3) how it should be used to assess treatment outcomes. Guidelines were provided to assist the contributors in addressing each of these areas. Many of the contributors adhered strictly to these guidelines; others modified the contents of their chapter to reflect and emphasize what they judged to be important to the reader to know about the instrument when using it for planning, monitoring, or outcome assessment purposes. Some may consider the chapters in Volumes 2 and 3 to be the "meat" of this revised work, because they provide "how to" instructions for tools that are commonly found in the clinician's armamentarium of assessment instruments. In fact, these chapters are no more or less important than those found in Volume 1. They are only extensions and are of limited value outside of the context of the chapters in Volume 1.

As was the case with the previous two editions, the third edition of *The Use of Psychological Testing for Treatment Planning and Outcomes Assessment* is not intended to be a definitive work on the topic. However, it is hoped that the reader will find its chapters useful in better understanding general and test-specific considerations and approaches related to treatment planning and outcomes assessment, and in effectively applying them in his or her daily practice. It also is hoped that it will stimulate further endeavors in investigating the application of psychological testing for these purposes.

—Mark E. Maruish
Burnsville, MN

# List of Contributors

Brian V. Abbott
Texas A&M University
College Station, TX

Thomas M. Achenbach
University of Vermont
Burlington, VT

Ross B. Andelman
Contra Costa Children's Mental
  Health Services
Concord, CA

Robert P. Archer
Eastern Virginia Medical School
Norfolk, VA

C. Clifford Attkisson
University of California
San Francisco, CA

Steven E. Bailley
University of Texas–Houston Health
  Sciences Center
Houston, TX

Thomas Beers
Kaiser Permanente San Diego
  Chemical Dependency Program
San Diego, CA

Albert J. Belanger
Harvard Medical School
Boston, MA

Larry E. Beutler
University of California
Santa Barbara, CA

Phillip J. Brantley
Pennington Biomedical Research Center
Baton Rouge, LA

Gary M. Burlingame
Brigham Young University
Provo, UT

James N. Butcher
University of Minnesota
Minneapolis, MN

David L. Carlston
Ohio University
Athens, OH

Antonio Cepeda-Benito
Texas A&M University
College Station, TX

Dianne L. Chambless
University of Pennsylvania
Philadelphia, PA

James A. Ciarlo
University of Denver
Denver, CO

Paul D. Cleary
Harvard Medical School
Boston, MA

James R. Clopton
Texas Tech University
Lubbock, TX

John D. Cone
Alliant International
    University
San Diego, CA

C. Keith Conners
Duke University School of Medicine
Durham, NC

Jonathan C. Cox
Brigham Young University
Provo, UT

William J. Culpepper
University of Maryland
Baltimore, MD

Constance J. Dahlberg
Alliant International University
San Diego, CA

Allen S. Daniels
Alliance Behavioral Care, University
    of Cincinnati
Cincinnati, OH

Edwin de Beurs
Leiden University Medical Center
Leiden, The Netherlands

Leonard R. Derogatis
Johns Hopkins University
    School of Medicine
Baltimore, MD

Kathy Dowell
Ohio University
Athens, OH

Gareth R. Dutton
Louisiana State University
Baton Rouge, LA

William W. Eaton
Johns Hopkins University, Bloomberg
    School of Public Health
Baltimore, MD

Susan V. Eisen
Center for Health Quality, Outcomes,
    and Economic Research, Edith Nourse
    Rogers Veterans Hospital
Boston, MA

Jeffery N. Epstein
Duke University School of Medicine
Durham, NC

Alex Espadas
University of Texas–Houston Health
    Sciences Center
Houston, TX

Laura E. Evison
Johns Hopkins University
    School of Medicine
Baltimore, MD

Kya Fawley
Northwestern University
Evanston, IL

Maureen Fitzpatrick
Johns Hopkins University
    School of Medicine
Baltimore, MD

Jenny Fleming
University of California
Santa Barbara, CA

Michael B. Frisch
Baylor University
Waco, TX

Anthony B. Gerard
Western Psychological Services
Los Angeles, CA

Sona Gevorkian
Massachusetts General Hospital
Boston, MA

David H. Gleaves
Texas A&M University
College Station, TX

Pamela Greenberg
American Managed Behavioral
  Healthcare Association
Washington, DC

Roger L. Greene
Pacific Graduate School of
  Psychology
Palo Alto, CA

Thomas K. Greenfield
University of California and Public
  Health Institute Berkeley
San Francisco, CA

Ann T. Gregersen
Brigham Young University
Provo, UT

Grant R. Grissom
Polaris Health Directions
Langhorne, PA

Seth D. Grossman
Institute for Advanced Studies in
  Personology and Psychopathology
Coral Gables, FL

Kurt Hahlweg
Technical University of
  Braunschweig
Braunschweig, Germany

Steven R. Hahn
Albert Einstein College of
  Medicine
New York, NY

Ashley E. Hanson
University of Alabama
Tuscaloosa, AL

Nancy M. Hatcher
University of Georgia
Athens, GA

Derek Hatfield
Ohio University
Athens, OH

Eric J. Hawkins
Brigham Young University
Provo, UT

Jena Helgerson
Northwestern University
Evanston, IL

Kay Hodges
Eastern Michigan University
Ann Arbor, MI

Elizabeth A. Irvin
Services Research Group, Inc. and
  Simmons College, Graduate School
  of Social Work
Boston, MA

Gary Jeager
Kaiser Permanente Harbor City
  Chemical Dependency Program
Harbor City, CA

R. W. Kamphaus
University of Georgia
Athens, GA

Jennifer M. Karpe
University of Alabama
Tuscaloosa, AL

Sangwon Kim
University of Georgia
Athens, GA

Kenneth A. Kobak
Dean Foundation for Health Research
  and Education
Madison, WI

Scott H. Kollins
Duke University School of Medicine
Durham, NC

Teresa L. Kramer
University of Arkansas for
  Medical Sciences
Little Rock, AR

Kurt Kroenke
Regenstrief Institute for Health Care,
  Indiana University School of
  Medicine
Indianapolis, IN

Samuel E. Krug
MetriTech, Inc.
Champaign, IL

David Lachar
University of Texas–Houston Health
  Sciences Center
Houston, TX

Michael J. Lambert
Brigham Young University
Provo, UT

Jeanne M. Landgraf
HealthAct
Boston, MA

William W. Latimer
Johns Hopkins University
Baltimore, MD

Jean-Philippe Laurenceau
University of Miami
Miami, FL

John S. Lyons
Northwestern University
Evanston, IL

Melanie Buddin Lyons
Buddin Praed Foundation
Winnetka, IL

Mary Malik
University of California
Santa Barbara, CA

John S. March
Duke University Medical Center
Durham, NC

Mark E. Maruish
Southcross Consulting
Burnsville, MN

Sarah E. Meagher
University of Miami
Miami, FL

Gregorio Melendez
Ohio University
Athens, OH

Theodore Millon
Institute for Advanced Studies
  in Personology and Psychopathology
Coral Gables, FL

Carla Moleiro
University of California
Santa Barbara, CA

Leslie C. Morey
Texas A&M University
College Station, TX

Carles Muntaner
University of Maryland School
  of Nursing
College Park, MD

Jack A. Naglieri
George Mason University
Fairfax, VA

Charles Negy
University of Central Florida
Orlando, FL

Frederick L. Newman
Florida International University
Miami, FL

Sharon-Lise T. Normand
Harvard Medical School and Harvard
  School of Public Health
Boston, MA

Benjamin M. Ogles
Ohio University
Athens, OH

Ashley E. Owen
University of South Florida
Tampa, FL

James D. A. Parker
Trent University
Peterborough, ON, Canada

Julia N. Perry
Veteran's Administration Hospital
Minneapolis, MN

Steven I. Pfeiffer
Duke University
Durham, NC

James O. Prochaska
Cancer Prevention Research Center
Kingston, RI

Janice M. Prochaska
Pro-Change Behavior Systems, Inc.
Kingston, RI

Eric C. Reheiser
University of South Florida
Tampa, FL

Leslie A. Rescorla
Bryn Mawr College
Bryn Mawr, PA

Cecil R. Reynolds
Texas A&M University
College Station, TX

William M. Reynolds
Humboldt State University
Arcata, CA

James M. Robbins
University of Arkansas for Medical
  Sciences
Little Rock, AR

Abram B. Rosenblatt
University of California
San Francisco, CA

Douglas Rugh
Florida International University
Miami, FL

Scott Sangsland
Kaiser Permanente
Southern California
  Permanente Medical Group
Pasadena, CA

Forrest R. Scogin
University of Alabama
Tuscaloosa, AL

James A. Shaul
Harvard Medical School
Boston, MA

Gill Sitarenios
Multi-Health Systems, Inc.
Toronto, ON, Canada

Corey Smith
Johns Hopkins University, Bloomberg
  School of Public Health
Baltimore, MD

G. Richard Smith
University of Arkansas
  for Medical Sciences
Little Rock, AR

Douglas K. Snyder
Texas A&M University
College Station, TX

Charles D. Spielberger
University of South Florida
Tampa, FL

Robert L. Spitzer
New York State Psychiatric Institute
New York, NY

Steven Stein
Multi-Health Systems, Inc.
Toronto, ON, Canada

Randy Stinchfield
University of Minnesota
Minneapolis, MN

Sumner J. Sydeman
Northern Arizona University
Flagstaff, AZ

Elana Sydney
Albert Einstein College of
  Medicine
New York, NY

Hani Talebi
University of California
Santa Barbara, CA

Manuel J. Tejeda
Barry University
Miami Shores, FL

Allen Tien
MDLogix, Inc.
Towson, MD

John E. Ware, Jr.
QualityMetric Inc. and Tufts
  University Medical School
Lincoln, RI

Dana Aron Weiner
Northwestern University
Evanston, IL

Irving B. Weiner
University of South Florida
Tampa, FL

M. Gawain Wells
Brigham Young University
Provo, UT

Douglas L. Welsh
University of Alabama
Tuscaloosa, AL

Janet B. W. Williams
New York State Psychiatric Institute
New York, NY

Kimberly A. Wilson
Stanford University Medical School
Palo Alto, CA

Ken C. Winters
University of Minnesota
Minneapolis, MN

Stephen E. Wong
Florida International University
Miami, FL

Karen B. Wood
Louisiana State University
Baton Rouge, LA

Michele Ybarra
Johns Hopkins University, Bloomberg
  School of Public Health
Baltimore, MD

# The Use of Psychological Testing for Treatment Planning and Outcomes Assessment

*Third Edition*

## Volume 1   General Considerations

# Introduction

Mark E. Maruish
*Southcross Consulting*

The cost of health care in the United States has reached astronomical heights. In 1995, approximately $1 trillion, or 14.9% of the gross domestic product (GDP), was spent on health care ("Future Targets," 1996). In 1998, these costs increased to $1.1 trillion and accounted for 13.5% of the GDP (see Levit et al., 2000). These costs rose to $1.31 trillion (13.3% of the GDP) in 2000, and then increased 8.7% to $1.42 trillion (14.1% of the GDP) in 2001 ("Health Care Costs," 2003). The most recent projections are that between 2001 and 2011 the national health expenditures will grow at an average annual rate of 7.3%, or 2.5% faster that the GDP (Centers for Medicare and Medicaid Services, 2002). Thus, it is estimated that by 2011, health care costs will reach $2.8 trillion, or approximately 17% of the GDP.

The costs of mental health and substance abuse problems also have risen over the past several years and are particularly disconcerting. A Substance Abuse and Mental Health Services Administration (SAMHSA) summary of various findings in the literature indicated that America's bill for mental health disorders in 1990 was $148 billion (Rouse, 1995). This compares to the 1983 direct and indirect mental health costs of $73 billion reported by Harwood, Napolitano, and Kristiansen (cited in Kiesler & Morton, 1988). The Surgeon General's report on mental health indicated that in 1996 $69 billion (7.3% of the total spending on health care) could be attributed to direct mental health services, $12.6 billion to substance abuse treatment, and $17.7 billion to treatment for Alzheimer's and other dementias (Surgeon General of the United States, 1999). All told, these expenditures represented 10.5% of the total health care cost of $943 billion for 1996. This does not include indirect costs, which most recently (1990) were estimated to be $78.6 billion for mental health disorders.

The high cost of treating behavioral health problems is not surprising, given the prevalence of psychiatric and substance use disorders in this country. Based on the findings from the Epidemiologic Catchment Area (ECA) study conducted in the early 1980s (Regier et al., 1993) and the National Comorbidity Study (NCS) of the early 1990s (Kessler et al., 1994), the Surgeon General (1999) estimated the following one-year prevalence rates for adults 18–54 years old:

- Nineteen percent have a mental health disorder.
- Nine percent have a mental health disorder accompanied by significant functional impairment.

- Six percent have an addictive disorder.
- Three percent have both mental health and addictive disorders.
- Twenty-eight to thirty percent have either a mental health or addictive disorder.

The Surgeon General also estimated that 20% of children 9–17 years old have a mental health or substance abuse disorder with at least mild functional impairment, while 20% of adults 55 years or older have a mental health disorder. Four percent of Americans 55 years or older were said to have a mental disorder accompanied by significant functional impairment.

The 2001 National Household Survey on Drug Abuse (NHSDA; Substance Abuse and Mental Health Services Administration [SAMHSA], 2002) reveals further details about the prevalence of mental health and substance abuse disorders. The results of this survey indicated that 7.3% of individuals 18 years or older had a DSM–IV disorder accompanied by functional impairment. In addition, 7.3% of individuals 12 years or older were classified with abuse of or dependence on alcohol or illicit drugs.

## THE VALUE OF BEHAVIORAL HEALTH CARE SERVICES

The need for behavioral health care services is great. Unsurprisingly, the demand for mental health and substance abuse services also is significant. According to the Surgeon General's (1999) report, 15% of the adult population and 21% of children and adolescents use mental health services in a given year. About half of the 15% of adults have a diagnosed mental health or addictive disorder, and the remainder are said to have a mental health "problem." The NHSDA report (SAMHSA, 2002) indicates that during the previous year, 11% of individuals 18 years or older and 18% of individuals 12–17 years old received mental health treatment. These represent significant ($p < .01$) increases from the previous year's estimates. Also, an estimated 1.4% of the population 12 years or older receive treatment for substance use. But what is the value of the services provided to those suffering from mental illness or substance abuse/dependency? Some might argue that the benefit from these services is either minimal or too costly to achieve if significant effects are to be gained. This claim, however, is at odds with data that indicate otherwise.

Numerous studies have demonstrated that treatment of mental health and substance abuse/dependency problems can result in substantial savings when viewed from a number of perspectives. This "cost offset" effect has been demonstrated most clearly in savings in medical care dollars. Given reports that 50–70% of typical primary care visits are for medical problems that involve psychological factors, the value of medical cost offset is significant (American Psychological Association, 1996). Moreover, the American Psychological Association also reported that 25% of patients seen by primary care physicians have a disabling psychological disorder and that depression and anxiety rank among the top six conditions dealt with by family physicians.

Following are just a few of the findings supporting the medical cost savings that can be achieved through the provision of behavioral health care treatment:

- Patients with diagnosable behavioral disorders who are seen in primary care settings use 2 to 4 times as many medical resources as patients without these disorders ("Leaders Predict," 1996).

• A study by Simon, Von Korff, and Barlow (1995) revealed that the annual health care costs of 6,000 primary care patients with identified depression were nearly twice those of the same number of primary care patients without depression ($4,246 vs. $2,371).

• Johnson, Weissman, and Klerman (1992) reported that depressed patients make 7 times as many visits to emergency rooms as nondepressed patients.

• Saravay, Pollack, Steinberg, Weinschel, and Habert (1996) found that cognitively impaired medical and surgical inpatients were rehospitalized twice as many times as cognitively unimpaired patients within a 6-month period. In the same study, depressed medical and surgical inpatients were found to have an average of approximately 12 days of rehospitalization over a 4-year follow-up period. During this same period, nondepressed inpatients averaged only 6 days of rehospitalization.

• Demonstrating the potential for additional costs that can accrue from the presence of a behavioral health problem, a longitudinal study found the health care costs of families with an alcoholic member to be twice that of families without alcoholic members (Holder & Blose, 1986).

• Sipkoff (1995) reported several conclusions drawn from a review of several studies conducted between 1988 and 1994 and listed in the "Cost of Addictive and Mental Disorders and Effectiveness of Treatment" report published by the Substance Abuse and Mental Health Services Administration (SAMHSA). One conclusion derived from a meta-analysis of the cost-offset effect was that treatment for mental health problems results in about a 20% reduction in the overall cost of health care. The report also concluded that although alcoholics were found to spend twice as much on health care as those without abuse problems, one-half of the cost of substance abuse treatment is offset within one year by subsequent reductions in the combined medical costs for the patient and his or her family.

• Strain et al. (1991) found that screening a group of 452 elderly hip-fracture patients for psychiatric disorders prior to surgery and then providing mental health treatment to the 60% of the sample needing treatment reduced total medical expenses by $270,000. The cost of the psychological/psychiatric services provided to this group was only $40,000.

• Simmons, Avant, Demski, and Parisher (1988) compared the average medical costs for chronic back pain patients at a multidimensional pain center (providing psychological and other types of intervention) incurred during the year prior to treatment to those costs incurred in the year following treatment. The pretreatment costs per patient were $13,284 while posttreatment costs were $5,596.

APA (1996) succinctly summarized what appear to be the prevalent findings of the medical cost–offset literature:

• Patients with mental disorders are heavy users of medical services, averaging twice as many visits to their primary care physicians as patients without mental disorders.

• When appropriate mental health services are made available, heavy use of the system often decreases, resulting in overall health savings.

• Cost-offset studies show a decrease in total health care costs following mental health interventions even when the cost of the intervention is included.

• In addition, offset increases over time, largely because . . . patients continue to decrease their overall use of the health care system, and don't require additional mental health services. (p. 2)

A more detailed discussion of various ways in which behavioral interventions can both maximize care to medical patients and achieve significant economic gains can be found in the work of Friedman, Sobel, Myers, Caudill, and Benson (1995).

The dollar savings that result from medical cost offset are relatively obvious and easy to measure. However, the larger benefits to the community—financial and otherwise—that can also accrue from the treatment of mental health and substance abuse/dependency problems may not be as obvious. One area in which treatment can have a tremendous impact is in the workplace. For example, note the following facts compiled by the American Psychological Association (1996):

- In 1985, behavioral health problems resulted in over $77 billion in lost income to Americans.
- California's stress-related disability claims totaled $380 million in 1989.
- In 1980, alcoholism resulted in over 500 million lost workdays in the United States.
- Major depression cost an estimated $23 billion in lost workdays in 1990.
- Individuals with major depression are 3 times more likely than nondepressed individuals to miss time from work and 4 times more likely to take disability days.
- Seventy-seven percent of all subjects from 58 psychotherapy effectiveness studies focusing on the treatment of depression received significantly better work evaluations than depressed subjects who did not receive treatment.
- Treatment resulted in a 150% increase in earned income for alcoholics and a 390% increase in income for drug abusers in one study of 742 substance abusers.

On another front, the former director of Office of National Drug Control Policy reported that for every dollar spent on drug treatment, America saves $7 in health care and criminal justice costs ("Brown Resigns," 1995). Also, SAMHSA's summary of the literature on 1990 behavioral health care costs indicated that crime, criminal justice activities, and property loss associated with crime stemming from substance use and mental disorders resulted in a total of $67.8 billion spent or lost (Rouse, 1995).

These and several other similar findings have been used to support the assertion that the costs associated with the identification and treatment of behavioral health problems is money well spent. At the same time, it appears that the case is not totally clear-cut, at least as far as *medical* cost offset is concerned. In fact, based on their review of over 25 mental health–offset cost studies published between 1965 and 1995, Sperry, Brill, Howard, and Grissom (1996) determined the following:

> The only conclusion to come from research on cost-offset due to mental health treatment is that there is no clear-cut indication of cost savings. Studies that claim such an effect are often methodologically flawed. The same design problems also cast doubt on the findings of studies that claim to find no cost-offset effect. Future research needs stronger methodology to be considered valid. (pp. 205–206)

The truth of the matter probably lies somewhere in the middle.

Society's need for behavioral health care services provides an opportunity for psychologists and other trained behavioral health service providers to become part of the solution to a major health care problem that shows no indication of decline. Each of the helping professions has the potential to make a contribution to this solution. Not the least are those contributions that can be made by psychologists and others trained in the use of psychological tests.

For decades, psychologists and other behavioral health care providers have come to rely on psychological assessment as a standard tool to assist diagnostic and treatment-planning activities. However, the care delivery system that has evolved within health care in general and behavioral health care services in particular has led to changes in how third-party payers, psychologists, and other service providers think about and/or use psychological assessment in day-to-day clinical practice. Some question the value of psychological assessment in the managed behavioral health care arena. Others argue that it is in just such an arena that the benefits of psychological assessment can be most fully realized and contribute significantly to the delivery of cost-effective treatment for behavioral health disorders (Maruish, 1999). Consequently, assessment could assist the health care industry in appropriately controlling or reducing the utilization and cost of health care over the long term. As Maruish (1990) observed well over a decade ago:

> Consider that the handwriting on the wall appears to be pointing to one scenario. With limited dollars available for treatment, the delivery of cost-efficient, effective treatment will be dependent on the ability to clearly identify the patient's problem(s). Based on this and other considerations, the most appropriate treatment modality ... must then be determined. Finally, the organization will have to show that it has met the needs of each client. ... It is in all of these functions—problem identification, triage/disposition, and outcome measurement—that psychological assessment can make a significant contribution to the success of the organization. (p. 5)

It is the latter side of the argument that is supported by this author and provides the basis for this and the subsequent chapters within this work.

As a final introductory note, it is important for the reader to understand that the term *psychological assessment*, as it is used in this chapter, refers to the evaluation of a patient's mental health status using psychological tests or related instrumentation. This evaluation may be conducted with or without the benefit of patient or collateral interviews, review of medical or other records, and/or other sources of relevant information about the patient.

## THE PRACTICE OF PSYCHOLOGICAL ASSESSMENT IN THE AGE OF MANAGED BEHAVIORAL HEALTH CARE

Probably in no other period has so much progress in the field of health care taken place than during the past century. Breakthroughs and technological advances in the diagnosis, treatment, and prevention of diseases abounded in this 100 years. On the other hand, never has there been so much controversy, debate, and upheaval surrounding this country's health care delivery system as during the past 2 decades. Out-of-control costs and the provision of inefficient and sometimes ineffective services have led to drastic changes in this delivery system, especially the introduction of "managed care," which has been aptly described as "one of the most significant changes to our nation's health care financing and delivery system in recent years (Davis, Collins, & Morris, 1994, p. 178). Managed care affects not only the way treatment for physical problems is delivered but also the way in which behavioral health care—mental health and substance abuse services—is provided. Indeed, managed care has become the dominant force in the delivery of mental health care services (Cushman & Gilford, 2000).

The general opinion about the effects of managed care seems to be a negative one. Reed, Levant, Stout, Murphy, and Phelps (2001) summarized the common perception of the current state of affairs in noting that

> the dramatic expansion and dominance of managed care in recent years have made the importance and potentially negative impact of market and policy forces on professional psychology abundantly clear. The health care system in which psychology currently finds itself is employer focused, market driven, and largely governed by the rules of free enterprise and big business, including a preoccupation with cost and short-term profitability. (p. 65)

However, depending on one's point of view, many of the effects of managed care might also be considered positive. The Surgeon General of the United States (1999), for instance, described managed care as representing "a confluence of several forces shaping the organization and financing of health care. These include the drive to deliver more highly individualized, cost effective care; a more health-promoting and preventive orientation; and a concern with cost containment to address the problem of moral hazard" (pp. 420–421).

### Effects on Mental Health Benefits

One of the most obvious effects of the widespread adoption of a managed system of health care delivery in the United States can be seen in changes in the spending for mental health benefits. Citing the work of the Hay Group (1998) and McCarthy (1998), Reed et al. (2001) noted that from 1988 to 1997 mental health benefits dropped 54%, from $154 per covered life to $69. This compares with a 7% decrease in the value of general health care benefits. During this same period, behavioral health care benefits as a percentage of the total health care benefits dropped 50%, from 6% to 3%. Reed et al. identified several reasons for the decrease in mental health benefits, including past abuse of these benefits, problems in mental health patients serving as advocates for themselves, and payers' and policymakers' limited understanding of mental health problems and the services that are employed to address those problems.

### Effects on Quality of Care

It is not surprising that a concern about the impact of managed care on quality of care would accompany the effects it has had on health care benefits in general and mental health benefits in particular. Indeed, the widespread perception that managed care has had a negative effect on the quality of mental health care can be seen in numerous surveys of mental health professionals (discussed later) and anecdotal managed care "horror stories" that appear in both the popular media and the professional literature. Limits to the number and type of psychotherapy sessions that are covered, authorization for psychological testing only for specific purposes under specific circumstances, level-of-care determinations being made according to strict criteria for medical necessity, prescriptions written according to approved formularies—these are but a few of the perceived obstacles and sources of quality-of-care concerns that practitioners must deal with on a daily basis. To some extent, these concerns are justified, particularly in cases where unique individual problems and circumstances demand unique approaches to care.

At the same time, there is much evidence of an increasing focus on quality since the advent of managed care. For example, Norquist (2002) identified a number of initiatives that arose on a national level with the advent of managed care. These included the creation of the President's Advisory Commission on Consumer Protection and Quality in the Health Care Industry to address the public's concerns about the quality of health care, the Department of Health and Human Services' establishment of the Quality Interagency Coordination Task Force to seek ways of improving federal health programs through interagency collaboration, and a request for recommendations from the Institute of Medicine for reporting on the quality of health care on a national level. In addition, many have observed a shift in managed care's focus from cost containment to value (Reed et al., 2001; Shaffer, 1997). Here, value can be viewed as the relationship between quality and cost (Bartlett, 1997). Employer concerns that limiting the availability of mental health services has increased the number of psychiatric disability claims (Reed et al., 2001) have likely had a significant influence on this change of focus. Moreover, accreditation bodies such as the National Committee for Quality Assurance (NCQA) and the Joint Commission for Accreditation of Healthcare Organizations (JCAHO), as well state and federal regulatory bodies such as the Center for Medicare and Medicaid Services (CMS), require managed care companies or the health plans they serve to meet numerous quality assurance/improvement standards in order maintain their accreditation (important for marketing purposes) or their license to do business and receive reimbursement for services. Overall, in spite of the shortcomings of managed care, the new "rules of the game" imposed by the dominance of this form of health care delivery have served to eliminate wasteful practices (e.g., open-ended psychotherapy, administration of psychological tests to every patient), promote more effective and efficient treatment strategies, and generally increase practitioner accountability.

## Effects on the Practice of Psychology

All behavioral health care professions have been affected by managed care, not least psychology. The extent to which the effects of managed care on psychology are perceived as threatening to its practice and the people who seek its services can seen in the American Psychological Association's support of legislative and judicial efforts that seek to curb managed care policies and practices. Kent and Hersen (2000) identified and grouped the challenges that psychologists must face under managed care into three general categories: clinical, administrative, and professional. Unsurprisingly, the greatest challenges posed by managed care in the clinical arena have to do with the bread-and-butter services that psychologists offer, that is, assessment and psychotherapy. In both areas, the psychologist's autonomy in deciding how best to assess and treat his or her patients has been curtailed. Indeed, psychological testing is the one truly unique and (some would argue) defining aspect of psychology distinguishing it from the other behavioral health care professions. Previously, psychologists have had the freedom to choose when to conduct psychological assessment, which tests to use, and how many tests to administer. Now, managed care demands justification for administering psychological tests. Sometimes, decisions to authorize testing are based on a cost-benefit analysis; in other words, one must determine whether the gain or value from the assessment warrants what it is going to cost the mental and behavioral health care organization (MBHO) for the testing.

## Current Status of Psychological Testing

For a number of decades, psychological assessment has been a valued and integral part of the services offered by psychologists and other mental health professionals trained in its use. However, its popularity has not been without its ups and downs. Megargee and Spielberger (1992) described a period of decreased interest in assessment that began in the 1960s. This decline in interest was attributed to a number of factors, including a shift in focus to those aspects of treatment where assessment was thought to contribute little (e.g., a growing emphasis on behavior modification techniques, an increased use of psychotropic medications, and an emphasis on the study of symptoms rather than personality syndromes and structures). At the time of their writing, Megargee and Spielberger also noted resurgence in the interest in assessment, including a new realization of how psychological assessment can assist in mental health care interventions today. But where does psychological assessment currently fit into the daily scope of activities for practicing psychologists? How has managed care affected the practice of psychological testing and assessment?

*Survey Findings.* The newsletter *Psychotherapy Finances* ("Fee, Practice, and Managed Care Survey," 1995) reported the results of a nationwide readership survey of 1,700 mental health providers. Sixty-seven percent of the psychologists participating in this survey reported that they provided psychological testing services. This represented about a 10% drop from the level indicated by a similar survey published in 1992 by the same newsletter. Also of interest in the 1995 survey was the percentage of professional counselors (39%), marriage and family counselors (16%), psychiatrists (21%), and social workers (13%) offering these same services.

Watkins, Campbell, Nieberding, and Hallmark (1995) surveyed 412 randomly selected APA members with a clinical specialty who were engaged in assessment services. This study essentially sought to replicate a study published 18 years earlier, and its purpose was to determine what, if any, changes in assessment practices had occurred in the intervening period of time. In fact, it found that the most frequently used assessment procedures had changed little over almost two decades. Among the most frequently used tests were those one might expect—MMPI, the Wechsler scales, Rorschach, TAT, Beck Depression Inventory, and so on. However, the most frequently used *procedure* was the clinical interview, reported by 391 of the 412 survey respondents. The implication is that, regardless of whatever tests they may employ in their assessment, most clinical psychologists rely on the clinical interview as part of their standard assessment procedures. In one sense, this supports MBHOs' view that interviews are all that are really required for diagnosis and treatment planning. However, as Groth-Marnat (1999a) pointed out, this may be true for dealing with "routine difficulties" but not so in other instances, such as those where the possibility of liability issues (e.g., a patient with suicidal or homicidal potential) or complex diagnostic questions come into play.

In a survey conducted in 1995 by the American Psychological Association's Committee for the Advancement of Professional Practice (CAPP), Phelps, Eisman, and Kohut (1998) found that assessment was the second most prevalent activity, occupying an average of 16% of the professional time of the nearly 16,000 respondents. Most of the respondents (55%) were practitioners whose primary work setting was a group or solo independent practice. The percentage of time spent in assessment activities varied considerably by setting ranging from 5% in academic settings to 15% in independent practices, 19% in government settings, and 23% in medical settings.

Phelps et al. also found that 29% of the respondents were involved in outcomes assessment, with those with the least number of years of postlicensure experience being more likely to report the use of outcomes measures than those with more postlicensure experience. The highest rate of use of outcomes measures (40%) was found for psychologists in medical settings. A random sample of 10% of the returned questionnaires revealed no consistency in the types of measures or criteria used for outcomes measurement.

Taking a closer look at the impact that managed care has had on assessment, Piotrowski, Belter, and Keller (1998) conducted a survey in the fall of 1996 that included mailings to 500 psychologists randomly selected from that year's *National Register of Health Service Providers in Psychology*. The purpose of the survey was to determine how managed care has affected assessment practices. One hundred thirty-seven usable surveys (32%) were returned. Sixty-one percent of the respondents saw no positive impact from managed care, and 70% saw managed care as negatively impacting clinicians or patients. The testing practices of 72% of the respondents were affected by managed care, as reflected in their doing less testing, using fewer instruments when they did test patients, and being reimbursed at lower rates. Overall, they reported less reliance on tests requiring much clinician time—such as the Wechsler scales, Rorschach, and TAT—along with a move toward the use of briefer, problem-focused tests. The results of their study led Piotrowski et al. to speculate on possible scenarios for the future of assessment—many of which are becoming realities. These included such things as providers' relying on briefer tests or briefer test batteries, changing the focus of their practice to more lucrative types of assessment activities (e.g., forensic assessment), using computer-based testing, or, in some cases, referring testing out to another psychologist.

Another large-scale testing-specific survey was conducted by Camara, Nathan, and Puente (1998; also published in 2000) to investigate which tests were most frequently used by 933 clinical psychologists and 567 neuropsychologists; the time required to administer, score, and interpret these tests; and other aspects of test use in the era of managed care. The neuropsychologists were selected from the membership of the National Academy of Neuropsychology, while the clinical psychologists included APA, doctoral-level independent practitioners whose primary or secondary employment involved the provision of mental health services. Perhaps one of the most telling of Camara et al.'s (2000) findings was the fact that 755 (81%) of the 933 clinical psychologists spent less than 5 hours in testing activities (administration, scoring, and interpretation) in a typical week. However, using only the results for the 179 clinical psychologists who spent 5 or more hours per week in these activities, Camara et al. found the following:

- Ninety-seven percent of this sample of psychologists performed testing for personality-psychopathology assessment, 88% for intellectual achievement assessment, and 47% for neuropsychological assessment.
- The annual mean and median for full-battery assessments conducted in each of these three areas were 80.4 and 50.0, respectively, for personality-psychopathology assessment; 87.3 and 50.0, respectively, for intellectual achievement assessment; and 63.6 and 30.0, respectively, for neuropsychological assessment.
- Across these three assessment areas and five other assessment areas (e.g., developmental assessment), test battery administration accounted for 45% of the total assessment time, scoring accounted for 36%, and interpretation accounted for 19%.

• The mean number of minutes to administer, score, and interpret the tests in a full-battery assessment in each of the same three areas was 241.7 minutes for a personality-psychopathology assessment, 211.3 minutes for an intellectual achievement assessment, and 366.5 minutes for a neuropsychological assessment. Mean and median administration, scoring, and interpretation times for the 50 most frequently used tests also were reported in this study.

• The 10 most frequently used tests were, in descending order, the WAIS–R, original MMPI/MMPI–2, WISC–III, Rorschach, Bender Visual-Motor Gestalt Test, TAT, WRAT–R/WRAT–III, House–Tree–Person, Wechsler Memory Scale–Revised, and Beck Depression Inventory and MCMI (tie).

• Computer services were infrequently used for assessment purposes; only 3.6% of tests were administered by computers, only 10.4% were scored by computers, and only 3.9% were interpreted by computer services.

Stout and Cook (1999) conducted a survey of 40 managed care companies regarding their viewpoints on reimbursement for psychological assessment. The good news is that the majority (70%) of these companies reported that they did reimburse for these services. At the same time, the authors pointed to the possible negative implications for the people enrolled in the 12 or so companies that did not reimburse for psychological assessment. These people may not be receiving the services they need because of missing information that might have been revealed through the psychological assessment.

Seventy-one percent of Murphy, DeBernardo, and Shoemaker's (1998) Division 42 respondents indicated that they provided psychological testing services, and 64% of these providers reported problems in getting reimbursed for these services. For neuropsychological testing, these figures were 18% and 29%, respectively. In addition, 70% of these respondents felt that managed care led to inadequate or inappropriate assessment. The study's authors saw this as an indication of the need for "continued study and concerted action." But somewhat surprisingly, Rothbaum, Bernstein, Haller, Phelps, and Kohout (1998) did not find "request for psychological testing denied" among the common complaints endorsed by their sample of New Jersey psychologists. Minimization of this as a problem area held up across 10 specific MBHOs.

A survey conducted by Pingitore, Scheffler, Haley, Sentell, and Schwalm (2001) revealed evidence of the practice and reimbursement patterns of 395 California Psychological Association (CPA) members. In this survey, 34% of the respondents indicated that they provided psychological assessment services on a weekly basis. For these psychologists, psychological assessment represented an average of 22% of their weekly caseload.

In another survey, Cashel (2002) explored the impact of managed care on a specific aspect psychological assessment. Her survey investigated the extent to which 162 child and adolescent psychologists perceived managed care as affecting their assessment practices. On average, the respondents reported that they spent 27% of their time conducting psychological assessment, with the median percentage being close to 15%. Approximately 35% of the respondents reported that managed care had no impact on their ability to conduct psychological testing, and 46% reported a negative impact. Only 1% of the respondents indicated a positive impact (the remaining 18% did not respond to the question).

Reported usage of 45 specific child and adolescent assessment instruments in the Cashel (2002) survey (selected for inquiry based on past child/adolescent test utilization studies) revealed that managed care most negatively affected the utilization of the lengthier or more time consuming instruments (e.g., WISC, Rorschach, and MMPI). At the same time, the most frequently used assessment instruments tended to be the same as those identified in pre–managed care surveys. Perhaps the most surprising survey finding was the frequency at which the respondents reported using assessment measures as treatment outcomes indices. Twenty percent indicated that they formally assessed treatment outcomes either "frequently" or "routinely," and another 48% indicated they did so "sometimes." In comparison, one survey of a single MBHO's providers indicated that only about 31% of these clinicians regularly use an outcomes measure ("Advances in Outcomes Measurement," 2001).

*Other Considerations.* Numerous articles (e.g., Ficken, 1995; Pingitore et al., 2001; Piotrowski, 1999) have commented on how the advent of managed care has limited the reimbursement for (and therefore the use of) psychological assessment. Certainly, no one would disagree with Ficken (1995), who saw the primary reason for this as a financial one. The amount of money available for behavioral health care treatment is limited. MBHOs therefore require a demonstration that the amount of money spent for testing will be more than offset by treatment cost savings. As of this writing, this author is unaware of any published or unpublished research to date that can provide this demonstration. In addition, Ficken (1995) noted that much of the information obtained from psychological assessment is not relevant to the treatment of patients within a managed care environment. And, understandably, MBHOs are reluctant to pay for gathering such information.

Werthman (1995) provided similar insights into this issue, noting that

> managed care . . . has caused [psychologists] to revisit the medical necessity and efficacy of their testing practices. Currently, the emphasis is on the use of highly targeted and focused psychological and neuropsychological testing to sharply define the "problems" to be treated, the degree of impairment, the level of care to be provided and the treatment plan to be implemented.
>
> The high specificity and "problem-solving" approach of such testing reflects MCOs' commitment to effecting therapeutic change, as opposed to obtaining a descriptive narrative with scores. In this context, testing is perceived as a strong tool for assisting the primary provider in more accurately determining patient "impairments" and how to "repair" them. (p. 15)

In general, Werthman viewed psychological assessment as no different from other forms of patient care, thus making it subject to the same scrutiny, the same demands for demonstrating medical necessity and/or utility, and the same consequent limitations imposed by MBHOs on other covered services.

Piotrowski (1999) best summed up the current state of psychological assessment:

> Admittedly, the emphasis on the standard personality battery over the past decade has declined due to the impact of brief therapeutic approaches with a focus on diagnostics, symptomatology, and treatment outcome. That is, the clinical emphasis has been on addressing referral questions and not psychodynamic defenses, character structure, and object relations. Perhaps the managed care environment has brought this issue to the forefront. Either way, the role of clinical assessment has, for the most part, changed. To the dismay of proponents of clinical methods, the future is likely to focus more on specific domain-based rather than comprehensive assessment. (p. 793)

Given the current state of affairs, it is important to ask how those responsible for the training of psychologists and other behavioral health practitioners are preparing their students for practice in the real world of the 21st century. The answer appears to be, not very well. In their survey of assessment training, Belter and Piotrowski (2001) found that 62% of the directors of training from 82 APA-approved clinical psychology doctoral programs were able to identify at least one factor that led to changes in their program's approach to assessment training. Of these, only 39% identified external, nonprogrammatic factors—for example, changes in the marketplace, decreased reimbursement for assessment, and a focus on brief assessment methods—as having influence on assessment training. Of greater interest is the fact that only 29% of the directors indicated that managed care affected their curriculum in assessment. As the authors point out, this finding stands in stark contrast to the results of Piotrowski et al's. (1998) survey of practicing psychologists, in which 72% of the respondents reported a "profound" effect of managed care on assessment practices. The training directors did report a decrease in training in time-consuming projective measures; at the same time, the authors observed that training in the use of several relatively brief tests that are popular in practice (e.g., SCL–90–R, WRAT, Wechsler Memory Scale) appeared to be lacking.

Looking at the issue more broadly, Daniels, Alva, and Olivares (2001) surveyed chairs of graduate programs in clinical psychology, counselor education or counseling psychology, and social work about the extent to which their programs train students to work in managed care settings. Of the 117 respondents, 60% reported that their programs provided at least some form of this type of training. For those offering it, the most common means of providing the training was through external practicums (60%) whereas the least common means was through a specific course (19%). The most common managed care training among those offering this training was in the areas of ethics (93%), diversity issues (89%), outcomes assessment (77%), and brief therapies (73%). The order of these rankings generally remained the same when the results of each of the three types of professional training programs were analyzed separately. Interestingly, a little over half (54%) of those offering managed care training indicated that their students were receiving "enough" of this type of training, and only 17% indicated current or planned curriculum changes to meet this training need.

## Reasons for the Decline in Psychological Assessment in MBHOs

It is apparent that the introduction of managed care has affected one of the chief professional activities of psychologists. They need to do much work in order to reclaim for psychological testing the level of acceptance and value it once held. But stepping back for a moment, it's important to ask why MBHOs are hesitant to authorize testing of their covered health plan members. Understanding this will be the key to regaining psychological testing's former status as a valuable component of behavioral health care services.

*General Emphasis on Streamlining Interventions and Containing Costs.* First and foremost among the reasons for the decline of psychological testing in MBHOs is their general emphasis on streamlining interventions and containing costs while maintaining value. MBHOs have adopted what Schreter (1997) referred to as the *principle of parsimony,* which holds that "each patient should receive the least intensive, least expensive treatment at the lowest level of care that will permit a return to health and function" (p. 653).

It is important to keep in mind that the managed care movement arose from the need to control health care costs. Managed care was and will continue to be (at least in the foreseeable future) a viable solution to runaway costs. It is therefore incumbent upon managed care organizations to trim as many unnecessary costs as possible without compromising quality of care. One way of doing this is to eliminate services that are not necessary for patient improvement. Given MBHOs' questions surrounding the validity and cost-effectiveness of testing (see below), as well as psychologists' sometimes indiscriminate or inappropriate use of testing in the past, it is not surprising that psychological testing has come under close scrutiny and is authorized by MBHOs only under certain circumstances. Moreover, because of the limited benefits and the fact that the typical patient terminates treatment after only four to six sessions anyway, it frequently doesn't make sense to devote an authorized visit or hour of time to an activity that may yield no long-term benefit for the patient. This is particularly the case when, for the reasons just cited, treatment tends to be problem focused.

*MBHOs' Attitude Toward Psychological Testing.*   Ambrose (1997) summarized what the American Psychological Association's Psychological Assessment Work Group (PAWG; Kubiszyn et al., 2000) concluded to be the typical attitude of MBHOs toward psychological assessment:

> Typically, when a clinician is asked why third-party payers should pay for personality assessment measures, their response generally falls into one of the following categories:
>
> • It improves diagnosis.
> • It improves treatment outcomes.
> • It shortens treatment.
> • I have children in college, and I need the money.
>
>    While these responses appear to be logical, there is no conclusive, unequivocal research that demonstrates that objective personality assessment in and of itself does any of the above. Intuitively, we anticipate that the more information we gather about a patient, the better likelihood we will be able to improve diagnosis. With a better diagnosis, we can increase treatment outcomes and shorten treatment durations. Yet, most research has never been aimed at a cost benefit analysis of objective personality assessment. Instead, most research is based on a goal of diagnostic or triage verification. (p. 66)

This is consistent with Schaefer, Murphy, Westerveld, and Gewirtz's (2000) observation that MBHOs find limited evidence for the claims that are made about the utility of psychological assessment. However, the PAWG contested the claims made by Ambrose (1997), stating that

> considerable empirical support exists for many important clinical health care applications of psychological assessment instruments. For such applications psychological assessment can enhance diagnosis and treatment. Health care cost savings would be expected to follow from enhanced diagnosis and treatment, an outcome that third-party payers would be expected to be seriously interested in. (Kubiszyn et al., 2000, p. 120)

The PAWG cites several studies and meta-analyses supporting its claims for the validity and utility of psychological testing for several applications. The applications that are noted include symptom description and differential diagnosis; description and prediction of role functioning; prediction of health, medical, mental health, psychotherapeutic, and forensic outcomes; identification of characteristics that can affect the outcomes of treatment; and psychological assessment as a treatment technique.

For the most part, this author is in agreement with the argument put forth by the PAWG. Why then do the findings reported in the professional literature seem to fall on deaf ears? The PAWG members contend that the profession has not done a good job of educating MBHOs and other third-party payers about the empirical support that exists for psychological testing and assessment. Taking some license with that famous saying from the movie *Jerry Maguire*, MBHOs are asking psychologists to *SHOW ME THE DATA!*

*Cost-Effectiveness and Value of Assessment Not Empirically Demonstrated.* One major claim made by the PAWG that this author disagrees with is its contention that psychological testing has been shown to be cost-effective (Kubiszyn et al., 2000). In truth, there really has not been an *empirical* demonstration of the direct value and (most importantly) the cost-effectiveness of psychological testing and assessment in MBHOs. This allegation is not new and, to the best of this author's knowledge, cannot be disputed at this time. Even the PAWG stops short of disputing it and instead makes statements that suggest the *possibility* or *likelihood* of cost-effectiveness. For example, the PAWG indicated that "health care costs would be *expected to follow* from enhanced diagnosis and treatment" (p. 120) stemming from psychological assessment, that "neuropsychological tests . . . are useful . . . for *facilitating* accurate diagnosis toward cost-effective treatment" (p. 120), that "psychological assessment instruments can identify who are *likely* to utilize health care services more often than average," and that "health care utilization *clearly influences* third-party payer 'bottom line' decision making" (p. 124; italics added throughout). But MBHOs are crying, *SHOW ME THE MONEY!* The industry will not accept a "trust me, it works" attitude by psychologists, particularly when other behavioral health care professionals render effective treatment without testing. Psychologists must show actual cost-effectiveness and/or treatment effectiveness *beyond* what treatment yields without using the same assessment process.

Why has the cost-effectiveness of psychological testing never been proven? One reason is the difficulty of implementing the type of methodology that would be required—particularly with regard to controlling for variables related to the psychologists' skill, the patients' symptoms, the instrumentation used, and the therapeutic process employed. Ambrose (1997) put the point this way:

> As distasteful as it sounds, the question that all health care providers face in this new health care environment is, "Why should managed care pay for these traditional services?"—especially since it is the responsibility of [the MBHOs] to ensure that benefits are expended in an appropriate fashion on behalf of the members they serve. While it is fairly easy to document benefits of the extrication of a cancerous tumor from the human body, or the utilization of an advanced radiological technique to identify cerebral malfunction, it is much more difficult to present a uniform cause-effect relationship between the uses of objective personality assessment, and treatment outcomes, given the uniqueness of instrument client-clinician variables. (p. 62)

A well-controlled study is not impossible, but it would be very difficult and quite costly to complete. Assuming the ability to implement the necessary methodology, the question then becomes, who would bear the cost of such a study? It is fairly certain that it would not be the MBHOs. To be sure, assessing the cost-effectiveness of testing would be more appropriately dealt with by the American Psychological Association or other professional groups that represent the practicing psychologists and promote their work to individuals, businesses, and organizations outside of the profession. In fact, the first step in this direction appears imminent. At the time of this writing, the Society for Personality Assessment announced its intention to commission and fund one or more preliminary studies that "address the applied value [i.e., benefits and costs] of clinical personality assessment for clients, therapists, and referral sources" (Finn, 2003, p. 2). It is hoped that other organizations will follow this lead.

*Use of Medication Trials to Arrive at Diagnoses.*   Another PAWG report (Eisman et al., 1998, 2000) identified an increase in the use of medication trials as one reason for the decline in psychological testing, at least for diagnostic purposes. Here, the fact that positive reactions to certain medications are expected in certain disorders but not in others could help differentiate between those disorders. A good example might be the use of Ritalin to differentiate ADHD from other possible disorders, such as anxiety, depression, or a psychotic disorder. However useful this might seem, the PAWG pointed out that it has a downside. For example, there is the possibility of serious medication side effects or of delaying or restricting a patient's access to other more appropriate types of treatment, such as psychotherapy.

## Opportunities for Psychologists

The current state of psychological assessment in behavioral health care delivery could be viewed as an omen of worse things to come. In this author's opinion, it should not be. Rather, the limitations that are being imposed on psychological assessment and the demand for justification of its use in clinical practice represent part of health care customers' dissatisfaction with the way that things were done in the past. In general, the tightening of the purse strings is a positive move for both behavioral health care and the profession of psychology. It is a wake-up call to those who have contributed to the health care crisis by uncritically performing costly psychological assessments, avoiding accountability, and generally not performing psychological assessment services in the most responsible, cost-effective way possible.

The current system of health care provides psychologists with an opportunity to reestablish the value of the contributions they can make to improve the quality of care delivery through their knowledge and skills in the area of psychological assessment. However, in order to do this, they must evaluate how they have used psychological assessment in the past and then determine the best way to use it in the future. Perhaps more importantly, they need to develop a new attitude and a new set of skills if they are to function efficiently, effectively, and with less frustration in MBHO systems. As Knapp and Keller (2001) and Maruish (2002) suggested, psychologists need to learn about the climate and demands of these organizations and then adapt to them.

There are several actions that psychologists can take in order to help achieve these goals. First, psychologists need to accept the fact that not everyone needs to be tested, especially in an environment where a typical episode of care is only four to six sessions long and that the typical approach taken is problem oriented and focused on achieving an attainable, measurable goal. In addition, when testing is called for (e.g., for diagnostic rule-out or clarification), an extensive battery of tests is not always required. In many cases, the results from one well-selected relevant test, along with data obtained from patient and collateral interviews and chart reviews, are sufficient for answering the question that led the MBHO to authorize the testing in the first place.

In addition, learning to use many of the good, validated, public domain or low-cost instruments that are available can lower the overhead for testing activities and thus make psychological assessment a more profitable enterprise. Finally, psychologists can acquire the expertise that is required for nontraditional applications of psychological testing in MBHO systems. Use of testing in outcomes management programs is a prime example, given the emphasis that many MBHOs now place on outcomes assessment activities. As Dorfman (2000) indicated:

> Psychologists are encouraged to develop a program of outcome evaluation within their own private practice, inpatient, or clinic settings. By providing outcome and patient satisfaction data to managed care companies psychologists gain the additional credibility of empirical validation of their work, increase the chance for authorization of services they request for their patients, and enhance their ability to obtain contracts from [managed care organizations]. The providing of data that documents the use of psychological testing reduced treatment length, resulted in the successful use of differential approaches with different types of patients, and improved patient satisfaction as a function of patients being more "understood" through testing will be critical in the future if psychological assessment is to play a major role in managed mental health care. (p. 36)

Mechanic (n.d.) described managed behavioral health care as being "very much a work in progress and its ultimate outcomes remain unclear. It offers considerable potential to better organize and rationalize services, and bring to them a more evidence-based culture, but it also presents risks, threatening innovation and appropriate provision of care" (p. 1). The sections that follow are intended to convey one vision of the present and future opportunities for psychological assessment in this era of managed behavioral health care and the means of best realizing them. They are also intended to establish the context for the remaining chapters of this work. The views advanced are based on the author's experience in working for an MBHO, his knowledge of current psychological assessment practices, and the directions provided by the current literature. Some likely will disagree with the author's view, given their own experience and thinking on the matters discussed. However, it is hoped that, even though in disagreement, these readers will be challenged to defend their position to themselves and as a result further refine their thinking and approach to the use of assessment within their practices.

## PSYCHOLOGICAL ASSESSMENT AS A TREATMENT ADJUNCT: AN OVERVIEW

According to Turner, DeMers, and Fox (2001), psychological tests are typically administered for one or more of five purposes, regardless of the setting in which they are administered. These purposes are *classification, description, prediction, intervention planning,* and *tracking.* However, the role of psychological assessment in therapeutic settings has been quite limited. Those who did not receive their clinical training within the past decade or so were probably taught that the value of psychological assessment is found only at the "front end" of treatment. That is, they were likely instructed in the power and utility of psychological assessment as a means of assisting a practitioner in identifying symptoms and their severity, personality characteristics, and other aspects of the patient (e.g., intelligence, vocational interests) that are important in understanding and describing the patient at a specific point in time. Based on the data and information obtained from patient and collateral interviews and from medical records and on the patient's stated goals for treatment, the practitioner would develop a diagnostic impression and formulate a treatment plan, then place the plan in the patient's chart—hopefully to be reviewed at various points during the course of treatment. In some cases, the patient would be assigned to another practitioner within the same organization or referred out, never to be seen or contacted again, much less be reassessed by the one who performed the original assessment.

Fortunately, during the past several years psychological assessment has come to be recognized for more than just its usefulness at the beginning of treatment. Consequently, its utility has been extended beyond being a mere tool for describing an individual's current state to being a means of facilitating treatment and understanding behavioral health care problems throughout the episode of care and afterwards. Generally speaking, several psychological tests now commercially available can be employed as tools to assist in *clinical decision-making* and *outcomes assessment* and, more directly, as *treatment techniques* in and of themselves. Each of these uses contributes value to the therapeutic process.

**Psychological Assessment for Clinical Decision-Making**

Traditionally, psychological assessment has been used to assist psychologists and other behavioral health care clinicians in making important clinical decisions. The types of decision making for which it has been used include those related to *screening, treatment planning,* and *monitoring of treatment progress.* Generally, screening may be undertaken to assist in (a) identifying the patient's need for a particular service or (b) determining the likely presence of a particular disorder or other behavioral/emotional problems. More often than not, a positive finding on screening leads to a more extensive evaluation of the patient in order to confirm with greater certainty the existence of the problem or further delineate the nature of the problem. The value of screening lies in the fact that it permits the clinician to quickly and economically identify, with a fairly high degree of confidence (depending on the particular instrument used), those who are likely to need care or at least further evaluation.

In many instances, psychological assessment is performed in order to obtain information that is deemed useful in the development of a specific treatment plan. Typically, this type of information is not easily (if at all) accessible through other means or sources. When combined with other information about the patient, information obtained from a psychological assessment can aid in understanding the patient, identifying the most important problems and issues that need to be addressed, and formulating recommendations about the best means of addressing them.

Psychological assessment also plays a valuable role in treatment monitoring. Repeated assessment of the patient at regular intervals during the treatment episode can provide the clinician with feedback regarding therapeutic progress. Based on the findings, the therapist will be encouraged to continue with the original therapeutic approach or, in the case of no change or exacerbation of the problem, modify or abandon the approach in favor of an alternate one.

**Psychological Assessment as a Treatment Technique**

The degree to which the patient is involved in the assessment process is changing. One reason for this can be found in the 1992 revision of the ethical standards of the American Psychological Association (1992). This revision includes a mandate for psychologists to provide feedback to clients whom they assess. According to ethical standard 2.09, "Psychologists ensure that an explanation of the results is provided using language that is reasonably understandable to the person assessed or to another legally authorized person on behalf of the client" (p. 8). APA elaborated further on this standard in the 2002 revision of their ethical principles (2002).

Finn and Tonsager (1992) offered other reasons for the interest in providing patients with assessment feedback. These include the recognition of the patients' right to see their medical and psychiatric health care records as well as clinically based and research-based findings and impressions that suggest that "therapeutic assessment" (described below) facilitates patient care. Finn and Tonsager also referred to Finn and Butcher's (1991) summary of potential benefits that may accrue from providing test results feedback to patients. The benefits cited include increased feelings of self-esteem and hope, reduced symptomatology and feelings of isolation, increased self-understanding and self-awareness, and increased motivation to seek or be more actively involved in their mental health treatment. In addition, Finn and Martin (1997) noted that the therapeutic assessment process provides a clinician-patient relationship model that can result in increased mutual respect, increased feelings of mastery and control, and decreased feelings of alienation.

Therapeutic use of assessment generally involves a presentation of assessment results (including assessment materials such as test protocols, profile forms, and other assessment summary materials) directly to the patient, an elicitation of the patient's reactions to them, and an in-depth discussion of the meaning of the results in terms of patient-defined assessment goals. In essence, assessment data can serve as a catalyst for the therapeutic encounter via (a) the objective feedback that is provided to the patient, (b) the patient self-assessment that is stimulated, and (c) the opportunity for patient and therapist to arrive at mutually agreed upon therapeutic goals.

*Therapeutic Assessment.*   The use of psychological assessment as a means of therapeutic intervention has received particular attention primarily through the work of Finn and his associates (Finn, 1996a, 1996b; Finn & Martin, 1997; Finn & Tonsager, 1992). In discussing what he terms *therapeutic assessment* using the MMPI-2, Finn (1996b) outlines a procedure with a goal to "gather accurate information about clients . . . and then use this information to help clients understand themselves and make positive changes in their lives" (p. 3). Elaborating on this procedure and extending it to the use of any test, Finn and Martin (1997) describe therapeutic assessment as

> collaborative, interpersonal, focused, time limited, and flexible. It is . . . very interactive and requires the greatest of clinical skills in a challenging role for the clinician. It is unsurpassed in respectfulness for clients: collaborating with them to address *their* concerns (around which the work revolves), acknowledging them as experts on themselves and recognizing their contributions as essential, and providing to them usable answers to their questions in a therapeutic manner. (p. 134)

Simply stated, Finn and his colleagues' therapeutic assessment procedure may be considered an approach to the assessment of mental health patients in which the patient not only is the primary provider of information needed to answer questions but also is actively involved in formulating the questions that are to be answered by the assessment. Feedback regarding the results of the assessment is provided to the patient and is considered a primary, if not *the* primary, element of the assessment process. Thus, the patient becomes a partner in the assessment process, and as a result therapeutic and other benefits accrue.

Finn's clinical and research work has primarily been focused on therapeutic assessment techniques using the MMPI–2. However, it appears that the same techniques can be employed with other instruments or batteries of instruments that provide information on multiple dimensions that are relevant to patients' concerns. Thus, the work of Finn and his colleagues can serve as a model for deriving direct therapeutic benefits from the psychological assessment experience using any of several commercially available and public domain instruments.

*Feedback Consultation.*   A lesser known approach to providing feedback to patients regarding assessment results is what Quirk, Strosahl, Kreilkamp, and Erdberg (1995) referred to as *feedback consultation*. It is viewed as a means to facilitate closure of a case and improve outcomes and is described as being "particularly useful . . . when a shared understanding between the therapist and the patient has been difficult to acquire or when the initial evaluation indicates that clinical or cost outcomes could be enhanced with this addition" (p. 28). In this approach, the "examining psychologist" is typically someone other than the individual treating the patient. Also, the consultation is provided both to the therapist and the patient.

There are three basic elements to feedback consultation (Quirk et al., 1995). *Paradigm thinking* refers to "each personality assessment measure possessing an underlying schema that can enrich our understanding of the client and that correspondingly influences the client's perceptions" (p. 28). *Data sampling* refers to the vast amount of data that assessment can provide to assist in the therapeutic process. The last element is the patient's *active participation,* which is thought to bring the benefits of both paradigm thinking and data sampling to the process of psychotherapy. The patient's participation may also help him to accept the findings of the assessment. The reader is referred to Quirk et al. (1995) as well as Erdberg (1979) and Fischer (1985) for more detailed information about feedback consultation.

### Psychological Assessment for Outcomes Assessment

Currently, one of the most common reasons for conducting psychological assessment in the United States is to assess the outcomes of behavioral health care treatment. A 1998 study conducted by the Center for Mental Health Services (CMHS) and reported by Manderscheid, Henderson, and Brown (n.d.) found that 85% of 676 ambulatory mental health facilities had systems in place to measure adult outcomes. In 1999, Merrick, Garnick, Horgan, and Hodgkin (2002) conducted a national survey of 434 managed care organizations (MCOs) offering 752 products (health maintenance organizations [HMOs], preferred provider organizations [PPOs], and point-of-service [POS]). They found that almost half of the products (48.9%) conducted behavioral health outcomes assessments. It is difficult to open a trade paper or health care newsletter or attend a professional conference without being presented with a discussion on how to "do outcomes" or what the results of a certain facility's outcomes study has revealed. The interest in and focus on outcomes assessment most probably can be traced to the continuous quality improvement (CQI) movement that was initially implemented in business and industrial settings. The impetus for the movement was a desire to produce quality products in the most efficient manner and thereby increase revenues and decrease costs. Currently, however, the importance of outcomes measurement may have more to do with identifying effective practices and their implications for financial efficiency (Manderscheid et al., n.d.) as well as enhancing clinical science and living up to the ethical responsibility to evaluate the quality of care that is provided (Ogles, Lambert, & Fields, 2002).

In health care, outcomes assessment has multiple purposes, not the least of which is to aid in marketing the organization's services. Related to this, those provider organizations vying for lucrative contracts from third-party payers frequently must present outcomes data demonstrating the effectiveness of their services. Equally important are data that demonstrate patient satisfaction. But perhaps the most important potential use of outcomes data within provider organizations (although not always recognized as such) is as a source of knowledge about what works and what doesn't. In this regard outcomes data can serve as a means for ongoing program evaluation. It is the knowledge obtained from outcomes data that, if acted upon, can lead to improvement in the services that an organization offers. When used in this manner, outcomes assessment can become an integral component of the organization's CQI initiative.

More importantly, however, for the individual patient, outcomes assessment provides a means of objectively measuring how much improvement he or she has made from the time of treatment initiation to the time of treatment termination, and in some cases extending to some time after termination. Feedback to this effect may serve to instill in the patient greater self-confidence and self-esteem and/or a more realistic view of where he or she is (from a psychological standpoint) at that point in time. It also may serve as an objective indicator to the patient of the need for continued treatment.

The purpose of the foregoing was to present a broad overview of psychological assessment as a multipurpose behavioral health care tool. Depending on the individual clinician or provider organization, it may be employed for one or more of the purposes just described. The preceding overview should provide a context for better understanding the following detailed discussion of each of these applications.

Prior to this discussion, however, it is important to briefly review the types of instrumentation most likely to be used in therapeutic psychological assessment as well as the significant considerations and issues related to the selection and use of these types. This should further facilitate the reader's understanding of the remainder of the chapter.

## GENERAL CONSIDERATIONS FOR THE SELECTION AND USE OF ASSESSMENT INSTRUMENTATION

Major test publishers regularly release new instruments for facilitating and evaluating behavioral health care treatment. Thus, the availability of instruments for these purposes is not an issue. However, the selection of the *appropriate* instrument(s) for one or more of the purposes described above is a matter requiring careful consideration. Inattention to an instrument's intended use, its demonstrated psychometric characteristics, its limitations, and other aspects related to its practical application can result in misguided treatment and potentially harmful consequences for a patient.

Several types of instruments could be used for the general assessment purposes described above. For example, neuropsychological instruments might be used to assess memorial deficits that could impact the goals established for treatment, the approach to treatment that is selected, and the clinician's decision to perform further testing. Tests designed to provide estimates of level of intelligence might be used for the same purposes. It is beyond the scope of this chapter (and this book) to address, even in the most general way, all of the types of tests, rating scales, and instruments that might be employed in a therapeutic environment. Instead, the focus here will be on general classes of instrumentation that have the greatest applicability in the service of patient screening as well as in the planning, monitoring, and evaluation of the outcomes of psychotherapeutic interventions. To a limited extent, specific examples of such instruments will be presented, followed by a brief overview of criteria and considerations that will assist clinicians in selecting the best instrumentation for their purposes. Newman, Rugh, and Ciarlo present a more detailed discussion of this topic in Chapter 6 of this volume.

### Instrumentation for Behavioral Health Assessment

The instrumentation required for any assessment application will depend on (a) the general purpose(s) for which the assessment is being conducted and (b) the level of informational detail that is required for those purpose(s). Generally, one may classify the types of instrumentation that would serve the purposes of the types of assessment specified above into one of four general categories. As mentioned above, other types of instrumentation are also frequently used in clinical settings for therapeutic purposes. However, the present discussion will be limited to the types more commonly used for screening, treatment planning, treatment monitoring, and outcome assessment.

*Psychological/Psychiatric Symptom Measures.* Probably the most frequently used instruments for each of the four stated purposes are measures of psychiatric symptomatology. These are the instruments on which the majority of the clinician's psychological assessment training has likely been focused. They were developed to assess the problems that typically prompt people to seek treatment.

There are several subtypes of measures of psychological/psychiatric symptomatology. The first is the *comprehensive multidimensional measure.* This is typically a lengthy, multiscale instrument that measures and provides a graphical profile of the patient on several psychopathological symptom domains (e.g., anxiety, depression) or disorders ( e.g., schizophrenia, antisocial personality). Summary indices sometimes are also available to provide a more global picture of the individual with regard to his or her psychological status or level of distress. Probably the most widely used and/or recognized of these measures are the Minnesota Multiphasic Personality Inventory (MMPI; Hathaway & McKinley, 1951) and its restandardized revision, the MMPI–2 (Butcher, Dahlstrom, Graham, Tellegen, & Kaemmer, 1989); the Millon Clinical Multiaxial Inventory–III (MCMI–III; Millon, 1994); and the Personality Assessment Inventory (PAI; Morey, 1991).

Multiscale instruments of this type can serve a variety of purposes. They may be used upon initial contact with the patient to screen for the need for service and, at the same time, yield information that is useful for treatment planning. Indeed, some such instruments (e.g., the MMPI–2) may make available supplementary, content-related, and/or special scales that can assist in addressing specific treatment considerations (e.g., motivation for treatment). Other multiscale instruments might be useful in identifying specific problems that may be unrelated to the patients' chief complaints (e.g., low self-esteem). They also can be administered numerous times during the course of treatment to monitor the patient's progress toward achieving established goals and to assist in determining what adjustments (if any) must be made to the clinician's approach. In addition, use of such an instrument in pre- and posttreatment can provide information related to the outcomes of the patient's treatment. Data obtained in this fashion can also be aggregated and analyzed with the results for other patients to evaluate the effectiveness of an individual therapist, a particular therapeutic approach, or an organization.

*Abbreviated multidimensional measures* are quite similar to the comprehensive multidimensional measure in many respects. First, by definition, they contain multiple scales for measuring a variety of symptom domains and disorders. They also may allow for the derivation of an index of the patient's general level of psychopathology or distress. In addition, they may be used for screening, treatment planning and monitoring, and outcomes assessment purposes just like the comprehensive instruments. The distinguishing feature of the abbreviated instrument is its length. By definition, these instruments are relatively short, easy to administer, and (usually) easy to score. Their brevity does not allow for an in-depth assessment of the patient and his or her problems, but this is not what these instruments were developed for.

Probably the most widely used of these brief instruments are Derogatis's family of symptom checklist instruments. These include the original Symptom Checklist–90 (SCL–90; Derogatis, Lipman, & Covi, 1973) and its revision, the SCL–90–R (Derogatis, 1983). Both of these instruments contain a checklist of 90 psychological symptoms, most of which score on the instruments' nine symptom scales. In the case of each, an even briefer version has been developed. The first to appear was the Brief Symptom Inventory (BSI; Derogatis, 1992), derived from the SCL–90–R. In a health care environment that is cost-conscious and unwilling to make too many demands on a patient's time, this 53-item instrument is gaining popularity over its longer 90-item parent. Similarly, a brief form of the original SCL–90 has been developed. Titled the Symptom Assessment–45 Questionnaire (SA–45; Strategic Advantage, Inc., 1996, 1998), its development did not follow Derogatis's approach to the development of the BSI; instead, cluster analytic techniques were used to select five items for assessing each of the nine symptom domains found on the other three Derogatis checklists.

The major strength of the abbreviated multiscale instruments is their ability to broadly and very quickly survey several psychological symptom domains and disorders relative to the patient. Their value is most clearly evident in settings where both time and dollars available for assessment services are limited. These instruments provide a lot of information quickly and inexpensively. Also, they are much more likely to be completed by patients than their lengthier counterparts. This last point is particularly important if one is interested in monitoring treatment or assessing outcomes, both of which require two or more assessments to obtain the necessary information.

*Measures of General Health Status and Role Functioning.* During the past decade, there has been an increasing interest in the assessment of health status in physical and behavioral health care delivery systems. Initially, this interest was shown primarily within those organizations and settings focused on the treatment of physical diseases and disorders (e.g., hospitals, medical specialty clinics). In recent years, behavioral health care providers have recognized the value of assessing the patient's general level of health. It is important to recognize that the term *health* means more than just the absence of disease or debility; it also implies a state of well-being throughout the individual's physical, psychological, and social spheres of existence (World Health Organization, 1948). Dickey and Wagenaar (1996) note how this concept of health recognizes the importance of eliciting the patient's point of view in assessing health status. They also point to similar conclusions reached by Jahoda (1958) specific to the area of mental health. Here, an individual's self-assessment relative to *how the individual feels he or she should be* is an important component of "mental health."

Measures of health status and physical functioning can be classified into one of two groups: *generic* and *condition or disorder specific*. Whereas generic measures typically measure aspects of *general* health, well-being, and functioning, condition-specific measures focus on assessing symptom severity, functioning, and sentinel indicators (Burnam, 1996). Probably the most widely used and respected generic health status measures are the 36-item SF–36 Health Survey (SF–36; 1 Ware, Snow, Kosinski, & Gandek, 1993; 2 Ware & Sherbourne, 1992) and the 39-item Health Status Questionnaire 2.0 (HSQ; Health Outcomes Institute, 1993; Radosevich, Wetzler, & Wilson, 1994). Aside from minor variations in the scoring of one of the instruments' scales (i.e., Bodily Pain) and the HSQ's inclusion of three depression-screening items, the two measures essentially are identical. Each assesses eight dimensions of health—four addressing mental health–related constructs and four addressing physical health–related constructs— that reflect the World Health Organization (WHO) concept of "health."

How the person's ability to work, perform daily tasks, or interact with others is affected by the disorder is important to know in devising a treatment plan and monitoring progress over time. Thus, role functioning has also gained attention as an important variable to address in the course of assessing the impact of a physical or mental disorder on an individual's life functioning. Sperry (1997) has noted that

> focused functional assessment is rapidly replacing [assessment of symptomatic distress and personality factors accounting for that distress] because clinicians and managed care organizations value evaluations that provide tangible and clinically relevant treatment targets and markers of therapeutic change. Assessment of life functioning reflects more of what individuals can or cannot do, rather than who they are as persons. It reflects the individual's coping skills and skill deficits rather than more abstract personality traits and dynamics. Furthermore, focused functional assessment is more relevant to the determination of medical necessity than are personality dynamics. Although the use of formal psychological testing . . . is declining, the use of functional assessment is increasing. (p. 96)

The SF–36 and HSQ both address these issues with scales designed for this purpose. In response to concerns that even these two relatively brief objective measures are too lengthy for regular administration in clinical and research settings, a 12-item version of each was constructed. The SF–12 (Ware, Kosinski, & Keller, 1995) was developed for use in large-scale population-based research where the monitoring of health status at a broad level is all that is required. Also, a 12-item version of the HSQ, the HSQ–12 (Radosevich & Pruitt, 1996), was developed for similar uses. (It is interesting that despite being derived from essentially the same instrument, there is only a 50% item overlap between the two abbreviated instruments.) The data supporting the use of each instrument that have been gathered to date are promising.

Condition- or disorder-specific measures of health status and functioning have been utilized for a number of years. Most have been developed for use with physical rather than mental disorders, diseases, or conditions. However, condition-specific measures of mental health status and functioning are beginning to appear. A major source of this type of instrument is the University of Arkansas' Center for Outcomes Research and Effectiveness (CORE). CORE has developed several condition-specific Technology of Patient Experience specifications (TyPEs). Among the available TyPEs that would be most useful to behavioral health care practitioners are those for depressive, phobic, and alcohol/substance use disorders.

Burnam (1996) identified several strengths and weaknesses of generic and condition-specific health status measures. These are summarized in Table 1.1. Use

TABLE 1.1
Common Characteristics of Generic and Condition-Specific Health Status Measures

| Type | Strengths | Weaknesses |
|------|-----------|------------|
| Generic | Assesses outcomes domains that patients are most concerned about | Limited information for treatment planning and monitoring |
| | Relevant to a broad range of patients | Limited number of versions available for use with children |
| | Appropriate for use among adults of all ages and racial/ethnic backgrounds | Limited meaning that is pertinent to clinical practice or specific life experience |
| | Possesses good psychometric properties | |
| | Self-report versions are low-cost and low-burden | |
| Condition-Specific | Directly relevant to clinical care | Less sensitive to what is important to the consumer (e.g., functioning, quality of life) |
| | Strongly grounded in clinical experience, thus facilitating clinical interpretation and use | Often provides information that is too complex for organization decision-making |
| | | Development limited to specific clinical populations |
| | | Seldom achieves the same level of validity and reliability as generic measures |
| | | Often is higher in cost and burden |

*Note.* From Burnam (1996), pp. 10–13.

of an instrument of one type over an instrument of the other often requires trade-offs. To deal with this issue, Burnam recommended administering instruments of both types, at least in assessing outcomes.

*Quality-of-Life Measures.*   Andrews, Peters, and Teesson (1994) indicated that most definitions of quality of life (QOL) describe a multidimensional construct encompassing physical, affective, cognitive, social, and economic domains. *Objective measures* of QOL focus on environmental resources required to meet one's needs, and the instruments can be completed by someone other than the patient. *Subjective measures* of QOL assess the patient's satisfaction with the various aspects of his or her life, and thus the instruments must be completed by the patient.

Andrews et al. (1994) pointed to other distinctions in the QOL arena. One has to do with the differences between QOL and health-related quality of life, or HRQL. According to Seid, Varni, and Jacobs (2000):

> Quality of life encompasses all aspects of an individual's life, including housing, environment, work, school, a safe neighborhood, and the like, which are traditionally beyond the scope of the health care system. [HRQL] refers specifically to those domains of an individual's health that are potentially within the influence of the health care system. (p. 18)

Similar to the case with health status measures, the other distinction that Andrews et al. (1994) made is between *generic* and *condition-specific* measures of QOL. QOL measures differ from HRQL measures in that the former assess the whole "fabric of life" whereas the latter assess quality of life as it is affected by a disease or disorder or by its treatment. Generic measures are designed to assess aspects of life that are generally relevant to most people; condition-specific measures are focused on aspects of the lives of those with a particular disease or disorder. However, as Andrews et al. stated, there tends to be a great deal of overlap between generic and condition-specific QOL measures.

Seid et al. (2000) pointed to the usefulness of HRQL in improving treatment practice through both treatment monitoring and evaluation. At the same time, they pointed to the paucity of empirical evidence supporting an association (a) between scores on HRQL measures and clinical signs and symptoms or (b) between the provision of HRQL assessment results to physicians and improved clinical practice. This state of affairs certainly would not bode well for incorporating HRQL assessment for whatever purpose in medical or other settings in which a medical model is used to understand and treat illness. And as Seid et al. indicated:

> Not until conceptual and empirical links are documented between [HRQL] assessments on the one hand and clinical signs and symptoms . . . and clinical practice change . . . , on the other, will clinicians begin thinking about the "genesis and pathogenesis of disorders of [HRQL]" (Wilson & Kaplan, 1995) . . . and designing interventions to ameliorate the biological, physiological, symptomatic, and functional status impairments underlying these disorders. (p. 23)

*Service Satisfaction Measures.*   With the expanding interest in assessing the outcomes of treatment, it is not surprising to see an accompanying interest in assessing the patient's and (in some instances) the patient's family's satisfaction with the services received. In fact, many professionals and organizations view satisfaction as an outcome, even the most important outcome. In one survey of 73 behavioral health care organizations, 71% of the respondents indicated that their outcomes studies included measures of patient satisfaction (Pallak, 1994). Merrick et al.'s (2002) sample of 434 MCOs indicated that 70% of their 752 products used patient satisfaction surveys as quality measures.

Although service satisfaction is frequently viewed as an outcome or an aspect of the total outcome (e.g., Ogles et al., 2002; Shaffer, 1997), it is this author's contention that it should not be classified as such. Rather, it should be considered a measure of the overall therapeutic process, encompassing the patient's (and, at times, others') view of how the services were delivered, the capabilities and attentiveness of the services provider, the benefits of the services (if any), and any of a number of other selected aspects of the services received. Patient satisfaction surveys *do not* answer the question, What was the result of the treatment rendered to the patient? They *do* answer the question, How did the patient feel about the treatment he or she received? Thus, they play an important role in program evaluation and improvement.

Ogles et al. (2002) identified many advantages and disadvantages tied to the collection and use of satisfaction data. The advantages include the fact that the data only need to be collected once (following treatment completion), there is a minimal cost and labor burden since the questionnaires are usually mailed out to patients, the questionnaires can elicit retrospective data about the patients' perceptions of the benefits derived from treatment, the results are usually very favorable (typical surveys yield an 80% satisfaction rating), and those who pay for services are quite interested in the types of information that satisfaction surveys deliver. On the other hand, the return rates for mail-out satisfaction surveys are usually low, at times so low as to limit the representativeness of the data; there is no way to objectify or validate the patients' perceptions of change due to treatment, especially since the reported degree of change tends to be overstated; they provide little information related to symptomatic change; and the data do not allow for improving care of the patients during the actual course of treatment. In short, although satisfaction information can be quite helpful and relatively easy to obtain for many purposes, collection of this information is not always trouble-free, and its use is of limited value for assessing the quality and effectiveness of the *clinical* services that patients have received.

The questionnaires currently being used to measure patient satisfaction are countless. This fact reflects the attempt of individual health care organizations to develop customized measures that assess variables important to their particular needs and at the same time respond to outside demands to "do something" to demonstrate the effectiveness of their services. Often, this "something" has not been evaluated to determine its basic psychometric properties. As a result, there exist numerous survey options to choose from but very few whose validity and reliability as measures of service satisfaction have been demonstrated.

Fortunately, there are a few instruments that have been investigated for their psychometric integrity. Probably the most widely used and researched patient satisfaction instrument designed for use in behavioral health care settings is the 8-item version of the Client Satisfaction Questionnaire (CSQ–8; Attkisson & Zwick, 1982; Nguyen, Attkisson, & Stegner, 1983). The CSQ–8 was derived from the original 31-item CSQ (Larsen, Attkisson, Hargreaves, & Nguyen, 1979), which also yielded two 18-item alternate forms, the CSQ–18A and CSQ–18B (LeVois, Nguyen, & Attkisson, 1981). The more recent work of Attkisson and his colleagues at the University of California at San Francisco has focused on the Service Satisfaction Scale–30 (SSS–30; Attkisson & Greenfield, 1996; Greenfield & Attkisson, 1989; see also chap. 28, Vol. 3). The SSS–30 is a 30-item, multifactorial scale that yields information about several aspects of satisfaction with the services received, such as perceived outcome and manner and skill of the clinician.

Another behavioral health care patient satisfaction survey that has recently been made available is the Experience of Care and Health Outcomes Survey (ECHO; "ECHO Survey: Homepage," n.d.). The ECHO was developed by NCQA for use in its accredited MBHO programs. It includes 33 items dealing with nine treatment-related areas, such as access, communication with clinicians, cultural competency, perceived improvement in functioning, and patient rights. Respondent demographics are also assessed by means of 7 additional items. More published information on the ECHO is sure to appear as this instrument becomes the standard for the measurement of patient satisfaction in managed behavioral health care settings.

### Guidelines for Instrument Selection

Regardless of the type of instrument being considered for use in the therapeutic environment, one frequently must choose between many product offerings. But what are the general criteria for the selection of an assessment instrument? What should guide the selection of an instrument for a specific purpose? As part of their training, psychologists and some other mental health professionals have been educated about the psychometric properties that are important to consider when determining the appropriateness of an instrument for a particular purpose. However, this is just one of several considerations that should be taken into account in evaluating an instrument for use.

Probably the most thorough and clinically relevant guidelines for the selection of psychological assessment instruments comes from work of Ciarlo, Brown, Edwards, Kiresuk, and Newman (1986) supported by the National Institute of Mental Health (NIMH). Newman, Rugh, and Ciarlo present an updated summary and synopsis of this work in chapter 6 of this volume. The criteria they describe generally concern applications, methods and procedures, psychometric features, and cost and utility considerations. Although these selection criteria were originally developed for use in evaluating instruments for outcomes assessment purposes, most also have relevance in the selection of instrumentation for screening, treatment planning, and treatment monitoring.

The work of Ciarlo and his colleagues provides more extensive instrument selection guidelines than most. Others who have addressed the issue have arrived at recommendations that serve to reinforce and/or complement those listed in the NIMH document. For example, Andrews' work in Australia has led to significant contributions to the body of outcomes assessment knowledge. As part of this, Andrews et al. (1994) identified six general "qualities of consumer outcome measures" that are generally in concordance with those from the NIMH study—*applicability, acceptability, practicality, reliability, validity,* and *sensitivity to change.* Ficken (1995) indicated that instruments used for screening purposes should (a) possess high levels of sensitivity and specificity with regard to diagnostic criteria from the *Diagnostic and Statistical Manual of Mental Disorders,* fourth edition (DSM–IV; American Psychiatric Association, 1994) or the most up-to-date version of the *International Classification of Diseases* (ICD); (b) focus on hard-to-detect (in a single office visit) but treatable disorders that are associated with imminent harm to self or others, significant suffering, and a decrease in productivity; (c) require no more than 10 minutes to administer; and (d) have an administration protocol that easily integrates into the organization's workflow.

It is important for readers to recognize that no single outcomes measure will meet the needs of all stakeholders in the care of a single patient or a patient population (Eisen & Dickey, 1996; Norquist, 2002; Ogles et al., 2002). Given this, Ogles et al. offer a few suggestions that should be heeded in selecting outcomes instrumentation:

1. Know the trade-offs. Identifying the pros and cons of the instrumentation for meeting your personal needs or those of your organization will allow you to make an informed decision.
2. Know your audience. Instrument selection should always take into consideration who will be the end users of the obtained information. When there are multiple audiences for this information (as is often the case), all of their needs must be balanced.
3. Recognize resource limitations. It is important to assess a given instrument's burden on your practice's financial and human resources or those of your organization. For an instrument under consideration, you might ask, Is the information the instrument yields worth the cost of obtaining it?

Before closing this discussion, I will make one last point. As Beutler Kim, Davison, Karno, and Fisher (1996) observed, psychologists are a relatively conservative group whose favorite assessment measures are over 50 years old. Those responsible for the selection of outcomes instrumentation for personal or organizational use must be willing to consider more than just the tried and proven instruments they have been using for many years. Indeed, many of these established instruments have solid psychometric underpinnings and work quite well for specific purposes. However, their cost, the burden they place on both staff and patients, and their original purpose (which may have been other than to be administered multiple times for treatment monitoring and outcomes assessment) may make them less than ideal for a given purpose in a given setting. Over the past several years, a number of instruments have been developed to address a variety of specific issues. Because these instruments are relatively new, they do not have the same amount of psychometric support or name recognition as the more established instruments. However, the initial findings for many of these new instruments are promising and confirm they should be given serious consideration for use either in individual practices or organizational settings. Chapters on several of these instruments are included in this edition of this book.

The reader is referred to other sources (Burlingame, Lambert, Reisinger, Neff, & Mosier, 1995; Burnam, 1996; Cone, 2001; Eisen & Dickey, 1996; Lohr et al., 1996; Ogles et al., 2002; Pfeiffer, Soldivera, & Norton, 1992; Schlosser, 1995; Sederer, Dickey, & Hermann, 1996) for further discussion of and recommendations for instrument selection.

## PSYCHOLOGICAL ASSESSMENT AS A TOOL FOR SCREENING

Among the most significant ways in which psychological assessment can contribute to the development of an economic and efficient behavioral health care delivery system is through its ability to quickly identify individuals in need of mental health or substance abuse treatment services and/or to determine the likelihood of the presence of a specific disorder or condition. The most important aspect of any screening procedure is the efficiency with which it can provide information that is useful in clinical decision-making.

In the field of psychology, the most efficient and thoroughly investigated screening procedures involve the use of psychological test instruments. The power or utility of a psychological screener lies in its ability to determine, with a high level of probability, whether the respondent has a particular disorder or condition or is a member of a group with clearly defined characteristics. The most commonly used screeners in daily clinical practice are those designed to identify some specific aspect of psychological functioning or disturbance or to provide a broad overview of the respondent's point-in-time mental status. Examples of problem-specific screeners include the Beck Depression Inventory–II (BDI–II; Beck, Steer, & Brown, 1996) and State–Trait Anxiety Inventory (STAI; Spielberger, 1983). Examples of screeners for more generalized psychopathology or distress include the SA–45 and BSI.

### Research-Based Use of Psychological Screeners

The establishment of a system for screening for a particular disorder or condition involves determining what it is one wants to screen in or screen out, the level of probability at which one feels comfortable in making a screening decision, and how many misclassifications (or what percentage of errors) one is willing to tolerate. Once it is decided what particular disorder or condition will be screened, one then must evaluate the instrument's classification efficiency statistics—sensitivity, specificity, positive predictive power (PPP), and negative predictive power (NPP)—to determine if a given instrument is suitable for the intended purpose(s). These statistics and related issues are described in detail in chapter 2 of this volume.

## Implementation of Screeners into the Daily Workflow of Service Delivery

The utility of a screening instrument is only as good as the degree to which it can be integrated into an organization's daily regimen of service delivery. This, in turn, depends on a number of factors. The first is the degree to which the administration and scoring of the screener is quick and easy and the amount of time required to train the staff to successfully incorporate the screener into the daily workflow.

The second factor relates to the instrument's use. Generally, screeners are developed to assist in determining the likelihood that the patient has the specific condition or characteristic the instrument is designed to identify. Using a screener for any other purpose (e.g., to assign a diagnosis based solely on screener results or to estimate the likelihood of the presence of other characteristics) only serves to undermine the integrity of the instrument in the eyes of staff, payers, and other parties with a vested interest in the screening process.

The third factor has to do with the ability of the clinician to act on the information obtained from the screener. It must be clear how the clinician should proceed once the information is available.

The final factor is staff acceptance and commitment to the screening process. This comes only with a clear understanding of the importance of the screening, the usefulness of the obtained information, and how the screening process is to be incorporated into the organization's daily workflow.

Ficken (1995) provided an example of how screeners can be integrated into an assessment system designed to assist primary care physicians in identifying patients with psychiatric disorders. This system (which also allows for the incorporation of practice guidelines) seems to take into account the first three utility-related factors just mentioned. It begins with the administration of a screener that is highly sensitive and specific to DSM- or ICD-related disorders. These screeners should require no more than 10 minutes to complete, and "their administration must be integrated seamlessly into the standard clinical routine" (p. 13). Like in the sequence described by Derogatis and Culpepper in chapter 2 of this volume, positive findings would lead to a second level of testing. Here, another screener that meets the same requirements as those for the first screener and also affirms or rules out a diagnosis would be administered. Positive findings would lead to additional assessment for treatment-planning purposes. Consistent with standard practice, Ficken recommended confirmation of screener findings by a qualified psychologist or physician. Figure 1.1 provides a flowchart showing the two-step screening process.

## PSYCHOLOGICAL ASSESSMENT AS A TOOL FOR TREATMENT PLANNING

Problem identification through the use of screening instruments is only one way in which psychological assessment can facilitate the treatment of behavioral health problems. When employed by a trained clinician, psychological assessment also can provide information that can greatly facilitate and enhance the planning of a specific therapeutic intervention for the individual patient. It is through the implementation of a tailored treatment plan that the patient's chances of problem resolution are maximized.

The importance of treatment planning has received significant attention during the past several years. The reasons for this recognition were summarized by Maruish (1990) as follows:

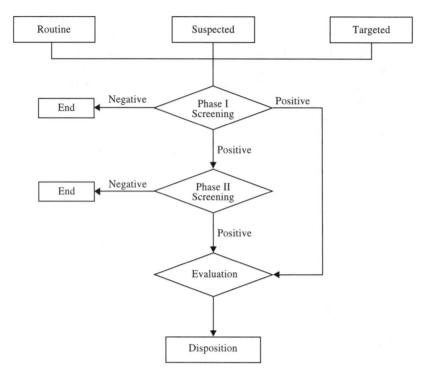

FIG. 1.1. Flowchart for a sequential screening process. From *Psychological Testing in the Age of Managed Behavioral Health Care* (p. 31), by M. E. Maruish, 2002, Mahwah, NJ: Lawrence Erlbaum Associates. Copyright 2002 by Lawrence Erlbaum Associates. Reproduced with permission.

Among important and interrelated reason . . . [are] concerted efforts to make psychotherapy more efficient and cost effective, the growing influence of "third parties" (insurance companies and the federal government) that are called upon to foot the bill for psychological as well as medical treatments, and society's disenchantment with open-ended forms of psychotherapy without clearly defined goals. (p. iii)

The role that psychological assessment can play in planning a course of treatment for behavioral health care problems is significant. Butcher (1990) indicated that information available from instruments such as the MMPI–2 not only can assist in identifying problems and in establishing communication with the patient but can help ensure that the plan for treatment is consistent with the patient's personality and external resources. In addition, psychological assessment may reveal potential obstacles to therapy, areas of potential growth, and problems that the patient may not be consciously aware of. Moreover, both Butcher (1990) and Appelbaum (1990) viewed testing as a means of quickly obtaining a second opinion. Other benefits of psychological assessment identified by Appelbaum include assistance in identifying patient strengths and weaknesses, identification of the complexity of the patient's personality, and establishment of a reference point during the therapeutic episode.

The type of treatment-relevant information that can be derived from patient assessment and the manner in which it is applied are quite varied—a fact that will become evident later in this chapter. Regardless, Strupp probably provided the best summary of the potential contribution of psychological assessment to treatment planning, stating that "careful assessment of patient's personality resources and liabilities is of inestimable importance. It will predictably save money and avoid misplaced therapeutic effort; it can also enhance the likelihood of favorable treatment outcomes for suitable patients" (Butcher, 1990, pp. v–vi).

### Assumptions About Treatment Planning

The introduction to this section presented a broad overview of ways in which psychological assessment can assist in the development and successful implementation of treatment plans for behavioral health care patients. These and other benefits are discussed in greater detail later. However, it is important to first clarify what treatment planning is and some of the general, implicit assumptions that one typically can make about this important therapeutic activity.

For the purpose of this discussion, the term *treatment planning* is defined as that part of a therapeutic episode in which a set of goals for an individual presenting with mental health or substance abuse problems is developed and the specific means by which the therapist and/or other resources will assist the individual in achieving those goals are identified. General assumptions underlying the treatment planning process are as follows:

1. The patient is experiencing behavioral health problems that have been identified either by him- or herself or another party. Common external sources of problem identification include the patient's spouse, parent, teacher, and employer and the legal system.
2. The patient experiences some degree of internal and/or external motivation to eliminate or reduce the identified problems. As an example of external motivation, the patient may face the potential loss of a job or dissolution of a marriage if the problems are not resolved to the satisfaction of the other party.
3. The treatment goals are tied directly or indirectly to the identified problems.
4. The treatment goals have definable criteria, are indeed achievable by the patient, and are developed by the patient in collaboration with the clinician.
5. The prioritization of goals is reflected in the treatment plan.
6. The patient's progress toward the achievement of the treatment goals can be tracked and compared against an expected path of improvement in a formal or an informal manner. This expected path of improvement might be based on the clinician's experience or (ideally) on objective data gathered on similar patients.
7. Deviations from the expected path of improvement will lead to a modification in the treatment plan, followed by subsequent monitoring to determine the effectiveness of the alteration.

These assumptions should not be considered exhaustive, nor are they likely to reflect what actually occurs in all situations. For example, some patients seen for therapeutic services have no motivation to change. In juvenile detention settings or when children are brought to treatment by their parents, the patients' participation in treatment may be forced, and they may exert no effort to change. In extreme cases, a patient may in fact engage in intentional efforts to sabotage the therapeutic intervention. In other cases, some clinicians may continue to identify and prioritize treatment goals without the direct input from the patient. Regardless, the assumptions above have a direct bearing on the manner in which psychological assessment can best serve treatment-planning efforts.

**The Benefits of Psychological Assessment for Treatment Planning**

As has already been touched upon, there are several ways in which psychological assessment can assist in the planning of treatment for behavioral health care patients. The more common and apparent contributions can be organized into four general categories: *problem identification, problem clarification, identification of important patient characteristics,* and *monitoring of treatment progress.*

*Problem Identification.* Probably the most common purpose of psychological assessment in the service of treatment planning is problem identification. Often, psychological testing per se is not needed to identify what problems patients are experiencing. They either will tell the clinician directly without questioning or will admit their problem(s) upon direct questioning during a clinical interview. However, this is not always the case.

The value of psychological testing becomes apparent in those cases where the patient is hesitant or unable to identify the nature of his or her problems. With a motivated and engaged patient who responds open and honestly to items on a well-validated and reliable test, the process of identifying what led the patient to seek treatment may be greatly facilitated. Cooperation shown during testing may be attributable to the nonthreatening nature of questions presented on paper or a computer monitor (as opposed with those posed by another human being); the subtle, indirect qualities of the questions themselves (compared with those asked by the clinician); or a combination of these reasons.

In addition, the nature of some of the more commonly used psychological test instruments allows for the identification of secondary but significant problems that might otherwise be overlooked. Multidimensional inventories such as the MMPI–2 and the PAI are good examples of these types of instruments. Moreover, these instruments may be sensitive to other patient symptoms, traits, or characteristics that may exacerbate or otherwise contribute to the patients' problems.

Note that the type of problem identification described here is different from that conducted during screening. Whereas screening is focused on determining the presence or absence of a single specific problem, problem identification generally takes a broader view and investigates the possibility of the presence of *multiple problem areas.* At the same time, there also is an attempt to determine problem severity and the extent to which one or more of the problem areas affect the patient's ability to function.

*Problem Clarification.* Psychological testing can often assist in the clarification of a known problem. Tests designed for use with populations presenting problems similar to those of the patient can elucidate aspects of identified problems. Information gained from these tests can improve the patient's and clinician's understanding of the problem and lead to the development of a better treatment plan. The three most important types of information that can be gleaned for this purpose concern the *severity* of the problem, the *complexity* of the problem, and the degree of *functional impairment* in one or more life roles.

The manner in which a patient is treated depends a great deal on the severity of his or her problem. In particular, problem severity plays a significant role in determining the proper level of care of the behavioral health care intervention. Those patients whose problems are so severe that they are considered a danger to themselves or others are often best suited for inpatient treatment, at least until dangerousness is no longer an issue. Similarly, problem severity may be a primary criterion that signals the necessity of evaluation for a medication adjunct to treatment. Severity also may have a bearing on the type of psychotherapeutic approach that is taken by the clinician. For example, it may be more productive for the clinician to take a supportive role with severe cases; all things being equal, a more confrontational approach may be more appropriate with patients whose problems are mild to moderate in severity.

As noted, the problems of patients seeking behavioral health care services are frequently multidimensional. Patient and environmental factors that play into the formation and maintenance of a psychological problem, along with the problem's relationship with other conditions, all contribute to its complexity. Knowing the complexity of the target problem is invaluable in developing an effective treatment plan. Again, multidimensional instruments or batteries of tests, each measuring specific aspects of psychological dysfunction, can serve this purpose well.

As with problem severity, knowledge of the complexity of a patient's problems can help the clinician and patient in many aspects of treatment planning, including determination of the appropriate level of care, the appropriate therapeutic approach, the need for medication, and other important decisions. However, possibly of equal importance to the patient and other concerned parties (wife, employer, school, etc.) is the extent to which the identified problems affect the patients' ability to function in his or her role as parent, child, employee, student, friend, and so on. Information gathered from the administration of instruments designed to assess role functioning clarifies the impact of the patient's problems and serves to establish role-specific goals. It also can help in identifying other parties who may serve as potential allies in the therapeutic process. In general, the most important role-functioning domains to assess are those related to work or school performance, interpersonal relationships, and activities of daily living (ADLs).

*Identification of Important Patient Characteristics.*  The identification and clarification of the patient's problems is of key importance in planning a course of treatment. However, there are numerous other types of patient information not specific to the identified problems that can be easily identified and will facilitate treatment planning and the use of psychological assessment instruments. The vast majority of treatment plans are developed or modified in light of at least some nonpathological characteristics. The exceptions are generally the result of taking a "one size fits all" approach to treatment.

Probably the most useful type of information that is not specific to the patient's problems but can be gleaned from psychological assessment consists of patient characteristics able to serve as assets or areas of strength for the patient in working to achieve his or her therapeutic goals. For example, Morey (1999) points to the utility of the PAI's Nonsupport scale in identifying whether the patient perceives there to be an adequate social support network, this being a predictor of positive therapeutic progress. Other examples include "normal" personality characteristics, such as those measurable by Gough, McClosky, and Meehl's Dominance (1951) and Social Responsibility (1952) scales developed for use with the MMPI and MMPI–2. Greene (1991) described individuals with high scores on the Dominance scale as "being able to take charge of responsibility for their lives. They are poised, self-assured, and confident of their own abilities" (p. 209). Gough and his colleagues interpreted high scores on the Social Responsibility scale as indicative of individuals who, among other things, trust the world, are self-assured and poised, and believe that each individual must carry his or her share of duties. Thus, scores on these and similar types of scales may reveal important aspects of patient functioning that can be useful to the patient in effecting positive change in his or her life.

Similarly, knowledge of the patient's weaknesses or deficits also may impact the type of treatment plan that is devised. Greene and Clopton (1999) provided numerous types of deficit-relevant information from the MMPI–2 content scales that have implications for treatment planning. For example, a clinically significant score ($T > 64$) on the Anger scale suggests the possible wisdom of including training in assertiveness and/or anger control as part of the patient's treatment. On the other hand, uneasiness in social situations, as indicated by a significantly elevated score on either the Low Self-Esteem or Social Discomfort scale, suggests that a supportive interventional approach would be beneficial, at least initially.

Moreover, use of specially designed scales and procedures can provide information related to the patient's ability to become engaged in the therapeutic process. For example, the Therapeutic Reactance Scale (Dowd, Milne, & Wise, 1991) and the MMPI–2 Negative Treatment Indicators Content Scale (Butcher, Graham, Williams, & Ben-Porath, 1989) may be useful in determining whether the patient is likely to resist therapeutic intervention. Morey (1999) presented rules for scoring and interpreting his Treatment Process Index, which utilizes $T$-scores from several PAI scales and can assist in the assessment of treatment amenability.

Other types of patient characteristics that can be identified through psychological assessment have implications for selecting the best therapeutic approach for a given patient and thus can contribute significantly to the treatment-planning process. For example, Moreland (1996) pointed out that psychological assessment can assist in determining if the patient deals with problems through internalizing or externalizing behaviors. He noted that all things being equal, internalizers would probably profit most from an insight-oriented approach rather than a behavioral approach. The reverse would be true for externalizers. And through their work over the years, Beutler and his colleagues (Beutler & Clarkin, 1990; Beutler, Goodrich, Fisher, & Williams, 1999; Beutler & Williams, 1995) have identified several patient characteristics that are important for matching patients and treatment approaches to achieve maximum therapeutic effectiveness. These are addressed in detail in chapter 3 of this volume.

*Monitoring of Progress Along the Path of Expected Improvement.* Information from repeated testing during the treatment process can help the clinician determine if the treatment plan is appropriate for the patient at a given point in time. From Howard, Martinovich, and Black's (1997) perspective, "The most useful clinical information . . . is about the progress of the individual patient assessed during the course of treatment. Is the patient 'on track' for a successful outcome?" (p. 110). Many clinicians use psychological assessment to determine whether their patients are showing the expected improvement as treatment progresses. If not, adjustments can be made. These adjustments may reflect the need for (a) more intensive or aggressive treatment (e.g., a higher level of care, an increased number of psychotherapeutic sessions each week, the addition of a medication adjunct), (b) less intensive treatment (e.g., a reduction or discontinuation of medication, a transfer from partial hospitalization to outpatient care), or (c) a different therapeutic approach (e.g., a switch from humanistic therapy to cognitive-behavioral therapy). Regardless, any modifications require later reassessment of the patient to determine if the treatment revisions have impacted patient progress in the expected direction. This process may be repeated any number

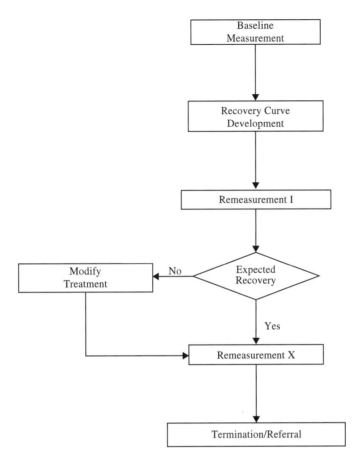

FIG. 1.2. Flowchart for a treatment-monitoring process. From *Psychological Testing in the Age of Managed Behavioral Health Care* (p. 43), by M. E. Maruish, 2002, Mahwah, NJ: Lawrence Erlbaum Associates. Copyright 2002 by Lawrence Erlbaum Associates. Reproduced with permission.

of times. "In-treatment" reassessments also can provide information relevant to the decision when to terminate treatment.

Figure 1.2 presents a general process for treatment monitoring. In this particular paradigm, the screening process may serve as the source of the baseline data against which data obtained at other points in treatment can be compared. This assumes, of course, that the screening instrument is what one wants to use to monitor treatment progress.

Once baseline data are obtained, the organization, assuming it has the necessary resources in place, can generate an expected recovery curve for the patient. This curve will enable the clinician to determine if the patient is on the expected track for recovery through the episode of care. Deviations noted on remeasurement should lead the clinician to consider modifying the treatment strategy.

The goal of monitoring is to determine whether treatment is "on track" with expected progress at a given point in time. When and how often to assess the patient is dependent on a few factors. One is the instrumentation selected for monitoring. Many instruments are designed to assess the patient's status at the time of testing. Items on these measures are generally worded in the present tense (e.g., "I feel tense and nervous," "I feel that my family loves and cares about me"). Changes from one day to the next on the construct(s) measured by these instruments should be reflected in the test results.

Other instruments, however, ask the patient to indicate if a variable of interest has been present, or how much or to what extent it has occurred, during a specific interval of time. The items usually begin thus: "During the past month, how often have you..." or "During the past week, to what extent has..." Readministration of these interval-of-time instruments or subsets of items within them should be undertaken only after the passing of a period of time equivalent to or longer than the time interval to be considered in responding to the items. For example, an instrument that asks the patient to consider the extent to which certain symptoms have been problematic during the past 7 days should not be readministered for at least 7 days. The responses from a readministration that occurs less than 7 days after the first administration would include the patient's consideration of his or her status during the previously considered time period. This may make interpretation of the change of symptom status (if any) from one administration to the next difficult if not impossible.

Aside from instrumentation considerations, Smith, Manderscheid, Flynn, and Steinwachs (1997) recommend that reassessment occur at those points in time that are clinically meaningful from the standpoint of the course of the disorder. That is, reassessment should occur at points at which clinical changes (e.g., remission, relapse) would be expected. They add that "assessment that is simply convenient for assessors will have little clinical utility" (p. 1036).

One might also consider the points at which clinically significant change is expected in deciding when to schedule remeasurement. For example, Kopta, Howard, Lowry, and Beutler (1994) found that for 50% of 850 patients clinically significant change (as measured by 18 items from the SCL–90–R) occurred after 11 sessions. Kadera, Lambert, and Andrews (1996) found that 50% of their 64 patients achieved clinically significant change (as measured by OQ–45 results) by the 16th session. Using survival analysis, Anderson and Lambert (2001) combined the results for the Kadera et al. study patients who started treatment in the dysfunctional range ($n = 47$) with the results for 53 other patients who also began treatment in the OQ–45 dysfunctional range; they found that 25% reached *clinically significant* change by Session 8, 50% by Session 13, and 75% by Session 25. This research suggests that, for similar patient populations, it might make sense to schedule remeasurement of all patients after Sessions 8 and 13. Anderson and Lambert also reported the percentage of patients showing *reliable* change by the number of sessions for the combined samples. Such data might be used instead of data on clinically significant change. Depending on the utility of the approach over a period of time, the schedule of remeasurement might be adjusted regardless of which type of data is used.

Methods to determine if clinically significant change has occurred from one point in time to another have been developed and can be used for treatment monitoring. These methods are discussed in chapters 8 and 9. However, another approach to monitoring therapeutic change, referred to as *patient profiling*, may be superior. Patient profiling is yet another contribution stemming from the work of Howard and his colleagues. It is the product of two of their theories: the *phase model of psychotherapy* (Howard, Lueger, Maling, & Martinovich, 1993; Howard, Moras, Brill, Martinovich, & Lutz, 1996) and the *dosage model of psychotherapeutic effectiveness* (Howard, Kopta, Krause, & Orlinsky, 1986; Howard et al., 1996). The phase model proposes a standard, consistent patient progression through distinct phases of psychotherapy: remoralization, remediation, and rehabilitation. The successful accomplishment of one phase permits the patient to move to the next phase and consequently to progress efficiently and effectively through the entire therapeutic process. The dosage model posits "a lawful linear relationship between the log of the number of sessions and the normalized probability of patient improvement" (Howard et al., 1996, p. 1060). Howard and his colleagues thought that a log-normal model would fit because the target of improvement changes during the course of treatment. In fact, this line of thinking led to their conceptualization of the phase model of psychotherapy. Using session-by-session data rather than mathematical extrapolations of pre- and posttreatment data, Kadera et al. (1996) derived dose-effect curves that were more conservative that those generated Howard et al. Those readers considering the use of dose-effect curves or patient profiling are encouraged to take note of the Kadera et al. findings.

Patient profiling essentially involves the generation of an expected curve of recovery over the course of psychotherapy along any measurable construct dimension that the clinician or investigator may choose (Howard et al., 1996; Leon, Kopta, Howard, & Lutz, 1999). Individual profiles are generated from selected patient clinical characteristics (e.g., severity and chronicity of the problem, attitudes toward treatment, scores on treatment-relevant measures) present at the time of treatment onset. Simply put, the measure of the construct of interest is modeled as a log-linear function of the session number, based on data from a large sample of therapy patients on the same clinical characteristics. Howard and his colleagues used scores from the Mental Health Index (MHI; Howard, Brill, Lueger, O'Mahoney, & Grissom, 1993; Sperry et al., 1996), a composite of scores from three instruments measuring well-being, symptomatology, and life functioning, to demonstrate the generation and tracking of individual patient profiles. (The MHI was developed to reflect the important dimensions of Howard's phase theory and thus provides an excellent measure for profiling purposes. However, one could choose to profile the patient only on a single domain, such as symptomatology, or on other global constructs using other appropriate instrumentation.) Hierarchical linear modeling is used to predict the course of improvement during treatment. Multiple administrations of the instrument during the course of treatment allow a comparison of the patient's actual score with that which would be expected from similar individuals after the same number of treatment sessions. The therapist thus knows when the treatment is working and when it is not working (and can then make necessary adjustments in the treatment strategy).

Recent support for Howard and his colleagues dose-effect and phase models can be found in a study by Lutz, Lowry, Kopta, Einstein, and Howard (2001). Using three samples of outpatients, Lutz et al. were able to demonstrate that the highest levels of improvement across phases for both predicted scores (based on one sample) and observed scores (based on another sample) were, in descending order, on measures of well-being, symptomatology, and functioning. There was a tendency to overestimate the dose-response relationship on measures of symptomatology. They also found that overall mental health improved at a rate consistent with previous research. Also consistent with previous research, the dose-response relationship was found to vary across disorders (e.g., anxiety, depression, bipolar disorder).

The work of Lambert and his colleagues (Lambert, Whipple, Smart, et al., 2001; Lambert, Whipple, Vermeesch, et al., 2001) and Azocar et al. (2003) lends support to the claim that benefits accrue from the use of assessment-based feedback provided to clinicians during treatment. At the same time, Lambert, Hansen, and Finch (2001) pointed out that, in order to be effective, the feedback needs to be timely and provide information that is action oriented. Also, the provision of clinical support tools (e.g., a diagnostic decision tree, a list of possible interventions, supplemental measures, a tracking form) with the feedback can increase its effectiveness (Whipple et al., in press).

Whether psychological test data obtained from treatment monitoring are used as fodder for generating complex statistical predictions or for simple point-in-time comparisons, the work of Howard, Lambert, and their colleagues demonstrates that such data can provide an empirically based means of determining the effectiveness of mental health and substance abuse treatment during an episode of care. Their value lies in their ability to support ongoing treatment decisions that must be made using objective means. Consequently, they can help improve patient care while supporting efforts to demonstrate accountability to the patient and interested third parties.

## PSYCHOLOGICAL ASSESSMENT AS A TOOL
## FOR OUTCOMES MANAGEMENT

Since the 1990s, the behavioral health care field has witnessed accelerating interest in and development of outcomes assessment programs. Cagney and Woods (1994) attributed this to four major factors. First, behavioral health care purchasers are asking for information regarding the value of the services they buy. Second, an increasing number of purchasers are requiring a demonstration of patient improvement and satisfaction. Third, MCOs need data to prove that their providers render efficient and effective services (Dorfman, 2000; Kent & Hersen, 2000; Manderscheid et al.; n.d., Speer & Newman, 1996). And fourth, outcomes information will be needed for the "quality report cards" that MCOs anticipate they will be required to provide in the future. In short, fueled by soaring health care costs, the need for providers to demonstrate that they deliver effective, high-quality health care has continued to increase (Busch & Sederer, 2000). Further, this trend has occurred within the context of the CQI movement, which has added to the level of interest and growth in outcomes assessment programs.

As noted previously, the need for outcomes measurement and accountability in this era of managed care provides a unique opportunity for psychologists to use their training and skills in assessment (Maruish, 1994, 1999, 2002). However, the extent to which psychologists and other trained professionals become key and successful contributors to an organization's outcomes initiative (whatever that might be) will depend on their understanding of what "outcomes" and their measurement and applications are all about.

### What Are Outcomes?

Before discussing outcomes, it is important to have a clear understanding of what is meant by the term. Experience has shown that its meaning varies, depending on the source. From the most basic perspective, outcomes can be defined as "the intermediate or final result of either the natural course of a disorder (that is, how an individual would do in the absence of any treatment) or the processes of medical or other interventions" (McGlynn, 1996, p. 20). However, outcomes are probably best understood as just one component of *quality of care*. Donabedian (1985) has identified three dimensions of quality of care. The first is *structure*. This encompasses various aspects of the organization providing the care, including how the organization is "organized," its physical facilities and equipment, and the number and professional qualifications of its staff. *Process* encompasses the specific types of services that are provided to a given patient (or group of patients) during a specific episode of care. These might include various tests and assessments (e.g., psychological tests, lab tests, magnetic resonance imaging), therapeutic interventions (e.g., group psychotherapy, medication), and discharge-planning activities. Processes that address treatment complications (e.g., drug reactions) also are included here. *Outcomes*, on the other hand, are the results of the specific treatment that was rendered. These results can include any number of variables that are relevant to stakeholders in the patient's care. For example, Seid et al. (2000) have identified three general categories of outcomes: clinical (e.g., signs, symptoms, indicators of disorders), financial (e.g., costs saved), and patient based (e.g., patient perceptions of quality of life).

Given the relationship between structure, process, and outcomes, which aspect(s) should be focused on to measure the quality of care being rendered to a patient or group of patients? Until relatively recently, the focus had primarily been on structures and processes (Sederer, Dickey, & Eisen, 1997). Early on, outcomes information was considered to be more difficult to obtain for several reasons (e.g., costs, limitations on available instrumentation). Over the years, however, the use of measures of structure has declined, as only a few have been shown to predict variation in processes or outcomes (Norquist, 2002). During this same time, the use of outcomes information for quality measurement has grown (Sederer et al., 1997). Many consider the measurement of outcomes as more important than the measurement of processes, and some might even question the need for gathering process information at all. Others view processes as more important than outcomes for the assessment of quality (Brook, McGlynn, & Cleary, 1996). Some have argued that understanding how outcomes are achieved can come only through knowledge of both structures and processes (Bartlett, 1997; McGlynn, 1996). Perhaps Brook et al. (1996) provide a means of determining the best way to judge which aspect of quality is most important to measure:

> If quality-of-care criteria based on structural or process data are to be credible, it must be demonstrated that variations in the attribute they measure lead to differences in outcome. If outcome criteria are to be credible, it must be demonstrated that differences in outcome will result if the processes of care under the control of health professionals are altered. (p. 966)

Hermann (2002) discusses the strengths and limitations of both process and outcomes measurement (summarized in Table 1.2) and notes that efforts toward quality improvement are best served by combining the measurement of these two aspects of quality of care.

The outcomes, or results, of treatment should be used to assess more than a single aspect of functioning. This is why the plural of the term is used throughout this chapter and in the title of this volume. Treatment may impact multiple facets of a patient's life. Stewart and Ware (1992) have identified five broad aspects of general health status: physical health, mental health, social functioning, role functioning, and general health perception. Treatment may affect each of these aspects of health in different ways, depending on the disease or disorder being treated and the effectiveness of the treatment. Some specific aspects of functioning related to these five areas of general health status that are commonly measured include feelings of well-being, psychological symptom status, use of alcohol and other drugs, functioning on the job or at school, marital/family relationships, utilization of health care services, and ability to cope.

In considering the types of outcomes that might be assessed in behavioral health care settings, a substantial number of clinicians probably would identify symptomatic

TABLE 1.2
Advantages and Limitations of Process and Outcomes Measurement

| Measure | Advantages | Disadvantages |
|---|---|---|
| Outcomes | Clinically relevant<br>Efficient: Can assess the aggregated impact of care | No national system of outcomes management<br>Some of the more commonly tracked outcomes are too rare or occur too far after the completion of treatment<br>Poor outcomes can result from factors other than treatment factors (e.g., clinical characteristics, environmental factors)<br>Does not provide information about how to improve care |
| Process | Treatment processes are more common than significant outcomes<br>Can be evaluated at the same time as care is being delivered<br>Can help identify actual practices that show significant variation from standards of care<br>Can reduce burden by relying on existing data (e.g., claims, pharmacy records)<br>Less susceptible to confounding variables | Provides information about only specific interventions<br>Little research into their validity<br>May promote micromanagement of practice by suggesting how to achieve the desired results |

*Note.* From Hermann (2002), pp. 25–28.

change in psychological status as the most important. However important change in symptom status may have been considered in the past, psychologists and other behavioral health care providers have come to realize that change in many other aspects of functioning identified by Stewart and Ware (1992) are equally important indicators of treatment effectiveness. As Sederer et al. (1996) noted:

> Outcome for patients, families, employers, and payers is not simply confined to symptomatic change. Equally important to those affected by the care rendered is the patient's capacity to function within a family, community, or work environment or to exist independently, without undue burden to the family and social welfare system. Also important is the patient's ability to show improvement in any concurrent medical and psychiatric disorder.... Finally, not only do patients seek symptomatic improvement, but also they want to experience a subjective sense of health and well being. (p. 2)

A much broader perspective is offered in Faulkner and Gray's *The 1995 Behavioral Outcomes and Guidelines Sourcebook* (Migdail, Youngs, & Bengen-Seltzer, 1995):

> Outcomes measures are being redefined from a vague "is the patient doing better?" to more specific questions, such as, "Does treatment work in ways that are measurably valuable to the patient in terms of daily functioning level and satisfaction, to the payer in terms of value for each dollar spent, to the managed care organization charged with administering the purchaser's dollars, and to the clinician charged with demonstrating value for hours spent?" (p. 1)

Thus, *outcomes* holds a different meaning for each of the different parties who have a stake in behavioral health care delivery, and what is measured generally depends on the purpose(s) for which outcomes assessment is undertaken. As shown in chapter 7, the aspects of care that are measured can vary greatly.

### Outcomes Assessment: Measurement, Monitoring, and Management

Just as it is important to be clear about what is meant by *outcomes*, it is equally important to clarify the three general purposes for which outcomes assessment may be employed. The first is outcomes *measurement*. This involves nothing more than pre- and posttreatment assessment of one or more variables to determine the amount of change that has occurred in these variables during the episode of care.

A more helpful approach is that of outcomes *monitoring*, "the use of periodic assessment of treatment outcomes to permit inferences about what has produced change" (Dorwart, 1996, p. 46). Like the earlier described treatment progress monitoring used for treatment planning, outcomes monitoring involves the tracking of changes in the status of one or more outcomes variables at multiple points in time. Assuming a baseline assessment at the beginning of treatment, reassessment may occur one or more times during the course of treatment (e.g., weekly, monthly), at the time of termination, and/or during one or more periods of posttermination follow-up. Whereas treatment progress monitoring is used to determine deviation from the expected course of improvement, outcomes monitoring focuses on revealing aspects of the therapeutic process that seem to affect change. As Brill and Sperry (1997) noted, "The more treatment relevant the data that the outcomes system feeds back to the clinician, the more likely the process and outcomes of treatment will be focused and effective" (p. 124). Callaghan (2001) presented a step-by-step approach to establishing an outcomes monitoring system.

The third and most useful purpose of outcomes assessment is outcomes *management*. Dorwart (1996) defined outcomes management as "the use of monitoring information in the management of patients to improve both the clinical and administrative processes for delivering care" (pp. 46–47). Whereas Dorwart appears to view outcomes management as relevant to the individual patient, this author views it as a means to improve the quality of services offered to the *patient population(s)* served by the provider, not to any one patient. Information gained through the assessment of patients can provide the organization with indications of what works best, with whom, and under what set of circumstances, thus helping to improve the quality of services for all patients. In essence, outcomes management can serve as a tool for any organization with an interest in implementing a CQI initiative.

In the outcomes assessment process, a baseline measurement is taken (see Fig. 1.3). In some cases, this may be followed by the treatment monitoring process discussed earlier. Frequently, the patient is assessed at the termination of treatment, although this may not always be the case. Posttreatment follow-up measurement may occur, with or without measurement at the termination of treatment. The follow-up measurement may involve more than one remeasurement at various points in time. Commonly used intervals include 3 months, 6 months, and 12 months posttermination. This process, which incorporates monitoring with pre- and posttreatment assessment, is what Sperry (1997) refers to as *concurrent measurement.*

Sperry treated measurement, monitoring, and management as "developmental" levels of outcomes assessment, with each level required for the next level. The higher the level of assessment that an organization employs, the more advanced it and its providers are likely to be.

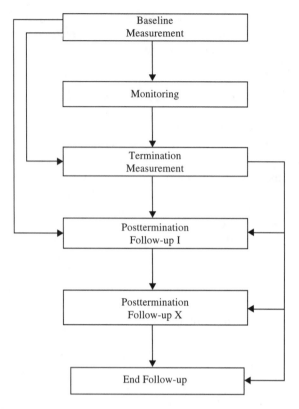

FIG. 1.3. Flowchart for an outcomes assessment process. From *Psychological Testing in the Age of Managed Behavioral Health Care* (p. 50), by M. E. Maruish, 2002, Mahwah, NJ: Lawrence Erlbaum Associates. Copyright 2002 by Lawrence Erlbaum Associates. Reproduced with permission.

### The Benefits of Outcomes Assessment

The implementation of any type of outcomes assessment initiative within an organization does not come without effort from and cost to the organization. However, if such an initiative is implemented properly, all interested parties—patients, clinicians, provider organizations, payers, and the health care industry as a whole—should find the yield from the outlay of time and money to be substantial. Cagney and Woods (1994) identified several benefits to patients, including enhanced health and quality of life, improved health care quality, and effective use of the dollars paid into benefits plans. For providers, the outcomes data can result in improved clinical skills, information related to the quality of care provided and to local practice standards, increased profitability, and decreased concerns over possible litigation.

Outside of the clinical context, benefits also can accrue to payers and MCOs. Cagney and Woods (1994) viewed the potential payer benefits as including healthier workers, improved health care quality, increased worker productivity, and reduced or contained health care costs. As for MCOs, the benefits include increased profits, information that can shape the practice patterns of their providers, and a decision-making process based on delivering quality care. Moreover, Seid et al. (2000) noted that outcomes assessment can help MCOs demonstrate accountability to a number of different stakeholders in the patient's treatment.

There is no one system or approach to the assessment of treatment outcomes for an individual patient that is appropriate for all providers of behavioral health care services. Because of the various types of outcomes one may be interested in, the reasons for assessing them, and the ways in which they may impact decisions, any successful and useful outcomes assessment approach must be customized. Customization should reflect the needs of the primary benefactor of the assessment information (i.e., patient, payer, or provider), with consideration given to the secondary stakeholders in the therapeutic endeavor. Ideally, the identified primary benefactor would be the patient. Only rarely would the patient not benefit from involvement in the outcomes assessment process.

A discussion of issues, considerations, and recommendations for the development and implementation of an outcomes assessment initiative by behavioral health care providers and organizations is presented in chapter 7 of this volume. The reader is also encouraged to seek other sources of information that specifically address that topic (e.g., Migdail et al., 1995; Ogles et al., 2002).

## PSYCHOLOGICAL ASSESSMENT AS A TOOL FOR CONTINUOUS QUALITY IMPROVEMENT

Implementing a regimen of psychological testing for planning treatment and/or assessing its outcomes has a place in all organizations where the delivery of cost-efficient, high-quality behavioral health care services is a primary goal. However, additional benefits can accrue from testing when it is incorporated within an ongoing program of service evaluation and continuous quality improvement (CQI). Simply put, CQI may be viewed as a process of continuously setting goals, measuring progress toward the achievement of those goals, and subsequently reevaluating them in light of the progress made. Depending on the findings, changes are made to the process, and evaluation occurs again. This cycle continues as ongoing process of improvement.

The CQI philosophy was initially implemented by the Japanese in rebuilding their economy after World War II. Today, many U.S. organizations have sought to balance quality with cost by implementing CQI procedures. The underlying assumption is that those organizations that can produce high-quality products or services at the lowest possible cost have the best chance of surviving and prospering in today's competitive market. Although initially implemented in a manufacturing environment, CQI has applicability to the production of goods *or* services and thus is relevant to improving the quality of behavioral and other health care services.

Berwick, Godfrey, and Roessner (1990) identified 10 basic principles of quality management. These are summarized in Table 1.3. The reader will note two important aspects of these principles. First, they have a distinct manufacturing flavor that may mask their applicability to health care and other service industries. In addition, the focus of quality management is on processes. This supports the contentions made in the earlier discussion on the role of processes in quality of care and their importance in understanding and improving outcomes. More information about CQI and quality management can be found in several sources (e.g., Berwick, 1989; Chowanec, 1994; Dertouzos, Lester, & Solow, 1989; Donabedian, 1980, 1982, 1985; Johnson, 1989; Rath & Strong Management Consultants, 2000; Scherkenback, 1987; Walton, 1986; Watson, 1993).

It is important to note that CQI activities do not constitue research as it is typically conceived (Dickey, 2002). The focus is more on improving the quality of care

TABLE 1.3
Basic Principles of Quality Management

---

1.  Productive work is accomplished through processes.
2.  Sound customer-supplier relationships are absolutely necessary for sound quality management.
3.  The main source of quality defects are problems in the process.
4.  Poor quality is costly.
5.  Understanding the variability of processes is a key to improving quality.
6.  Quality control should focus on the most vital processes.
7.  The modern approach to quality is thoroughly grounded in scientific and statistical thinking.
8.  Total employee involvement is critical.
9.  New organizational structures can help achieve quality improvement.
10. Quality management employs three basic, closely interrelated activities: quality planning, quality control, and quality improvement.

---

*Note.* From Berwick, Godfrey, & Roessner (1990), pp. 32–43.

provided by the individual clinician or organization involved in these activities, with little regard to their external generalizability or applicability. The continuous setting, measurement, and reevaluation of goals, characteristic of the CQI process, is employed by many health care organizations as part of their efforts to survive in a competitive, changing market. At least in part, the move toward CQI also reflects what InterStudy (1991) described as a "shifting from concerns about managing costs in isolation to a more comprehensive view that supplements an understanding of costs with an understanding of the quality and value of care delivered" (p. 1). InterStudy identified quality as the value that should lead all processes within a system. In the case of the health care system, the most crucial of these processes is that of patient care. Inter-Study pointed out that, with a CQI orientation, these processes must be well defined, agreed upon, and implemented unvaryingly when delivering care. Consistent with the earlier discussion, they also should provide measurable results that will subsequently lead to conclusions about how the processes might be altered to improve the results of care.

In behavioral health care, as in other arenas of health care, CQI is concerned with the services delivered to customers. Here, the "customers" may include not only the patient being treated but also the employer through whom the health care plan is offered and the third-party payer who selects or approves the service providers who can be accessed by individuals seeking care under the plan. From the discussion presented throughout this chapter, it should be evident that psychological testing can help the provider focus on delivering the most efficient and effective treatment in order to satisfy the needs of all customers. It thus can contribute greatly to the CQI effort.

Perhaps the most obvious way in which testing can augment the CQI process is through its contributions in the area of outcomes assessment. Through the repeated administration of tests to all patients at intake and later at one or more points during or after the treatment process, an organization can obtain a good sense of how effective individual clinicians, treatment programs or units, and/or the organization as a whole are in providing services to their patients. This testing might include the use of problem-oriented measures and also measures of patient satisfaction. Considered in light of other, nontest data, the results may lead to changes in service delivery goals such as the implementation of more effective problem-identification and treatment-planning procedures. For example, Newman's (1991) graphic demonstration of how data are used to support treatment decisions can be extended to indicate how various levels of depression (as measured by the original BDI) may be best served by different types of treatment (e.g., inpatient vs. outpatient).

## FUTURE DIRECTIONS

The ways in which psychologists and other behavioral health care clinicians conduct the types of psychological assessment described in this chapter are continuing to undergo dramatic changes. This should come as no surprise to anyone who spends a few minutes a day skimming the newspaper or watching the evening news. The health care revolution started gaining momentum in the early 1990s and has not slowed down since that time—and there are no indications that it will subside in the foreseeable future. From the beginning, there was no real reason to think that behavioral health care would be spared the effects of the health care revolution, and there is no good reason why it *should* have been spared. The behavioral health care industry certainly has contributed its share of waste, inefficiency, and lack of accountability to the problems that led to the revolution. Now, like other areas of health care, it is forced to "clean up its act." Although some consumers of mental health or chemical dependency services have benefited from the revolution, others have not. Regardless, the way in which health care is delivered and financed has changed, and psychologists and other behavioral health care professionals must adapt to survive in the marketplace.

Some of those involved in the delivery of psychological assessment services may wonder (with some fear and trepidation) where the revolution is leading the behavioral health care industry and, in particular, how it will affect their ability to practice. At the same time, others are eagerly awaiting the inevitable advances in technology and other resources that will come with the passage of time. What ultimately will occur is open to speculation. However, close observation of the practice of psychological assessment and the various industries that support it has led this author to arrive at a few predictions as to where the field of psychological assessment is headed and the implications for patients, clinicians, and provider organizations.

### What the Industry Is Moving Away From

One way of discussing what the field is moving toward is to first talk about what it is moving away from. In the case of psychological assessment, two trends are becoming quite clear. First, beginning in the early 1990s, the use of (and reimbursement for) psychological assessment has gradually been curtailed. In particular, the indiscriminate administration of lengthy and expensive psychological test batteries has been reduced. Payers began to demand evidence that the knowledge gained from the administration of these instruments in fact contributes to the delivery of cost-effective, efficient care to patients. There are no indications that this trend will stop.

Second, there is a move away from the lengthy, multidimensional objective instruments (e.g., MMPI) or time-consuming projective techniques (e.g., Rorschach) that previously represented the standard in practice. The type of assessment now usually authorized involves the use of brief, inexpensive, yet well-validated problem-oriented instruments. This change reflects modern behavioral health care's time-limited, problem-oriented approach to treatment. Today, the clinician can no longer afford to spend a great deal of time in assessment when the patient is only allowed a limited number of payer-authorized sessions. Thus, brief instruments will become more commonly employed for problem identification, progress monitoring, and outcomes assessment in the foreseeable future.

## Trends in Instrumentation

In addition to the move toward the use of brief, problem-oriented instruments, there is an increasing use of public domain tests, questionnaires, rating scales, and other measurement tools. In many cases, these "free-use" instruments have not been developed with the same rigor that is applied by commercial test publishers in the development of psychometrically sound instruments. Consequently, they commonly lacked the validity and reliability data that are necessary to judge their psychometric integrity.

Recently, however, there has been significant improvement in the quality and documentation of the public domain tests and licensed-use tests that are available. The CESD is an example of the former, and the SF–36/SF–12 health status measures are good examples of the latter. These and instruments such as the Behavior and Symptom Identification Scale (BASIS–32; Eisen, Grob, & Klein, 1986) and the Outcome Questionnaire (OQ–45.1; Lambert, Lunnen, Umphress, Hansen, & Burlingame,1994) have undergone psychometric scrutiny and have gained widespread acceptance as a result. Although copyrighted, many of these types of instruments may be used for an annual licensing fee. In the future, one can expect that other high-quality, useful instruments will be made available for use at a nominal cost.

As for the types of instruments administered, some changes can be expected. Accompanying the increasing focus on outcomes assessment is a recognition by patients, payers, and other stakeholders that positive changes in several areas of functioning are at least as important as change in level of symptom severity when evaluating treatment effectiveness. For example, a patient's employer is interested in the patient's ability to resume the functions of his or her job, whereas family members are concerned with the patient's ability to resume his or her role as spouse or parent. Increasingly, measurement of the patient's functioning in areas other than psychological/mental status has come to be included as part of behavioral health care outcomes systems. Probably the most visible indication of this is the incorporation of the SF–36 or similar types of instrument in various behavioral health care studies. One will likely see other public domain and commercially available nonsymptom-oriented instruments, especially those emphasizing social and occupational role functioning, in increasing numbers over the next several years.

Other types of instrumentation will also become prominent. These may well include measures of variables that support outcomes assessment and other assessment initiatives undertaken by provider organizations. What one organization or provider believes is important, or what payers determine is important for reimbursement or other purposes, will dictate what is measured. Instrumentation also may include measures that will be useful in predicting outcomes for individuals seeking specific psychotherapeutic services from those organizations.

## Trends in Technology

Looking back to the mid-1980s and early 1990s, the cutting-edge technology for psychological testing included desktop personal computers linked to an optical mark reader (OMR) as well as those "little black boxes" that facilitated the per-use sale and security of test administration, scoring, and interpretive reports for test publishers while making computer-based testing convenient for practitioners. As has always been the case, someone has applied current technological advances to the practice of psychological testing. Just as at one time the personal computer held the power of facilitating the assessment process, Internet, fax, and interactive voice response (IVR) technologies are being developed to make the assessment process easier, quicker, and more cost-effective. These technologies support the increasing popularity of *telehealth* "the use of electronic and communications technology to accomplish health care over distance" (Jerome et al., 2000, p. 407). In addition to assessment, telehealth can enable or support the provision of other clinical services, including crisis response, triage, treatment planning, care management, and even psychotherapy.

*Internet Technology.*  The Internet has changed the way we do many things, so the application of Internet technology for the administration, scoring, and interpretation of psychological instruments should not be a surprise to anyone. An Internet-based process is straightforward. The clinician accesses the Web site on which the instrumentation resides. Once the desired test is selected for administration, the patient completes the test online (the patient may also have the option of completing a paper-and-pencil version of the instrument, in which case the administrative staff would key-enter the responses on the Web site). The data are scored and entered into the Web site's database, and a report is generated and transmitted back to the clinician through the Web. Turn-around time for receiving the report can be only a matter of minutes. The archived data can later be used for any of a number of purposes, such as regularly scheduled reporting of aggregated data to the MBHO or the individual clinician. Data from repeated testing can be used for treatment monitoring and report card generation. These data can also be used for psychometric test development or other statistical purposes.

A good example of an Internet-based outcomes management system is that available through CORE, the University of Arkansas Medical Sciences Center for Outcomes Research and Effectiveness (2002). The NetOutcomes Solutions system provides a package of behavioral health outcomes tools that can benefit not only the organization in its mission but also the individual clinician in the delivery of quality services to the individual patient (see http://www.netoutcomes.net/NO_Solutions/NO_Main/NO_Home.asp?menu=nethome, retrieved November 6, 2002). At the time of this writing, the CORE was making available to MBHOs and providers its outcomes "modules" for depression, schizophrenia, substance abuse, and adolescent treatment through the NetOutcomes Solutions system, which includes capabilities for administering, scoring, and reporting baseline and multiple follow-up assessment results. The instruments can be administered online or data from completed paper forms can be key-entered into the system through the Internet.

The NetOutcomes System can generate an individual patient report with tabular and graphic summaries of the data and transmit it back to the provider almost immediately. Results from any previous assessments of the patient are presented along with the current findings, assisting in the determination of the progress the patient has made over time and enhancing the assessments' overall clinical utility. The system also enables the creation of quarterly reports generated from the aggregation of data from patients seen by a given provider or data from all patients seen by all providers in a program or multiple programs in one facility. Included in the reporting is case-mix information and disease severity indexing that enhances the meaningfulness of the information. Benchmarking also is possible through the system's database capabilities.

The advantages of an Internet-based assessment system are clear-cut. It allows for online administration of tests that include branching logic for item selection. Instruments accessible through a Web site can be easily updated and made available to users immediately. This is in contrast with disk-distributed software, where updates and fixes are sometimes long in coming. The results of an Internet-based test can be made available almost immediately. In addition, data from multiple sites can easily be aggregated and used for the purpose of normative comparisons, test validation, risk adjustment, benchmarking, generating recovery curves, and any number of other statistically based activities that require large data sets. Moreover, test administration can take place anytime, anywhere, and under secure conditions (Gershon, 2001).

There are only a few major disadvantages to an Internet-based system. The first and most obvious is that it requires access to the Internet. In this day and age, many would probably be surprised to know that, by some estimates, less than 50% of clinicians have computers in their offices. And it is probably safe to say that the percentage who have access to the Internet in their offices is even less. This percentage will increase over time. The second disadvantage has to do with data security on the Internet. Again, this will likely become less of a concern as advances in Internet security software and procedures continue to take place. Finally, as Tsacoumis (2000) noted, Internet-based testing can be costly, especially when fees for Internet access, test administration scoring and reporting services from a reputable vendor, and equipment maintenance and upgrading are taken into account. How costly it may become will vary from one provider or organization to another, depending on the particular services and vendors that are used.

*Faxback Technology.*   The development of facsimile and faxback technology that has taken place during the last decade has made available an important application for psychological testing. At the same time, it probably has dealt a huge blow to the low-volume customer base of scanning technology companies.

The process for implementing faxback technology is fairly simple. The patient completes a paper-and-pencil answer sheet for a test available through the faxback system. In a system in which several tests are available, the answer sheet for a given test contains numbers or other types of code that tell the scoring and reporting software which test is being submitted. When the answer sheet is completed, it is faxed in—usually through a toll-free number that the scoring service has provided—to the central scoring facility, where the data are entered into a database and then scored. A report is generated and faxed back to the clinician within a few minutes, depending on the number of phone lines that vendor has made available and the volume of submissions at that particular time of day. At the scoring end of the process, the whole system remains paperless. Later, the stored data can be used in the same ways as data gathered by an Internet-based system.

Like Internet-based systems, faxback systems allow for immediate access to software updates and fixes. They also can incorporate the same statistical and benchmarking capabilities. Like the computer-based testing products that are offered through most test publishers, their paper-and-pencil format allows for great flexibility as regards the time and place of administration. In addition to the types of security issues that come with Internet-based testing, the biggest disadvantage of or problem with faxback testing centers around test identification and the linkage of data obtained from an individual patient. Separate answer sheets are required for each instrument that can be scored through the faxback system. The system must also be able to link data from multiple tests or multiple administrations of the same test to a single patient. At first glance, this may not seem to be a challenging task for 21st-century technology. But there are issues related to the need to maintain confidentiality while ensuring the accuracy of patient identifiers that link data over a single episode or multiple episodes of care, and these issues may be difficult to resolve. If data cannot be linked, then they will be limited in their usefulness. Overcoming this challenge can therefore be the key to success for any faxback system.

An example of how faxback technology can be implemented for screening purposes can be found in a project described by Maruish, Bershadsky, and Goldstein (1998) and Goldstein, Bershadsky, and Maruish (2000). In this project, the SA–45 and SF–12 were scored and reported in a primary care practice through the use of faxback technology. The project had several interesting results, not the least of which were the barriers to successful implementation that arose during its course.

*IVR Technology.*   One of the more recent applications of new technology to the administration, scoring, and reporting of results of psychological tests can be found in the use of IVR systems. In essence, IVR test administration is similar to the automated online administration of psychological instruments. However, as Kobak, Greist, Jefferson and Katzelnick (1996) pointed out, the advantages of IVR over computer-based testing include the typical patient's comfort with the technology (i.e., touch-tone telephone), the easy availability of that technology, and the ability of the patient to complete the test outside of the practitioner's office at any time of the day or week.

We are all familiar with IVR technology. Anyone calls to order products, address billing problems, find out a checking account balance, or conduct other phone-enabled activities will probably be asked to provide information to an automated system in order to facilitate the meeting of the request. This is IVR, and its applicability to test administration, data processing, and data storage is simple. What may not be obvious is how the data can be accessed and used.

An example of the use of an IVR system for data gathering and reporting for the purpose of improving the quality of care can be seen in a project that was conducted by one MBHO. Patients were asked to take an intake assessment test at the time of treatment initiation. The instrument used was one that was designed by the MBHO staff and its external project partner to assess the key aspects of functioning identified by Howard and his colleagues: well-being, symptomatology, and social and work functioning. The CAGE–AI (Brown & Rounds, 1995) was also included as part of the instrument. All items were either taken from public domain instruments or were developed in-house. When calling in to the MBHO, patients were either connected directly to the IVR system by the intake coordinator or were given a toll-free number and patient code to access the system at their convenience later on (the system was available 7 days a week, 24 hours a day).

After a patient completed the questionnaire, the data were processed, and a report was generated and either faxed or mailed to the patient's care provider. This report could give the clinician a head start on the assessment of the patient's problems and needs, sometimes before the first therapy session. A copy of the report was also automatically faxed to the patient's care manager. This was intended to assist the care manager in making utilization and other care-related decisions.

Six weeks after the initial assessment, the patient was sent a notice that it was time for him or her to complete the assessment instrument again. The notice contained the dial-up number and patient-specific code so that the patient could access the system once again. The patient code also tied the patient's data from the current follow-up administration to those of the previous administration of the IVR instrument. Using the same process, the patient was reassessed again 6 months after the initial assessment. The outcomes data from this assessment could be used for predictive modeling, for the generation of recovery curves, or simply as outcomes information to demonstrate that the standards of accreditation agencies (e.g., JCAHO, NCQA) were being met.

IVR technology's utility for test delivery has been reported in a number of published studies. Over the years, Kobak and his colleagues have conducted several studies on the use of IVR technology for administration of various types of psychological instruments. In their review of 10 studies that included the administration of both clinician- and IVR-administered versions of the Hamilton Depression Rating Scale (HDRS; Kobak, Reynolds, Rosenfeld, & Greist, 1990), Kobak, Mundt, Greist, Katzelnick, and Jefferson (2000) found the IVR version to generally yield data with comparable or better psychometric properties than those yielded by the clinician version. The combined data across all 10 studies yielded an overall correlation of .81 ($p < .001$) between the scores resulting from the administration of the HRSD in both formats. In another study, Kobak, Taylor, Dottl, Greist, Jefferson, Burroughs, Katzelnick, et al. (1997) found support for the overall validity and use of both IVR-administered and desktop computer–administered versions of the PRIME–MD (Spitzer et al., 1994) as instruments for gathering information from behavioral health patients. Here, the results from the clinician-administered SCID–IV (First et al., 1995) were used as the diagnostic gold-standard criteria.

Moreover, in their HRDS and other studies, Kobak et al. (2000) reported that up to 90% of patients being assessed by IVR systems reported moderate to very strong acceptance in regard to clarity and ease of use. These results, in turn, are consistent with Kobak, Taylor, Dottl, Greist, Jefferson, Burroughs, Katzelnick, et al.'s (1997) findings in the PRIME–MD study. Findings from these and other studies led Kobak, Taylor, Dottl, Greist, Jefferson, Burroughs, Mantle, et al. (1997) to observe that "several decades of research have shown that people often report more problems of greater severity to computer applications than to clinicians, especially when such problems concern personally sensitive topics" (p. 152). Millard and Carver (1999) arrived at a similar conclusion in their comparison of results obtained from the administration of the SF–12 via the IVR and live telephone interview formats.

IVR technology is attractive from many standpoints. It requires no extra equipment beyond a touch-tone telephone for administration. It is available for use anytime. The patient's reading ability is not a concern, although oral comprehension levels need to be taken into account when determining which instruments are appropriate for administration via the IVR (or any other audio) administration format. As with faxback- and Internet-based assessment, branching logic can be used in the administration of the instrument. Updates and fixes are easily implemented systemwide. Also, the ability to store data allows for comparison of results from previous testings, aggregation of data for statistical analyses, and all the other data analytic capabilities available through faxback- and Internet-based assessment.

Moreover, Kobak, et al. (2000) cited the following methodological benefits of IVR:

1. Completely standardized, structured assessment,
2. Elimination of inter-rater unreliability,
3. Remote patient evaluation 24 hours a day, 7 days a week,
4. Thorough and complete error checking of data at the time of collection,

5. Elimination of possible data transcription or scoring errors,
6. Immediate real-time access to analyzable data,
7. Patient-determined pace of assessment,
8. Increased honesty on sensitive questions, and
9. Independent, reliable assessments that cannot be influenced by exogenous information, such as functional unblinding of human raters. (p. 153)

As for the downside of IVR assessment, probably the biggest issue is that in many instances the patient must be the one to initiate the testing. Thus, control of the test administration is relinquished to a party that may not be interested in or otherwise amenable to psychological testing. With less cooperative patients, costly follow-up efforts may be required to encourage full participation in the process.

### Psychological Testing in Primary Care Settings

The U.S. health care industry has undergone dramatic changes during the past 2 decades. What once was a loosely monitored system of care with skyrocketing costs has turned into a system that has tight controls and provides only limited services and choice of providers. The efforts to keep costs down have been particularly obstructive for those seeking help for mental health and substance abuse problems. For these and other reasons (e.g., the stigma associated with mental illness), a considerable number of individuals with behavioral health problems have turned to their primary care providers (PCPs) for help—help that is often not provided or does not adequately meet the patients' needs.

Fortunately, the winds of change are now blowing in favor of the types of reform advocated by behavioral health care proponents. The enactment of the Mental Health Parity Act of 1996, the industry's realization of the benefits of one-stop health care, NCQA and JCAHO accreditation standards, the growing belief that potential long-term health care cost savings can result from the appropriate treatment of behavioral disorders, and other circumstances bode well for greater access to more and/or better behavioral health care services. They also serve as the impetus for a more pervasive integration of primary and behavioral health care services throughout the United States. Goldstein et al. (2000) summarized the current state of these affairs by noting the following:

1. A large portion of patients who seek services from primary care providers experience significant psychological distress or symptomatology.
2. Primary care providers, in general, are not sufficiently skilled to identify or provide appropriate treatment to these patients.
3. Consequently, patients with behavioral health problems consume a large portion of the available primary care resources.
4. Identifying and adequately treating the behavioral health problems of primary care patients in the primary care setting has been shown to result in significant cost savings.
5. Consultation, liaison, and educational services offered by behavioral health professionals can be instrumental in ensuring the success of these intervention efforts in the primary care setting. (p. 735)

The alliance of primary and behavioral health care providers is not a new phenomenon; it has existed in one form or another for decades. The value the behavioral health care professional brings to the primary care setting—either as an off-site con-sultant or as an on-site collaborative member of the primary care team—is attested to daily in primary care practices throughout the country. Moreover, there is every indication that the picture of interdisciplinary cooperation in the primary care setting will become more commonplace as the move to reintegrate behavioral and primary care gains momentum (Cummings, 2000; Kent & Hersen, 2000; Kiesler, 2000). The extent to which these two services will become integrated will, of course, depend on any number of factors (e.g., reimbursement structures, funding, available office space, staff interest and motivation) that will vary from setting to setting.

Psychologists and other trained behavioral health care professionals have unique contributions to make toward fully integrating their services in primary care and other health care settings. Levant et al. (2001) suggested that

> psychologists' core skills in assessment and treatment can be integrated into roles in supervision, administration, program design, program evaluation, and research. As a consequence, psychologists are uniquely positioned to assume a greater role in the man-agement of health and disease. . . . Further, psychologists' strong research background—a unique qualification among health care professionals—prepares psychologists to play key roles in the design, implementation, and evaluation of prevention and intervention programs at the individual, system, and community level. (p. 80)

Levant et al.'s opinion is consistent with that expressed by Knapp and Keller (2001). It is also consistent with this author's opinion that one of the most significant con-tributions that psychologists can make to the integration of medical and behavioral health care is through the establishment and use of psychological testing services. Information obtained from psychometrically sound self-report tests and other report instruments (e.g., clinician rating scales, parent-completed instruments) can assist the primary care provider in several types of clinical decision-making activities, including screening for the presence of mental health or substance abuse problems, planning a course of treatment, and monitoring patient progress. Testing can also be used to measure the outcome of treatment that has been provided to patients with mental health or substance abuse problems, thus assisting in determining what works for whom.

There are a number of psychological test instruments that are appropriate for use in primary care settings (see Maruish, 2000). Some were originally developed for use in behavioral health settings but have been found useful in primary and other medical care practices (e.g., SCL–90–R); others were designed specifically for use in primary care settings (e.g., PRIME–MD). In all, the psychologist has a large array of tools that are psychometrically sound, efficient, economical, easy to use, and provide the type of information needed to help complete the various measurement tasks that may be required in a busy primary care practice.

The degree to which psychological testing services can become part of a package of primary behavioral health care services will depend on the value they bring to the integrated service delivery system. The key to the success of this endeavor lies in the psychologists' ability to demonstrate to primary care providers that psychological testing can be a cost-effective means of helping to serve the needs of a significant portion of their patient population. But as is the case with any of the new oppor-tunities presented in this era of managed care, incorporating psychological testing into the service delivery system will depend on the psychologists' receiving relevant training—in this case, training in working in primary care or other health care settings

(Levant et al., 2001) and surviving in a service delivery culture that most psychologists will find quite different than that found in behavioral health care.

## A CAVEAT

Before concluding this chapter, I want to address one important issue: the money available for psychological testing services. It is difficult to imagine that any practice, facility, or MBHO would not find value in at least one or two of the previously described testing applications. The question is whether there are budgeted funds for such applications. These might include funds for testing materials, the reimbursement of network providers or other third-party contractors (e.g., disease management companies) for the testing they perform, and/or salary compensation for an in-house staff position responsible for conducting or overseeing psychological testing. Regardless, it is highly unlikely that any MBHO is going to spend money on any service that is not considered essential for the proper care of patients *unless that service can demonstrate either short-term or long-term cost savings or cost offset*. The current restrictions on authorizing assessment in many MBHOs are a reflection of this fact.

All of the applications of psychological testing that were discussed in the previous sections of this chapter may seem obviously beneficial to both patients and providers—if one is looking at the issue from the perspective of a clinician. Frequently, academic and internship training, in which cost considerations typically take a back seat to teaching the art and skills of the profession, has influenced this perspective. In some instances, even lack of empirical support for the validity and/or usefulness of a particular test, technique, or application has been overlooked for the sake of teaching student clinicians what the instructor feels has been useful for him or her in the past, or at least what he or she feels every student should know. And unfortunately, the students thus taught commonly propagate this flawed line of thinking during their professional careers, perhaps as teachers or supervisors themselves. As Hunsley (2002) noted:

> As with so many aspects of psychological practice, psychologists lack scientific evidence that bears on assessment's value. Psychologists must build a science of assessment, not just a body of research on tests and test subscales. If psychological assessment is to be promoted on the basis of science, it must be on the basis of relevant studies of assessment, not on extrapolations from the literature on test validity. (p. 140)

Invalid and otherwise useless instruments and wasteful procedures (e.g., testing every patient seeking services) are among the many contributors to the health care crisis. These are just the types of things that MBHOs and the health care industry are now trying to control. Thus, MBHOs tend to view things from the perspective of *demonstrated utility and value*. As Dorfman (2000) succinctly put it:

> Until the value of testing can be shown unequivocally, support and reimbursement for evaluation and testing will be uneven with [MBHOs] and frequently based on the psychologist's personal credibility and competence in justifying such expenditures. In the interim, it is incumbent on each psychologist to be aware of the goals and philosophy of the managed care industry, and to understand how the use of evaluation and testing with his or her patients not only is consistent with, but also helps to further, those goals. To the extent that these procedures can be shown to enhance the value of the managed care

product by ensuring quality of care and positive treatment outcome, to reduce treatment length without sacrificing that quality, to prevent overutilization of limited resources and services, and to enhance patient satisfaction with care, psychologists can expect to gain greater support for their unique testing skill from the managed care company. (pp. 24–25)

One way to win support for psychological assessment is to use it in the most cost-effective ways. Groth-Marnat (1999b) provided a set of rationally derived guidelines for demonstrating the financial efficacy of clinical assessment to MBHOs. He recommended that clinicians do the following:

1. Focus on those domains that are most relevant for treatment planning and optimizing patient outcomes. In particular, clinicians should address referral questions and relevant diagnostic issues and patient characteristics.
2. Use formal assessment to reduce legal risk to both themselves and the MBHO, especially in situations, for example, where patients present a danger to themselves or others or where complex differential diagnostic issues are involved.
3. Assess those conditions most likely to result in the greatest cost savings. Being able to identify and refer somatizing patients to appropriate treatment, for example, could result in tremendous cost savings.
4. Use computer-assisted assessment in cases where it will result in time savings. Time savings will lead to cost savings.
5. Along the same line of reasoning, use instruments that require less clinician time. (Many such instruments are discussed in this work.)
6. Provide a close linkage between assessment, feedback, and intervention. Finn's (1996b) therapeutic assessment procedure is a good example.
7. Provide a close linkage between assessment undertaken at the time of treatment initiation and assessment conducted for the purpose of treatment monitoring and outcomes measurement.

Note that Groth-Marnot's guidelines are consistent with the contents of this and other chapters of this work. Many are also consistent with the recommendations provided by Belar (1997), although Belar stressed in addition the importance of being able to empirically demonstrate the value-added aspect of testing, of considering the potential negative side effects of testing, of becoming involved in the development of health policy, and of improving one's research skills.

Ficken (1995), in his discussion of the role of assessment in an MBHO environment, concluded that the difficulties clinicians are experiencing in demonstrating the utility of psychological assessment to payers lie in the fact the instruments and objectives of traditional psychological assessment do not fit the needs of managed care. The solution to the problem appears simple:

The underlying objectives of testing must be aligned with the values and processes of [MBHOs]. In short, this means identifying decision points in managed care processes that could be improved with objective, standardized data. There are two avenues in which these can be pursued: through facilitation/objectification of clinical-decision processes and through outcome assessment. (p. 12)

Even if they convince an MBHO or other third-party payer of the utility of a particular test or a specific application of a program of testing (e.g., screening all new patients for substance abuse), clinicians still can administer a specific test or initiate a program of testing for their patients. The difference, of course, is that they may not be reimbursed for their efforts. Some clinicians might not offer any clinical service unless it is reimbursed. Others may feel that what they want to do is important for the quality of care and will go ahead and test patients without any guarantee of reimbursement. It is especially for these individuals that I have drawn attention to Groth-Marnat's (1999b) guidelines. For this same reason, as editor I have included discussion of no-cost or low-cost instrumentation in this work. The clinician may not be reimbursed for his or her time, but at least implementation of testing will not necessarily involve large outlay of money for the instruments and associated materials required to do what the clinician thinks is best for the patient.

## SUMMARY

The health care revolution has brought mixed blessings to those in the behavioral health care professions. It has limited reimbursement for services rendered and has forced many to change the way they practice their profession. At the same time, it has led to revelations about the cost savings that may accrue from the treatment of mental health and substance abuse disorders. This has been the bright spot in an otherwise bleak picture for some behavioral health care professionals. But for psychologists and others trained in psychological assessment procedures, the picture appears to be somewhat different. They now have additional opportunities to contribute to the positive aspects of the revolution and to gain from the "new order" it has imposed. By virtue of their training, they are uniquely qualified to support or otherwise facilitate multiple aspects of the therapeutic process.

Earlier in this chapter, some of the types of psychological assessment instruments commonly used in therapeutic endeavors were identified. These included both brief and lengthy instruments for symptom identification as well as for assessing general health status, quality of life, role functioning, and patient satisfaction. Also identified were different sets of general criteria that can be applied when selecting instruments for use in therapeutic settings. The main purpose of this chapter, however, was to present an overview of the various ways in which psychological assessment can be used to facilitate the selection, implementation, and evaluation of appropriate therapeutic interventions in behavioral health care settings.

Generally, psychological assessment can assist the clinician in three important clinical activities: clinical decision-making, treatment (when used as a specific therapeutic technique), and treatment outcomes evaluation. As the first of these, three important clinical decision-making functions can be facilitated by psychological assessment: screening, treatment planning, and treatment monitoring. The first can be served by the use of brief instruments designed to identify, within a high degree of certainty, the likely presence (or absence) of a particular condition or characteristic. Here, the diagnostic efficiency of the instrument used (as indicated by its PPP and NPP) is of great importance. Through their ability to identify and clarify problems as well as other important treatment-relevant patient characteristics, psychological assessment instruments also can be of great assistance in planning treatment. In addition, treatment monitoring, or the periodic evaluation of the patient's progress during the course of treatment, can be served well by the application psychological assessment instruments.

Second, assessment may be used as part of a therapeutic technique. In what Finn terms "therapeutic assessment," situations in which patients are evaluated via psychological testing are used as opportunities for the process itself to serve as a therapeutic

intervention. This is accomplished through involving the patient as an active participant in the assessment process, not just as the object of the assessment.

Third, psychological assessment can be employed as the primary mechanism by
which the outcomes or results of treatment can be measured. However, use of assessment for this purpose is not a cut-and-dry matter. Issues pertaining to what to
measure, how to measure, and when to measure require considerable thought prior
to undertaking a plan to assess outcomes. Guidelines for resolving these issues and
determining if the measured outcomes of treatment are indeed "significant" are presented in chapter 7. The role that outcomes assessment can have in an organization's
CQI efforts was discussed in the current chapter.

In the final section of the chapter, some thoughts were shared about where psychological assessment likely is headed. Ogles et al. (2002) observed that "the field has
gradually moved from a reliance on global therapist ratings of improvement to the
use of more specific, multidimensional outcome instruments that are quantified from
a variety of viewpoints, including those of the patient, outside observers, therapists,
family members, and so on" (p. 10). In general, what is foreseen is the appearance of
higher quality, more affordable instrumentation designed to assess various aspects of
a patient's functioning.

There is no doubt that the practice of psychological assessment has been dealt a
blow within recent years. However, as this chapter indicates, clinicians trained in
the use of psychological tests and related instrumentation have the skills to take these
powerful tools, apply them in ways that will benefit those suffering from mental health
and substance abuse problems, and demonstrate their value to patients and payers.
Seid et al. (2000) concisely summarized the current situation and its opportunities,
particularly with regard to outcomes assessment:

> Providers are increasingly pressured to document the quality of their care to healthcare
> payers and purchasers. . . . Health care decision makers able to harness health outcomes
> measurement technology will have a powerful tool to evaluate the effectiveness of their
> interventions and to drive performance improvement projects.
>
> The marketplace also demands provider accountability. The increased competition
> among managed care companies has forced providers to [increasingly] distinguish them-
> selves from the marketplace at large . . . on the basis of value, a function of both cost and
> quality. Patient-based health outcomes are means by which providers can document the
> quality and thus the value they provide to consumers of their health care services (Peskin,
> 1995). Providers with the technology to measure and document with precision patient-
> based outcomes that are important to consumers of their health care services will survive
> and thrive in a highly competitive health care marketplace. (p. 21)

Only time will tell whether providers will be successful in demonstrating the value of
psychological assessment. Meanwhile, the field will continue to make advancements
that will facilitate and improve the quality of its work.

## A FINAL WORD

As suggested, training in psychological testing should provide practitioners with an
edge in the evolving revolution in behavioral health service delivery. Maximizing their
ability to use the "tools of the trade" to facilitate problem identification, subsequent
planning and monitoring of appropriate treatment, and measuring and documenting the effectiveness of their efforts can only aid clinicians in their quest for optimal

efficiency and quality in service. It is hoped that the information and guidance provided by the many distinguished contributors to the third edition of this work will assist practicing psychologists, psychologists in training, and other behavioral health care providers in maximizing the resources available to them and thus prospering in the emerging new health care arena.

This is a time of uncertainty and perhaps some anxiety. It is also a time of great opportunity. How one deals with the current state of affairs is a matter of personal and professional choice.

## ACKNOWLEDGMENTS

Portions of this chapter were adapted with permission from the following sources:

M. E. Maruish, "Therapeutic Assessment: Linking Assessment and Treatment," in M. Hersen & A. Bellack (Series Eds.) and C. R. Reynolds (Vol. Ed.), *Comprehensive Clinical Psychology, Volume 4. Assessment* (in press), with permission from Elsevier Science LTD., The Boulevard, Langford Lane, Kidlington OX5 1GB, UK.

M. E. Maruish, *Psychological Testing in the Age of Managed Behavioral Health Care* (2002), with permission of Lawrence Erlbaum Associates, Mahwah, NJ.

## REFERENCES

Advances in outcomes measurement. (2001, 4th Quarter). *Data Points, 4*, 1.

Ambrose, P. A. (1997). Challenges for mental health service providers: The perspective of managed care organizations. In J. N. Butcher (Ed.), *Personality assessment in managed health care* (pp. 61–72). New York: Oxford University Press.

American Psychiatric Association. (1994). *Diagnostic and statistical manual of mental disorders* (4th ed.). Washington, DC: Author.

American Psychological Association. (1992). *Ethical principles.* Washington, DC: Author.

American Psychological Association. (1996). *The costs of failing to provide appropriate mental health care.* Washington, DC: Author.

American Psychological Association. (2002). Ethical principles of psychologists and code of conduct. *American Psychologist, 57*, 1060–1073.

Anderson, E. M., & Lambert, M. J. (2001). A survival analysis of clinically significant change in outpatient psychotherapy. *Journal of Clinical Psychology, 57*, 875–888.

Andrews, G., Peters, L., & Teesson, M. (1994). *The measurement of consumer outcomes in mental health.* Canberra, Australia: Australian Government Publishing Service.

Appelbaum, S. A. (1990). The relationship between assessment and psychotherapy. *Journal of Personality Assessment, 54*, 791–801.

Attkisson, C. C., & Greenfield, T. K. (1996). The Client Satisfaction Questionnaire (CSQ) scales and the Service Satisfaction Scale–30 (SSS–30). In L. I. Sederer & B. Dickey (Eds.), *Outcomes assessment in clinical practice* (pp. 120–127). Baltimore: Williams & Wilkins.

Attkisson, C. C., & Zwick, R. (1982). The Client Satisfaction Questionnaire: Psychometric properties and correlations with service utilization and psychotherapy outcome. *Evaluation and Program Planning, 6*, 233–237.

Azocar, F., Cuffel, B., McCabe, J., McCulloch, J., Tani, S., Maruish, M., et al. (2003). *Monitoring patient progress and its relation to treatment outcomes in managed behavioral heal thcare organizations.* Manuscript submitted for publication.

Bartlett, J. (1997). Treatment outcomes: The psychiatrist's and health care executive's perspectives. *Psychiatric Annals, 27*, 100–103.

Beck, A. T., Steer, R. A., & Brown, G. K. (1996). *Manual for the Beck Depression Inventory–II.* San Antonio, TX: The Psychological Corporation.

Belar, C. D. (1997). Psychological assessment in capitated care. In J. N. Butcher (Ed.), *Personality assessment in managed health care: Using the MMPI–2 in treatment planning* (pp. 73–80). New York: Oxford University Press.

Belter, R. W., & Piotrowski, C. (2001). Current status of doctoral-level training in psychological testing. *Journal of Clinical Psychology, 57,* 717–726.

Berwick, D. M. (1989). Sounding board: Continuous improvement as an ideal in health care. *New England Journal of Medicine, 320,* 53–56.

Berwick, D. M., Godfrey, A. B., & Roessner, J. (1990). *Curing health care: New strategies for quality improvement.* San Francisco: Jossey-Bass.

Beutler, L. E., & Clarkin, J. (1990). *Systematic treatment selection: Toward targeted therapeutic interventions.* New York: Brunner/Mazel.

Beutler, L. E., Goodrich, G., Fisher, D., & Williams, R. E. (1999). Use of psychological tests/instruments for treatment planning. In M. E. Maruish (Ed.), *The use of psychological testing for treatment planning and outcomes assessment* (2nd ed., pp. 81–113). Mahwah, NJ: Lawrence Erlbaum Associates.

Beutler, L. E., Kim, E. J., Davison, E., Karno, M., & Fisher, D. (1996). Research contributions to improving managed health care outcomes. *Psychotherapy, 33,* 197–206.

Beutler, L. E., & Williams, O. B. (1995). Computer applications for the selection of optimal psychosocial therapeutic interventions. *Behavioral Health care Tomorrow, 4,* 66–68.

Brill, P. L., & Sperry, L. (1997). Using treatment outcomes information in clinical practice. *Psychiatric Annals, 27,* 124–126.

Brook, R. H., McGlynn, E. A., & Cleary, P. D. (1996). Quality of health care: Part 2. Measuring quality of care. *New England Journal of Medicine, 335,* 966–970.

Brown resigns drug post. (1995, December 22). *Substance Abuse Findings News,* p. 7.

Brown, R. L., & Rounds, L. A. (1995). Conjoint screening questionnaires for alcohol and other drug abuse: Criterion validity in a primary care practice. *Wisconsin Medical Journal, 94,* 135–140.

Burlingame, G. M., Lambert, M. J., Reisinger, C. W., Neff, W. M., & Mosier, J. (1995). Pragmatics of tracking mental health outcomes in a managed care setting. *Journal of Mental Health Administration, 22,* 226–236.

Burnam, M. A. (1996). Measuring outcomes of care for substance use and mental disorders. In D. M. Steinwachs, L. M. Flynn, G. S. Norquist, and E. A. Skinner (Eds.), *Using client outcomes information to improve mental health and substance abuse treatment* (pp. 3–17). San Francisco: Jossey-Bass.

Busch, A. B., & Sederer, L. I. (2000). Assessing outcomes in psychiatric practice: Guidelines, challenges, and solutions. *Harvard Review of Psychiatry, 8,* 323–327.

Butcher, J. N. (1990). *The MMPI–2 in psychological treatment.* New York: Oxford University Press.

Butcher, J. N., Dahlstrom, W. G., Graham, J. R., Tellegen, A. M., & Kaemmer, B. (1989). *MMPI–2: Manual for administration and scoring.* Minneapolis, MN: University of Minnesota Press.

Butcher, J. N., Graham, J. R., Williams, C. L., & Ben-Porath, Y. (1989). *Development and use of the MMPI–2 content scales.* Minneapolis, MN: University of Minnesota Press.

Cagney, T., & Woods, D. R. (1994). Why focus on outcomes data? *Behavioral Health care Tomorrow, 3,* 65–67.

Callaghan, G. M. (2001). Demonstrating clinical effectiveness for individual practitioners and clinics. *Professional Psychology, 32,* 289–297.

Camara, W., Nathan, J., & Puente, A. (1998). *Psychological test usage in professional psychology: Report to the APA Practice and Science Directorates.* Washington, DC: American Psychological Association.

Camara, W. J., Nathan, J. S., & Puente, A. E. (2000). Psychological test usage: Implications in professional psychology. *Professional Psychology: Research and Practice, 31,* 141–154.

Cashel, M. L. (2002). Child and adolescent psychological assessment: Current clinical practices and the impact of managed care. *Professional Psychology: Research and Practice, 33,* 446–453.

Centers for Medicare and Medicaid Services. (2002). *National health expenditures projections: 2001–2011.* Retrieved October 8, 2002, from http://cms.hhs.gov/statistics/nhe/projections-2001/highlights.asp

Chowanec, G. D. (1994). Continuous quality improvement: Conceptual foundations and application to mental health care. *Hospital and Community Psychiatry, 45,* 789–793.

Ciarlo, J. A., Brown, T. R., Edwards, D. W., Kiresuk, T. J., & Newman, F. L. (1986). *Assessing mental health treatment outcomes measurement techniques* (DHHS Pub. No. [ADM], 86-1301). Washington, DC: U.S. Government Printing Office.

Cone, J. D. (2001). *Evaluating outcomes: Empirical tools for effective practice.* Washington, DC: American Psychological Association.

Cummings, N. A. (2000). A psychologist's proactive guide to managed care: New roles and opportunities. In A. J. Kent & M. Hersen (Eds.), *A psychologist's proactive guide to managed mental health care* (pp. 141–161). Mahwah, NJ: Lawrence Erlbaum Associates.

Cushman, P., & Gilford, P. (2000). Will managed care change our way of being? *American Psychologist, 55,* 985–996.

Daniels, J. A., Alva, L. A., & Olivares, S. (2001, August). *Graduate training for managed care: A national survey of psychology and social work programs.* Poster session presented at the annual meeting of the American Psychological Association, San Francisco.

Davis, K., Collins, K. S., & Morris, C. (1994). Managed care: Promise and concerns. *Health Affairs (Millwood), 13,* 179–185.

Derogatis, L. R. (1983). *SCL-90-R: Administration, scoring and procedures manual-II.* Baltimore: Clinical Psychometric Research.

Derogatis, L. R. (1992). *BSI: Administration, scoring and procedures manual–II.* Baltimore: Clinical Psychometric Research.

Derogatis, L. R., Lipman, R. S., & Covi, L. (1973). SCL–90: An outpatient psychiatric rating scale: Preliminary report. *Psychopharmacology Bulletin, 9,* 13–27.

Derogatis, L. R., & Lynn, L. L. (1999). Psychological tests in screening for psychiatric disorder. In M. E. Maruish (Ed.), *The use of psychological testing for treatment planning and outcomes assessment* (2nd ed., pp. 41–79). Mahwah, NJ: Lawrence Erlbaum Associates.

Dertouzos, M. L., Lester, R. K., & Solow, R. M. (1989). *Made in America: Regaining the productive edge.* Cambridge, MA: MIT Press.

Dickey, B. (2002). Outcome measurement from research to clinical practice. In W. W. IsHak, T. Burt, & L. I. Sederer (Eds.), *Outcome measurement in psychiatry: A critical review* (pp. 15–22). Washington, DC: American Psychiatric Publishing.

Dickey, B., & Wagenaar, H. (1996). Evaluating health status. In L. I. Sederer & B. Dickey (Eds.), *Outcomes assessment in clinical practice* (pp. 55–60). Baltimore: Williams & Wilkins.

Donabedian, A. (1980). *Explorations in quality assessment and monitoring: Vol. 1. The definition of quality and approaches to its assessment.* Ann Arbor, MI: Health Administration Press.

Donabedian, A. (1982). *Explorations in quality assessment and monitoring: Vol. 2. The criteria and standards of quality.* Ann Arbor, MI: Health Administration Press.

Donabedian, A. (1985). *Explorations in quality assessment and monitoring: Vol. 3. The methods and findings in quality assessment: An illustrated analysis.* Ann Arbor, MI: Health Administration Press.

Dorfman, W. I. (2000). Psychological assessment and testing under managed care. In A. J. Kent & M. Hersen (Eds.), *A psychologist's proactive guide to managed mental health care* (pp. 23–39). Mahwah, NJ: Lawrence Erlbaum Associates.

Dorwart, R. A. (1996). Outcomes management strategies in mental health: Applications and implications for clinical practice. In L. I. Sederer & B. Dickey (Eds.), *Outcomes assessment in clinical practice* (pp. 45–54). Baltimore: Williams & Wilkins.

Dowd, E. T., Milne, C. R., & Wise, S. L. (1991). The Therapeutic Reactance Scale: A measure of psychological reactance. *Journal of Counseling and Development, 69,* 541–545.

*ECHO survey: Homepage.* (n.d.). Retrieved April 1, 2003, from http://www.hcp.med.harvard.edu/echo/home.html

Eisen, S. V., & Dickey, B. (1996). Mental health outcome assessment: The new agenda. *Psychotherapy, 33,* 181–189.

Eisen, S. V., Grob, M. C., & Klein, A. A. (1986). BASIS: The development of a self-report measure for psychiatric inpatient evaluation. *The Psychiatric Hospital, 17,* 165–171.

Eisman, E. J., Dies, R. R., Finn, S. E., Eyde, L. D., Kay, G. G., Kubiszyn, T. W., et al. (1998). *Problems and limitations in the use of psychological assessment in contemporary health care delivery: Report to the Board of Professional Affairs, Psychological Assessment Work Group, Part II.* Washington, DC: American Psychological Association.

Eisman, E. J., Dies, R. R., Finn, S. E., Eyde, L. D., Kay, G. G., Kubiszyn, T. W., et al. (2000). Problems and limitations in using of psychological assessment in contemporary health care delivery. *Professional Psychology: Research and Practice, 31,* 131–140.

Erdberg, P. (1979). A systematic approach to providing feedback from the MMPI. In C. S. Newmark (Ed.), *MMPI clinical and research trends* (pp. 328–342). New York: Praeger.

Fee, practice and managed care survey. (January, 1995). *Psychotherapy Finances, 21.*

Ficken, J. (1995). New directions for psychological testing. *Behavioral Health Management, 20,* 12–14.

Finn, S. E. (1996a). Assessment feedback integrating MMPI–2 and Rorschach findings. *Journal of Personality Assessment, 67,* 543–557.

Finn, S. E. (1996b). *Manual for using the MMPI–2 as a therapeutic intervention.* Minneapolis, MN: University of Minnesota Press.

Finn, S. E. (2003). 2003 Presidential address: SPA Board calls for research on utility of clinical personality assessment. *SPA Exchange, 15,* 1–2.

Finn, S. E., & Butcher, J. N. (1991). Clinical objective personality assessment. In M. Hersen, A. E. Kazdin, & A. S. Bellack (Eds.), *The clinical psychology handbook* (2nd ed., pp. 362–373). New York: Pergamon.

Finn, S. E., & Martin, H. (1997). Therapeutic assessment with the MMPI–2 in managed health care. In J. N. Butcher (Ed.), *Objective personality assessment in managed health care: A practitioner's guide* (pp. 131–152). Minneapolis, MN: University of Minnesota Press.

Finn, S. E., & Tonsager, M. E. (1992). Therapeutic effects of providing MMPI–2 test feedback to college students awaiting therapy. *Psychological Assessment, 4,* 278–287.

First, M. B., Spitzer, R. L., Gibbon, M., & Williams, J. B. W. (1995). *Structured Clinical Interview for DSM-IV Axis I Disorders–Patient Edition (SCID-I/P, Version 2.0).* New York: New York State Psychiatric Institute.

Fischer, C. T. (1985). *Individualizing psychological assessment.* Monterey, CA: Brooks/Cole.

Friedman, R., Sobel, D., Myers, P., Caudill, M., & Benson, H. (1995). Behavioral medicine, clinical health psychology, and cost offset. *Health Psychology, 14,* 509–518.

Future targets behavioral health field's quest for survival. (1996, April 18). *Mental Health Weekly,* pp. 1–2.

Gershon, R. C. (2001, August). The future of computerized adaptive test for psychological assessment. In L. A. Frumkin (Chair), *Internet-based assessment: State of the art in testing.* Symposium conducted at the meeting of the American Psychological Association, San Francisco.

Goldstein, L., Bershadsky, B., & Maruish, M. E. (2000). The INOVA primary behavioral health care pilot project. In M. E. Maruish (Ed.), *Handbook of psychological testing in primary care settings* (pp. 735–760). Mahwah, NJ: Lawrence Erlbaum Associates.

Gough, H. G., McClosky, H., & Meehl, P. E. (1951). A personality scale for dominance. *Journal of Abnormal and Social Psychology, 46,* 360–366.

Gough, H. G., McClosky, H., & Meehl, P. E. (1952). A personality scale for social responsibility. *Journal of Abnormal and Social Psychology, 47,* 73–80.

Greene, R. L. (1991). *The MMPI–2/MMPI: An interpretive manual.* Boston: Allyn & Bacon.

Greene, R. L., & Clopton, J. R. (1999). Minnesota Multiphasic Personality Inventory–2 (MMPI-2). In M. E. Maruish (Ed.), *The use of psychological testing for treatment planning and outcomes assessment* (2nd ed., pp. 1023–1049). Mahwah, NJ: Lawrence Erlbaum Associates.

Greenfield, T. K., & Attkisson, C. C. (1989). Progress toward a multifactorial service satisfaction scale for evaluating primary care and mental health services. *Evaluation and Program Planning, 12,* 271–278.

Groth-Marnat, G. (1999a). Current status and future directions of psychological assessment: Introduction. *Journal of Clinical Psychology, 55,* 781–795.

Groth-Marnat, G. (1999b). Financial efficacy of clinical assessment: Rational guidelines and issues for future research. *Journal of Clinical Psychology, 55,* 813–824.

Hathaway, S. R., & McKinley, J. C. (1951). *MMPI manual.* New York: The Psychological Corporation.

The Hay Group. (1998). *The Hay Group study on health care plan design and cost trends: 1988–1997.* Philadelphia: Author.

Health Outcomes Institute. (1993). *Health Status Questionnaire 2.0 manual.* Bloomington, MN: Author.

Health care costs soared during 2001, federal report says. (2003, January 8). *Minneapolis Star Tribune,* p. A10.

Hermann, R. C. (2002). Linking outcome measurement with process measurement for quality improvement. In W. W. IsHak, T. Burt, & L. I. Sederer (Eds.), *Outcome measurement in psychiatry: A critical review* (pp. 23–34). Washington, DC: American Psychiatric Publishing.

Holder, H. D., & Blose, J. O. (1986). Alcoholism treatment and total health care utilization and costs: A four-year longitudinal analysis of federal employees. *Journal of the American Medical Association, 256,* 1456–1460.

Howard, K. I., Brill, P. L., Lueger, R. J., O'Mahoney, M. T., & Grissom, G. R. (1993). *Integra outpatient tracking assessment.* Philadelphia: Compass Information Services.

Howard, K. I., Kopta, S. M, Krause, M. S., & Orlinsky, D. E. (1986). The dose-effect relationship in psychotherapy. *American Psychologist, 41,* 159–154.

Howard, K. I., Lueger, R. J., Maling, M. S., & Martinovich, Z. (1993). A phase model of psychotherapy outcome: Causal mediation of change. *Journal of Consulting and Clinical Psychology, 61,* 678–685.

Howard, K. I., Martinovich, Z., & Black, M. (1997). Outpatient outcomes. *Psychiatric Annals, 27,* 108–112.

Howard, K. I., Moras, K., Brill, P. B., Martinovich, Z., & Lutz, W. (1996). Evaluation of psychotherapy: Efficacy, effectiveness, and patient progress. *American Psychologist, 51,* 1059–1064.

Hunsley, J. (2002). Psychological testing and psychological assessment: A closer examination [Comment]. *American Psychologist, 57,* 139–140.

InterStudy (1991). Preface. *The InterStudy Quality Edge, 1,* 1–3.

Jahoda, M. (1958). *Current concepts of mental health.* New York: Basic Books.

Jerome, L. W., DeLeon, P. H., James, L. C., Folen, R., Earles, J., & Gedney, J. J. (2000). The coming of age in telecommunications in psychological research and practice. *American Psychologist, 55,* 407–421.

Johnson, J., Weissman, M., & Klerman, G. J. (1992). Service utilization and social morbidity associated with depressive symptoms in the community. *Journal of the American Medical Association, 267,* 1478–1483.

Johnson, P. L. (1989). *Keeping score: Strategies and tactics for winning the quality war.* New York: Harper & Row.

Kadera, S. W., Lambert, M. J., & Andrews, A. A. (1996). How much therapy is really enough? A session-by-session analysis of the psychotherapy dose-effect relationship. *Journal of Psychotherapy Practice and Research, 5,* 132–151.

Kent, A. J., & Hersen, M. (2000). An overview of managed mental health care: Past, present, and future. In A. J. Kent & M. Hersen (Eds.), *A psychologist's proactive guide to managed mental health care* (pp. 3–19). Mahwah, NJ: Lawrence Erlbaum Associates.

Kessler, L. G., McGonagle, K. M., Zhao, S., Nelson., C. B., Hughes, M., Eshelman, et al. (1994). Lifetime and 12-month prevalence of DSM–III–R disorders in the U.S.: Results from the National Comorbidity Study. *Archives of General Psychiatry, 51,* 8–20.

Kiesler, C. A. (2000). The next wave of change for psychology and mental health services in the health care revolution. *American Psychologist, 55,* 481–487.

Kiesler, C. A., & Morton, T. L. (1988). Psychology and public policy in the "health care revolution." *American Psychologist, 43,* 993–1003.

Knapp, S., & Keller, P. A. (2001). Professional associations' strategies for revitalizing professional psychology. *Professional Psychology: Research and Practice, 32,* 71–78.

Kobak, K. A., Greist, J. H., Jefferson, J. W., & Katzelnick, D. J. (1996). Decision support for patient care: Computerized rating scales. *Behavioral Healthcare Tomorrow, 5,* 25–29.

Kobak, K. A., Mundt, J. C., Greist, J. H., Katzelnick, D. J., & Jefferson, J. W. (2000). Computer assessment of depression: Automating the Hamilton Depression Rating Scale. *Drug Information Journal, 34,* 145–156.

Kobak, K. A., Reynolds, W. M., Rosenfeld, R., & Greist, J. H. (1990). Development and validation of a computer-administered version of the Hamilton Depression Rating Scale. *Journal of Consulting and Clinical Psychology, 58,* 56–63.

Kobak, K. A., Taylor, L. V., Dottl, S. L., Greist, J. H., Jefferson, J. W., Burroughs, D., Katzelnick, D.J., et al. (1997). Computerized screening for psychiatric disorders in an outpatient community mental health clinic. *Psychiatric Services, 48,* 1048–1057.

Kobak, K. A., Taylor, L. V., Dottl, S. L., Greist, J. H., Jefferson, J. W., Burroughs, D., Mantle, J. M., et al. (1997). A computer-administered telephone interview to identify mental disorders. *Journal of the American Medical Association, 278,* 905–910.

Kopta, S. M., Howard, K. I., Lowry, J. L., & Beutler, L. E. (1994). Patterns of symptomatic recovery in psychotherapy. *Journal of Consulting and Clinical Psychology, 62,* 1009–1016.

Kubiszyn, T. W., Meyer, G. J., Finn, S. E., Eyde, L. D., Kay, G. G., Moreland, K. L., et al. (2000). Empirical support for psychological assessment in clinical health care settings. *Professional Psychology: Research and Practice, 31,* 119–130.

Lambert, M. J., Hansen, N. B., & Finch, A. E. (2001). Patient-focused research using patient outcome data to enhance treatment effects. *Journal of Consulting and Clinical Psychology, 69,* 159–172.

Lambert, M. J., Hansen, N. B., Umphress, V., Lunnen, K., Okiishi, J., Burlingame, G., et al. (1996). *Administration and scoring manual for the Outcome Questionnaire (OQ–45.2).* Wilmington, DL: American Professional Credentialing Services.

Lambert, M. J., Lunnen, K., Umphress, V., Hansen, N. B., & Burlingame, G. M. (1994). *Administration and scoring manual for the Outcome Questionnaire (OQ–45.1).* Salt Lake City, UT: IHC Center for Behavioral Healthcare Efficacy.

Lambert, M. J., Whipple, J. L., Smart, D. W., Vermeesch, D. A., Nielsen, S. L., & Hawkins, E. J. (2001). The effects of providing therapists with feedback on patient progress during psychotherapy: Are outcomes enhanced? *Psychotherapy Research, 11,* 49–68.

Lambert, M. J., Whipple, J. L., Vermeesch, D. A., Smart, D. W., Hawkins, E. J., Nielsen, S. L., et al. (2001). Enhancing psychotherapy outcomes via providing feedback on client progress: A replication. *Clinical Psychology and Psychotherapy, 9,* 91–103.

Larsen, D. L., Attkisson, C. C., Hargreaves, W. A., & Nguyen, T. D. (1979). Assessment of client/patient satisfaction: Development of a general scale. *Evaluation and Program Planning, 2,* 197–207.

Leaders predict integration of MH, primary care by 2000. (1996, April 8). *Mental Health Weekly,* pp. 1, 6.

Leon, S. C., Kopta, S. M., Howard, K. I., & Lutz, W. (1999). Predicting patients' responses to psychotherapy: Are some more predictable than others? *Journal of Consulting and Clinical Psychology, 67,* 698–704.

Levant, R. F., Reed, G. M., Ragusea, S. A., DiCowden, M., Murphy, M. J., Sullivan, F., et al. (2001). Envisioning and accessing new roles for professional psychology. *Professional Psychology: Research and Practice, 32,* 79–87.

Levit, K., Cowan, C., Lazenby, H., Sensenig, A., McDonnell, P., Stiller, J., et al. (2000). Health spending in 1998: Signals of change. *Health Affairs, 19,* 124–132.

LeVois, M., Nguyen, T. D., & Attkisson, C. C. (1981). Artifact in client satisfaction assessment: Experience in community mental health settings. *Evaluation and Program Planning, 4*, 139–150.

Lohr, K. N., Aaronson, N. K., Alonso, J., Burnam, M. A., Patrick, D. L., Perrin, E. B., et al. (1996). Evaluating quality-of-life and health status instruments: Development of scientific review criteria. *Clinical Therapeutics, 18*, 979–992.

Lutz, W., Lowry, J., Kopta, S. M., Einstein, D. A., & Howard, K. I. (2001). Prediction of dose-response relations based on patient characteristics. *Journal of Clinical Psychology, 57*, 889–900.

Manderscheid, R. W., Henderson, M. J., & Brown, D. Y. (n.d.). Status of national accountability efforts at the millennium. In R. W. Manderscheid & M. J. Henderson (Eds.), *Mental health, United States, 2000. Section 2: Decision support 2000+* (pp. 1–10). Retrieved December 19, 2001, from http://mentalhealth.org/publication/allpubs/sma01-3537/chapter6.asp

Maruish, M. (1990, Fall). Psychological assessment: What will its role be in the future? *Assessment Applications*, pp. 7–8.

Maruish, M. E. (1994). Introduction. In M. E. Maruish (Ed.), *The use of psychological testing for treatment planning and outcomes assessment* (pp. 3–21). Hillsdale, NJ: Lawrence Erlbaum Associates.

Maruish, M. E. (1999). Introduction. In M. E. Maruish (Ed.), *The use of psychological testing for treatment planning and outcomes assessment* (2nd ed., pp. 1–39). Mahwah, NJ: Lawrence Erlbaum Associates.

Maruish, M. E. (Ed.). (2000). *Handbook of psychological assessment in primary care settings.* Mahwah, NJ: Lawrence Erlbaum Associates.

Maruish, M. E. (2002). *Psychological testing in the age of managed behavioral health care.* Mahwah, NJ: Lawrence Erlbaum Associates.

Maruish, M. E., Bershadsky, B., & Goldstein, L. (1998). Reliability and validity of the SA–45: Further evidence from a primary care setting. *Assessment, 4*, 407–420.

McCarthy, R. (1998, August). Behavioral health: Don't ignore, integrate. *Business and Health*, pp. 46, 51.

McGlynn, E. A. (1996). Setting the context for measuring patient outcomes. In D. M. Steinwachs, L. M. Flynn, G. S. Norquist, and E. A. Skinner (Eds.), *Using client outcomes information to improve mental health and substance abuse treatment* (pp. 19–32). San Francisco: Jossey-Bass.

Mechanic, D. (n.d.). Mental health policy at the millennium: Challenges and opportunities. In R. W. Manderscheid & M. J. Henderson (Eds.), *Mental health, United States, 2000. Section 3: Status of mental health services at the millennium* (pp. 1–15). Retrieved December 19, 2001, from http://mentalhealth.org/publication/allpubs/sma01-3537/chapter7.asp

Megargee, E. I., & Spielberger, C. D. (1992). Reflections on fifty years of personality assessment and future directions for the field. In E. I. Megargee & C. D. Spielberger (Eds.), *Personality assessment in America* (pp. 170–190). Hillsdale, NJ: Lawrence Erlbaum Associates.

Merrick, E. L., Garnick, D. W., Horgan, C. M., & Hodgkin, D. (2002). Quality measurement and accountability for substance abuse and mental health services in managed care organizations. *Medical Care, 40*, 1238–1248.

Migdail, K. J., Youngs, M. T., and Bengen-Seltzer, B. (Eds.). (1995). *The 1995 behavioral outcomes and guidelines sourcebook.* New York: Faulkner & Gray.

Millard, R. W., & Carver, J. R. (1999). Cross-sectional comparison of live and interactive voice recognition administration of the SF–12 Health Status Survey. *American Journal of Managed Care, 5*, 153–159.

Millon, T. (1994). *MCMI–III manual.* Minneapolis, MN: National Computer Systems.

Moreland, K. L. (1996). How psychological testing can reinstate its value in an era of cost containment. *Behavioral Healthcare Tomorrow, 5*, 59–61.

Morey, L. C. (1991). *The Personality Assessment Inventory professional manual.* Odessa, FL: Psychological Assessment Resources.

Morey, L. C. (1999). Personality Assessment Inventory. In M. E. Maruish (Ed.), *The use of psychological testing for treatment planning and outcomes assessment* (2nd ed., pp. 1083–1121). Mahwah, NJ: Lawrence Erlbaum Associates.

Murphy, M. J., DeBernardo, C. R., & Shoemaker, W. E. (1998). Impact of managed care on independent practice and professional ethics: A survey of independent practitioners. *Professional Psychology: Research and Practice, 29*, 43–51.

Newman, F. L. (1991, Summer). Using assessment data to relate patient progress to reimbursement criteria. *Assessment Applications*, pp. 4–5.

Norquist, G. S. (2002). Role of outcome measurement in psychiatry. In W. W. IsHak, T. Burt, & L. I. Sederer (Eds.), *Outcome measurement in psychiatry: A critical review* (pp. 3–13). Washington, DC: American Psychiatric Publishing.

Nguyen, T. D., Attkisson, C. C., & Stegner, B. L. (1983). Assessment of patient satisfaction: Development and refinement of a service evaluation questionnaire. *Evaluation and Program Planning, 6*, 299–313.

Ogles, B. M., Lambert, M. J., & Fields, S. A. (2002). *Essentials of outcomes assessment.* New York: Wiley.

Pallak, M. S. (1994). National outcomes management survey: Summary report. *Behavioral Health care Tomorrow, 3,* 63–69.

Peskin, S. R. (1995). Applications of quality of life measurements: A managed care perspective. *Oncology, 9,* 127–128.

Pfeiffer, S. I., Soldivera, S., & Norton, J. A. (1992). *A consumer's guide to mental health outcome measures.* Devon, PA: The Devereux Foundation.

Phelps, R., Eisman, E. J., & Kohut, J. (1998). Psychological practice and managed care: Results of the CAPP practitioner survey. *Professional Psychology: Research and Practice, 29,* 31–36.

Pingitore, D., Scheffler, R., Haley, M., Sentell, T., & Schwalm, D. (2001). Professional psychology in a new era: Practice-based evidence from California. *Professional Psychology: Research and Practice, 6,* 585–596.

Pingitore, D., Scheffler, R., Sentell, T., Haley, M., & Schwalm, D. (2001). Psychologist supply, managed care, and the effects of income: Fault lines beneath California psychologists. *Professional Psychology: Research and Practice, 6,* 597–606.

Piotrowski, C. (1999). Assessment practices in the era of managed care: Current status and future directions. *Journal of Clinical Psychology, 55,* 787–796.

Piotrowski, C., Belter, R. W., & Keller, J. W. (1998). The impact of "managed care" on the practice of psychological testing: Preliminary findings. *Journal of Personality Assessment, 70,* 441–447.

Quirk, M. P., Strosahl, K., Krielkamp, T., & Erdberg, P. (1995). Personality feedback consultation in a managed mental health care practice. *Professional Psychology: Research and Practice, 26,* 27–32.

Radosevich, D., & Pruitt, M. (1996). *Twelve-item Health Status Questionnaire (HSQ–12) Version 2.0 user's guide.* Bloomington, MN: Health Outcomes Institute.

Radosevich, D. M., Wetzler, H., & Wilson, S. M. (1994). *Health Status Questionnaire (HSQ) 2.0: Scoring comparisons and reference data.* Bloomington, MN: Health Outcomes Institute.

Rath & Strong Management Consultants. (2000). *Rath & Strong's six sigma pocket guide.* Lexington, MA: Author.

Reed, G. M., Levant, R. F., Stout, C. E., Murphy, M. J., & Phelps, R. (2001). Psychology in the current mental health marketplace. *Professional Psychology: Research and Practice, 32,* 65–70.

Regier, D. A., Narrow, W. E., Rae, D. S., Manderscheid, R. W., Locke, B., & Goodwin, F. K. (1993). The de facto US mental and addictive disorders service system: Epidemiologic Catchment Area prospective 1-year prevalence rates of disorders and services. *Archives of General Psychiatry, 50,* 85–94.

Rothbaum, P. A., Bernstein, D. M., Haller, O., Phelps, R., & Kohout, J. (1998). New Jersey psychologists' report on managed mental health care. *Professional Psychology: Research and Practice, 29,* 37–42.

Rouse, B. A. (Ed.). (1995). *Substance abuse and mental health statistics sourcebook* (DHHS Publication No. [SMA] 95-3064). Washington, DC: Superintendent of Documents, U.S. Government Printing Office.

Saravay, S. M., Pollack, S., Steinberg, M. D., Weinschel, B., & Habert, M. (1996). Four-year follow-up of the influence of psychological comorbidity on medical rehospitalization. *American Journal of Psychiatry, 153,* 397–403.

Schaeffer, M., Murphy, R., Westerveld, M., & Gewirtz, A. (2000, August). *Psychological assessment and managed care: Guidelines for practice with children and adolescents.* Continuing education workshop presented at the annual meeting of the American Psychological Association, Washington, DC.

Scherkenback, W. W. (1987). *The Deming route to quality and productivity: Road maps and roadblocks.* Rockville, MD: Mercury Press/Fairchild Publications.

Schlosser, B. (1995). The ecology of assessment: A "patient-centric" perspective. *Behavioral Healthcare Tomorrow, 4,* 66–68.

Schreter, R. K. (1997). Essential skills for managed behavioral health care. *Psychiatric Services, 48,* 653–658.

Sederer, L. I., Dickey, B., & Eisen, S. V. (1997). Assessing outcomes in clinical practice. *Psychiatric Quarterly, 68,* 311–325.

Sederer, L. I., Dickey, B., & Hermann, R. C. (1996). The imperative of outcomes assessment in psychiatry. In L. I. Sederer & B. Dickey (Eds.), *Outcomes assessment in clinical practice* (pp. 1–7). Baltimore: Williams & Wilkins.

Seid, M., Varni, J. W. , & Jacobs, J. R. (2000). Pediatric health-related quality-of-life measurement technology: Intersections between science, managed care, and clinical care. *Journal of Clinical Psychology in Medical Settings, 7,* 17–27.

Shaffer, I. A. (1997). Treatment outcomes: Economic and ethical considerations. *Psychiatric Annals, 27,* 104–107.

Simmons, J. W., Avant, W. S., Demski, J., & Parisher, D. (1988). Determining successful pain clinic treatment through validation of cost effectiveness. *Spine, 13,* 34.

Simon, G. E., Von Korff, M., & Barlow, W. (1995). Health care costs of primary care patients with recognized depression. *Archives of General Psychiatry, 52*, 850–856.

Sipkoff, M. Z. (1995, August). Behavioral health treatment reduces medical costs: Treatment of mental disorders and substance abuse problems increase productivity in the workplace. *Open Minds*, p. 12.

Smith, G. R., Manderscheid, R. W., Flynn, L. M., & Steinwachs, D. M. (1997). Principles for assessment of patient outcomes in mental health care. *Psychiatric Services, 48*, 1033–1036.

Speer, D. C., & Newman, F. L. (1996). Mental health services outcome evaluation. *Clinical Psychology: Science and Practice, 3*, 105–129.

Sperry, L. (1997). Treatment outcomes: An overview. *Psychiatric Annals, 27*, 95–99.

Sperry, L., Brill, P. L., Howard, K. I., & Grissom, G. R. (1996). *Treatment outcomes in psychotherapy and psychiatric interventions*. New York: Brunner/Mazel.

Spielberger, C. D. (1983). *Manual of the State–Trait Anxiety Inventory: STAI (Form Y)*. Palo Alto, CA: Consulting Psychologists Press.

Spitzer, R. L., Williams, J. B., Kroenke, K., Linzer, M., deGruy, F. V., Hahn, S. R., et al. (1994). Utility of a new procedure for diagnosing mental disorders in primary care: The PRIME-MD 1000 study. *Journal of the American Medical Association, 272*, 1749–1756.

Stewart, A. L., & Ware, J. E., Jr. (1992). *Measuring functioning and well-being*. Durham, NC: Duke University Press.

Stout, C. E., & Cook, L. P. (1999). New areas for psychological assessment in general health care settings: What to do today to prepare for tomorrow. *Journal of Clinical Psychology, 55*, 797–812.

Strain, J. J., Lyons, J. S., Hammer, J. S., Fahs, M., Lebovits, A., Paddison, P. L., et al. (1991). Cost offset from a psychiatric consultation-liaison intervention with elderly hip fracture patients. *American Journal of Psychiatry, 148*, 1044–1049.

Strategic Advantage, Inc. (1996). *Symptom Assessment–45 Questionnaire manual*. Minneapolis, MN: Author.

Strategic Advantage, Inc. (1998). *Symptom Assessment–45 Questionnaire technical manual*. Toronto, On: Multi-Health Systems.

Substance Abuse and Mental Health Services Administration (2002). *2001 National Household Survey on Drug Abuse (NHSDA)*. Rockville, MD: Author.

Surgeon General of the United States. (1999). *Mental health: A report of the Surgeon General*. Rockville, MD: U.S. Department of Health and Human Services, Substance Abuse and Mental Health Services Administration.

Tsacoumis, S. (2000, August). Industrial and organizational assessment in the 21st century. In M. E. Maruish (Chair), *Clinical, school, industrial and organizational psychology, and educational assessment in the 21st century*. Symposium conducted at the annual meeting of the American Psychological Association, Washington, DC.

Turner, S. M., DeMers, S. T., & Fox, H. R. (2001). APA's guidelines for test user qualifications. *American Psychologist, 56*, 1099–1113.

University of Arkansas Medical Sciences Center for Outcomes Research and Effectiveness. (2002). *NetOutcomes Solutions: A confidential, low-cost Internet solution for behavioral health outcomes assessment*. Available: http://www.netoutcomes.net/NO_Solutions/NO_Main/NO_Home.asp?menu=nethome

Walton, M. (1986). *The Deming management method*. New York: Dodd, Mead & Company.

Ware, J. E., Kosinski, M., & Keller, S. D. (1995). *SF–12: How to Score the SF–12 Physical and Mental summary scales* (2nd ed.). Boston: New England Medical Center, The Health Institute.

Ware, J. E., & Sherbourne, C. D. (1992). The MOS 36-Item Short Form Health Survey (SF–36): I. Conceptual framework and item selection. *Medical Care, 30*, 473–483.

Ware, J. E., Snow, K. K., Kosinski, M., & Gandek, B. (1993). *SF–36 Health Survey manual and interpretation guide*. Boston: New England Medical Center, The Health Institute.

Watkins, C. E., Campbell, V. L., Nieberding, R., & Hallmark, R. (1995). Contemporary practice of psychological assessment by clinical psychologists. *Professional Psychology: Research and Practice, 26*, 54–60.

Watson, G. H. (1993). *Strategic benchmarking*. New York: Wiley.

Werthman, M. J. (1995). A managed care approach to psychological testing. *Behavioral Health Management, 15*, 15–17.

Whipple, J. L., Lambert, M. J., Vermeesch, D. A., Smart, D. W., Nielsen, S. L., & Hawkins, E. J. (in press). Improving the effects of psychotherapy: The use of early identification of treatment failure and problem solving strategies in routine practice. *Journal of Counseling Psychology*.

Wilson, I. B., & Kaplan, S. (1995). Clinical practice and patients' health status: How are the two related? *Medical Care, 33*, AS209–214.

World Health Organization. (1948). Constitution. In *Basic Documents*. Geneva: Author.

# Screening for Psychiatric Disorders

Leonard R. Derogatis
*Johns Hopkins University School of Medicine*

William J. Culpepper
*University of Maryland, Baltimore*

The data from recent comprehensive epidemiologic studies emphatically underscore the fact that psychiatric disorders are highly prevalent in contemporary society. The benchmark NIMH Epidemiologic Catchment Area (ECA) Study (Myers et al., 1984; Regier et al., 1988; Robins et al., 1984) demonstrated conclusively that psychiatric disorders are pervasive throughout the United States. Similar high rates have been documented in Europe and in Australia (Regier et al., 1988). In the context of primary care, which in recent years has been characterized as "the de facto mental health services system in the United States" (Burns & Burke, 1985; Regier, Goldberg, & Taube, 1978), the prevalence of psychiatric conditions is measurably higher, ranging between 20% and 30% (Barrett, Barrett, Oxman, & Gerber, 1988; Derogatis & Wise, 1989). These rates have been confirmed by Hansson, Nettelbladt, Borgquist, and Nordstrom (1994), Olfson et al. (1995), and Ustun and Sartorius (1995).

The most prevalent of these conditions are anxiety and depressive disorders (Derogatis et al., 1983; Von Korff, Dworkin, LeResche, & Kruger, 1988), which are often obscured in their presentation and difficult to detect. *American Medical News* (2002) recently reported that this year an estimated 19 million Americans will experience a depressive disorder that will go unrecognized in spite of the fact that many of these individuals have regular contact with a physician. It is estimated that by the year 2020 depression will become the second leading cause of disability in the United States after heart disease (Murray & Lopez, 1997), and its economic significance to society is underscored by estimated costs of over $43 billion annually (Pennix et al., 1998).

These facts have led the American Medical Association to strongly endorse National Depression Screening Day for the fifth consecutive year and encourage their members to use the event as an impetus to investigate and incorporate screening methodology into their practices. In addition, currently the U.S. Preventive Services Task Force, based on their extensive review, has recommended that every primary care provider screen all adult patients for depression (Pignone et al., 2002).

Because the majority of screening for psychiatric disorders occurs in primary care and other more specialized medical settings, this chapter looks at the topic from somewhat of a primary care perspective. This strategy is intended, not to abrogate the importance of community-based screening programs, but rather to facilitate an appreciation of screening methods by presenting them in a familiar and realistic context.

Psychiatric disorders represent a significant public health problem with high associated health care liability. This liability is magnified by the presence of comorbid medical disorders. Comorbid conditions have a long list of undesirable features associated with them, including increased utilization rates, failure to adhere to treatment regimens, atypical responses to treatment, high side-effect rates, a higher frequency of medical events, longer hospital stays, and significantly higher costs (Allison et al., 1995; Katon et al., 1990; Saravay, Pollack, Steinberg, Weinschel, & Habert, 1996).

This being the case, there are multiple incentives to develop and systematically implement effective psychiatric screening systems in community and primary care settings, not the least of which is the goal of decreasing the morbidity and mortality associated with undetected psychiatric disorders (Hawton, 1981; Kamerow, Pincus, & MacDonald, 1986; Regier, Roberts, et al., 1988). It is well established that the majority of individuals with psychiatric disorders, if not completely untreated, are treated by health care workers without comprehensive mental health training. These individuals are never seen by a certified mental health professional (Dohrenwend & Dohrenwend, 1982; Regier et al., 1978; Weissman, Myers, & Thompson, 1981; Yopenic, Clark, & Aneshensel, 1983). In addition, although there is a significant correlation between physical illness and psychiatric disorder (Barrett et al., 1988; Fulop & Strain, 1991; Rosenthal et al., 1991), rates of detection by primary care workers of the most prevalent psychiatric disorders (i.e., anxiety and depressive disorders) has been consistently disappointing (Linn & Yager, 1984; Nielson & Williams, 1980). Historically, it has not been unusual to find recognition rates in medical cohorts falling below 50%. Given the documented increases in rates of health care utilization and health care costs associated with undetected cases of psychiatric disorder, the efficient implementation of psychiatric screening systems in primary care settings, colleges, and geriatric sites would almost certainly result in a significant savings in health care expenditures. Finally, the implementation of effective screening systems could significantly aid those individuals in our communities who are afflicted with psychiatric disorders and who currently go undetected. They could be identified earlier in the course of their illnesses, which hopefully would enable earlier initiation of treatment and avert the pervasive morbidity associated with chronic mental conditions.

## PROBLEMS IN THE RECOGNITION OF PSYCHIATRIC DISORDERS

The prototypic psychiatric disorder is a construct, with few pathognomonic clinical or laboratory signs and a pathophysiology and an etiology that are obscure. For these reasons, unique problems arise in the detection of psychiatric disorders. A prominent source of confusion arises from the fact that the highly prevalent anxiety and depressive disorders often present with multiple associated somatic symptoms, manifestations that are difficult to differentiate from those arising from verifiable medical causes. Schurman, Kramer, and Mitchell (1985) indicated that in 72% of visits to primary care doctors resulting in a psychiatric diagnosis the patient presented with somatic symptoms as the primary complaint. Katon et al. (1990) and Bridges and Goldberg (1984) both specified that presentation with somatic symptoms is a key reason for misdiagnosis of psychiatric disorders in primary care. Consistent with this observation, Katon et al. (1990) reported that a high health care utilization group in their study revealed elevated SCL–90–R scores of almost a full standard deviation, not only on the anxiety and depression subscales but on the *somatization* subscale as well.

Another problem has to do with the misappreciation of clinical status (Derogatis & Wise, 1989). Many chronic illnesses, particularly those that inevitably result in

TABLE 2.1
Factors Responsible for Clinicians' Failure to Detect Anxiety and
Depressive Disorders in Primary Care Patients

---

Affective syndrome masked by predominantly *somatic symptoms*.
Affective syndrome judged to be a *demoralization reaction*.
Affective syndrome missed because of *incomplete diagnostic workup*.
Affective syndrome *minimized* relative to medical disorder.
Affective syndrome *misdiagnosed as dementia* in elderly patients.
Affective syndrome misunderstood as *negativistic attitude*.

---

mortality, are characterized by periods of disaffection and demoralization. These negative affect states are a natural reaction to the loss of vitality and well-being associated with chronic illness and, in some cases, to the anticipated loss of life itself. Health care professionals familiar with caring for such patients (e.g., cancer, emphysema, renal disease patients) sometimes misperceive true clinical depressions (for which effective treatments are available) as reactive states of demoralization that are a natural part of the illness. As a result, effective therapeutic regimens are not initiated on the grounds that such mood states are a natural part of the primary medical condition. There is good evidence that such reactive states can be reliably distinguished from major clinical depressions (Snyder, Strain, & Wolf, 1990), which should reinforce our efforts to adequately identify, diagnose, and appropriately treat these conditions.

Since most health care professionals have limited training in psychiatric diagnosis, another impediment to the accurate identification of these cases can arise from an incomplete diagnostic workup. Physicians and other health care professionals are already responsible for considerable amounts of information concerning the diagnosis and treatment of medical conditions that may be present; given that time with the patient is very limited, it is not surprising that many primary care professionals do not feel confident in their abilities to also detect and identify psychiatric disorders. An additional problem can arise from the fact that primary care providers sometimes minimize the importance of concomitant psychiatric problems relative to primary medical disorders. Table 2.1 lists a series of factors found to often underlie the failure to detect anxiety and depressive disorders in primary care patients.

Evidence suggests that approximately one fifth to one third of primary care patients suffer from at least one psychiatric disorder. This fact highlights that the proficiency with which primary care physicians recognize these conditions is an important issue for our health care system. Unfortunately, current evidence also suggests that accurate detection of prevalent psychiatric disorders in primary care is only a fraction of what it could be. Obviously, the low rate of detection has considerable implications for the physical and psychological health of our patients (Seltzer, 1989).

**Unaided Clinician Recognition**

Over the past several decades, a substantial number of studies have documented both the magnitude and nature of the problem of undetected psychiatric disorder in primary care (Davis, Nathan, Crough, & Bairnsfather, 1987; Jones, Badger, Ficken, Leeper, & Andersen, 1987; Kessler, Amick, & Thompson, 1985; Schulberg et al., 1985). The data from these studies reveal a wide span of rates of accurate diagnosis of psychiatric conditions, ranging from a low of 8% (Linn & Yager, 1984) to a high of 53% (Shapiro et al., 1987). In additional primary care studies, Gerber et al. (1989) reported that physicians correctly identified 57% of patients who were independently

TABLE 2.2
Recent Research on Rates of Accurate Identification of Psychiatric Morbidity
in Primary Care

| Investigators | Study Sample | Criterion | Correct Dx |
|---|---|---|---|
| Andersen & Harthorn, 1989 | 120 primary care physicians | DKI | 33% affective disorder, 48% anxiety disorder |
| Davis et al., 1987 | 377 family practice patients | Zung, SDS | 15% mild symptoms 30% severe symptoms |
| Gerber et al., 1989 | 1,068 rural primary care patients | HSCL | 57% |
| Jones et al., 1987 | 20 family physicians, 51 patients | DIS | 21% |
| Kessler et al., 1985 | 1,452 primary care patients | GHQ | 19.7% |
| Linn & Yager, 1980 | 150 patients in a general medicine clinic | Zung | 8% |
| Rand et al., 1988 | 36 family practice residents, 520 points | GHQ | 16% |
| Schulberg et al., 1985 | 294 primary care patients | DIS | 44% |
| Shapiro et al., 1987 | 1,242 points at a university internal medicine clinic | GHQ | 53% |
| Simon & Von Korff, 1995 | 1,952 primary care patients | GHQ | 64% |
| Zung et al., 1983 | 41 family medicine patients | Zung, SDS | 15% |

diagnosed with depression, Simon and Von Korff (1995) reported a 64% rate of accurate diagnosis of major depression, and Yelin et al. (1996) found that 44% of a cohort of 2,000 primary care patients who screened positive for clinical anxiety on the SCL–90–R had been independently assigned a mental health diagnosis. These findings represent an improvement over rates observed in earlier studies, but they also underscore the fact that significant proportions of patients with psychiatric morbidity go undiagnosed. Although the methodology and precision of studies of this phenomenon continue to improve (Anderson & Harthorn, 1989; Rand, Badger, & Coggins, 1988), rates of accurate diagnosis have remained for the most part lower than we wish them to be. A summary of these investigations, along with their characteristics and detection rates, is presented in Table 2.2.

## Aided Clinician Recognition

The data from the investigations outlined above strongly suggest that we should proceed in a proactive fashion to facilitate the accurate recognition of psychiatric conditions by health care professionals. This is particularly the case in light of the consensus that in the future, primary care physicians will be playing a greater role in the detection of psychiatric conditions. If these health care professionals cannot correctly identify psychiatric conditions, they can neither adequately treat them personally nor refer the patients to appropriate mental health professionals. Such a situation will ultimately degrade the quality of our health care systems further and deny effective treatment to those who in many ways need it most.

Evidence suggests that many primary care physicians have an accurate appreciation of both the nature and the prevalence of psychiatric disorders. They estimate prevalence to be between 20% and 25% in their patient populations and perceive anxiety and depressive disorders to be the most prevalent conditions they encounter (Fauman, 1983; Orleans, George, Haupt, & Brodie, 1985). In an effort to identify and overcome deficiencies in psychiatric diagnosis in primary care, a number of investigators have studied the effects of introducing diagnostic aids in the primary care setting, in the form of psychological screening tests. Although not unanimous in all their conclusions, the studies completed during the past several decades have generally found that in appropriate situations, screening tests can improve detection of psychiatric conditions in primary care.

Linn and Yager (1984) used the Zung SDS and reported an increase from 8% correct diagnosis to 25% in a cohort of 150 general medical patients. Similarly, Zung, Magill, Moore, and George (1983) reported an increase in correct identification from 15% to 68% in family medicine outpatients with depression using a similar intervention. Moore, Silimperi, and Bobula (1978) observed an increase in correct diagnostic identification from 22% to 56% working with family practice residents, and Magruder-Habib, Zung, and Feusnner (1990) reported a threefold increase in accurate identification in a VA sample of 800 primary care patients using feedback from the Zung SDS. Finally, Williams, Hitchcock, Cordes, Ramirez, and Pignone (2002) found a 10% increase in accurate identification of depression (39% versus 29%) among physicians receiving feedback from CESDs administered to their patients.

Not all studies have shown such dramatic improvements in diagnostic accuracy, however. Hoeper, Nyczi, and Cleary (1979) found essentially no improvement in diagnosis associated with making GHQ results available to doctors, and Shapiro et al. (1987) reported only a 7% increase in accuracy when GHQ scores were made accessible. Reifler, Kessler, Berhard, Leon, and Martin (1996) evaluated 358 primary care patients using the Symptom Driven Diagnostic System for Primary Care (SDDSP) and found no difference in outcomes at 9 months between patients of physicians who received feedback and those who did not. The issue of aided recognition of psychiatric disorders is a complicated one, for numerous patient and clinician variables affect results. Nonetheless, as suggested by Anderson and Harthorn (1990), the results of studies on aided recognition do offer some promise .

## OVERVIEW OF SCREENING

### The Concept of Screening

Screening has been defined as "the presumptive identification of unrecognized disease or defect by the application of tests, examinations or other procedures which can be applied rapidly to sort out apparently well persons who probably have a disease from those who probably do not" (Commission on Chronic Illness, 1957). Screening is an operation conducted in an ostensibly well population in order to identify occult instances of the disease or disorder in question. Some authorities make a distinction between screening and case finding, which is specified as the ascertainment of disease in populations composed of patients with other disorders. Under such a distinction, the detection of psychiatric disorders among primary care or other medical patients would more precisely fit the criteria for case finding than screening. In actual implementation there are few operational differences between the two processes, so in the current review we have chosen to use the term *screening* for both methods.

Regardless of its specific manifestation, the screening process represents a relatively unrefined sieve designed to segregate the cohort under assessment into "positives," who presumptively have the condition, and "negatives," who are ostensibly free of it. Screening is not a diagnostic procedure per se. Rather, it is a preliminary filtering operation that identifies those individuals with the highest probability of having the disorder in question so that they can undergo subsequent specific diagnostic evaluation. Those screened negative are usually not subjected to further evaluation.

The justification for screening rests on the premise that the early detection of unrecognized disease in apparently healthy individuals carries with it a discernable advantage in achieving effective treatment and/or cure of the condition. Although logical, this assumption is not always well founded. In certain conditions, early detection does not measurably improve our capacity to alter morbidity or mortality, either because the diagnostic procedures are unreliable or because effective treatments for the condition are not yet available.

In an attempt to foster a better appreciation of the particular health problems that lend themselves to effective screening systems, the World Health Organization (WHO) has published guidelines for effective health screening programs (Wilson & Junger, 1968). A version of these criteria is given here.

1. The condition should represent an important health problem that carries with it notable morbidity and mortality.
2. Screening programs must be cost-effective (i.e., the incidence or significance of the disorder must be sufficient to justify the costs of screening).
3. Effective methods of treatment must be available for the disorder.
4. The test(s) for the disorder should be reliable and valid so that detection errors (i.e., false positives or false negatives) are minimized.
5. The test(s) should have high cost-benefit ratio (i.e., the time, effort, and personal inconvenience to the patient associated with taking the test(s) should be substantially outweighed by the potential benefits).
6. The condition should be characterized by an asymptomatic or benign period during which detection will significantly reduce morbidity and/or mortality.
7. Treatment administered during the asymptomatic phase should demonstrate significantly greater efficacy than that dispensed during the symptomatic phase.

Some authorities are not convinced that psychiatric disorders and the screening systems designed to detect them conclusively meet all of the above criteria. For example, the efficacy of our treatments for certain psychiatric conditions (e.g., schizophrenia) is arguable, and we have not definitively demonstrated for some conditions that treatments initiated during asymptomatic phases (e.g., "maintenance" antidepressant treatment) are more efficacious than treatment initiated during acute episodes of manifest symptoms. Nevertheless, it is generally understood that psychiatric conditions and the screening paradigms designed to identify them do meet the WHO criteria in the large majority of instances and that the consistent implementation of screening systems in primary care populations can substantially improve the quality and cost-efficiency of our health care.

### The Epidemiologic Screening Model

Because many readers do not possess detailed familiarity with screening paradigms, we briefly review the basic epidemiologic screening model. Essentially, a cohort of individuals who are apparently well—or in the instance of case finding, present with a condition distinct from the index disorder—are evaluated by a "test" to determine if they are at high risk for a particular disorder or disease. As noted, the disorder must have sufficient incidence or consequence to be considered a serious public health

TABLE 2.3
Epidemiologic Screening Model

| Screening Test | Actual | |
| --- | --- | --- |
| | Cases | Noncases |
| Test positive | a | b |
| Test negative | c | d |

*Note.* Sensitivity (Se) = $a/(a+c)$; false negative rate $(1-Se)$ = $c/(a+c)$; specificity (Sp) = $d/(b+d)$; false positive rate $(1-Sp)$ = $b/(b+d)$; positive predictive value (PPV) = $a/(a+b)$; negative predictive value (NPV) = $d/(c+d)$.

problem and be characterized by a distinct early or asymptomatic phase during which detection could substantially improve the results of treatment.

The screening test itself (e.g., pap smear, Western blot) should be both *reliable*, that is, consistent in its performance from one administration to the next, and *valid*, that is, capable of identifying those with the index disorder and eliminating individuals who do not have the condition. In psychometric terms, this form of validity has traditionally been referred to as "predictive" or "criterion-oriented" validity. In epidemiologic models, the predictive validity of the test is apportioned into two distinct partitions: the degree to which the test correctly identifies those individuals who actually have the disorder, termed its *sensitivity*, and the extent to which those free of the condition are correctly identified as such, its *specificity*. Correctly identified individuals with the index disorder are referred to as *true positives*, and those accurately identified as being free of the disorder are termed *true negatives*. Healthy individuals misidentified as affected are labeled *false positives*, and affected individuals missed by the test are referred to as *false negatives*. Note that each type of prediction error carries with it a socially determined value or significance, termed its *utility*, and note also that the utilities need not be equal. The basic fourfold epidemiologic model, as well as the algebraic definitions of each of the validity indices, is presented in Table 2.3.

Sensitivity and specificity are a screening test's most fundamental validity indices; however, other parameters can markedly affect a test's performance. In particular, the *prevalence* or *base rate* of the disorder in the population under evaluation can have a powerful effect on the results of screening. Two other indicators of test performance, *predictive value of a positive* and *predictive value of a negative*, reflect the interactive effects of test validity and prevalence. These indices are also defined in Table 2.3, although their detailed discussion is postponed until a later section.

## PSYCHOMETRIC PRINCIPLES THAT APPLY TO SCREENING FOR PSYCHIATRIC DISORDERS

A realistic appreciation of the psychometric basis for psychiatric screening rests on the realization that we are involved in *psychological measurement*. Basically, the general principles underlying psychological measurement are no different from those that govern any other form of scientific measurement; however, a major characteristic that distinguishes psychological measurement from other forms resides in the object of measurement: it is usually a *hypothetical construct*. By contrast, measurement in the physical sciences usually involves tangible entities, which are measured via ratio scales with true zeros and equal intervals and ratios throughout the scale continuum (e.g., weight, distance, velocity). In quantifying hypothetical constructs (e.g., anxiety, depression, quality of life ), measurement occurs on ordinal-approaching-interval scales, which by their nature are less sophisticated and have substantially larger errors of measurement (Luce & Narens, 1987). Psychological measurement is no less scientific because of this distinction; it is, however, less precise than measurement in the physical sciences.

## Reliability

All scientific measurement is based on consistency or replicability; reliability concerns the degree of replicability inherent in measurement. To what degree would a screening measure provide the same results upon readministration one week later? To what extent do two clinicians making judgments on a psychiatric rating scale agree? Conceived differently, reliability can be thought of as the converse of measurement error. It represents that proportion of variation in measurement that is due to true variation in the attribute under study as opposed to random or systematic error variance. Reliability can be conceptualized as the ratio of *true score variation* to the total measurement variance. It specifies the precision of measurement and thereby sets the theoretical limit of measurement validity.

## Validity

Just as reliability indicates the consistency of measurement, validity reflects the *essence* of measurement, the degree to which an instrument measures what it is designed to measure. It specifies how well an instrument measures a given attribute or characteristic of interest, and it communicates the extent to which an inventory is capable of discriminating those individuals who possess the characteristic from those in whom it is absent. Establishing the validity of a screening instrument is more complex and programmatic than determining its reliability and rests on more elaborate theory. Although the validation process involves many types of validity, the most central to the screening process is *predictive validity*.

The predictive validity of an assessment device hinges on its degree of correlation or agreement with an external reference criterion—a "gold standard" of some sort. With screening tests, the external criterion usually takes the form of a comprehensive laboratory and/or clinical diagnostic evaluation that definitively establishes the presence or absence of the index condition. Critical to a genuine understanding of predictive validity is the realization that it is highly specific in nature. To say that a particular screening test is valid in general has little or no scientific meaning; tests are valid only for specific predictive purposes. Psychological tests employed in screening for psychiatric disorder(s) must be validated specifically in terms of the diagnostic conditions they are designed to predict. As an example, a specific test for depression should be validated in terms of its ability to accurately predict clinical depressions; it should be of little value in screening for other psychiatric disorders except by virtue of the high comorbidity of certain other conditions with depression (Maser & Cloninger, 1990).

## Generalizability

Like reliability and validity, *generalizability* is a fundamental psychometric characteristic of test instruments used for psychiatric screening. Many clinical conditions and manifestations are systematically altered as a function of parameters such as age, sex, race, and the presence or absence of comorbid medical illnesses. Once validity coefficients (i.e., sensitivity and specificity) are established for a particular test relative to a specific diagnostic condition, they may vary considerably in a new sample if the demographic and health characteristics of the new cohort are significantly different from the cohort upon which the instrument was originally validated.

To cite examples, it is well established that men are more constrained than women in reporting emotional distress. Well-constructed tests measuring symptomatic distress should provide distinct norms for the two genders to reflect this effect (Nunnally, 1978). As another example, consider the change in the phenomenologic characteristics of depression across age: Depression in the very young tends toward less dramatic affective display and progresses through the classic clinical picture of young and middle adult years to the geriatric depressions of the elderly, which are more likely to be characterized by dementia-like cognitive dysfunctions. Any single test is unlikely to perform with the same degree of validity across shifts in relevant parameters; therefore, generalizability must be established empirically and cannot merely be assumed. Consistent with this fact, an essay by Messick (1995) on modernizing our conceptualization of validity in psychological assessment explicitly identifies generalizability, along with external criterion validity, as one of six discernable aspects of construct validity.

## METHODOLOGICAL ISSUES IN SCREENING FOR PSYCHIATRIC DISORDERS

### Assessment Modality: Self-Report Versus Clinician Rating

Although advocates argue the different merits of self-report versus clinician ratings, a great deal of evidence suggests that the two techniques have strengths and weaknesses of roughly the same magnitude. Neither approach can be said to function more effectively overall in screening for psychiatric disorder. The circumstances of each screening situation must be independently assessed and weighed to determine which modality is best suited for a particular screening implementation.

Traditionally, self-report inventories have been more frequently used as screening tests than clinical rating scales. This is probably because the self-report modality of measurement fits very well with the task of screening. Self-report measures tend to be brief, inexpensive, and well tolerated by the individuals being screened. These features improve the cost-efficiency and the cost-benefit ratio of such measures. Self-report scales are also transportable; they may be used in a variety of settings and tend to minimize the expenditure of professional time and effort. In addition, their administration, scoring, and evaluation requires little or no professional input. The advent of personal computers has also facilitated the adoption of the self-report approach, as computer administration and scoring markedly reduces both the professional and technical time involved. Finally, perhaps the greatest advantage of the self-report approach resides in the fact that a self-report test is completed by the only person experiencing the phenomena, the respondent him- or herself. A clinician, no matter how skilled , can never know the actual experience of the respondent but rather must be satisfied with an *approximate* or *deduced* representation of the phenomena.

This last feature of self-report measures also represents one of their greatest potential sources of error: patient bias in reporting. Because the test respondent is providing the data, the opportunity exists for the respondent to consciously or unconsciously distort the responses given. Although patient bias does represent a potential difficulty for self-report, empirical studies have indicated that response distortions represent a problem only in situations where there is obvious personal gain to be derived from such distortions. Otherwise, patient bias is usually not a major source of bias (Derogatis, Lipman, Rickles, Uhlenhuth, & Covi, 1974a). There is also the possibility that response sets such as acquiescence or attempts at impression management may result in systematic response distortions, but such effects tend to add little error variance in most realistic clinical screening situations.

Probably the greatest limitation of self-report arises from the inflexibility of the format. With the exception of a very few online tests with branching logics, a line of questioning cannot be altered or modified as a result of how the individual responds to previous questions. In addition, only denotative responses can be appreciated; facial expression, tone of voice, attitude and posture, and the cognitive/emotional status of the respondent are not integral aspects of the test data. This inflexibility extends to the fact that the respondent must be literate in order to read and understand the questions.

The brief psychiatric rating scale or clinical interview is a viable alternative to self-report instruments in designing a screening paradigm. The clinical rating scale introduces professional judgment into the screening process and is intrinsically more flexible than self-report. The clinician has both the expertise and freedom to delve in more detail into any area of history, thought, or behavior that will deliver relevant information on the respondent's mental status. The clinician also retains the capacity to clarify ambiguous answers and probe areas of apparent contradiction. In addition, because of the clinician's sophistication in psychopathology and human behavior, there is the theoretical possibility that more complex and sophisticated instrument design may be utilized in developing psychiatric rating scales.

On the negative side, just as self-report is subject to patient bias, clinical rating scales are subject to interviewer bias, which can be equally powerful. Training sessions and videotaped interviews may be utilized in an attempt to reduce systematic errors of this type; however, interviewer bias can never be completely eliminated. Furthermore, the very fact that a professional clinician is required to do the interview significantly increases the costs of screening. Lay interviewers have been trained as evaluators in some cases, but they are rarely as skilled as professionals, and the costs of their training and participation must be weighed into the equation as well. Finally, the more flexibility designed into the interview, the more time it is likely to take. At some point, the procedure will cease to resemble a screening instrument and begin to take on the characteristics of a comprehensive diagnostic interview.

Both self-report instruments and brief clinical interviews can be designed to define the respondent's status in a way that facilitates the evaluation of his or her "caseness." Both approaches lend themselves to quantitative methods that allow for a normative framework to be established within which to evaluate individuals. Most importantly, both approaches "work." Which will work best in any particular situation depends on the nature of the screening task, the resources at hand, and the experience of the clinicians or investigators involved.

### The Problem of Low Base Rates

Almost 50 years ago, Meehl and Rosen (1955) published a report in a psychology journal that sensitized psychologists to the dramatic impact of low base rates on the

TABLE 2.4
Predictive Values of Positive and Negative Tests at Varying
Prevalence (Base) Rates

| Prevalence or Base Rate (%) | Predictive Value of a Positive (%) | Predictive Value of a Negative (%) |
|---|---|---|
| 1 | 16.1 | 99.9 |
| 2 | 27.9 | 99.9 |
| 5 | 50.0 | 99.7 |
| 10 | 67.9 | 99.4 |
| 20 | 82.6 | 98.7 |
| 50 | 95.0 | 95.0 |
| 75 | 98.3 | 83.7 |
| 100 | 100 | — |

*Note.* Synopsis of data originally presented by Vecchio (1966). Sensitivity and specificity = 95%.

predictive validity of psychological tests. The authors showed that attempts to predict a rare attribute or event, even with highly valid tests, would result in substantially more misclassifications than correct classifications if the prevalence of the attribute or event was sufficiently low. Knowledge and understanding of this important but poorly appreciated relationship remained limited to a few specialists at that time. Eleven years later, Vecchio (1966) published a report in the *New England Journal of Medicine* dealing with essentially the same phenomenon. In Vecchio's report, because the substantive aspects of the report dealt with screening tests in medicine, the information reached a much wider audience. As a result, knowledge of the special relationship between low base rates and the predictive validity of screening tests has since become widespread.

To be precise, low prevalence does not affect all aspects of a test's validity equally; its impact is felt only in the validity partition that deals with correctly classifying positives, or "cases." Predictive validity concerning negatives, or "noncases," is minimally affected, because with extremely low prevalence even a test with moderate validity will perform the task of identifying negatives adequately. This relationship is summarized by the statistics in Table 2.4, which presents a synopsis of data originally given by Vecchio (1966).

In the example developed by Vecchio, the sensitivity and specificity of the screening test are given as .95, values which do not represent realistic validity coefficients for a psychological screening test. Table 2.5 provides a more realistic example of the relationship between prevalence and positive predictive value, based on a hypothetical cohort of $N = 1,000$, and it contains validity coefficients (i.e., sensitivity and specificity) more consistent with those that might be genuinely anticipated for such tests.

The data in Tables 2.4 and 2.5 make it clear that, as the prevalence drops below 10%, the predictive value of a positive undergoes a precipitous decline. In the example presented in Tables 2.4, when the prevalence reaches 1%, the predictive value of a positive is only 16%, which means in practical terms that in such situations 5 out of 6 positives will be *false positives*. The predictive value of a negative remains extremely high throughout the range of base rates depicted and is essentially unaffected by low prevalence situations. The example presented in Tables 2.5 is more realistic in that the validity coefficients are more analogous to those commonly reported for psychological screening tests. In the screening situation depicted here, the predictive value of a

TABLE 2.5
Relationship of Prevalence (Base Rate) and Positive Predictive Value

| | Assumed Test Sensitivity = 0.80 Assumed Test Specificity = 0.90 | | | | | | | | | | |
|---|---|---|---|---|---|---|---|---|---|---|---|
| | Prevalence = 0.30 Actual Disorder | | | | Prevalence = 0.05 Actual Disorder | | | | Prevalence = 0.01 Actual Disorder | | |
| T | Pos. | Neg. | | T | Pos. | Neg. | | T | Pos. | Neg. | |
| E + | 240 | 70 | 310 | E + | 40 | 95 | 135 | E + | 8 | 99 | 107 |
| S − | 60 | 630 | 690 | S − | 10 | 855 | 865 | S − | 2 | 891 | 893 |
| T | | | | T | | | | T | | | |
| | 300 | 700 | | | 50 | 950 | | | 10 | 990 | |

Pos. Predict. Val. = 240/310 = 77%  Pos. Predict. Val. = 40/135 = 30%  Pos. Predict. Val. = 8/107 = 7.5%

positive drops from 77% when the prevalence equals 30% (the percentage of psychiatric disorders among specialized medical patients) to 7.5% when the prevalence falls to 1%. In the latter instance, 12 out of 13 positives would be *false positives*.

### Sequential Screening: A Technique for Low Base Rates

Although screening for psychiatric disorders is not usually affected by problems of low base rates, there are specific mental health phenomena (e.g., suicide) and diagnostic categories (e.g., panic disorder) for which the prevalences are quite low. In addition, as Baldessarini, Finklestein, and Arana (1983) noted, the nature of the population being screened can markedly affect the quality of screening outcomes. A good example of this is provided by the dexamethasone suppression test (DST) when used as a screen for major depressive disorder (MDD). The DST functions relatively effectively as a screen for MDD on inpatient affective disorder units, where the prevalence of the disorder is quite high. In general medical practice, however, where the prevalence of MDD is estimated to be about 5%, the DST results in unacceptable rates of misclassification. The validity of the DST is insufficient to support effective screening performance in populations with low base rates of MDD.

One method designed to help overcome low base rate problems is commonly referred to as *sequential screening*. In a sequential screening paradigm, there are two screening phases and two screening tests. Phase I involves a less refined screen, whose primary purpose is to correctly identify individuals without the condition and eliminate them from consideration in Phase II. The initial screening also has the important effect of raising the prevalence of the index condition in the remaining cohort. In Phase II, a separate test of equal or superior sensitivity is then utilized. Because the base rate of the index condition has been significantly raised by the Phase I screening, use of the Phase II screen results in much lower levels of false positive misclassification than it would otherwise. A hypothetical example of sequential screening is presented in Table 2.6.

In Phase I of the hypothetical screening, a highly valid instrument with sensitivity and specificity equal to .90 is used in a large population cohort ($N = 10,000$) with a prevalence of 4% for the index condition. Because of the low base rate, the predictive value of a positive is only 27.2%, meaning essentially that less than 1 out of every 3 positives will be true positives. The 1,320 individuals screened positive from the original cohort of 10,000 subsequently become the cohort for the Phase II screening. With an equally valid, independent test (sensitivity and specificity are both .90) and

TABLE 2.6
Hypothetical Example of Sequential Screening as a Strategy for Dealing With Low
Base Rates

| Phase 1 | Phase II |
|---|---|
| $N = 10,000$; Sensitivity $= .90$; Specificity $= .90$ | $N = 1,320$; Sensitivity $= .90$; Specificity $= .90$ |
| Prevalence (Base Rate) $= 4\%$ | Prevalence (Base Rate) $= 27.2\%$ |
| Predictive Value of a Positive $=$ | Predictive Value of a Positive $=$ |
| $\dfrac{360}{360 + 960} = 0.272 \text{ or } 27.2\%$ | $\dfrac{(.272)(.90)}{(.272)(.90) + (.728)(.10)} = 0.77 \text{ or } 77\%$ |

a base rate of 27.2%, the predictive value of a positive in Phase II rises to 77%, a substantial increase in the level of screening performance.

Sequential screening essentially zeros in on a high-risk subgroup of the population of interest by virtue of a series of consecutive sieves. These have the effect of eliminating from consideration individuals with low likelihood of having the disorder and simultaneously raise the base rate of the condition in the remaining sample. Sequential screening can become expensive because of the increased number of screening tests that must be administered. However, in certain situations where prevalence is low (e.g., HIV screening in the general population) and the validity of the screening test is already close to maximum, it may be the only method available to minimize errors in classification.

## Receiver Operating Characteristic Analysis

Although some screening tests operate in a qualitative fashion (i.e., depend on the presence or absence of a key indicator), psychological screening tests function, as do many others, along a quantitative continuum. The individual being screened must obtain a probability or score above some criterion threshold (or "cutoff") to be considered a positive (or a "case"). The cutoff value is usually that value that has been determined to maximize correct classification and minimize misclassification relative to the index disorder. If the consequences of one type of error are considered more costly than those of the other (i.e., the consequences have dramatically different utilities, as might occur if a false negative would result in missing a fatal but potentially curable disease), the cutoff value will often be adjusted to take the difference utilities into account. Although quantitative methods exist to estimate optimal threshold values (e.g., Weinstein et al., 1980), traditionally the threshold values have been selected by simple inspection of cutoff tables and their associated sensitivities and specificities.

The selection of a cutoff value automatically determines both the sensitivity and specificity of the test because it defines the rates of correct identification and misclassification. Actually, an entire distribution of cutoffs is possible, with corresponding sensitivities and specificities. Further, as touched on in the previous section, test performance (i.e., the errors associated with a particular cutoff value) is highly affected by the prevalence or base rate of the disorder under study. Viewed from this perspective, a test should not be characterized by *a* sensitivity and *a* specificity; rather it should be seen as possessing *distributions* of sensitivities and specificities associated with the distribution of possible threshold values and the distribution of possible sample prevalences.

Receiver operating characteristic (ROC) analysis is a method that enables the visualization of the entire distribution of sensitivity-specificity combinations for all possible

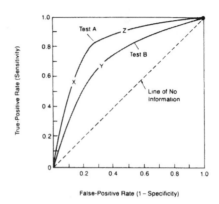

FIG. 2.1.  ROC curves for two hypothetical screening tests.

cutoff values and prevalences. As such, it enables the selection of a criterion threshold based on substantially more information and represents a much more sophisticated clinical decision process. ROC analysis was first developed by Swets (1964) in the context of signal detection paradigms in psychophysics. Subsequently, applications of the technique were developed in the areas of radiology and medical imaging (Hanley & McNeil, 1982; Metz, 1978; Swets, 1979). Madri and Williams (1986) and Murphy et al. (1987) introduced and applied ROC analysis to the task of screening for psychiatric disorders. Subsequently, Somoza and his colleagues (Somoza, 1994, 1996; Somoza & Mossman, 1990a, 1991; Somoza, Steer, Beck, & Clark, 1994) published an extensive series of in-depth reports integrating ROC analysis with information theory to optimize the performance of diagnostic and screening tests. In their informative series, these investigators reviewed the topics of construction of tests (Somoza & Mossman, 1990), the effects of prevalence (Mossman & Somoza, 1991), the optimization of information yield (Somoza & Mossman, 1992a), and the maximization of expected utility (Mossman & Somoza, 1992), among others.

Typically, an ROC curve is developed by plotting corresponding values of a test's sensitivity (true-positive rate) on the vertical axis against the complement of its specificity (false-positive rate) on the horizontal axis for the entire range of possible cutoff scores from lowest to highest (see Fig. 2.1). A number of computer programs (e.g., Somoza, 1991; Vida, 2001) are available to generate and plot ROC curves. The ROC curve demonstrates the discriminative capacity of the test at each possible definition of threshold (cutoff score) for the particular psychiatric disorder. If the discriminative capacity of the test is no better than chance, the curve will follow a diagonal straight line from the origin of the graph (lower left) to its upper right corner. This line is termed the *line of no information*. The ROC curve rises from the origin (point 0,0) to its termination point (1,1) on a plane defined as above. To the extent that a test has discriminative ability, the curve will bow in a convex manner toward the upper left corner of the graph. The greater the deviation toward the upper left corner, the greater discriminative ability the test has for the particular application at hand. Generally, the cutoff score corresponding to the upper-left-most point on the ROC curve is the empirically determined best score—the one that optimizes the balance between the true-positive rate (sensitivity) and the false-positive rate (1 − specificity). In other words, this is the cutoff score that yields the greatest discriminative efficiency for the test in the current sample.

An ROC summary statistic describing the overall discriminative capacity of a test is termed the *area under the curve* (AUC). The AUC may be thought of as a probability estimate that at each cutoff score a randomly chosen positive (or case) will demonstrate a higher score than a randomly chosen negative. When the ROC curve follows the line of no information, the AUC equals .50. In the situation of theoretically optimal discrimination, the ROC curve would follow the outline of the ordinate of the graph from point 0,0 to point 1,0 and then move at right angles to point 1,1. In this situation, the AUC would equal 1.0.

ROC analysis was introduced to the area of screening for psychiatric disorders only within the past decade or so; however, investigators have found numerous applications for the technique. In addition to simply describing the distribution of validity coefficients for a single test, ROC analysis has been used to compare various screening tests (Somoza et al., 1994; Weinstein, Berwick, Goldman, Murphy, & Barsky, 1989), aid in the validation of new tests, compare different scoring methods for a particular test (Birtchnell, Evans, Deahl, & Master, 1989), contrast the screening performance of a test in different populations (Burnam, Wells, Leake, & Lanverk, 1988; Hughson, Cooper, McArdle, & Smith, 1988), and assist in validating a foreign language version of a standard test (Chong & Wilkinson, 1989). ROC analysis has also been effectively integrated with paradigms from information theory to maximize information yield in screening (Somoza & Mossman, 1992b) and with decision-making models to optimize expected utilities of screening outcomes (Mossman & Somoza, 1992). Although ROC analysis does not by itself resolve the complex problems of psychiatric screening, it does significantly increase the information available to the decision makers and provides a relatively precise and sophisticated method for reaching decisions.

## SCREENING TESTS FOR PSYCHIATRIC DISORDERS

### A Brief History

The predecessors of modern psychological screening instruments date back to the late 19th and early 20th centuries. Sir Francis Galton (1883) created the prototype psychological questionnaire as part of an exposition for the World Fair. The first self-report symptom inventory, the *Personal Data Sheet*, was developed by Robert Woodworth (1918) as part of the effort to screen American soldiers for psychiatric disorders. At approximately the same time, the psychiatrist Adolph Meyer constructed the first psychiatric rating scale, the Phipps Behavior Chart at Johns Hopkins (Kempf, 1914). Since these pioneering efforts, many hundreds of analogous tests and rating scales have been developed and published. A number of them have become well validated and widely used. Here we briefly review a small number of these instruments in an effort to familiarize the reader with the nature of screening measures available. This chapter is not the appropriate place for a comprehensive review of psychological screening tests (see Sederer & Dickey, 1996; Spilker, 1996; Zalaquett & Wood, 1997); rather, our goal is to familiarize the reader with a number of instruments that are judged to be representative of their class.

In this section we provide a brief synopsis of each of a number of popular inventories and rating scales that are frequently employed as screening instruments. We outline each measure and provide some information about its background and

TABLE 2.7
Psychiatric Screening Tests in Common Use With Medical and Primary Care Populations

| Instrument | Author | Mode | Description | Time | Applications | Sensitivity Specificity |
|---|---|---|---|---|---|---|
| SCL–90–R | Derogatis, 1977 | Self | 90 items, multidim-ensional | 15–20 min. | 1–4, 7 | .73/.91 |
| BSI | Derogatis & Spencer, 1982 | Self | 53 items, multidim-ensional | 10–15 min. | 1–4, 7 | .72/.90 |
| GHQ | Goldberg, 1972 | Self | 60, 30, and 12 items, multidimensional | 5–15 min. | 1–5 | .69–1.0/ .75–.92 |
| CESD | Radloff, 1977 | Self | 20 items, unidim-ensional | 10 min. | 1–4 | .83–.97/ .61–.90 |
| BDI | Beck et al., 1961 | Self | 21 items, unidim-ensional | 5–10 min. | 2–4 | .76–.92/ .64–.80 |
| PRIME–MD | Spitzer et al., 1994 | Clinician | 26 items, multidim-ensional | 5–15 min. | 4 | .75/.90 |
| HRDS | Hamilton, 1960 | Clinician Rated | 21 items, unidim-ensional | 30+ min. | 1–5, 7 | .94–1.0/ 1.0 |

*Note.* 1 = community adults; 2 = community adolescents; 3 = inpatients/outpatients; 4 = medical patients; 5 = elderly patients; 6 = children; 7 = college students.

psychometric characteristics. In the case of proprietary tests (e.g., SCL–90–R, BSI/BSI–18, GHQ, BDI, PRIME–MD/PHQ), detailed discussions and comprehensive psycho-metric data are available from published manuals and associated materials. Scholarly reviews provide analogous information in the cases of the others (CESD, HRDS). Five of the screening tests discussed here are self-report, one is clinician rated, and one has versions in both modalities (PRIME–MD/PHQ). Table 2.7 provides a brief summary of instrument characteristics.

**Popular Instruments**

*SCL–90–R/BSI/BSI–18.* The SCL–90–R (Derogatis, 1977, 1983, 1994) is a 90-item multidimensional self-report symptom inventory derived from the Hopkins Symp-tom Checklist (Derogatis, Lipman, Rickles, Uhlenhuth, & Covi, 1974b) and first pub-lished in 1975. The inventory measures symptomatic distress in terms of nine primary dimensions and three global indices of distress. The dimensions include somatization, obsessive-compulsive, interpersonal sensitivity, depression, anxiety, hostility, phobic anxiety, paranoid ideation, and psychoticism. Several matching clinical rating scales, such as the Derogatis Psychiatric Rating Scale and the SCL–90 Analogue Scale, which measure the same nine dimensions, are also available. Gender-keyed norms for the SCL–90–R have been developed for adult community nonpatients, psychiatric outpa-tients, psychiatric inpatients, and adolescent nonpatients.

The Brief Symptom Inventory (BSI; Derogatis, 1993; Derogatis & Melisaratos, 1983; Derogatis & Spencer, 1982) is the brief form of the SCL–90–R. The BSI measures the same nine symptom dimensions and three global indices using only 53 items. Dimen-sion scores on the BSI correlate highly with comparable SCL–90–R scores (Derogatis, 1993), and the brief form shares most of the psychometric characteristics of the longer scale. Recently, an 18-item version of the BSI was developed and normed (Derogatis,

2000). The BSI–18 retains items from the depression, anxiety, and somatization dimensions, plus it delivers a total score. It was designed specifically to function as a screening instrument.

Both the SCL–90–R and the BSI have been used as outcome measures in an extensive array of research studies, among them a number of investigations focusing specifically on screening ( Derogatis et al., 1983; Kuhn, Bell, Seligson, Laufer, & Lindner, 1988; Royse & Drude, 1984; Zabora, Smith-Wilson, Fetting, & Enterline, 1990). The BSI–18 was also utilized effectively as a screen in a comprehensive study with over 1,500 cancer patients (Zabora et al., 2001), and it demonstrated high sensitivity to the traumatically induced stress of 9/11 in a large community sample ($N = 2,729$; Silver, Holman, McIntosh, Poulin, & Gil-Rivas, 2002). The SCL–90–R has served as an outcomes measure in over 1,000 published research studies, with over 500 listed in a published bibliography (Derogatis, 1990). The BSI has also demonstrated sensitivity to psychological distress in numerous clinical and research contexts (Cochran & Hale, 1985; O'Hara, Ghonheim, Heinrich, Metha, & Wright, 1989; Piersma, Reaume, & Boes, 1994). All of the scales in the series have been translated into numerous languages in addition to English.

*General Health Questionnaire (GHQ).* The GHQ was originally developed as a 60-item multidimensional self-report symptom inventory by Goldberg (1972). Subsequent to its publication (Goldberg & Hillier, 1979), four subscales were factor-analytically derived: somatic symptoms, anxiety and insomnia, social dysfunction, and severe depression. The GHQ is one of the most widely used screening tests for psychiatric disorder internationally, its popularity arising in part from the fact that several brief forms of the test are available (e.g., the GHQ28 and GHQ12). The more recent brief forms retain the basic four-subscale format of the longer parent scale but avoid including physical symptoms as indicators of distress (Malt, 1989). The GHQ has been validated for use in screening and outcome assessment in numerous populations, including the traumatically injured, cancer patients, geriatric populations, and many community samples (Goldberg & Williams, 1988). Mulrow et al. (1995) did a broad review of the performance of the GHQ and several other case-finding instruments in detecting depression in primary care populations, and Furukawa, Goldberg, Rabe-Hesketh, and Ustun (2001) explored the use of stratum-specific likelihood ratios to improve the performance of the GHQ, using data from the WHO Psychological Problems in General Health Care study (Ustun & Sartorious, 1995).

*Center for Epidemiologic Studies Depression Scale.* The Center for Epidemiological Studies Depression Scale (CESD) was developed by Radloff and her colleagues (Radloff, 1977). It is a brief unidimensional self-report depression scale composed of 20 items that assess the respondent's perceived mood and level of functioning within the past 7 days. Four fundamental dimensions—*depressed affect, positive affect, somatic problems,* and *interpersonal problems*—have been identified as basic to the CESD. The CESD also delivers a total aggregate score.

The CESD has been used effectively as a screening test with a number of community samples (Comstock & Helsing, 1976; Frerichs, Aneshensel, & Clark, 1981; Radloff & Locke, 1985) as well as medical (Parikh, Eden, Price, & Robinson, 1988) and clinic populations (Roberts, Rhoades, & Vernon, 1990). Shrout and Yager (1989) demonstrated that the CESD could be shortened to 5 items and would still maintain adequate sensitivity and specificity as long as prediction was limited to traditional two-class categorizations. Generally, an overall score of 16 has been used as a cutoff score for depression, with approximately 15% to 20% of community populations scoring 16 or above.

*Beck Depression Inventory (BDI).* The original BDI is a unidimensional self-report depression inventory that employs 21 items to measure the severity of depression. Pessimism, guilt, depressed mood, self-deprecation, suicidal thoughts, insomnia, somatization, and loss of libido are some of the symptom areas covered by the BDI. The BDI was developed by Beck et al. in 1961. A short (13-item) version of the BDI was introduced in 1972 (Beck & Beck, 1972), with additional psychometric evaluation accomplished subsequently (Reynolds & Gould, 1981). More recently, in response to the significant nosological revisions inherent in the DSM-IV, a revised version of the BDI (the BDI–II) has been published (Beck, Steer, & Brown, 1996). The BDI–II does differ substantially from the original BDI in that 4 items have been changed completely and 2 others have been modified.

The BDI has been characterized by Beck as most appropriate for measuring severity of depression in patients who have been clinically diagnosed with depression. It has been utilized to assess depression worldwide with numerous community and clinical populations (Steer & Beck, 1996). Each of the items represents a characteristic symptom of depression on which the respondent is to rate him- or herself on a 4-point scale (0–3). The scores are then summed to yield a total depression score. Beck's rationale for this system is that the frequency of depressive symptoms is distributed along a continuum from "nondepressed" to "severely depressed." In addition, the *number* of symptoms is viewed as correlating with intensity of distress and severity of depression.

The BDI has been used as a screening device with renal dialysis patients as well as with medical inpatients and outpatients (Craven, Rodin, & Littlefield, 1988). Subsequently, Whitaker et al. (1990) used the BDI with a group of 5,108 community adolescents and noted that it performed validly in screening for major depression in this previously undiagnosed population. In screening community populations, scores in the 17–20 range are generally considered suggestive of dysphoria, and scores greater than 20 are felt to indicate the presence of clinical depression (Steer & Beck, 1996).

*Primary Care Evaluation of Mental Disorders (PRIME–MD).* The PRIME–MD is a multistage case-finding instrument developed by Spitzer et al. (1994) for use by primary care physicians to aid in the identification of psychiatric disorders in general medical populations. The PRIME–MD differs from most screening and case-finding instruments by virtue of the fact that it not only enables the clinician to assess risk potential (caseness) but also facilitates the assignment of a DSM diagnosis in the instance of positives. Consistent with this declared dual purpose, the instrument incorporates two evaluative modalities: Screening is accomplished through a self-report inventory, the Patient Questionnaire (PQ), and diagnostic assignment is made as a result of a clinician interview, carried out in accordance with the Clinician Evaluation Guide (CEG). Mood disorders, anxiety disorders, alcohol abuse, and somataform and eating disorders are reflected in the modules of the CEG. In an effort to reduce administration time even further, the group developed a new totally self-report version of the CEG segment called the *Patient Problem Questionnaire (PPQ)* (Spitzer, Williams, & Kroenke, 1997). Subsequently, a completely self-report version of the PRIME–MD, termed the *Patient Health Questionnaire (PHQ)*, was developed and validated (Spitzer et al., 1999).

In addition to the original validation studies done by Spitzer et al. (1994), other validation research has been done with the various versions of the instrument. Kobak and associates (1997) developed a version of the PRIME–MD utilizing interactive voice response (IVR) technology and found that the IVR–PRIME–MD was comparable to the face-to-face interview version in terms of diagnostic efficiency. Whooley, Avins, Miranda, and Browner (1997) also used the instrument with a large VA sample and found it to perform well. Spitzer et al. (1999) also completed a validation study of the newer self-report PHQ and found study physicians reported high levels of utility for the instrument when used in treatment planning.

Recently, Williams, et al. (2002) published an excellent review of the performance of the CESD, the BDI, the PRIME–MD, the SDSS-PC, and the HSCL (progenitor of the SCL–90–R) across 28 published studies involving 25,550 patients screened for major depression. The authors concluded that the majority of these instruments possess "reasonable performance characteristics" that make them helpful to clinicians in identifying cases of major depression.

*Hamilton Rating Scale for Depression (HRDS/HAM-D).* The HRDS is designed to provide quantitative assessments of the severity of a clinical depression. The HRDS was developed in 1960 by Hamilton and revised in 1967 (Hamilton, 1967). It consists of 21 items, each measuring a depressive symptom. Hamilton has recommended using only 17 items when scoring because of the rarity of the symptoms measured by the remaining items (e.g., depersonalization).

Hedlund and Vieweg (1979) reviewed the psychometric and substantive properties of the HRDS in two dozen studies and gave it a very favorable evaluation. More recently, Bech (1987) completed a similar review and concluded that the HRDS is an extremely useful scale for measuring depression. A *Structured Interview Guide for the HRDS (SIGH–D)* also is available (Williams, 1988). It provides standardized instructions for administration and has been shown to improve inter-rater reliability. The HRDS has become a standard outcomes assessment instrument in antidepressant clinical drug trials.

## PSYCHIATRIC SCREENING IN SPECIFIC SETTINGS

### Community Settings

By far the most comprehensive source data on the prevalence of psychiatric disorders in local communities is the NIMH Epidemiologic Catchment Area (ECA) investigation, a study of psychiatric disorders involving nearly 20,000 individuals. These results make explicit the fact that psychiatric disorders are highly prevalent in our society. This is so regardless of whether we assess lifetime (Robins et al., 1984), 6-month (Blazer et al., 1984; Myers et al., 1984), or 1-month (Regier et al., 1988) prevalence estimates. The 1-month prevalence for any psychiatric disorder, across all demographic parameters, was 15.4%, similar to European and Australian estimates, which ranged from 9% to 16% (Regier et al., 1988).

In terms of specific diagnoses, the overall rate for affective disorders was 5.1%, and that for anxiety disorders was 7.3% (Regier et al., 1988). Six-month prevalence estimates for affective disorders ranged from 4.6% to 6.5% across the five ECA sites (Myers et al., 1984), and 6-month estimates for anxiety disorders, subsequently updated by Weissman and Merikangas (1986), reveal rates for panic disorder ranging from 0.6% to 1.0%. Agoraphobia showed prevalences from 2.5% to 5.8% across the various ECA sites.

These data demonstrate unequivocally that psychiatric disorders are a persistent and demonstrable problem and affect substantial numbers of people within our society. Unfortunately, there is no currently effective system for screening individuals per se; we must wait until they seek medical advice or treatment for a disorder and formally enter the health care system. At that point, primary care "gatekeepers" have the first, and in most instances the only, opportunity to identify psychiatric morbidity.

## Medical Settings

In medical populations, prevalence estimates of psychiatric disorder are substantially higher than community rates. This is particularly true of anxiety and depressive disorders, which account for the vast majority of psychiatric diagnoses assigned to medical patients (Barrett et al., 1988; Derogatis et al., 1983; Von Korff et al., 1988). In recent reviews of psychiatric disorder prevalence in medical populations, Barrett et al. (1988) observed prevalence rates of 25% to 30%, and Derogatis and Wise (1989) reported prevalence estimates ranging from 22% to 33% for a broad range of medical cohorts. Derogatis and Wise concluded, "In general, it appears that up to one-third of medical inpatients reveal symptoms of depression, while 20 to 25% manifest more substantial depressive symptoms" (p.101). Concerning anxiety, Kedward and Cooper (1966) observed a prevalence rate of 27% in their study of a London general practice, and Schulberg and his colleagues (1985) observed a combined rate of 8.5% for phobic and panic disorders among American primary care patients. In another contemporary review, Wise and Taylor (1990) concluded that 5% to 20% of medical inpatients suffer the symptoms of anxiety and 6% receive formal anxiety diagnoses. They further determined that depressive phenomena are even more prevalent among medical patients, citing reported rates of depressive syndromes of 11% to 26% in inpatient samples.

Given prevalence rates such as these, along with the acknowledged escalations in morbidity and mortality associated with psychiatric disorders, there is little doubt that screening programs for psychiatric disorders in medical populations could achieve impressive utility. Potential therapeutic gains associated with psychiatric screening would be further enhanced by the fact that related problems such as substance abuse, inappropriate diagnostic tests, and high utilization of health care services also would be minimized. Particularly dramatic gains could be realized in specialty areas where estimated prevalence rates are over 50%, such as HIV infection (Lyketsos, Hutton, Fishman, Schwarz, & Trishman, 1996) and obesity/weight reduction (Goldstein, Goldsmith, Anger, & Leon, 1996). In general, early and accurate identification of occult mental disorders in individuals with primary medical conditions would lead to a significant improvement in their well-being. It would also help relieve the fiscal and logistic strain on the health care system.

## Academic Settings

Recollections of college days often bring to mind idyllic images of youthful abandon, unencumbered by the tedious demands and stresses of everyday adult life. However, the realities of contemporary student life paint a different portrait. The period of undergraduate and graduate studies represents a phase in the life cycle of rapid change, high stress, and previously unparalleled demands on an individual's coping resources. In the light of this reality, it is not surprising that it also represents a phase of life associated with a high incidence of psychiatric morbidity.

Numerous studies have reported prevalence rates of psychological disorders in university populations. Telch, Lucas, and Nelson (1989) investigated panic disorder in a sample of 2,375 college students and found that 12% reported at least one panic attack in their lifetime. Furthermore, 2.36% of the sample met DSM–III–R criteria for panic disorder. Craske and Krueger (1990) reported lifetime prevalence of nocturnal panic attacks in 5.1% of their 294 undergraduates. Prevalence of daytime panic attacks was also 5.1%, but only 50% of those reporting nocturnal panic also reported daytime panic.

Disorders that are especially salient in college populations include addictions, eating disorders, and depression. West, Drummond, and Eames (1990) found that, of 270 college students, 25.6% of men and 14.5% of women reported drinking large quantities of alcohol weekly. This same sample included 20% of men and 6% of women who damaged property after drinking in the past year. Seay and Beck (1984) administered the Michigan Alcohol Screening Test to 395 undergraduates and observed that 25% scored as problem drinkers and 7% as alcoholics. However, only 1% considered themselves to have a problem.

Eating disorders, especially bulimia, are relatively common in college populations, since the average age at onset is between adolescence and early adulthood (American Psychiatric Association, 1987). In a study of 1,040 college students, Striegel-Moore, Silberstein, Frensch, and Rodin (1989) found rates of bulimia of 3.8% for females and 0.2% for males. In another cohort of 69 college women, Schmidt and Telch (1990) studied the prevalence of personality disorders in three distinct groups. In a group defined as bulimic, 61% met criteria for at least one personality disorder, and "nonbulimic binge eaters" had a 13% prevalence. The prevalence of personality disorders in the control group was only 4%. Most bulimics (57%) who exhibited personality disorders met criteria for borderline personality disorder.

Wells, Klerman, and Deykin (1987) reported that 33% of their sample of 424 adolescents met the standard criteria for depression using the CESD. When more stringent duration criteria were applied, the rate fell to 16%. Even more troubling are the results of a study by McDermott, Hawkins, Littlefield, and Murray (1989) which revealed that 65% of the 331 college women and 51% of the 241 college men they surveyed met criteria for depression using the CESD. Furthermore, 10% of this sample reported contemplating self-injurious behavior during the previous week. Suicidal ideation was reported by 8%, and 1% said they thought about suicide "most or all of the time" during the past week. The results of these studies make it apparent that university students suffer from considerable levels of psychiatric morbidity. A critical question then becomes, to what degree is this morbidity detected by university health centers?

University physicians carry much of the burden for detecting psychological disorders because of the nature of their contacts with students. These physicians, like those in community settings, invariably treat many patients who present with somatic complaints that are actually manifestations of an underlying psychological disorder. The relative homogeneity of the age of the student group does carry some advantages with it, but beyond that fact university physicians are essentially in the same position as their primary care counterparts when it comes to recognizing psychological disorders. There is only a small amount of published data regarding the accuracy of university physicians' diagnoses; however, it is probably safe to assume that they are as precise as their primary care colleagues, which means the level of detection is unsatisfactory given the prevalence of psychiatric disorders in college populations.

The high prevalence of psychiatric disorders in university populations is well documented, and there are a variety of instruments currently available that can improve detection rates in university students. It is now incumbent upon academic decision makers to formally integrate such instruments into university mental health care systems.

## SCREENING FOR SPECIALIZED PROBLEMS

### Screening for Alcohol Abuse/Alcoholism

Approximately 7.4% of the adult population (14 million individuals) meet the DSM–IV diagnostic criteria for alcohol abuse/alcoholism, and the estimated "cost of illness" is nearly $185 billion (NIAAA, Tenth Special Report to the U.S. Congress on Alcohol and Health, 2001). Kessler et al. (1994) found a lifetime prevalence of alcoholism in the general adult population of 14%. In primary care and community hospital settings, where less severe forms of alcohol use (e.g., hazardous drinking) are included, the prevalence of problem drinking has been reported to be as high as 20% (Bradley, 1992; Muller, 1996; Saunders, Aasland, Babor, de la Fuente, & Grant, 1993; Schloring, Klas, Willems, & Everett, 1994). Additionally, alcohol use and abuse is strongly related to violent crime, motor vehicle accidents, and lost productivity (NIAAA, Tenth Special Report to the U.S. Congress on Alcohol and Health, 2001).

Clearly, alcohol-related problems present a major public health concern. Routine screening for alcoholism and hazardous drinking, by enabling early intervention, could help lessen the burden of alcohol-related consequences. However, alcoholism is a disease that many physicians feel unprepared to diagnose and treat. Israel et al. (1996) noted that 30% to 40% of physicians feel unprepared to diagnose alcoholism, and Chang (1997) reported that only 19% of physicians felt that they had adequate preparation for treating alcohol-related disorders. Physicians often lack knowledge about the disorders and their symptoms, which can impede treatment and may contribute to further medical problems. Hopkins, Zarro, and McCarter (1994) observed that physicians accurately identified only 37% of problem drinkers. Other barriers to routine screening for problematic alcohol use and dependence include unfamiliarity of physicians with available screening instruments (Bradley, Curry, Koepsell, & Larson, 1995; Wenrich, Paauw, Carline, Curtis, & Ramsey, 1995) and time constraints (Stange, Flocke, & Goodwin, 1998). For example, Ford, Klag, Whelton, Goldsmith, and Levine (1994) noted that, although 45% of physicians had heard of the CAGE, only 14% could recite all four questions needed.

The routine use of alcohol screens would help primary care physicians and other health professionals to identify alcohol-related disorders quickly and accurately so that they could initiate timely treatment or referral. Three of the most commonly used screening instruments are the Michigan Alcoholism Screening Test (MAST; Selzer, 1971), the CAGE questionnaire (Ewing, 1984), and the Alcohol Use Disorders Identification Test (AUDIT; Babor, de la Fuente, Saunders, & Grant, 1989). In addition to these, several reports have noted the utility of a single item (quantity and/or frequency of drinking) as a screen for problem drinking (Gordon et al., 2001; Taj, Devera Sales, & Vinson, 1998; Williams & Vinson, 2001). Each of the three screening instruments mentioned is briefly outlined below. For a more detailed analysis and comparison of the utility of these instruments, see the recent review by Fiellin, Reid, and O'Connor (2000).

*Michigan Alcoholism Screening Test (MAST).* The MAST (Selzer, 1971) was designed to detect alcohol dependence and is composed of 24 yes/no weighted questions. The weighted scores are summed to yield a total score. Individuals with total scores of 0 to 3 are considered to be "non-alcohol dependent," those with scores of 4 or 5 are considered to be "probably alcohol dependent," and those with scores greater than 5 are considered to be "definitely alcohol dependent." The MAST takes about 20 minutes to administer, and another minute or two is needed to compute the total score. There are two revised versions designed to shorten the administration time. The Brief MAST (BMAST; Pokorny, Miller, & Kaplan, 1972) consists of 10 or the original MAST items, and the Short MAST (SMAST; Selzer, Vinokur, & van Rooijen, 1975) consists of 13 of the original items.

The reliability of the MAST and the SMAST has been documented by Selzer et al. (1975). For the MAST, internal consistency ranged from .83 to .95, and for the SMAST from .76 to .93. The diagnostic accuracy of the MAST has been assessed in a variety of patient populations, with reported sensitivities from 71% to 100% and specificities from 81% to 96% (Bernadt, Mumford, Taylor, Smith, & Murray, 1982; Cleary et al., 1988; Ross, Gavin, & Skinner, 1990). Studies that used unweighted scoring of the SMAST and a cutoff of 2 or more found sensitivities of 82% and 100% and specificities of 96% and 85% for lifetime and current alcohol abuse/dependence, respectively (Fiellin et al., 2000). Other studies have reported sensitivities from 48% to 80% and specificities from 80% to 97%, with variations related to referent diagnostic category (lifetime vs. current abuse/dependence), scoring method (unweighted and cutoff equal to 2 or more vs. weighted and cutoff equal to 5 or more), and the population being studied (see Fiellin et al., 2000).

*CAGE Questionnaire.* One of the simpler tools physicians can use is the CAGE questionnaire (Ewing, 1984), which consists of four questions designed to screen for alcohol abuse/dependence. The four questions are these:

1. Have you ever felt the need to **C**ut down on your drinking?
2. Have you ever felt **A**nnoyed by someone criticizing your drinking?
3. Have you ever felt **G**uilty about your drinking?
4. Have your ever felt the need of an **E**ye opener (a drink first thing in the morning)?

The sensitivity of the CAGE ranged from 53% to 91% and the specificity from 77% to 97% (Fiellin et al., 2000) when used to screen for alcohol abuse/dependence. When used to screen for hazardous/harmful alcohol use, the CAGE had a sensitivity between 49% and 69% and a specificity between 75% and 95% (Fiellin et al., 2000; Israel et al., 1996). As with the MAST, performance of the CAGE has varied with differences in the patient population (gender and ethnic differences) and whether current or lifetime alcohol use was being screened.

*Alcohol Use Disorders Identification Test (AUDIT).* The AUDIT was developed by the World Health Organization to screen for less severe forms of alcohol use (hazardous/harmful drinking) in addition to alcohol abuse/dependence (Saunders, Aasland, Babor, et al., 1993). The audit consists of 10 questions that cover the quantity and frequency of alcohol use, symptoms of alcohol dependence, and alcohol-related problems. Questions are scored 0 to 4 (maximum score = 40), with a higher score indicating more problematic alcohol use. A cutoff score of 8 or more is commonly used to indicate hazardous/harmful alcohol use that may lead or be related to alcohol dependence (Saunders, Aasland, Amundsen, et al., 1993; Saunders, Aasland, Babor, et al., 1993).

Used as a screen for harmful or heavy drinking (cutoff ≥ 8), the AUDIT has a sensitivity of 95% or better and a specificity of 78% or better (Fiellin et al., 2000). Similar results were reported by Saunders, Aasland, Amundsen, et al. (1993) and Saunders, Aasland, Babor, et al. (1993) in the original publications for the AUDIT. The performance characteristics of the AUDIT have not been as consistently good when it has been used to screen for alcohol abuse/dependence. In the review by Fiellin et al. (2000), the AUDIT had a sensitivity of 38% to 61% and a specificity of 91% to 96%. The performance of the AUDIT varied depending on whether the focus was on detecting current or lifetime alcohol abuse/dependence. Results also varied depending on gender and ethnic group.

*Other Alcohol Use Screening Instruments.* Recently there have been several reports on the utility of single-item screens for problematic alcohol use. Taj et al. (1998) asked patients in a primary care setting the following question: "On any single occasion during the past 3 months, have you had more than 5 drinks containing alcohol?" For detecting problem drinkers, the sensitivity of this single item was 62% and the specificity 93%. Williams and Vinson (2001) revised the single-item screen of Taj et al. by using different thresholds for men and women and asking, "When was the last time you had more than $x$ drinks in 1 day?" ($x = 5$ for men and $x = 4$ for women). In this patient population (with a prevalence of hazardous drinking or alcohol use disorder of 35%), a response of "within the past 3 months" was considered positive for problematic drinking. The sensitivity and specificity were each 86%, and the ROC area under the curve was 0.90.

In a similar effort to condense alcohol-screening instruments, Gordon et al. (2001) took the first three questions of the AUDIT (AUDIT–C) and the third question alone (AUDIT–3) and compared their performance with that of the full AUDIT. Additionally, all three AUDIT scores were compared to a criterion of hazardous drinking based on quantity and frequency of drinking (≥16 drinks per week for men and ≥12 drinks per week for women). Cutoff scores were 8 or higher for the AUDIT, 3 or higher for the AUDIT–C, and 1 or higher for the AUDIT–3. Compared with the quantity-frequency criterion for hazardous drinking, the sensitivity and specificity for the AUDIT were 76% and 92%, respectively. The sensitivity and specificity for the AUDIT–C and AUDIT–3 were 99.6% and 48.3% and 89.1% and 64.7%, respectively. When compared with the full AUDIT, the AUDIT–C had a sensitivity and specificity of 94.9% and 68.1%, respectively, and the AUDIT–3 had a sensitivity and specificity of 99.6% and 51.1%, respectively.

These findings suggest that questions assessing quantity, frequency, and binge drinking are comparable to the full AUDIT and CAGE. In fact, Fleming (2001) and Gordon et al. (2001) advocate using one of the above-mentioned abbreviated instruments to identify patients with hazardous drinking and then administering the full AUDIT or CAGE to those with a score above the cutoff to more thoroughly define the nature and severity of their alcohol use/abuse.

To summarize, practitioners now have several valid instruments and effective strategies available to screen for alcohol abuse/dependence. The recent review by Fiellin et al. (2000) provides an excellent review of the most commonly used screening instruments and the factors known to influence their accuracy and utility. Some of these factors include the target condition the screen is designed to detect, the criterion standard used to compare the screening instrument, and the study sample/population (e.g., gender, ethnicity, and setting, such as primary care vs. emergency department). All of these factors influence the performance and accuracy of the instruments and thus will determine the utility of a given screen. Also, the approach recommended by Fleming (2001) and Gordon et al. (2001), to use an initial abbreviated screen, then a more comprehensive screen for initial positives, shows promise as a way of increasing effectiveness.

### Screening for Suicidal Behavior

*Suicidal behavior* is a phrase that strongly affects most physicians, psychologists, and other health care professionals. Suicidal behavior has always been a perplexing subject for members of the health care community because of its perceived unpredictability and its inherent life-threatening nature. Chiles and Strosahl (1995) define suicidal behavior as a "broad spectrum of thoughts, communications, and acts . . . ranging from the least common, completed suicide, . . . to the more frequent, suicidal communications, . . . and the most frequent, suicidal ideation and verbalizations" (pp. 52). Chiles and Strosahl report that for the past 20 years the rate of suicide has remained stable in the United States at approximately 12.7 deaths per 100,000, and suicide ranks as the eighth leading cause of death in the general population. Suicide ranks as the third leading cause of death for individuals 18–24 years old, and the suicide rate among the elderly (i.e., those over 65) is approximately double the rate of suicide in the 18- to 24-year-old population.

Suicidal behavior is generally broken down into three categories. The first encompasses *suicidal ideation*, which involves thoughts about suicide. Relatively little is known about the predictive value of suicidal ideation. The second category consists of *suicide attempts*, which tend to be more common in females and younger individuals. Chiles and Strosahl (1995) stated that approximately 50% of those who attempt suicide have no formal mental health diagnosis. The last category consists of cases of *completed suicide*, which is more common in males and older individuals, many of whom have formal psychiatric diagnoses. Evidence also suggests that whites and divorced or separated persons are at increased risk for suicide, as are individuals with diagnoses of depression, drug abuse, panic disorder, generalized anxiety disorder, phobias, posttraumatic stress disorder, obsessive-compulsive disorder, somatoform disorder, and dysthymic disorder (Lish et al., 1996). Other risk factors include loss of a spouse (increases risk for up to 4 years), unemployment, physical illness, bereavement, and physical abuse. Some personality traits associated with suicide include poor problem solving, dichotomous thinking, and feelings of helplessness (Chiles & Strosahl, 1995).

Lish et al. (1996) noted that 82% of the people who commit suicide have visited a primary care physician within 6 months, 53% within 1 month, and 40% within 1 week prior to the suicide. This fact makes it imperative for primary care physicians to be able to screen for and recognize the risk factors involved in suicidal behavior. Because medical illness is itself a risk factor for suicide, primary care physicians are more likely to see patients exhibiting suicidal behavior in its initial stage than are mental health professionals such as psychologists or psychiatrists. Because they are usually not well trained in the identification of mental disorders, these physicians frequently miss the risk factors associated with suicidal behavior.

A major problem that affects screening for suicidal behavior is the phenomenon of *low base rates*, discussed previously, for there is indeed a low prevalence of suicide in the general population. Chiles and Strosahl (1995) reported a lifetime prevalence of suicide between 1% and 12%, and Lish et al. (1996) reported a 7.5% prevalence of suicidal behavior in a VA hospital sample. As pointed out earlier, with prevalences this low, even the most valid screening tests will produce an unacceptably high number of false positives for every true positive identified.

One of the most common ways of estimating or predicting suicidal behavior is to construct a *profile of risk factors*. As already mentioned, *age* (younger and older individuals are at higher risk for suicidal behavior) and *race* (whites, Hispanics, and Asians are 2 times more likely to attempt suicide than African-Americans [Lish et al., 1996]) have significant predictive value. In addition, those with a mental health diagnosis are 12 times more likely, those who have had previous mental health treatment are 7 times more likely, and those in poor physical health are 4 times more likely to attempt suicide. Even with these ratios, Chiles and Strosahl (1995) noted that profiling is not sufficiently powerful to accurately predict suicide in individuals but is better suited to documenting differential rates of occurrence of suicidal behavior across groups. Some key risk factors addressed by these authors as part of an overall evaluation of suicidal behavior include a positive evaluation of suicidal behavior, a low tolerance of emotional pain, a high level of hopelessness, sense of the inescapability of suicide, and low survival and coping beliefs.

Although a clinical interview that elicits a detailed history of treatment and previous suicidal behaviors appears to be the most effective predictor of current suicidal behavior, comprehensive interviewing can often be very time consuming and is not cost-effective or practical for screening purposes. Several brief instruments have been found to be useful in predicting suicidal behavior, including the Beck Hopelessness Scale (BHS; Beck, Kovacs, & Weissman, 1975). In addition, Westefeld and Liddel (1994) noted that the 21-item BDI may be particularly useful for screening for suicidal behavior in college students. Derogatis and Derogatis (1996) have documented the utility of the SCL–90–R and the BSI in screening for suicidal behavior. A number of investigators have reported that the primary symptom dimensions and the global scores of the SCL–90–R/BSI are capable of identifying those likely to engage in suicidal behavior among individuals diagnosed with depression and panic disorder (Bulik, Carpenter, Kupfer, & Frank, 1990; Noyes, Chrisiansen, Clancy, Garvey, & Suelzer, 1991). Similarly, Swedo et al. (1991) found that all SCL–90–R subscales successfully distinguished suicide attempters from controls in an adolescent population and that the majority of subscales were effective in discriminating attempters from members of an intermediate at-risk group. Adolescents and adults who attempted suicide tended to perceive themselves as more distressed and hopeless on the SCL–90–R than the at-risk group, a finding confirmed by Cohen, Test, and Brown (1990) using the BSI.

Several other instruments have been used to screen for suicidal behavior, including the SCREENER and the College Student Reasons for Living Inventory. Lish et al. (1996) used the SCREENER to screen for psychiatric disorders and to determine the possibility of suicidal behavior. The SCREENER screens for DSM–IV Axis I conditions and is available in 96-item and 44-item versions. It contains three questions that address death or suicide and one that addresses suicidal ideation directly. The authors state that clinicians should screen for substance abuse and anxiety disorders as well as major depression because all of these disorders increase the risk of suicidal behavior in a primary care setting.

The College Student Reasons for Living Inventory (CSRLI) is a college student version of the 47-item Reasons for Living Inventory (Westefeld, Cardin, & Deaton, 1992). The CSRLI produces a total score as well as scores for six subscales: Survival and

Coping Beliefs, College and Future-Related Concerns, Moral Objections, Responsibility to Friends and Family, Fear of Suicide, and Fear of Social Disapproval. Westefeld, Bandura, Kiel, and Scheel (1996) collected additional data on the CSRLI and found that college students who were at higher risk for suicidality endorsed fewer reasons for living. The authors stated that the data support using the CSRLI as screening tool in a college setting.

Two other methods for screening suicidal behavior are worth a brief mention. In the first, a computer interview program developed by Greist et al. (1974) is used to assess suicide risk. The interview consists of both open-ended and multiple-choice questions, and the program uses a "branching" system of questions based on answers previously given. The method was well received by the patients and correctly predicted 70% of suicide attempts whereas clinicians predicted only 40%. The second is a form of profiling, but unlike traditional profiling it uses "manifest predictors." Bjarnason and Thorlindsson (1994) suggested that predictors such as school posture (two questions), leisure time (two questions about music and two about the use of leisure time), peer and parent relations (eight questions), consumption (five questions about smoking, alcohol, caffeine, and skipping meals), and contact with suicidal behavior (three questions) should be used to complement the more common "latent" predictors, such as depression and hopelessness.

### Screening for Cognitive Impairment

Screening for cognitive impairment, especially when dealing with geriatric populations, is extremely important, as it is estimated that up to 70% of patients with an organic mental disorder (OMD) go undetected (Strain et al., 1988). Because some OMDs are reversible if discovered early enough, screening programs in high-risk populations can have a very high utility. Even for conditions that are irreversible, early detection and diagnosis can help in the development of a treatment plan and the education of family members.

There are several instruments available that provide quick and efficient screening of cognitive functioning. Most of these address the general categories of cognitive functioning covered in the standard mental status examinations, including attention, concentration, intelligence, judgment, learning ability, memory, orientation, perception, problem solving, psychomotor ability, reaction time, and social intactness (McDougall, 1990). However, not all of the instruments include items from all of these categories. These general instruments can be contrasted with cognitive screening instruments that have a more specific focus. For example, the Stroke Unit Mental Status Examination (SUMSE) was designed specifically to identify cognitive deficits and assist in developing rehabilitation programs for stroke patients (Hajek, Rutman, & Scher, 1989). Another example of a screening instrument with a specific focus is the Dementia of Alzheimer's Type Inventory (DAT), designed to distinguish Alzheimer's disease from other dementias (Cummings & Benson, 1986). Previously, instruments with a specific focus tended to be less common, owing to their limited range of applicability. They have become more popular and are now often used in conjunction with general instruments.

Unlike other screening tests, the great majority of cognitive impairment scales are administered by an examiner. Of the instruments reviewed here, none are self-reporting. There are no pencil-and-paper inventories that can be completed by the respondent alone. Instead, these screening instruments are designed to be administered by a professional and require a combination of oral and written responses. Most

TABLE 2.8
Screening Instruments for Cognitive Impairment

| Instrument | Author | Description | Applications | Sensitivity/ Specificity |
|---|---|---|---|---|
| MMSE | Folstein et al., 1975 | 11 items; designed to determine level of cognitive impairment | 1, 3, 4 | .83/.89 |
| CCSE | Jacobs et al., 1977 | 30 items; designed to detect presence of organic mental disorder | 2–5 | .73/.90 |
| SPMSQ | Pfeiffer, 1975 | 10 items; designed to detect presence of cognitive impairment | 1 | .55–.88/ .72–.96 |
| HSCS | Faust & Fogel, 1989 | 15 items; designed to estimate presence, scope, and severity of cognitive impairment | 2 | .94/.92 |
| MSQ | Kahn et al., 1960 | 10 items; designed to quantify dementia | 1–6 | .55–.96/NA |

*Note.* 1 = community populations; 2 = cognitively intact patients; 3 = hospital inpatients; 4 = medical patients; 5 = geriatric patients; 6 = long-term care patients.

of the tests are highly transportable, however, and can be administered by a wide variety of health care workers.

Following is a description of nine cognitive impairment screening instruments. The purpose is merely to provide some data on the nature of each measure and its psychometric properties (see also Table 2.8).

*Mini-Mental State Examination (MMSE).* The MMSE was developed by Folstein, Folstein, and McHugh (1975) to determine the *level* of cognitive impairment. It is an 11-item scale measuring six aspects of cognitive function: orientation, registration, attention and calculation, recall, language, and praxis. Scores can range from 0 to 30, with lower scores indicating greater impairment.

The MMSE has proved successful at assessing levels of cognitive impairment in many populations, including community residents (Kramer, German, Anthony, Von Korff, & Skinner, 1985), hospital patients (Teri, Larson, & Reiffler, 1988), residents of long-term care facilities (Lesher & Whelihan, 1986), and neurological patients (Dick et al., 1984). However, Escobar et al. (1986) suggested using another instrument with Spanish-speaking individuals, as the MMSE may overestimate dementia in this population. For similar reasons, Roca et al. (1984) recommended other instruments for patients with less than 8 years of schooling. In contrast, the MMSE may underestimate cognitive impairment in psychiatric populations (Faustman, Moses, & Cernansky, 1990). The MMSE appears to have a lower sensitivity with mildly impaired individuals, who are more likely to be labeled as demented (Doyle, Dunn, Thadani, & Lenihan, 1986). Consequently, the MMSE is most useful for patients with moderate to moderately severe dementia. Fuhrer and Ritchie (1993) more recently confirmed that the MMSE was more discriminating for moderate dementias than milder cases but did not find a significant difference associated with education. They also noted that cutoff scores for the MMSE require adjustment when comparisons involve clinical samples with base rates higher than the 6% prevalence observed in the general population.

*Cognitive Capacity Screening Examination (CCSE).*   The CCSE is a 30-item scale designed to detect diffuse organic disorders, especially delirium, in medical populations. The instrument was developed by Jacobs, Berhard, Delgado, and Strain (1977) and is recommended if delirium is suspected. The items include questions involving orientation, digit recall, serial sevens, verbal short-term memory, abstractions, and arithmetic, all of which are helpful in detecting delirium (Baker, 1989).

The CCSE has been used with geriatric patients (McCartney & Palmateer, 1985) as well as hospitalized medico-surgical patients (Foreman, 1987). In a comparison study of several brief screening instruments, the CCSE was shown to be the most reliable and valid (Foreman, 1987). Like the MMSE, the CCSE is also influenced by the educational level of the subject. However, unlike the MMSE, the CCSE cannot differentiate levels of cognitive impairment or types of dementias, and it is most appropriate for cognitively intact patients (Judd et al., 1986).

*Short Portable Mental Status Questionnaire (SPMSQ).*   The SPMSQ (Pfeiffer, 1975) is a 10-item scale for use with community and/or institutional residents. This scale is unique in that it has been used with rural and less educated populations (Baker, 1989). The items assess orientation and recent and remote memory; however, visuospatial skills are not tested. The SPMSQ is a reliable detector of organicity (Haglund & Schuckit, 1976) but should not be used to predict the progression or course of the disorder (Berg et al., 1987).

*High Sensitivity Cognitive Screen (HSCS).*   This scale was designed to be as sensitive and comprehensive as lengthier instruments while still being clinically convenient. It was developed by Faust and Fogel (1989) for use with 16-to 65-year-old native English-speaking subjects who have at least an eighth grade education and are free from gross cognitive dysfunction. The 15 items include reading, writing, immediate and delayed recall, and sentence construction tasks, among others. The HSCS has shown adequate reliability and validity and is best used to estimate the presence, scope, and severity of cognitive impairment (Faust & Fogel, 1989). The HSCS cannot pinpoint specific areas of involvement, and as most of these scales, its use should be a first step toward cognitive evaluation, not a substitute for a standard neuropsychological assessment.

*Mental Status Questionnaire (MSQ).*   The MSQ is a 10-item scale developed by Kahn, Goldfarb, Pollock, and Peck (1960). It has been used successfully with medical geriatric patients (LaRue, D'Elia, Clark, Spar, & Jarvik, 1986), community residents (Shore, Overman, & Wyatt, 1983), and long-term care patients (Fishback, 1977). Disadvantages of this measure include its sensitivity to the education and ethnicity of the subject; its reduced sensitivity with mildly impaired individuals; and its omission of tests of retention, registration, and cognitive processing (Baker, 1989).

*Other Instruments.*   Three measures have been developed that are particularly appropriate for primary care use, since their main function is to simply detect or rule out the presence of dementia. FROMAJE (Libow, 1981) classifies individuals into normal, mild, moderate, and severe dementia groups and has been used successfully with long-term care patients (Rameizl, 1984). The Blessed Dementia Scale (Blessed, Tomlinson, & Roth, 1968) measures changes in activities and habits, personality, interests, and drives and is useful for determining the presence of dementia, though not its progression. Finally, the Global Deterioration Scale (GDS; Reisberg, Ferris, DeLeon, & Crook, 1982) can be used to distinguish between normal aging, age-associated memory impairment, and primary degenerative disorder (such as Alzheimer's disease). The GDS is useful for assessing the magnitude and progression of cognitive decline (Reisberg, 1984).

Recently, other innovative approaches have been proposed. With specific reference to Alzheimer's disease, Steffens et al. (1996) proposed using the Telephone Interview for Cognitive Status in conjunction with a videotaped mental status exam. These researchers believe that the use of a telephone-based methodology shows some promise and may help physicians deal with time constraints. Another innovative new scale is the Chula Mental Test (CMT), developed by Jitapunkul, Lailert, Worakul, Srikiatkhachorn, and Ebrahim (1996) for use with elderly respondents from underdeveloped countries. The authors comment that most cognitive screening measures have been based on highly developed Western notions of cognitive dysfunction. Consequently, they may not be culturally or linguistically relevant in other countries. The CMT is a 13-item scale that is less biased toward education and literacy, than other scales and results in fewer false positives when used for screening in underdeveloped countries. The CMT tests for remote memory, orientation, attention, language, abstract thinking, judgment, and general knowledge.

Two other instruments of particular interest to the field of psychiatry are the Neurobehavioral Cognitive Status Examination (NCSE; Mitrushina, Abara, & Blumenfeld, 1995) and the Cognitive Levels Scale (Allen & Allen, 1987). The Cognitive Levels Scale is designed to measure cognitive impairment and social dysfunction in patients with mental disorders. Cognitive impairment is classified according to six levels (profoundly disabled to normal) and has implications for patients' functioning at home and at work. The NCSE samples 10 cognitive domains: orientation, attention, comprehension, repetition, naming, construction, memory, calculation, similarities, and judgment. It is capable of screening intact individuals as negative within approximately 5 minutes, due to its design, which introduces a demanding item at the beginning of each substantive domain. It has been applied with neurological, medical and psychiatric patients and has been found capable of discriminating patients with an organic mental disorder from those free of the disorder. Although the NCSE has established a record of high sensitivity, it often exhibits low specificity (Mitrushina et al., 1995).

## Cognitive Screening in Geriatric Populations

As mentioned at the beginning of the chapter, an important consideration in any screening paradigm is the prevalence of the index disorder in the population under investigation. The prevalence of cognitive disorders is relatively dramatic in elderly populations. Furher and Ritchie (1993) noted a 6% prevalence rate for dementia in the general patient population, but the rate may rise to as high as 18% in the elderly (Jagger, Clark, & Anderson, 1992). In studying delirium, Hart et al. (1995) noted a prevalence of 10% to 13% in the general patient population, which they estimated may rise to as high as 15% to 30% in the elderly.

Screening geriatric patients is often a challenge for a number of diverse reasons. First, these patients often present with sensory, perceptual, and motor problems that seriously constrain the use of standardized tests. Poor vision, diminished hearing, and other physical handicaps can undermine the appropriateness of tests that are dependent on particular perceptual or physical abilities. Similarly, required medications can cause drowsiness or inalertness or in other ways interfere with optimal cognitive functioning. Illnesses such as heart disease and hypertension, common in the elderly, have also been shown to affect cognitive functioning (Libow, 1977). These limitations require screening instruments that are flexible enough to be adapted to patients with handicaps or illnesses and yet be sufficiently standardized to allow normative comparisons.

Another difficulty with this population involves distinguishing cognitive impairment from aging-associated memory loss and from characteristics of normal aging. Distinguishing these requires a sensitive screening instrument, as the differences between these conditions are often subtle. Normal aging and dementia can be differentiated through their different effects on such functions as language, memory, perception, attention, information processing, and intelligence (Bayles & Kaszniak, 1987). The Global Deterioration Scale is designed for this specific purpose. It has been shown to describe the magnitude of cognitive decline and predict functional ability (Reisberg et al., 1988).

A final problem encountered when screening in geriatric populations is the comorbidity of depression. Depression is one of several disorders in the elderly that may imitate dementia, resulting in a syndrome known as *pseudodementia*. Patients with pseudodementia have no discernable organic impairment, and the symptoms of dementia will usually remit when the underlying affective disorder is treated. Variability of task performance can distinguish these patients from truly demented patients, who tend to have a lowered performance level on every task (Wells, 1979). If depression is suspected, it should be the focus of a distinct diagnostic workup.

Recently, a number of new instruments have been developed that help address these problems. One of these, the Cognitive Test for Delirium (CTD; Hart et al., 1995), appears promising. The CTD is a 9-item, examiner-administered instrument that evaluates orientation, attention span, memory, comprehension, and vigilance. The CTD is completely nonverbal and requires only 10 to 15 minutes administration time. Through the application of ROC analysis, the authors were able to establish an optimal cutoff score of less than 19 to discriminate delirium from other disorders (Hart et al., 1995). The authors also reported that the CTD correlates highly with the MMSE in delirium and dementia patients and that it achieved a sensitivity and specificity of 100% and 95%, respectively, in the assessment of dementia in ICU patients.

## Cognitive Screening Among Inpatient Medical Populations

When attempting to screen for cognitive impairment in medical populations, clinicians will face several of the limitations mentioned earlier as pertaining to geriatric populations, since the groups often overlap. Medical patients are often constrained by their illness and may not be able to respond to the test in the required manner. In addition, these patients are often bedridden, necessitating the use of a portable bedside instrument.

Perhaps the most demanding issue when evaluating this population is discriminating between the dementing patient and the patient with acute confusional states, or delirium. This is particularly important not only because of the increased occurrence of delirium in medical patients but because, if left untreated, delirium can progress to an irreversible condition. Delirium can have multiple etiologies, such as drug intoxication, metabolic disorders, fever, cardiovascular disorders, or effects of anesthesia. Elderly people and medical patients are both susceptible to misuse or overuse of prescription drugs as well as metabolic or nutritional imbalances. Hypothyroidism, hyperparathyroidism, and diabetes are a few of the medical conditions that are often mistaken for dementia (Albert, 1981). In addition, cognitive impairment can also be caused by infections, such as pneumonia.

Fortunately, three cardinal characteristics enable us to distinguish dementia from delirium. First is the *rate of onset of symptoms*. Delirium is marked by acute or abrupt onset of symptoms, whereas dementia has a more gradual progression. Second is the *impairment of attention*. Delirious patients have special difficulty sustaining attention on tasks such as serial sevens and digit span. Third is *nocturnal worsening*, which is a characteristic of delirium but not dementia (Mesulam & Geschwind, 1976).

### Cognitive Screening in Primary Care Settings

As mentioned, many cases of cognitive impairment go undetected. The low rate of diagnosis may be due to the fact that the early stages of cognitive dysfunction are often quite subtle and that cases of cognitive dysfunction often first present to primary care physicians (Mungas, 1991), who tend to have their principal focus on other systems. Also, many physicians are unfamiliar with the available procedures for detecting cognitive impairment, and others are reluctant to add a formal cognitive screening to their schedule of procedures. Although brief, the 10 to 30 minutes required for most cognitive screening instruments remains a formidable obstacle considering that on average a family practice physician spends from 7 to 10 minutes with each patient. Because cognitive screening techniques are highly transportable and actuarial in nature and may be administered by a broad range of health care professionals, the solution to introducing such screening in primary care may be to train nurses or physician's assistants to conduct screening. Such an approach would not add to the burden of physicians and would at least effect an initiation of such programs so that their utility could be realistically evaluated.

## CONCLUSION

Currently, little doubt remains that psychiatric disorders meet the WHO criteria for conditions appropriate for the development of effective health screening programs (Wilson & Junger, 1968). These conditions represent a health problem of substantial magnitude, and the morbidity, mortality, and costs associated with these conditions are imposing. We currently possess valid, cost-efficient, psychological screening tests to effectively identify these conditions in medical and community settings, and the efficacy of our treatment regimens is consistently improving (Regier et al., 1988). Although confirmation of the incremental treatment advantage of early detection remains somewhat equivocal, the evidence is compelling that, left to their natural courses, such conditions will result in chronic, compound morbidities of both a physical and psychological nature (Derogatis & Wise, 1989; Katon et al., 1990; Regier et al., 1988).

Paradoxically, however, it will be of little ultimate consequence to develop effective systems of treatment planning and outcomes assessment for these conditions if the majority of individuals who would benefit from their utilization are lost to the system.

In large measure, this undesirable reality has to do with the fact that a substantial majority of patients with psychiatric conditions are never seen by mental health professionals and that up to 20% are never seen by any health care professional. Even when engaged by the health care system, the majority of individuals with psychiatric morbidity are seen by professionals who have been insufficiently trained to recognize or effectively treat these conditions. A substantial plurality of these cases go unrecognized, and of those who recieve a correct diagnosis, only a minority are referred to mental health professionals for treatment. Often, primary care physicians prefer to treat these cases personally, even though many indicate that they do not feel confident in doing so.

The major implication of these facts is that, although we now possess highly efficient methods to identify individuals suffering from psychological disintegration, these are essentially being addressed to the "tip of the iceberg." These assessment methods are irrelevant for a large majority of those who would derive benefit from their utilization because the psychiatric disorders of these individuals are rarely recognized by their primary care providers.

In our health care system, primary care physicians and other health care providers are continuing to play a prominent role as "gatekeepers" for behavioral health care as well as other kinds of care, and all evidence points toward their expanding this role in the future. Therefore, it seems imperative that we introduce and adopt effective methods to help these professionals make appropriate diagnostic and treatment decisions concerning psychiatric disorders. Available psychological screening techniques can deliver valid, cost-effective identification of these conditions now; given their numerous benefits and demonstrated cost savings, it is our belief that such techniques should be extensively implemented as soon as possible.

## REFERENCES

Adams, W. L., Barry, K. L., & Fleming, M. F. (1996). Screening for problem drinking in older primary care patients. *Journal of the American Medical Association, 276,* 1964–1967.
Albert, M. (1981). Geriatric neuropsychology. *Journal of Consulting and Clinical Psychology, 49,* 835–850.
Allen, C., & Allen, R. (1987). Cognitive disabilities: Measuring the social consequences of mental disorders. *Journal of Clinical Psychiatry, 48,* 185–190.
Allison, T. G., Williams, D. E., Miller, T. D., Patten, C. A., Bailey, K. R., Squires, R. W., & Gau, G. T. (1995). Medical and economic costs of psychologic distress in patients with coronary artery disease. *Mayo Clinic Proceedings, 70,* 734–742.
*American Medical News.* (2002, Sept. 23–30). Editorial.
American Psychiatric Association. (1987). *Diagnostic and statistical manual of mental disorders* (3rd ed.). Washington, DC: Author.
American Psychiatric Association. (1994). *Diagnostic and statistical manual of mental disorders* (4th ed.). Washington, DC: Author.
Anderson, S. M., & Harthorn, B. H. (1989). The recognition, diagnosis, and treatment of mental disorders by primary care physicians. *Medical Care, 27,* 869–886.
Anderson, S. M., & Harthorn, B. H. (1990). Changing the psychiatric knowledge of primary care physicians: The effects of a brief intervention on clinical diagnosis and treatment. *General Hospital Psychiatry, 12,* 177–190.
Association for the Advancement of Automotive Medicine. (1990). Abbreviated Injury Scale. Des PLaines, IL: Author.
Babor, T. F., de la Fuente, J. R., Saunders, J. B., & Grant, M. (1989). *The Alcohol Use Disorders Identification test: Guidelines for use in primary health care.* Geneva, Switzerland: World Health Organization.
Baker, F. (1989). Screening tests for cognitive impairment. *Hospital and Community Psychiatry, 40,* 339–340.
Baldessarini, R. J., Finklestein S., & Arana, G. W. (1983). The predictive power of diagnostic tests and the effect of prevalence of illness. *Archives of General Psychiatry, 40,* 569–573.
Barrett, J. E., Barrett, J. A., Oxman, T. E., Gerber, P. D. (1988). The prevalence of psychiatric disorders in a primary care practice. *Archives of General Psychiatry, 45,* 1100–1106.

Barry, K. L., & Fleming, M. F. (1990). Computerized administration of alcoholism screening tests in a primary care setting. *Journal of the American Board of Family Practice, 3*, 93–98.

Barry, K. L., & Fleming, M. F. (1993). The Alcohol Use Disorders Identification Test: Predictive validity in a rural primary care sample. *Alcohol and Alcoholism, 28*, 33–42.

Bayles, K., & Kaszniak, A. (1987). *Communication and cognition in normal aging and dementia.* Boston: Little, Brown.

Bech, P., Grosby, H., Husum, B., et al. (1984). Generalized anxiety and depression measured by the Hamilton Anxiety Scale and the Melancholia Scale in patients before and after cardiac surgery. *Psychopathology, 17*, 253–263.

Bech, P. (1987). Observer rating scales of anxiety and depression with reference to DSM–III for clinical studies in psychosomatic medicine. *Advances in Psychosomatic Medicine, 17*, 55–70.

Beck, A. T., & Beck, R. W. (1972). Screening depressed patients in family practice: A rapid technic. *Postgraduate Medicine, 52*, 81–85.

Beck, A. T., Kovacs, M., & Weissman, A. (1975). Hopelessness and suicidal behavior: An overview. *Journal of the American Medical Association, 234*, 1146–1149.

Beck, A. T., Steer, R. A., & Brown, G. K. (1996). *Manual for the Beck Depression Inventory–II.* San Antonio, TX: The Psychological Corporation.

Beck, A. T., Ward, C., Mendelson, M., et al. (1961). An inventory for measuring depression. *Archives of General Psychiatry, 4*, 53–63.

Beck, A. T., & Steer, (1993). Manual for the Beck Depression Inventory. San Antonio, TX: Psychological Corp.

Benjamin, G., Kaszniak, A., Sales, B., & Shanfield, S. (1986). The role of legal education in producing psychological distress among law students and lawyers. *American Bar Foundation Research Journal, 2*, 225–252.

Berg, G., Edwards, D., Danzinger, W., & Berg, L. (1987). Longitudinal change in three brief assessments of SDAT. *Journal of the America Geriatrics Society, 35*, 205–212.

Bernadt, M. W., Mumford, J., Taylor, C., Smith, B., & Murray, R. M. (1982). Comparison of questionnaire and laboratory tests in the detection of excessive drinking and alcoholism. *Lancet, 1*, 325–328.

Bien, T. H., Miller, W. R., & Tonigan, J. S. (1993). Brief interventions for alcohol problems: A review. *Addiction, 88*, 315–336.

Birtchnell, J., Evans, C., Deahl, M., & Master, N. (1989). The Depression Screening Instrument (DSI): A device for the detection of depressive disorders in general practice. *Journal of Affective Disorders, 16*, 269–281.

Bjarnason, T., & Thorlindsson, T. (1994). Manifest predictors of past suicide attempts in a population of Icelandic adolescents. *Suicide and Life-Threatening Behavior, 24*, 350–357.

Blazer, D., George, G. K., Landerman, R., Pennybacker, M., Melville, M. L., Woodbury, M., et al. (1984). Psychiatric disorders: A rural/urban comparison. *Archives of General Psychiatry, 41*, 959–970.

Blessed, G., Tomlinson, B., & Roth, M. (1968). The association between quantitative measures of dementia and of senile change in the cerebral gray matter of the elderly. *British Journal of Psychiatry, 114*, 797–811.

Bradley, K. A. (1992). Screening and diagnosis of alcoholism in the primary care setting. *Western Journal of Medicine, 156*, 166–171.

Bradley, K. A., Curry, S. J., Koepsell, T. D., & Larson, E. B. (1995). Primary and secondary prevention of alcohol problems: US internist attitudes and practices. *Journal of General Internal Medicine, 10*, 67–72.

Bradley, K. A., McDonell, M. B., Bush, K., Kivlahan, D. R., Diehr, P., & Film, S. D. (1998). The AUDIT alcohol consumption questions: Miability, viability, and responsiveness to change in older male primary care patients. *Alcoholism, Clinical and Experimental Research, 22*, 1842–1849.

Bradley, K. A., Bush, K. R., McDonell, M. B., Malone, T., & Fihn, S. D. (1998). Screening for problem drinking: Comparison of CAGE and AUDIT. *Journal of General Internal Medicine, 13*, 379–388.

Bridges, K., & Goldberg, D. (1984). Psychiatric illness in in-patients with neurological disorders: Patient's view on discussions of emotional problems with neurologists. *British Medical Journal, 289*, 656–658.

Broadhead, W. E., Leon, A. C., & Weissman, M. M., et al. (1995). Development and validation of the SDDS–PC screen for multiple mental disorders in primary care. *Archives of Family Medicine, 4*, 211–219.

Brown, R. L., & Rounds, L. A. (1995). Conjoint screening questionnaires for alcohol and other drug abuse: Criterion validity in a primary care practice. *Western Medical Journal, 94*, 135–140.

Buchsbaum, D. G., Buchanan, R. G., Centor, R. M., Schnoll, S. H., & Lawton, M. J. (1991). Screening for alcohol abuse using CAGE scores and likelihood ratios. *Annals of Internal Medicine, 115*, 774–777.

Buchsbaum, D. G., Buchanan, R. G., Welsh, J., Centor, R. M., & Schnoll, S. H. (1992). Screening for drinking disorders in the elderly using the CAGE questionnaire. *Journal of the American Geriatrics Society, 40*, 662–665.

Buchsbaum, D. G., Buchanan, R. G., Poses, R. M., Schnoll, S. H., & Lawton, M. I. (1992). Physician detection of drinking problems in patients attending a general medicine practice. *Journal of General Internal Medicine, 7,* 517–521.

Buchsbaum, D. G., Welsh, J., Buchanan, R. G., & Elswick, R. K., Jr. (1995). Screening for drinking problems by patient self report: even "safe" levels may indicate a problem. *Archives of Internal Medicine, 155,* 104–108.

Bulik, C. M., Carpenter, L. L., Kupfer, D. J., & Frank, E. (1990). Features associated with suicide attempts in recurrent major depression. *Journal of Affective Disorders, 18,* 27–29.

Burnam, M. A., Wells, K. B., Leake, B., & Lanverk, J. (1988). Development of a brief screening instrument for detecting depressive disorders. *Medical Care, 26,* 775–789.

Burns, B. J., & Burke, J. D. (1985). Improving mental health practices in primary care. *Public Health Reports, 100,* 294–299.

Bush, K., Kivlahan, D. R., McDonell, M. B., Film, S. D., & Bradley, K. A. (1998). The AUDIT alcohol consumption questions (AUDIT): An effective brief screening test for problem drinking. *Archives of Internal Medicine, 158,* 1789–1795.

Chang, G. (1997). Primary Care: Detection of newman with alcohol use Disorders, Harvaro Review of Psychiatry, *4,* 334–337.

Center for Disease Control. (1999). Behavioral Risk Factor Surveillance System online prevalence data. Retrieved December 5, 2000, from http://www2.cdc.gov/nccd_brfss/index.asp

Chan, A. W., Pristach, E. A., & Welte, J. W. (1994). Detection by the CAGE of alcoholism or heavy drinking in primary care outpatients and the general population. *Journal of Substance Abuse, 6,* 123–135.

Cherpitel, C. J. (1998). Performance of screening instruments for identifying alcohol dependence in the general population, compared with clinical populations. *Alcoholism, Clinical and Experimental Research, 22,* 1399–1404.

Cherpitel, C. J. (1998). Differences in performance of screening instruments for problem drinking among blacks, whites and Hispanics in an emergency room population. *Journal of Studies of Alcohol, 59,* 420–426.

Cherpitel, C. J. (2000). Screening for alcohol problems in the emergency room: A rapid alcohol problems screen. *Drug and Alcohol Dependence.* Retrieved, from http://gateway2.ovid.com/ovidweb.cgi

Chiles, J. A., & Strosahl, K. D. (1995). *The suicidal patient: Principles of assessment, treatment, and case management.* Washington DC: American Psychiatric Press.

Chong, M., & Wilkinson, G. (1989). Validation of 30- and 12-item versions of the Chinese Health Questionnaire (CHQ) in patients admitted for general health screening. *Psychological Medicine, 19,* 495–505.

Clark, L., Levine, M., & Kinney, N. (1988). A multifaceted and integrated approach to the prevention, identification, and treatment of bulimia on college campuses. *Journal of College Student Psychotherapy, 3,* 257–298.

Cleary, P. D., Miller, M., Bush, B. T., Warburg, M. M., Delbanco, T. L., & Aronson, M. D. (1988). Prevalence and recognition of alcohol abuse in a primary care population. *American Journal of Medicine, 85,* 466–471.

Cochran, C. D., & Hale, W. D. (1985). College students norms on the Brief Symptom Inventory. *Journal of Clinical Psychology, 31,* 176–184.

Cohen, L. J., Test, M. A., & Brown, R. L. (1990). Suicide and schizophrenia: Data from a prospective community treatment study. *American Journal of Psychiatry, 47,* 602–607.

Commission on Chronic Illness. (1957). *Chronic illness in the United States.* Cambridge, MA: Commonwealth Fund, Harvard University Press.

Comstock, G. W., & Helsing, K. J. (1976). Symptoms of depression in two communities. *Psychological Medicine, 6,* 551–564.

Craske, M., & Krueger, M. (1990). Prevalence of nocturnal panic in a college population. *Journal of Anxiety Disorders, 4,* 125–139.

Craven, J. L., Rodin, G. M., & Littlefield, C. (1988). The Beck Depression Inventory as a screening device for major depression in renal dialysis patients. *International Journal of Psychiatry in Medicine, 18,* 365–374.

Cummings, J., & Benson, F. (1986). Dementia of the Alzheimer Type: An inventory of diagnostic clinical features. *Journal of the American Geriatrics Society, 34,* 12–19.

Davis, T. C., Nathan, R. G., Crough, M. A., & Bairnsfather, L. E. (1987). Screening depression with a new tool: Back to basics with a new tool. *Family Medicine, 19,* 200–202.

Dawson, D. A. (1994). Consumption indicators of alcohol dependence. *Addiction, 89,* 345–350.

Depue, R., Krauss, S., Spoont, M., & Arbisi, P. (1989). General Behavior Inventory identification of unipolar and bipolar affective conditions in a nonclinical university population. *Journal of Abnormal Psychology, 98,* 117–126.

Derogatis, L. R. (1977). *SCL–90–R: Administration, scoring and procedures manual–I.* Baltimore: Clinical Psychometric Research.

Derogatis, L. R. (1983). SCL–90–R: *Administration, scoring and procedures manual–II*. Baltimore: Clinical Psychometric Research.

Derogatis, L. R. (1990). *SCL–90–R: A bibliography of research reports 1975–1990*. Baltimore: Clinical Psychometric Research.

Derogatis, L. R. (1992). *BSI: Administration, scoring and procedures manual for the Brief Symptom Inventory II* (2nd ed.). Baltimore: Clinical Psychometric Research.

Derogatis, L. R. (1993). *BSI: Administration, scoring and procedures manual for the Brief Symptom Inventory* (3rd ed.). Minneapolis, MN: National Computer Systems.

Derogatis, L. R. (1994). *SCL–90–R: Administration, scoring and procedures manual* (3rd ed.). Minneapolis, MN: National Computer Systems.

Derogatis, L. R. (1997). *The Brief Symptom Inventory–18 (BSI–18)*. Minneapolis, MN: National Computer Systems.

Derogatis, L. R. (2000.) *The Brief Symptom Inventory–18 (BSI–18): Administration, scoring and procedures manual*. Minneapolis, MN : National Computer Systems.

Derogatis, L., DellaPietra, L., & Kilroy, V. (1992). Screening for psychiatric disorder in medical populations. In M. Fava, G. Rosenbaum, & R. Birnbaum (Eds.), *Research designs and methods in psychiatry* (pp. 145–170). Amsterdam: Elsevier.

Derogatis, L. R., & Derogatis, M. F. (1996). SCL-90-R and the BSI. In B. Spilker (Ed.), *Quality of life and pharmacoeconomics* (pp. 323–335). Philadelphia: Lippincott-Raven.

Derogatis, L. R., Lipman, R. S., Rickels, K., Uhlenhuth, E. H., & Covi, L. (1974a). The Hopkins Symptom CheckList (HSCL): A self-report symptom inventory. *Behavioral Science, 19*, 1–15.

Derogatis, L. R., Lipman, R. S., Rickels, K., Uhlenhuth, E. H., & Covi, L. (1974b). The Hopkins Symptom Checklist (HSCL). In P. Pinchot (Ed.), *Psychological measurements in psychopharmacology* (pp. 79–111). Basel: Karger.

Derogatis, L. R., & Melisaratos, N. (1983). The Brief Symptom Inventory: An introductory report. *Psychological Medicine, 13*, 595–605.

Derogatis, L. R., Morrow, G. R., Fetting, J., Penman, D., Piasetsky, S., Schmale, A. M., et al. (1983). The prevalence of psychiatric disorders among cancer patients. *Journal of the American Medical Association, 249*, 751–757.

Derogatis, L. R., & Spencer, P. M. (1982). *BSI administration and procedures manual I*. Baltimore: Clinical Psychometric Research.

Derogatis, L. R., & Wise, T. N. (1989). *Anxiety and depressive disorders in the medical patient*. Washington, DC: American Psychiatric Press.

Dick, J., Guiloff, R., Stewart, A., Blackstock, J., Bielawska, C., Paul, E., et al. (1984). Mini-Mental State Examination in neurological patients. *Journal of Neurology, Neurosurgery, and Psychiatry, 47*, 496–499.

Dohrenwend, B. P., & Dohrenwend, B. S. (1982). Prespectives on the past and future of psychiatric epidemiology. *American Journal of Public Health, 72*, 1271–1279.

Doyle, G., Dunn, S., Thadani, I., & Lenihan, P. (1986). Investigating tools to aid in restorative care for Alzheimer's patients. *Journal of Gerontological Nursing, 12*, 19–24.

Eisen, S. V. (1996). Behavior and Symptom Identification Scale (BASIS-32). In L. I. Sederer, & B. Dickey (Ed.), *Outcomes assessment in clinical practice* (pp. 65–69). Baltimore: Williams & Wilkins.

Eisen, S. V., & Dickey, B. (1996). Mental health outcome assessment: The new agenda. *Psychotherapy, 33*, 181–189.

Eisen, S. V., Grob, M. C., & Klein, A. A. (1986). BASIS: The development of a self-report measure for psychiatric inpatient evaluation. *Psychiatric Hospitalization, 17*, 165–171.

Emhart, C. B., Sokol, R. J., & Martier, S., et al. (1987). Alcohol teratogenicity in the human: A detailed assessment of specificity, critical period, and threshold. *American Journal of Obstetrics and Gynecology, 156*, 33–39.

Erikkson, J. (1988). Psychosomatic aspects of coronary artery bypass graft surgery: A prospective study of 101 male patients. *Acta Psychiatrica Scandinavica, 77*(Suppl. 340), 112.

Escobar, J., Burnam, A., Karno, M., Forsythe, A., Landsverk, J., & Golding, J. (1986). Use of the Mini-Mental State Examination (MMSE) in a community population of mixed ethnicity: Cultural and linguistic artifacts. *Journal of Nervous and Mental Disease, 174*, 607–614.

Escobar, F., Espi, F., & Canteras, M. (1995). Diagnostic tests for alcoholism in primary health care: Compared efficacy of different instruments. *Drug and Alcohol Dependence, 40*, 151–158.

Ewing, J. A. (1984). Detecting alcoholism: The CAGE questionnaire. *Journal of the American Medical Association, 252*, 1905–1907.

Fauman, M. A. (1983). Psychiatric components of medical and surgical practice: II. Referral and treatment of psychiatric disorders. *American Journal of Psychiatry, 140*, 760–763.

Faust, D., & Fogel, B. (1989). The development and initial validation of a sensitive bedsider cognitive screening test. *Journal of Nervous and Mental Disease, 177*, 25–31.

Faustman, W., Moses, J., & Csernansky, J. (1990). Limitations of the Mini-Mental State Examination in predicting neuropsychological functioning in a psychiatric sample. *Acta Psychiatrica Scandinavica, 81*, 126–131.

Feinstein, A. R. (1985). *Clinical epidemiology: The architecture of clinical research.* Philadelphia: Saunders.

Fiellin, D. A., Reid, M. C., & O'Connor, P. G. (2000). Screening for alcohol problems in primary care: A systematic review. *Archives of Internal Medicine, 160*, 1977–1989.

First, M. B., Spitzer, R. L., Gibbon, M., & Williams, J. B. (1995). *Structured Clinical Interview for DSM–IV Axis I Disorders.* New York: Biometrics Research Department, New York State Psychiatric Institute.

Fishback, D. (1977). Mental Status Questionnaire for Organic Brain Syndrome, with a new visual counting test. *Journal of the American Geriatrics Society, 35*, 167–170.

Fleming, M. F. (2001). In search of the holy grail for the detection of hazardous drinking. *Journal of Family Practice, 50*, 321–322.

Fleming, M. F., & Barry, K. L. (1991). The effectiveness of alcoholism screening in an ambulatory care setting. *Journal of Studies on Alcoholism, 52*, 33–36.

Fleming, M. F., Barry, K. L., Manwell, L. B., Johnson, K., & London, R. (1997). Brief physician advice for problem alcohol drinkers. *Journal of the American Medical Association, 277*, 1039–1044.

Fleming, M. F., Manwell, L. B., Barry, K. L., & Johnson, K. (1998). At-risk drinking in an HMO primary care sample: Prevalence and health policy implications. *American Journal Public Health, 88*, 90–91.

Fleming, W., & Barry, K. L. (1991). A three-sample test of a masked alcohol screening questionnaire. *Alcohol and Alcoholism, 26*, 81–91.

Folstein, M., Folstein, S., & McHugh, P. (1975). Mini-Mental State. *Journal of Psychiatric Research, 12*, 189–198.

Ford, D. E., Klag, M. J., Whelton, P. K., Goldsmith, M., & Levine, D. (1994). Physician knowledge of the CAGE alcohol screening questions and its impact on practice. *Alcohol and Alcoholism, 29*, 329–336.

Foreman, M. (1987). Reliability and validity of mental status questionnaires in elderly hospitalized patients. *Nursing Research, 36*, 216–220.

Frerichs, R. R., Aneshensel, C. S., & Clark, V. A. (1981). Prevalence of depression in Los Angeles County. *American Journal of Epidemiology, 113*, 691–699.

Friedmann, P. D., Saitz, R., & Samet, J. H. (1998). Management of adults recovering from alcohol or other drug problems. *Journal of the American Medical Association, 279*, 1227–1123.

Fulop, G., & Strain, J. J. (1991). Diagnosis and treatment of psychiatric disorders in medically ill inpatients. *Hospital and Community Psychiatry, 42*, 389–394.

Furher, R., & Ritchie, K. (1993) RE: C. Jagger et al.'s article "Screening for dementia—A comparison of two tests using Receiver Operating Characteristic (ROC) analysis" 1992 (7) 659–665. *International Journal of Geriatric Psychiatry, 8*, 867–868.

Furukawa, T. A., Goldberg, D. P., Rabe-Hesketh, S., & Ustun, T. B. (2001). Stratum-specific likelihood ratios of two versions of the General Health Questionnaire. *Psychological Medicine, 31*, 519–529.

Gabrynowicz, J. W., & Watts, D. J. (1981). Early diagnosis of alcoholism: A quick and reliable technique. *Australian Family Physician, 10*, 893–898.

Galton, F. (1883). *Inquiries into human faculty and its development.* New York: Macmillan.

Gardner, S. B., Winter, P. D., & Gardner, M. J. (1989). *Confidence interval analysis.* London: British Medical Journal.

Gentilello, L. M., Rivara, F. P., & Donovan, D. M., et al. (1999). Alcohol interventions in a trauma center as a means of reducing the risk of injury recurrence. *Annals of Surgery, 230*, 473–480.

Gerber, P. D., Barrett, J., Barrett, J., Manheimer, E., Whiting, M. D., & Smith, R. (1989). Recognition of depression by internists in primary care: A comparison of internist and "gold standard" psychiatric assessments. *Journal of Internal Medicine, 4*, 7–13.

Gibbs, E. (1983). Validity and reliability of the Michigan Alcoholism Screening Test. *Drug and Alcohol Dependence, 12*, 279–285.

Goldberg, D. (1972). *The detection of psychiatric illness by questionnaire.* Oxford: Oxford University Press.

Goldberg, D., & Hillier, V. F. (1979). A scaled version of the General Health Questionnaire. *Psychological Medicine, 9*, 139–145.

Goldberg, D., & Williams, P. (1988). *A user's guide to the General Health Questionnaire.* Windsor, Ontario: Nfer-Nelson.

Goldstein, L. T., Goldsmith, S. J., Anger, K., & Leon, A. C. (1996). Psychiatric symptoms in clients presenting for commercial weight reduction treatment. *International Journal of Eating Disorders, 20*, 191–197.

Gordon, A. J., Maisto, S. A., McNeil, M., Kraemer, K. L., Conigliaro, R. L., Kelley, M. E., et al. (2001). Three questions can detect hazardous drinkers. *Journal of Family Practice, 50*, 313–320.

Grant, B. F., Harford, T. C., Dawson, D. A., Chou, P., Dufour, M., & Pickering, R. (1994). Prevalence of DSM–IV alcohol abuse and dependence: United States, 1992. *Alcoholism Health Research World, 18,* 243–248.

Griest, J. H., Gustafson, D. H., Stauss, F. F., Rowse, G. L., Laughren, T. P., & Chiles, J. A. (1974). A computer interview for suicide-risk prediction. *American Journal of Psychiatry, 130,* 1327–1332.

Haglund, R., & Schuckit, M. (1976). A clinical comparison of tests of organicity in elderly patients. *Journal of Gerontology, 31,* 654–659.

Hajek, V., Rutman, D., & Scher, H. (1989). Brief assessment of cognitive impairment in patients with stroke. *Archives of Physical Medicine and Rehabilitation, 70,* 114–117.

Hamilton, M. (1959). The assessment of anxiety states by rating. *British Journal of Medical Psychology, 32,* 50–55.

Hamilton, M. (1960). A rating scale for depression. *Journal of Neurosurgery Psychiatry, 23,* 50–55.

Hamilton, M. (1967). Development of a rating scale for primary depressive illness. *British Journal of Social and Clinical Psychology, 6,* 278–296.

Hanley, J. A., & McNeil, B. J. (1982). The meaning and use of the area under a receiver operating characteristic (ROC) curve. *Diagnostic Radiography, 143,* 29–36.

Hansson, L., Nettleblad, P., Borquist, L., & Nordstrom, G. (1994) Screening for psychiatric illness in primary care. *Social Psychiatry and Psychiatric Epidemiology, 29,* 83–87.

Hart, R. P., Levenson, J. L., Sessler, C. N., Best, A. M., Schwartz, S. M., & Rutherford, L. E. (1995). Validation of a cognitive test for delerium in medical ICU patients. *Psychosomatics, 37,* 533–546.

Hasin, D., & Paykin, A. (1999). Alcohol dependence and abuse diagnoses: Concurrent validity in a nationally representative sample. *Alcoholism, Clinical and Experimental Research, 23,* 144–150.

Hawton, K. (1981). The long term outcome of psychiatric morbidity detected in general medical paitents. *Journal of Psychosomatic Research, 25,* 237–243.

Hedlund, J. L., & Vieweg, M. D. (1979). The Hamilton Rating Scale for Depression: A comprehensive review. *Journal of Operational Psychiatry, 10,* 149–165.

Hoeper, E. W., Nyczi, G. R., & Cleary, P. D. (1979). Estimated prevalence of RDC mental disorders in primary care. *International Journal of Mental Health, 8,* 6–15.

Hopkins, T. B., Zarro, V. J., & McCarter, T. G. (1994). The adequacy of screening, documenting, and treating diseases of substance abuse. *Journal of Addictive Diseases, 13,* 81–87.

Hore, B. D., Alsafar, J., & Wilkins, R. H. (1977). An attempt at criterion-oriented validation of an alcoholism questionnaire in general practice. *British Journal of Addiction of Alcohol and Other Drugs, 72,* 19–22.

Hughson, A. V. M., Cooper, A. F., McArdle, C. S., & Smith, D. C. (1988). Validity of the General Health Questionnaire and its subscales in patients receiving chemotherapy for early breast cancer. *Journal of Psychosomatic Research, 32,* 393–402.

Isaacson, J. H., Butler, I., Zacharek, M., & Tzelepis, A. (1994). Screening with the Alcohol Use Disorders Identification Test (AUDIT) in an inner-city population. *Journal of General Internal Medicine, 9,* 550–553.

Israel, Y., Hollander, O., Sanchez-Craig, M., Booker, S., Miller, V., Gingrich, R., et al. (1996). Screening for problem drinking by the primary care physician–nurse team. *Alcoholism, Clinical and Experimental Research, 20,* 1443–1450.

Jacobs, J., Berhard, M., Delgado, A., & Strain, J. (1977). Screening for organic mental syndromes in the medically ill. *Annals of Internal Medicine, 86,* 40–46.

Jaeschke, I. T., Guyatt, G. H., & Sackett, D. L. (1994). [For the Evidence Based Medicine Working Group.] Users' guides to the medical literature: III: How to use an article about a diagnostic test. B. What are the results and will they help me in caring for my patients? *Journal of the American Medical Association, 271,* 703–707.

Jagger, C., Clarke, M., & Anderson, J. (1992). Screening for dementia: A comparison of two tests using receiver operating characteristic (ROC) analysis. *International Journal of Geriatric Psychiatry, 7,* 659–665.

Jefferson, J. W. (1988). Biologic systems and their relationship to anxiety. *Psychiatric Clinics of North America, 11,* 463–472.

Jitapunkul, S., Lailert, C., Worakul, P., Srikiatkhachorn, A., & Ebrahim, S. (1996). Chula Mental Test: A screening test for elderly people in less developed countries. *International Journal of Geriatric Psychiatry, 11,* 715–720.

Johnson, R., Ellison, R., & Heikkinen, C. (1989). Psychological symptoms of counseling center clients. *Journal of Counseling Psychology, 36,* 110–114.

Jones, L. R., Badger, L. W., Ficken, R. P., Leepek, J. D., & Anderson, R. L. (1987). Inside the hidden mental health network: Examining mental health care delivery of primary care physicians. *General Hospital Psychiatry, 9,* 287–293.

Judd, B., Meyer, J., Rogers, R., Gandhi, S., Tanahashi, N., Mortel, K., et al. (1986). Cognitive performance correlates with cerebrovascular impairments in multi-infarct dementia. *Journal of the American Geriatrics Society, 34,* 355–360.

Kahn, R., Goldfarb, A., Pollack, M., & Peck, A. (1960). Brief objective measures for the determination of mental status in the aged. *American Journal of Psychiatry, 117,* 326–328.

Kamerow, D. B., Pincus, H. A., & MacDonald, D. I. (1986). Alcohol abuse, other drug abuse, and mental disorders in medical practice: Prevalence, cost, recognition, and treatment. *Journal of the American Medical Assocation, 255,* 2054–2057.

Kane, M. T., & Kendall, P. C. (1989). Anxiety disorders in children: A multiple-baseline evaluation of a cognitive-behavioral treatment. *Behavior Therapy, 20,* 499–508.

Katon, W., Von Korff, M., Lin, E., Lipscomb, P., Russo, J., Wagner, E., et al. (1990). Distressed high utilizers of medical care: DSM–III–R diagnoses and treatment needs. *General Hospital Psychiatry, 12,* 355–362.

Kedward, H. B., & Cooper, B. (1966). Neurotic disorders in urban practice: A 3 year follow-up. *Journal of the College of General Practice, 12,* 148–163.

Kempf, E. J. (1914). The behavior chart in mental diseases. *American Journal of Insanity, 7,* 761–772.

Kessler, L. G., Amick, B. C., & Thompson, J. (1985). Factors influencing the diagnosis of mental disorder among primary care patients. *Medical Care, 23,* 50–62.

Kessler, L. G., McGonagle, K. A., & Zhao, S., et al. (1994). Lifetime and 12-month prevalence of DSM–III–R psychiatric disorders in the United States: Results from the National Comorbidity Survey. *Archives of General Psychiatry, 51,* 8–19.

King, M. (1986). At risk drinking among general practice attenders: Validation of the CAGE questionnaire. *Psychological Medicine, 16,* 213–217.

Kitchens, J. M. (1994). Does this patient have an alcohol problem? *Journal of the American Medical Association, 272,* 1782–1787.

Kobak, K. A., Taylor, L. H., Dottl, S. L., et al. (1997). A computer-administered telephone interview to identify mental disorders. *Journal of the American Medical Association, 278,* 905–910.

Kramer, M., German, P., Anthony, J., Von Korff, M., & Skinner, E. (1985). Patterns of mental disorders among the elderly residents of eastern Baltimore. *Journal of the American Geriatrics Society, 11,* 236–245.

Kuhn, W. F., Bell, R. A., Seligson, D., Laufer, S. T., & Lindner, J. E. (1988). The tip of the iceberg: Psychiatric consultations on an orthopedic service. *International Journal of Psychiatry in Medicine, 18,* 375–378.

LaRue, A., D'Elia, L., Clark, E., Spar, J., & Jarvik, L. (1986). Clinical tests of memory in dementia, depression, and healthy aging. *Psychology and Aging, 1,* 69–77.

Leon, A. C., Olfson, M., & Weissman, M. M., et al. (1996). Brief screens for mental disorders in primary care. *Journal of General Internal Medicine, 11,* 426–430.

Lesher, E., & Whelihan, W. (1986). Reliability of mental status instruments administered to nursing home residents. *Journal of Consulting and Clinical Psychology, 54,* 726–727.

Libow, L. (1977). Senile dementia and pseudosenility: Clinical diagnosis. In C. E. R. Friedel (Ed.), *Cognitive and emotional disturbance in the elderly* (pp. 200–214). Chicago: Year Book Medical Publishing.

Libow, L. (1981). A rapidly administered, easily remembered mental status evaluation: FROMAJE. In L. S. Libow & F. T. Sherman (Eds.), *The core of geriatric medicine* (pp. 85–91). St. Louis: Mosby.

Linn, L., & Yager, J. (1984). Recognition of depression and anxiety by primary care physicians. *Psychosomatics, 25,* 593–600.

Lish, J. D., Zimmerman, M., Farber, N. J., Lush, D. T., Kuzma, M. A., & Plescia, G. (1996). Suicide screening in a primary care setting at a Veterans Affairs medical center. *Psychosomatics, 37,* 413–424.

Luce, R. D., & Narens, L. (1987). Measurement scales on the continuum. *Science, 236,* 1527–1532.

Lyketsos, C. G., Hutton, H., Fishman, M., Schwartz, J., & Trishman, G. J. (1996). Psychiatric morbidity on entry to an HIV primary care clinic. *Aids, 10,* 1033–1039.

Madri, J. J., & Williams, P. (1986). A comparison of validity of two psychiatric screening questionnaires. *Journal of Chronic Disorders, 39,* 371–378.

Magruder-Habib, K., Zung, W. W., & Feussner, J. R. (1990). Improving physicians' recognition and treatment of depression in general medical care: Results from a randomized clinical trial. *Medical Care, 28,* 239–250.

Malt, U. F. (1989). The validity of the General Health Questionnaire in a sample of accidentally injured adults. *Acta Psychiatrica Scaninavica, 80,* 103–112.

Maser, J. D., & Cloninger, C. R. (1990). *Comorbidity of mood and anxiety disorder.* Washington, DC: American Psychiatry Press.

Mayfield, D., McLeod, G., & Hall, P. (1974). The CAGE questionnaire: Validation of a new alcohol screening instrument. *American Journal of Psychiatry, 131,* 1121–1123.

McCartney, J., & Palmateer, L. (1985). Assessment of cognitive deficit in geriatric patients: A study of physician behavior. *Journal of the American Geriatrics Society, 33,* 467–471.

McDermott, R., Hawkins, W., Littlefield, E., & Murray, S. (1989). Health behavior correlates of depression among university students. *Journal of the American College of Health, 38,* 115–119.

McDougall, G. (1990). A review of screening instruments for assessing cognition and mental status in older adults. *Nurse Practitioner, 15,* 18–28.

McGinnis, J. M., & Foege, W. H. (1993). Actual causes of death in the United States. *Journal of the American Medical Association, 270,* 2207–2212.

Meade, M. O., & Richardson, W. S. (1997). Selecting and appraising studies for a systematic review. *Annals of Internal Medicine, 127,* 531–537.

Meehl, P. E., & Rosen, A. (1955). Antecedent probability and the efficiency of psychometric signs, patterns, or cutting scores. *Psychological Bulletin, 52,* 194–216.

Messick, S. (1995). Validity of psychological assessment: Validation of inferences from persons' responses and performances as scientific inquiry into score meaning. *American Psychologist, 50,* 741–749.

Mesulam, M., & Geschwind, N. (1976). Disordered mental status in the postoperative period. *Urologic Clinics of North America, 3,* 199–215.

Metz, C. E. (1978). Basic principles of ROC analysis. *Seminars in Nuclear Medicine, 8,* 283–298.

Mitrushina, M., Abara, J., & Blumenfeld, A. (1995). Cognitive screening of psychiatric patients. *Journal of Psychiatric Research, 29,* 13–22.

Moore, J. T., Silimperi, D. R., & Bobula, J. A. (1978). Recognition of depression by family medicine residents: The impact of screening. *Journal of Family Practice, 7,* 509–513.

Moran, M. B., Naughton, B. J., & Hughes, S. L. (1990). Screening elderly veterans for alcoholism. *Journal of General Intenal Medicine, 5,* 361–364.

Morton, J. L., Jones, T. V., & Manganaro, M. A. (1996). Performance of alcoholism screening questionnaires in elderly veterans. *American Journal of Medicine, 101,* 153–159.

Mossman, D., & Somoza, E. (1991). Neuropsychiatric decision making: The role of disorder prevalence in diagnostic testing. *Journal of Neuropsychiatry and Clinical Neurosciences, 3,* 84–88.

Mossman, D., & Somoza, E. (1992). Balancing risks and benefits: Another approach to optimizing diagnostic tests. *Journal of Neuropsychiatry and Clinical Neurosciences, 4,* 331–335.

Muller, A. (1996). Alcohol consumption and community hospital admissions in the United States: A dynamic regression analysis, 1950–1992. *Addiction, 91,* 231–242.

Mulrow, C. D., Williams, J. W., Jr., Gerety, M. B., Ramirez, G., Montiel, O. M., & Kerber, C. (1995). Case-finding instruments for depression in primary care settings. *Annals of Internal Medicine, 122,* 913–921.

Mungas, D. (1991). In-office mental status testing: A practical guide. *Geriatrics, 46,* 54–66.

Murphy, J. M., Berwick, D. M., Weinstein, M. C., Borus, J. F., Budman, S. H., & Klerman, G. L. (1987). Performance of screening and diagnostic tests. *Archives of General Psychiatry, 44,* 550–555.

Murray, C. J., & Lopez, A. D. (1997) Global mortality, disability and the contribution of risk factors: Global burden of disease study. *Lancet 349,* 1436–1442.

Myers, J. K., Weissman, M. M., Tischler, G. L., Holzer, C. E., Leaf, P. J., Orvaschel, H., et al. (1984). Six-month prevalence of psychiatric disorders in three communities. *Archives of General Psychiatry, 41,* 959–970.

National Institute on Alcohol Abuse and Alcoholism. (1995). *The physician's guide to helping patients with alcohol problems.* Retrieved from http://www.silk.nih.gov/silk/niaaa_I/publication/physicn.htm

Nielson, A. C., & Williams, T. A. (1980). Depression in ambulatory medical patients. *Archives of General Psychiatry, 37,* 999–1009.

Noyes, R., Christiansen, J., Clancy, J., Garvey, M. J., & Suelzer, M. (1991). Predictors of serious suicide attempts among patients with panic disorder. *Comprehensive Psychiatry, 32,* 261–267.

Nunnally, J. (1978). *Psychometric theory.* New York: McGraw-Hill.

Office of National Drug Control Policy. (2001). *The economic costs of drug abuse in the United States, 1992–1998* (Publication No. NCJ-190636). Washington, DC: Executive Office of the President.

O'Hara, M. N., Ghonheim, M. M., Hinrich, J. V., Metha, M. P., & Wright, E. J. (1989). Psychological consequences of surgery. *Psychosomatic Medicine, 51,* 356–370.

Orleans, C. T., George, L. K., Houpt, J. L., & Brodie, H. (1985). How primary care physicians treat psychiatric disorders: A national survey of family practitioners. *American Journal of Psychiatry, 142,* 52–57.

Parikh, R. M., Eden, D. T., Price, T. R., & Robinson, R. G. (1988). The sensitivity and specificity of the center for epidemiologic studies depression scale in screening for post-stroke depression. *International Journal of Psychiatry in Medicine, 18,* 169–181.

Pennix, B. W., Guralnik, J. M., Ferrucci, L., Simonsick, E. M., Deeg, D. J., & Wallace, R. B. (1998). Depressive symptoms and physical decline in community-dwelling older persons. *Journal of the American Medical Association, 279,* 1720–1806.

Pfeiffer, E. (1975). A short portable mental status questionnaire for the assessment of organic brain deficit in elderly patients. *Journal of the American Geriatrics Society, 23,* 433–441.

Piccinelli, M., Tessari, E., Bortolomasi, M., et al. (1997). Efficacy of the Alcohol Use Disorders Identification Test as a screening tool for hazardous alcohol intake and related disorders in primary care: A validity study. *British Medical Journal, 314*, 420–424.

Piersma, H. L., Reaume, W. M., & Boes, J. L. (1994). The Brief Symptom Inventory (BSI) as an outcome measure for adult psychiatric inpatients. *Journal of Clinical Psychology, 50*, 555–563.

Pignone, M. Gaynes, B. N., Ruston, J. L., Mulrow, C., Orleans, C. T., Whitener, B. L., et al. (2002). *Screening for depression* (Systematic evidence review for the research triangle Institute–University of North Carolina's Evidence-based Practice Center). Research Triangle Institute, Raleigh, NC.

Pokorny, A. D., Miller, B. A., & Kaplan, H. B. (1972). The brief MAST: A shortened version of the Michigan Alcoholism Screening Test. *American Journal of Psychiatry, 129*, 342–348.

Radloff, L. S. (1977). The CES–D scale: A self-report depression scale for research in the general population. *Applied Psychological Measurement, 1*, 385–401.

Radloff, L. S., & Locke, B. Z. (1985). The community mental health assessment survey and the CES–D scale. In M. M. Weissman, J. K. Myers, & C. G. Ross (Eds.), *Community survey of psychiatric disorders*. New Brunswick, NJ: Rutgers University Press.

Rameizl, P. (1984). A case for assessment technology in long-term care: The nursing perspective. *Rehabilitation Nursing, 9*, 29–31.

Rand, E. H., Badger, L. W., & Coggins, D. R. (1988). Toward a resolution of contradictions: Utility of feedback from the GHQ. *General Hospital Psychiatry, 10*, 189–196.

Regier, D. A., Boyd, J. H., Burke, J. D., Rae, D. S., Myers, J. K., Kramer, M., et al. (1988). One month prevalence of mental disorders in the United States. *Archives of General Psychiatry, 45*, 977–986.

Regier, D. A., Goldberg, I. D., Burns, B. J., Hankin, J., Hoeper, E. W., & Nyez, G. R. (1982). Specialist/generalist division of responsibility for patients with mental disorders. *Archives of General Psychiatry, 39*, 219–224.

Regier, D., Goldberg, I., & Taube, C. (1978). The defacto US mental health services system: A public health perspective. *Archives of General Psychiatry, 35*, 685–693.

Regier, D. A., Roberts, M. A., Hirschfeld, R. M. A., Goodwin, F. K., Burke, J. D., Lazar, J. B., et al. (1988). The NIMH depression awareness, recognition, and treatment program: Structure, aims, and scientific basis. *American Journal of Psychiatry, 145*, 1351–1357.

Reid, M. C., Fiellin, D. A., & O'Connor, P. G. (1999). Hazardous and harmful drinking in primary care. *Archives of Internal Medicine, 159*, 1681–1689.

Reid, M. C., Lachs, M. S., & Feinstein, A. R. (1995). Use of methodological standards in diagnostic test research: Getting better but still not good. *Journal of the American Medical Association, 274*, 645–651.

Reid, M. C., Tinetti, M. E., Brown, C. J., & Concato, J. (1998). Physician awareness of alcohol use disorders among older patients. *Journal of General Internal Medicine, 13*, 729–734.

Reifler, D. R., Kessler, H. S., Bernhard, E. J., Leon, A. C., & Martin, G. J. (1996). Impact of screening for mental health concerns on health service utilization and functional status in primary care patients. *Archives of Internal Medicine, 156*, 2593–2599.

Reisberg, B. (1984). Stages of cognitive decline. *American Journal of Nursing, 84*, 225–228.

Reisberg, B., Ferris, S., deLeon, M., & Crook, T. (1982). The Global Deterioration Scale for assessment of primary degenerative dementia. *American Journal of Psychiatry, 139*, 1136–1139.

Reisberg, B., Ferris, S., deLeon, M., & Crook, T. (1988). Global Deterioration Scale (GDS). *Psychopharmacology Bulletin, 24*, 661–663.

Reynolds, W. M., & Gould, J. W. (1981). A psychometric investigation of the standard and short form Beck Depression Inventory. *Journal of Consulting Clinical Psychology, 49*, 306–307.

Riskind, J. H., Beck, A. T., Brown, G., & Steer, R. A. (1987). Taking the measure of anxiety and depression: Validity of the reconstructed Hamilton scales. *Journal of Nervous and Mental Disease, 175*, 474–479.

Ritchie, K., & Furher, R. (1992). A comparative study of the performance of screening tests for senile dementia using receiver operating characteristics analysis. *Journal of Clinical Epidemiology, 45*, 627–637.

Roberts, R. E., Rhoades, H. M., & Vernon, S. W. (1990). Using the CES–D scale to screen for depression and anxiety: Effects of language and ethnic status. *Psychiatry Research, 31*, 69–83.

Robins, L. N., Helzer, J. E., Weissman, M. M., Orvaschel, H., Greenberg, E., Burke, J. D., et al. (1984). Lifetime prevalence of specific psychiatric disorders in three sites. *Archives of General Psychiatry, 41*, 949–958.

Roca, P., Klein, L., Kirby, S., McArthur, J., Vogelsang, G., Folstein, M., et al. (1984). Recognition of dementia among medical patients. *Archives of Internal Medicine, 144*, 73–75.

Rosenthal, T. L., Miller, S. T., Rosenthal, R. H., Sadish, W. R., Fogleman, B. S., & Dismuke, S. E. (1992). Assessing emotional interest at the internist's office. *Behavioral Research and Therapy, 29*, 249–252.

Ross, H. E., Gavin, D. R., & Skinner, H. S. (1990). Diagnostic validity of the MAST and Alcohol Dependence Scale in the assessment of DSM–III alcohol disorders. *Journal of Studies on Alcohol, 51*, 506–513.

Rounsaville, B. J., Bryant, K., Babor, T., Kranzler, H., & Kadden, R. (1993). Cross system agreement for substance use disorders: DSM–III–R, DSM–IV and ICD–10. *Addiction, 88,* 337–348.

Royse, D., & Drude, K. (1984). Screening drug abuse clients with the Brief Symptom Inventory. *International Journal of Addiction, 19,* 849–857.

Rumpf, H. J., Hapke, U., Hill, A., & John, U. (1997). Development of a screening questionnaire for the general hospital and general practices. *Alcoholism, Clinical and Experimental Research, 21,* 894–898.

Rydon, P., Redman, S., Sanson Fisher, R. W., & Reid, A. L. (1992). Detection of alcohol related problems in general practice. *Journal of Studies on Alcohol, 53,* 197–202.

Sackett, D. L., Haynes, R. B., Guyatt, G. H., & Tugwell, P. (1991). *Clinical epidemiology: A basic science for clinical medicine* (2nd ed.). Boston: Little, Brown.

Samet, J. H., Rollnick, S., & Barnes, H. (1996). Beyond CAGE: A brief clinical approach after detection of substance abuse. *Archives of Internal Medicine, 156,* 2287–2293.

Sanchez, C. M. (1995). Empirically based guidelines for moderate drinking: I year results from three studies with problem drinkers. *American Journal of Public Health, 85,* 823–828.

Saravay, S. M., Pollack, S., Steinberg, M. D., Weinschel, B., & Habert, B. A. (1996). Four-year follow-up of the influence of psychological comorbidity on medical rehospitalization. *American Journal of Psychiatry, 153,* 397–403.

Saunders, J. B., Aasland, O. G., Amundsen, A., & Grant, M. (1993). Alcohol consumption and related problems among primary health care patients: WHO Collaborative Project on Early Detection of Persons With Harmful Alcohol Consumption. *Addiction, 88,* 349–362.

Saunders, J. B., Aasland, O. G., Babor, T. F., de la Fuente, J. R., & Grant, M. (1993). Development of the Alcohol Use Disorders Identification Test (AUDIT): WHO Collaborative Project on Early Detection of Persons With Harmful Alcohol Consumption. *Addiction, 88,* 791–804.

Schmidt, A., Barry, K. L., & Fleming, M. F. (1995). Detection of problem drinkers: The Alcohol Use Disorders Identification Test (AUDIT). *Southern Medical Journal, 88,* 52–59.

Schmidt, N., & Telch, M. (1990). Prevalence of personality disorders among bulimics, nonbulimic binge eaters, and normal controls. *Journal of Psychopathology and Behavioral Assessment, 12,* 160–185.

Schorling, J. B., Klas, P. T., Willems, J. P., & Everett, A. S. (1994). Addressing alcohol use among primary care patients: Differences between family medicine and internal medicine residents. *Journal of General Internal Medicine, 9,* 248–254.

Schorling, J. B., Willems, J. P., & Klas, P. T. (1995). Identifying problem drinkers: Lack of sensitivity of the two question drinking test. *American Journal of Medicine, 98,* 232–236.

Schulberg, H. C., Saul, M., McClelland, M., Ganguli, M., Christy, W., & Frank, R. (1985). Assessing depression in primary medical and psychiatric practices. *Archives of General Psychiatry, 42,* 1164–1170.

Schurman, R. A., Kramer P. D., & Mitchell, J. B. (1985). The hidden mental heath network. *Archives of General Psychiatry, 42,* 89–94.

Seay, T., & Beck, T. (1984). Alcoholism among college students. *Journal of College Student Personnel, 25,* 90–92.

Sederer, L. I., & Dickey, B. (1996). *Outcomes assessment in clinical practice.* Baltimore: Williams & Wilkins.

Seltzer, A. (1989). Prevalence, detection and referral of psychiatric morbidity in general medical patients. *Journal of the Royal Society of Medicine, 82,* 410–412.

Selzer, M. L. (1971). The Michigan Alcoholism Screening Test: The quest for a new diagnostic instrument. *American Journal of Psychiatry, 127,* 1653–1658.

Selzer, M. L., Vinokur, A., & van Rooijen, M. A. (1975). A self administered Short Michigan Alcoholism Screening Test (SMAST). *Journal of Studies on Alcohol, 36,* 117–126.

Shapiro, S., German, P., Skinner, E., Von Korff, M., Turner, R., Klein, L., et al. (1987). An experiment to change detection and management of mental morbidity in primary care. *Medical Care, 25,* 327–339.

Shore, D., Overman, C., & Wyatt, R. (1983). Improving accuracy in the diagnosis of Alzheimer's disease. *Journal of Clinical Psychiatry, 44,* 207–212.

Shrout, P. E., & Yager, T. J. (1989). Reliability and validity of screening scales: Effect of reducing scale length. *Journal of Clinical Epidemiology, 42,* 69–78.

Silver, R. C., Holman, E. A., McIntosh, D. N., Poulin, M., & Gil-Rivas, V. (2002). Nationwide longitudinal study of psychological responses to September 11. *Journal of the American Medical Association, 288,* 1235–1244.

Simon, G. E., & Von Korff, M. (1995). Recognition, management and outcomes of depression in primary care. *Archives of Family Medicine, 4,* 99–105.

Skinner, H. A., Schuller, R., Roy, J., & Israel, Y. (1984). Identification of alcohol abuse using laboratory tests and a history of trauma. *Annals of Internal Medicine, 101,* 847–885 841.

Snyder, S., Strain, J. J., & Wolf, D. (1990). Differentiating major depression from adjustment disorder with depressed mood in the medical setting. *General Hospital Psychiatry, 12,* 159–165.

Soderstrom, C. A., Smith, G. S., Kufer, J. A., Dischinger, P. C., Hebel, J. R., McDuff, D. R., et al. (1997). The accuracy of the CAGE, the Brief Michigan Alcoholism Screening Test, and the Alcohol Use Disorders Identification Test in screening trauma center patients for alcoholism. *Journal of Trauma, 43,* 962–969.

Sokol, R. J., Martier, S. S., & Ager, J. W. (1989). The T-ACE questions: Practical prenatal detection of risk drinking. *American Journal of Obstetrics and Gynecology, 160,* 863–868.

Somoza, E. (1994). Classification of diagnostic tests. *International Journal of Biomedical Computing, 37,* 41–55.

Somoza, E. (1996). Eccentric diagnostic tests: Redefining sensitivity and specificity. *Medical Decision Making, 16,* 15–23.

Somoza, E., & Mossman, D. (1990a). Introduction to neuropsychiatric decision making: Binary diagnostic tests. *Journal of Neuropsychiatry and Clinical Neurosciences, 2,* 297–300.

Somoza, E., & Mossman, D. (1990b). Optimizing REM latency as a diagnostic test for depression using ROC analysis and information theory. *Biological Psychiatry, 27,* 990–1006.

Somoza, E., & Mossman, D. (1991). Biological markers and psychiatric diagnosis: Risk-benefit analysis using ROC analysis. *Biological Psychiatry, 29,* 811–826.

Somoza, E., & Mossman, D. (1992a). Comparing and optimizing diagnostic tests: An information-theoretic approach. *Medical Decision Making, 12,* 179–188.

Somoza, E., & Mossman, D. (1992b). Comparing diagnostic tests using information theory: The INFO-ROC technique. *Journal of Neuropsychiatry and Clinical Neurosciences, 4,* 214–219.

Somoza, E., Steer, R. A., Beck, A. T., & Clark, D. A. (1994). Differentiating major depression and panic disorders by self-report and clinical rating scales: ROC analysis and information theory. *Behavioral Research and Therapy, 32,* 771–782.

Spilker, B. (1996). *Quality of life and pharmacoeconomics in clinical trials.* Philadelphia: Lippincott-Raven.

Spitzer, R. L., Kroenke, K., Williams, J. B., & the Patient Health Questionnaire Primary Care Study Group. (1999). *Journal of the American Medical Association, 282,* 1737–1744.

Spitzer, R. L., Williams, J. B., Gibbon, M., & First, M. B. (1990). *Structure Clinical Interview for DSM–III–R: Non-patient edition (SCTD–NP, Version 1.0).* Washington, DC: American Psychiatric Press.

Spitzer, R. L., Williams, J. B. W., Korenke, K., et al. (1994). Utility of a new procedure for diagnosing mental disorders in primary care: The PRIME–MD 1000 study.

Stange, K. C., Flocke, S. A., & Goodwin, M. S. (1998). Opportunistic preventive services delivery: Are time limitations and patient barriers? *Journal of Family Practice, 46,* 419–424.

Steer, R. A., & Beck, A. T. (1996). Beck Depression Inventory. In L. I. Sederer & B. Dickey (Eds.), *Outcomes assessment in clinical practice.* Baltimore: Williams & Wilkins.

Steffens, D. C., Welsh, K. A., Burke, J. R., Helms, M. J., Folstein, M. F., Brandt, J., et al. (1996). Diagnosis of Alzheimer's disease in epidemiologic studies by staged review of clinical data. *Neuropsychiatry, Neuropsychology and Behavioral Neurology, 2,* 107–113.

Steinbauer, J. F., Cantor, S. B., Holzer, C. E., III, & Volk, R. J. (1998). Ethnic and sex bias in primary care screening tests for alcohol use disorders. *Annals Internal Medicine, 129,* 353–362.

Strain, J. J., Fulop, G., Lebovits, A., Ginsberg, B., Robinson, M., Stern, A., et al. (1988). Screening devices for diminished cognitive capacity. *General Hospital Psychiatry, 10,* 16–23.

Striegel-Moore, R., Silberstein, L., Frensch, P., & Rodin, J. (1989). A prospective study of disordered eating among college students. *International Journal of Eating Disorders, 8,* 499–509.

Swedo, S. E., Rettew, D. C., Kruppenheimer, M., Lum, D., Dolan, S., & Goldberger, E. (1991). Can adolescent suicide attempters be distinguished from at-risk adolescents? *Pediatrics, 88,* 620–629.

Swets, J. A. (1964). *Signal detection and recognition by human observers.* New York: Wiley.

Swets, J. A. (1979). ROC analysis applied to the evaluation of medical imaging techniques. *Investigatory Radiology, 14,* 109–121.

Szulecka, T., Springett, N., & De Pauw, K. (1986). Psychiatric morbidity in first-year undergraduates and the effect of brief psychotherapeutic intervention: A pilot study. *British Journal of Psychiatry, 149,* 75–80.

Taj, N., Devera Sales, A., & Vinson, D. C. (1998). Screening for problem drinking: Does a single question work? *Journal of Family Practice, 46,* 328–335.

Telch, M., Lucas, J., & Nelson, P. (1989). Nonclinical panic in college students: An investigation of prevalence and symptomatology. *Journal of Abnormal Psychology, 98,* 300–306.

Teri, L., Larson, E., & Reifler, B. (1988). Behavioral disturbance in dementia of the Alzheimer type. *Journal of the American Geriatrics Society, 36,* 1–6.

Tollefson, G. D. (1990). Differentiating anxiety and depression. *Psychiatric Medicine, 8,* 27–39.

Tucker, M. A., Ogle, S. J., Davison, J. G., & Eilenberg, M. D. (1987). Validation of a brief screening test for depression in the elderly. *Age and Aging, 16,* 139–144.

US Department of Health and Human Services. (2001). *Tenth special report to the U.S. Congress on alcohol and health from the Secretary of Health and Human Services, September 2001.* U.S. Department of Health and

Human Services, Public Health Service, National Institutes of Health, National Institute on Alcohol Abuse and Alcoholism. Retrieved from http://www.niaaa.nih.gov/publications/10report.pdf

Ustun, T. B., & Sartorius, N. (Eds.). (1995). Mental illness in general health care: An international study. New York: Wiley.

Vecchio, T. J. (1966). Predictive value of a single diagnostic test in unselected populations. *New England Journal of Medicine, 274*, 1171.

Vida, S. (2001). AccuROC for Windows 95/98/NT. Montreal: Accumetric Corporation.

Volk, R. J., Cantor, S. B., Steinbauer, J. R., & Cass, A. R. (1997). Item bias in the CAGE screening test for alcohol use disorders. *Journal of General Internal Medicine, 12*, 763–769.

Volk, R. J., Steinbauer, J. F., Cantor, S. B., & Holzer, C. E. (1997). The Alcohol Use Disorders Identification Test (AUDIT) as a screen for at-risk drinking in primary care patients of different racial/ethnic backgrounds. *Addiction, 92*, 197–206.

Von Korff, M., Dworkin, S. F., LeResche, L., & Kruger, A. (1988). An epidemiologic comparison of pain complaints. *Pain, 32*, 173–183.

Waterson, E. J., & Murray Lyon, I. M. (1989). Screening for alcohol related problems in the antenatal clinic: An assessment of different methods. *Alcohol and Alcoholism, 24*, 21–30.

Weinstein, M. C., Fineberg, H. V., Elstein, A. S., Neuhauser, D., Neutra, R. R., & McNeil, B. J. (1980). *Clinical decision analysis*. Philadelphia: Saunders.

Weinstein, M. C., Berwick, D. M., Goldman, P. A., Murphy, J. M., & Barsky, A. J. (1989). A comparison of three psychiatric screening tests using receiver operating characteristic (ROC) analysis. *Medical Care, 27*, 593–607.

Weissman, M. M., Myers, J. K., & Thompson, W. D. (1981). Depression and its treatment in a U. S. urban community. *Archives of General Psychiatry, 38*, 417–421.

Weissman, M. M., & Merikangas, K. R. (1986). The epidemiology of anxiety and panic disorder: An update. *Journal of Clinical Psychiatry, 47*, 11–17.

Wells, C. (1979). Pseudodementia. *American Journal of Psychiatry, 136*, 895–900.

Wells, K. B., Golding, J. M., & Burnam, M. A. (1988). Psychiatric disorders in a sample of the general population with and without chronic medical conditions. *American Journal of Psychiatry, 145*, 976–981.

Wells, V., Klerman, G., & Deykin, E. (1987). The prevalence of depressive symptoms in college students. *Social Psychiatry, 22*, 20–28.

Wenrich, M. D., Paauw, D. S., Carline, J. D., Curtis, J. R., & Ramsey, P. G. (1995). Do primary care physicians screen patients about alcohol intake using the CAGE questions? *Journal of General Internal Medicine, 10*, 631–634.

West, R., Drummond, C., & Eames, K. (1990). Alcohol consumption, problem drinking and anti-social behaviour in a sample of college students. *British Journal of Addiction, 85*, 479–486.

Westefeld, J. S., Bandura, A., Kiel, J. T., & Scheel, K. (1996). The College Student Reason for Living Inventory: Additional psychometric data. *Journal of College Student Development, 37*, 348–350.

Westefeld, J. S., Cardin, D., & Deaton, W. L. (1992). Development of the College Student Reasons for Living Inventory. *Suicide and Life-Threatening Behavior, 22*, 442–452.

Westefeld, J. S., & Liddell, D. L. (1994). The Beck Depression Inventory and its relationship to college student suicide. *Journal of College Student Development, 35*, 145–146.

Whitaker, A., Johnson, J., Shaffer, D., Rapoport, J., Kalikow, K., Walsh, B., et al. (1990). Uncommon trouble in young people: Prevalence estimates of selected psychiatric disorders in a nonreferred adolescent population. *Archives of General Psychiatry, 47*, 487–496.

Whooley, M. A., Avins, A. L., Miranda, J., & Browner, W. S. (1997). Case-finding instruments for depression. *Journal of General Internal Medicine, 12*, 439–445.

Williams, J. B. (1988). A structured interview guide for the Hamilton Depression Rating Scale. *Archives of General Psychiatry, 45*, 742–747.

Williams, J. W., Hitchcock, P., Cordes, J. A., Ramirez, G., & Pignone, M. (2002). Is this patient clinically depressed? *Journal of the American Medical Association, 287*, 1160–1170.

Williams, R., & Vinson, D. C. (2001). Validation of a single question for problem drinking. *Journal of Family Practice, 50*, 307–312.

Wilson, J. M., & Jungner, F. (1968). Principles and practices of screening for diseases. *Public Health Papers* (Geneva), *34*, 1968.

Wise, M. G., & Taylor, S. E. (1990). Anxiety and mood disorders in mentally ill patients. *Journal of Clinical Psychiatry, 51*, 27–32.

Woodworth, R. S. (1918). *Personal data sheet*. Chicago: Stoelting.

World Health Organization. (1992). *The ICD-10 classification of mental and behavioral disorders: Clinical descriptions and diagnostic guidelines*. Geneva: Author.

Yelin, E., Mathias, S. D., Buesching, D. P., Rowland, C., Calucin, R. Q., & Fifer, S. (1996). The impact of the employment of an intervention to increase recognition of previously untreated anxiety among primary care physicians. *Social Science in Medicine, 42,* 1069–1075.

Yopenic, P. A., Clark, C. A., & Aneshensel, C. S. (1983). Depression problem recognition and professional consultation. *Journal of Nervous and Mental Disease, 171,* 15–23.

Zabora, J. R., Smith-Wilson, R., Fetting, J. H., & Enterline, J. P. (1990). An efficient method for psychosocial screening of cancer patients. *Psychosomatics, 31,* 1992–1996.

Zabora, J., Brintzenhofeszoc, K., Jacobsen, P., Curbow, B., Piantadosi, S., Hooker, C., et al. (2001). A new psychosocial screening instrument for use with cancer patients. *Psychosomatics, 42,* 241–246.

Zalaquett, C. P., & Wood, R. J. (1997). *Evaluating stress: A book of resources.* Lanham, MD: Scarecrow Press.

Zung, W. K. W. (1965). A self-rating depression scale. *Archives of General Psychiatry, 12,* 63–70.

Zung, W., Magill, M., Moore, J., & George, D. (1983). Recognition and treatment of depression in a family practice. *Journal of Clinical Psychology, 44,* 3–6.

# Use of Psychological Tests/Instruments for Treatment Planning

Larry E. Beutler, Mary Malik, Hani Talebi, Jenny Fleming, and Carla Moleiro
*University of California, Santa Barbara*

The advent of the descriptive diagnostic system of DSM–III, biological psychiatry, and managed health care have conspired to produce a decline of third-party support for the use of formal psychological tests as routine diagnostic procedures in mental health. Descriptive diagnosis and the symptom focus of biological treatments eliminated the need for complex tests to identify covert and highly abstract psychic processes, as had previously been required in the diagnosis of such disorders as schizophrenia and neurosis. It is paradoxical that the same psychiatric and managed care forces that voiced initial concern about maintaining reliable and valid diagnostic data have consistently preferred the use of subjective and unreliable unstructured clinical interviews to gather this data over empirically established, reliable, and valid psychological tests. The virtual exclusion of formal tests from routinely approved intake procedures underlines the signal failure of psychological assessment to establish itself as a meaningful contributor to treatment planning.

To capitalize on the empirical advantages of psychological tests over unstandardized clinical methods, the nature and goals of the assessment process must change. The omnibus, broad-ranging instruments that have long served this tradition must give way to assessment procedures that are short, practical, and treatment centered. The clinician presented with a new patient would be greatly assisted by the use of reliable and empirically based assessment procedures: Is this condition treatable? Is psychotherapy or pharmacotherapy an appropriate treatment modality? What about family therapy? Should treatment focus on the immediate symptoms, on the broader symptoms of depression and anxiety, or on the resolution of underlying, dynamic conflicts? Should the patient be hospitalized for further evaluation or be seen by a neurologist or other medical specialist? What will tell us when treatment can be safely terminated?

Clinicians must immediately decide on the most productive intervention with which to commence treatment and engage the client. Simultaneously, they must devise a treatment plan that is maximally effective in addressing the client's needs. In pursuing these objectives, it is implicitly acknowledged that treatments effective for one client or problem may be ineffective for another. Recognizing this fact, health care researchers have attempted to develop guidelines to assist clinicians by identifying both treatments with the highest likelihood of success and those either inappropriate or minimally effective. The emerging field of prescriptive treatment planning is devoted to the prescription of effective treatments and the proscription of ineffective ones (Beutler & Clarkin, 1990; Beutler & Harwood, 1995; Frances, Clarkin, & Perry, 1984).

Because of their psychometric qualities and their adaptability to complex statistical manipulations, psychological tests are ideal for developing standardized procedures for differentially assigning or recommending psychosocial treatments (e.g., Beutler & Berren, 1995; Beutler & Groth-Marnat, 2003; Butcher, 1990; Graham, 1987, 1993; Groth-Marnat, 1997). However, most indicators and signs employed by clinicians using psychological tests to make mental health treatment decisions are based on clinical experiences and conjectures rather than evidence of improved treatment effectiveness. Therefore, this chapter is devoted to providing the clinician with a representative overview of some of the growing body of research that suggests that test performance may predict both treatment outcome and, more importantly, a differential response to available treatments. We also report an initial effort to develop a method that consolidates, in one measurement device, information currently available only by using a large battery of contemporary tests.

## PREDICTIVE DIMENSIONS IN DIFFERENTIAL THERAPEUTICS

Psychological tests have traditionally been used to address questions within five domains: (1) diagnosis, (2) etiology or causes of behavior, (3) prognosis and course, (4) treatment planning, and (5) functional impairment (Beutler & Rosner, 1995). Of these questions, as noted, questions of diagnosis and differential diagnosis have always been primary.

Psychological tests like the Rorschach and TAT were developed and came to be relied on to uncover covert thought disorder, underlying dynamic conflicts, and pathological ideation and impulses associated with various diagnoses. Since these tests purported to be able to reveal these hidden processes with much more validity than unstructured interviews, diagnoses came to frequently depend on them. As the diagnostic system became less reliant on evidence of covert, underlying processes with the advent of the third edition of the *Diagnostic and Statistical Manual* (DSM–III) of the American Psychiatric Association (1983), weaknesses of projective tests became apparent (Butcher, 1995; Groth-Marnat, 1997; Nezworski & Wood, 1995).

Even beyond the contributions of DSM-III, the seemingly unbridled expansion and growing complexity of the diagnostic system has raised concerns about the processes of constructing psychiatric diagnoses. Contemporary disorders and their criteria (DSM–IV; American Psychiatric Association, 1994) represent a consensual opinion of a committee of psychiatric experts the majority of whom determine whether a pattern of symptoms is accorded the status of a socially viable "syndrome" or "disorder." The recognition of a cluster of symptoms as a diagnosable condition has traditionally been based on (a) the presence and frequency of the symptoms; (b) an analysis of the symptom's social significance and interpersonal effects, where the empirical evidence has warranted; and (c) the specificity of the symptomatic response to various classes of drugs.

Committees responsible for the development of the *Diagnostic and Statistical Manuals*, however, have largely ignored empirical information about patient characteristics and traits (e.g., coping styles, resistance, conflicts, etc.) that have been found useful in selecting psychotherapeutic procedures. Consequently, even a reliable diagnosis (still debated, e.g., Beutler & Malik, 2002; Follette & Houts, 1996; Wells & Sturm, 1996) provides little information upon which to develop a differentially sensitive psychotherapeutic program.

Though a patient with a diagnosis of major depression with vegetative signs can be expected to respond better to tricyclic antidepressants than to anxiolytics (e.g., Wells & Sturm, 1996), the diagnostic label does not allow a clinician to select among cognitive, interpersonal, or relationship psychotherapies. Symptoms that determine diagnosis are quite insensitive to qualities and characteristics that determine how well prospective patients will respond. Treatments themselves are cross-cutting. Their use is not bound by or specific to patient diagnoses, and in fact diagnoses may be poor indicators for their implementation. It is unlikely that a cognitive therapy can be constructed to be so specific that it would work well for patients with major depression but not for those with anxiety, personality disorders, minor depression, or eating disorders. Cognitive therapy has been applied to all these disorders as well as to such widely different conditions as tics, sexual dysfunctions, sleep disorders, impulse control disorders, substance abuse disorders, adjustment disorders—virtually any condition in which thought and/or behavior is disrupted. Such theoretically diverse treatments as cognitive, behavioral, psychodynamic, and interpersonal therapy have all been advocated as treatments for the same multitude of diagnostic conditions.

This cross-diagnostic application of psychotherapies does not mean that specific treatment indicators are not available. Indeed, some such indicators are present, but many of these were ignored in constructing the diagnostic criteria.

Most clinicians realize the weaknesses and limitations of diagnosis and develop a rich array of treatment possibilities as they seek and obtain extradiagnostic information. This information is consolidated into both a patient formulation and a treatment plan. However, patient formulations and resulting treatment plans vary widely from clinician to clinician, even within a given theoretical framework (e.g., Caspar, 1995; Horowitz et al., 1984; Luborsky, 1996; Masterson, Tolpin, & Sifneos, 1991; Vaillant, 1997). The uniqueness of the diverse formulations reflects the amalgamation and influence both of therapists' personal theories of psychopathology and formal variations that exist among different formal systems. The failure of clinicians to rely on empirically derived dimensions of personality and prediction in constructing their formulations of patients and treatments probably reflects the absence of knowledge about how to define and use such empirical predictors and also the absence of discriminating measures simply administered to reliably capture some of the patient characteristics related to treatment outcomes.

Many authors have attempted to define the extradiagnostic dimensions that may allow a clinician to predict the differential effects of applying different therapeutic procedures. Most of these efforts have provided guidelines for the application of different procedures within a single theoretical framework, and few have attempted to incorporate the breadth of interventions that characterize widely different theories. For example, Hollon and Beck (1986) suggested the conditions under which cognitive therapy might be directed to schematic change versus changes in automatic thoughts, and Strupp and Binder (1984) suggested guidelines within which the psychodynamic therapist may differentially offer interpretations or support. However, since any single theoretical framework will not fully encompass the many foci, procedures, and strategies advocated by the available array of psychotherapies, these monotheoretical guidelines are necessarily incomplete and are weaker than they would be if more comprehensive constructs were included.

Recognizing the limitations that exist when only procedures advocated by a single theory can be selected for use, practitioners and researchers alike have in recent years been swayed toward "technical eclecticism" (Norcross & Goldfried, 1992; Striker & Gold, 1993). The approaches associated with this movement, diverse in type, share the objective of developing guidelines for the selection of maximally effective interventions from the broadest array of proven procedures regardless of the theories generating them. These guidelines specify the characteristics of patients and therapeutic situational demands that, according to theories of intervention, best fit one another.

The various models differ in their level of technical specificity and in the nature of constructs selected as most important. For example, Lazarus (1981) developed one of the more widely recognized integrative models, Multi-Modal Therapy (MMT). MMT offers a general framework that not only helps define a patient's experience and problems but relates these dimensions to the use of different models and techniques of treatment. Specifically, MMT provides a structured means for assessing the relative and absolute levels of problems in seven general domains of experience—domains captured in the acronym BASIC–ID: *B*ehaviors, *A*ffects, *S*ensory experiences, *I*magery, *C*ognitions, *I*nterpersonal relationships, and need for *D*rugs. The clinician observes the levels of disturbance in each domain and then elucidates their interrelationships by determining their firing or triggering order: the pattern of behavior that occurs when the problems arise. Then the model proposes classes of interventions that correspond to the dimensions of patient experience affected by the problems. Thus, experiential procedures may be used when sensory and affective experiences are disturbed, behavioral interventions when behavioral symptoms are disruptive, cognitive change procedures when dysfunctional thoughts are observed, and so forth.

In contrast to the focus on problem activation that defines the integration of procedures within MMT, other approaches have emphasized alternative methods for integrating procedures. In some cases, this has resulted in a less specific relationship being posited between patient dimensions and the nature of treatment techniques than that proposed by Lazarus. Some, for example, have identified stages of problem development or resolution as an organizing principle. These stage models vary from one to another by virtue of the degree of emphasis they place on patient variables (Prochaska & DiClemente, 1984) or intervening therapy goals (Beitman, 1987) as the stage indicators.

Prochaska and DiClemente (1984), more specifically, identified broad classes of intervention that may be recommended as a function of the patient's stage of problem resolution. Thus, behavioral strategies are recommended when the patient is in a stage of active problem resolution, strategies that raise awareness when the patient is in a preconceptual (precontemplative) stage of problem resolution, insight strategies when the patient is in the process of problem contemplation and cognitive exploration; and so forth.

Beitman (1987), on the other hand, applied the concept of stages to the course of psychotherapy rather than to the stage of problem resolution achieved by the patient. Accordingly, he advocated that the early sessions should focus on relationship development and that the therapist should then proceed through helping the patient recognize patterns, changing these patterns, and preparing for termination.

Beutler and Clarkin (1990; Beutler, Clarkin, & Bongar, 2000) suggested a resolution of these viewpoints, offering the possibility that there may be interrelationships between the patient and the treatment stages. The resolution of such differences are dependent on success in developing psychological tests that can reliably identify patient and problem information that is directly usable in planning treatments.

## PATIENT PREDISPOSING VARIABLES

Psychometrically stable measurements of treatment-relevant patient dimensions (i.e., predisposing variables) could be used to identify markers for the application of different interventions. Unavoidably, however, patient, treatment, and matching dimensions correlated with treatment effects are virtually limitless (Beutler, 1991).[1]

To bring some order to the diverse hypotheses associated with several models of differential treatment assignment and to place them in the perspective of empirical research, Beutler and Clarkin (1990) grouped patient characteristics presented by different theories into a series of superordinate and subordinate categories. This classification included seven specific classes of patient variables, distinguished both by their susceptibility to measurement using established psychological tests and by their ability to predict differential responses to psychosocial treatment (Beutler & Groth-Marnat, 2003; Beutler & Hodgson, 1993; Gaw & Beutler, 1995). These categories included (a) Functional Impairment, (b) Subjective Distress, (c) Problem Complexity, (d) Readiness for/Stage of Change, (e) Potential to Resist Therapeutic Influences, (f) Social Support, and (g) Coping Styles. To these, we add in this review an eighth category based on the results of a task force organized by Division 29 of the American Psychological Association. This eighth category is closely related to Coping Style but is considered here separately in the interests of clarity. It is identified as patient Attachment Style.

Collectively, these eight "patient predisposing" dimensions provide points of reference for organizing the topics of this chapter as we consider the use of psychological tests for treatment planning. Table 3.1 summarizes some representative instruments that may be used for assessing these various dimensions.

### Functional Impairment

Traditionally, the literature on the role of problem severity in treatment success has confounded two aspects of patient functioning, level of impairment and subjective distress (e.g., Beutler, Wakefield, & Williams, 1994). Not surprisingly, therefore, research on this topic has produced mixed results. To clarify the differing roles of impairment and distress, we have followed the suggestions of Strupp, Horowitz, and Lambert (1997) and distinguish between external ratings of social functioning (i.e., observed impairment) and self-reports of unhappiness and subjective distress. With this distinction, measures of functional impairment reflect reduced levels of functioning in such areas as self-care, social responsibility, interpersonal relationships, work activity, and intimacy (Sperry, Brill, Howard, & Grissom, 1996).

Level of patient impairment in social functioning is a variable of considerable importance to treatment studies. It is typically measured by the General Assessment of Functioning (GAF) scale from DSM–IV or by specific problem-centered measures such as the Anxiety Disorders Interview Schedule (ADIS; DiNardo, O'Brien, Barlow,

---

[1] Because of space constraints the discussion here is restricted to psychological interventions and initial disposing variables. We give only limited attention to how tests have been used for the selection of medical or somatic treatments (e.g., hospitilization, ECT, medication, etc.), for establishing DSM diagnoses, or for the purposes of making treatment alterations in midcourse. Likewise, the discussion does not include differential treatment planning for children and adolescents. The reader is referred to Beutler and Clarkin (1990) and Beutler, Clarkin, and Bongar (2000) for further information about these topics.

TABLE 3.1
Representative Tests for Measuring Patient/Problem Dimensions

| Test | Functional Impairment | Subjective Distress | Readiness for Change | Problem Complexity | Resistance Potential | Social Support | Coping Style | Attachment Style |
|---|---|---|---|---|---|---|---|---|
| ADIS[a] | X | | | | | | | |
| BDI[b] | | X | | | | | | |
| HRSD[a] | X | | | | | | | |
| SCL–90–R[b] | | X | | X | | | | |
| STAI[b] | X | | | | | | | |
| Stages of Change[b] | | | X | | | | | |
| TRS[b] | | | | X | | | X | |
| CCRT[a] | | | X | | | | | |
| MMPI[b] | | | | X | | | | |
| CPI[b] | | | | | | | | X |
| FES[b] | | | | | | X | | |
| NEO–PI[b] | | | | | | | | X |
| IES[b] | | X | | | | | | |
| BAADS[b] | | X | | | | | | |
| BASIS–32[b] | | X | | | | | | |
| MBSS[b] | | | | | | | X | |
| WCQ[b] | | | | | | | X | |
| AAI[a] | | | | | | | | X |

Note. ADIS = Anxiety Disorders Interview Schedule; BDI = Beck Depression Inventory; HRSD = Hamilton Rating Scale for Depression; SCL-90R = Symptom Checklist 90–Revised; STAI = State–Trait Anxiety Inventory; TRS = Therapeutic Reactance Scale; CCRT = Core Conflictual Relationship Theme; MMPI = Minnesota Multiphasic Personality Inventory; CPI = California Personality Inventory; FES = Family Environment Scale; NEO–PI = NEO Personality Inventory; IES = Impact of Events Scale; BAADS = Behavioral Approach-Avoidance and Distress Scale; BASIS-32 = Behavior and Symptom Identification Scale; MBSS = Miller Behavioral Style Scale; WCQ = Ways of Coping Questionnaire; AAI = Adult Attachment Interview.
[a] Observer-report instrument.
[b] Self-report instrument.

Waddell, & Blanchard, 1983) and the Hamilton Rating Scale for Depression (HRSD; Hamilton, 1967). Changes in these impairment indices reflect treatment improvement, but the initial level of impairment may also be a valuable index in treatment planning.

There is modest but relatively consistent direct evidence that level of functional impairment is negatively related to treatment outcome. This finding has been obtained in such diverse conditions as bulimia (Fahy & Russell, 1993), obsessive-compulsive disorder (Keijsers, Hoogduin, & Schaap, 1994), major depression (Beutler, Kim, Davison, Karno, & Fisher, 1996), dysthymia (Ravindran et al., 1999), and substance abuse (McLellan, Woody, Luborsky, O'Brien, & Druley, 1983). Indeed, McLellan et al. (1983) determined that measures of functional impairment were the single best (negative) predictors of treatment outcome. Moreover, patients with high functional impairment show less improvement with all kinds of treatment, including pharmacotherapy (e.g., Hoencamp, Haffmans, Duivenvoorden, Knegtering, & Dijken, 1994). The Beutler, Kim, et al. (1996) study, found that the negative relationship between impairment level and improvement in treatment was virtually independent of the type of treatment used.

However, a measure of functional impairment has more value to the clinician than merely as a prognostic indicator. Assessment of patient functional impairment can aid in three important dimensions of treatment planning: treatment intensity, type of psychosocial treatment, and the consideration of pharmacological treatment.

As regards treatment intensity, there is evidence that persistent treatment may eventually induce an effect among moderately impaired patients (Gaw & Beutler, 1995; Keijsers et al., 1994). Beutler, Harwood, Alimohamed, & Malik (2002) reviewed 10 studies that evaluated whether more intense treatment differentially benefited those with higher impairment; 8 of the 10 studies found a complex differential relationship. In a representative study, Shapiro et al. (1994) compared behavioral and psychodynamic-interpersonal therapies that were applied over a format that varied the level of treatment intensity—either 8 or 16 weeks' duration. The more intensive and lengthy treatment showed the most positive effects among those with high levels of impairment, regardless of the model or type of treatment implemented. More intensive treatment did not benefit those with low levels of impairment.

Research on relapse provides some indirect evidence that more intense treatment may be needed to maintain treatment gains among those with higher functional impairment. Brown and Barlow (1995) demonstrated both initial therapeutic gains among patients with panic disorder and a negative relationship between impairment and maintenance of benefit two years later. They concluded that even when treatment is able to induce an initial positive effect among those with high levels of initial impairment, the improvements are not as well maintained as improvements experienced by patients less severely impaired. Interestingly, the good results obtained by Shapiro et al. (1994), which favored more intensive treatment among more impaired individuals, largely disappeared after one year (Shapiro et al., 1995).

In all these studies, unfortunately, even the most intensive treatment was short term and infrequent compared with conventional standards for treating those with severe problems. The "intensive" treatment studied by Shapiro and his group consisted of only 16 sessions and certainly would not be endorsed as being intense by most practitioners. Studying a treatment whose length and frequency was more typical of the intensity applied to such problems in usual practice might have improved the results, both by facilitating the initial gains and by maintaining the effects of treatment longer than the short-term treatments studied in these investigations.

Next, there is promising evidence that functional impairment may be a mediator of differential effects attributed to various psychosocial models of treatment (e.g., Fremouw & Zitter, 1978; Joyce & Piper, 1996; McLellan et al., 1983; Shoham-Salomon & Rosenthal, 1987; Woody et al., 1984). Of special note, unimpaired object (interpersonal) relations (Joyce & Piper, 1996) and absence of comorbid personality disorders (Woody et al., 1984) have been found to enhance the power of dynamically oriented psychotherapy. The opposite may also hold—poor interpersonal relationships and complex personality disorders may respond poorly to psychodynamic and insight treatments, compared with other psychosocial interventions. For example, Kadden, Cooney, Getter, & Litt (1989) found that patients exhibiting sociopathic personality patterns responded better to cognitive-behavioral coping skills training than to an insight-oriented, interpersonal, interactional group therapy. Likewise, in a study of acutely impaired psychiatric inpatients, Beutler, Frank, Scheiber, Calvert, and Gaines (1984) concluded that, for this population, experiential-expressive interventions are not as effective as interactive, process-oriented, or behaviorally oriented therapies. Patients treated with experiential-expressive therapies showed increased symptoms and deterioration at the end of treatment, but these negative effects were not found among those treated with the other interventions.

Finally, the conventional wisdom that pharmacotherapy is indicated for more severely impaired patients has received mixed empirical support. In recent years, coinciding with the discovery of evidence that impaired functioning may be related to various central nervous system impairments, researchers have found evidence suggesting that high levels of functional impairment may potentiate the effects of pharmacological interventions (Beutler, Harwood, et al., 2002). For example, Fountaoulakis, Tsolaki, and Kazis (2000) reported that older depressed patients were responsive to antidepressant medications, particularly if they also suffered cognitive impairment related to depression.

Beutler, Harwood, et al. (2002) reviewed 12 studies that included pharmacotherapy in comparing different types of treatment; 8 of the 12 favored the use of medication among more severely impaired patients. These studies provide evidence that pharmacotherapy is more effective than placebo and that medication is differentially more effective for those patients with high levels of functional impairment (Basoglu, Marks, & Swinson, 1994; Eldridge, Locke, & Horowitz, 1998; McLean & Taylor, 1992; Mintz, Mintz, Arruda, & Hwang, 1992; Shea et al., 1992; Sotsky et al., 1991; Woody et al., 1984).

## Subjective Distress

Patient distress is a cross-cutting, cross-diagnostic index of well-being. It is poorly correlated with external measures of impairment and is a transitory or changeable symptom state (Lambert, 1994; Strupp et al., 1997). In clinical research, the Beck Depression Inventory (BDI; Beck, Ward, Mendelson, Mock, & Erbaugh, 1961), the SCL–90–R[2] (Derogatis, 1994), and the State–Trait Anxiety Inventory (STAI; Spielberger, Gorsuch, & Lushene, 1970) are most often used for assessing subjective distress. Additional assessment measures for appraising a patient's level of distress include the Impact of Events Scale (IES; Flett, Madorsky, Hewitt, & Heisel, 2002; Horowitz, Wilner, & Alvarez, 1979), the Behavioral Approach-Avoidance and Distress Scale (BAADS; Bachanas & Blout, 1996), and the Behavior and Symptom Identification Scale (BASIS–32; Eisen, Grob, & Klein, 1986; Eisen, Wilcox, Leff, Shaefer, & Culhane, 1999).

Interestingly, theoretical perspectives have emphasized the importance of distress as a motivating variable in keeping a patient engaged in treatment (Frank & Frank, 1991) as well as a measure of improvement. There is at least modest support for the proposition that distress can act as such a measure, and unlike patient level of impairment, moderate amounts of subjective distress have generally been found to positively correlate with subsequent improvement (Lambert, 1994). Specifically, there is reasonably consistent evidence that psychosocial treatments achieve their greatest effects among those with relatively high initial levels of subjective distress (e.g., Klerman, 1986; Klerman, DiMascio, Weissman, Prusoff, & Paykel, 1974; Lambert & Bergin, 1983; McLean & Taylor, 1992). These findings are especially strong among those with ambulatory depressions, general anxiety, and diffuse medical symptoms. Using the BDI as a measure of distress, for example, Parker, Holmes, and Manicavasager (1986) found that initial depression severity correlated positively with treatment response among general medical patients. Likewise, Mohr et al. (1990) observed that the likelihood (though not the magnitude) of response to treatment was positively and linearly associated with general symptom severity on the SCL–90–R among patients with moderately severe depression. Even further, among patients with mild and moderate impairment levels, research evidence suggests that psychosocial interventions are as

---

[2] For purposes of this discussion, we use the preferred acronym for the Symptom Checklist–90-Revised, as it is not distributed by a more formal name.

effective as antidepressant and antianxiety medications (Elkin et al., 1989; Robinson, Berman, & Neimeyer, 1990; Nietzel, Russell, Hemmings, & Gretter, 1987).

These findings are not entirely uniform, however, and some evidence indicates that subjective distress may relate to outcome in a curvilinear fashion, particularly when personality disturbance or somatic symptoms are present. Hoencamp et al. (1994), for example, found that, whereas a positive linear relationship existed between distress and improvement among depressed and anxious patient groups, a curvilinear relationship characterized those who had a comorbid personality disorder (with the exception of obsessive-compulsive personality disorder) and those whose complaints were weighted heavily in the direction of somatic symptoms.

Among nonsomatic patients, subjective distress has been implicated in the prediction of differential responses to various forms of psychotherapeutic treatment. For example, in the National Institute of Mental Health (NIMH) collaborative study of moderate depression, subjective distress, as measured by the BDI, differentiated the efficacy of the psychotherapeutic treatments (Imber et al., 1990). Patients with the most severe distress were more effectively treated by interpersonal psychotherapy than by cognitive therapy. Beutler, Kim, et al. (1996), employing a similar sample, demonstrated that level of subjective distress was positively related to the efficacy of self-directed, supportive forms of treatment but was not substantially related to the effects of cognitive and experiential treatments.

The consistency of the foregoing relationship is mitigated by the response among patients with prominent somatic symptoms. Blanchard, Schwarz, Neff, and Gerardi (1988) determined that subjective distress (measured by the STAI) was negatively, rather than positively, associated with improvement among patients with irritable bowel syndrome. Patients whose subjective anxiety did not exceed moderate limits were most likely to benefit from behavioral and self-regulatory treatment.

Similarly, using the BDI as a subjective measure of distress/depression, Jacob, Turner, Szekely, and Eidelman (1983) suggested that those with low distress levels were more likely than those with high levels of distress to benefit from self-monitored relaxation as a treatment for headaches. Patients with moderate and high levels of subjective distress most inconsistently benefited from behavioral and psychotherapeutic treatments.

Contemporary research conducted on distress has produced mixed results in another psychological arena: acute stress and debriefing. More specifically, there is growing agreement that early intervention for trauma, most often referred to as psychological debriefing, does not necessarily prevent consequent psychopathology (Bisson, McFarlane, & Rose, 2000; Gist & Woodall, 2000). Nevertheless, psychological debriefing is consistently provided following exposure to events that could be considered potentially traumatizing (Raphael, Wilson, Meldrum, & McFarlane, 1996). Clearly, some studies have indicated debriefing is effective in preventing the detrimental effects of exposure to disaster and trauma (Chemtob, Nakashima, & Carlson, 2002; Saunter, 1993). However more significantly, research intimates that the symptoms an individual experiences after a traumatic occurrence may be aggravated by psychological debriefing (Bisson, Jenkins, Alexander, & Bannister, 1997).

Litz, Gray, Bryant, and Adler (2002) found that single-session psychological debriefing applied to individuals who had experienced moderate to severe levels of potentially traumatizing events was no more useful in reducing posttraumatic stress disorder symptoms than would naturally occur with the passage of time. Litz et al. (2002) also demonstrated the importance of prescreening patients to assess their former levels of distress, their suitability for active intervention, and myriad other risk factors affecting treatment outcomes—information rarely collected in most potentially traumatic treatment milieus. Acute stress and psychological debriefing unmistakably bring to the fore an additional domain where distress is variably conducive and disadvantageous to the therapy process. In the end, although most theories assume that there is a clear fixed association between distress and progress in treatment, there are numerous instances where this relationship is reversed, resulting in both linear negative and linear positive relationships across interventions (Beutler, 2002).

**Problem Complexity**

In addition to the severity of symptomatic presentation and the stage of problem resolution achieved, problems also vary in their complexity (Beutler, 1983; Beutler & Clarkin, 1990). Complexity is indexed by a variety of things, including the concomitant presence of multiple personality disorders, comorbid diagnoses, and the chronicity of major disorders, and by evidence that interpersonal and conflictual patterns recur in persistent and pervasive ways. Recurrent patterns that indicate complex, problematic behavior are thought to be evoked by the similarity of symbolic meanings given to evoking cues rather than by obvious similarities in overt stimulus characteristics (Barber, 1989; Crits-Christoph & Demorest, 1991). Complex patterns are expressed in a similar way across a large variety of social systems, transcending specific events and situations.

The issue of assessing problem complexity is intimately related to treatment, as, almost by definition, complex issues might be expected to require either quantitative or qualitative differences in treatment approach. In this section, we first briefly address issues related to the assessment and treatment of two specific instances of complexity: comorbid diagnoses and personality disorders. We then elaborate on several of the more broadly based approaches to assessing problem complexity as well as the relationship between these measures of complexity and treatment outcome.

The concept of comorbidity has become more prevalent in the clinical literature with the increasing awareness that many people seeking help for emotional or behavioral problems meet the criteria for more than one diagnosis. The very use of the term *comorbidity* illustrates some of these real-world complexities in that it is used to describe individuals with both physical and psychiatric diagnoses (e.g., Saravay & Lavin, 1994), with combined substance-related and other Axis I diagnoses (e.g., Goldsmith, 1999), and with at least one diagnosis on both Axis I and Axis II. With respect to psychiatric comorbidity, assessment is typically carried out by means of structured or semistructured interviews based on the most recent version of the American Psychiatric Association's *Diagnostic and Statistical Manual of Mental Disorders*, which assigns a separate diagnosis for each constellation of symptoms. Thus, the vast number of potential diagnostic combinations presents a formidable challenge to those who study comorbidity, aside from complications such as the potential for causal interactions between disorders (Greenberg, 1997). This variation also makes it difficult to devise strong recommendations for the best approaches to the treatment of comorbid conditions. In a recent review, Greenberg (1997) concluded that the evidence to date supports the idea that comorbidity appears to be associated with poor treatment outcome. However, he cautions that the research literature on comorbidity is beset with statistical and methodological flaws, making it difficult to have confidence in the causal nature of these findings.

Like comorbidity, personality disorders can also be seen as representing complex psychiatric problems. Indeed, the idea of a personality disorder as consisting of long-standing problematic modes of functioning that cut across situations is consistent with psychodynamically derived ideas of problem complexity. As with many studies of comorbidity, most contemporary studies of personality disorder utilize DSM-based interviews for assessment purposes, an approach necessary for funding purposes but one that potentially results in large heterogeneity within a given diagnostic category as well as multiple diagnoses for individuals with more than one Axis II diagnosis.

Perhaps for this reason, the impact of personality disorders on treatment outcome is not entirely clear. In a recent review, Piper and Joyce (2001) concluded that the presence of personality disorder appears to be generally associated with relatively poor outcomes. In contrast, Tyrer, Gunderson, Lyons, and Tohen (1997) argued that individuals with personality disorders tend to appear worse at the end of treatment than those without personality disorders because the former have higher levels of distress and impairment at the beginning of treatment. They asserted that the rates of change are similar for those with and without personality disorders, a corollary of which is that treatments are equally effective in the presence and absence of Axis II diagnoses and that equal results can presumably be obtained by extending the treatment period for individuals with personality disorders. Thus, Tyrer et al.'s argument suggests that the presence of a personality disorder is predictive of quantitative (but not qualitative) differences in treatment approach.

In contrast to these diagnosis-based approaches to problem complexity are studies that seek to predict treatment outcome using broader definitions of complexity. One approach utilizes the Minnesota Multiphasic Personality Inventory (MMPI; Butcher, 1990) and other omnibus personality measures to assess problem complexity, especially with respect to the relationship between more severe disorder and differential treatment outcome. Much of this work has involved a general search for predictors of termination and outcome, with results often showing a relationship between elevations on some MMPI or MMPI–2 subscales and poorer treatment response (e.g. Chisholm, Crowther, & Ben-Porath, 1997). Other approaches have sought to predict the value of symptom-focused interventions for individuals whose MMPI profiles suggest chronicity. For example, Knight-Law, Sugerman, and Pettinati (1988) found that the effectiveness of behavioral symptom–focused interventions was highest among patients whose MMPIs indicated that their problems were reactive and situational in nature. Similar evidence that situation-specific problems are more responsive to behavioral treatments than chronic and recurrent ones has accrued from studies of individuals who abuse alcohol (Sheppard, Smith, & Rosenbaum, 1988) and patients with chronic back pain (Trief & Yuan, 1983).

Although omnibus personality tests are useful in assessing chronicity, they are limited in identifying the significance of pervasive dynamic conflicts. Among the instruments designed to determine the presence and pervasiveness of interpersonal, conflictual themes, the Core Conflictual Relationship Theme (CCRT) method (Barber, 1989; Crits-Christoph & Demorest, 1988; Crits-Christoph, Demorest, & Connolly, 1990; Crits-Christoph et al., 1988; Luborsky, 1996; Luborsky, Crits-Christoph, & Mellon, 1986) is one of the most promising. Based either on clinician ratings or self-reports, the CCRT defines patterns related to complex, dynamically oriented problems and identifies three sequential aspects of recurring interpersonal behaviors: (1) organizing wishes that motivate the interaction, (2) acts anticipated from others if these wishes are expressed, and (3) acts of self that either follow or prevent these acts of others. The pervasiveness of a given theme across a variety of interpersonal relationships can be viewed as an index of problem complexity.

Treatment objectives vary widely, ranging from symptomatic to thematic. These variations in breadth are reminiscent of corresponding variations in problem complexity, suggesting a link between the two. For example, psychosocial interventions, as a rule, are aimed at broader objectives than medical ones (DeRubeis et al., 1990; Simons, Garfield, & Murphy, 1984), and treatments oriented toward insight and awareness focus on broader themes than behavioral and cognitive ones (e.g., Caspar, 1995; Luborsky, 1996; Strupp & Binder, 1984). The similarity between problem complexity and treatment focus suggests an optimal fit between problem complexity and the treatment focus applied. High problem complexity should favor psychosocial over pharmacological interventions and systemic or dynamic treatments over symptom-focused ones (Beutler et al., 2000; Gaw & Beutler, 1995).

In the absence of research directly on this hypothesis, evidence for its validity is, necessarily, indirect. One approach to assessing the importance of problem complexity in treatment planning is to evaluate the importance of recurrent themes as guides in psychodynamic interventions. In an early study, Crits-Christoph, Cooper, & Luborsky (1988) found that treatment outcomes were enhanced as a function of the level of correspondence between the interpretation offered and the most pervasive (independently determined) theme. However, in a review of research during the past decade, Beutler et al. (2000) found the effects of therapist interpretations on client outcomes to be inconsistent, possibly due to the existence of multiple moderating variables. Such inconsistency has also been noted in other studies. For example, an evaluation of data from the Vanderbilt II psychotherapy project found that changes in the pervasiveness of patients' CCRT themes were not related to self-reported changes in symptoms or interpersonal dependence (Lunnen, 2000). In contrast, an analysis of 27 clients participating in a process-experiential therapy found a positive relationship between changes in self-representation (based in part on the CCRT) and outcome (McMain, 1996).

Another line of investigation has provided evidence of a negative relationship between problem complexity and the impact of narrowband treatments. Using comorbidity (coexisting personality or somatic disorders) as an index of complexity, several studies (e.g., Fahy & Russell, 1993) have found that, in treating patients with cognitive-behavioral therapy (a symptom-focused treatment), complexity was a negative indicator of improvement. Supportive of this conclusion, a recent meta-analysis by Weston and Morrison (2001) found that improvements due to short-term psychotherapies (most of which were cognitive or behavioral) tended to be lost within a year or two of the end of treatment for clients with major depressive disorder (MDD) or generalized anxiety disorder (GAD), causing the authors to remark that these treatments may be more effective at treating states than traits. Wilson (1996) conceded that cognitive-behavioral treatment has been observed to have poor effects on such patients, but he pointed out that such complexity is a negative prognostic factor for all interventions. Though this point is well taken and indicates the need to standardize the means of identifying problem complexity, the research results suggest a promising mediating role of problem complexity in predicting (or controlling) the benefit of treatments that vary in breadth of focal objectives.

The inconsistent findings noted in the preceding paragraphs suggest the presence of unidentified, additional moderators of treatment. There are promising approaches to addressing this level of complexity in the hope of resolving the inconsistencies. For example, the Operationalized Psychodynamic Diagnostic System (OPD), a multiaxial system that integrates a variety of information, including assessments of relational issues, internal and external conflicts, and structural disorder, is gaining popularity in Europe, and initial studies support the system's predictive validity (Schneider et al., 2002). Thus, more studies are needed to determine whether more complex problems are indeed more responsive to broadband psychodynamic interventions than to symptom-focused treatments.

## Readiness for Change

Prochaska and colleagues (Prochaska & DiClemente, 1984; Prochaska, DiClemente, & Norcross, 1992; Prochaska & Norcross, 2002a) have suggested that a patient's progress in treatment is a function of how well the intervention method used fits the patient's position along a progressive series of stages reflecting personal readiness and efforts to change. He and his colleagues have identified five phases through which a person progresses while seeking to change an aspect of his or her life. It is thought that, in the course of intentionally implementing change, an individual normally proceeds sequentially through the stages, sometimes recycling several times in a spiral process. These stages of readiness include *precontemplation, contemplation, preparation, action,* and *maintenance.* The Stages of Change Questionnaire (McConnaughy, DiClemente, & Velicer, 1983) is designed to assess these stages of readiness and differential receptivity to different interventions.

Prochaska and his colleagues posed two hypotheses regarding the stage of readiness achieved by a patient: (1) More advanced stages of readiness are associated with a greater likelihood of improvement, and (2) the stage of readiness serves as an indicator for the use of specific therapeutic interventions (i.e., different processes of change are differently effective in certain stages of change). In support of the first of these propositions, they demonstrated that, among patients seeking help to quit smoking, those who progressed to a higher stage of readiness during the early phase of treatment also doubled the likelihood of making improvement within the subsequent 6 months (Prochaska et al., 1992; Prochaska & Norcross, 2002a).

Research support for the proposition that a patient's pretreatment stage of readiness predicts a differential response to specific interventions has been more difficult to obtain but has increased in the last few years. Prochaska and DiClemente (1984) initially postulated that symptom- or action-oriented therapies (behavior-focused therapies) were best suited to patients who had reached the preparation and action stages of readiness but would be less suited to patients in the precontemplation or contemplation stages of readiness. In turn, they postulated that consciousness-raising and motivation-enhancement techniques (e.g., insight-oriented interventions) would be most effective for patients in these early stages of readiness.

Prochaska's proposals have stimulated a good deal of research on how people prepare themselves for making changes and how to use these processes for treatment planning (e.g., O'Connor, Carbonari, & DiClemente, 1996; Prochaska, Rossi, & Wilcox, 1991). Findings initially modestly supported the value of fitting some intervention strategies to the patient's stage of readiness.

Project MATCH (Project MATCH Research Group, 1997) compared the patient's pretreatment readiness for change to the effectiveness of various types of intervention. The findings were partially supportive of Prochaska's predictions: Patients identified as having little readiness for change (i.e., those in the precontemplative and contemplative stages) responded better to procedures designed to enhance motivation and encourage contemplation than to the more action-oriented procedures of cognitive-behavioral therapy. Patients at the action stage, however, did not show the expected preference for cognitive therapy, and the significant fit between stage and therapy strategy proved to be time dependent, emerging only during the last month of follow-up.

More recently, Rosen (2000) published a meta-analysis of 47 studies involving smoking behaviors, substance abuse, exercise, dieting, and psychotherapy. These studies examined relationships between stages and processes of change. This author found mean effect sizes of .11 and .14 for variation in cognitive-affect processes by stage and for variation in behavioral processes by change, respectively. These constitute small but significant effects that support the presence of a modest link between stages and processes of change as they relate to outcome. This meta-analysis, in addition to other recent reviews (Prochaska & Norcross, 2002a, 2002b), supported the conclusion of the Task Force on Empirically Supported Therapy Relationships (Norcross, 2002) that customizing therapy interventions to individual patients on the basis of stage of change is promising and probably effective in maximizing treatment.

**Reactant/Resistance Tendencies**

Several investigations have explored the predictive role of patient resistance to psychosocial interventions in selecting therapy procedures. The research diverges according to whether resistance is seen as a statelike quality, as in a response to a specific therapeutic intervention, or a traitlike quality, reflecting individual differences in resistance proneness. Although statelike resistance is an important and related concept, the measurement of traitlike resistance has the most salient implications for treatment planning (Beutler et al., 2000).

Designed specifically to predict resistance to treatment, the Therapeutic Reactance Scale (TRS; Dowd, Milne, & Wise, 1991) is the best known measure of reactance traits. A self-report measure derived from the reactance theory of Brehm and Brehm (1981), the TRS describes individuals' response in oppositional ways to perceived loss of choice. To broaden the applicability of the TRS and to define the correlates of resistance traits, Dowd, Wallbrown, Sanders, and Yesenosky (1994) compared this test to established measures of personality traits. For example, they regressed their own and a German language measure of resistance traits (*Fragebogen zur Messung der psychologischen Reactanz* [Questionnaire for the Measurement of Psychological Reactance]; Merz, 1983) on scores from the California Psychological Inventory–Revised (CPI–R; Gough, 1987) scales. Results indicated that resistance-prone individuals were relatively less concerned about "impression management" and relatively more likely to resist rules and social norms than people with low resistance-potential. Moreover, highly trait reactant individuals preferred work settings that allow them to exercise personal freedom and initiative.

Another common way of measuring traitlike resistance is to use various subscales and subscale combinations from personality tests. For example, the average of the Taylor Manifest Anxiety scale and the Edwards Social Desirability scale from the MMPI–2 (Butcher, Dahlstrom, Graham, Tellegen, & Kaemmer, 1989) has demonstrated validity in measuring the construct of reactance (Beutler, Engle, et al., 1991; Karno, 1997; Karno, Beutler, & Harwood, 2002).

Traitlike resistance has been particularly promising both as an indicator of poor prognosis and as a mediator of differential treatment response (Arkowitz, 1991). Beutler, Moleiro, and Talebi (2002) identified 11 studies that specifically investigated resistance in psychotherapy in controlled research designs. Nine of these studies found a negative relationship between level of patient resistance and treatment outcome. For example, Khavin (1985) compared the psychological characteristics of 50 young adult males being treated for stuttering with psychosocial interventions and concluded that resistance-prone patients did poorly in all forms of intervention. However, there is strong evidence that the type of psychotherapy intervention implemented can moderate the effect of patient resistance on outcome.

Following theory, researchers proposed that highly resistant individuals would respond poorly to highly therapist controlled and directive therapies (Beutler, 1983; 1991; Shoham-Salomon & Hannah, 1991). Beutler et al. (2002) reviewed 20 studies inspecting the differential effect of therapist directiveness as moderated by patient resistance. Eighty percent of the studies ($N = 16$) supported the hypothesis that directive interventions work best with mildly resistant patients and nondirective interventions work best with highly resistant patients.

A prospective test of the hypothesis that clients who varied on measures of resistance potential would respond in an opposite way to directive and nondirective therapies was undertaken by Beutler, Engle, et al. (1991) using a combination of MMPI subscales as an index of defensive anxiety. They demonstrated that manualized therapies that differed in level of therapist directiveness were differentially effective for reducing depressive symptoms. Among highly resistance prone depressed subjects, the nondirective therapies surpassed the directive ones in effecting change in depressive symptoms, but the reverse was true among mildly resistant patients. This result was cross-validated at a 1-year follow-up of depression severity and relapse (Beutler, Machado, Engle, & Mohr, 1993) and was confirmed in a cross-cultural sample of several alternative measures of resistance (Beutler, Mohr, Grawe, Engle, & MacDonald, 1991).

Karno et al.'s (2002) study of interactions between patient attributes and therapist interventions on alcoholism treatment outcomes used observer ratings rather than relying on the model of therapy (e.g. cognitive-behavioral vs. supportive/self-directed) to measure the level of in-session therapist directiveness. Patients with high levels of resistance improved more with nondirective therapy, and patients with lower levels of resistance more with directive therapy.

Several researchers extended the hypothesis that resistant individuals react negatively to therapist directiveness, postulating that highly resistance prone individuals would respond to paradoxical interventions that capitalize on their oppositional tendencies (e.g., Shoham-Salomon, Avner, & Neeman, 1989; Swoboda, Dowd, & Wise, 1990). The findings of Horvath and Goheen (1990) support this hypothesis. In their study, clients whose TRS scores indicated high levels of traitlike resistance responded well to a paradoxical intervention and maintained their improvements beyond the period of active treatment. Less reactant clients exposed to the same treatment deteriorated after active treatment stopped. The reverse pattern was found among those treated with a nonparadoxical, stimulus control intervention.

Interaction between patient resistance and therapist directiveness in influencing treatment outcome is one of the best supported aptitude-by-treatment interactions theorized thus far. The value of guidelines originally proposed by Beutler, Sandowicz, Fisher, and Albanese (1996) to the clinician planning treatment has been confirmed:

1. Minimally structured, self-directed interventions, nondirective procedures, or paradoxical directives are effective among patients highly prone to interpersonal resistance.
2. Directive treatment interventions and clinician guidance are advantageous to patients with low resistance tendencies.

## Social Support

The level of social and interpersonal support from others has also been widely postulated as a predictor of therapeutic outcome and maintenance. Numerous studies have found that the presence of social support can improve outcomes in psychotherapy and decrease the likelihood of relapse (e.g., Sherbourne, Hays, & Wells, 1995; Vallejo, Gasto, Catalan, Bulbena, & Menchon, 1991). However, a close inspection of this literature suggests that some methods of measuring social support are better than others.

Measures of social support either rely on external evidence of resource availability (objective support) such as proximity of family members, marriage, social network participation, and so forth (e.g., Ellicott, Hammen, Gitlin, Brown, & Jamison, 1990), or on self-reports (e.g., Moos & Moos, 1986) by patients themselves (subjective support). These two measurement methods play different roles in predicting response to treatment. For example, using the Family Environment Scale (FES; Moos & Moos, 1986), Moos (1990) found that the satisfaction levels derived from the proximal availability of at least one objectively identified confidant and at least one objectively identified family support member each significantly and independently increased the likelihood of improvement among depressed patients.

Comparing the predictive power of subjective and objective measures of support, Hooley and Teasdale (1989) found that the impact of subjective social support exceeded the impact of objective measures in the treatment of depressed patients. The quality of the marital relationship rather than its presence predicted relapse rates, for example. Nor were all indices of marital quality of equivalent importance. In fact, the level of perceived personal criticism from spouses accounted for more of the variance in relapse rates than did the presence of less personal marital conflict.

The relative importance of subjective social support as a predictor of outcome also found support in a study by Hoencamp et al. (1994). Perceived lack of family support had a significant negative association with treatment outcome with moderately depressed outpatients. This study surprisingly found that the quality of perceived contact with children was negatively related to outcome, however. Patients reporting a poor relationship with their children improved more than those who felt support from their children. An interesting finding but one whose proper interpretation is uncertain.

One should not prematurely reject the role of objective social support, however. Billings and Moos (1984) investigated the relationship between the availability of social support networks and the chronicity and impairment associated with depression. Though both chronic and nonchronic patients reported fewer available social resources than nondepressed controls, only among patients with nonchronic depression was the severity of the problem related to the availability of social resources. These findings raise some interesting questions about the role of social support in the etiology of chronically depressed individuals and about the possibility of a differential effect of activating support systems within the treatment of depression along the continuum of chronicity.

Pursuing this point, one of the most interesting aspects of social support may be its potential for playing a role in the differential assignment of intensive and short-term treatments. Moos (1990), for example, found social support availability to be related to the optimal duration of treatment, the level serving as either an indicator or a contraindicator for the application of long-term treatment, depending on its level. Depressed patients lacking social support continued to improve as a direct function of the number of weeks of treatment, whereas patients with satisfying support systems achieved an asymptotic level of benefit early in treatment and failed to benefit from continuing treatment. Interestingly, these latter patients were at risk for deterioration during long-term therapy.

Another line of social support research suggests that the use of available resources by patients may also be important, independent of resource availability. Longabaugh, Beattie, Noel, Stout, and Malloy (1993) compared conventional measures of objective or subjective social support with the patient's level of social investment—the effort expended in maintaining involvement with others. Measured by the amount of time spent close to another person (an aspect of objective support) and by the patient's perception of the quality of that relationship, social investment incorporates both objective and subjective social support.

The authors compared the independent roles of social support and social investment both in prognosis and differential response to psychotherapies. They found that both predicted a differential response to relationship-enhancement and cognitive-behavioral therapies, but social investment played a more central and pervasive mediating role. Cognitive-behavioral therapy was more effective than relationship-enhancement therapy among those experiencing little satisfying support from others but not among those who felt supported by others. However, these effects were partially moderated by the high social investment of the therapies. Among those individuals, regardless of the level of available social support, relationship-enhancement therapy was more effective than cognitive therapy. A correspondent match between social investment and type of therapy also improved maintenance effects.

### Coping Style

People adopt characteristic ways of responding to distress. Coping styles embody both conscious and nonconscious behaviors that endure across situations and times (Butcher, 1990). These traitlike qualities go by various titles but generally range from extroversion and impulsivity to self-constraint and emotional withdrawal (Eysenck & Eysenck, 1969). This dimension of external to internal patterns of behavior can be assessed with omnibus personality measures, including such instruments at the Eysenck Personality Inventory (EPI; Eysenck & Eysenck, 1964), the MMPI, the California Personality Inventory (CPI), the NEO Personality Inventory (NEO-PI; Costa & McCrae, 1985) of personality, and the Millon Clinical Multiaxial Inventory–III (MCMI–III; Millon, 1994). Besides extant personality inventories, two additional direct measures of coping strategy reliably utilized in psychotherapeutic contexts are the Miller Behavioral Style Scale (MBSS; Miller, 1987; Myers & Derakshan, 2000) and the Ways of Coping Questionnaire (WCQ; Folkman & Lazarus, 1980; Hatton, Knussen, Sloper, & Turner, 1995).

The CPI and MMPI have been most often used in the study of differential response to psychotherapy. Research of this type suggests that the effects of behavioral and insight-oriented psychotherapies are differentially moderated by patient coping style, ranging from externalized and impulsive to internalized and seclusive. For example, in a well-controlled study of interpersonal and behavioral therapies, Kadden et al. (1989) determined that a high rating and a low rating on the CPI Socialization subscale, a measure of sociopathic impulsivity, were predictive of the response of alcoholic subjects to treatments based on behavioral and interpersonal insight models, respectively. Continued improvement over a 2-year follow-up period was also found to be greatest among compatibly matched client-therapy dyads (Cooney, Kadden, Litt, & Getter, 1991).

Other studies have also confirmed this relationship and expanded the role of patient coping style as a predictor of differential response to various psychotherapies. For example, Beutler and his colleagues (e.g., Beutler, Engle, et al., 1991) found that depressed patients who scored high on the MMPI externalization subscales responded better to cognitive-behavioral treatment than to insight-oriented therapies, and the reverse was found with patients who scored low. Beutler and Mitchell (1981) and Calvert, Beutler, and Crago (1988), also using the MMPI, found a similar pattern among mixed psychiatric in- and outpatients. Similarly, Longabaugh et al. (1994) found that alcoholics characterized as impulsive and aggressive (externalizing behaviors) drank less frequently and with less intensity after receiving cognitive-behavioral treatment than after receiving relationship-enhancement therapy. The reverse was found with alcoholic clients who did not have these traits.

Similarly, Barber and Muenz (1996) found cognitive therapy more effective than interpersonal therapy among patients employing direct avoidance (externalization) as a coping mechanism, whereas interpersonal therapy was more effective among obsessively constricted (internalization) patients. The authors noted the similarity to the findings of Beutler et al. and advanced an interpretation based on the theory of opposites: Individuals respond to interventions that are counter to, and therefore undermine, their own customary styles. Avoidant clients are pushed by cognitive therapy to confront anxiety-provoking situations through homework and specific instructions, and obsessive clients, who tend toward rigidity and intellectualization, are encouraged to depart from these defenses by advancing interpersonal, insight-oriented interpretations.

This latter interpretation has received interesting albeit indirect support in studies of patient preferences for treatment type. Tasca, Russell, and Busby (1994) found that externalizers preferred a process-oriented psychodynamic group over a structured activity-oriented group when allowed to choose and that internalizers preferred a cognitive-behavioral intervention. In each case, the therapy that was preferred was the treatment that had been found to be *least effective* in outcomes research, indicating that patients may prefer the treatment that poses the least threat to their normal defenses. Further research is called for on this interesting paradox.

Blatt, Shahar, & Zuroff (2001) advanced a theory of personality that is designed to explain the mechanisms associated with the research findings encountered within the domain of coping style. Their research identifies two rationally derived personality types: anaclitic (or sociotropic) and introjective (or autonomous). Anaclitic patients are concerned with obtaining and maintaining close and nurturing interpersonal relations, whereas introjective patients are more preoccupied with securing a positive sense of self. When analyzing the therapeutic responses of anaclitic and introjective patients in three different settings (intensive, inpatient psychoanalytically oriented therapy; psychoanalysis, long-term supportive-expressive therapy; and manualized brief treatments for depression), their findings bolster the hypothesis that idiosyncratic coping traits play an integral role in treatment effectiveness. Specifically, they infer that anaclitic patients improve more in long-term supportive-expressive therapy than in psychoanalysis. As expected, the opposite occurs with introjective patients, who also experienced poor outcomes in brief manualized treatment for depression. In the end, a patient's personality style can augment the therapist's understanding of the patient's responses to treatment and to demanding events.

**Attachment Style**

Descriptions of coping styles, particularly as defined by Blatt et al. (2001), bear a striking resemblance to explorations of patients' interpersonal attachment styles. Research on attachment style has additional significance because of its possible relevance to the therapeutic relationship. Meta-analyses have repeatedly uncovered empirical evidence supporting the belief that relationship or alliance is implicated in treatment outcomes (Horvath & Symonds, 1991; Martin, Garske, & Davis, 2000). Evidence is also accumulating on the benefit of adapting and tailoring the therapy relationship to specific characteristics and needs of the patient in addition to the diagnosis (Norcross, 2002). Given that the patient's attachment style affects his or her ability to feel comfortable and safe in close relationships, it is not surprising that some authors (e.g., Meyer & Pilkonis, 2002) have investigated the affect of the patient's attachment style on the quality of the alliance and on the treatment outcomes.

Since John Bowlby's and Mary Ainsworth's pioneer work on attachment (Bowlby, 1969; Ainsworth, Blehar, Waters, & Wall, 1978), attachment theory has inspired considerable work in child development (e.g., Ainsworth et al., 1978), personality and individual differences (e.g., Hazan & Shaver, 1987, 1994), evolutionary psychology (e.g., Belsky, 1999), and research methods (e.g., George, Kaplan, & Main, 1985), among other areas. However, not until recently has literature and research based on attachment theory focused on clinical groups and their treatment (Holmes, 1996), especially in adult populations. The theory postulates that early relational experiences lead to the development of internal models of oneself and of others in a relational context and that specific interpersonal expectations and behaviors are formed based on those models. These attachment patterns constitute self-perpetuating developmental schemas that maintain some predictability in a quite uncertain relational world (Holmes, 1996).

As in the case of children, adult attachment is understood as the mental representation of one's capacity to form close bonds, to be alone, to achieve balance between autonomy and separation, and to enjoy intimacy. Adult attachment is often classified as secure, anxious-ambivalent (or preoccupied), and avoidant (Holmes, 1996). This latter category has been subdivided by some authors (Bartholomew & Horowitz, 1991) into fearful-avoidant and dismissive-avoidant, creating four adult attachment styles based on two dimensions, anxiety and avoidance:

1. Secure (positive self and other models).
2. Preoccupied (negative self and positive other models).
3. Fearful (negative self and other models).
4. Dismissive (positive self and negative other models).

There have been two main approaches to the measurement of adult attachment styles, the first marked by the development of the Adult Attachment Interview (AAI; George et al., 1985). A semi-structured interview, the AAI elicits and explores the patient's current perceptions of his or her childhood experiences, including the quality of the relationship with caregivers, separation experiences such as losses, and how the patient coped with them. After transcription, the scoring system rates not only the content but the form and structure of the patient's narrative. Three classification categories arise:

1. Free-autonomous (coherent valuing of attachments).
2. Dismissive (idealizing, derogatory, and cut off from attachment experiences).
3. Preoccupied (passive, angry, and enmeshed; Fonagy et al., 1996).

A second approach to the assessment of adult attachment styles involves using self-report questionnaires. In one of the first attempts to assess the applicability of

Ainsworth's attachment concepts to adults, Hazan and Shaver (1987) proposed a simple instrument containing three paragraphs describing the feelings, beliefs, and relational behaviors expected in secure, ambivalent, and avoidant attachment styles, respectively. Respondents were asked to identify the paragraph that best described their relational experiences. Other brief multi-item questionnaires have been developed in the last decade (e.g., Brennan, Clark, & Shaver, 1998; Mallinckrodt, Gantt, & Coble, 1995), including some translated into several languages (e.g., Hoges, 1999; Moreira et al., 1998). However, one should note that the convergent validity among all proposed measures of adult attachment style has been only moderate, which suggests that these instruments may be assessing relatively different facets of attachment (Meyer & Pilkonis, 2002). For instance, though some focus on adult experiences of close or romantic relationships, others examine early attachment experiences with parental figures and still others apply directly to the therapeutic context.

Recent studies have explored the complex relationships between adult attachment and personality, psychopathology, and psychotherapy. In one area of research, authors have explored the link between patient attachment and the quality of the therapeutic alliance, a variable that many believe is causally implicated in treatment outcome. Not surprisingly, most studies have found that securely attached patients tend to form stronger and more stable alliances throughout treatment (e.g., Eames & Roth, 2000) and tend to perceive the therapist as more responsive, accepting, and caring (Mallinckrodt et al., 1995). Conversely, fearful-avoidant patients tend to experience problems in the alliance, a preoccupied attachment style has been shown to relate to a poor alliance in the middle of treatment and a strong alliance in later stages of therapy, and patients with a dismissive attachment style have reported deterioration of the alliance toward the end of treatment (see Meyer & Pilkonis, 2002). However, among those with an insecure attachment style, the results are sometimes contradictory, and further empirical data are needed. Furthermore, it has been noted that the therapists themselves respond differently to patients with different attachment styles. For example, Hardy et al. (1999) noted that therapists responded to preoccupied patients with reflection and used more interpretations with patients with a dismissive attachment style. This makes it difficult to disentangle the link between patient attachment and treatment outcome. Nevertheless, using reliable clinical change measures (as proposed by Jacobson, Follette, & Revenstorf, 1984), Fonagy et al. (1996) found evidence to support the claim that securely attached patients tend to function better than insecurely attached patients both at admission and discharge and that those patients with a dismissive attachment style experience the greatest clinical improvement.

In sum, there is substantial evidence that patient attachment style is an important variable in psychotherapy. It appears to affect the patient's assessment of the quality of the therapeutic alliance, the treatment outcome, and even the therapist's intervention responses. Not surprisingly, the evidence points to the benefits of a secure attachment style (Meyer & Pilkonis, 2002). Still, a number of areas need further investigation. First, if instruments are used to assess attachment style and plan effective treatments, it is important to examine the constructs being measured by the currently available instruments. As pointed out by Meyer and Pilkonis (2002), the weak correlations among narrative approaches, self-report questionnaires of romantic relationships or of early attachments, and self-reports of attachment to therapists warrant further exploration.

Second, researchers are just beginning to explore possible moderators and mediators between attachment style and outcome (e.g., cultural background). This literature must begin to define the relationship between attachment styles and the concepts of coping style described earlier. It is likely that they are related, and uncovering this relationship should assist in predicting effects associated with different interventions.

Finally, the Task Force on Empirically Supported Therapy Relations (Norcross, 2002) concluded that current research is still insufficient and that further investigation is needed to support the conclusion that customizing the therapy alliance to attachment style improves treatment outcomes.

### Combinations of Matching Dimensions

Theoretical literature suggests that matching patients to treatments by simultaneously using a number of patient-treatment dimensions at once may enhance outcomes more than by using any single dimension (Beutler & Clarkin, 1990). Some evidence supports this suggestion and reveals that various matching dimensions may add independent predictive power to the forecasting of treatment outcomes (e.g., Beutler et al., 2000; Beutler, Moleiro, et al., in press; Karno, 1997; Karno et al., 2002).

Our research program is designed to test the independent and collective contributions of several of the matching dimensions discussed in this chapter across samples of patients with depression and substance abuse. Both individual and joint effects of various matching dimensions have been revealed in an initial study that included cohabitating couples each of which had a problem drinker (Karno et al., 2002). The Couples Alcoholism Treatment (CAT) program employed an attribute × treatment interaction (ATI) design, manualized cognitive therapy (Wakefield, Williams, Yost, & Patterson, 1996), and family systems therapy (Rohrbaugh, Shoham, Spungen, & Steinglass, 1995), and it carefully monitored outcomes to test the mediating roles of patient variables on treatment response. The separate and combined effects of matching four client characteristics with corresponding treatments were assessed:

1. Level of functional impairment with the number and frequency of treatment sessions.
2. Level of patient initial subjective distress with therapist focus on increasing or decreasing level of arousal.
3. Level of patient traitlike resistance with level of therapist directiveness.
4. Patient coping style with the relative therapeutic focus on symptom change or insight.

For the major analysis, the model of psychotherapy was ignored in favor of looking more specifically at actual in-therapy therapist behaviors using various models. We reasoned from prior research that models overlap in the particular procedures and therapeutic styles represented, so the distinctiveness of the model is less sensitive to different therapist behaviors than direct observations (Beutler, Machado, & Neufeldt, 1994). Thus, all four matching variables were studied by measuring patient variables before treatment and directly observing the nature of the therapy sessions.

Patient variables were assessed by using standardized tests (e.g., MMPI, BSI, etc.), as suggested in the foregoing sections. Ratio scores reflecting the amount of a given therapeutic activity relative to a corresponding patient quality (e.g., amount of directiveness per patient nondefensiveness, amount of behavioral focus relative to patient externalization, amount of emotional focus relative to patient initial distress level, intensity of treatment relative to level of functional impairment, etc.) were used to assess the degree of correspondence between each patient and treatment dimension. Hierarchal linear modeling was used to assess the contributions of each patient and therapy dimension separately and the four matching dimensions. Effects were assessed and modeled over time (20 treatment sessions and 1-year follow-up).

To ensure a wide distribution of therapeutic procedures, the two treatments were designed to differ in two dimensions. Cognitive therapy was symptom focused whereas family systems therapy was system focused; cognitive therapy was therapist directed whereas family systems therapy was patient directed. By chance, they also differed in intensity or concentration (the number of weeks required to complete weekly and biweekly sessions), with the 20 sessions of family systems therapy taking longer to complete than the 20 sessions of cognitive therapy. Individual therapists also differed, both within and between treatments, in their levels of directiveness, the application of insight-oriented procedures, and their success in raising patient emotions and arousal.

The sample consisted of 62 male and 12 female alcoholics and their partners. The outcome measures reflected the substance abuse status and general psychiatric functioning of the identified alcoholic patients. All patients were alcohol dependent, most (85%) were Euro-American, and they had been partnered for an average of 8.3 years. Nearly half of the patients also used illicit drugs.

The growth curve modeling procedure revealed a steady decline of symptoms throughout treatment independent of treatment type or level of fit between patient and treatment qualities. Estimated abstinence rates were quite low, but mean rates were consistent with other substance abuse treatment research (Bellack & Hersen, 1990). At termination, the abstinence rates were 42.9% and 37.5% for clients who had received cognitive therapy and family systems therapy, respectively, and 39.3% and 29.7% at follow-up. An even lower rate of change was noted on general symptoms independent of alcoholic symptoms. These low average rates of change, along with wide variations of outcomes, were not unexpected, and they precisely underline the need to match patients with the best suited treatments.

Analyses of the independent effects of patient and therapy variables indicated that the level of patient distress and patient impulsivity were inhibitors of treatment benefit and that treatment intensity and level of behavioral/symptom orientation were both associated with the level of improvement. In all instances, wide differences from patient to patient indicated the presence of patient variables that were selectively determining treatment response. The analysis of the matching dimensions revealed that by the 6-month posttreatment three of the four matching dimensions studied proved to be related to desirable changes in alcohol usage:

1. The match between level of initial severity (functional impairment) and level of care (average time to complete 20 planned sessions) predicted improvement in substance abuse. Patients whose level of care corresponded with the amount of impairment in functioning (high functioning with low-intensity therapies and low functioning with high-intensity procedures) tended to show more alcohol-related improvements than those whose level of care and amount of impairment did not correspond.

2. The match between patient resistance and treatment directiveness predicted change in alcohol use. Resistant patients who received nondirective interventions and nonresistant patients who received directive interventions reduced consumption and abuse more than those patients who were matched otherwise.

3. When patients were separated into two groups, abstinent and nonabstinent, the relationship between therapist activation of affect and patient initial distress emerged as a significant predictor. Patients with low levels of distress who were treated with emotional activating procedures and patients with high levels of distress who were treated with emotional reduction procedures were more likely to benefit than their counterparts matched otherwise.

Collectively, the matching dimensions alone accounted for 76% of the variance in alcohol-related changes. Therapist directiveness was also a positive predictor of treatment benefit, independent of its fit with patient qualities. Likewise, low level of patient impairment was a predictor of positive change. By adding these two independent effects to the equation, we were able to account for 82% of the variance in outcome, an astonishingly high rate of prediction.

In comparison to changes in alcohol abuse, general changes in psychiatric functioning were not as efficiently predicted. This is not to say that the patient, treatment, and matching variables were unimportant, however. One patient variable (impulsivity), two treatment variables (arousal induction and symptom-focused interventions), and a matching dimension (distress × stress-reduction procedures) accounted for nearly 50% of the variance in outcomes. Improvement was significantly but negatively related to initial patient impulsivity/externalization and positively related to the use both of arousal induction procedures and symptom-focused interventions. At the same time, the level of initial patient distress and the corresponding amount of emphasis on procedures that reduced or raised distress predicted improved psychiatric functioning.

A subsequent study of these relationships among comorbid depressed and chemically abusing patients provided independent confirmation of (a) the benefits to be derived from the overall fit of the treatment and patient qualities and (b) the strength of this relationship (Beutler, Moleiro, et al., in press). In this study, patient variables, treatment variables, relationship quality, and degree of fit all provided independent contributions to outcome and maintenance of gains. Overall predictive efficiency was very high when patient, treatment, relationship, and matching variables were considered together. Changes in depression were predicted, and at long-term follow-up over 90% of the variance was accounted for by treatment planning and matching variables, while over 50% of the variance in drug use was accounted for by these variables. These percentages and accuracy of prediction are very high, compared with others in the literature, and suggest the extremely promising nature of predictions that give extra value to variables within the categories of patient factors, treatment strategies, relationship quality, and patient-therapist fit.

Specifically, when the foregoing findings are taken collectively, they provide support for the conclusion that patient distress and impairment, coping style, and resistance behaviors are important factors that may help determine the most appropriate and effective psychotherapeutic strategies for treating depression, substance abuse, or both. Patient coping style, therapist emotional focus, and treatment intensity and support all can be identified as valuable qualities, regardless of the nature of the patient and his or her problems. An ideal treatment would do the following:

1. Directly focus on particularly disruptive social symptoms, such as those involved in drug abuse or acting-out behaviors.
2. Attempt to enhance emotional arousal and processing.
3. Adapt the level of emotional focus to the patient's level of subjective distress.

4. Adapt the symptomatic versus insight/awareness focus of treatment to the patient's level of externalization.
5. Adapt the level of confrontation and directiveness to patient's level of resistance.

## SELECTION OF APPROPRIATE INSTRUMENTS

The selection of appropriate instruments to measure the patient's presenting symptoms, personality traits, and transitional states is an important concern for the clinician. Each of the previous sections has mentioned representative instruments whose use has empirical support. The clinician must keep in mind several important considerations when selecting and using instruments for treatment-planning purposes (see Cattell & Johnson, 1986; Goldstein & Hersen, 1990).

First, the clinician must select instruments that together measure a variety of dimensions of potential importance in making required treatment decisions (see Table 3.1). Some instruments measure more than one dimension but few measure all the dimensions recommended here. Even if every instrument did, it would still be necessary to consider the advantages and costs of including multiple instruments, for these instruments generally embody different perspectives and viewpoints. Both observer ratings and self-report measures should be used whenever possible to prevent the unchecked influence of a single perspective from biasing the results.

Clinicians require focused tools specific to the task of assessing relevant patient qualities to guide treatment decisions. Hayes, Nelson, and Jarrett (1987) argued that "the role of clinical assessment in treatment utility has been buried by conceptual confusion, poorly articulated methods, and inappropriate linkage to structural psychometric criteria" (p. 973). Over the past 8 years, we have been developing a clinician-based, research-informed method of identifying traits and relatively enduring states of patients to allow clinicians to select psychotherapeutic strategies that best fit different patients (Beutler, 2001; Beutler & Groth-Marnat, 2003; Beutler & Williams, 1999; Harwood & Williams, 2003). This effort has been based on the method of Systematic Treatment Selection (STS) originally outlined by Beutler and Clarkin (1990) and subsequently revised by Gaw and Beutler (1995) and by Harwood and Williams (2003).

The STS software program[3] is available in both Spanish and English versions and can be administered as both a clinician rating procedure and as a patient self-report. In turn, it can be administered via a Web-based system or a telephonic response system (see Beutler & Groth-Marnat, 2003, and Harwood & Williams, 2003, for details).

The STS assessment system is designed to help clinicians develop empirically based and validated treatment plans. Clinicians enter patient information obtained through their usual assessment procedures using an interactive computer interface. They can include information gained from clinical observation as well as results from standardized psychological tests. Patient self-reports, likewise, call for patients to identify both objective and subjective experiences.

Output includes an intake report consisting of a proposed treatment program, including recommendations about level of care and treatment intensity, format, and modality; medical considerations; a risk assessment; and a variety of appropriate research-based treatment packages. It allows a clinician to project the course and

---

[3] The STS treatment planning software is available from the Center for Behavioral Health Technology, Inc. Information is available at the following Web site: www.systematictreatmentselection.com

length of treatment, and through subsequent patient monitoring, the projections can be calculated that will reveal the degree to which the patient's gains are within the limits expected within that particular clinic. The program will flag nonresponders for further treatment refinement. Additional features include clinician profiling, assistance in therapist selection, and problem charting.

Although standardized instruments are available for assessing the various patient dimensions identified by the STS model, these instruments frequently are unnecessarily long and provide a good deal of superfluous information. Hence, a single instrument whose subscales are designed to reveal treatment-relevant characteristics promises to be more time efficient than those conventionally used in patient diagnostic assessment. Current psychometric studies of the STS dimensions are promising for both English-language (Fisher, Beutler, & Williams, 1999) and Spanish-language (Corbella et al., 2003) versions.

The studies using the STS system (e.g., Beutler et al., 2000; Beutler, Moleiro, et al., in press; Corbella et al., in press; Fisher, Beutler, & Williams, 1999) have relied on several of the dimensions described in this chapter for constructing treatment plans: functional impairment, subjective distress, problem complexity, resistance potential, social support, and coping style. Satisfactory construct and predictive validity data have been obtained in the use of these dimensions, as derived from the STS, and these are reported in the studies cited.

## CONCLUSION

Psychological tests have been used widely in the prediction of response to treatment. In this chapter, we summarized the status of research on some of the more promising of these dimensions and their associated measures. Eight dimensions appear to be promising for use in planning treatment: (1) functional impairment, (2) subjective distress, (3) readiness for (or stage) of change, (4) problem complexity, (5) resistance potential or inclination, (6) social support, (7) coping style, and (8) attachment style. Some of these dimensions, such as social support and coping style, have individual components that appear promising as well.

To summarize, the following conclusions appear to be justified:

1. *Functional Impairment.* Impairment level serves as an index of progress in treatment as well as a predictor of outcome. High impairment may also serve as a contraindicator for the use of insight- and relationship-oriented psychotherapies. Very impairing symptoms seem to indicate the value of pharmacological interventions or problem-oriented approaches, and mild to moderate levels of impairment may be conducive to or predictive of a positive response to a variety of psychotherapy models.

2. *Subjective Distress.* Subjective distress is directly related to improvement among nonsomatic depressed and anxious patients. Distress is more complexly related to improvement among those with somatic complaints. Distress level may be a particular marker for the differential application of self-directed and traditional therapies and may indicate the need to use procedures that either lower or raise distress to enhance patient motivation. High distress serves as a positive marker for self-directed treatment among nonsomatic patients whereas low distress may serve such a function among somatically disturbed patients. Still, more controlled research trials are necessary to better isolate and understand the multifaceted function of distress in the psychotherapeutic context.

3. *Readiness for Change.* Contemporary studies on patient stages of change are very promising. The higher the readiness level of the patient, the more positive the outcomes of treatment. In addition, evidence suggests that those at the precontemplative (preconceptual) and contemplative (conceptual) stages may be particularly suited for interventions that raise consciousness and facilitate self-exploration. Conversely, patients at the preparation and action stages may benefit from more symptom- and action-oriented interventions.

4. *Problem Complexity.* Complexity has been defined both in terms of multiple diagnoses (i.e., the presence of comorbidity and/or personality disorders) and more generally in terms of the chronicity and cross-situational prevalence of problems. Diagnostically based complexity studies have stressed the need for longer terms of treatment for individuals with multiple diagnoses. In contrast, studies utilizing omnibus personality assessments or psychodynamically derived measures of complexity have been more likely to suggest the need for qualitatively different treatment approaches depending on differences in problem complexity. For example, these studies suggest that both symptom-focused psychopharmacological interventions and symptom-focused psychological interventions may be indicated most clearly for patients whose conditions are acute or relatively uncomplicated by concomitant personality disorders, interpersonal conflicts, or dynamic conflicts associated with symbolic internal conflicts. At the same time, comparisons across treatment models suggest that treatment efficacy is enhanced when the breadth of interventions used corresponds to the complexity of the problem. More studies are needed to explicitly examine the potential of problem complexity as a moderator of outcomes for symptom-focused versus dynamic interventions.

5. *Resistance Potential.* Traitlike resistance is a reasonably good predictor of the differential effects of directive and nondirective therapies. Therapist guidance, use of status, and control are contraindicated for resistance-prone individuals. On the other hand, these patients respond quite well to paradoxical and nondirective interventions, whereas mildly resistant patients respond well to directive interventions and therapist guidance. State reactions that suggest the presence of resistance also may be indicators for how to present material is in treatment session.

6. *Social Support.* Dimensions of objective social support, subjectively experienced support, and social investment have implications for treatment planning, even serving as indices and predictors of differential response to various psychosocial interventions. Some aspects of support even serve as contraindicators for long-term treatment. Patients who have low levels of objective social support or feel unsupported by those around them are candidates for long-term or intensive treatment. Their level of improvement corresponds with the intensity of treatment. However, those with good support systems do not respond well to intensive or long-term treatments. Their improvement appears to reach an asymptote and may even decline with continuing treatment. The level of social investment may outweigh actual support availability, however, and it may be a mediator that increases the value of relationship-oriented psychotherapy over behavioral and symptom-oriented treatments.

7. *Coping Style.* Patient level of impulsivity, or what we have called *coping style*, has consistently been found to be a differential predictor of the value of cognitive-behavioral and relationship- or insight-oriented treatments. Comparatively, externalizing, impulsive patients respond better to behaviorally oriented therapies whereas constricted and introspective patients tend to respond better to and relationship- and insight-oriented therapies.

8. *Attachment Style.* A patient's attachment style has been found both to influence his or her ability to establish a therapeutic relationship and to impact treatment outcome. Though secure attachment, not surprisingly, appears associated with overall better functioning or prognosis, pre- to posttreatment improvement may be greater among dismissive patients. Further data are needed to clarify how treatment can be tailored to patient attachment style for greatest efficacy.

The tests used to assess these various dimensions often have implications for the assessment of outcome. Measures of functional impairment, subjective distress, and problem complexity may be especially valuable for assessing outcome or predicting prognosis. In contrast, both the statelike measures of resistance and readiness for change and the trait measures of resistance potential, complexity, and coping style appear promising for selecting treatments that vary in directiveness and insight focus, respectively. Measures used to assess these patient dimensions are often drawn from omnibus personality instruments, and in the case of coping style measures, they may reflect complex processes that encompass both unconscious and conscious experience.

Taken together, the research reported in this brief and selective review suggests that various combinations of dimensions allow discrimination among treatment variables and may point to directions in which the development and applications of treatments may evolve in clinical practice. Accordingly, we have reported the initial development of the STS, a Web-based measure (systematictreatmentselection.com) designed to tap six of the eight dimensions reviewed here in providing assistance to clinicians in treatment planning and patient monitoring. Research on the potential of this instrument to enhance the efficiency of treatment has been promising. Alternatively, clinicians can apply some combination of the standardized tests reviewed in this chapter, along with an interview, to develop treatment-planning hypotheses.

## ACKNOWLEDGMENT

The authors wish to thank Ms. Harrianne Mills for her valuable assistance in editing this chapter. Correspondence regarding this chapter should be addressed to the first author, Larry E. Beutler, Clinical Psychology Program, Pacific Graduate School of Psychology, Palo Alto, CA 94303.

## REFERENCES

Ainsworth, M. D. S., Blehar, M. C., Waters, E., & Wall, S. (1978). *Patterns of attachment: A psychological study of the strange situation.* Hillsdale, NJ: Lawrence Erlbaum Associates.

American Psychiatric Association. (1983). *Diagnostic and statistical manual of mental disorders* (3rd ed.). Washington, DC: Author.

American Psychiatric Association. (1994). *Diagnostic and statistical manual of mental disorders* (4th ed.). Washington, DC: Author.

Arkowitz, H. (1991, August). *Psychotherapy integration: Bringing psychotherapy back to psychology.* Paper presented at the annual meeting of the American Psychological Association, San Francisco.

Bachanas, P. J., & Blount, R. L. (1996). The Behavioral Approach-Avoidance and Distress Scale: An investigation for reliability and validity during painful medical procedures. *Journal of Pediatric Psychology, 21,* 671–681.

Barber, J. P. (1989). *The Central Relationship Questionnaire (version 1.0).* Unpublished manuscript, University of Pennsylvania, School of Medicine.

Barber, J. P., & Muenz, L. R. (1996). The role of avoidance and obsessiveness in matching patients to cognitive and interpersonal psychotherapy: Empirical findings from the Treatment of Depression Collaborative Research Program. *Journal of Consulting and Clinical Psychology, 64*, 951–958.

Bartholomew, K., & Horowitz, L. M. (1991). Attachment styles among young adults: A test of a four-category model. *Journal of Personality and Social Psychology, 61*, 226–244.

Basoglu, M., Marks, I. M., & Swinson, R. P. (1994). Pre-treatment predictors of treatment outcome in panic disorder and agoraphobia treated with alprazolam and exposure. *Journal of Affective Disorders, 20*, 123–132.

Beck, A. T., Ward, C. H., Mendelson, M., Mock, J., & Erbaugh, J. (1961). An inventory for measuring depression. *Archives of General Psychiatry, 4*, 561–569.

Beitman, B. D. (1987). *The structure of individual psychotherapy*. New York: Guilford.

Bellack, A. S., & Hersen, M. (Eds.). (1990). *Handbook of comparative treatments for adult disorders*. New York: Wiley.

Belsky, J. (1999). Modern evolutionary theory and patterns of attachment. In J. Cassidy and P. R. Shaver, (Eds.), *Handbook of attachment: Theory, research, and clinical applications* (pp. 141–161). New York: Guilford.

Beutler, L. E. (1983). *Eclectic psychotherapy: A systematic approach*. New York: Pergamon.

Beutler, L. E. (1991). Have all won and must all have prizes? Revisiting Luborsky, et al.'s verdict. *Journal of Consulting and Clinical Psychology, 59*, 226–232.

Beutler, L. E. (2001). Comparisons among quality assurance systems: From outcome assessment to clinical utility. *Journal of Consulting and Clinical Psychology, 69*, 197–204.

Beutler, L. E. (2002, August). *The complex role of emotional arousal as a motivational variable in psychotherapy*. An invited address (EMPathy Symposium). Presented at the annual meeting of the American Psychological Association, Chicago.

Beutler, L. E., & Berren, M. (1995). *Integrative assessment of adult personality*. New York: Guilford Press.

Beutler, L. E., & Clarkin, J. (1990). *Systematic treatment selection: Toward targeted therapeutic interventions*. New York: Brunner/Mazel.

Beutler, L. E., Clarkin, J. F., & Bongar, B. (2000). *Guidelines for the systematic treatment of the depressed patient*. New York: Oxford University Press.

Beutler, L. E., Engle, D., Mohr, D., Daldrup, R. J., Bergan, J., Meredith, K., et al. (1991). Predictors of differential and self-directed psychotherapeutic procedures. *Journal of Consulting and Clinical Psychology, 59*, 333–340.

Beutler, L. E., Frank, M., Scheiber, S. C., Calvert, S., & Gaines, J. (1984). Comparative effects of group psychotherapies in a short-term inpatient setting: An experience with deterioration effects. *Psychiatry, 47*, 66–76.

Beutler, L. E., & Groth-Marnat, G. (Eds.). (2003). *Integrative assessment of adult personality*. New York: Guilford Press.

Beutler, L. E., & Harwood, T. M. (1995) Prescriptive psychotherapies. *Applied and Preventive Psychology, 4*, 89–100.

Beutler, L. E., Harwood, T. M., Alimohamed, S., & Malik, M. (2002). Functional impairment and coping style. In J. C. Norcross (Ed.), *Psychotherapy relationships that work: Therapists' relational contributions to effective psychotherapy* (pp. 140–165). New York: Oxford University Press.

Beutler, L. E., & Hodgson, A. B. (1993). Prescriptive psychotgherapy. In G. Stricker & J. R. Gold (Eds.), *Comprehensive handbook of psychotherapy integration* (pp. 151–163). New York: Plenum.

Beutler, L. E., Kim, E. J., Davison, E., Karno, M., & Fisher, D. (1996). Research contributions to improving managed health care outcomes. *Psychotherapy, 33*, 197–206.

Beutler, L. E., Machado, P. P. P., Engle, D., & Mohr, D. (1993). Differential patient × treatment maintenance of treatment effects among cognitive, experiential, and self-directed psychotherapies. *Journal of Psychotherapy Integration, 3*, 15–32.

Beutler, L. E., Machado, P. P. P., & Neufeldt, S. (1994). Therapist variables. In A. E. Bergin & S. L. Garfield (Eds.), *Handbook of psychotherapy and behavior change* (4th ed., pp. 229–269), New York: Wiley.

Beutler, L. E., & Malik, M. L. (Eds.). (2002). *Rethinking the DSM*. Washington, DC: American Psychological Association.

Beutler, L. E., Malik, M. L., Alimohammed, S., Harwood, M. T., Talebi, H., Noble, S., & Wong, E. (in press). Therapist variables. In S. L. Garfield & A. E. Bergin (Eds.), *The handbook of psychotherapy and behavior change* (5th ed.)

Beutler, L. E., & Mitchell, R. (1981). Psychotherapy outcome in depressed and impulsive patients as a function of analytic and experiential treatment procedures. *Psychiatry, 44*, 297–306.

Beutler, L. E., Mohr, D. C., Grawe, K., Engle, D., & MacDonald, R. (1991). Looking for differential effects: Cross-cultural predictors of differential psychotherapy efficacy. *Journal of Psychotherapy Integration, 1*, 121–142.

Beutler, L. E., Moleiro, C., Malik, M., Harwood, T. M., Romanelli, R., Gallagher-Thompson, D., et al. (in press). A comparison of the Dodo, EST, and ATI factors among co-Morbid stimulant dependent, depressed patients. *Clinical Psychology and Psychotherapy.*

Beutler, L. E., Moleiro, C., & Talebi, H. (2002). Resistance. In J. C. Norcross (Ed.), *Psychotherapy relationships that work: Therapists' relational contributions to effective psychotherapy.* New York: Oxford University Press.

Beutler, L. E., & Rosner, R. (1995). Introduction. In L. E. Beutler & M. Berren (Eds.), *Integrative assessment of adult personality* (pp. 1–24). New York: Guilford.

Beutler, L. E., Sandowicz, M., Fisher, D., & Albanese, A. L. (1996). Resistance in Psychotherapy: What can be concluded from empirical research? *In Session: Psychotherapy in Practice, 2,* 77–86.

Beutler, L. E., Wakefield, P., & Williams, R. E. (1994). Use of psychological tests/instruments for treatment planning. In M. Maruish (Ed.), *Use of psychological testing for treatment planning and outcome assessment* (pp. 55–74). Hillsdale, NJ: Lawrence Erlbaum Associates.

Beutler, L. E., & Williams, O. B. (1999). *Systematic treatment selection.* Ventura, CA: Center for Behavioral Health Technology.

Billings, A. G., & Moos, R. H. (1984). Chronic and nonchronic unipolar depression: The differential role of environmental stressors and resources. *Journal of Nervous and Mental Disease, 172,* 65–75.

Bisson, J. I., Jenkins, P. L., Alexander, J., & Bannister, C. (1997). Randomized controlled trial of psychological debriefing for victims of acute burn trauma. *British Journal of Psychiatry, 171,* 78–81.

Bisson, J. I., McFarlane, A., & Rose, S. (2000). Psychological debriefing. In E. B. Foa, T. M. Keane, et al. (Eds.), *Effective treatments for PTSD: Practice guidelines from the International Society for Traumatic Stress Studies* (pp. 317–319). New York: Guilford Press.

Blanchard, E. B., Schwarz, S. P., Neff, D. F., & Gerardi, M. A. (1988). Prediction of outcome from the self-regulatory treatment of irritable bowel syndrome. *Behavior, Research and Therapy, 26,* 187–190.

Blatt, S. J., Shahar, G., & Zuroff, D. C. (2001). Anaclitic (sociotropic) and introjective (autonomous) dimensions. *Psychotherapy: Theory, Research, Practice, Training, 38,* 449–454.

Bowlby, J. (1969). *Attachment and loss.* New York: Basic.

Brehm, S. S., & Brehm, J. W. (1981). *Psychological reactance: A theory of freedom and control.* New York: Wiley.

Brennan, K. A., Clark, C. L., & Shaver, P. R. (1998). Self-report measurement of adult attachment: An integrative overview. In J. A. Simpson & W. S. Rhodes (Eds.), *Attachment theory and close relationships* (pp. 46–76). New York: Guilford.

Brown, T. A., & Barlow, D. H. (1995). Long-term outcome in cognitive-behavioral treatment of panic disorder: Clinical predictors and alternative strategies for assessment. *Journal of Consulting and Clinical Psychology, 63,* 754–765.

Butcher, J. N. (1990). *The MMPI–2 in psychological treatment.* New York: Oxford University Press.

Butcher, J. N. (Ed.). (1995). *Clinical personality assessment: Practical approaches.* New York: Oxford University Press.

Butcher, J. N., Dahlstrom, W. G., Graham, J. R., Tellegen, A., & Kaemmer, B. (1989). *Minnesota Multiphasic Personality Inventory–2 (MMPI–2): Manual for administration and scoring.* Minneapolis, MN: University of Minnesota Press.

Calvert, S. J., Beutler, L. E., & Crago, M. (1988). Psychotherapy outcome as a function of therapist-patient matching on selected variables. *Journal of Social and Clinical Psychology, 6,* 104–117.

Caspar, F. (1995). *Plan analysis: Toward optimizing psychotherapy.* Seattle: Hogrefe & Huber.

Cattell, R. B., & Johnson, R. C. (Eds.). (1986). *Functional psychological testing.* New York: Brunner/Mazel.

Chemtob, C. M., Nakashima, J., & Carlson, J. G. (2002). Brief treatment for elementary school children with disaster-related posttraumatic stress disorder: A field study. *Journal of Clinical Psychology, 58,* 99–112.

Chisholm, S. M., Crowther, J. H., & Ben-Porath, Y. S. (1997). Selected MMPI–2 scales' ability to predict premature termination and outcome from psychotherapy. *Journal of Personality Assessment, 69*: 127–144.

Cooney, N. L., Kadden, R. M., Litt, M. D., & Getter, H. (1991). Matching alcoholics to coping skills or interactional therapies: Two-year follow-up results. *Journal of Consulting and Clinical Psychology, 59,* 598–601.

Corbella, S., Beutler, L. E., Fernandeq-Alvarez, H., Botella, L., Malik, M. L., Lane, G., & Wagstaff, N. (2003). Measuring coping style and resistance among Spanish and Argentine samples: Development of the Systematic Treatment Selection Self-Report (STS–SR) in Spanish. *Journal of Clinical Psychology.*

Costa, P. T., & McCrae, R. R. (1985). *The NEO Personality Inventory manual.* Odessa, FL: Psychological Assessment Resources.

Crits-Christoph, P., Cooper, A., & Luborsky, L. (1988). The accuracy of therapists' interpretations and the outcome of dynamic psychotherapy. *Journal of Consulting and Clinical Psychology, 56,* 490–495.

Crits-Christoph, P., & Demorest, A. (1988, June). *The development of standard categories for the CCRT method.* Paper presented at the Society for Psychotherapy Research, Santa Fe, NM.

Crits-Christoph, P., & Demorest, A. (1991). Quantitative assessment of relationship theme components. In M. J. Horowitz (Ed.), *Person schemas and maladaptive interpersonal patterns* (pp. 197–212). Chicago: University of Chicago Press.

Crits-Christoph, P., Demorest, A., & Connolly, M. B. (1990). Quantitative assessment of interpersonal themes over the course of psychotherapy. *Psychotherapy, 27*, 513–521.

Crits-Christoph, P., Luborsky, L., Dahl, L., Popp, C., Mellon, J., & Mark, D. (1988). Clinicians can agree in assessing relationship patterns in psychotherapy. *Archives of General Psychiatry, 45*, 1001–1004.

Derogatis, L. R. (1994). *SCL–90–R: Administration, scoring and procedures manual* (3rd ed.). Minneapolis, MN: National Computer Systems.

DeRubeis, R. J., Evans, M. D., Hollon, S. D., Garvey, M. J., Grove, W. M., & Tuason, V. B. (1990). How does cognitive therapy work? Cognitive change and symptom change in cognitive therapy and pharmacotherapy for depression. *Journal of Consulting and Clinical Psychology, 58*, 862–869.

DiNardo, P. A., O'Brien, G. T., Barlow, D. H., Waddell, M. T., & Blanchard, E. B. (1983). Reliability of DSM–III anxiety disorder categories using a new structured interview. *Archives of General Psychiatry, 40*, 1070–1075.

Dowd, E. T., Milne, C. R., & Wise, S. L. (1991). The Therapeutic Reactance Scale: A measure of psychological reactance. *Journal of Counseling and Development, 69*, 541–545.

Dowd, E. T., Wallbrown, F., Sanders, D., & Yesenosky, J. M. (1994). Psychological reactance and its relationship to normal personality variables. *Cognitive Therapy and Research, 18*, 601–612.

Eames, V., & Roth, A. (2000). Patient attachment orientation and the early working alliance: A study of patient and therapist reports of alliance quality and ruptures. *Psychotherapy Research, 10*, 421–434.

Eisen, S. V., Grob, M. C., & Klein, A. A. (1986). BASIS: The development of a self-report measure for psychiatric inpatient evaluation. *Psychiatric Hospital, 17*, 165–171.

Eisen, S. V., Wilcox, M., Leff, H. S., Schaefer, E., & Culhane, M. A. (1999). Assessing behavioral health outcomes in outpatient programs: Reliability and validity of the BASIS–32. *Journal of Behavioral Health Services and Research, 26*, 5–17.

Eldridge, K. L., Locke, K. D., & Horowitz, L. M. (1998). Patterns in interpersonal problems associated with binge eating disorder. *International Journal of Eating Disorders, 23*, 383–389.

Elkin, I., Shea, T., Watkins, J. T., Imber, S. D., Sotsky, S. M., Collins, J. F., et al. (1989). National Institute of Mental Health Treatment of Depression Collaborative Research Program. *Archives of General Psychiatry, 46*, 971–982.

Ellicott, A., Hammen, C., Gitlin, M., Brown, G., & Jamison, K. (1990). Life events and the course of bipolar disorder. *American Journal of Psychiatry, 147*, 1194–1198.

Eysenck, H., & Eysenck, S. B. G. (1964). *Manual of the Eysenck Personality Inventory.* London: University of London Press.

Eysenck, H. J., & Eysenck, S. B. G. (1969). *Personality structure and measurement.* San Diego, CA: Knapp.

Fahy, T. A., & Russell, G. F. M. (1993). Outcome and prognostic variables in bulimia nervosa. *International Journal of Eating Disorders, 14*, 135–145.

Fisher, D., Beutler, L. E., & Williams, O. B. (1999). Making assessment relevant to treatment planning: The STS Clinician Rating Form. *Journal of Clinical Psychology, 55*, 825–842.

Flett, G. L., Madorsky, D., Hewitt, P. L., & Heisel, M. J. (2002). Perfectionism cognitions, rumination, and psychological distress. *Journal of Rational-Emotive and Cognitive Behavior Therapy, 20*, 33–47.

Folkman, S., & Lazarus, R. S. (1980). An analysis of coping in a middle-aged community sample. *Journal of Health and Social Behavior, 21*, 219–239.

Follette, W. C., & Houts, A. C. (1996). Models of scientific progress and the role of theory in taxonomy development: A case study of the DSM. *Journal of Consulting and Clinical Psychology, 64*, 1120–1132.

Fonagy, P., Leigh, T., Steele, M., Steele, H., Kennedy, R., Matton, G., et al. (1996). The relation of attachment status, psychiatric classification, and response to psychotherapy. *Journal of Consulting and Clinical Psychology, 64*, 22–31.

Fountoulakis, K. N., Tsolaki, M., & Kazis, A. (2000). Target symptoms for fluvoxamine in old age depression. *International Journal of Psychiatry in Clinical Practice, 4*, 127–134.

Frances, A., Clarkin, J., & Perry, S. (1984). *Differential therapeutics in psychiatry.* New York: Brunner/Mazel.

Frank, J. D., & Frank, J. B. (1991). *Persuasion and healing* (3rd ed.). Baltimore: Johns Hopkins University Press.

Fremouw, W. J., & Zitter, R. E. (1978). A comparison of skills training and cognitive restructuring-relaxation for the treatment of speech anxiety. *Behavior Therapy, 9*, 248–259.

Gaw, K. F., & Beutler, L. E. (1995). Integrating treatment recommendations. In L. E. Beutler & M. Berren (Eds.), *Integrative assessment of adult personality* (pp. 280–319). New York: Guilford.

George, C., Kaplan, N., & Main, M. (1985). *Adult attachment interview* (2nd ed.). Berkeley, CA: University of California–Berkeley.

Gist, R., & Woodall, S. (2000). There are no simple solutions to complex problems. In J. M. Violanti & P. Douglas (Eds.), *Posttraumatic stress intervention: Challenges, issues, and perspectives* (pp. 81–95). Springfield, IL: Charles C Thomas.

Goldsmith, R. J. (1999). Overview of psychiatric comorbidity: Practical and theoretic considerations. *Psychiatric Clinics of North America, 22*, 331–349.

Goldstein, G., & Hersen, M. (Eds.). (1990). *Handbook of psychological assessment* (2nd ed.). New York: Pergamon.

Gough, H. G. (1987). *California Psychological Inventory administrator's guide.* Palo Alto, CA: Consulting Psychologists Press.

Graham, J. R. (1987). *The MMPI: A practical guide* (2nd ed.). New York: Oxford University Press.

Graham, J. R. (1993). *The MMPI–2: Assessing personality and psychopathology.* New York: Oxford University Press.

Greenberg, M. D. (1997). Treatment implications of psychiatric comorbidity. In S. Fisher & R. P. Greenberg (Eds.), *From placebo to panacea: Putting psychiatric drugs to the test* (pp. 57–97). New York: Wiley.

Groth-Marnat, G. (1997). *Handbook of psychological assessment* (3rd ed.). New York: Wiley.

Hamilton, M. (1967). Development of a rating scale for primary depressive illness. *British Journal of Social and Clinical Psychology, 6*, 278–296.

Hardy, G. E., Aldridge, J., Davidson, C., Rowe, C., Reilly, S., & Shapiro, D. A. (1999). Therapist responsiveness to patient attachment styles and issues observed in patient-identified significant events in psychodynamic-interpersonal psychotherapy. *Psychotherapy Research, 9*, 36–53.

Harwood, T. M., & Williams, O. B. (2003). Identifying treatment relevant assessment: The STS. In L. E. Beutler & G. Groth-Marnat (Eds.), *Integrative assessment of adult personality* (2nd ed.). New York: Guilford.

Hatton, C., Knussen, C., Sloper, P., & Turner, S. (1995). The stability of the Ways of Coping (Revised) Questionnaire over time in parents of children with Down's syndrome: A research note. *Psychological Medicine, 25*, 419–422.

Hayes, S. C., Nelson, R. O., & Jarrett, R. B. (1987). The treatment utility of assessment: A functional approach to evaluating assessment quality. *American Psychologist, 42*, 963–974.

Hazan, C., & Shaver, P. R. (1987). Romantic love conceptualized as an attachment process. *Journal of Personality and Social Psychology, 52*, 511–524.

Hazan, C., & Shaver, P. R. (1994). Attachment as an organizational framework for research on close relationships. *Psychological Inquiry, 5*, 1–22.

Hoencamp, E., Haffmans, P. M. J., Duivenvoorden, H., Knegtering, H., & Dijken, W. A. (1994). Predictors of (non-)response in depressed outpatients treated with a three-phase sequential medication strategy. *Journal of Affective Disorders, 31*, 235–246.

Hoges, D. (1999). The Bielefeld Questionnaire on Client Expectations: A method for assessing attachment styles among therapy patients. *Psychotherapeutics, 44*, 159–166.

Hollon, S. D., & Beck, A. T. (1986). Research on cognitive therapies. In S. L. Garfield & A. E. Bergin (Eds.), *Handbook of psychotherapy and behavior change* (3rd ed., pp. 443–482). New York: Wiley.

Holmes, J. (1996). *Attachment, intimacy, autonomy: Using attachment theory in adult psychotherapy.* Northvale, NJ: Jason Aronson Inc.

Hooley, J. M., & Teasdale, J. D. (1989). Predictors of relapse in unipolar depressives: Expressed emotion, marital distress, and perceived criticism. *Journal of Abnormal Psychology, 98*, 229-235.

Horowitz, M., Marmar, C., Krupnick, J., Wilner, N., Kaltreider, N., & Wallerstein, R. (1984). *Personality styles and brief psychotherapy.* New York: Basic Books.

Horowitz, M. J., Wilner, N., & Alvarez, W. (1979). Impact of Event Scale: A measure of subjective stress. *Psychosomatic Medicine, 41*, 209–218.

Horvath, A. O., & Goheen, M. D. (1990). Factors mediating the success of defiance- and compliance-based interventions. *Journal of Counseling Psychology, 37*, 363–371.

Horvath, A. O., & Symonds, B. D. (1991). Relation between working alliance and outcome in psychotherapy: A meta-analysis. *Journal of Counseling Psychology, 38*, 139–149.

Imber, S. D., Pilkonis, P. A., Sotsky, S. M., Elkin, I., Watkins, J. T., Collins, J. F., et al. (1990). Mode-specific effects among three treatments for depression. *Journal of Consulting and Clinical Psychology, 58*, 352–359.

Jacob, R. G., Turner, S. M., Szekely, B. C., & Eidelman, B. H. (1983). Predicting outcome of relaxation therapy in headaches: The role of "depression." *Behavior Therapy, 14*, 457–465.

Jacobson, N. S., Follette, W. C., & Revenstorf, D. (1984). Psychotherapy outcome research: Methods of reporting variability and evaluating clinical significance. *Behavior Therapy, 15*, 336–352.

Joyce, A. S., & Piper, W. E. (1996). Interpretive work in short-term individual psychotherapy: An analysis using hierarchical linear modeling. *Journal of Consulting and Clinical Psychology, 64*, 505–512.

Kadden, R. M., Cooney, N. L., Getter, H., & Litt, M. D. (1989). Matching alcoholics to coping skills or interactional therapies: Posttreatment results. *Journal of Consulting and Clinical Psychology, 57,* 698–704.

Karno, M. (1997). *Identifying patient attributes and elements of psychotherapy that impact the effectiveness of alcoholism treatment.* Unpublished doctoral dissertation, University of California at Santa Barbara.

Karno, M. P., Beutler, L. E., & Harwood, T. M. (2002). Interactions between psychotherapy procedures and patient attributes that predict alcohol treatment effectiveness: A preliminary report. *Addictive Behaviors, 27,* 779–797.

Keijsers, G. P. J., Hoogduin, C. A. L., & Schaap, C. P. D. R. (1994). Predictors of treatment outcome in the behavioural treatment of obsessive-compulsive disorder. *British Journal of Psychiatry, 165,* 781–786.

Khavin, A. B. (1985). Individual-psychological factors in prediction of help to stutterers. *Voprosy-Psikhologii, 2,* 133–135.

Klerman, G. L. (1986). Drugs and psychotherapy. In S. L. Garfield & A. E. Bergin (Eds.), *Handbook of psychotherapy and behavior change* (3rd ed., pp. 777–818). New York: Wiley.

Klerman, G. L., DiMascio, A., Weissman, M. M., Prusoff, B., & Paykel, E. S. (1974). Treatment of depression by drugs and psychotherapy. *American Journal of Psychiatry, 131,* 186–191.

Knight-Law, A., Sugerman, A. A., & Pettinati, H. M. (1988). An application of an MMPI classification system for predicting outcome in a small clinical sample of alcoholics. *American Journal of Drug and Alcohol Abuse, 14,* 325–334.

Lambert, M. J. (1994). Use of psychological tests for outcome assessment. In M. E. Maruish (Ed.), *The use of psychological testing for treatment planning and outcome assessment* (pp. 75–97). Hillsdale, NJ: Lawrence Erlbaum Associates.

Lambert, M. J., & Bergin, A. E. (1983). Therapist characteristics and their contribution to psychotherapy outcome. In C. E. Walker (Ed.), *The handbook of clinical psychology* (Vol. 1, pp. 205–241). Homewood, IL: Dow Jones-Irwin.

Lazarus, A. A. (1981). *The practice of multimodal therapy.* New York: McGraw-Hill.

Litz, B. T., Gray, M. J., Bryant, R. A., & Adler, A. B. (2002). Early intervention for trauma: Current status and future directions. *Clinical Psychology: Science and Practice, 9,* 112–134.

Longabaugh, R., Beattie, M., Noel, N., Stout, R., & Malloy, P. (1993). The effect of social investment on treatment outcome. *Journal of Studies on Alcohol, 54,* 465–478.

Longabaugh, R., Rubin, A., Malloy, P., Beattie, M., Clifford, P. R., & Noel, N. (1994). Drinking outcomes of alcohol abusers diagnosed as antisocial personality disorder. *Alcoholism, Clinical and Experimental Research, 18,* 778–785.

Luborsky, L. (1996). *The symptom-context method.* Washington, DC: American Psychological Association.

Luborsky, L., Crits-Christoph, P., & Mellon, J. (1986). The advent of objective measures of the transference concept. *Journal of Consulting and Clinical Psychology, 54,* 39–47.

Lunnen, K. M. (2000). An evaluation for CCRT pervasiveness in the Vanderbilt II Psychotherapy project. *Dissertation Abstracts International, 60* (9-B), 4895.

Machado, P. P. P., Beutler, L. E., Engle, D., & Mohr, D. (1983). Differential patient × treatment maintenance among cognitive, experiential, and self-directed therapies. *Journal of Psychotherapy Integration, 3,* 15–32.

Mallinckrodt, B., Gantt, D. L., & Cole, H. M. (1995). Attachment patterns in the psychotherapy relationship: Development of the Patient Attachment to Therapist Scale. *Journal of Consulting Psychology, 42,* 307–317.

Martin, D. J., Garske, J. P., & Davis, M. K. (2000). Relation of the therapeutic alliance with outcome and other variables: A meta-analytic review. *Journal of Consulting and Clinical Psychology, 68,* 438–450.

Masterson, J. F., Tolpin, M., & Sifneos, P. E. (1991). *Comparing psychoanalytic psychotherapies.* New York: Brunner/Mazel.

McConnaughy, E. A., DiClemente, C. C., & Velicer, W. F. (1983). Stages of change in psychotherapy: Measurement and sample profiles. *Psychotherapy, 20,* 368–375.

McLean, P. D., & Taylor, S. (1992). Severity of unipolar depression and choice of treatment. *Behavior Research and Therapy, 30,* 443–451.

McLellan, A. T., Woody, G. E., Luborsky, L., O'Brien, C. P., & Druley, K. A. (1983). Increased effectiveness of substance abuse treatment: A prospective study of patient-treatment "matching." *Journal of Nervous and Mental Disease, 171,* 597–605.

McMain, S. F. (1996). Relating changes in self-other schemas to psychotherapy outcome. *Dissertation Abstracts International, 56* (10-B), 5775.

Merz, J. (1983). Fragenbogen zur Messung der psychologischen Reactanz [Questionnaire for the measurement of psychological reactance]. *Diagnostica, 29,* 75–82.

Meyer, B., & Pilkonis, P. A. (2002). Attachment style. In J. C. Norcross (Ed.), *Psychotherapy relationships that work.* New York: Oxford.

Miller, S. M. (1987). Monitoring and blunting: Validation of a questionnaire to assess styles of information seeking under threat. *Journal of Personality and Social Psychology, 52,* 345–353.

Millon, T. (1994). *Millon Clinical Multiaxial Inventory–III (MCMI–III) manual.* Minneapolis, MN: National Computer Systems.

Mintz, J., Mintz, L. I., Arruda, M. J., & Hwang, S. S. (1992). Treatments of depression and the functional capacity to work. *Archives of General Psychiatry, 49,* 761–768.

Mohr, D. C., Beutler, L. E., Engle, D., Shoham-Salomon, V., Bergan, J., Kaszniak, A. W., et al. (1990). Identification of patients at risk for non-response and negative outcome in psychotherapy. *Journal of Consulting and Clinical Psychology, 58,* 622–628.

Moos, R. H. (1990). Depressed outpatients' life contexts, amount of treatment and treatment outcome. *Journal of Nervous and Mental Disease, 178,* 105–112.

Moos, R. H., & Moos, B. S. (1986). *Family Environment Scale manual* (2nd ed.). Palo Alto, CA: Consulting Psychologists Press.

Moreira, J. M., Bernardes, S., Andrez, M., Aguiar, P., Moleiro, C., & Silva, M. F. (1998). Social competence, personality and adult attachment style in a Portuguese sample. *Personality and Individual Differences, 24,* 565–570.

Myers, L. B., & Derakshan, N. (2000). Monitoring and blunting and an assessment of different coping styles. *Personality and Individual Differences, 28,* 111–121.

Nezworski, M. T., & Wood, J. M. (1995). Narcissism in the comprehensive system for the Rorschach. *Clinical Psychology: Science and Practice, 2,* 179–199.

Nietzel, M. T., Russell, R. L., Hemmings, K. A., & Gretter, M. L. (1987). Clinical significance of psychotherapy for unipolar depression: A meta-analytic approach to social comparison. *Journal of Consulting and Clinical Psychology, 55,* 156–161.

Norcross, J. C. (Ed.). (2002). *Psychotherapy relationships that work.* New York: Oxford University Press.

Norcross, J. C., & Goldfried, M. R. (Eds.). (1992). *Handbook of psychotherapy integration.* New York: Basic Books.

O'Connor, E. A., Carbonari, J. P., & DiClemente, C. C. (1996). Gender and smoking cessation: A factor structure comparison of processes of change. *Journal of Consulting and Clinical Psychology, 64,* 130–138.

Parker, G., Holmes, S., & Manicavasagar, V. (1986). Depression in general practice attenders: "Caneness," natural history and predictors of outcomes. *Journal of Affective Disorders, 10,* 27–35.

Piper, W. E., & Joyce, A. S. (2001). Psychosocial treatment and outcome. In J. Livesley (Ed.), *Handbook of personality disorders: Theory, research, and treatment* (pp. 323–343). New York: Guilford Press.

Prochaska, J. O., & DiClemente, C. C. (1984). *The transtheoretical approach: Crossing traditional boundaries of change.* Homewood, IL: Dow Jones-Irwin.

Prochaska, J. O., DiClemente, C. C., & Norcross, J. C. (1992). In search of how people change: Applications to addictive behaviors. *American Psychologist, 47,* 1102–1114.

Prochaska, J. O., & Norcross, J. C. (2002a). *Systems of psychotherapy: A transtheoretical analysis* (5th ed.). Pacific Grove, CA: Brooks/Cole.

Prochaska, J. O., & Norcross, J. C. (2002b). Stages of change. In J. C. Norcross (Ed.), *Psychotherapy relationships that work.* New York: Oxford University Press.

Prochaska, J. O., Rossi, J. S., & Wilcox, N. S. (1991). Change processes and psychotherapy outcome in integrative case research. *Journal of Psychotherapy Integration, 1,* 103–120.

Project MATCH Research Group. (1997). Matching alcoholism treatments to client heterogeneity: Project MATCH posttreatment drinking outcomes. *Journal of Studies on Alcohol, 58,* 7–29.

Raphael, B., Wilson, J., Meldrum, L., & McFarlane, A. C. (1996). Acute preventative interventions. In B. A. van der Kolk, & A. C. McFarlane (Eds.), *Traumatic stress: The effects of overwhelming experience on mind, body, and society* (pp. 463–479). New York: Guilford.

Ravindran, A. V., Anisman, H., Merali, Z., Charbonneau, Y., Telner, J., Bialik, R. J., et al. (1999). Treatment of primary dysthymia with group cognitive therapy and pharmacotherapy: Clinical symptoms and functional impairment. *American Journal of Psychiatry, 156,* 1608–1617.

Robinson, L. A., Berman, J. S., & Neimeyer, R. A. (1990). Psychotherapy for the treatment of depression: A comprehensive review of controlled outcome research. *Psychological Bulletin, 108,* 30–49.

Rohrbaugh, M., Shoham, V., Spungen, C., & Steinglass, P. (1995). Family systems therapy in practice: A systemic couples therapy for problem drinking. In B. Bongar & L. E. Beutler (Eds.), *Comprehensive textbook of psychotherapy: Theory and practice* (pp. 228–253). New York: Oxford University Press.

Rosen, C. S. (2000). Is the sequencing of change processes by stage consistent across health problems? A meta-analysis. *Health Psychology, 19,* 593–604.

Saravay, S. M., & Lavin, M. (1994). Psychiatric comorbidity and length of stay in the general hospital: A critical review of outcome studies. *Psychosomatics, 35,* 233–252.

Saunter, L. (1993). Debriefing from military origin to therapeutic application. *Journal of Psychosocial Nursing, 31*, 23–27.

Schneider, W., Buchheim, P., Cierpka, M., Dahlbender, R. W., Freyberger, H. J., Grande, T., et al. (2002). Operationalized psychodynamic diagnostics: A new diagnostic approach in psychodynamic psychotherapy. In L. E. Beutler & M. L. Malik (Eds.), *Rethinking the DSM: Psychological perspectives* (pp. 177–200). Washington, DC: American Psychological Association.

Shapiro, D. A., Barkham, M., Rees, A., Hardy, G. E., Reynolds, S., & Startup, M. (1994). Effects of treatment duration and severity of depression on the effectiveness of cognitive-behavioral and psychodynamic-interpersonal psychotherapy. *Journal of Consulting and Clinical Psychology, 62*, 522–534.

Shapiro, D. A., Rees, A., Barkham, M., Hardy, G., Reynolds, S., & Startup, M. (1995). Effects of treatment duration and severity of depression on the maintenance of gains after cognitive-behavioral and psychodynamic-interpersonal therapy. *Journal of Consulting and Clinical Psychology, 63*, 378–387.

Shea, M. T., Elkin, I., Imber, S. D., Sotsky, S. M., Watkins, J. T., Collins, J. F., et al. (1992). Course of depressive symptoms over follow-up: Findings from the National Institute of Mental Health Treatment of Depression Collaborative Research Program. *Archives of General Psychiatry, 49*, 782–787.

Sheppard, D., Smith, G. T., & Rosenbaum, G. (1988). Use of MMPI subtypes in predicting completion of a residential alcoholism treatment program. *Journal of Consulting and Clinical Psychology, 56*, 590–596.

Sherbourne, C. D., Hays, R. D., & Wells, K. B. (1995). Personal and psychosocial risk factors for physical and mental health outcomes and course of depression among depressed patients. *Journal of Consulting and Clinical Psychology, 63*, 345–355.

Shoham-Salomon, V., Avner, R., & Neeman, K. (1989). "You are changed if you do and changed if you don't": Mechanisms underlying paradoxical interventions. *Journal of Consulting and Clinical Psychology, 57*, 590–598.

Shoham-Salomon, V., & Hannah, M. T. (1991). Client-treatment interactions in the study of differential change processes. *Journal of Consulting and Clinical Psychology, 59*, 217–225.

Shoham-Salomon, V., & Rosenthal, R. (1987). Paradoxical interventions: A meta-analysis. *Journal of Consulting and Clinical Psychology, 55*, 22–28.

Simons, A. D., Garfield, S. L., & Murphy, G. E. (1984). The process of change in cognitive therapy and pharmacotherapy for depression. *Archives of General Psychiatry, 41*, 45–51.

Sotsky, S. M., Glass, D. R., Shea, M. T., Pilkonis, P. A., Collins, J. F., Elkin, I., et al. (1991). Patient predictors of response to psychotherapy and pharmacotherapy: Findings in the NIMH Treatment of Depression Collaborative Research Program. *American Journal of Psychiatry, 148*, 997–1008.

Sperry, L., Brill, P. L., Howard, K. L., & Grissom, F. R. (1996). *Treatment outcomes in psychotherapy and psychiatric interventions.* New York: Brunner/Mazel.

Spielberger, C. D., Gorsuch, R. L., & Lushene, R. E. (1970). *The State-Trait Anxiety Inventory (STAI) test manual for form X.* Palo Alto: Consulting Psychologists Press.

Striker, G., & Gold, J. R. (Eds.). (1993). *Comprehensive handbook of psychotherapy integration.* New York: Plenum.

Strupp, H. H., & Binder, J. L. (1984). *Psychotherapy in a new key.* New York: Basic Books.

Strupp, H. H., Horowitz, L. M., & Lambert, M. J. (1997). *Measuring patient changes in mood, anxiety, and personality disorders: Toward a core battery.* Washington, DC: American Psychological Association.

Swoboda, J. S., Dowd, E. T., & Wise, S. L. (1990). Reframing and restraining directives in the treatment of clinical depression. *Journal of Counseling Psychology, 37*, 254–260.

Tasca, G. A., Russell, V., & Busby, K. (1994). Characteristics of patients who choose between two types of group psychotherapy. *International Journal of Group Psychotherapy, 44*, 499–508.

Trief, P. M., & Yuan, H. A. (1983). The use of the MMPI in a chronic back pain rehabilitation program. *Journal of Clinical Psychology, 39*, 46–53.

Tyrer, P., Gunderson, J., Lyons, M., & Tohen, M. (1997). Special feature: Extent of comorbidity between mental state and personality disorders. *Journal of Personality Disorders, 11*, 242–259.

Vaillant, L. M. (1997). *Changing character.* New York: Basic Books.

Vallejo, J., Gasto, C., Catalan, R., Bulbena, A., & Menchon, J. M. (1991). Predictors of antidepressant treatment outcome in melancholia: Psychosocial, clinical, and biological indicators. *Journal of Affective Disorders, 21*, 151–162.

Wakefield, P. J., Williams, R. E., Yost, E. B., & Patterson, K. M. (1996). *Couple therapy for alcoholism: A cognitive-behavioral treatment manual.* New York: Guilford.

Wells, K. B., & Sturm, R. (1996). Informing the policy process: From efficacy to effectiveness data on pharmacotherapy. *Journal of Consulting and Clinical Psychology, 64*, 638–645.

Welsh, G. S. (1952). An anxiety index and an internalization ratio for the MMPI. *Journal of Consulting Psychology, 16*, 65–72.

Weston, D., & Morrison, K. (2001). A multidimensional meta-analysis of treatments for depression, panic, and generalized anxiety disorder: An empirical examination of the status of empirically supported therapies. *Journal of Consulting and Clinical Psychology, 69*, 875–899.

Wilson, T. G. (1996). Treatment of bulimia nervosa: When CBT fails. *Behavioral Research Therapy, 34*, 197–212.

Woody, G. E., McLellan, A. T., Luborsky, L., O'Brien, C. P., Blaine, J., Fox, S., et al. (1984). Severity of psychiatric symptoms as a predictor of benefits from psychotherapy: The Veterans Administration–Penn Study. *American Journal of Psychiatry, 141*, 1172–1177.

# Assessment as Intervention Within the Transtheoretical Model

James O. Prochaska
*Cancer Prevention Research Center*

Janice M. Prochaska
*Pro-Change Behavior Systems, Inc.*

The major causes of chronic disease, disability, and premature death are all behaviors. Addictive behaviors, like alcohol abuse, obesity, and smoking, for example, and distressing behaviors, like anxiety, depression, chronic hostility, and stress, are major killers and cripplers of our time. This fact has been known for decades, but that did not lead health care systems to treat such behaviors seriously.

More recently, it has been clear that behaviors are also the major cost drivers of health care. Pharmaceuticals account for about 10% of total health care costs, and behavior accounts for about 60% (Prochaska, 1997). If health care systems are to begin to treat seriously the major killers, cripplers, and cost drivers, then psychological and behavioral assessments must be used to plan treatments—and not just for individual patients but for entire populations. Many experts know how to plan treatments for individual patients with depression or addictions. Few specialists are prepared to plan treatment programs for entire populations with depression or addictions.

From the perspective of the transtheoretical model (TTM), treatment planning for entire populations requires interventions that can be matched to people at each stage of change and not just the small minority who are prepared to take action on their problems. In this chapter, we first review the stages of change, then we look at how a stage paradigm can be applied to help many more people than were ever imagined could be helped.

## A STAGE PARADIGM FOR INDIVIDUAL PATIENTS AND ENTIRE POPULATIONS

### Stages of Change

Historically, behavior change was taken as equivalent to taking action. Patients were assessed as having changed, for example, when they quit abusing substances like alcohol, food, or tobacco. According to the TTM, change is a process that unfolds over time and involves progress through a series of stages: precontemplation, contemplation, preparation, action, maintenance, and termination.

*Precontemplation* is the stage in which people are not intending to take action in the foreseeable future, usually measured as the next 6 months. People may be in this stage because they are uninformed or underinformed about the consequences of their behavior. Or they may have tried to change a number of times and become demoralized about their abilities to change. People of both types tend to avoid reading, talking, or thinking about their high-risk behaviors. They are often characterized in other theories as resistant or unmotivated clients or as not ready for therapy or health promotion programs. The fact is, traditional treatment programs were not ready for such individuals and were not motivated to match their needs.

People in the precontemplation stage underestimate the benefits of changing and overestimate the costs. But they typically are not aware that they are making such mistakes. If they are not conscious of making such mistakes, it will be difficult for them to change. So, many remain stuck in the precontemplation stage for years, doing considerable damage to themselves and others. We have found no inherent motivation for people to progress from one stage of change to the next. These are not like stages of human development, where children have inherent motivation to progress from crawling to walking even though crawling works very well and even though learning to walk can be painful and embarrassing.

We have identified two major forces that can move people to progress. The first consists of developmental events. In our research, the *mean* age of smokers reaching longer term maintenance is 39. Those of us who are older than 39 suspect why. It is an age at which people reevaluate how they have been living and decide whether they want to die from the way they have been living or whether they want to enhance the quality and quantity of the second half of their lives.

The other naturally occurring force consists of environmental events. One of my favorite examples is a couple whom we followed and who were both heavy smokers. Their dog of many years died of lung cancer. This eventually moved the wife to quit smoking. The husband bought a new dog. So even the same events can be processed differently by different people. There has been a common belief that people with addictions must hit bottom before they will be motivated to change. So family, friends, and physicians wait helplessly for a crisis to occur. But how often do people turn 39 or have a dog die? When people show the first signs of a serious physical illness, like cancer or cardiovascular disease, others around them can become mobilized to help them seek early intervention. We know that early interventions are often lifesaving, and we wouldn't wait for such patients to hit bottom. We shall see that we have created a third force to help addicted patients in precontemplation to progress. It is called planned interventions.

*Contemplation* is the stage in which people are intending to take action in the next 6 months. They are more aware of the pros of changing but are also acutely aware of the cons. When people begin to seriously contemplate giving up their favorite substances, their awareness of the costs of changing can increase. There is no free change. This balance between the costs and benefits of changing can produce profound ambivalence. This profound ambivalence can reflect a type of love-hate relationship with an addictive substance, and it can keep people stuck in this stage for long periods of time. We often characterize this phenomena as chronic contemplation or behavioral procrastination. These folks are not ready for traditional action-oriented programs.

*Preparation* is the stage in which people are intending to take action in the immediate future, usually measured as the next month. They have typically taken some significant action in the past year. These individuals have a plan of action, such as going to a recovery group, consulting a counselor, talking to their physician, buying a self-help book, or relying on a self-change approach. These are the people we should recruit for action-oriented treatment programs.

*Action* is the stage in which people have made specific overt modifications in their lifestyles within the past 6 months. Since action is observable, behavior change often has been equated with action. But in the TTM, action is only one of six stages. Not all modifications of behavior count as action in this model. People must meet a criterion that scientists and professionals agree is sufficient to reduce the risk of disease. In smoking, for example, only total abstinence counts. With alcoholism and alcohol abuse, many believe that only total abstinence can be effective, but some accept controlled drinking as an effective action.

*Maintenance* is the stage in which people are working to prevent relapse, but they do not apply change processes as frequently as people in the action stage. They are less tempted to relapse and increasingly more confident that they can continue their changes. Based on temptation and self-efficacy data, we estimate that maintenance lasts from 6 months to about 5 years. One of the common reasons that people relapse early is that they are not well prepared for the prolonged effort needed to progress to maintenance. Many think the worst will be over in a few weeks or a few months. If they ease up on their efforts too early, they are at great risk for relapse.

To prepare people for what is to come, we encourage them to think of overcoming an addiction as like running a marathon rather than a sprint. They may have wanted to enter the 100th running of the Boston Marathon. But if they had little or no preparation, they know they would not succeed, so would not enter the race. If they had done some preparation, they might make it for several miles before failing to finish the race. Only those well prepared could maintain their efforts mile after mile.

People who enter the Boston Marathon know they have to be well prepared if they are to survive Heartbreak Hill, which confronts runners after 20 some miles. What is the behavioral equivalent of Heartbreak Hill? The best evidence we have across addictions is that the majority of relapses occur at times of emotional distress. Times of depression, anxiety, anger, boredom, loneliness, stress, and distress are the times when we are at our emotional and psychological weakest. How does the average American cope with such troubling times? The average American drinks more, eats more, smokes more, and takes more drugs to cope with such distressing times (Mellinger, Balter, Uhlenhuth, Cisin, & Parry, 1978). It is not surprising, therefore, that people struggling to overcome addictions will be at greatest risk of relapse when they face distress without their substance of choice. We cannot prevent emotional distress from occurring. But we can help prevent relapse if our patients have been prepared for how to cope with distress without falling back on addictive substances.

If so many Americans rely on oral consumptive behavior as a way to manage their emotions, what is the healthiest oral behavior they could use? Talking with others about one's distress is a means of seeking support that can help prevent relapse. A second healthy alternative that can be relied on by large numbers of people is exercise. Not only does physical activity help manage moods, stress, and distress, but by exercising 60 minutes a week a recovering addict can receive over 75 health and mental health benefits (Reed, Velicer, Prochaska, Rossi, & Marcus, 1997). These benefits include better stress management, better mood management, improved sleep, increased self-esteem, more energy, and a healthier heart. Exercise should be prescribed to all sedentary patients with addictions as the bargain basement of behaviors. A third healthy alternative is some form of deep relaxation, like meditation, yoga, prayer, massage, or deep muscle relaxation. Letting the stress and distress drift away from one's muscles and one's mind helps one keep progressing at the most tempting of times.

*Termination* is the stage in which individuals have zero temptation and 100% self-efficacy. No matter whether they are depressed, anxious, bored, lonely, angry, or stressed, they are sure they will not return to their old unhealthy habit as a way of coping. It is as if they never acquired the habit in the first place. In a study of former smokers and alcoholics, we found that fewer than 20% of each group met the criteria of no temptation and total self-efficacy (Snow, Prochaska, & Rossi, 1992). Although the ideal goal is to be cured or totally recovered, we recognize that for many people the best they can do is live a lifetime of maintenance.

## Assessing Stages in Entire Populations

Health risk assessments (HRAs) are among the most widely used assessment tools for assessing the behavioral risks of chronic disease and disability in entire populations, such as employees in worksites or patients in health care systems (e.g., Eddington, 2001). These tools provide feedback to individuals about their risk profiles and what each individual needs to change. They also can provide a needs assessment for treatment planners. Reports on the population can indicate the prevalence of each behavioral risk. A major limitation of HRAs is that, though they help assess what major behavioral problems need to be changed, they provide little guidance on how treatments should be planned to facilitate change in both individuals and populations.

A recent innovation called the health risk intervention (HRI) assesses not only the presence of particular problems but also assesses what stage of change each individual is in for such problems as smoking, alcohol abuse, depression/stress, high-fat diet, and sedentary behavior. Also, this assessment immediately generates stage-matched computer guidance about the most important steps individuals can take to progress on each of their behavioral problems. Individuals in the precontemplation stage, for example, are encouraged to set a realistic goal of progressing to the contemplation stage rather than being pressured to take immediate action. They are also informed that their next assessments can provide expert guidance on how they can begin progressing to the next stage.

The HRI also generates computer-based guidance for treatment planners. Planners might be informed that 25% of the population in question are not managing stress effectively and 70% of these are not prepared to pursue stress management, 20% are at risk for depression and 65% of these are not prepared to take action, 25% are at risk for alcohol abuse and 70% of these are in the precontemplation stage, and 25% are smokers and 80% of these are not prepared to quit. Just from this brief example, it is clear that providing only action-oriented treatments would not match the needs of the vast majority of the at-risk population. The treatment planning report would guide the planners to provide interventions that would match the needs of all of the at-risk population and not just the small minority prepared to take action. As a real-life example, the Centers for Disease Control and Prevention found through such assessments that 75% of the population at highest risk for HIV and AIDS were in the precontemplation stage, but 75% of the intervention programs were action oriented. No wonder their treatment programs were assessed as having little impact.

## Assessing Stages in Individual Patients

The most widely used assessments for stage of change have been brief algorithms. The fundamental structure of these algorithms is as follows:

1. Precontemplation: Not at criterion and not intending to be in the next 6 months.
2. Contemplation: Not at criterion but intending to be in the next 6 months.

3. Preparation: Not at criterion but intending to be in the next month.
4. Action: At criterion for less than 6 months.
5. Maintenance: At criterion for 6 to 60 months.
6. Termination: At criterion for more than 5 years.

With smoking, this algorithm is easy, as there is almost total agreement that total abstinence is the only acceptable action. With alcohol problems, there is more controversy. Those influenced most by the recovery movement would argue that abstinence is the only healthy criterion for successful behavior change. Those influenced more by a harm reduction approach would use alcohol abuse criteria like not drinking five or more drinks on any occasion for males and four or more for females.

For all too many traditional mental health problems, like depression, stress, and anxiety disorders, there is little or no consensus as to what are appropriate or acceptable criteria for successful change. For such problems, considerable research is needed to identify behavior markers for effective management. These markers typically include a series of behavior criteria such as (a) engaging in pleasant activities daily, (b) controlling negative thinking, (c) daily physical activity, (d) practicing stress management, and (e) receiving professional help when prescribed.

Though brief and simple, these stage algorithms can have considerable predictive power. The *stage effect* predicts that clients in precontemplation will take less effective action than those in contemplation, who will take less action than those in preparation. Stage assessments on smokers at the start of treatment predicted 66 out of 70 possible stage effects in 11 different treatment groups at 6-, 12-, and 18-month follow-ups (Prochaska, Velicer, Prochaska, & Johnson, in press).

### Assessing Stages in Special Needs Patients

More complex assessments can be used with patients with special needs, such as patients in mandated treatments, who often experience considerable pressure to misreport what stage of change they are in. These patients may believe that, if they report they are in the precontemplation stage, courts, social services, employers, health care systems, or spouses may punish them for not being prepared to take action.

With such patient populations, we recommend using assessments modeled after the University of Rhode Island Change Assessment Inventory (URICA; McConnaughy, Prochaska, & Velicer, 1982; McConnaughy, DiClemente, Prochaska, & Velicer, 1989). More recently the URICA has been used with domestic violence and vocational rehabilitation clients (Levesque, Gelles, & Velicer, 2000; Mannock, Levesque, & Prochaska, 2002). This instrument has four scales (*PC, C, A,* and *M*) that unfortunately were named after specific stages. The original test development predicted five scales, but factor analysis only produced four, and the stage between contemplation and action was dropped from the TTM for 7 years. Because the TTM is evidence based, the evidence from the factor analyses led to modification of the theory.

Years later, research based on algorithm measures of stage clearly supported the preparation stage, including data showing that smokers in preparation were more abstinent at 6, 12, and 18 months than those in contemplation (Prochaska et al., in press). Recurring research on the URICA showed that there was evidence for the preparation stage, but it came from cluster analyses rather than factor analyses. A cluster of psychiatric patients who scored high on both the contemplation and action scales had the profile of patients in preparation. Contrast them with the cluster of

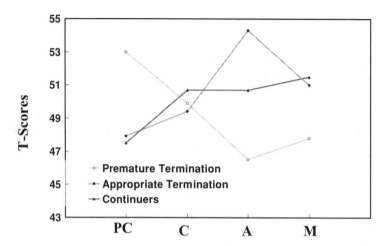

FIG. 4.1. Stage profiles for three treatment groups (premature termination, appropriate termination, and continuation).

patients who scored high on the precontemplation scale and low on the other three scales; here you see the profile of patients in precontemplation.

Such clear profiles occur, however, only when standardized scores are used rather than raw scores. Standardized scores help correct for ease of responding. It is much easier for patients to agree with contemplation or action items than with precontemplation items (e.g., "I don't have a problem" or "I don't need to be here"). Clusters of patients with precontemplation profiles typically mildly disagree with all of the precontemplation items and still are assessed as being in the precontemplation stage. Such subtle and more sophisticated assessments are likely to be more valid than simple algorithms, which can more easily be faked.

This discussion of URICA-type tests reflects several important rules to keep in mind when applying the more subtle and sophisticated assessments. First, standardized scores need to be used rather than raw scores, as standardized scores correct for ease of responding. It is easier for clients to agree with contemplation or action items than with precontemplation items. Second, individual scales cannot be used to stage clients, and profiles across the scales are needed instead. The four scales (of eight items typically) each have adequate reliabilities (e.g., alphas ranging from .65 to .90). They also have appropriate construct validity, such as predictable simplex patterns in which adjacent scales correlate more highly than nonadjacent scales (e.g., precontemplation correlates higher with contemplation than with action, and contemplation correlates higher with action than with maintenance; McConnaughy et al., 1982, 1989).

But valid staging requires profile analyses based on cluster analysis. Patients in precontemplation, for example, are high on the precontemplation scale and low on the other three scales (Fig. 4.1 contains such a profile for a group of patients who terminated therapy prematurely). Patients in the contemplation stage are typically somewhat elevated on the contemplation scale and lower on the other scales but not as dramatically lower as those with a precontemplation profile. As indicated earlier, patients in the preparation stage are elevated on the contemplation and action scales and low on the precontemplation and maintenance scales. Patients in the action stage are elevated on the action scale and lower on the other scales (Fig. 4.1 also presents an example of patients who had this profile and completed treatment quickly but appropriately). The maintenance scale is trickier and tends to reflect struggling to keep from relapsing rather than maintaining change without much struggle. So, patients with profiles that are elevated on maintenance are likely to enter therapy with a concern that they are at risk for relapsing rather than confidence that their changes are stable. Stable maintainers typically have no need to enter therapy unless they want to work on a different problem behavior.

Sometimes we encourage clinicians to just go with the base rates if they are likely to be so high that scientific assessments cannot outperform them. For example, when speaking to psychotherapists who do marital therapy, we ask, "If a husband and wife enter therapy together, what stage is the husband likely to be in?" The audience laughs knowingly: precontemplation. And what stage is the wife likely to be in? They laugh again: action or preparation. They give the same response when asked about a mother bringing an adolescent to therapy. No wonder such clients are having conflict, and unknowing clinicians can be caught in the middle.

## THE FIVE PHASES OF TREATMENT

Let us apply the stages of change model to see how we can help many more people at each phase of planned treatment. The five phases are (1) reach, (2) retain, (3) progress, (4) process, and (5) outcomes. The phases follow a rational planning approach for treating entire populations. The first concern has to be the application of protocols that can reach as high a percentage of the target population as possible. Once a high percentage enter treatment, the next challenge is to have protocols that will retain as many participants as possible until they complete the treatment program. The next concern is to help as many participants progress while in the treatment program and to have a process that can help continue that progress once time-limited treatment has ended. The final phase is producing long-term outcomes with as many people as possible being free from the high-risk target behavior.

### Reach

Too few studies have paid attention to one of the skeletons in the closet of professional treatment programs. The fact is, these programs recruit or reach too few people. Across all *DSM–IV* diagnoses, less than 25% of populations with these disorders ever enter professional therapy programs (Veroff, Douvan, & Kulka, 1981). In the case of smoking, the most deadly of addictions, less than 10% ever participate in professional programs (U.S. Department of Health and Human Services, 1990).

Given that such behaviors are currently among the most costly, we must reach many more people with appropriate programs. These behaviors are costly to the individuals, their families and friends, their employers, their communities, and their health care systems. We can no longer be satisfied with treating such behaviors on a case basis. We must develop programs that can deal with them on a population basis.

Of course, there are some governments and health care systems that are seeking to treat costly conditions on a population basis. But when they turn to the biggest and best relevant clinical trials, what do they discover? Trial after trial is reporting troubling outcomes (e.g., COMMIT, 1995; Ennett, Tabler, Ringwolt, & Fliwelling, 1994; Glasgow, Terborg, Hollis, Severson, Boles, 1995; Luepker et al., 1994). Whether the trials were done at worksites, at schools, or in entire communities, the results are remarkably similar: no significant effects compared with the control conditions.

If we examine more closely one of these trials, the Minnesota Heart Health Study (Lando et al., 1995), we can find hints of what went wrong. Smoking was one of the targeted behaviors, and nearly 90% of the smokers in the treated communities reported seeing media stories about smoking. But the same was true of smokers in the control communities. Only about 12% of smokers in the treatment and control conditions said their physicians talked to them about smoking in the past year. Looking at participation in the most powerful behavior change programs—clinics, classes, and counseling—we find only 4% of the smokers participated over the 5 years of planned interventions. When managed care organizations offer free state-of-the-science cessation clinics, only 1% of smokers are recruited (Lichtenstein & Hollis, 1992). We simply cannot have much impact on the health of our nation if our best treatment programs reach so few of the people who engage in the deadliest of behaviors.

How do we help many more people to seek appropriate help? By changing our paradigms and our practices. There are two paradigms that we need to contemplate changing. The first is an action-oriented paradigm that construes behavior change as an event that can occur quickly, immediately, discretely, and dramatically. Treatment programs designed to have people take immediate action are implicitly or explicitly designed for the portion of the population who are in the preparation stage.

The problem here is that, across 15 unhealthy behaviors, typically less than 20% of the people who engage in one of these behaviors are prepared to take action (Rossi, 1992). The general rule of thumb is 40, 40, 20: 40% in precontemplation, 40% in contemplation, and 20% in preparation. When we offer action-oriented interventions, we are implicitly recruiting from less than 20% of the at-risk population. If we are to meet the needs of entire populations with addictions, then we must design interventions for the 40% in precontemplation and the 40% in contemplation. By offering stage-matched interventions and applying proactive or outreach recruitment methods in three large-scale clinical trials, we have been able to motivate 80% to 90% of smokers to enter our treatment programs (Prochaska, Velicer, Fava, Rossi, & Tsoh, 2001; Prochaska, Velicer, Fava, Ruggiero, et al., 2001). This is a quantum increase in our ability to move people to take the action of starting therapy.

The second paradigm change that this approach requires is a switch from a passive-reactive approach to a proactive approach. Most professionals have been trained to be passive-reactive: to passively wait for patients to seek services and then react. The biggest problem with this approach is that the majority of people with behavior problems never seek such services. The passive-reactive paradigm is designed to serve populations with acute conditions. The pain, distress, or discomfort of such conditions can motivate people to seek the services of health professionals. But the major killers of our time are chronic conditions caused in large part by chronic lifestyle disorders.

If we are to treat such behaviors seriously, we simply must learn to reach out to entire populations and offer them stage-matched therapies. There are regions of the National Health Service in Great Britain that are training health professionals in these new paradigms. Over 6,000 physicians, nurses, counselors and health educators have been trained to proactively interact at each stage of change with all of their patients who smoke or abuse alcohol, drugs, or food.

What happens if professionals change only one paradigm and proactively recruit entire populations to action-oriented interventions. This experiment has been tried in one of the largest managed care organizations in the United States (Lichtenstein & Hollis, 1992). Physicians spent time with all smokers to get them to sign up for a state-of-the-art action-oriented clinic. If that did not work, nurses spent up to 10 minutes to get them to sign up, followed by 12 minutes of discussion with health educators and a counselor call to the home. The base rate was 1% participation.

This intensive recruitment protocol motivated 35% of the smokers in precontemplation to sign up. But only 3% showed up, 2% finished up, and 0% ended up better off.

Of the smokers in the combined contemplation and preparation group, 65% signed up, 15% showed up, 11% finished up, and some percentage ended up better off.

Given the growing evidence to date, we believe we can provide an innovative and probably definitive answer to the question, what can move a majority of people to start a professional treatment program? One answer is, professionals who are motivated and prepared to proactively reach out to entire populations and offer them interventions that match whatever stage of change they are in.

## Retain

What motivates people to continue in therapy? Or conversely, what moves clients to terminate counseling quickly and prematurely as judged by their counselors? A meta-analysis of 125 studies found that nearly 50% of clients drop out of treatment (Wierzbicki & Pekarik, 1993). Across studies, there were few consistent predictors of premature termination; only substance abuse, minority status, and lower level of education predicted dropouts. Though important, these variables did not account for much of the variance in dropouts.

There are now at least five studies done from a stage model perspective that focus on dropping out from treatment for substance abuse, smoking, obesity, and a broad spectrum of psychiatric disorders. These studies found that stage-related variables outpredicted demographics, type of problem, severity of problem, and other problem-related variables. Figure 4.1 presents stage profiles of three groups of patients with a broad spectrum of psychiatric disorders (Brogan, Prochaska, & Prochaska, 1999). In this study, we were able to predict 93% of the three groups: premature terminators, early but appropriate terminators, and continuers in therapy.

Figure 4.1 shows that the pretherapy profile of the entire group who dropped out quickly and prematurely (40%) was a URICA profile of people in the precontemplation stage. The 20% who finished quickly but appropriately had the profile of patients who were in the action stage when entering therapy. Those who continued in longer term treatment were a mixed group, with the majority in the contemplation stage.

We cannot treat people in the precontemplation stage as if they were starting in the same place as those in the action stage and expect them to continue in therapy. If we try to pressure them to take action when they are not prepared, should we expect to retain them in therapy? Or do we drive them away and then blame them for not being motivated enough or not being ready enough for our action-oriented interventions?

With patients entering therapy in the action stage, what would be an appropriate approach? One alternative would be to provide relapse prevention strategies such as that developed by Marlatt and Gordon (1985). But would relapse prevention strategies make any sense for the 40% of patients who enter in the precontemplation stage? What might be a good match here? We would recommend a dropout prevention approach, since we know that those patients are likely to leave early if we do not help them to continue.

With clients starting therapy in precontemplation, I typically share with them my key concerns: "I'm concerned that therapy may not have a chance to make a significant difference in your life because you may be tempted to leave early." I might then explore whether they have been pressured to enter therapy. How do they react when someone tries to pressure or coerce them into quitting an addiction when they are not ready? Can they let me know if they feel that I am trying to pressure or coerce them? I do want to help them but will only encourage them to take steps where they are most ready to succeed.

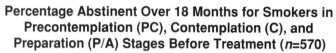

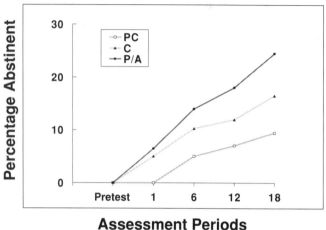

FIG. 4.2. Stage effects over 18 months for three groups of smokers (precontemplation, contemplation, and preparation).

Fortunately, we now have a series of studies on stage-matched interventions that provide data on the retention rates of people entering interventions in the precontemplation stage (Prochaska, DiClemente, Velicer, & Rossi, 1993; Prochaska, Velicer, Fava, Rossi, et al., 2001; Prochaska, Velicer, Fava, Ruggiero, et al., 2001; Prochaska, Velicer, et al., 2002). What is clear is that when treatment is matched to stage, people in the precontemplation stage continue at the same high rates as those who started in the preparation stage. That result held for clinical trials where people were recruited proactively (we reached out to them to offer help) as well as trials with participants recruited reactively (they called us for help).

### Progress

What moves people to progress in therapy and to continue to progress after therapy? Figure 4.2 presents examples of the *stage effects*. A stage effect predicts that the amount of successful action taken during treatment and after treatment is directly related to the stage people are in at the start of treatment (Prochaska, DiClemente, & Norcross, 1992). In this example, the interventions with smokers end at 6 months. The smokers who started in the precontemplation stage show the least amount of progress, as measured by abstinence at each assessment point. Those who started in the contemplation stage made significantly more progress. And those who entered treatment already prepared to take action were the most successful at every assessment.

Stage effects have been found across a variety of problems and populations, including rehabilitative success for brain injury and recovery from anxiety and panic disorders following random assignment to placebo or medication (Beitman et al., 1994; Lam, McMahon, Priddy, & Gehred-Schultz, 1988). In the latter clinical trial, the psychiatrist leading the trial concluded that patients will need to be assessed for their stage of readiness to benefit from the medication and will need to be helped through the stages so that they are well prepared prior to being placed on the medication.

Here is one strategy for applying stage effects clinically. We have already seen that if we try to move all people with addictions to immediate action, we are likely to have the majority of them not show up for therapy or not finish up. An alternative is to set a realistic goal for brief encounters with clients at each stage of change. A realistic goal is to help clients progress one stage during a brief period of therapy. If the client moves relatively quickly, then we can help the client progress two stages. The results to date indicate that if clients progress one stage in 1 month, they almost double their chances of taking effective action by 6 months. If they progress two stages, they triple their chances of taking effective action (Prochaska et al., in press). Setting realistic goals can enable many more people to enter therapy, continue in therapy, progress in therapy, and continue to progress after therapy.

The first results reported from England, where the 6,000 health professionals have been trained in this approach, show a dramatic increase in the morale of the health professionals. They can now see progress with the majority of their patients instead of the failure they saw when immediate action was the only criterion of success. They are much more confident that they have treatments that can match the stage of all of their patients rather than just the 20% or so who are prepared to take immediate action. As I teach my students, the models of therapy that we choose should be good for our mental health as well as the mental health of our clients. After all, we are involved in therapy for a lifetime whereas most of our clients are involved for only a brief time.

As managed care organizations move toward briefer and briefer therapies, there is a danger that most health professionals will feel pressured to produce immediate action. If the pressure they feel is then transferred to patients who are not prepared for action, we will repeat the past: reaching few patients and retaining even fewer. We can help move a majority of patients to progress in relatively brief encounters but only if we set realistic goals for them and for us. Otherwise we risk demoralizing and demotivating both them and ourselves.

**Process**

If we are to help motivate patients to move from one stage to the next, we need to know principles and processes of change that can produce such progress.

*Principle 1.*  The pros of changing must increase in order for people to progress from the precontemplation stage. We found that in 12 out of 12 studies the pros were higher in the contemplation stage than in the precontemplation stage (Prochaska et al., 1994). The pros were assessed using standardized scores from a three- or four-item pros scale contained in a decisional balance measure specific to each of 12 behaviors. This pattern held true across 12 problem behaviors: cocaine, use, smoking, delinquency, obesity, inconsistent condom use, unsafe sex, sedentary lifestyle, high-fat diet, sun exposure, radon testing, mammography screening, and the practice of behavioral medicine (by physicians). It also held true for the views of psychotherapy among patients with behavioral problems amenable to psychotherapeutic treatment. Those in the precontemplation stage perceived the cons of psychotherapy as outweighing the pros. Those in the contemplation stage perceived the pros and cons as about equal, reflecting their ambivalence. Those in action or maintenance stage were convinced the pros of therapy clearly outweighed the cons.

Here is a technique we use in our population-based programs. Ask patients in the precontemplation stage to tell you all the benefits or pros of making a change, such as starting to exercise. They typically can list four or five. Let them know there are 8 to 10 times that amount. Challenge them to double or triple their list for your next meeting. If they find many more motives, like a healthier heart, healthier lungs, more energy, a healthier immune system, better moods, less stress, a better sex life, and enhanced self-esteem, they will be more motivated to seriously contemplate changing.

*Principle 2.* The cons of changing must decrease for people to progress from contemplation to action. In 12 out of 12 studies, we found that the cons of changing were lower in the action than in the contemplation stage (Prochaska et al., 1994). The cons were assessed using standardized scores from a three- or four-item cons scale contained in a decisional balance measure specific to each of the 12 behaviors.

*Principle 3.* The pros and cons must cross over for people to be prepared to take action. In 12 out of 12 studies, the cons of changing were higher than the pros in the precontemplation stage, but in 11 out of 12, the pros were higher than the cons in the action stage. The one exception was a study on quitting cocaine, and that study's population was the only one to contain a large percentage of inpatients. We interpret this exception to mean that the actions of inpatient cocaine addicts may be more under the social controls of residential care than under their self-control. At a minimum, their pattern would not bode well for immediate discharge.

It should be noted that if we used raw scores to assess the patterns of pros and cons, we would often find that the pros of changing were higher than the cons, even for people in precontemplation. It is only when we used standardized scores that we found a clear pattern in which the cons of changing were always higher than the pros for those people. This means that, compared with their peers in other stages, people in the precontemplation stage underestimate the pros and overestimate the cons. Of course, they are not likely to be particularly conscious of making these mistakes, as they do not know how they compare with their peers.

It should also be noted that as soon as the pros and cons of changing are assessed by means of three or four pro items and three or four con items, clients are immediately given intervention feedback on these key principles. Such feedback is tailored by computers to match the assessment of the particular individual. One patient in precontemplation may be told of the need to increase his or her appreciation of the pros of changing. Another might be told that his or her estimation of the pros is sufficiently high to warrant progression to the contemplation stage. These show how TTM assessments are integral aspects of TTM treatments.

*Principle 4.* The strong principle of progress holds that, for an individual to progress from precontemplation to effective action, the pros of changing must increase one standard deviation (Prochaska, 1994a).

*Principle 5.* The weak principle of progress holds that, for an individual to progress from contemplation to effective action, the cons of changing must decrease one half standard deviation.

Because the pros of changing must increase twice as much as the cons decrease, we place twice as much emphasis on the benefits of changing as on the costs. What is striking here is that we believe we have discovered mathematical principles for how much positive motivations must increase and how much negative motivations must decrease. Such principles can produce much more sensitive assessments for guiding our interventions, giving us and our patients feedback that accurately indicates when

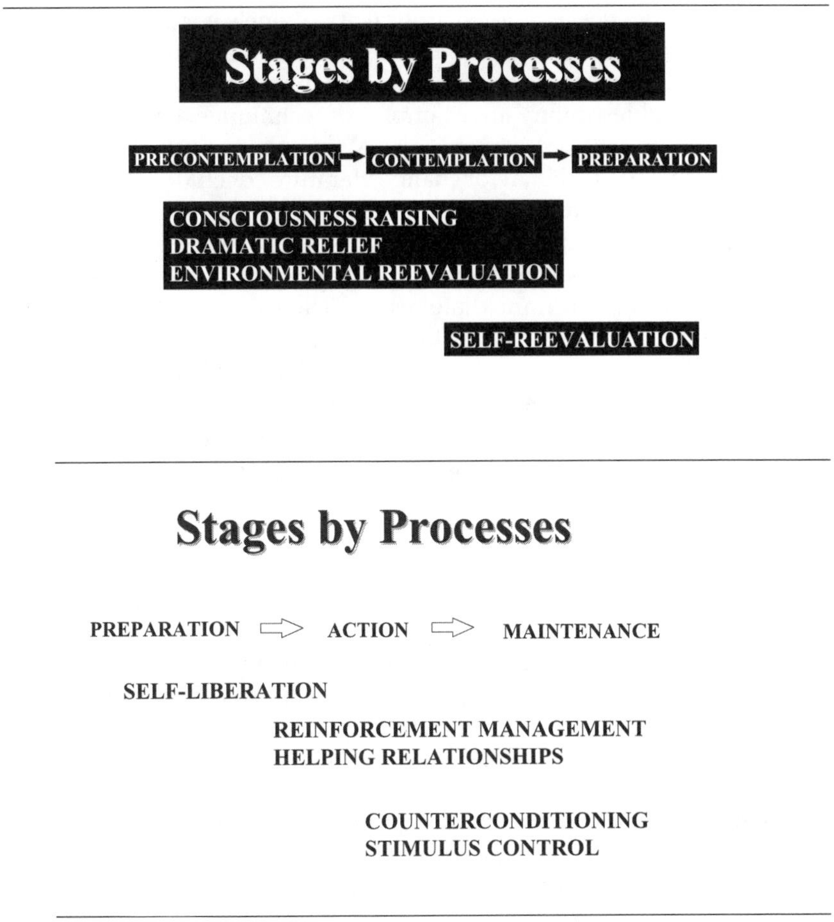

# Stages by Processes

PRECONTEMPLATION → CONTEMPLATION → PREPARATION

CONSCIOUSNESS RAISING
DRAMATIC RELIEF
ENVIRONMENTAL REEVALUATION

SELF-REEVALUATION

# Stages by Processes

PREPARATION ⇨ ACTION ⇨ MAINTENANCE

SELF-LIBERATION

REINFORCEMENT MANAGEMENT
HELPING RELATIONSHIPS

COUNTERCONDITIONING
STIMULUS CONTROL

FIG. 4.3. Stages by processes of change.

therapeutic efforts are producing progress and when they are failing. Together we can modify our methods if we are not seeing as much movement as is needed for becoming adequately prepared for action.

*Principle 6.* We need to match particular processes of change to specific stages of change. Figure 4.3 presents the empirical integration that we have found between processes and stages of change. Guided by this integration we would apply the following processes with patients in precontemplation.

1. *Consciousness raising* involves increased awareness about the causes, consequences, and cures for a particular problem. Interventions that can increase awareness include observations, confrontations, interpretations, feedback, and education (e.g., bibliotherapy). Some techniques, like confrontation, are high risk in terms of retention and are not recommended as much as motivational enhancement methods, like personal feedback about the current and long-term consequences of continuing with the addiction. Increasing the cons of not changing is the corollary of raising the pros of changing. Clearly, therefore, consciousness raising is partly designed to increase the pros of changing.

2. *Dramatic relief* involves emotional arousal about one's current behavior and relief that can come from changing. Fear, inspiration, guilt, and hope are some of the emotions that can move people to contemplate changing. Psychodrama, role-playing, grieving, and personal testimony are examples of techniques that can move people emotionally.

We should note that earlier behavior change literature concluded that interventions like education and fear arousal did not motivate behavior change. Unfortunately, many interventions were evaluated by their ability to move people to immediate action. Processes like consciousness raising and dramatic relief are intended to move people to contemplation, not immediate action. Therefore, we should assess their effectiveness by whether they produce the progress they are expected to produce. Fortunately, practitioners never stopped believing that education and emotion can move people to action, in spite of what some studies said.

3. *Environmental reevaluation* combines both affective and cognitive assessments of how an addiction impacts one's social environment and how changing would influence that environment. Empathy training, value clarification, and family or network interventions can facilitate such reevaluation.

Here is brief media intervention aimed at smokers in precontemplation. A man clearly in grief says, "I always feared that my smoking would lead to an early death. I always worried that my smoking would cause lung cancer. But I never imagined it would happen to my wife." Beneath his grieving face appears this statistic: "50,000 deaths per year are caused by passive smoking. The California Department of Health." In 30 seconds we have consciousness raising, dramatic relief, and environmental reevaluation. No wonder such media interventions have been shown to be an important part of California's successful reduction of smoking. Brief therapists need to learn how to communicate such poignant messages to help patients apply appropriate change processes and make progress.

4. *Self-reevaluation* combines both cognitive and affective assessments of one's self-image free from a chronic problem. Imagery, presenting healthier role models, and value clarification are techniques that can move people evaluatively. Clinically, we find people first looking back and reevaluating how they have been as troubled individuals. As they progress into preparation, they begin to develop more of a future focus, imagining more how their life will be free from particular problems.

5. *Self-liberation* is both the belief that one can change and the commitment and recommitment to act on that belief. Techniques that can enhance willpower include making a public rather than merely a private commitment. Motivational research also suggests that people are not as motivated if they only have one choice rather than two (Miller, 1985). Three choices are even better, but the addition of a fourth does not seem to enhance motivation. Wherever possible, we try to provide people with three of the best choices for applying each process. With smoking cessation, for example, we used to believe only one commitment really counted, and that was the commitment to quit cold turkey. We now know there are at least three good choices: (1) cold turkey, (2) nicotine replacement, and (3) nicotine fading. Asking clients to choose which alternative they believe would be most effective for them and which they would be most committed to can enhance their motivation and their self-liberation.

6. *Counterconditioning* requires the learning of healthier behaviors that can substitute for problem behaviors. We just discussed three healthier alternatives to smoking. Earlier we discussed three healthier alternatives for coping with emotional distress

rather than relapsing. Counterconditioning techniques tend to be specific to a particular behavior and include desensitization, assertion, and cognitive counters to irrational self-statements that can elicit distress.

7. *Contingency management* involves the systematic use of reinforcements and punishments to move the person in a particular direction. Because we find that successful self-changers rely much more on reinforcement than punishment, we emphasize reinforcements for progressing rather than punishments for regressing. Contingency contracts, overt and covert reinforcements, and group recognition can be used to increase the probability that healthier responses will be repeated.

To prepare people for the longer term, we teach them to rely more on self-reinforcements then social reinforcements. We find clinically that many clients expect much more reinforcement and recognition from others than what others actively provide. Relatives and friends often take improvement for granted too quickly. Acquaintances typically generate only a couple of positive consequences early in the action stage. Self-reinforcements are obviously much more under self-control and can be given more quickly and consistently when temptations to lapse or relapse are resisted.

8. *Stimulus control* involves modifying the environment to increase cues that prompt healthier responses and decrease cues that are tempting. Avoidance, environmental reengineering (e.g., removal of addictive substances and paraphernalia), and attending self-help groups can provide stimuli that elicit healthier responses and reduce the risk of relapse.

9. *Helping relationships* combine caring, openness, trust, and acceptance as well as support for changing. Rapport building, a therapeutic alliance, counselor calls, buddy systems, sponsors, and self-help groups can be excellent resources for social support. If people become dependent on such support for maintaining change, we need to take care in fading out such support lest termination of therapy becomes a condition for relapsing.

10. *Social liberation* involves giving people more choices and more freedom to live their lives the way they choose. Acceptance of and support for groups that were once stigmatized, such as gay individuals, minority groups, and individuals with mental illness, can help many people live their lives more fully and freely.

Competing theories of therapy have implicitly or explicitly advocated alternative processes for enhancing the motivation to change. Do cognitions move people or do emotions? Are values, decisions, or dedication the most help? Are contingencies what motivate us or are we controlled by environmental conditions or conditioned habits? Or is it the therapeutic relationship that is the common healer across all therapeutic modalities?

Our answer to each of these questions is yes. Therapeutic processes originating from competing theories can be compatible when they are combined in a stage-matched paradigm. Figure 4.3 presents an integration of the stages and processes of change (Prochaska & DiClemente, 1983). With patients in earlier stages of change, we can enhance progress through more experiential processes that produce healthier cognitions, emotions, evaluations, decisions, and commitments. In later stages, we seek to build on such solid preparation by emphasizing more behavioral processes, which can help condition healthier habits, reinforce these habits, and provide physical and social environments that support healthier lifestyles freer from problems.

## Outcomes

What happens when we combine all of these principles and processes of change to help patients and entire populations to move toward action on their problems? We now examine a series of clinical trials applying stage-matched interventions to see what lessons we might learn about the future of behavioral health care.

In our first large-scale clinical trial, we compared four treatments: (1) one of the best home-based, action-oriented cessation programs (standardized); (2) stage-matched manuals (individualized); (3) expert system computer reports plus manuals (interactive); and (4) counselors plus computers and manuals (personalized). We randomly assigned by stage 739 smokers to one of the four treatments (Prochaska et al., 1993).

In the computer condition, participants completed by mail or telephone 40 questions that were entered into our central computers and generated feedback reports. The 40 questions included measures of each of the TTM constructs (stage, decisional balance, temptations, and processes of change), demographics, and problem history. The reports informed participants about their stage of change, their pros and cons of changing, and their use of change processes appropriate to their stages. At baseline, participants were given positive feedback on what they were doing correctly and guidance on which principles and processes they needed to apply more in order to progress. In two progress reports delivered over the next 6 months, participants also received positive feedback on any improvement they made on any of the variables relevant to progressing. So, demoralized and defensive smokers could begin progressing without having to quit and without having to work too hard. Smokers in the contemplation stage could begin taking small steps, like delaying their first cigarette in the morning for an extra 30 minutes. They could choose small steps that would increase their self-efficacy and help them become better prepared for quitting.

In the personalized condition, smokers received four proactive counselor calls over the 6-month intervention period. Three of the calls were based on the computer reports. Counselors reported much more difficulty in interacting with participants without any progress data. Without scientific assessments, it was much harder for both clients and counselors to tell whether any significant progress had occurred since their last interaction.

Figure 4.4 presents point prevalence abstinence rates for each of the four treatment groups over 18 months (treatment ended at 6 months). The two self-help manual conditions paralleled each other for 12 months. At 18 months, the stage-matched manuals moved ahead. This is an example of a *delayed action effect*, which we often observe with stage-matched programs specifically and which others have observed with self-help programs generally. It takes time for participants in early stages to progress all the way to action. Therefore, some treatment effects as measured by action will be observed only after considerable delay. But it is encouraging to find treatments producing therapeutic effects months and even years after treatment ended.

The computer alone and computer plus counselor conditions paralleled each other for 12 months. Then, the effects of the counselor condition flattened out whereas the computer condition effects continued to increase. We can only speculate as to the delayed differences between those two conditions. Participants in the personalized condition may have become somewhat dependent on the social support and social control of the counselor calling. The last call was after the 6-month assessment, and benefits would be observed at 12 months. Termination of the counselors could result in no further progress because of the loss of social support and control. The classic pattern in smoking cessation clinics is rapid relapse beginning as soon as the treatment is

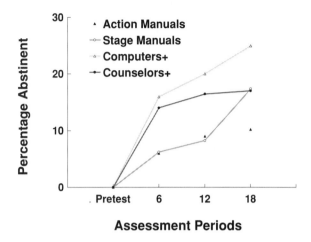

FIG. 4.4.  Abstinence outcomes for four treatment groups over 18 months.

terminated. Some of this rapid relapse could well be due to the sudden loss of social support or social control provided by the counselors and other participants in the clinic.

The next test was to demonstrate the efficacy of the expert system when applied to an entire population recruited proactively. With over 80% of 5,170 smokers participating and fewer than 20% in the preparation stage, we demonstrated significant benefit of the expert system at each 6-month follow-up (Prochaska, Velicer, Fava, Rossi, et al., 2001). Furthermore, the advantages over proactive assessment alone increased at each follow-up for the full 2 years assessed. The implications here are that an expert system intervention in a population can continue to demonstrate benefits long after the intervention has ended.

We then showed remarkable replication of the expert system's efficacy in an HMO population of 4,000 smokers with 85% participation (Prochaska, Velicer, Fava, Ruggiero, et al., 2001). In the first population-based study, the expert system was 34% more effective than assessment alone; in the second, it was 31% more effective. Those replicated differences were clinically significant as well. While working on a population basis, we were able to produce the level of success normally found only in intense clinic-based programs with low participation rates of much more selected samples of smokers. The implication is that once expert systems are developed and show effectiveness with one population, they can be transferred at much lower cost and produce replicable changes in new populations.

The next challenge was to extend the assessment-based expert systems to provide treatments for individuals and populations with alternative problems, like stress. With a national population suffering from stress symptoms, we proactively recruited over 70% ($N = 1,085$) to a single behavior change program for effective stress management (Evers, Johnson, Padula, Prochaska, & Prochaska, 2002). The TTM program involved assessments on each of the TTM constructs to derive each of three expert system–tailored communications over 6 months and a stage-based self-help manual. At the 18-month follow-up, the TTM group had over 60% of the at-risk sample reaching action or maintenance, whereas the control group had only 40%. Compared with studies on smoking cessation, this study produced much more effective action at 6 months in the TTM group (about 60%), and this outcome was maintained over the next 12 months.

*Enhancing Interactive Interventions.* In recent benchmarking research, we have been trying to create enhancements to our expert system to produce even better outcomes. In the first enhancement in our HMO population of smokers, we added a personal handheld computer designed to bring the behavior under stimulus control (Prochaska, Velicer, Fava, Ruggiero, et al., 2001). This commercially successful innovation was an action-oriented intervention that did not enhance our expert system program on a population basis. In fact our expert system alone was twice as effective as the system plus the enhancement. There are two major implications here: (1) More is not necessarily better; and (2) providing interventions that are mismatched to stage can make outcomes markedly worse.

*Counselor Enhancements.* In our HMO population, counselors plus expert system computers outperformed expert systems alone at 12 months. But at 18 months the effectiveness of the counselor enhancement had declined and the effectiveness of the computers alone had increased. Both interventions were producing identical outcomes of 23.2% abstinence, which are excellent for an entire population. Why did the effectiveness of the counselor condition drop after the intervention? Our leading hypothesis is that people can become dependent on counselors for the social support and social monitoring that they provide. Once those social influences are withdrawn, people may do worse. The expert system computers, on the other hand, may maximize self-reliance. In a current clinical trial, we are fading out counselors over time as a method for dealing with dependency on them. If fading is effective, it will have implications for how counseling should be terminated: gradually over time rather than suddenly.

We believe that the most powerful change programs will combine the personalized benefits of counselors and consultants with the individualized, interactive, and data-based benefits of expert system computers. But to date we have not been able to demonstrate that counselors, who are costly but had been our most powerful change agents, can actually add value over computers alone. These findings have clear implications for the cost-effectiveness of expert systems for entire populations needing behavior change programs.

*Interactive Versus Noninteractive Interventions.* Another important aim of the HMO project was to assess whether interactive interventions (computer-generated expert systems) are more effective than noninteractive communications (self-help manuals) when controlling for number of intervention contacts (Velicer, Prochaska, Fava, Laforge, & Rossi, 1999). The interactive programs require scientific assessments at each intervention point and therefore are more costly and demanding than noninteractive interventions. It is essential, therefore, that such assessment-driven interventions be more effective to justify the additional costs and demands. At 6, 12, and 18 months for groups of smokers receiving a series of 1, 2, 3, or 6 interactive versus noninteractive contacts, the interactive interventions (expert system) outperformed the noninteractive manuals in all four comparisons. In three of the comparisons (1, 2, and 3), the difference at 18 months was at least five percentage points, a difference between treatment conditions assumed to be clinically significant. Those results clearly support the hypothesis that interactive interventions will outperform noninteractive interventions when the number of contacts is the same.

Those results support our assumption that the most powerful behavior change programs for entire populations will be interactive. In the reactive clinical literature, it is clear that interactive interventions like behavioral counseling produce greater long-term abstinence rates (20% to 30%) than do noninteractive interventions such as self-help manuals (10% to 20%). It should be kept in mind that these traditional action-oriented programs were implicitly or explicitly recruiting for populations in the preparation stage. Our results indicate that, even with proactively recruited smokers with less than 20% in the preparation stage, the long-term abstinence rates are in the 20% to 30% range for the interactive interventions and in the 10% to 20% range for the noninteractive interventions. The implications are clear. Providing assessment-driven interactive interventions via computers is likely to produce greater outcomes than relying on noninteractive communications, such as newsletters, the media, or self-help manuals.

## Multiple Behavior Change

More than a decade of efforts failed to increase the impact on smoking cessation by increasing the efficacy of the best practice of tailored communications for smoking cessation. Doubling the number of tailored communication contacts and adding telephone counselors, nicotine fading computers, NRT, and tale-communications all failed to increase abstinence.

Faced with a real ceiling on recruitment and a practical ceiling on efficacy, the impact has not improved since the first population-based clinical trial more than a decade ago. One potential alternative was to treat multiple behaviors in a population, since populations with multiple behavior risks are at greatest risk for chronic disease, disability, and premature death. These populations also account for a disproportionate percentage of health care costs. The best estimates are that about 60% of health care costs are due to about 15% of the population, all of whom have multiple behavior risks (Eddington, 2001).

The research literature indicates that changing multiple behaviors on a population basis would be a particularly risky test. A thorough literature review funded by the Robert Wood Johnson Foundation failed to find adequate evidence for the consistent efficacy of treating multiple behaviors (Orleans et al., 2002). Ebrahim & Smith (1997) also failed to find support for multiple behavior interventions, and they concluded that "such interventions implemented through standard health channels have limited use in the general population" (p. 1666). The established wisdom in disease management has been that it is not possible to successfully treat multiple behaviors simultaneously because it places too many demands on a population (Patterson, 2001).

The literature to date, however, was limited by reliance on the action paradigm, the frequent use of quasi-experimental designs, and the lack of applying the most promising interventions, such as interactive and individualized, stage-based, tailored communications (Orleans et al., 2002). Applying the action paradigm to multiple behaviors would indeed risk overwhelming populations, since the action stage is the most demanding, and taking action on two or more behaviors at once could be too difficult. Also, among individuals with four risky behaviors, like smoking, high-fat diet, sun exposure, and sedentary lifestyle, fewer than 10% are ready to take action on two or more behaviors (Prochaska & Velicer, 1997). The same thing is true of populations with diabetes who need to change four behaviors (Ruggiero et al., 1997).

Applying the best practices of a stage-based multiple behavior manual and three assessment-driven expert system feedback reports over 12 months, we proactively intervened in a population of parents of teens who were participating in parallel projects at school (Prochaska, Velicer, et al., 2002). First, the study had to demonstrate that it could proactively recruit a high percentage of parents (necessary if the impacts were to be high). This study recruited 83.6% ($N = 2,460$) of the available parents. The treatment group received up to three expert system reports at 0, 6, and 12 months. At 24-month follow-up, the smoking cessation rate was significantly greater in the treatment group (22% abstinent) than in the control group (17%). The parents did even better on diet, with 33.5% progressing to the action or maintenance stage and going from high-fat to low-fat diets, compared with 25.9% of the controls. With sun exposure, 29.7% of the at-risk parents had reached the action or maintenance stage, compared with 18.1% of the controls.

From a population of 5,545 patients from primary care practices, we proactively recruited 65% for a multiple behavior change project. This low recruitment rate, the lowest among all the studies, appeared to be due to patient concerns that project leaders had received their names and phone numbers from their managed care company, which many did not trust.

In this population, mammography screening was also targeted, but most of the women over 50 were in the action or maintenance stage, so the focus was on relapse prevention. Of the four targeted behaviors, significant treatment effects were found for all four. At 24 months, the smoking cessation rate for the treatment group was 25.4% compared with 18% for the controls. With diet, 28.8% of the treatment group had progressed from high-fat to low-fat diets, compared with 19.5% of the control group (Redding et al., 2002). As regards sun exposure, 23.4% of the treatment group were in the action or maintenance stage, compared with 14.4% of the controls. And as for mammography screening, twice as many in the control had relapsed (6%) as in the treatment group (3%).

From a population of patients in Canada with Type 1 and Type 2 diabetes, we proactively recruited 1,040 patients to enter a multiple behavior change program for diabetes self-management (Jones et al., in press). With this population, self-monitoring for blood glucose (SMBG), diet, and smoking were targeted. Patients were randomly assigned to standard care or TTM. The TTM program involved monthly contacts that included three assessments, three expert system reports, three counseling calls, and three newsletter mailings targeted to the participant's stage of change. At the 12-month assessment, the TTM group had significantly more patients in the action or maintenance stage for diet (40.6% vs. 31.8%) and for SMBG (38% vs. 25%). With smoking, 25% of the TTM group were abstinent, compared with 15% of the usual care group. This was not significant because of the statistical power, but the abstinence rate fell within the 22% to 25% range for single and multiple behavior change programs for disease prevention.

From a population of patients in Hawaii with Type 1 and 2 diabetes, we proactively recruited 400 patients to enter a multiple behavior change program for diabetes self-management (Rossi et al., 2002). The same three behaviors were targeted as in the Canada study. The TTM program, however, did not include counselor contacts but did have monthly contacts. At the 12-month assessment, the TTM group had significantly more patients in the action or maintenance stage for diet (24.1% vs. 11.5%) and for SMBG (28% vs. 18%). There were too few smokers to do statistical comparisons, but the abstinence rates were 25.9% for TTM versus 15.9% for the controls.

Though the absolute levels of change for TTM in the Hawaii study were less than those in the Canada study using counselors, the differences compared with usual care were actually greater in the Hawaii study. These informal comparisons across studies suggest that with diabetes management telephone counselors do not by themselves increase the efficacy of tailored communications, a finding consistent with the results of our previous studies on disease prevention.

## Proactive Versus Reactive Results

We believe that the future of behavior change programs lies with stage-matched, proactive, and interactive interventions driven by sensitive assessments. Much greater impacts can be generated by proactive programs because of the much higher participation rates, even if efficacy rates are lower. But we also believe that proactive programs can produce comparable outcomes to traditional reactive programs. It is counterintuitive to believe that comparable outcomes can be produced with people whom we reach out to help as with people who call us for help. But that is what informal comparisons strongly suggest. Comparing 18-month follow-ups for all subjects who received our three expert system reports in our previous reactive study and in our proactive study with a representative population of smokers, we found the abstinence curves to be remarkably similar (Prochaska et al., 1993; Prochaska, Velicer, Fava, Rossi, et al., 2001).

The results with our counseling plus computer conditions were even more impressive. Proactively recruited smokers working with counselors and computers had higher abstinence rates at each follow-up than did the smokers who had called for help (Prochaska et al., 1993, vs. Prochaska, Velicer, Fava, Ruggiero, et al., 2001). Part of the explanation may be that our proactive counseling protocol had been revised and hopefully improved based on previous data and experience. But the main point is that if we reach out and offer people improved behavior change programs that are appropriate for their stage, we probably can produce efficacy or abstinence rates at least equal to those we achieve with people who reach out to us for help. Unfortunately, there is no experimental design that could permit us to randomly assign people to proactive versus reactive recruitment programs. We are left with informal but provocative comparisons.

## APPLICATION TO OTHER PROBLEMS

We presently have behavior change programs in clinical trials funded by the National Institutes of Health. The programs utilize TTM-based expert systems for weight management, depression prevention and management, adherence to lipid-lowering medication, adherence to antihypertensive medication, and domestic violence prevention. Assessments are a key part of all of these programs.

To give a sense of the work involved in developing a validated measure, we here describe the development of the weight management assessments. Six hundred and seventy study participants were recruited from a list of 2,050 adults provided by a market research company. The list included healthy adults (i.e., those without a diagnosis of a chronic disease) between the ages of 18 and 86 years and were representative of the population with respect to age, income, geographic region, population density, and number of household members. A 16-page questionnaire assessed a range of demographic variables and TTM constructs, including stage of change and behavioral indicators for four different health-related behaviors: regular moderate exercise, calorie reduction, dietary fat reduction, and emotional distress management. Principle component analyses of variance and follow-up tests were used to assess the concurrent and construct validity of the measures for each of the TTM constructs (Sarkin, Johnson, Prochaska, & Prochaska, 2001).

Assessments are given at each of the three participant time points in the clinical trials, and the findings determine the individualized normative and ipsative TTM feedback. If the results generated with stress, smoking, and multiple behaviors continue to be replicated and extended to new behaviors, we will be able to produce therapeutic programs that have unprecedented impacts on entire populations.

## CONCLUSION

Assessments based on the TTM are designed for interventions not just for individual patients but for entire populations. This population approach to health requires reliable and valid assessments for each of the core constructs of TTM: the stages of change, the pros and cons of changing, the 10 processes of change, temptations, and self-efficacy. Assessments begin with evaluating the needs of entire at-risk populations to be sure that intervention resources are available for at-risk groups at each stage of change and not just the small minority who are prepared to take action.

Reaching a high percentage of a population requires proactive assessments and a program that reaches out to at-risk people rather than waits for them to come to it, as people in the early stages of change do not typically ask for help. Retaining a high percentage of people who enter treatment requires interventions that can be individually and scientifically matched to the needs of the participants.

Helping participants progress through a program requires repeated assessments over time that generate normative and ipsative feedback about how they are progressing compared with their peers and what steps they can take to continue to progress. The process of behavior change involves applying a series of principles and processes of change that are scientifically assessed and that very with the stage of change. That is, different principles and processes of change have to be assessed and applied at different stages of change. This strategy requires tailored assessments that generate expert feedback appropriate for the needs of each individual. At long-term follow-up, the process has to be assessed by looking at the percentage of participants who have reached the action and maintenance stages and are relatively free from the problem.

Based on clinical and population trials to date, we conclude that unprecedented impacts on entire populations can be produced if the following scientific and professional shifts occur:

- From an action paradigm to a stage paradigm.
- From reactive recruitment to proactive recruitment.
- From expecting participants to match the characteristics of the program to using scientific assessments to match interventions to the needs of each individual.
- From clinic-based programs to population-based programs that still apply the field's most powerful individualized and interactive assessments and treatment strategies.
- From interventions based on clinical judgments to treatments based on scientific assessments and statistical decision-making.

## REFERENCES

Beitman, B. D., Beck, N. C., Deuser, W., Carter, C., Davidson, J., & Maddock, R. (1994). Patient stages of change predicts outcome in a panic disorder medication trial. *Anxiety, 1,* 64–69.

Brogan, M. M., Prochaska, J. O., & Prochaska, J. M. (1999). Predicting termination and continuation status in psychotherapy by using the transtheoretical model. *Psychotherapy, 36,* 105–113.

COMMIT Research Group. (1995). COMMunity Intervention Trial for Smoking Cessation (COMMIT): 1. Cohort results from a four-year community intervention. *American Journal of Public Health, 85*, 183–192.

Ebrahim, S., & Smith, G. D. (1997). Systematic review of randomized controlled trials of multiple risk factor interventions for preventing coronary heart disease. *British Medical Journal, 314*, 1666–1674.

Eddington, D. W. (2001). Emerging research: A view from one research center. *American Journal of Health Promotion, 15*, 341–369.

Ennett, S. T., Tabler, N. S., Ringwolt, C. L., & Fliwelling, R. L. (1994). How effective is drug abuse resistance education? A meta-analysis of Project DARE outcome evaluations. *American Journal of Public Health, 84*, 1394–1401.

Evers, K. E., Johnson, J. L., Padula, J. A., Prochaska, J. M., & Prochaska, J. O. (2002). Stress management development for transtheoretical constructs of decisional balance and confidence. *Annals of Behavioral Medicine*, S24.

Glasgow, R. E., Terborg, J. R., Hollis, J. F., Severson, H. H., & Boles, S. M. (1995). Take Heart: Results from the initial phase of a work-site wellness program. *American Journal of Public Health, 85*, 209–216.

Jones, J., Edwards, L., Vallis, M. T., Ruggiero, L., Rossi, S., Rossi, J. S., Greene, G., Prochaska, J.O., and Zinman, B. (in press). Changes in diabetes self-care behaviors make a difference to glycemic control: The Diabetes Stages of Change (DiSC) study. *Health Education*.

Lam, C. S., McMahon, B. T., Priddy, D. A., & Gehred-Schultz, A. (1988). Deficit awareness and treatment performance among traumatic head injury adults. *Brain Injury, 2*, 235–242.

Lando, H. A., Pechacek, T. F., Pirie, P. L., et al. (1995). Changes in adult cigarette smoking in the Minnesota Heart Health Program. *American Journal of Public Health, 85*, 201–208.

Levesque, D. A., Gelles, R. J., & Velicer, W. F. (2000). Development and validation of stages of change measure for men in battered treatment. *Cognitive Therapy and Research, 24*, 175–199.

Lichtenstein, E., & Hollis, J. (1992). Patient referral to smoking cessation programs: Who follows through? *Journal of Family Practice, 34*, 739–744.

Luepker, R. V., Murray, D. M., Jacobs, D. R., et al. (1994). Community education for cardiovascular disease prevention: Risk factor changes in the Minnesota Heart Health Program. *American Journal of Public Health, 84*, 1383–1393.

Mannock, T. J., Levesque, D. A., & Prochaska, J. M. (2002). Assessing readiness of clients with disabilities to engage in job seeking behavior. *Journal of Rehabilitation, 68*, 16–23.

Marlatt, G. A., & Gordon, J. R. eds. (1985). Relapse Prevention, New York: Guilford Press.

McConnaughy, E. A., DiClemente, C. C., Prochaska, J. O., & Velicer, W. F. (1989). Stages of change in psychotherapy: A follow–up report. *Psychotherapy, 26*, 494–503.

McConnaughy, E. A., Prochaska, J. O., & Velicer, W. F. (1982). Stages of change in psychotherapy: Measurement and sample profiles. *Psychotherapy: Theory, Research and Practice, 20*, 358–357.

Mellinger, G. D., Balter, M. B., Uhlenhuth, E. H., Cisin, I. H., & Parry, H. J. (1978). Psychic distress, life crisis, and use of psychotherapeutic medicines: National Household Survey data. *Archives of General Psychiatry, 35*, 1045–1052.

Miller, W. R. (1985). Motivation for treatment: a review with special emphasis on alcoholism. *Psychological Bulletin, 98*, 84–107.

Orleans, C. T., Prochaska, J. O., Redding, C. A., Rossi, J. S., & Rimer, B. (2002, April). *Multiple behavior change for cancer prevention and diabetes management*. Symposium presented at the Society for Behavior Medicine, Washington, DC.

Patterson, R. (2001). *Changing patient behavior: Improving outcomes in health and disease management*. San Francisco: Jossey-Bass.

Prochaska, J. O. (1994a). Strong and weak principles for progressing from precontemplation to action based on twelve problem behaviors. *Health Psychology, 13*, 47–51.

Prochaska, J. O. (1994b). Why do we behave the way we do? *Canadian Journal of Cardiology, 11*(Suppl. A), 20A–25A.

Prochaska, J. O. (1996). A stage paradigm for integrating clinical and public health approaches to smoking cessation. *Addictive Behaviors, 21*, 721–732.

Prochaska, J. O. (1997). A Revolution in health promotion: Smoking cessation as a case study. In R. J. Resnick & R. H. Rozensky (Eds.), *Health psychology through the lifeSpan: Practice and research opportunities*. (pp. 361–376). Washington, DC: American Psychological Association.

Prochaska, J. O., & DiClemente, C. C. (1983). Stages and processes of self-change of smoking: Toward an integrative model of change. *Journal of Consulting and Clinical Psychology, 51*, 390–395.

Prochaska, J. O., DiClemente, C. C., & Norcross, J. C. (1992). In search of how people change: Applications to the addictive behaviors. *American Psychologist, 47*, 1102–1114.

Prochaska, J. O., DiClemente, C. C., Velicer, W. F., & Rossi, J. S. (1993). Standardized, individualized, interactive and personalized self-help programs for smoking cessation. *Health Psychology, 12*, 399–405.

Prochaska, J. O., & Velicer, W. F. (1997). The transtheoretical model of health behavior change. *American Journal of Health Promotion, 12*, 38–48.

Prochaska, J. O., Velicer, W. F., Fava, J. L., Rossi, J. S., & Tsoh, J. Y. (2001). Evaluating a population-based recruitment approach and a stage-based expert system intervention for smoking cessation. *Addictive Behaviors, 26*, 583–602.

Prochaska, J. O., Velicer, W. F., Fava, J., Ruggiero, L., Laforge, R., & Rossi, J. S. (2001). Counselor and stimulus control enhancements of a stage matched expert system for smokers in a managed care setting. *Preventive Medicine, 32*, 23–32.

Prochaska, J. O., Velicer, W. F., Prochaska, J. M., & Johnson, J. (in press). Size, consistency and stability of stage effects for smoking cessation. *Addictive Behaviors.*

Prochaska, J. O., Velicer, W. F., Rossi, J. S., Goldstein, M. G., Marcus, B. H., Rakowski, W., et al. (1994). Stages of change and decisional balance for twelve problem behaviors. *Health Psychology, 13*, 39–46.

Prochaska J. O., Velicer, W. F., Rossi, J. S., Redding, C. A., Greene, G. W., Rossi, S. R., et al. (2002). Impact of simultaneous stage-matched expert systems for multiple behaviors in a population of parents [Abstract]. *Annals of Behavioral Medicine, 24*, S191.

Redding, C. A., Prochaska, J. O., Goldstein, M., Velicer, W. F., Rossi, J. S., Sun, X., et al. (2002). Efficacy of stage-matched expert systems in primary care patients to decrease smoking, dietary fat, sun exposure and relapse from mammography [Abstract]. *Annals of Behavioral Medicine, 24*, S191.

Reed, G. R., Velicer, W. F., Prochaska, J. O., Rossi, J. S., & Marcus, B. H. (1997). What makes a good staging algorithm: Examples from regular exercise. *American Journal of Health Promotion, 12*, 57–67.

Rossi, J. S. (1992). *Stages of change for 15 health risk behaviors in an HMO population.* Paper presented at 13th meeting of the Society for Behavioral Medicine, New York.

Rossi, J. S., Ruggiero, L., Rossi, S., Greene, G., & Prochaska, J. O. (2002). Multiple behaviors changes for diabetes self-management. *Annals of Behavioral Medicine, 24*, S191 (abstract).

Ruggiero, L., Glasgow, R. E., Dryfoos, J. M., Rossi, J. S., Prochaska, J. O., Orleans, C. T., et al. (1997). Diabetes self-management. *Diabetes Care, 4*, 568–576.

Sarkin, J. A., Johnson, S. S., Prochaska, J. O., & Prochaska, J. M. (2001). Applying the transtheoretical model to regular moderate exercise in an overweight population: Validation of a stage of change measure. *Preventive Medicine, 33*, 462–464.

Snow, M. G., Prochaska, J. O., & Rossi, J. S. (1992). Stages of change for smoking cessation among former problem drinkers: A cross-sectional analysis. *Journal of Substance Abuse, 4*, 107–116.

U.S. Department of Health and Human Services. (1990). *The health benefits of smoking cessation: A report of the Surgeon General* (DHHS Publication No. CDC 90-8416). Washington, DC: U.S. Government Printing Office.

Velicer, W. F., Prochaska, J. O., Fava, J., Laforge, R., & Rossi, J. (1999). Interactive versus non-interactive and dose response relationships for stage matched smoking cessation programs in a managed care setting. *Health Psychology, 18*, 21–28.

Veroff, J., Douvan, E., & Kulka, R. A. (1981). *Mental health in America.* New York: Basic Books.

Wierzbicki, M., & Pekarik, G. (1993). A meta-analysis of psychotherapy dropout. *Professional Psychology: Research and Practice, 29*, 190–195.

# Use of Psychological Tests for Assessing Treatment Outcomes

Michael J. Lambert
Eric J. Hawkins
*Brigham Young University*

The assessment of treatment outcomes is a branch of applied psychology that measures the effectiveness of therapeutic strategies and interventions. Though outcomes assessment has been done since the inception of psychotherapy in one form or another (e.g., case study), there has been a considerable focus on it during the 1990s. In response to policy and financial pressures, the beneficial effects of mental health services have been subjected to scrutiny. Although historically the measurement of therapeutic interventions was left mostly to outcome researchers, such measurement has recently become the responsibility of clinical agencies in order to support their efforts and demonstrate their effectiveness. A critical component of the assimilation of this information is the selection of an appropriate instrument.

To introduce this discussion, we provide a brief history of outcomes assessment that highlights the major changes that have occurred in the measurement of psychological distress. We end the introduction with an evaluation of the current status of outcome measures. Much of this chapter is devoted to the principle factors that inform the selection of an appropriate instrument. The very diversity and abundance of available outcome measures makes such a choice challenging. Additionally, because not all assessment instruments measure the same way, a user must carefully consider which instrument is selected for estimating patient change. To facilitate the selection process, we offer a scheme to conceptualize outcome measures that includes the following test characteristics: content, level of assessment, source, technology, and time orientation. Following the discussion of this conceptual scheme, we provide strategies for evaluating the estimates of change. We conclude the chapter with a discussion of particular advances made in the history of outcomes assessment and areas that deserve further attention.

## AN OVERVIEW OF OUTCOMES ASSESSMENT

The problems associated with assessing the changing psychological status of patients are, as Luborsky (1971) suggested, a "hardy perennial" in the field of psychotherapy. Historically, psychotherapists have devoted themselves to defining and perfecting treatments rather than systematically assessing the consequences of these treatments.

In contrast, personality psychologists have been more interested in static traits and stability than in change. Although occasional exceptions to this trend can be found (e.g., Worchel & Byrne, 1964), minimal effort has been expended on developing measures for the purpose of measuring change. Moreover, there was little scientific rigor in the earliest attempts to quantify treatment gains. The field has gradually moved from complete reliance on therapist ratings of gross and general improvement to the use of outcome indices of specific symptoms that are quantified from a variety of viewpoints, including the patient, outside observers, relatives, physiological indices, and environmental data such as employment records. Although the data generated from these multiple perspectives are not impervious to methodological limitations, this approach represented an improvement over previous measurement methods. The use of operational definitions and the systematic collection of data signified an additional advancement. This improvement not only fostered replications of studies but also allowed researchers to demonstrate the generality of previous findings. Psychotherapy outcomes assessment, with some recent notable exceptions such as the *Consumer Reports* satisfaction survey (Seligman, 1995), has moved from simple posttherapy ratings to complex, multifaceted assessments of change.

In the past, attempts at measuring change reflected the zeitgeist of the period. The assessments used in the early studies were developed from Freudian psychology. These instruments (e.g., Rorschach and TAT) largely have been discarded as measures of outcome because of their poor psychometric qualities, reliance on inference, and emphasis on unconscious processes. Although scoring systems such as Exner's for the Rorschach have reduced some of the psychometric problems associated with projective testing (Wood, Lilienfeld, Garb, & Nezworski, 2000), the time-intensive nature of these measures prohibits repeated use. The employment of these measures was followed by the advent of instruments consistent with client-centered theory (e.g., the Q-sort technique), behaviorism (behavioral monitoring), and, more recently, cognitive theory.

Though prevailing theoretical perspectives are likely to continue to influence the assessment of outcomes, a legacy of the theoretically based examination of change was a seemingly diverse and plentiful pool of measures that made comparison between treatment theories a serious challenge. An outcome measures project sponsored by the Clinical Research Branch of the National Institute of Mental Health (NIMH) attempted to solve this problem. The purpose of this project was to compare the effectiveness of various treatments using a uniform or core battery of instruments (Waskow & Parloff, 1975). The relatively meager results of this attempt led to a resurgence of the core battery notion many years later.

In 1994, the American Psychological Association supported a conference at Vanderbilt University with a similar objective in mind. Three panels of experts convened with the purpose of developing a core battery to measure progress and outcomes in anxiety, mood, and personality disordered individuals. Despite individual panel differences, there were many common themes endorsed by the groups. All three groups supported the use of multiple perspectives. Additionally, each concluded that severity of patient distress, degree of patient impairment, and frequency of specific and critical symptoms represent the domains that are essential for measuring outcomes (Horowitz, Strupp, Lambert, & Elkin, 1997). Moreover, the groups agreed that instruments making up the battery should be psychometrically sound, appropriately normed, theory free, and efficiently adapted to use in clinical settings. Finally, they deemed administration of the battery before, during, and after treatment to be important.

The history of outcomes assessment suggests several recommendations for the use of tests in future research and practice. Some of the more important of these are as follows:

1. Clearly define the construct measured.
2. Measure change from multiple perspectives.
3. Employ different types of rating scales and methods.
4. Employ symptom-based atheoretical measures.
5. Examine, to some extent, patterns of change over time.

These recommendations, which represent an improvement over the past, are discussed in the sections that follow.

## THE CURRENT STATE OF OUTCOMES ASSESSMENT

### Common Measures of Outcome

Although all measures of outcome have inherent weaknesses, one advantage of utilizing widely used instruments is that comparisons between studies examining different interventions are possible. The use of identical measures across studies allows for accurate comparisons of treatment change while controlling for pretreatment levels of distress. Despite this and the recommendations of experts, the application of a core battery remains elusive. In a review of 21 American journals published between 1983 and 1988, Froyd, Lambert, and Froyd (1996) summarized instrument usage data from 334 outcome studies. The most frequently used self-report scales were the Beck Depression Inventory (BDI; Beck, Ward, Mendelson, Mock, & Erbaugh, 1961), the State–Trait Anxiety Inventory (STAI; Spielberger, Gorsuch, Lushene, & Jacobs, 1978), the Symptom Checklist–90–Revised (SCL–90–R; Derogatis, 1983), the Locke-Wallace Marital Adjustment Test (MAI; Locke & Wallace, 1959), and the Minnesota Multiphasic Personality Inventory–2 (MMPI–2; Butcher, Dahlstrom, Graham, Tellegen, & Kaemmer, 1989). A more recent review of studies measuring outcome in the *Journal of Consulting and Clinical Psychology* from 1995 to 2000 reported that the BDI, STAI, SCL–90–R, and Inventory of Interpersonal Problems (IIP; Horowitz, Rosenberg, Baer, Ureno, & Villasenor, 1988) were, in that order, the most commonly used self-report instruments (Farnsworth, Hess, & Lambert, 2001). The results of this review are presented in Table 5.1. They and the results of Froyd et al. (1996) indicate there are some popular measures within the category of self-report instruments.

Although on the surface the results of these reviews suggest some uniformity in instrument choice, further scrutiny reveals a startling conclusion. Of a total of 1,430 outcomes assessment instruments identified by Froyd et al. (1996), 840 were used just once. Unfortunately, the heterogeneous nature of the studies included in this review (e.g., studies on patient diagnosis, treatment modality, and therapy approach) cannot account for the diversity of the measures used. Reviews of studies with similar patient populations and treatment interventions suggest a similar conclusion. For example, Ogles, Lambert, Weight, and Payne (1990) conducted a review of the agoraphobia outcomes literature during the 1980s. Though a majority of the 106 studies included in their review utilized behavioral and cognitive-behavioral interventions, 98 unique

TABLE 5.1

Commonly Used Inventories and Methods of Assessments

| Self-Report (N = 384) | No. of Times Used | % of Total |
|---|---|---|
| Beck Depression Inventory | 40 | 10.4 |
| Experimentor-created scales or questionnaires | 37 | 9.6 |
| Diary behavior and/or thoughts | 27 | 7.0 |
| State–Trait Anxiety Inventory | 14 | 3.6 |
| SCL-90-R | 12 | 3.1 |
| Minnesota Multiphasic Personality Inventory | 6 | 1.6 |
| Dysfunctional Attitude Scale | 6 | 1.6 |
| Hassles Scale | 5 | 1.3 |
| Schedule for Affective Disorders and Schizophrenia | 5 | 1.3 |

| Instrumental (N = 50) | No. of Times Used | % of Total |
|---|---|---|
| Heart rate | 9 | 18 |
| Blood pressure | 7 | 14 |
| Weight | 5 | 10 |
| Saliva composition | 5 | 10 |
| $CO_2$ level | 3 | 6 |
| Respiration rate | 2 | 4 |

| Significant Others | No. of Times Used | % of Total |
|---|---|---|
| Information of specific behavior | 5 | 33 |
| Problem checklist by informant | 6 | 40 |
| Single use of measure of family functioning (e.g., Family Life Symptom Checklist, Family Environment Scale, Family Adjustment Questionnaire) | 3 | 20 |

| Trained Therapist (N = 66) | No. of Times Used | % of Total |
|---|---|---|
| Interview: global or level-of-functioning ratings | 35 | 53 |
| Hamilton Rating Scale for Depression[a] | 14 | 21 |

| Observer (N = 67) | No. of Times Used | % of Total |
|---|---|---|
| Frequency of specific behavior | 13 | 19 |
| Rating of behavior or subject characteristics | 27 | 40.3 |
| Interview of subject | 12 | 17.9 |

Note. From Farnsworth, Hess, & Lambert (2001) by permission of the authors.

[a]This scale also was counted as a trained observer measure when it was administered by someone other than the therapist.

outcome measures were used to assess outcomes. Wells, Hawkins, and Catalano (1988) reported similar conclusions, identifying more than 25 ways to measure drug usage in addiction outcomes research.

The seeming disarray of instruments is partly a function of the complex and multifaceted nature of psychotherapy outcomes, which are influenced by a wide range of clients and problems, a diversity of treatments and underlying assumptions and techniques, and the multidimensionality of the change process itself. The lack of consensus is also indicative of the inability of scientists and practitioners to agree on valued outcomes. The result, it appears, is that measuring the outcomes of psychotherapy promises to be a hardy perennial for years to come.

## Change Is Complex

Regardless of the diagnostic criteria patients meet, most patients in therapy experience a varied set of problems. For example, it is not uncommon for patients diagnosed with depression to also have interpersonal difficulties, anxiety, physical ailments, functional impairment, and quality-of-life concerns. As a result, it is virtually impossible for any single measure to fully assess changes that occur in these domains. Because of the inherent complexity, we can only suggest that researchers begin studying outcomes by identifying major targets of treatment while accepting that the resulting picture of change will be far from complete.

The implications of our incomplete understanding of change are important to acknowledge. First, those who produce as well as consume psychotherapy research, such as the insurance industry and government policymakers, are advised to draw modest conclusions from outcomes research. Second, because of the complexity of psychological distress and its consequences, we believe it is important to employ a conceptual scheme that addresses the primary characteristics of instruments that are developed to measure outcomes.

## CONCEPTUALIZING MEASURES AND METHODS

A number of conceptual frameworks have been proposed to integrate the complex facets relevant to the assessment of outcomes (e.g., Lambert, Ogles, & Masters, 1992; McGlynn, 1996; Rosenblatt & Attkisson, 1993; Schulte, 1995). For example, McLellan and Durell (1996) suggested four areas for assessment: (1) reduction of symptoms; (2) improvement in health and personal and social functioning; (3) cost of care; and (4) reduction in public health and safety threats. On the other hand, Docherty and Streeter (1996) proposed a total of seven dimensions: (1) symptomatology, (2) social/interpersonal functioning, (3) work functioning, (4) satisfaction, (5) treatment utilization, (6) health status/global well-being, and (7) health-related quality of life. These two frameworks are based on a rather broad view of the topic, and include outcome domains related to the delivery and associated cost of mental health services. Though these dimensions of outcome are no doubt important, the conceptual framework discussed in this chapter emphasizes factors more central to the measurement of patient outcomes. We prefer this focus for two reasons. First, the conceptual framework delineated here is presented as a guide to choosing an outcome measure among the many that exist. Outcome instruments, typically, are not the best measures of treatment resources expended, and many alternative indicators exist that can more accurately estimate treatment utilization and related costs (e.g., payroll records, patient

TABLE 5.2
Scheme for Organizing and Conceptualizing Outcome Measures

| Content | Social Level | Source | Technology | Time Orientation |
|---|---|---|---|---|
| Intrapersonal | Self | Global | Cognition | Trait |
| 1 | 1 | 1 | 1 | 1 |
| 2 | 2 | 2 | 2 | 2 |
| * | * | * | * | * |
| Interpersonal | Therapist | Specific | Affect | State |
| 1 | 1 | 1 | 1 | 1 |
| 2 | 2 | 2 | 2 | 2 |
| * | * | * | * | * |
| Social Role | Trained Observer | Observation | Behavior | |
| 1 | 1 | 1 | 1 | |
| 2 | 2 | 2 | 2 | |
| * | * | * | * | |
| | Relevant Other | Status | | |
| | 1 | 1 | | |
| | 2 | 2 | | |
| | * | * | | |

*Note.* The numbers and asterisks below each area represent the notion that there can be subcategories such as types of intrapersonal events, types of interpersonal measures, and so on.

records, and emergency room expenditures). Second, our primary interest is in the assessment of patient outcomes rather than the administrative concerns of treatment providers.

Despite the above difference, the conceptual scheme introduced here has much in common with the frameworks mentioned in the preceding paragraph. Like these, it is absent a theoretical model. The history of outcomes assessment revealed the limitations of theory-based assessments; comparisons between various treatment outcomes were difficult and inconclusive. Moreover, in the purest sense, the assessment of outcomes has little interest in supporting the instruments preferred by specific theoretical backgrounds. Rather, its primary purpose is the empirical evaluation of the efficacy of therapy and the accurate measurement of meaningful change. The merit of an instrument is determined by the extent to which it can accomplish these goals.

To assist in the assessment selection process, Ogles, Lambert, and Masters (1996) introduced a broad conceptual model that proposed that measures can be characterized by their content, social level, source, methodology or technology of data collection, and time frame (see Table 5.2). The remainder of this section discusses each of these factors in detail.

## Content

Outcome measures are typically designed to assess specific domains, traits, or characteristics of individuals that are of interest. In the case of psychotherapy outcomes assessment, these constructs are generally of a psychological nature, such as depression, anxiety, or interpersonal difficulties. The domain that an instrument assesses is referred to as its content. Depending on the scope of the psychological areas of interest, a measure may address a broad area of content (e.g., symptoms of many of the most common psychological disorders) or a rather specific domain (e.g., symptoms relevant to a single disorder). Regardless of the primary content area, three broad domains of interest are represented in most outcomes assessment: cognition, affect, and behavior. Thus, although unique measures of depression and anxiety exist, for example, it is likely that these have in common items that address the cognition, affect, and behavior of depressed and anxious individuals.

Selecting an outcomes assessment instrument is contingent on the constructs that one wishes to measure. In addition to choosing a measure that emphasizes a psychological domain of interest, the user must determine the components of this domain that are important. Are cognition, affect, and behavior of equal interest or would a measure that emphasizes behavior be more useful. In general, and to the extent possible, all three areas should be considered essential to a complete study of change.

## Level of Social Focus

The second dimension listed in Table 5.2 is entitled *Social Level,* and this term refers to areas of social functioning that are often addressed by outcome measures. This dimension is divided into intrapersonal, interpersonal, and social role performance. Thus, social level reflects changes that occur within the client, in the client's interpersonal relationships, and in the client's participation in the community through social roles. It can be considered a continuum, ranging from qualities inherent in the individual (e.g., subjective discomfort, intrapsychic attributes, and bodily experiences) to characteristics of the individual's participation in the interpersonal world of intimate contacts and the degree to which the individual participates in work and leisure activities. The results of outcome studies are generally considered more impressive when multiple levels of social focus are measured, in part, because changes in social functioning can help determine whether individual progress is deemed meaningful in the context of society.

Social level has important implications for the measure of change in outcomes assessment because it tends to be a reflection of the values and interests of clients, mental health providers, third-party payers, government agencies, and society at large (Strupp & Hadley, 1977). A resulting weakness of these influences is that outcome measures have overwhelming emphasized the intrapersonal level (74%) at the expense of the interpersonal (17%) and social role performance level (9%; Froyd et al., 1996).

Like for the content dimension, users must determine which level or levels of social assessment matter most. Although the literature suggests that most instruments target individual change, it is important to understand the social level actually assessed and the inherent value-judgments associated with this level. In addition to limiting the conclusions one can make about treatment gains, the social level of assessment provides support for the merits of treatment. Having addressed the components that define the social level of outcomes assessment, we turn to a discussion of the specific sources that can contribute to the measurement of change.

## Source

In the ideal study of change, all of the parties who have information about a client's progress are represented, including the client, therapist, relevant (significant) others, trained judges (or observers), and societal agencies that collect information, such as employment and educational data. A multiplicity of sources is considered superior because of the validity it lends to the estimates of change. Two or more judgments of improvement are more credible than a single one. Furthermore, there is less concern about the potential bias of independent sources of data, such as ratings provided by individuals independent of the therapeutic intervention (Smith, Glass, & Miller, 1980). Based on the extant literature, there is good reason to be cautious about interpreting the results of outcome studies employing single and potentially biased perspectives.

The practice of applying multiple measures in research studies has made it clear that multiple measures from different sources do not yield unitary results (Lambert, 1983). Indeed, relying on different sources of assessment can result in questionable conclusions. For example, a specific treatment used to reduce fears may result in a decrease in behavioral avoidance of the feared object (information provided by observers) while having seemingly little effect on the self-reported level of discomfort associated with the feared object (Mylar & Clement, 1972; Ross & Proctor, 1973; Wilson & Thomas, 1973). Conversely, despite marked improvement in self-reported fear, an intervention may have no effect on a physiological indicator of fear (Ogles et al., 1990). In a review of the effects of relaxation training, Glaister (1982) found a similar departure from agreement. Compared to exposure techniques, relaxation training primarily affected physiological indices of change, proving superior to other treatments in 11 of 12 outcome comparisons. In contrast, according patients' verbal reports of self-improvement, exposure techniques were superior in 28 of 38 comparisons. However, behavioral assessments of change that included assessor ratings revealed no differences between the relaxation and exposure conditions.

The lack of convergence between measurement methods is further supported by factor analytic studies that have examined the agreement between numerous outcome measures (Cartwright, Kirtner, & Fiske, 1963; Forsyth & Fairweather, 1961; Gibson, Snyder, & Ray, 1955; Shore, Massimo, & Ricks, 1965). Pilkonis, Imber, Lewis, and Rubinsky (1984) collected trait and symptom data from clients, therapists, expert judges, and significant others using 15 different scales. A factor analysis of these data reduced to three factors more closely representing the source of the data rather than the content of the scales.

Having made a case for multiple sources and methods, we acknowledge that the implementation of such an approach is unrealistic in many settings. Although obtaining ratings from therapists, trained raters, significant others, and those removed from the therapeutic setting is ideal, there are considerable associated costs. Moreover, it is often impractical to obtain assessments from others given the additional effort required from already burdened parties (e.g., therapists). Finally, it is arguably the patients' perspective that matters most (Ogles, Lambert, & Fields, 2002). Thus, it is perhaps not surprising that the most popular source for outcome data has been the client.

Lambert and McRoberts (1993) examined the assessment sources of 116 outcome studies reported in the *Journal of Consulting and Clinical Psychology* between 1986 and 1991. The outcome measures used in these studies were classified into five source categories: self-report, trained observer, significant other, therapist, and instrumental (e.g., societal records and physiological recording devices). A self-report scale was used alone or in combination in over 90% of the studies (25% employed client self-report data as the single source for evaluation). Combinations of 2 data sources—self-report and observer ratings, self-report and therapist ratings, self-report and instrumental— were utilized in 20%, 15%, and 8% of the studies, respectively. Significant other ratings were rarely employed; they were used alone or in combination with other data sources in approximately 9% of the reviewed studies. In contrast to the general pattern, 30% of the studies used 6 or more instruments to assess changes in patients. The most ambitious effort used a combination of 12 distinct measures to assess changes following psychotherapy.

The agreement in findings appears to rely more on the source of the obtained data than the constructs purportedly measured by the outcome instruments. The lack of consensus between sources of outcome measures coupled with the financial and practical consequences associated with implementing multiple sources of data presents a challenging dilemma. Thus, it is important for researchers and clinicians alike to consider the advantages of diverse perspectives while acknowledging the consequences of using a single source. Given the importance of assessing the patients' perspective of change, we believe the essential issue is not whether the patients' perspective is obtained but whether additional sources are included in the assessment. The development of easily administered, inexpensive, and multiple sourced measures of outcome is a task for future research.

### Technology of Change Measures

In addition to selecting different sources to evaluate change, the technology (methodology) used to develop measures impacts the assessment of change (Smith et al., 1980). Table 5.2 lists several different technologies or procedures that have been employed in the measurement of outcomes. These include procedures to gather global information (e.g., global ratings that inclde measures of client satisfaction), specific information (e.g., specific symptom indexes), observational information (e.g., behavioral counts), and status information (e.g., physiological and institutional measures).

Because procedures for collecting data on patient change vary simultaneously on several dimensions, it is difficult to isolate the aspect of the measurement approach that may be the most important. However, our intent in this chapter is to address technological factors in isolation. Consequently, we purposely ignore the complex relationship that often exists between technology and the other dimensions used to categorize outcome measures. An underlying limitation relevant to the technology of measures is the extent to which raters of outcomes are able to consciously manipulate their responses. We use this characteristic to provide a context to address the advantages and disadvantages inherent in global, specific, behavioral, and institutional assessments of outcome.

Traditionally, global ratings of outcome consisted of a general construct that reflects the overall severity of patient distress. Generally, patients are requested to respond to questions that broadly assess their progress in treatment, but therapists and significant others can also provide these ratings. Moreover, global ratings typically provide a summary evaluation of a complex area of patient functioning such as treatment improvement or general well-being using one or a few items. (e.g., "Therapy helped me feel less distressed"). There are number of advantages of using a global approach. First, complex constructs can be assessed with a few items. Because global ratings are easily designed, they serve as a flexible approach to measure nearly any construct of interest (Kazdin, 1998). In addition, global ratings are adaptable to various sources of outcome data.

However, global measures are not without their limitations. Because global measures are usually face valid (questions ask specifically about improvement), it is not difficult for respondents to consciously manipulate their responses. Furthermore, because the construct of interest is global, only general conclusions can be drawn from the findings. The lack of psychometric qualities is an additional limitation of most global ratings. As a result, it is frequently unclear whether a global rating is measuring what it purports to measure. A survey completed by Consumer Reports (1995) represents a typical global measure. The findings of this survey indicated that respondents benefited greatly from psychotherapy; however, the psychometric properties, or lack thereof, of the items used in this survey prevent definitive conclusions about the meaning of the findings (Jacobson & Christensen, 1996). Although historically many of these deficiencies have been relevant, more recently a number of measures meeting the global rating objective of an overall assessment of outcome have been developed. Unlike the traditional development of global ratings, these instruments utilize a number of items, usually 30 to 70, to address the severity of patient distress. Furthermore, these newer instruments have been subjected to the scrutiny of psychometric testing (Ogles et al., 2002).

In contrast to global measures, specific ratings assess particular or multiple psychological constructs of interest. In addition, they tend to use a number of items to measure the construct of interest, and there is usually psychometric information demonstrating their reliability and validity. Although they are somewhat longer than global ratings, their brevity facilitates the administration procedure. The mode of assessment for many of these specific scales is self-report, which is conducive to the accumulation of information that only patients can provide. Consequently, specific assessments typically provide clinically relevant and meaningful information (Ogles et al., 2002).

Like global scales, specific scales of outcome are subject to distortion. Many of these instruments are face valid and rely on self-report. However, because these scales focus the raters' attention on the status of specific symptoms and signs, as opposed to general questions about the benefits of therapy, there is likely less risk of patients' distorting their responses. They also produce more complicated assessment of functioning because patient ratings across many items can show areas of improvement and deterioration within a single scale.

The frequency with which specific behaviors are performed is often of relevance to treatment goals. Provided that observer ratings have little influence on the behavior of those watched, such ratings offer an objective assessment of the individual's behavior. An advantage of observational procedures is that the actual behavior of the person can be observed in the context of realistic situations, allowing generalization of the effects of treatment to the person's natural environment. In addition, behaviors of interest can be formally defined and customized to the individual's presenting concerns.

Although observational approaches to outcomes assessment remain among the most relevant, there are limitations to their use. Change in cognition and affect is frequently of interest as well, two constructs that are essentially unobservable by others. Furthermore, some overt behaviors occur infrequently (e.g., particular phobias) or are not typically performed in public (e.g., sexual performance). In addition, it is not always accurate to assume that the performance of an individual in a single situation is representative of how that person customarily interacts.

The last approach to be introduced involves the use of procedures to gather status information, which for the sake of this discussion will be taken to include physiological and institutional information. For example, devices that measure physiological arousal (e.g., heart rate, blood pressure) can be used to determine the effectiveness of treatments designed to reduce symptoms of anxiety. Status information is only minimally subject to distortion, but the cost of assessment equipment and the expertise required to operate it are obstacles to the use of this approach. Also, though individuals are less able to consciously manipulate their responses to physiological measuring devices, care must be taken to ensure that the measurement setting has not affected estimates of outcome. Furthermore, as with many measures of outcome, it is important to scrutinize the construct validity of physiological assessments (Tomarken, 1995).

Institutional outcome information is perhaps least subject to distortion. An example is the information in agency records that is relevant to the construct of interest. For instance, juvenile criminal records subsequent to a therapeutic intervention can be reviewed to evaluate the success of treatment. A particular advantage of using institutional information is that overt behavior can be evaluated in the absence of purposeful distortion. In addition to being relevant to the individual receiving treatment, such information is often relatively simple to generalize to society. However, in the case of institutional assessments, specific indicators of outcome are subject to the data collected and may represent a combination of many related constructs, including the accuracy of the data (e.g., arrest records).

The four approaches described in this section were presented in order of their susceptibility to manipulation by the individual being rated. The discussion also included a description of strengths and limitations of these four basic approaches for measuring outcomes. These approaches also differ in their degree of flexibility. The global rating approach provides the evaluator with the most freedom, requiring only the construction of a few items that purportedly measure the desired construct. In contrast, the status rating approach is the least flexible, as the evaluator is confined to the precision of developed instruments or the availability and relevancy of collected data. A careful weighing of the procedural strengths and limitations of these approaches will facilitate the selection of an appropriate outcome measure and strengthen the credibility of the resulting data.

## Time Orientation

The final characteristic introduced to conceptualize instruments is time orientation. An instrument's time orientation determines whether the instrument measures psychological traits or states. Traits are enduring characteristics that tend to distinguish one individual from another whereas states are temporary. Instruments that assess less malleable individual qualities (traits) are designed for infrequent use, for example, pre- and posttreatment, provided that the length of the time between measurements allows for change in these qualities. In contrast, more frequent assessments are possible with instruments developed to measure states. Such instruments also allow researchers to study patterns of change over time, as they can be used repeatedly during psychotherapy.

The preceding discussion introduced five dimensions that characterize outcome instruments. The content dimension encompasses the psychological constructs measured by an instrument, whereas the social dimension concerns the level of social focus, which ranges from an emphasis on self to an emphasis on general social roles. The source of the data and the type of procedure used to develop outcome measures, along with its susceptibility to distortion, are also important. Finally, we proposed a dimension, time orientation, that represents the stability of the constructs measured. Whereas enduring psychological constructs are not conducive to the assessment of change, more transitory constructs can be measured repeatedly to evaluate progress.

A consideration of the strengths and limitations of these dimensions can facilitate the selection of an outcomes assessment instrument. Furthermore, we believe that they can help the user of an instrument make accurate and meaningful interpretations of the test data. Because of the importance of the last dimension introduced, time orientation, we include a related discussion regarding the sensitivity of outcome instruments.

## Sensitivity to Change

A central issue in outcomes assessment is the degree to which different measures and measurement methods are likely to reflect changes that actually occur as a result of participation in therapy. Many factors influence the sensitivity of the items composing a measure, including the relevancy, scaling approach, stability of constructs assessed, and ability of individual items to detect change at the extremes of the construct of interest (Vermeersch, Lambert, & Burlingame, 2000).

In general, not all items in an outcomes assessment instrument are relevant to each individual. However, the sensitivity of a specific instrument is contingent on the endorsement of a sufficient number of items. Consequently, a sensitive instrument is likely to have few irrelevant items. Additionally, the scale used to document responses determines the change sensitivity of an instrument. Categorical (e.g., yes/no) questions or a limited scale range minimizes the potential for detecting change (Lipsey, 1990). As mentioned earlier, the static nature of some constructs prohibits the measurement of change. For example, Kopta, Howard, Lowry, and Beutler (1994) reported the propensity of specific items to change during the course of treatment. Items representing symptoms of psychological distress were the most susceptible to change in the early stages of treatment, and items measuring characterological traits were more susceptible in the later stages. Lastly, it is important that instruments have few items subject to floor or ceiling effects, as an instrument's ability to detect change is negatively impacted by the existence of these scale limitations.

Although these factors increase the utility of a particular instrument, two additional criteria further demonstrate the sensitivity of individual items (Vermeersch et al., 2000). First, for the purposes of psychotherapeutic assessment, change that occurs on a specific item during the course of treatment should reflect an improvement in functioning. Second, the positive change measured in treated samples of patients should exceed the positive change measured in untreated patients. In essence, items that fail to distinguish the improvement made in patients and nonpatients are lacking in change sensitivity.

A more common approach to determining the sensitivity of an instrument is to focus on the global index it produces. From pre- and posttest assessments, one can calculate an effect size within a group of individuals. One advantage of effect sizes is that they transform the magnitude of the difference between assessments into standard deviation units, allowing comparisons between independent measures. A growing body of meta-analytic literature suggests that there are reliable differences in the change sensitivity of instruments (Lambert, Hatch, Kingston, & Edwards, 1986; Ogles et al., 1990).

For example, Table 5.3 presents data from the Ogles et al. (1990) review of agoraphobia outcome studies published in the 1980s. This table appears to illustrate the remarkable disparity in estimates of improvement that can occur with different instruments or methods of measurement. The two extremes, which are based on the Fear Survey Schedule ($M = .99$) and Phobic Anxiety and Avoidance Scale ($M = 2.66$), suggest different conclusions. The average patient taking the Fear Survey Schedule moved from the mean (50th percentile) of the pretest group to the 16th percentile after treatment. In contrast, the average patient assessed with measures of the Phobic Anxiety and Avoidance Scale moved from the 50th percentile of the pretest group to the zero percentile following treatment.

Comparisons between the measures depicted in Table 5.3 are confounded somewhat by the fact that the data were aggregated across all studies that used either

TABLE 5.3
Overall Effect Size (*ES*), Mean (*M*), and Standard Deviation (*SD*) by Scale

| Scale | N[a] | M | SD |
|---|---|---|---|
| Phobic anxiety and avoidance | 65 | 2.66 | 1.83 |
| Global Assessment Scale | 31 | 2.30 | 1.14 |
| Self-rating severity | 52 | 2.12 | 1.55 |
| Fear Questionnaire | 56 | 1.93 | 1.30 |
| Anxiety during BAT[b] | 48 | 1.36 | .85 |
| Behavioral Approach Test | 54 | 1.15 | 1.07 |
| Depression measures | 60 | 1.11 | .72 |
| Fear Survey Schedule | 26 | .99 | .47 |
| Heart rate | 21 | .44 | .56 |

*Note.* Based on Ogles, Lambert, Weight, and Payne (1990).
[a] N = the number of treatments whose effects were measured by each scale.
[b] BAT = Behavioral Avoidance Test.

measure. However, similar results can be found when only studies that gave both measures to a patient sample were aggregated. Table 5.4 presents data from a comparison of three frequently employed measures of depression: the Beck Depression Inventory (BDI) and the Zung Self-Rating Scale for Depression (ZSRS), both self-report inventories, and the Hamilton Rating Scale for Depression (HRSD), an expert judge–rated instrument (Lambert et al., 1986). Meta-analytic results suggest that the most popular dependent measures used to assess depression following treatment provide reliably different pictures of change. It appears that the HRS–D, as employed by trained professional interviewers, provides a significantly larger index of change than the BDI and ZSRS. Because the amount of actual improvement that patients experience after treatment is never known, these findings are subject to several different interpretations. They may mean that the HRSD overestimates patient improvement, but the HRSD might in fact accurately reflect improvement, in which case the BDI and ZSRS would underestimate the amount of improvement. It is also possible that the actual amount falls somewhere between the HRSD estimate and the estimates provided by the BDI and ZSRS.

Regardless of the reason for these discrepant findings, it is clear that not all instruments of outcome measure change equally. Many test characteristics influence the

TABLE 5.4
Matched Pairs of Mean Effect Size (*ES*) Values

| Scale Pair | N[a] | M[b] | SD | t |
|---|---|---|---|---|
| HRSD/ZSRS | 17 | 0.94*/0.62* | 0.61/0.30 | 1.88 |
| BDI/HRS-D | 49 | 1.16**/1.57** | 0.86/1.08 | 2.11 |
| ZSRS/BDI | 13 | 0.70/1.03 | 0.46/0.52 | 1.65 |

*Note.* HRSD = Hamilton Rating Scale for Depression; ZSRS = Zung Self-Rating Scale; BDI = Beck Depression Inventory. Reprinted with permission of the American Psychological Association and the authors.
[a] N = the number of treatments whose effects were measured by each pair of depression scales.
[b] Values derived from studies in which subjects' depression was measured on two scales at a time. Effect size represents within-study comparisons.
*$p < .05$.
**$p < .25$.

magnitude of change detected. From a number of meta-analytic reviews (Miller & Berman, 1983; Ogles et al., 1990; Shapiro & Shapiro, 1982; Smith et al., 1980), the following tentative conclusions have been reached:

1. Therapist and expert judge–based data (where the judges are aware of the treatment status of the clients) produce larger effect sizes than self-report data, data produced by significant others, institutional data, or instrumental data.
2. Gross ratings of change produce larger estimates of change than ratings on specific dimensions or symptoms.
3. Change measures based on the specific targets of therapy (e.g., measures based on individualized goals or anxiety-based measures used in specific situations) produce larger effect sizes than more distal measures, including tests of personality.
4. Life adjustment measures that tap social role performance in the natural setting (e.g., GPA) produce smaller effect sizes than more laboratory based measures.
5. Measures collected soon after therapy show larger effect sizes than measures collected at a later date.
6. Physiological measures such as heart rate usually show relatively small treatment effects.

Although it is virtually impossible to eliminate the various challenges that are faced when measuring outcome, or to choose the perfect instrument to measure change, we believe that by understanding how content, social level, source, technology, and time orientation affect the estimates of patient improvement, a user of outcomes assessment instruments is better positioned to select the best available instrument from the many that exist. Moreover, because not all instruments are equivalent in their ability to reflect change, an awareness of the complexity inherent in measuring change can aid in choosing an appropriate instrument.

## EVALUATING THE MEANINGFULNESS OF CHANGE

### Statistical Versus Clinical Significance

Much psychotherapy research is aimed at answering questions of theoretical interest, such as whether dynamic therapy is more effective than cognitive therapy or whether exposure in vivo is necessary for fear reduction. These and a host of similar questions have given rise to research designs that emphasize the use of statistical tests of significance. Typically, the within-group variability and the between-group variability are estimated, the group means are compared, and the resulting numerical result is compared to a preset critical value. The occurrence of a sufficiently large difference, defined as one that is unlikely to occur as frequently as the predetermined critical value (e.g., $p < .05$), demonstrates statistical significance.

Although this common approach is an essential part of the scientific process, it has its limitations (Jacobson, Roberts, Berns, & McGlinchey, 1999). First, a statistically significant result may have little practical meaning. For example, a behavioral method of treatment for obesity may create a statistically significant difference between treated and untreated groups if all treated subjects lost 10 pounds and all untreated subjects lost 5 pounds. However, the clinical utility of an extra 5 pounds of weight loss is debatable, especially in clinically obese patients. Second, the focus on group averages that arises from using statistical techniques makes it difficult to generalize the results to the outcomes for a specific individual. Third, statistical significance does not clarify the strength of a demonstrated effect (Kazdin, 1998). A less commonly used statistic, effect size, aims to address this limitation, but effect size is unable to convey the meaningfulness of an effect. For instance, in the weight loss example, the intervention is likely to have a moderate effect size despite the practical insignificance of the extra 5 pounds shed.

We believe that these limitations are not lost on practicing clinicians. The question "How likely is it that a client with a particular problem will leave therapy without that problem?" (Jacobson, Roberts, Berns, & McGlinchey, 1999, p. 306) remains of central importance to most therapists. Clinical significance is a concept that was introduced to provide a solution to this dilemma (Jacobson, Follette, & Revenstorf, 1984; Jacobson & Truax, 1991). In the last two decades, a number of methods have been proposed to determine the clinical significance of interventions (e.g., Blanchard & Schwarz, 1988; Gladis, Gosch, Dishuk, & Crits-Christoph, 1999; Kendall, 1999; Kendall & Grove, 1988; Kendall & Norton-Ford, 1982), and a broader approach referred to as *social validity* has its proponents as well (Kazdin, 1977; Wolf, 1978). Whereas the former approach evaluates meaningfulness of change based on criteria identified by clinicians-researchers through the use standardized assessment instruments, the latter method defines the practicality of change using the perspectives of clients and societal members (Ogles, Lunnen, & Bonesteel, 2001). For the remainder of this discussion, we focus on the clinical significance method.

Clinical significance is equivalent to return to normal functioning (Jacobson et al., 1999). To be labeled *clinically significant*, an outcome must meet two criteria: (1) The magnitude of change must be considered reliable, and (2) as a result of the improvement, the client must be indistinguishable from individuals defined as having normal function. The purpose of the first criterion is to ensure that measured change exceeds what is possible from chance or measurement error. Alone, it is referred to as the *reliable change index* (RCI; Jacobson et al., 1984; Jacobson & Truax, 1991), and it identifies clients who have reliably improved but not recovered following treatment (Jacobson et al., 1999). When both of the criteria are met, the change is referred to as *clinically significant* and the client is considered to be recovered.

Like any methodological approach, the concept of clinical significance is associated with numerous assumptions and issues. For example, the very use of the two criteria is contingent on the availability of an instrument that has been psychometrically tested and normed. Reliability coefficients are necessary for the calculation of the RCI, and normative data corresponding to functional and dysfunctional populations are required for the calculation of a cutoff value that discriminates between these two groups (Jacobson et al., 1984, 1999; Jacobson & Truax, 1991). Given the magnitude of change necessary for a client to achieve recovered status, it is conceivable that some groups of individuals (e.g., those with schizophrenia) may only rarely meet the criteria, suggesting the need for samples representing a continuum of improvement (Tingey, Lambert, Burlingame, & Hansen, 1996). The complexity of these issues are beyond the scope of this chapter; however, there are many sources that readers may find interesting (e.g., Bauer, Lambert, & Nielsen, in press; Beckstead et al., 2003; Kendall & Grove, 1988; Kendall, Marrs-Garcia, Nath, & Sheldrick, 1999; Ogles et al., 1996, 2001; Tingey et al., 1996). Presumably, with the availability of test manuals, users can either obtain or calculate cutoff and reliable change scores corresponding to clinically significant criteria.

Having presented the criteria for clinical significance, we provide an example showing how such an approach can be used in practice. The Beck Depression Inventory

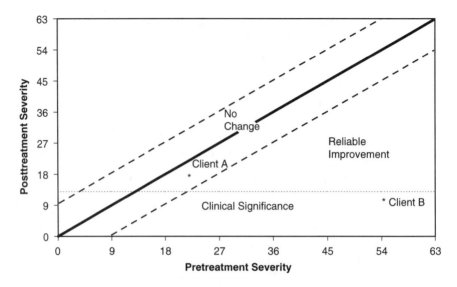

FIG. 5.1. Graphical example of using reliable change index and clinically significant change criteria to evaluate meaningfulness of patient progress.

(BDI; Beck et al., 1961) has an RCI of 9 points and a cutoff score of 14 that separates the dysfunctional and functional population (Seggar, Lambert, & Hansen, 2002). By means of these criteria and pre- and posttreatment assessments using the BDI, a client's final outcome status can be categorized. For example, assume that Client A began treatment with a score of 25 and ended treatment with a score of 18. A change score of 7 represents the client's improvement, suggesting that reliable improvement was not attained. Suppose that Client B began treatment with a score of 54 and ended treatment with a score of 10. In this case, Client B has recovered: In addition to achieving 44 points of improvement (many more than the RCI), Client B ended treatment in the range of functional clients (below the cutoff score of 14). This example is presented graphically in Fig. 5.1.

### Similar and Related Procedures

Additional examples of estimating clinically significant change have been published in recent years. The methods used have emphasized the role of normative comparison. For instance, social drinking behaviors have been used as outcome criteria in the treatment of problem drinking, and both the ratio of orgasms to attempts at sex and the time to orgasm following penetration have been used as criteria of adequate sexual performance (Sabalis, 1983). These criteria are based on data on the normal functioning of individuals and can be applied easily and meaningfully to a number of disorders where normal or ideal functioning is readily apparent and easily measured (e.g., obesity, suicidal behavior).

Normative comparisons also can be used to evaluate the clinical significance of treatment by comparing treated clients with samples of nondistressed individuals. For example, Trull, Nietzel, and Main (1988) reviewed 19 studies of agoraphobia that used the Fear Questionnaire (Marks & Mathews, 1978). The normative samples included one consisting of university students and one consisting of individuals randomly selected from the community. Because the community sample appeared more distressed than the university sample, the estimate of clinically significant change varied with the sample used for comparison. When the university sample was used, the average agoraphobic patient began treatment at the 99th percentile and ended treatment at the 98.7 percentile. When the community sample was used, the average agoraphobic patient began treatment at the 97th percentile but progressed to the 68th percentile at the end of treatment.

Using a similar methodology, Nietzel, Russell, Hemmings, and Gretter (1987) studied the clinical significance of psychotherapy for unipolar depression. In all, 28 published studies were used to calculate composite BDI norms for three groups: a nondistressed group, a general population group (consisting mostly of collegiate subjects), and a situationally distressed group (e.g., pregnant women), which turned out to be very similar to the general population group. These norms were then applied to data from 31 studies, yielding 60 effect sizes. Comparisons of the depressed patients and the normative samples suggested that the various treatments (all of which appeared similar in their effectiveness) produced clinically significant changes in relation to the general population norms. In fact, the average depressed patient moved from the 99th percentile of the general population norms to the 76th percentile. These gains were maintained at follow-up. In reference to the nondistressed group, the same improvements were much less remarkable. The average depressed patient only moved from the 99th percentile to the 95th percentile.

Normative comparison approaches provide a number of advantages. Numerous measures have normative data that facilitate comparisons between distressed and nondistressed groups of individuals, relieving researchers and clinicians alike from the need to collect data on normal individuals. Additionally, provided that specific normative samples exist, finer comparisons between treatment progress are possible, particularly for psychological disorders that are somewhat resistant to change (e.g., schizophrenia). However, the meaningfulness of these narrower comparisons becomes less clear as well. As the examples show, the extent of improvement depends on the comparison group used. Additional methodological weaknesses of such an approach deserve mention. Inherent in this approach is a reliance on the distribution of the normative sample. Consequently, samples that are not normally distributed (and suffer from floor and ceiling effects) present serious difficulties. Also, many tests are developed to measure psychological disorders and thus are not as effective at measuring less severely distressed individuals.

Nevertheless, clinicians preferring to evaluate the meaningfulness of patient gains using a normative comparison approach have available a number of instruments with published normative data. Brief lists of some of the more common measures, along with norms, have been made available. These measures include the Beck Depression Inventory, Symptom Checklist 90–R, Fear Questionnaire, Child Behavior Checklist, Hamilton Depression Rating Scale, Outcome Questionnaire–45, and Inventory for Interpersonal Problems. Cutoffs and reliable change indexes for these instruments and others have been reported in Ogles, Lambert, and Masters (1996) and Ogles, Lambert, and Fields (2002).

## ISSUES IN NEED OF FURTHER RESEARCH

There are many topics related to the assessment of therapy improvement that require additional research. However, we complete our discussion by highlighting the status of three distinct areas of assessment-related research that perhaps have promising information to provide to clinicians and researchers alike. Because of the recent and likely future pressure to restrain the costs of providing mental health services, the use of cost-effective treatment as a potential measure of outcome seems pertinent. The notion of provider profiling is the second topic presented. Although the profiling of providers is undoubtedly a controversial topic, there is evidence that therapists contribute to the gains of therapy as well. Lastly, we introduce some of the earliest results regarding a relatively new research area, patient-focused research, which offers a strategy for enhancing outcomes for treatment nonresponders.

### Cost-Effective Care as an Outcome

Among the outcomes that can be monitored, the cost-effectiveness of treatments is an interesting but rarely studied phenomenon. In a society that is becoming more preoccupied with cost-containment, the cost-effectiveness of treatment is an important outcome. The value of care is often defined as the trade-off between quality of care (or traditional clinical outcomes) in relation to dollars spent on care. To health plans and employers (if not patients), the value of care, or the cost-effectiveness of care, should be as important as absolute costs for deciding on a treatment. Cost-effectiveness data are particularly important when the effects of different treatments are equal—a state of affairs that is common in psychotherapy and pharmacotherapy (Lambert & Ogles, 2004).

Perhaps the best example of research on this topic is that provided by the Rand medical outcome study that examined outcomes in depression (Wells, Strum, Sherbourne, & Meredith, 1996). This study examined systems of care, patient case-mix, processes of care, utilization, and clinical outcomes using an indirect structural analysis in order to develop models to inform policy and treatment decisions. The authors found that treatment increases mental health services utilization and costs regardless of provider specialty (general practitioner, psychiatrist, or other mental health specialist). The lowest cost but also the worst outcomes for depression were found in the general medical sector; the highest costs, but also the best outcomes, occurred in psychiatry. When cost-effectiveness ratios were calculated, the greatest "value" was to be found in the other mental health specialist provider group (psychologists, etc.). The authors also estimated that quality improvement programs or decisions could make substantial improvements in cost-effectiveness. Without quality improvement efforts that take into account the cost-benefit ratios of different treatments, the current tendency to shift treatment toward general medical practitioners may continue simply because it reduces costs, not because it is cost-effective.

Although the results of the Rand study are highly complex (they reflect type of depression, follow-up time period, etc.), it is obvious that they constitute a rich source of data. Using the data analytic procedures utilized by Wells and colleagues, it is possible to calculate the amount of money it costs to reduce a single symptom by a particular amount (e.g., what it costs to reduce the number of headaches a person has by one per week through the use of medication versus biofeedback). It would also be possible to estimate the cost of bringing a depressed patient into a normal state of functioning (and keep him or her there) and to compare the costs associated with specific treatment strategies—say, the cost-effectiveness of group versus individual cognitive behavior therapy.

The Rand study of depression was a large-scale effort that cost approximately 4 million to complete (Wells, Strum, Sherbourne, & Meredith, 1996). Numerous other studies have been conducted on a variety of other disorders, such as chronic pain (Texidor &

Taylor, 1991) and psychosomatic disorders (Pautler, 1991), but none has reached the scope of the Rand study. The limited number and diversity of studies makes it difficult to identify the best methods of estimating costs. As in the area of clinical outcomes measurement, there are few agreed methods of estimating treatment costs.

The Rand study defined health as the number of serious functioning limitations. Costs were based on the "direct" costs of providing services to treat depression, and the value of care was estimated by calculating the cost of reducing one or more functioning limitations. Other researchers estimate the average cost of providing treatment for an episode of illness by adding up staff expenses (including benefits) and then dividing by the number of patients treated in a year (Melson, 1995). Researchers have also attempted to estimate social costs, such as those that arise from lost productivity, use of social services and the criminal justice system, use of other health services, and the like. Cost-benefit analysis combined with estimates of outcome based on clinical significance could be usefully applied in the managed mental health setting to understand the consequences of rationing treatment. What is the "value" of fewer sessions versus more sessions in terms of their effect on the long-term adjustment of patients?

The complexity of these issues is beyond the scope of this chapter. Suffice it to say that estimating the cost, cost-effectiveness, and medical cost offsets of psychotherapy is important for the assessment of psychotherapeutic outcomes. McKenzie (1995), for example, argued that the relative equivalence of outcomes in group and individual psychotherapy can be a powerful argument for the use of group therapy when the relative costs of delivering individual treatment and group therapy are considered. At the very least, this finding emphasizes the importance of research aimed at selecting patients who are most suitable for group treatment.

### The Importance of Tracking Outcomes for Improving Quality: The Case for Provider Profiling

Considerable research on psychotherapeutic outcomes shows that a major contributor to patient improvement and deterioration is the individual therapist (Lambert & Ogles, 2004). Despite the current emphasis on "empirically validated" treatments (Task Force, 1996), manual-based therapy (Lambert, 1998; Wilson, 1998), and treatment guidelines that assume the curative power of therapy rests on treatment techniques, ample evidence suggests the importance of particular therapists for positive outcomes (Garfield 1996; Lambert & Okiishi, 1997; Okiishi, Lambert, Ogles, & Nielsen, in press). One clear implication of this finding is that it is important to use psychological tests to track patient outcomes (by provider) for the purpose of increasing the quality of services (Clement, 1996; Lambert & Brown, 1996). This type of research can be expected to modify the practices of clinicians directly whereas research on specific disorders (clinical trials) will be much slower in having a real impact on clinical practice. It is important to use outcome measures that can provide clinicians with information about the effectiveness of their practices. Okiishi, Lambert, Ogles, and Nielsen (in press) analyzed session-by-session outcome data on clients who sought treatment in a large outpatient clinic. The data presented suggest clear differences in average pretherapy levels of disturbance and also in the average amount of change associated with particular therapists. Three of the therapists analyzed saw clients whose response to treatments were exceptionally positive, whereas two therapists had clients whose outcomes were on average negative! Such data should alert clinicians to the fact that they have different outcomes and may suggest the need for a particular clinician to explore the reasons for poor outcomes in her or his patients (relative to those of other clinicians).

Figure 35.7, from chapter 35, suggests an unusual rapidity of improvement in patients treated by the therapist L. J. This provider profile, based on repeated measurement of patient progress, shows an unusual pattern of improvement and calls for exploration of the methods used by L. J. Without the use of a reliable tracking device, along with criteria for successful outcomes, it would be far more difficult to compare clinician success rates. It is not difficult to see the advantages of this methodology for clinicians, health systems, and, most importantly, patients. Tracking patient outcomes through the use of meaningful outcome measures can result in improved clinical decision making and patient care.

**Patient-Focused Research: A New Approach to Assessing Outcomes**

In much of the recent psychotherapy literature, there is a focus on retrospective assessments of outcome. Typically, the progress of groups of individuals receiving theoretically distinct interventions is compared to determine the efficacy of their unique approaches. The primary aim of these studies is to determine the average success of these specific interventions rather than the individual results of the patients receiving treatment. Consequently, the assessment of outcomes used in these studies generally follows a pre- and posttreatment pattern of rating. With such a design, it is not possible to identify patients who are not responding to treatment and implement corrective procedures in time to prevent a treatment failure (Lambert, Hansen, & Finch, 2001; Mash & Hunsley, 1993). Howard, Moras, Brill, Martinovich, and Lutz (1996) introduced an alternative psychotherapeutic outcome research paradigm to address these limitations. Referred to as *patient-focused research*, this paradigm involves systematically monitoring a patient's progress during the course of therapy to provide treatment progress information, in the form of feedback, to clinicians or case managers as well as to generate data on outcomes.

Since the introduction of the client-focused research paradigm, several quality assurance systems have been developed for monitoring and providing client progress information (e.g., Barkham et al., 2001; Beutler, 2001; Kordy, Hannover, & Richard, 2001; Lambert, Hansen, et al., 2001). Despite unique system differences, the underlying goal of each approach is to enhance an individual client's treatment outcomes (Beutler, 2001). In general, each approach favors continuous monitoring of client treatment progress and providing feedback to clinicians during treatment.

Some of the earliest findings from a program of patient-focused research that emphasizes the early identification of and response to treatment failure have been promising. Lambert and colleagues (Lambert et al., 2002; Lambert, Whipple, et al., 2001; Whipple et al., 2003) found that providing client progress information to therapists of clients identified as "at risk" for treatment failure resulted in increased lengths of treatment and improved outcomes at termination. Outcome comparisons between the at-risk clients in the feedback and treatment-as-usual conditions revealed moderate effect sizes (approximately .40). Also, significantly fewer deteriorators were found among the clients of therapists receiving feedback information.

Although these initial findings were statistically significant and clinically meaningful, a majority of the clients predicted to have poor outcomes failed to return to a functional state despite the positive effects of the feedback intervention. To address the insufficient impact of the feedback intervention in prior studies, additional components were added to the feedback (Lambert et al., 2002; Lambert, Whipple, et al.,

2001). Two avenues of research have been pursued. In the first approach, Whipple et al. (2003) combined the provision of client progress information to therapists and the use of clinical support tools based on an empirically derived problem-solving strategy. Clinical variables with demonstrated relevance to psychotherapy outcome were arranged in a hierarchy to produce clinical strategies for therapists treating clients identified as potential treatment failures. Clients in the feedback-plus-clinical-support condition showed larger treatment gains than those in the control and feedback-only conditions. As an additional measure of the impact of the strengthened intervention, significantly fewer clients in this treatment group met criteria for deterioration at termination.

## CONCLUSION

Outcomes assessment has evolved as a result of decades of scientific research. Much of the focus has been on general procedures for measuring outcomes. Complicating the process of choosing an outcome instrument is the availability of myriad measures that assess progress and outcomes. To aid in the selection process, several characteristics were presented as a means to characterize the various tests that exist. Assessment instruments are generally distinguished by their content, level of social assessment, and contributing source. As described in this chapter, they also vary in the procedures they use to collect outcome information and the extent to which they measure psychological states or traits. The sensitivity of an instrument to change during the therapeutic process is equally important and deserves attention as well. We encourage interested users of outcome instruments to carefully consider the importance of these test qualities, along with related issues, before selecting a measure.

In our discussion, we also presented two strategies for evaluating the meaningfulness of change estimates for individual patients. The first included the use of two criteria, whether the patient has made reliable improvement and whether the improvement brings the patient into the normal range of functioning. The second strategy involved a direct comparison between the patient's final assessment of outcome and an instrument's normative data. Lastly, we highlighted three assessment-related topics that deserve further examination. It is our hope that future researchers will benefit by lessons learned and will not repeat past mistakes, even though these have provided ample guidance to best practices.

It is obvious that the quality of clinical services offered to clients can be enhanced if client treatment response is monitored through the repeated administration of standardized tests. It is doubtful that clinicians can gain an adequate awareness of low-quality care without the use of such tests. It is time to select and use outcome measures for the purpose of improving patient outcomes and further understanding best therapeutic practices.

## REFERENCES

Barkham, M., Margison, F., Leach, C., Lucock, M., Mellowr-Clark, J., Evans, C., et al. (2001). Service profiling and outcomes benchmarking using the CORE–OM: Toward practice-based evidence in the psychological therapies. *Journal of Consulting and Clinical Psychology, 69*, 184–196.

Bauer, S., Lambert, M. J., & Nielsen, S. L. (in press). Clinical significant methods: A comparison of statistical techniques. *Journal of Personality Assessment.*

Beck, A. T., Ward, C. H., Mendelson, M., Mock, J., & Erbaugh, J. (1961). An inventory for measuring depression. *Archives of General Psychiatry, 4*, 561–571.

Beckstead, D. J., Hatch, A. L., Lambert, M. J., Eggett, D. L., Goates, M. K., & Vermeersch, D. A. (2003). Clinical significance of the Outcome Questionnaire (OQ-45). *The Behavior Analyst Today, 4*, 749.

Beutler, L. E. (2001). Comparisons among quality assurance systems: From outcome assessment to clinical utility. *Journal of Consulting and Clinical Psychology, 69*, 197–204.

Blanchard, E. B., & Schwarz, S. P. (1988). Clinically significant changes in behavioral medicine. *Behavioral Assessment, 10*, 171–188.

Butcher, J. N., Dahlstrom, W. G., Graham, J. R., Tellegen, A., & Kaemmer, B. (1989). *Minnesota Multiphasic Personality Inventory-2 (MMPI-2): Manual for administration and scoring.* Minneapolis, MN: University of Minnesota Press.

Cartwright, D. S., Kirtner, W. L., & Fiske, D. W. (1963). Method factors in changes associated with psychotherapy. *Journal of Abnormal and Social Psychology, 66*, 164–175.

Clement, P. W. (1996). Evaluation in private practice. *Clinical Psychology: Science and Practice, 3*, 146–159.

Consumer Reports. (1995, November). Mental health: (Does therapy help?). *Consumer Reports, 734*–739.

Derogatis, L. R. (1983). SCL–90–R: Administration, scoring, and procedures manual–II. Towson, MD: Clinical Psychometric Research.

Docherty, J. P., & Streeter, M. J. (1996). Measuring outcomes. In L. I. Sederer & B. Dickey (Eds.), *Outcome assessment in clinical practice* (pp. 8–18). Baltimore: Williams & Wilkins.

Farnsworth, J., Hess, J., & Lambert, M. J. (2001, April). A review of outcome measurement practices in the *Journal of Consulting and Clinical Psychology.* Paper presented at the annual meeting of the Rocky Mountain Psychological Association, Reno, NV.

Forsyth, R. P., & Fairweather, G. W. (1961). Psychotherapeutic and other hospital treatment criteria: The dilemma. *Journal of Abnormal and Social Psychology, 62*, 598–604.

Froyd, J. E., Lambert. M. J., & Froyd, J. D. (1996). A review of practices of psychotherapy outcome measurement. *Journal of Mental Health, 5*, 11–15.

Garfield, S. L. (1996). Some problems associated with validated forms of psychotherapy. *Clinical Psychology: Science and Practice, 3*, 245–250.

Gibson, R. L., Snyder, W. U., & Ray, W. S. (1955). A factor analysis of measures of change following client-centered psychotherapy. *Journal of Counseling Psychology, 2*, 83–90.

Gladis, M. M., Gosch, E. A., Dishuk, N. M., & Crits-Christoph, P. (1999). Quality of life: Expanding the scope of clinical significance. *Journal of Consulting and Clinical Psychology, 67*, 320–331.

Glaister, B. (1982). Muscles relaxation training for fear reduction of patients with psychological problems: A review of controlled studies. *Behavior Research and Therapy, 20*, 493–504.

Horowitz, L. M., Rosenberg, S. E., Baer, B. A., Ureno, G., & Villasenor, V. S. (1988). Inventory of Interpersonal Problems: Psychometric properties and clinical applications. *Journal of Consulting and Clinical Psychology, 56*, 885–892.

Horowitz, L. M., Strupp, H. H., Lambert, M. J., & Elkin, I. (1997). Overview and summary of the core-battery conference. In H. H Strupp, L. M Horowitz, & M. J. Lambert (Eds.), *Measuring patient changes in mood, anxiety, and personality disorders: Toward a core battery* (pp. 11–54). Washington, DC: American Psychological Association.

Howard, K. I., Moras, K., Brill, P. L., Martinovich, Z., & Lutz, W. (1996). Evaluation of psychotherapy: Efficacy, effectiveness, and patient progress. *American Psychologist, 51*, 1059–1064.

Jacobson, N. S., & Christensen, A. (1996). Studying the effectiveness of psychotherapy: How well can clinical trials do the job. *American Psychologist, 51*, 1031–1039.

Jacobson, N. S., Follette, W. C., & Revenstorf, D. (1984). Psychotherapy outcome research: Methods for reporting variability and evaluating clinical significance. *Behavior Therapy, 15*, 336–352.

Jacobson, N. S., Roberts, L. J., Berns, S. B., & McGlinchey, J. B. (1999). Methods for defining and determining the clinical significance of treatment effects: Description, application, and alternatives. *Journal of Consulting and Clinical Psychology, 67*, 300–307.

Jacobson, N. S., & Truax, P. (1991). Clinical significance: A statistical approach to defining meaningful change in psychotherapy research. *Journal of Consulting and Clinical Psychology, 59*, 12–19.

Kazdin, A. E. (1977). Assessing the clinical or applied importance of behavior change through social validation. *Behavior Modification, 1*, 427–452.

Kazdin, A. E. (1998). *Research design in clinical psychology.* Boston: Allyn & Bacon.

Kendall, P. C. (1999). Clinical significance. *Journal of Consulting and Clinical Psychology, 67*, 383–384.

Kendall, P. C., & Grove, W. M. (1988). Normative comparisons in therapy outcome. *Behavioral Assessment, 10*, 147–158.

Kendall, P. C., Marrs-Garcia, A., Nath, S. R., & Sheldrick, R. C. (1999). Normative comparisons for the evaluation of clinical significance. *Journal of Consulting and Clinical Psychology, 67*, 285–299.

Kendall, P. C., & Norton-Ford, J. D. (1982). *Clinical psychology: Scientific and professional dimensions.* New York: Wiley.

Kopta, S. M., Howard, K. I., Lowry, J. L., & Beutler, L. E. (1994). Patterns of symptomatic recovery in time-unlimited psychotherapy. *Journal of Consulting and Clinical Psychology, 62*, 1009–1016.

Kordy, H., Hannover, W., & Richard, M. (2001). Computer-assisted feedback-driven quality management for psychotherapy: The Stuttgart-Heidelberg model. *Journal of Consulting and Clinical Psychology, 69*, 173–183.

Lambert, M. J. (1983). Introduction to assessment of psychotherapy outcome: Historical perspective and current issues. In M. J. Lambert, E. R. Christensen, & S. S. DeJulio (Eds.), *The assessment of psychotherapy outcome* (pp. 3–32). New York: Wiley Inter-science.

Lambert, M. J. (1998). Manual-based treatment and clinical practice: Hangman of life or promising development? *Clinical Psychology: Science and Practice, 5*, 391–395.

Lambert, M. J., & Bergin, A. E. (1994). The effectiveness of psychotherapy. In A. E. Bergin and S. L. Garfield (Eds.), *Handbook of psychotherapy and behavior change* (4th ed., pp. 143–189). New York: Wiley.

Lambert, M. J., & Brown, G. S. (1996). Data-based management for tracking outcome in private practice. *Clinical Psychology: Science and Practice, 3*, 172–178.

Lambert, M. J., Hansen, B. S., & Finch, A. E. (2001). Patient-focused research: Using patient outcome data to enhance treatment effects. *Journal of Consulting and Clinical Psychology, 69*, 159–172.

Lambert, M. J., Hatch, D. R., Kingston, M. D., & Edwards, B. C. (1986). Zung, Beck, and Hamilton rating scales as measures of treatment outcome: A meta-analytic comparison. *Journal of Consulting and Clinical Psychology, 54*, 54–59.

Lambert, M. J., & McRoberts, C. H. (1993, April). *Outcome measurement in JCCP 1986–1991.* Paper presented at the meeting of the Western Psychological Association. Phoenix, AZ.

Lambert, M. J., & Ogles, B. M. (2004). The efficacy and effectiveness of psychotherapy. In M. J. Lambert (Ed.), *Bergin and Garfield's handbook of psychotherapy and behavior change* (5th ed., pp. 139–193). New York: Wiley.

Lambert, M. J., Ogles, B. M., & Masters, K. S. (1992). Choosing outcome assessment devices: An organizational and conceptual scheme. *Journal of Counseling and Development, 70*, 527–532.

Lambert, M. J., & Okiishi, J. C. (1997). The effects of the individual psychotherapist and implications for future research. *Clinical Psychology: Science and Practice, 4*, 66–75.

Lambert, M. J., Whipple, J. L., Smart, D. W., Vermeersch, D. A., Nielsen, S. L., & Hawkins, E. J. (2001). The effects of providing therapists with feedback on patient progress during psychotherapy: Are outcomes enhanced? *Psychotherapy Research, 11*, 49–68.

Lambert, M. J., Whipple, J. L., Vermeersch, D., Smart, D. W., Hawkins, E. J., Nielsen, S. L., et al. (2002). Enhancing psychotherapy outcomes via providing feedback on client progress: A replication. *Clinical Psychology and Psychotherapy, 9*, 91–103.

Lipsey, M. W. (1990). *Design sensitivity.* Newbury Park, CA: Sage.

Locke, H. J., & Wallace, K. M. (1959). Short-term marital adjustment and prediction tests: Their reliability and validity. *Marriage and Family Living, 21*, 251–255.

Luborsky, L. (1971). Perennial mystery of poor agreement among criteria for psychotherapy outcome. *Journal of Consulting and Clinical Psychology, 37*, 316–319.

Marks, I. M., & Mathews, A. M. (1978). Brief standard self-rating for phobic patients. *Behavior Research and Therapy, 17*, 263–267.

Mash, E. J., & Hunsley, J. (1993). Assessment considerations in the identification of failing psychotherapy: Bringing the negatives out of the darkroom. *Psychological Assessment, 5*, 292–301.

McGlynn, E. A. (1996). Domains of study and methodological challenges. In L. I. Sederer & B. Dickey (Eds.), *Outcome assessment in clinical practice* (pp. 19-24). Baltimore: Williams & Wilkins.

McKenzie, K. R. (1995). *Effective use of group therapy in managed care.* Washington, DC: American Psychiatric Press.

McLellan, A. T., & Durell, J. (1996). Outcome evaluation in psychiatric and substance abuse treatments: Concepts, rationale, and methods. In L. J. Sederer & B. Dickey (Eds.), *Outcome assessment in clinical practice* (pp. 34–44). Baltimore: Williams & Wilkins.

Melson, S. J. (1995). Brief day treatment for nonpsychotic patients. In K. R. McKenzie (Ed.), *Effective use of group therapy in managed care* (pp. 113–128). Washington, DC: American Psychiatric Press.

Miller, R. C., & Berman, J. S. (1983). The efficacy of cognitive behavior therapies: A quantitative review of the research evidence. *Psychological Bulletin, 94*, 39–53.

Mylar, J. L., & Clement, P. W. (1972). Prediction and comparison of outcome in systematic desensitization and implosion. *Behavior Research and Therapy, 10,* 235–246.

Nietzel, M. T., Russell, R. L., Hemmings, K. A., & Gretter, M. L. (1987). Clinical significance of psychotherapy for unipolar depression: A meta-analytic approach to social comparison. *Journal of Consulting and Clinical Psychology, 55,* 156–161.

Ogles, B. M., Lambert, M. J., & Fields, S. A. (2002). *Essentials of outcome assessment.* New York: Wiley.

Ogles, B. M., Lambert, M. J., & Masters, K. S. (1996). *Assessing outcome in clinical practice.* Boston: Allyn & Bacon.

Ogles, B. M., Lambert, M. J., Weight, D. G., & Payne, I. R. (1990). Agoraphobia outcome measurement: A review and meta-analysis. *Psychological Assessment: A Journal of Consulting and Clinical Psychology, 2,* 317–325.

Ogles, B. M., Lunnen, K. M., & Bonesteel, K. (2001). Clinical significance: History, application, and current practice. *Clinical Psychology Review, 21,* 421–446.

Okiishi, J., Lambert, M. J., Ogles, B. M., & Nielsen, S. L. (in press). In search of supershrink: Using patient outcome data to identify effective and ineffective psychotherapists. *Clinical Psychology and Psychotherapy, 10,* .

Pautler, T. (1991). A cost effective mind-body approach to psychosomatic disorders. In K. N. Anchor (Ed.), *The handbook of medical psychotherapy: Cost effective strategies in mental health* (pp. 231–248). Toronto: Hogrefe & Huber.

Pilkonis, P. A., Imber, S. D., Lewis, P., & Rubinsky, P. (1984). A comparative outcome study of individual, group, and conjoint psychotherapy. *Archives of General Psychiatry, 41,* 431–437.

Polkinghorne, D. E. (1991). Two conflicting calls for methodological reform. *The Consulting Psychologist, 19,* 103–114.

Rosenblatt, A., & Attkisson, C. C. (1993). Assessing outcomes for sufferers of severe mental disorder: A conceptual framework and review. *Evaluation and Program Planning, 16,* 347–363.

Ross, S. M., & Proctor, S. (1973). Frequency and duration of hierarchy item exposure in a systematic desensitization analogue. *Behavior Research and Therapy, 11,* 303–312.

Sabalis, R. F. (1983). Assessing outcome in patients with sexual dysfunctions and sexual deviations. In M. J. Lambert, E. R. Christensen, & S. S. DeJulio (Eds.), *The assessment of psychotherapy outcome* (pp. 205–262). New York: Wiley.

Schulte, D. (1995). How treatment success could be assessed. *Psychotherapy Research, 5,* 281–296.

Seggar, L., Lambert, M. J., & Hansen, N. B. (2002). Assessing clinical significance: Application to the Beck Depression Inventory. *Behavior Therapy, 33,* 253–269.

Seligman, M. E. P. (1995). The effectiveness of psychotherapy: The Consumer Reports study. *American Psychologist, 50,* 965–974.

Shapiro, D. A., & Shapiro, D. (1982). Meta-analysis of comparative therapy outcome studies: A replication and refinement. *Psychological Bulletin, 92,* 581–604.

Shore, M. F., Massimo, J. L., & Ricks, D. F. (1965). A factor analytic study of psychotherapeutic change in delinquent boys. *Journal of Clinical Psychology, 21,* 208–212.

Smith, M. L., Glass, G. V., & Miller, T. (1980). *The benefits of psychotherapy.* Baltimore: Johns Hopkins University Press.

Spielberger, C. D., Gorsuch, R. L., Lushene, P. R., & Jacobs, G. A. (1983). *Manual for the State-Trait Anxiety Inventory (Form Y).* Palo Alto, CA: Consulting Psychologists Press.

Strupp, H. H., & Hadley, S. W. (1977). A tripartite model of mental health and therapeutic outcomes: With special reference to negative effects in psychotherapy. *American Psychologist, 32,* 187–196.

Strupp, H. H., Horowitz, L. M., & Lambert, M. J. (1997). *Measuring patient changes in mood, anxiety, and personality disorders: Toward a core battery.* Washington, DC: American Psychological Association.

Task Force in Promotion and Dissemination of Psychological Procedures. (1996). An update on empirically validated therapies. *The Clinical Psychologist, 49,* 5–22.

Texidor, M., & Taylor, C. (1991). Chronic pain management: The interdisciplinary approach and cost effectiveness. In K. N. Anchor (Ed.), *The handbook of medical psychotherapy: Cost effective strategies in mental health* (pp. 89–100). Toronto: Hogrefe & Huber.

Tingey, R. C., Lambert, M. J., Burlingame, G. M., & Hansen, N. B. (1996). Assessing clinical significance: Proposed extensions to method. *Psychotherapy Research, 6,* 109–123.

Tomarken, A. J. (1995). A psychometric perspective on psychophysiological measures. *Psychological Assessment, 7,* 387–395.

Trull, T. J., Nietzel, M. T., & Main, A. (1988). The use of meta-analysis to assess the clinical significance of behavior therapy for agoraphobia. *Behavior Therapy, 19,* 527–538.

Vermeersch, D. A., Lambert, M. J., & Burlingame, G. M. (2000). Outcome Questionnaire: Item sensitivity to change. *Journal of Personality Assessment, 74*, 242–261.

Wampold, B. E., & Jenson, W. R. (1986). Clinical significance revisited. *Behavioral Therapy, 17*, 302–305.

Waskow, I. E., & Parloff, M. B. (1975). *Psychotherapy change measures.* Rockville, MD: National Institute of Mental Health.

Wells, E. A., Hawkins, J. D., & Catalano, R. F. (1988). Choosing drug use measures for treatment outcome studies: The influence of measurement approach on treatment results. *International Journal of Addictions, 23*, 851–873.

Wells, K. B., Strum, R., Sherbourne, C. D., & Meredith, L. A. (1996). Caring for depression: A Rand study. Cambridge, MA: Harvard University Press.

Whipple, J. L., Lambert, M. J., Vermeersch, D. A., Smart, D. W., Nielsen, S. L., & Hawkins, E. J. (2003). Improving the effects of psychotherapy: The use of early identification of treatment failure and problem solving strategies in routine practice. *Journal of Counseling Psychology, 58*, 59–68 .

Wilson, G. T. (1998). Manual-based treatment and clinical practice. *Clinical Psychology: Science and Practice, 5*, 363–375.

Wilson, G. T., & Thomas, M. G. (1973). Self versus drug-produced relaxation and the effects of instructional set in standardized systematic desensitization. *Behavior Research and Therapy, 11*, 279–288.

Wolf, M. M. (1978). Social validity: The case for subjective measurement or how applied behavior analysis is finding its heart. *Journal of Applied Behavior Analysis, 11*, 203–214.

Wood, J. M., Lilienfeld, S. O., Garb, H. N., & Nezworski, M. T. (2000). The Rorschach test in clinical diagnosis: A critical review, with a backward look at Gasfield (1997). *Journal of Clinical Psychology, 56*, 395–430.

Worchel, P., & Byrne, D. (Eds.). (1964). *Personality change.* New York: Wiley.

# Guidelines for Selecting Psychological Instruments for Treatment Planning and Outcomes Assessment

Frederick L. Newman and Douglas Rugh
*Florida International University*

James A. Ciarlo
*University of Denver*

A primary aim of this chapter is to assist mental health programs with making decisions about improving treatment services with psychological testing procedures that fit smoothly into the delivery of mental health services. One problem faced by practitioners when arguing for a particular level or mode of care is that little evidence exists in the research literature to guide decisions that link both type and amount (or dosage) of an intervention (Hermann et al., 2002; Mumma, 2001; Newman, & Tejeda, 1996). Traditional clinical research designs contrast an experimental condition with a control condition by fixing the treatment dosage level for each of the conditions and comparing the outcomes with that dosage between groups over time. This research model works well when the purpose is to determine baselines for therapeutic dose ranges. Mental health services do not work that way. In practice, mental health clinicians work with the client to achieve an agreed level of functioning or reduction in symptom distress, or both. The modification of research strategies for guiding clinical decisions begins with a shift toward use of psychological tests (or assessments) measures that support the demands of clinical decision-making. The following sections provide guidelines for selecting one or more such instruments most suitable for treatment planning, mapping client progress, and measuring treatment outcome.

## ASSESSMENT GUIDELINES

Finding agreement among a group of professionals is always a challenge. Finding agreement among professionals on an assessment procedure based on psychological criteria has not yet been accomplished. Fortunately, well-designed psychological assessments are better recognized in managed care settings for determining eligibility and level of care (see reviews by Owen, Klapow, Hicken, & Tucker, 2001; and Gavin & Henderson, 2000). Additionally, many employers and behavioral health insurers understand that simplistic notions of cost-containment often lead to greater long-term expense. This is particularly true for the growing number of behavioral managed care programs that serve persons with severe and persistent mental illnesses. The challenge lies in agreeing on this basic question: Who is eligible for what level of care? In

TABLE 6.1
Guidelines for the Development, Selection, and/or Use of Progress-Outcome Measures

---

Applications
  1. Relevance to target group independent of specific treatment provided
     although sensitive to treatment-related changes
Methods and procedures
  2. Simple, teachable methods
  3. Use of measures with objective referents
  4. Use of multiple respondents
  5. Process-identifying outcome measures
Psychometric features
  6. Psychometric strengths: reliability, validity, sensitivity to treatment-related
     change, and nonreactivity
Cost considerations
  7. Low costs relative to uses
Utility considerations
  8. Understandability by nonprofessional audiences
  9. Easy feedback and uncomplicated interpretation
  10. Usefulness in clinical services
  11. Compatibility with clinical theories and practices

---

this chapter, level of care is defined as the amount and type of resources allocated to achieve a satisfactory outcome. For example, inpatient or residential care for 21 days is certainly a different level of care than that of 21 outpatient psychotherapy sessions of 45 minutes. Clinical decision-making begins with the assessment, and it is our hope that the framework in this section will help clinicians create standard protocols to match individual clinical contexts.

The 11 guidelines to assist in such clinical decisions were originally developed by a panel of experts assembled by the National Institute of Mental Health (Ciarlo, Brown, Edwards, Kiresuk, & Newman, 1986).[1] This chapter provides updates to the guidelines as a result of two demands on the clinical community: managed care philosophy and operations that control consumer choice of service provider in the effort to control costs, and consumer demand for greater choice of service provider (Newman & Carpenter, 1997). Often managed care controls and consumer choice are considered diametrically opposed, but they do not have to be. Consumer choice can be seen as offering a feedback mechanism toward greater accountability and efficiency. Proper selection of psychological assessment techniques is thus critical to both managed care and consumer choice. The 11 guidelines are summarized in Table 6.1. Each focuses on unique concerns that will assist the reader in considering the demands of his or her own situation.

## Guideline 1: Relevance to Target Group

An outcome measure or set of measures should be relevant and appropriate to the target group(s) whose treatment is being studied; that is, the most important and frequently observed symptoms, problems, goals, or other domains of change for the group(s) should be addressed by the measure(s). . . . Other factors being equal, use of a measure appropriate

---

[1] Members of the expert panel were A. Broskowski, J. A. Ciarlo, G. B. Cox, H. H. Goldman, W. A. Hargreaves, I. Elkins, J. Mintz, F. L. Newman, and J. W. Zinober.

to a wider range of client groups is preferred.... Measures ... independent of the type of treatment service provided are to be preferred. (Ciarlo et al., 1986, p. 26)

Common wisdom supports the opinion that treatment selection, and a person's probable response to treatment, should be based on both clinical and demographic characteristics (Vavaeke & Emmelkamp, 1998). A target group can be described as a cluster of persons who possess similar clinical and demographic characteristics and are expected to have a similar response to treatment. Epidemiological needs assessments combined with expert panels have identified target groups requiring similar systems of services for persons with a severe mental illness (Helzer & Hudziak, 2002; Uehara, Smukler, & Newman, 1994). Another approach to defining target groups is to link the epidemiological data with historic levels of care or a combination of both.

A second feature of a target group that must be considered consists of the personal characteristics that are known to influence how the information is collected. Differences in age, ethnicity (related to language and meaning), comorbidity with a physical illness or developmental disability, and past experience all influence the collection of information. This becomes important, for example, when a clinician considers a scale for the measurement of cognitive functioning. It will provide skewed results if it is given to clients who are younger than the age intended for that scale. The instruments discussed in this volume provide an excellent platform for selecting measures based on clinical-demographic characteristics and personal characteristics.

### Guideline 2: Simple, Teachable Methods

The development of computer-assisted assessments has enhanced the reliability and validity of implementation by standardizing the way in which queries are presented (Butler et al., 2001). However, even with the development of computer-assisted methods, training and the controlling of administrative quality must still occur (Nunnally & Burnstein, 1994). Self-report measures (e.g., SCL–90–R, Basis–32, Beck Depression Inventory, MMPI–2) or measures completed by a family member that have adequate psychometric quality usually have good instructions and administration manuals. If the recommended guidelines for administration are ignored, the effects on measure reliability and validity are potentially disastrous. For example, the instructions for most self-report instruments strongly recommend their completion independent of guidance or advice from others, preferably in isolation. This basic requirement is not always adequately respected. People within a group will likely bias their responses in the direction of how they want to present themselves or relate to others rather than how they would specifically respond in relation only to themselves. Computers help collect accurate information in other ways besides presenting standardized queries.

It is possible that the use of computers to collect self-report information will also increase the integrity of how the data are collected. The integrity of the data is increased because people typically use computers alone and therefore group biases are reduced. This is one area where computer-assisted applications are particularly useful. Many people are becoming accustomed to interacting with a machine that asks them questions, often of a quite personal nature (Butler et al., 1998, 2001).

Measures completed by an independent clinical observer or by the treating clinician can be very useful, but they pose their own challenges. Often the instructions on the instrument's use, training, and quality control procedures fail to account for judgment bias. On the one hand, such measures seek to make use of the professional's trained observations. On the other hand, such scales tend to be more reactive to clinician judgment bias (Newman, 1983; Petkova, Quitkin, McGrath, Stewart, & Klein, 2000). Useful procedures for identifying judgment biases in a staff-training format are discussed in Newman (1983) and detailed in Newman and Sorensen (1985).

When an assessment instrument is used as the basis for determining the level of need and reimbursement eligibility in a managed care environment, controls over training and use are necessary to prevent improper use of the instrument. A good example of where such controls are currently employed is in Indiana Division of Mental Health's implementation of a managed care program, the Hoosier Assurance Plan (HAP DeLiberty, Newman, & Ward, 2001). HAP provides state funds to cover services to adults with a serious mental illness or a chronic addiction and to children and adolescents with a severe emotional disorder. Two key features of the plan are as follows: The consumer is to have informed choice[2] of service provider, and the level of reimbursement is determined by the level of need demonstrated by the array of factor scores on an assessment instrument—one instrument for children and adolescents and another for adults (DeLiberty et al., 2001).

Based on our experience with this plan, we suggest two additional controls. First, all clinicians must be trained in the use of the instrument, with evidence of meeting the established criteria available for an audit. To support the local service program training efforts, each program is expected to have one or more clinical staff trained as trainers of other clinical or service staff. The training program includes handouts, vignettes, and guidelines on how to conduct the staff training. Second, a trained independent audit team should conduct a review of a random sample of cases on-site at each service provider location. A report of the audits goes both to the service program and to the State Office of Mental Health. Training in the use of the instrument and audits of both the local program's application of training procedures and the assessment instruments are seen as necessary controls. In the example cited, these controls were employed in the pilot work, and high levels of reliability and validity were observed (Deliberty et al., 2001). An assessment plan that includes consumer informed choice of service provider, scoring based on an array of factor scores, on-site trainers for consistent instruction, and regular audits provides a solid foundation for measuring a program's response to clients' care needs.

### Guideline 3: Use of Measures with Objective Referents

An objective referent is a concrete observable, or at least describable, example given at key points on the rating scale. The major advantage of objective referents is that they support the development of reliable norms, and such norms are particularly critical when applied to managed care eligibility and level-of-care decisions. One example of a scale with objective referents is the Child Adolescent Functional Assessment Scale (CAFAS; Hodges & Gust, 1995). Examples of behaviors are provided at the four levels of impairment for each of 35 categories of behavior. For example, under

---

[2] Informed choice is supported by an annual Hoosier Assurance Plan Provider Profile Report Card that contains information on the performance of each service provider as measured by data from two data sources. The first contains the results of telephone interviews of a random sample of consumers asking about the impact of the services on their functioning and quality of life. The sample is stratified by service program, and the survey is conducted by the University of Indiana Survey Research Unit. The second source is the reported baselines and the 90-day changes in factor scores from the clinical assessments performed on all consumers covered by the Hoosier Assurance Plan (Indiana's managed care program). A copy of the report card, the adult instrument, and the training manual can be obtained from Indiana Division of Mental Health.

the most severe level of impairment (Unsafe/Potentially Unsafe Behavior), there are five examples of behaviors, two of which are "Dangerous behavior caused harm to household member" and "Sexually assaulted/abused another household member, or attempted to (e.g., sibling)." Another approach involves the development of multiple items within a class of behaviors. The rater is provided one referent behavior in an item and then requested to identify (a) the behavior's frequency (e.g., $x$ times in last 24 hours, in the last week, or in the last 30 days), (b) the similarity of the observed behavior to the referent behavior (e.g., most like to least like the referent behavior), or (c) the intensity of the referent behavior (e.g., from not evident to severe). Which approach is best suited to each particular program is an empirical issue (see Guidelines 6–11).

Many clinicians are attracted to instruments that are individualized to the client, partly because the instruments can be linked more directly to the consumer's own behaviors and life situation and partly because treatment selection, course, and outcome can be individualized to the consumer. In fact, a consistent finding in the literature is that when the client and the clinician have agreed on the problems and goals, there is a significant improvement in outcome (Tryon & Winograd, 2001). Individualized measures include severity of target complaints, goal-attainment scaling, problem-oriented records, and global improvement ratings. The major problem with individualized measures involves generalizability across clients. In other words, is the change in the severity of one person's complaint or problem comparable to a like degree of change in another person's? If such changes are not generalizable across a group of clients, funding of the treatment(s) involved becomes more difficult to justify. Even though no measure is perfectly generalizable, without objective referents the distribution of outcomes becomes free-floating across settings or clinical groups, thereby limiting its utility in making decisions.

Besides focusing on referent behaviors, an alternative method of measurement exists. Local conditions, including statewide funding practices or community standards of "normal functioning," will transform the distributions of any measure, with or without objective referents (Newman, 1980; Ruggeri, Bisoffi, Fontecedro, & Warner, 2001). Several meta-analytic studies in which effect size was standardized have been very informative without specifically identifying the behaviors that have been modified (e.g., Morris & DeShon, 2002). Shadish, Navarro, Matt, and Phillips (2000) studied the relationship of the number of visits to outcome across studies. The measure of outcome was simply whether improvement was observed. However, this application is only useful for addressing research and policy questions and does not satisfy the need of a clinician or a clinical service to communicate with a client or an insurer about an individual client's eligibility for care. Doing studies that identify local "norms" should become standard practice for any measure intended to help set funding guidelines, set standards for treatment review, or conduct evaluation research (Bierman et al., 2002; Newman, Kopta, McGovern, Howard, & McNeilly, 1988).

Both individualized problem identification and goal setting are needed for a holistic perspective when serving a client within a community program. This can be accomplished by using an individualized instrument and an instrument with national norms with objective referents. By using both, one can satisfy two demands. The first demand is to identify the individual client's characteristics in terms that are most useful in the local situation. The other is to relate these characteristics to the client's performance on a standardized instrument. In both cases, the guidelines that support reliable and valid application of either assessment technique also must be applied.

## Guideline 4: Use of Multiple Respondents

A number of theorists note that measures representing the principal stakeholders—the client, therapist, family, and research evaluator—should be obtained in order to capture their different perspectives (Ciarlo et al., 1986; Sobell, Agrawal, & Sobell, 1997). For example, a second respondent is helpful when assessing behaviors that are embarrassing to the client. In the assessment of children, Mesman and Koot (2000) consider both parents and teachers valid observers of psychologically troubled children. Similar issues are being addressed in the development of assessment scales for the elderly, where the adult children of the frail elderly would be considered major stakeholders whose assessments are considered primary over self-reports (Salamon, 1999). Researchers' perspectives have often been contrasted with respondents' views. Turner, McGovern, and Sandrock (1982) found a high level of agreement across different respondents (high canonical correlations) in the use of measures originally designed specifically for one of the respondent groups. Higher coefficients were obtained when observers described specific behaviors (objective referents), while lower coefficients were obtained when observers described how another person felt (e.g., he or she felt "happy" or "sad"). Again, the measure's characteristics directly affect its validity, and when measuring stakeholders, it is prudent to anchor the scale with objective referents.

The advantages of obtaining measures from multiple observers include these: (a) Each observer's experiences result in a unique view of the client, (b) concurrent validation of behavioral status and changes can be obtained, (c) responses are likely to be more honest if all of the respondents are aware of the other respondents' involvement, and (d) discrepancies between informants can alert the clinician to potential problem areas. For instance, a client might claim to be sleeping soundly whereas the spouse reports that the client's nights are restless. This type of disagreement is an excellent starting point for a therapeutic session. Disadvantages of using multiple sources include (a) higher assessment costs, particularly in terms of the time and effort of data collection and analysis; (b) the added logistical problem of attempting to collect the functional status data on the client from multiple respondents at the same time so that the same states are being observed; and (c) the need to resolve discrepant responses in an attempt to isolate the actual behavior. However, time and effort costs are becoming more manageable with the widespread use of computer-based administration of measures.

## Guideline 5: Process-Identifying Outcome Measures

> Measure(s) that provide information regarding the means or processes by which treatments may produce positive effects are preferred to those that do not. (Ciarlo et al., 1986, p. 28)

A process measure focuses on the behaviors of the parties involved in the treatment during individual sessions or over the course of treatment. Two examples of process measures are development of a therapeutic alliance (e.g., Diamond, Liddle, Hogue, & Dakof, 1999; Horvath & Luborsky, 1993; Tolan, Hanish, McKay, & Dickey, 2002) and adherence to therapeutic technique (e.g., Henggeler, Melton, Brondino, Scherer, & Hanley, 1997). The relationship between the scores on therapeutic alliance measures and outcome has been found to be statistically significant but not strong, with indications of positive correlations between alliance measure scores and outcome measures (typically that of day-to-day functioning) of under .30. For this reason, and for reasons of time and expense in collecting process measure data, such measures are not routinely performed in the day-to-day delivery of services. However, Henggeler et al. (1997) argued in favor of their use, as they found that the degree to which scores on a measure of adherence to Multi Systemic Treatment (MST) significantly predicted the number of arrests and days of detention for violent substance-abusing youth over the 20 months following treatment. To our knowledge, Henggeler et al.'s call for the further development and routine use of such process measures has not been widely acted on. However, he and his colleagues are attempting to have the adherence measure used as a routine part of the application of MST for all programs that seek assistance from his group to train staff and implement MST in their agency (personal communication, February 2002).

Process measures are to be distinguished from progress measures used regularly over the course of the treatment to gather data on behavioral markers of progress or risk behaviors that are the target of the treatment. Examples of behavioral markers include signs of suicidality, depression, anxiety, substance abuse, interpersonal functioning, or community functioning (Lambert, & Co. Author, this edition; Lucki, 1998). Such behavioral progress markers do not necessarily describe the actual therapeutic process. Instead, they describe whether the client is functioning adequately with regard to treatment objectives, and they are used to consider continuing versus altering the ongoing treatment. Certainly, programs serving consumers with serious and persistent illnesses should adopt a strategy of regularly collecting data on progress markers.

The basic strategy of using more process-identifying measures, however, is still somewhat controversial. On one side, researchers (e.g., Constantino, 2000) have argued that a relationship between process and progress should exist. Cognitive behavioral treatments employing self-management, homework assignments, and self-help group feedback often use measures with objective behavioral referents as both process and progress measures. On the other side, Stiles and Shapiro (1995) argued that the most important interpersonal and relationship ingredients (processes) that occur during psychotherapy are not expected to correlate with progress. Adequate empirical support for either side of the argument is still lacking, and the different sides of the arguments appear to be theory related (Newman, 1995).

It may be best to consider process in terms of treatment progress or attainment of intermediate goals of the treatment plan. Steady progress toward these goals should be an integral part of the conversation between client and clinician. Howard, Moras, Brill, Martinovich, & Lutz (1996) described mapping of individual client's progress on a standardized measure. The mapping relates the expected progress to a database that includes a large sample of consumers with similar clinical characteristics at the start of their therapeutic episode. Since it is thus possible to empirically describe when a consumer's progress is or is not satisfactory in a timely fashion, this approach is particularly attractive to managed care companies. If the observed progress matches the expected progress, continue treatment; if not, it may be advisable to alter the treatment strategy.

### Guideline 6: Psychometric Strengths

The measure used should meet minimum criteria of psychometric adequacy, including: a) reliability (test-retest, internal consistency, or inter-rater agreement where appropriate); b) validity (content, concurrent, and construct validity); c) demonstrated sensitivity to treatment-related change; and d) freedom from response bias and non-reactivity (insensitivity) to extraneous situational factors that may exist (including physical settings, client expectation, staff behavior, and accountability pressures). The measure should be difficult to intentionally fake, either positively or negatively. (Ciarlo et al., 1986, p. 27)

Two issues are important when considering psychometric features. The first is intuitive. When trying to measure an attribute, use measures of high psychometric quality. The second seems bold. The psychometric quality of the local application of an instrument is related to the management and the quality of services.

On the surface, no one should argue for lowering the standards for an instrument's psychometric qualities. Yet, the more reactive, less psychometrically rigorous global measures (e.g., global improvement ratings, global level-of-functioning ratings) are popular with upper-level management. These less rigorous measures have a place. However, the instrument used is not the only aspect of a quality evaluation. The environment and the training of observers are crucial to the success of the evaluation. A similar issue arises when measures are applied within an environment of competing objectives such as improving care and meeting funding needs. It is possible to exert reasonable control over the application of these measures to ensure psychometric quality (Newman, 1980), but if such control is not enforced, then psychometric quality suffers (DeLiberty et al., 2001).

A second aspect of this guideline is that the psychometric quality of the local application of an instrument is related to the quality of services. Consider an example in which the popular Global Assessment of Functioning (GAF) score (AXIS V on DMS–IV) or a multidimensional measure (e.g., the HAPI–Adult scale; DeLiberty et al., 2001) is employed to rate clients at intake and at termination from treatment and the ratings are to be used for treatment planning, determining service eligibility, and indicating program performance on a statewide report card. It is possible that some clinical staff will adjust their ratings of clients in a manner that will help the organization justify services and "look good" on the report card. Specifically, these clinicians may believe that it is best to rate clients at a low level of functioning at the start of treatment (to show a need for and justify the reimbursement of services) and then rate the clients at a higher level of functioning at the end of treatment in order to demonstrate positive results. Other staff in the same agency may not be inclined to do this. As a consequence of this disparity in rating styles (biases), the reliability of the instrument would be decreased to below that of the published results of well-controlled studies. But it is a sad result if such misinformation about a client is communicated to other staff also involved in treating the client either at that time or on some future occasion (e.g., upon readmission).

Here we are making a double-edged assertion. On the one hand, the selection and use of an instrument of poor psychometric quality could lower the apparent quality of care being delivered. It is likely that the wrong information about a person would be transmitted to program managers and third-party payers. On the other hand, it is also probable that a service providing poor quality of care would itself reduce the psychometric quality of the assessment techniques. If local data collection produces low reliability and validity estimates and the instrument has been demonstrated to have adequate reliability and validity in another context, then one of two possibilities should be considered. The results could be a matter of poor data collection and management, but if the psychometric quality of the instrument is lower in its local application than in national norms, it would make sense to question the quality and effectiveness of the clinical services.

Another concern is an instrument's validity within its local application. If locally established estimates of instrument validity (among services or within a service) deviate from established norms, the service staff's concept of "normal" should be examined. Classical examples of differences in estimates can occur when inpatient and outpatient staff evaluate community functioning (Newman, Heverly, Rosen, Kopta,

& Bedell, 1983). Kopta, Newman, McGovern, and Sandrock (1986) also found that multiple frames of reference among clinicians from different theoretical orientations produced differing syntheses of the clinical material within a session and resulted in different intervention strategies and treatment plans proposed. Researchers also found that differences in attributions of problem causality and treatment outcome responsibility were related to judgments regarding the clinicians' choice of treatment strategies (McGovern, Newman, & Kopta, 1986). A more recent review of this issue can be found in Horwitz and Scheid (1999). Different frames of reference most likely reduce the estimates of concurrent validity of measures as well as interrater reliability. However, reduced coefficients of reliability and validity are not as serious as the potential negative impact on services that occurs when service staff are unclear about and lack agreement on purpose, language, and meaning.

There are three conditions that, when satisfied, increase both the quality of care and the psychometric quality of assessment data. First, a clinical service should clearly define target groups for specific services. Second, the service should clearly define observable progress and outcome goals for each target group. Third, the leadership should identify one or more instruments whose interpretative language is useful for supporting clinical communication about client status. When one or more instruments are selected in a situation where the first two conditions are met, the instruments can support reliable and useful communication that in turn promotes a high quality of care.

To illustrate the relationship between the quality of care and the quality of an instrument as implemented, consider psychometric reliability in relation to program quality. The prime function of a measure is to communicate information about clients and services. If the reliability of a measure (communication) is low, it is likely that there is inconsistent communication or understanding about the clients' psychological and functional status, the treatment goals, and/or the clients' progress and outcomes. Such inconsistent communication or understanding between clients and therapists or among clinical staff will very probably lead to poorer outcomes (Tryon & Winograd, 2001).

However, measures can fit into clinical communication. First, careful selection of the progress-outcome measures must be preceded by and based on a clear statement of the program's purpose and goals. Second, the language describing the functional domains covered by the instruments should represent an agreed vocabulary for staff to use when communicating with and about clients. If the language of communication is related to the language of the instruments, then any inconsistency in the use of the instruments will reflect an inconsistency in the communication with clients and among staff.[3]

A two-part strategy is recommended here. First, the leadership of a service program should implement or refine operations to satisfy the three conditions identified above: obtainment of a clear target group definition by service staff, provision of operational definitions of treatment goals and objectives, and selection of instruments

---

[3] Work with several colleagues has focused on both the methods and results of studies identifying factors influencing differences in clinicians' perceptions. The theoretical arguments and historical research basis for this line of work are discussed in Newman (1983). The procedures for conducting these studies as staff development sessions are detailed in Newman and Sorensen (1985) and Heverly, Fitt, and Newman (1987). Studies on factors influencing clinical assessment and treatment decisions include Heverly and Newman (1984); Kopta, Newman, McGovern, and Angle (1989); Kopta, Newman, McGovern, and Sandrock (1986); McGovern, Newman, and Kopta (1986); Newman, Fitt, and Heverly (1987); Newman, Heverly, Rosen, Kopta, and Bedell (1983); and Newman, Kopta, McGovern, Howard, and McNeilly (1988).

whose structure and language reflect the first two conditions. The program should also incorporate staff supervision and procedures that will help identify when and how differences in frames of reference and language meaning may be occurring. Staff development exercises can also serve to document the level of measure reliability (Newman & Sorensen, 1985). Such exercises contrast staff assessments and treatment plans for the same set of client profiles. The client profiles could be presented via taped interviews or written vignettes. Green and Gracely (1987) found that a two-page profile was as effective as a taped interview (and a lot less costly) when estimating interrater reliability. Methods for constructing such profiles and analyzing the results are described in Newman and Sorensen (1985). Data from these exercises can also be used to assess the degree to which the local use of the instruments matches the national norms.

## Guideline 7: Low Costs Relative to Uses

How much should be spent on collecting, editing, storing, processing, and analyzing process, progress, or outcome information? How large is the investment needed to ensure a positive return on these functions? The answer can be considered in terms of five important functions that the data support: screening and treatment planning, quality assurance, program evaluation, cost-containment (utilization review), and revenue generation.

There are several pressures on both mental and physical health services that could make an investment in the use of progress-assessment instruments cost-beneficial. First, third-party payers usually require an initial assessment to justify the provision of services and the development of a treatment plan for reimbursable clients. For the seriously and persistently mentally ill, funded placement in extended community services depends on the performance of a diagnostic and functional assessment. Most third-party payers will cover the cost of judicious testing if it can be shown to be a cost-effective means of making screening and utilization review decisions. Justification for continued care is also required by both public and private third-party payers. Again, the cost of the assessment can often be underwritten by the cost-containment/quality assurance agreement with the third-party payer.

Second, increasing levels of accountability for treatment interventions are being demanded. Our own experience is that the legal profession is divided on this issue. According to one view, the less "hard data" a service program has, the less liability it would have for its actions. The credo can be stated thus: Do not put anything in writing unless required to do so by an authority that will assume responsibility. The other view holds that a service program increases its liability if it does not have concrete evidence to justify its actions. There is little doubt that the former view has been the more popular one until recently. Additionally, because of increased legal actions by consumer groups on the issue of "right to treatment" and the call for "evidence-based treatment," there is likely to be an increased need for data that can justify the types and levels of treatment provided.

A force in the opposite direction is being exerted by the increased budgetary constraints imposed by both private and public sources of revenues for mental health services. Pressure to enforce the application of cost-containment/utilization review guidelines appears to be stronger than pressure to ensure quality of care. Although the literature has indicated the efficacy of many mental health interventions, empirical research supporting the cost-effectiveness and cost-benefits of these services still lags (Newman & Howard, 1986; Yates, 1998). At the time that Ciarlo assembled the panel of experts for National Institute of Mental Health, in 1986, 0.5% of an agency's total budget was considered a fair estimate of the cost of collecting and processing progress and outcome data. This was to include the costs of test materials and training of personnel as well as collecting and processing the data. The estimate was made at a time when the public laws governing the disbursements of federal block grant funds required that 5% of the agency's budget be directed toward the evaluation of needs and program effectiveness.

Three notable changes in service delivery have occurred since the panel produced its report. One is that the Health Care Financing Agency (HCFA) and other third-party payers now require an assessment procedure that will identify and deflect those who do not require care or identify the level of care required for clients applying for service. They offer limited reimbursement for such assessment activities. The second change focuses on the use of assertive case management or continuous-treatment team approaches for the seriously and persistently mentally ill and for substance abusers. Here client-tracking procedures can be part of the reimbursed overhead costs. The third and perhaps the most powerful impetus for change is the new National Committee on Quality Assurance (NCQA) standards for accrediting managed behavioral health organizations; there is a standard requiring more clinical and quality studies than in the past. Managed care contractors can expect to face rising expectations for outcome data collection and analysis, auditing of medical records, and adherence to practice guidelines.

Assessment and client-tracking procedures are logically compatible activities. The requirement for initial and progress assessments to justify levels of care can be integrated with the client-tracking system requirement for case management or treatment team approaches. If a cost-effective technique for integrating the assessment and the client-tracking procedures is instituted, then the costs for testing become part of the costs of coordinating and providing services. It is possible that if the costs considered here were restricted to just the costs of purchasing the instrument and the capacity to process the instrument's data (and not the professionals' time), the costs would not exceed the 0.5% estimate. Proper cost estimation studies should be done to provide an empirical basis for identifying the appropriate levels of costs.

### Guideline 8: Understandability by Nonprofessional Audiences

The scoring procedures and presentation of the results should be understandable to stakeholders at all levels. These stakeholders include the consumer, the family, and other third parties. The analysis and interpretation of the results should be understandable by the consumers themselves. Two lines of reasoning support this. First, there is increased belief in and legal support for the consumer's right to know about assessment results and the selection of treatment and services. Second an understandable descriptive profile of the client can be used in a therapeutically positive fashion. Questions asked by the client might include the following:

- Do the assessment scores indicate the need for treatment, progress in treatment, or the need for continued treatment?
- Do my assessment scores over time describe how I functioned in the past relative to how I am doing now?
- Do the assessment scores help me to communicate how I feel or function with those who are trying to serve, treat, or assist me (including my family)?
- Does the assessment help me understand what I can expect in the future?

Another advantage of understandable test results is that they can be aggregated over groups of consumers in order to communicate evaluation research to influential stakeholders (e.g., regulators, funders, legislators, and employers). This includes needs assessment results used for program- and budget-planning purposes (Uehara et al., 1994). It also includes evaluating program effectiveness and/or cost-effectiveness among service alternatives for policy analysis and decision-making (Newman & Howard, 1986; Yates, 1998). Finance and policy executives require data relevant to their decision-making. They are often reticent to rely solely on expert opinion to interpret the data, and some even prefer to do the interpretation themselves. Questions that the data should be able to address include these:

- Do the scores show whether a client has improved functioning to a level where he or she requires less restrictive care or no longer requires care?
- Do the measures assess and describe the client's functioning in socially significant areas, such as independent living, vocational productivity, and appropriate interpersonal and community behaviors?
- Would the measures permit comparisons of relative program effectiveness among similar programs that serve similar clients?

In summary, it is important to ensure not only that the test results are understandable to those at the front-line level (consumers, their families, and service staff) but that the aggregate data are understandable to budget planners and policymakers.

## Guideline 9: Easy Feedback and Uncomplicated Interpretation

The discussion under Guideline 8 is also relevant to this guideline, but the focus here is on presentation measure results or findings. Does the instrument and its scoring procedures provide reports that are easily interpreted? Does the report stand on its own without further explanation or the training of recipients? For example, complex tables are less desirable than a graphic display describing the characteristics of a client or a group of clients relative to a recognizable norm. Also, narrative and graphic formats are becoming more common.

Another recent development is the trend toward developing report cards on mental health services for use by consumers, their families, or funding agencies (Dewan & Carpenter, 1997). In the past, such report cards focused on the types of consumers served and their level of satisfaction. The assessment techniques used by managed care to determine eligibility, level of care, progress, and outcome should also be used as part of a delivery system report card to inform consumers and other purchasers of mental health services. Consumer groups are requesting that report cards go beyond satisfaction with the way services are provided (although that is also important) and incorporate the quality and long-term effects of the services themselves. Recently, there has been a movement to provide report cards that describe the impact of the services on the consumers' quality of life and functioning (DeLiberty et al., 2001; Eisen, 2001). The use of report cards is sufficiently new that systematic research on the quality and impact of instruments when used as part of a report card has yet to be done. Nevertheless, report cards of Health Maintenance Organizations in mental health care are substantial enough to reach wide distribution in the popular press and can be found on websites (three examples are www.mhmr.state.tx.us/CentralOffice/MentalHealth/PIMHpub.html, www.odmhsas.org/statisticsother.htm, and www.in.gov/fssa/servicemental/pub/profile.pdf).

There is an important cautionary note that concerns the relationship between what is communicated by a report and the actual underlying dimensions or variables assessed by the measures involved: The language of the presentation should not be so "user-friendly" that it misrepresents the data. The language used to label figures and tables must be carefully developed so that the validity of the instruments' underlying constructs are not violated. A related problem arises when it is assumed that the language used in the report matches the language used by the client or family members in their effort to understand and cope with their distress. For example, an elevated depression scale score might not match the client's verbalized experience of elevated depression. It is essential to not allow the language of test results to mask issues that are clinically important as well as important to the client.

## Guideline 10: Usefulness in Clinical Services

The assessment instruments should support the clinical processes of a service with minimum interference. As we have argued in this chapter, it is important that any the instrument's language, scoring, and presentation of results support clinical decision-making and communication. The list of those who need to communicate with each other includes not only the clinical and service staff working with the clients but also the clients themselves and their families. Several clinically relevant questions might be considered when discussing an instrument's utility:

- Will the test results describe the likelihood that the client needs services and be appropriately responsive to available services?
- Do the test results help in planning the array and levels of services, treatments, and intervention styles that might best meet service goals?
- Do the test results provide sufficient justification for the planned treatment to be reimbursed by third-party payers?
- Is the client responding to treatment as planned, and if not, what areas of functioning are not improving as expected?

An ideal instrument for meeting this guideline would be sufficiently supportive of these processes without requiring a burdensome effort to collect and process the data. The logic here is the same as for Guideline 7. The measure should have low costs relative to its use in screening and treatment planning, quality assurance, cost control, and revenue generation. The more the instrument is seen as supporting these functions, the less unduly expensive and interfering the instrument will be perceived to be by clinical staff.

## Guideline 11: Compatibility with Clinical Theories and Practices

An instrument that is compatible with a variety of clinical theories and practices should gain the interest and acceptance of a broader range of clinicians and stakeholders than one based on only one concept of treatment improvement. Such assessments could also provide a base for evaluative research by contrasting the relative effectiveness of different treatment approaches or strategies.

How does one evaluate the level of compatibility? A first step is to investigate the context in which it was developed and the samples used in developing norms. For example, if the only normative sample available on a measure consisted of clients on inpatient units, the instrument would probably be too limited for wide use, as inpatient care is now seen as the most restrictive and infrequently used type of care in the continuum of care. The broader the initial sampling population used in the measure's development, the more generalizable the instrument is to different clinical populations. Ideally, norms for both clinical and nonclinical populations would be available. For example, if an instrument is intended for a population with a chronic physical disability (e.g., wheelchair-bound patients), then for sampling purposes, the definition of a normal functioning population might change to persons with the chronic physical disability who function well in the community (Saunders, Howard, & Newman, 1988).

Another indicator of measure compatibility is whether there is evidence that the measure's use in treatment and service planning and review matches the research results published in formal scientific journals. This is especially important when a measure's data are used to contrast the outcomes of two or more therapeutic (or service) interventions. In reviewing this type of research, one should first review the types of clients served, the setting, and the diagnoses and problems treated. One should also note the differences in the range and distribution of scores (often assessed via standard deviations) among the groups studied. Evidence of compatibility would be indicated by similar (homogeneous) variations among the treatment groups. Such homogeneity would indicate that errors of measurement (and/or individual differences and/or item difficulty) were not biased by the therapeutic intervention that was employed. One note of caution here: It is possible for a measure to have homogeneity of variance within and across treatment groups and still lack equal sensitivity to the treatment effects for these groups. If a measure is not sufficiently sensitive to treatment effects for any particular group, its use as a progress or outcome assessment instrument is ill advised. Methods for assessing these features are discussed in Newman and Tejeda (1996) and in chapter 9 of this volume.

This guideline, of course, should never be considered in isolation, regardless of its attractiveness in terms of theory and practice. To be effective (and cost-effective) in selecting an instrument or instruments, one must systematically address an additional series of questions covered in other guidelines. For example, what psychological and community functioning domains do we wish to assess for this client or this group of clients? What are the behaviors that we expect to impact? What clinical or program decisions will be supported by an assessment of the person's psychological state or functional status? What is the most cost effective means for performing these assessments?

## CONCLUSION

The 11 guidelines are intended to set the stage for characterizing a mental health client's intake, progress, and outcome through the use of systematic, reliable assessments. These guidelines are designed to support the evaluation, selection, and application of assessment instruments and are not presented as firm rules. Few if any existing instruments could fully meet all the guidelines. But it is expected that if the guidelines are used as a means of drawing together available and relevant information on an instrument under consideration, they will decrease the number of unexpected or unpleasant surprises in its adoption (or adaptation) and use. For example, how different does a person's measured behavior have to be from those who are called asymptomatic to be described as symptomatic, and vice versa? The role that measure reliability and sensitivity play in determining whether a person's assessment status represents normal or abnormal functioning further confuses the issue. There is also the question whether the persons seeking or being referred for treatment actually consider their behavior to substantially impair their daily functioning and to thus signal a problem.

Addressing these issues requires not only an evaluation of the person's health or physical status but also an appreciation of the person's social context. For example, a person with a white-collar job may consider a certain class of events or objects to be so threatening and anxiety provoking that avoidance is a solution that allows him or her to function quite well. Such a person would probably not seek a therapeutic intervention to deal with anxiety. However, a commercial pilot might have to regularly cope with life-threatening events, and hence anxiety might impair his or her ability to function. Although the scores on a standardized measure of anxiety might be quite similar for the white-collar worker and the commercial pilot, the latter (at least) would be well advised to seek help from a professional.

Even a person's health or physical status must be considered in that person's historical and environmental context. For example, as described by Saunders et al. (1988), a person with diabetes might need to attend carefully to psychosomatic signals to monitor blood sugar level in a timely manner. Such individuals must also acknowledge helplessness to control the disease without the aid of an external agent (insulin) and the need to monitor exercise and food intake in a way that could isolate them from others in their social milieu. Thus, they might respond positively to items on an instrument measuring emotion-laden concern about attention to bodily functioning ("always"), feelings of helplessness ("often"), or feelings about being socially isolated ("sometimes"). Although all of these behaviors may be quite adaptive for persons with diabetes, these same measures can be construed as signs of an affective disorder, namely, depression. Thus, both researchers and clinicians must understand the social environmental context as well as the health and physical status of the individuals they study and/or treat (Kendall, Flannery-Shroeder, & Ford, 1999; Saunders et al, 1988).

The application of the 11 guidelines has its own costs. Although a master's degree level of psychometric training is normally sufficient background to assemble the basic information on an instrument's ability to meet these guidelines, a full application of the guidelines requires broader input. Some of the guidelines require clinical supervisors and managers to review clinical standards, program procedures, and policies. Others require an interchange among clinical supervisory and fiscal management personnel in areas where they have had little prior experience (e.g., the costs and worth of psychological testing). Our experience with involving clients and family members as participants in the selection or modification of instruments has been extremely useful (DeLiberty et al., 2001). For example, Teague (1995) found that the development of self-management skills was as important an outcome concern as reduction in the level of symptom distress across all subgroups—clients, family members, and clinical service providers. This finding was confirmed in our work in Indiana, where the advisory panel that guided the development of the assessment instruments (which included both professionals and consumer representatives) insisted that both self-management skills and level of problem severity be considered together in the assessment of each problem area (DeLiberty et al., 2001).

It is our contention, therefore, that the ultimate benefits to clients and stakeholders of applying these guidelines are well worth the costs. Although there are few controlled studies on whether timely feedback of client assessment information positively influences the decision making of clients, clinicians, and managers, research has reported on the anticipation of regret caused by expected feedback (Zeelenberg, 1999).

Much of this research looks at risk taking and risk avoidance in gambling situations. Zeelenberg (1999) reports findings that suggest people are motivated to make choices that shield them from threatening feedback and that this regret aversion influences their decisions. More research is needed before we fully understand the effects of feedback within social services, but by providing honest results and timely feedback, we do influence the process and in all likelihood increase the chances of better program outcomes.

## REFERENCES

Bierman, K. L., Coie, J. D., Dodge, K. A., Greenberg, M. T., Lochman, J. E., McMahon, R. J., et al. (2002). The implementation of the Fast Track program: An example of a large-scale prevention science efficacy trial. *Journal of Abnormal Child Psychology, 30,* 1–17.

Butler, S. F., Budman, S. H., Goldman, R. J., Newman, F. L., Beckley, K. E., Trottier, D., et al. (2001). Initial validation of a computer-administered addiction severity index: The ASIBMV *Psychology of Addictive Behaviors, 15,* 4–12.

Butler, S. F., Newman, F. L., Cacciola, J. S., Frank, A., Budman, S. H., McLellan, A. T., et al. (1998). Predicting Addiction Severity Index (ASI) interviewer severity rating for a computer administered ASI. *Psychological Assessment, 10,* 399–407.

Ciarlo, J. A., Brown, T. R., Edwards, D. W. Kiresuk, T. J., & Newman, F. L. (1986). *Assessing mental health treatment outcome measurement techniques* (DHHS Pub. No. [ADM] 86–1301). Washington, DC: Superintendant of Documents, U.S. Government Printing Office.

Constantino, M. J. (2000). Interpersonal process in psychotherapy through the lens of the structural analysis of social behavior. *Applied and Preventative Psychology, 9,* 153–172.

DeLiberty, R. N., Newman, F. L., & Ward, E. (2001). Risk Adjustment in the Hoosier Assurance Plan: Impact on providers. *Journal of Behavioral Health Services & Research, 28,* 301–318.

Dewan, N., & Carpenter, D. (1997). Value account of health care services. *American Psychiatric Press Review of Psychiatry, 16,* V 81–101.

Diamond, G. M., Liddle, H. A., Hogue, A., & Dakof, G. A. (1999). Alliance-building interventions with adolescents in family therapy: A process study. *Psychotherapy: Theory, Research, Practice, Training, 36,* 355–368.

Eisen, S. U. (2001). Toward a national report card: Measuring consumer experiences. In B. Dickey & L. Sederer (Eds.), *Improving mental health care: Commitment to quality* (pp. 115–134). Washington, DC: American Psychiatric Press.

Gavin, A., & Henderson, S. (Eds.). (2000). *Unmet need in psychiatry: Problems, resources, responses.* New York: Cambridge University Press.

Green R. S., & Gracely, E. J. (1987). Selecting a rating scale for evaluating services to the chronically mentally ill. *Community Mental Health Journal 23,* 91–102.

Helzer, J. E., & Hudziak, J. J. (Eds.). (2002). *Defining psychopathology in the 21st century: DSM–V and beyond* (American Psychopathological Association Series). Washington DC. American Psychiatric Press.

Henggeler, S. W., Melton, G. B., Brondino, M. J., Scherer, D. G., & Hanley, J. H. (1997). Multisystemic therapy with violent and chronic juvenile offenders and their families: The role of treatment fidelity in successful dissemination. *Journal of Consulting and Clinical Psychology, 65,* 821–833.

Hermann, R. C., Finnerty, M., Provost, S., Palmer, R. H., Chan, J., Lagodmos, G., Teller, T., et al. (2002). Process measures for the assessment and improvement of quality of care for schizophrenia. *Schizophrenia Bulletin, 28,* 95–104.

Heverly, M. A., & Newman, F. L. (1984). Evaluating the influence of day treatment program orientation on clinicians' judgments. *International Journal of Partial Hospitalization, 2,* 239–250.

Heverly, M. A., Fitt, D., & Newman, F. L. (1987). Influences of client, service program and clinician characteristics on judgments of functioning and treatment recommendations. *Evaluation and Program Planning, 10,* 260–267.

Hodges, K., & Gust, J. (1995). Measures of impairment for children and adolescents. *Journal of Mental Health Administration, 22,* 403–413.

Horvath, A. O., & Luborsky, L. (1993). The role of the therapeutic alliance in psychotherapy. *Journal of Consulting and Clinical Psychology ,61,* 561–573.

Horwitz, A. V., & Scheid, T. L. (Eds.). (1999). *Handbook for the study of mental health: Social contexts, theories, and systems.* New York: Cambridge University Press.

Howard, K. I., Moras, K., Brill, P., Martinovich, Z., & Lutz, W. (1996). Evaluation of psychotherapy: Efficacy, effectiveness, and client progress. *American Psychologist, 51*, 1059–1964.

Kendall, P. C., Flannery-Shroeder, E. C., & Ford, J. D. (1999). Therapy outcome research methods. In P. C. Kendall, J. N. Butcher, & G. N. Holmbeck (Eds.), *Handbook of research methods in clinical psychology* (pp. 330–363). New York: Wiley.

Kopta, S. M., Newman, F. L., McGovern, M. P., & Sandrock, D. (1986). Psychotherapeutic orientations: A comparison of conceptualizations, interventions and recommendations for a treatment plan. *Journal of Consulting and Clinical Psychology, 54*, 369–374.

Kopta, A. M., Newman, F. L., McGovern, M. P., & Angle, R. S. (1989). The relationship between years of psychotherapy experience and conceptualizations, interventions, and treatment plan costs, *Professional Psychology, 29*, 59–61.

Lambert, M. J. & Co-author (this edition). Use of psychological tests for outcome assessment. In Maruish, M. (Ed.), *Use of psychological testing for treatment planning and outcome assessment (2nd ed.).* Mahwah, NJ: Lawrence Erlbaum Associates.

Lucki, I. (1998). The spectrum of behaviors influenced by serotonin. *Biological Psychiatry, 44*, 151–162.

McGovern, M. P., Newman, F. L., & Kopta, S. M. (1986). Meta-theoretical assumptions and psychotherapy orientation: Clinician attributions of clients' problem causality and responsibility for treatment outcome. *Journal of Consulting and Clinical Psychology, 54*, 476–481.

Mesman, J., & Koot, H. M. (2000). Child-reported depression and anxiety in pre-adolescence: Associations with parent and teacher-reported problems. *Journal of the American Academy of Child and Adolescent Psychiatry, 39*(11), 1371–1378.

Morris, S. B., & DeShon, R. P. (2002). Combining effect size estimates in meta-analysis with repeated measures and independent-group designs. *Psychological Methods, 7*, 105–125.

Mumma, G. H. (2001). Increasing accuracy in clinical decision making: Toward an integration of nomothetic-aggregate and intraindividual-idiographic approaches. *Behavior Therapist, 24*(4), 77–94.

Newman, F. L. (1980). Global scales: Strengths, uses and problems of global scales as an evaluation instrument. *Evaluation and Program Planning, 3*, 257–268.

Newman, F. L. (1983). Therapists' evaluations of psychotherapy. In M. Lambert, E. Christensen, & R. DeJulio (Eds.), *The assessment of psychotherapy outcome* (pp. 497–534). New York: Wiley.

Newman, F. L. (1995). Disabuse of the drug metaphor in psychotherapy: An editorial dilemma. *Journal of Consulting and Clinical Psychology, 62*, 940–941.

Newman, F. L., & Carpenter, D. (1997). A primer on test instruments. In John F. Clarkin and John Docherty (Section Eds) *Psychologic and Biologic Testing: Issues for Psychiatrists* in Leah J. Dickstein, Michelle B. Riba, & John M. Odham (Eds) *Annual Review of Psychiatry, Vol. 16.*

Newman, F. L., Fitt, D., & Heverly, M. A. (1987). Influences of Patient, Service Program and Clinician Characteristics on Judgments of Functioning and Treatment Recommendations. *Evaluation and Program Planning, 10*, 260–267.

Newman, F. L., Heverly, M. A., Rosen, M., Kopta, S. M., & Bedell, R. (1983). Influences on internal evaluation data dependability: Clinicians as a source of variance. In A. J. Love (Ed.), *Developing effective internal evaluation: New directions for program evaluation* (No. 20). San Francisco: Jossey-Bass.

Newman, F. L., & Howard, K. I. (1986). Therapeutic effort, outcome and policy. *American Psychologist, 41*, 181–187.

Newman, F. L., Hunter, R. H., & Irving, D. (1987). Simple measures of progress and outcome in the evaluation of mental health services. *Evaluation and Program Planning, 10*, 209–218.

Newman, F. L., Kopta, S. M., McGovern, M. P., Howard, H. I., & McNeilly, C. (1988). Evaluating the conceptualizations and treatment plans of interns and supervisors during a psychology internship. *Journal of Consulting and Clinical Psychology, 56*, 659–665.

Newman, F. L., & Sorensen, J. E. (1985). *Integrated clinical and fiscal management in mental health: A guidebook.* Norwood, NJ: Ablex.

Newman, F. L., & Tejeda, M. J. (1996). The need for research designed to support decisions in the delivery of mental health services. *American Psychologist, 51*, 1040–1049.

Nunnally, J. C., & Burnstein, I. (1994). *Psychometric theory* (3ed ed.). New York: McGraw-Hill.

Owen, J. E., Klapow, J. C., Hicken, B., & Tucker, D. C. (2001). Psychosocial interventions for cancer: Review and analysis using a three-tiered outcomes model. *Pscyho-Oncology, 10*, 218–230.

Petkova, E., Quitkin, F. M., McGrath, P. J., Stewart, J. W., & Klein, D. F. (2000). A method to quantify rater bias in antidepressant trials. *Neuropharmacology, 22*, 559–565.

Ruggeri, M., Bisoffi, G., Fontecedro, L., & Warner, R. (2001). Subjective and objective dimensions of quality of life in psychiatric clients: A factor analytical approach: The South Verona Outcome Project 4. *British Journal of Psychiatry, 178,* 268–275.

Salamon, M. J. (1999). Evaluating functional and behavioral health. In P. A. Lichtenberg (Ed.), *Handbook of assessment in clinical gerontology* (pp. 203–242). New York: Wiley.

Saunders, S. M., Howard, K. I., & Newman, F. L. (1988). Evaluating the clinical significance of treatment effects: Norms and normality. *Behavioral Assessment, 10,* 207–218.

Shadish, W. R., Navarro, A. M., Matt, G. R., & Phillips, G. (2000). The effects of psychological therapies under clinically representative conditions: A meta-analysis. *Psychological Bulletin, 126,* 512–529.

Sobell, L. C., Agrawal, S., & Sobell, M. B. (1997). Factors affecting agreement between alcohol abusers and their collateral reports. *Journal of Studies on Alcohol, 58,* 405–413.

Stiles, W. B., & Shapiro, D. A. (1995). Disabuse of the drug metaphor: Psychotherapy process-outcome correlations. *Journal of Consulting and Clinical Psychology, 62,* 942–948.

Teague, G. B. (1995, May). *Outcome assessment in New Hampshire.* Presentation at the National Conference on Mental Health Statistics, Washington, D.C.

Tolan, P. H, Hanish, L. D., McKay, M. M., & Dickey, M. H. (2002). Evaluating process in child and family interventions: Aggression prevention as an example. *Journal of Family Psychology, 16,* 220–236.

Tryon, G. S., & Winograd, G. (2001). Goal consensus and collaboration. *Psychotherapy: Theory, Research, Practice, Training, 38,* 385–389.

Turner, R. M., McGovern, M. P., & Sandrock, D. (1982). A multiple perspective analysis of schizophrenic symptomatology and community functioning. *American Journal of Community Psychology, 11,* 593–607.

Uehara, E., Smukler, M., & Newman, F. L. (1994). Linking resource use to consumer level of need in a local mental health system: Field test of the "LONCA" case mix method. *Journal of Consulting and Clinical Psychology, 62,* 695–709.

Vavaeke, G. A., & Emmelkamp, P. M. (1998). Treatment selection: What do we know? *European Journal of Psychological Assessment, 14,* 50–59.

Yates, B. T. (1998). Formative evaluation of costs, cost-effectiveness, and cost-benefit: Toward cost, procedure, process, and outcome analysis. In L. Bickman & D. Rog (Eds.), *Handbook of applied social research methods* (pp. 285–337). Thousand Oaks, CA: Sage.

Zeelenberg, M. (1999). Anticipated regret, expected feedback and behavioral decision making. *Journal of Behavioral Decision Making, 12,* 93–106.

# Development and Implementation of a Behavioral Health Outcomes Program

Mark E. Maruish
*Southcross Consulting*

The interest in and need for behavioral health treatment outcomes measurement, management, and accountability in this era of managed care provides a unique opportunity for psychologists to use their training and skills in testing. However, the extent to which clinicians and other behavioral health care professionals become key and successful contributors to outcomes initiatives will depend on their understanding of what outcomes and their measurement and applications are all about. It is hoped that the reader has gained at least a basic level of this understanding from the information presented in the preceding chapters of this volume. Following from this, the purpose of the present chapter is twofold. First, it is intended to provide a deeper level of detail and understanding of the contexts, issues, and considerations that must be taken into account in developing a test-based outcomes management program. Second, it is also meant to provide specific steps and recommendations for designing and implementing an outcomes assessment and management program. The information and issues present in this chapter are important not only from the viewpoints of large behavioral health care delivery systems, such as managed behavioral health care organizations (MBHOs), hospitals, clinics, and community mental health centers, they are also relevant to those providing services through solo or group practices.

## WHAT ARE OUTCOMES?

Before discussing the basis and recommendations for establishing an outcomes management system, it is important to have a clear understanding of what is meant by the term. An extensive discussion of what outcomes are and how they are viewed by those with a stake in a patient's treatment is presented in chapter 1 of this volume and will not be repeated here. In summary, however, Donabedian (1985) has identified outcomes, along with structure and process, as the three dimensions of quality. More concretely, the term refers to the results of the specific treatment that was rendered to a patient or group of patients. Berman, Hurt, and Heiss (1996) defined outcomes as the change in the clinical, functional, or subjective state of a patient, or in his or her utilization of services over a specific time period.

*Outcomes* holds a different meaning for each of the different parties who have a stake in behavioral health care delivery. As will be shown below, what is measured generally depends on the purpose(s) for which outcomes assessment is undertaken. However, Bieber, Wroblewski, and Barber (1999) have identified commonalties of existing definitions of outcomes, such that outcomes are (a) results that may be favorable or unfavorable to the individual, (b) can be applied to individuals, subpopulations, or populations, and (c) can cover various lengths of time. The outcomes, or results, of treatment should not imply a change in only a single aspect of functioning. Thus, the term is commonly used in the plural form (i.e., outcomes) to convey that interventions typically affect or result in change in multiple domains of functioning.

## INTEREST IN BEHAVIORAL HEALTH CARE OUTCOMES

The tremendous interest in the assessment of outcomes that has developed in behavioral health care settings over the past decade is somewhat of a phenomenon. Those who were in the behavioral health care field prior to the 1990s can recall a time when the term *outcomes*, at least as it pertained to the treatment of mental health and substance abuse patients, was rarely mentioned. Now, it's even rarer to *not* hear the term in workshops, conference presentations, and published articles and newsletters having to do with psychological or behavioral interventions. What has led to the interest in this particular aspect of intervention? How do the different stakeholders in a patient's care vary in their interests in treatment outcomes? How do individual providers and organizations such as MBHOs use outcomes information? Answers to these questions will provide the foundation necessary for considering the more "nuts and bolts" issues that must be addressed in developing a systematic approach to assessing and managing outcomes.

### Impetus for Outcomes Assessment Initiatives

The movement to initiate programs for measuring, monitoring, and managing behavioral health care outcomes has undergone a period of dramatic growth. What accounts for this? It appears to be born out of a number of separate but interrelated circumstances that have emerged with some prominence at approximately the same time. Alone, each does not present itself as an overpowering force in physical or behavioral health care; together, however, these forces have acted as a formidable impetus to change in the way health care is provided.

*Need to Control Costs.* The rising costs for health care services in the United States have been addressed in chapter 1. Overall health care costs have risen to $1.42 trillion (14.1% of the gross domestic product) in 2001 ("Health care costs," 2003). Perhaps a more impressive statistic comes from the surgeon general, who reported that in 1996, the combined direct mental health and substance abuse cost was $81 billion (Surgeon General of the United States, 1999). This does not include indirect costs or costs for the treatment of dementias. What do these costs mean for the consumer? Ceridian Benefits Services (cited in "Monthly change," 2000) indicated that at that time, single-coverage monthly medical premiums for health maintenance organizations (HMOs) and non-HMOs were $194 and $213, respectively, whereas HMO and non-HMO monthly family premiums were $536 and $580, respectively.

*CQI Efforts to Manage Quality.* In chapter 1, it was noted that the health care industry has embraced the continuous quality improvement (CQI) principles which have long been in place in the business and manufacturing industries. The key to the successful implementation of any CQI program is the gathering and analysis of data—outcomes data—on an ongoing basis (Berman et al., 1996). These data provide the feedback that is necessary to determine if efforts toward improving the quality of the provided services have had a positive impact; if not, further interventions would be warranted.

*Accreditation and Regulatory Requirements.* Berman, Rosen, Hurt, and Kolarz (1998) indicated that possibly the greatest impetus for the assessment of outcomes on an ongoing basis has come from accreditation bodies such as the Joint Commission on Accreditation of Healthcare Organizations (JCAHO) and the National Committee for Quality Assurance (NCQA). Accreditation from one or both of these bodies infers that the organization has passed fairly stringent structure, process, and outcomes measurement standards. Thus, it helps ensure that the health care consumer is receiving services that meet or exceed at least a minimally acceptable level of quality. Accreditation by one or both of these organizations commonly is required for a health care organization to compete in the marketplace.

Both JCAHO and NCQA have been involved in the accreditation of health care organizations for a number of years. In the past, MBHOs were subject to the same requirements as nonbehavioral managed care organizations (MCOs), either as an independent organization or a delegate of another organization that was responsible for all of the consumer's health care needs. It has not been until recently that JCAHO and NCQA have each established a separate set of requirements, review processes, and expectations for the accreditation of MBHOs. Within each of these sets of requirements are standards that require the MBHO to be involved in some form of outcomes assessment activities. Because gaining and maintaining accreditation status from either of these organizations is essential for most MBHOs to be competitive, it is imperative for these organizations to have an ongoing program of outcomes assessment in some form or another.

*Pressures for Accountability.* The push toward accountability with regard to the quality and value of health care services has been noted numerous times in the literature (e.g., Andrews, 1995; Schlosser, 1996). Lyons, Howard, O'Mahoney, and Lish (1997) pointed out the particular importance accountability in the behavioral health field, given that this field has had greater price elasticity (i.e., its cost affects its consumption), has favored an open-ended (unlimited) approach to treatment and has a history of more unpredictable service utilization than what might have been found in the general health care arena previously. As Lyons et al. (1997) have indicated

> The task of making the mental health delivery system more accountable involves: (a) making use of the best scientific evidence from the mental health services literature on effectiveness and efficacy, (b) creating best-practice protocols, and (c) developing benchmark and feedback mechanisms that allow practitioners to improve their practice. (p. 13)

This, of course, necessitates the use of outcomes assessment information.

*Advances in Technology.* Any useful outcomes management system requires that data be gathered and analyzed easily, and the resulting information be fed back to consumers of that information in a timely manner. Only within the past decade or so has this been possible. The availability of inexpensive, efficient microcomputers and networking capabilities has made this possible. The burgeoning of the Internet and intranet systems has made available additional resources for establishing workable systems of outcomes assessment and management. Now, it is relatively easy to obtain, process, and disseminate outcomes and other quality improvement data. Patient and collateral questionnaires can be administered online, and the resulting data can be automatically entered into a database; alternately, data can be gathered via paper-and-pencil questionnaires and subsequently scanned, key entered, or faxed into the database. In addition, other data can be useful for outcomes management purposes, and these are commonly accessible from claims databases. Available software allows for regular generation of generic or customized reports of outcomes information scheduled to meet the needs of the organization (e.g., monthly or quarterly). After their generation, these reports can be automatically sent to other relevant stakeholders in the patient's care via e-mail, fax, or post.

Beyond the electronic technology, one must also consider the development of assessment tools that fit well into outcomes assessment programs. This is no small consideration. As Schlosser (1996) had noted:

> Instruments designed from the earlier era of pure psychotherapy research are nowadays being called into service for clinical "outcomes assessment" purposes, the appropriateness of which is a matter of debate. One problem with using older instruments for outcomes assessment is that they may not be well suited to the task. Most of these instruments were designed and normed years before the advent of managed care and the widespread adoption of brief psychotherapy. They are typically too lengthy or focused on variables of little salience to modern behavioral healthcare. (p. 285)

Thus, the development of instruments such as the SF–36/SF–12, OQ–45, BASIS–32, and other instruments that are brief and measure domains that are important to the various stakeholders in the patient's treatment surely must be considered another technological advance.

*Other Reasons.*  Other reasons for the push toward assessing outcomes have been observed over the years. For example, in addition to developments related to requirements for accountability, Schlosser (1996) attributed the interest in outcomes assessment to (a) the development of measurement tools required for research in health producing factors and health care interventions, (b) advancement in the acquisition and understanding of psychotherapy-related data, and (c) outcomes assessment filling the void left by the demise of routine administration of test batteries. Questions about medical decision-making that arose from regional variations in behavioral health care practice patterns, as well as the need for MBHOs to decrease their provider panel size, were noted by Berman et al. (1996). Moreover, Lyons et al. (1997) pointed to the growing movements by consumer groups such as the National Alliance for the Mentally Ill (NAMI) and their concern about choice, quality, and value in mental health as yet another factor in the increasing interest in outcomes.

## STAKEHOLDERS' RECOGNITION OF THE IMPORTANCE OF OUTCOMES MEASUREMENT IN MBHOs

The implementation of any type of outcomes assessment initiative does not come without effort from and cost to the organization. However, if implemented properly, all interested parties should find the yield from the outlay of time and money to be

TABLE 7.1
The Tripartite View of Mental Health and Therapy Outcomes

| Category | Configuration* B | W | S | Mental Health Status |
|---|---|---|---|---|
| 1 | + | + | + | Well-functioning, adjusted individual; optimal mental health. |
| 2 | + | − | + | Basically healthy person; troubled by dysphoric mood, perhaps due to minor trauma affecting self-esteem, temporary reverses, discouragement, loss, grief reaction. |
| 3 | + | + | − | May have fragile ego (borderline condition, schizoid personality, etc.) but functions well in society and feels content. Underlying psychotic process may be present, but defenses may be reasonably effective. |
| 4 | + | − | − | Similar to Category 3, but affect may be labile or dysphoric. Has basic ego weakness but functions adequately in society. |
| 5 | − | + | + | Society judges person's behavior as maladaptive (e.g., unconventional lifestyle), but his or her sense of well-being and personality structure are sound. |
| 6 | − | − | + | Similar to Category 2, except that social performance is considered maladaptive (e.g., as part of a grief reaction, person may withdraw, give up job, etc.). |
| 7 | − | + | − | Person with ego defects, psychopaths, character disorders, conversion reactions (*la belle indifférence*), and individuals who have poor reality testing and poor insight. |
| 8 | − | − | − | Clearly mentally ill. |

*$B$ = adaptive behavior (society); $W$ = sense of well-being (individual); $S$ = personality structure (professional).

*Note.* From Strupp, 1996, Table 1, p. 1020. Copyright 1996 by the American Psychological Association. Reprinted with permission.

substantial. But just who is interested in the behavioral health care outcomes, and what specifically are they interested in?

Strupp and Hadley (1977; Strupp, 1996) have formulated what they refer to as the *tripartite model* of mental health and therapeutic outcomes. This model basically states that the judgment of the mental health of an individual and the degree to which change in mental health is brought to bear by therapeutic intervention must be considered from the vantage points of the patient, the treating professional, and society. Table 7.1 presents an overview of the possible mixtures and implications of the types of tripartite judgments that may be made about an individual's mental health or the outcomes of therapeutic intervention for him or her.

Based on this model, Strupp and Hadley (1977; Strupp, 1996) concluded that (a) a given individual's level of mental health or therapeutic change may be judged differently, depending on the which of the three vantage points are taken; (b) the differences in judgment result from each party's individual interests; (c) one must recognize the limited utility of judgments made from a single perspective; (d) a comprehensive description of the patient's mental health can come only from assessing and integrating the affect, psychological structure, and behavior of the patient, which represent the three facets of the tripartite model; and (e) judgment of treatment outcomes ultimately becomes an issue of human values and public policy rather than a research issue.

The importance of Strupp's and Hadley's model here is that it brings to the forefront the fact that there is no single perspective from which to judge outcomes, because that judgment will reflect only the judging stakeholder's specific vested interest in the patient's status. *Stakeholders* can be defined as "those individuals and groups for whom the results of these [outcomes] data will potentially have an impact, including consumers/patients, family members, clinicians, administrators, employers, politicians, and insurance and managed care companies" (Berman, Rosen, Hurt, & Kolarz, 1998). Thus, the interest in, importance, and benefit of any particular type of treatment outcome will vary from one stakeholder to another.

*Patients' Interests.* Strupp (1996) and Oss and Sloves (2000) see the patient's outcomes interest as achieving happiness and contentment, thus experiencing highly subjective feelings of well-being. But patients' interests extend beyond just feeling good. Cagney and Woods (1994) identified several benefits to patients, including enhanced health and quality of life, improved health care quality, and effective use of the dollars paid into benefits plans. Put another way, patients may be most interested in the degree to which they have recovered, as might be reflected in measures of their ability to work or live independently and, again, quality of life (Bartlett, 1997). Outcomes information can also help patients identify preferred providers, track their treatment progress, and discuss treatment options with their providers (Berman et al., 1998; Bieber et al., 1999).

*Providers' Interests.* For providers, the outcomes data can result in improved clinical skills, important information related to the quality of care and local practice standards, increased profitability, and decreased concerns over possible litigation (Cagney & Woods, 1994). Bieber et al. (1999) noted that outcomes information can help the provider support treatment decisions, track patient progress, and assess the effectiveness of his or her methods. Bartlett (1997) saw providers' interests lying in the care that was delivered (i.e., process), its link to the outcomes of that care, or both. This information can also help to identify areas of service requiring change and to develop strategies for increasing the quality of care. For Strupp (1996), outcomes information afforded insights into patients' personality structure relative to the intervention provided.

*Interests of Service Delivery Systems.* From a general perspective, all health care delivery systems can use outcomes information to monitor outcomes and quality of care across providers (Bieber et al., 1999). The benefits derived from its use include increased profits, retention of accreditation status, information that can shape the practice patterns of their providers, and a decision-making process based on delivering quality care (Cagney & Woods, 1994). Bartlett (1997), however, felt that in most cases the interests of organizational administrators lie in how many resources (financial or service) are being used.

In addition, outcomes information can assist care managers in MBHOs and other service delivery systems in assessing the progress of individual patients during an episode of care. It can also be helpful in making decisions about the need for additional services beyond those that were initially authorized. In aggregate, this information can also provide a means of determining the effectiveness of individual providers for the various types of problems. This, in turn, can help ensure that patients are referred to those providers who are best suited for treating the presenting problem.

*Payers' Interests.* Cagney and Woods (1994) saw the potential payer benefits as including healthier workers, improved health care quality, increased worker productivity, and reduced or contained health care costs. Berman et al. (1998) and McLellan and Durell (1996) saw outcomes information as important in decreasing or controlling utilization and reducing costs (see chapter 1). This information can also be used by payers to select individual providers or to evaluate entire organizations (Bieber et al., 1999).

*Other Third-Party Interests.* There are numerous other parties that potentially could be considered stakeholders and thus have an interests in the outcomes of a given patient. The patient's family, for example, may want to be sure that the patient is progressing toward his or her premorbid level of role functioning. Employers also are interested in the patient's return to a level of functioning necessary to perform his or her job and increased productivity. They also are interested in decreasing absenteeism, on-the-job accidents, and turnover rates (Lyons et al., 1997). Other important stakeholders may include groups such as researchers and government agencies, all of which will have their own specific agenda and will view outcomes data accordingly.

The interests of all stakeholders for a given outcomes initiative are extremely important. They should provide the context in which outcomes assessment takes place. As Berman et al. (1998) put it, "it is the starting point which should frame all other aspects of the evaluation" (p. 121).

## Common Reasons for Implementing Outcomes Systems

There are numerous reasons why an organization might wish to establish and maintain a system for assessing and managing treatment outcomes. In a survey of 73 behavioral health care organizations, the top five reasons identified by the participants as to why they had conducted an outcomes program were (in descending order): evaluation of patients with specific disorders, evaluation of provider effectiveness, evaluation of integrated treatment programs, management of individual patients, and support of sales and marketing efforts (Pallak, 1994). All are very legitimate reasons for expending the time, effort, and resources necessary for establishing and maintaining an outcomes assessment system. But there are also many other reasons.

*Assistance in Real-Time Clinical Decision-Making.* It is not uncommon for one to view an outcomes system as something that provides information at the back end of treatment. But as the Pallak (1994) survey has shown, many value information that is gathered as part of an outcomes management system for what it can contribute to the ongoing management of patients. In that survey, 44% of the respondents indicated that they conducted outcomes studies to "manage individual patients," and 31% said that it was used for "settings triage/level-of-care decisions."

Going beyond these two rather broad categorizations, there is any number of real-time uses for the type of information that one might gather in support of an outcomes initiative. For example, data obtained at the time of treatment initiation can be used for problem identification, treatment planning, and development of individualized treatment recovery curves. Ongoing tracking of patient progress through readministration of outcomes instruments can assist in determining whether adjustment in the treatment plan is required and in the determination of the need for continued treatment. However, it is important to note that none of this is possible unless the outcomes system in place provides a means of feeding the information back to the provider on a timely basis. This information must be made available at a time when it can make a difference, not only after the patient's episode of care has been completed. Providing this type of real-time information can be a key factor or incentive to getting clinicians to "buy in" to an outcomes program and thus can be a key factor in the success of all outcomes programs.

Moreover, data obtained from outcomes assessment can help demonstrate the patient's need for therapeutic services beyond that which is typically covered by the patient's health care benefits (when this is indeed the case). When assessment is conducted for this reason, both the patient and the clinician may benefit from the outcomes data. However, the type of information that a third-party payer requires for authorization of extended benefits may not always be useful, relevant, or beneficial to the patient or the clinician.

*Determination of Treatment Outcomes.* Clinicians can employ outcomes assessment to obtain a direct measure of how much patient improvement has occurred as the result of a completed course of treatment. Here, the findings are more beneficial to the clinician than to the patient because a pre- and posttreatment approach to the assessment is utilized. The information will not lead to any change in the patient being assessed, but the feedback it provides to the clinician could assist him or her in the treatment of other patients in the future.

*Development of "Best Practices" and Treatment Guidelines.* Andrews (1995) has indicated that the aggregation of the outcomes research results provides "the underpinnings for practice guidelines" (p. 19). There sometimes is confusion over the use of "guideline" and related terms. To clarify, *guidelines* (sometimes also referred to as *clinical pathways*)

> provide a set of steps to guide patient care through an extended illness episode. Tight *protocols* focus in on a specific, high-leverage, complicated subprocess of care.... [Guidelines] are based on the premise that standardization of care process around best-known methods will tend to produce the best health results.... Protocols tend to contrast with pathways and guidelines by being narrower in scope and more directive as to what to do when. (Nelson, 1996, pp. 113–114)

The Committee on Quality Assurance and Accreditation Guidelines stated that "outcomes research is vitally important to improve the base of evidence related to treatment effectiveness. Outcomes research is needed to provide explicit direction in identifying performance indicators associated with good outcomes for different patient characteristics, types of treatment programs, and types of managed care organizations" (Institute of Medicine, 1997, p. 5). Indeed, it is only with outcomes data that a professional organization (e.g., American Psychological Association, American Psychiatric Association), governmental agency (e.g., Centers for Medicare and Medicaid Services), or specific health care organizations can begin to answer questions related to what type of treatment works best for whom, what type of patients receive the most benefit from the provider, and other questions related to improving the quality and effectiveness of care.

At this time, the use of guidelines in organizations appears limited. Thirty-one percent of Pallak's (1994) survey respondents reported their use of outcomes information to evaluate the effectiveness of different treatments, and 32% to evaluate or compare treatment guidelines. Berman et al.'s (1998) observation of newsletter and trade paper reports suggested that only about 20% of health care organizations used guidelines, and only 12% planned to do so. A recent survey of 417 MCOs revealed that 48.9% of their 752 product offerings utilized clinical outcomes assessment (Merrick, Garnick, Horgan, & Hodgkin, 2002). This rate will likely increase in the future but not as a matter of choice. Accreditation through NCQA and JCAHO now requires the measurement of an MBHO's compliance with treatment guidelines.

*Development of Predictive Models and Treatment Recovery Curves.*  The value of predictive models and treatment recovery curves was discussed at length in chapter 1. Recall that development of these tools for planning and monitoring treatment requires outcomes data. It is unlikely that an organization would implement an outcomes assessment system solely for these purposes. On the other hand, being able to use outcomes data for predictive modeling and generating treatment recovery curves can provide added value to the organization beyond whatever the primary purpose of the system might be. This can increase the payback to the organization and thus help justify the cost of implementing an outcomes system.

*Development of an Objectively Based Provider Profiling System.*  Provider (clinician) profiling is the process by which service providers (psychiatrists, psychologists, social workers, nurses, etc.) are evaluated and usually ranked based on some objective criteria (Berman et al., 1996). Pallak (1994) found that 57% of his sample used outcomes data to evaluate or compare provider effectiveness. In addition to improvement in symptomatology, functioning, well-being, and other outcomes data, profiling can be based on any number of clinical and nonclinical variables, such as data-related patient demographics and treatment satisfaction, claims, average length of treatment, service utilization, transition of patients to higher or lower levels of care, recidivism, and compliance with contractual obligations. Of course, the accuracy and utility of the profiling will depend on the case-mix adjustment procedures that are implemented to "level the playing field" and permit valid comparisons of providers (see below; also see Sperry, Brill, Howard, & Grissom, 1996).

Indeed, provider profiling can be another extremely useful tool for organizations in their efforts to improve the quality of the care they offer to health plan members. Through profiling, areas of strength, training needs, and problematic support processes can be identified and appropriate interventions designed. On the other hand, profiling is not without its limitations. As Eisen and Dickey (1996) have observed, there is no consensus regarding the selection of samples and the outcomes measures that would be used, and there are variations across patient samples that must be addressed. There also are data quality and availability issues that must be resolved. Moreover, it can be quite threatening to providers if profiling is used to determine rewards (e.g., bonuses, promotions) or punishments (e.g., lower rates of referral, termination from provider panels; Berman et al., 1998). Thus, the success of any profiling system will be dependent on the degree to which it is used to increase provider abilities and enhance processes, and its purpose is perceived as such by the providers.

*Support for CQI Efforts.*  The importance of CQI programs in organizations, and the importance of outcomes assessment information to those programs, are addressed in chapter 1 and other chapters of this book. Suffice it to say here that treatment outcomes information powers the engine of the CQI process by providing the fuel for the evaluation of current performance, the determination of means of improving that performance, evaluation of those improvement efforts, and so on. In addition, the more an outcomes initiative is consistent with other CQI initiatives within the organization, the more it is likely to be "bought into" and supported by the organization.

One specific type of CQI effort that has appeared in literature is that of *treatment redesign*. Treatment redesign "refers to changes in the specific interventions and treatment techniques that comprise the client's full episode of care: the initial interview, the therapy and the medications" (Bologna & Feldman, 1995, p. 60; see also Bologna & Feldman, 1994). Bologna, Barlow, Hollon, Mitchell, and Huppert (1998) identified the interest in treatment redesign as one of the responses to the challenges that MBHOs and other health care organizations must face in this "era of accountability." Here, Bologna and her colleagues refer to changes in the provision of treatment that begin at the level of a specific intervention for a specific patient during a specific episode of care and proceed to wider coverage within a system of care. The initiation of programmatic changes for specific diagnostic groups is given as an example. As with any other CQI effort, this approach requires the use of outcomes information to drive the redesign efforts.

*Fulfillment of Regulatory and Accreditation Requirements.* This is yet another area that has been covered in chapter 1 and elsewhere in this book. The reader is referred to these discussions for further information.

*Generation of a Report Card of Organization or Provider Performance.* Another result of the move toward accountability in health care delivery has been the development of report cards. For many, the term may conjure up memories of an earlier time in a person's life when a report card was a vehicle for reporting a student's school performance to a third party, such as the student's parents. In the context of health care—behavioral or otherwise—the report is usually of the performance an organization's system of health care delivery against predefined measures. The audience is the purchasers of health care services and other stakeholders. In considering report cards and their utility, one must take into consideration (a) the content of the report card (e.g., the outcomes, cost, and/or access to care), (b) the point of view of the organization that published the report card, and (c) the intended audience (Manderscheid, Henderson, & Brown, n.d.). In contrast to the one-time nature of program evaluations, report cards are designed to be used as a continuous activity that provides information at various points in time (Bartlett, 1997).

In some cases, the report card is oriented only to reporting the results of a single organization on any number of variables. Data may be trended to allow a display of the results of the organization's quality improvement efforts across two or more points in time. Internal or external benchmark data might also accompany the organization's trended data. Unless this information allows a comparison of the publishing organization's results to those of other organizations, this type of report card is limited in its utility to health care purchasers.

In other cases, the report card presents the results of several participating organizations (usually competitors) on a set of mutually agreed on measures using specific scoring and reporting methodologies. This enables purchasers of health care services to compare each organization's performance against other organizations, a benchmark, or both, thus permitting more informed conclusions about the value they are getting for their health care dollar. Probably the best known report card is the annual report of data for NCQA's Health Plan Employer Data and Information Set (HEDIS; NCQA, 2000). Most of the HEDIS measures are oriented to reporting the performance of medical health care delivery systems. The HEDIS measures do include some behavioral health care performance measures, such as average length of inpatient stay and percent of depressed patients on antidepressant medication who had three or more follow-up visits within 12 weeks of the initial diagnosis. Much more relevant sets of report card measures are contained in the Consumer-Oriented Mental Health Report Card, developed by the Center for Mental Health Statistics Improvement Program

(MHSIP, 1996) Task Force, and the Performance Measures for Managed Behavioral Healthcare Programs 1.0 (PERMS 1.0) and PERMS 2.0, developed by the American Managed Behavioral Healthcare Association (AMBHA, 1995, 1998).

Unfortunately, much needs to be done to increase the utility of report cards. The first order of business would be to refocus the content of these reporting instruments. Reports cards tend to rely or report on process measures more than outcomes measures (Steinwachs, Fischer, & Lehman, 1996). Also, they tend to have the same limitations as provider profiling (Eisen & Dickey, 1996).

*Generation of a Score Card of Organization's Performance.*  Unlike report cards, score cards are intended for internal use by the organization. As Bieber et al. (1999) indicated, they

> provide information at the systems level and key processes within the system, determined by a leadership group within a health care organization. A key feature of such measures is that they provide critical, real-time information to management, which supports action-oriented decision-making. These decision-support tools provide performance rankings for overall health care systems or specific processes or outcomes, such as patient access, clinical processes, and customer satisfaction. . . . [They] are put in place to help identify and manage *variation* in the system. (p. 178)

It is not uncommon for some types of performance measures and monitors to be reported on both report cards and score cards. Examples here could be change in symptom severity level from intake to discharge and patient satisfaction with the quality of care for all inpatients hospitalized during a reporting period. However, data related to 30-day (recidivism) rates, hospitalization rates per 1,000 covered lives; average length of stay; access rates to emergent, urgent and routine care; and so forth are likely to be of greater interest and utility to the organization than to its customers. It therefore is more likely to be reported in a score card than in a report card.

*Other Support of Marketing Efforts.*  Report cards can serve as a powerful marketing tool for organizations. They can succinctly convey to their existing and prospective customers information about the structure, processes, and outcomes of the care that they offer. What may not be offered (at least in regularly reported results) is information related to the value of their services. In this context, value can be broadly defined as the amount of improvement per dollar spent. Value estimates answer the customer's question, "How much bang am I getting for my buck?" Improvement could be expressed in many ways, such as average changes in scores on outcomes measures (e.g., average decrease in SCL–90–R GSI T scores during an episode of care), movement from one level of functioning to another (e.g., number of patients that displayed clinically significant improvement on the OQ–45, number of patients unemployed at the time of treatment initiation who secured gainful employment), or substantial decrease in negative behaviors (e.g., number of patients that maintained sobriety for 1 month). Value here might be determined by calculating the cost of attaining the criteria for improvement on the specified variable(s) for a single patient or group of patients over a period of time.

Another means of determining value has received quite a bit of attention over the past several years. This has to do with *cost offset*. Cost-offset studies seek to determine to what extent (if any) savings in other areas of his or her functioning can offset the cost of a patient's treatment. These studies commonly focus on cost savings in one of two areas. The first is medical expenditures. Medical cost-offset studies look at the savings in nonpsychiatric medical expenses (inpatient treatment, outpatient and emergency room visits, medication, lab work, etc.) that result from the treatment of a behavioral health problem or disorder. The literature is replete with studies demonstrating that individuals with behavioral health problems utilize more nonpsychiatric medical resources that those with no such disorders (see Friedman, Sobel, Meyers, Caudill, & Benson, 1995). Medical cost-offset information is particularly useful in systems that provide or manage both the medical and behavioral health care benefits of a health plan, because the savings will be reflected in the organization's bottom line and lowered health care premiums. One complication in pursuing this type of investigation is that medical cost-offset effects usually appear after an extended period of time; consequently, they are not likely to be demonstrated when patients switch to other plans before the offset effect can take place.

The other area of cost offset, and a major focus of related studies, is that related to employment. According to the American Psychological Association (1996), the health conditions most limiting the ability to work are mental disorders. For example, major depression resulted in $23 billion in lost work days in 1990, and in 1985, behavioral health problems resulted in over $77 billion in lost income. Also, the National Depressive and Manic-Depressive Association (as cited in "Depression still undertreated," 1997) reported that depression costs employers $4,200 per depressed worker, or $250 per employee, with only 28% of these costs going toward actual treatment. Here, the financial effects of improvement in such areas as rates of productivity and absenteeism can be easily calculated and compared against the cost of providing behavioral health care to employees. Obviously, data on work productivity cost offset is of particular interest when the purchaser of the behavioral health care benefits is an employer or employer group.

*Additional Reasons.* McGlynn (1996) identified other purposes or uses of outcomes assessment information, including: providing information to consumers so that they can make informed choices about their health care, improving the quality of care, evaluating changes in treatment or policy, and designing financial incentives. In addition to monitoring treatment, evaluating programs, and providing information to consumers and third-party payers, Ogles, Lambert, and Fields (2002) indicated that outcomes assessment can also be used to enhance the supervision of services. At a broader level, Dickey (2002) identified four types of studies in which outcomes information might be required. The focus of these studies would be to investigate the efficacy of a specific treatment, determine the effectiveness of treatment, supply information for CQI purposes, or to gather information related to performance measures.

There may be many other, idiosyncratic reasons why an organization or individual clinician wishes to initiate an outcomes system. Because of the range of questions and needs that the outcomes system might be asked to address, there is no one system or approach to the assessment of treatment outcomes that is appropriate for all organizations. Any successful and useful outcomes assessment approach must be customized, because of the various types of outcomes one may be interested in, the reasons for assessing them, and the manner in which they may impact decisions. Customization should reflect the needs of the primary benefactor of the assessment information (e.g., patient, payer, provider), with consideration to the secondary stakeholders in the therapeutic endeavor. Ideally, the identified primary benefactor would be the patient. After all, as Andrews (1995) noted, "Outcomes measurement is the cornerstone of good clinical care" (p. 21). Only rarely would the patient not benefit from involvement in the outcomes assessment process. Finally, as Docherty and Dewan (1995) have pointed out:

> Although survival is and should be the key motivating factor for an organization's involvement in outcomes measurement, there are even stronger reasons for this involvement. A health care network that chooses to respond solely to the immediate demands of regulatory agencies or the perceived marketplace, without regard to the medical necessity and theoretical justification for this work, does so at its own social and economic peril.
>
> Such a superficial system would miss the main benefit to be derived from outcomes assessment and measurement; namely, the ability to address the major problems that now affect our field and undermine its credibility and, hence, its fundability. A sophisticated, comprehensive outcomes measurement system will allow us to effectively remedy the root causes of those problems and thus move our entire system of care to a new and more effective mode of functioning. We would not think of trying to conduct a business enterprise without a careful financial accounting system. "Guesstimates" of costs and profitability are unacceptable. It makes quite as little sense not to demand the same kind of careful accounting and accountability with regard to the *quality* of health care. Just as we have quantitative financial management, we require quantitative clinical management. (p. 2)

## WHAT TO MEASURE

Deciding to assess outcomes in a systematic fashion, and then committing to that decision, is the first hurdle that must be passed in the development of an outcomes initiative. This can be a difficult process. Once it is passed, the organization must make another difficult decision, that is, which outcomes to measure. As discussed in chapter 1, probably the most frequently measured variable is that of symptomatology, or psychological or mental health status, because disruption in this dimension is probably the most common reason why people seek behavioral health care services in the first place. Moreover, McGlynn (1996) noted that "it represents how most disorders are defined and how the effectiveness of existing and new treatments is evaluated" (p. 24). Thus, in the vast majority of the cases seen for behavioral health care services, the assessment of the patient's overall level of psychological distress or disturbance will yield the most singularly useful information. This is regardless of whether it is used for outcomes measurement, outcomes monitoring, outcomes management, or to meet the requirements of third-party payers. Indexes such as the Positive Symptom Total (PST) or Global Severity Index (GSI), which are part of both the SA–45 and the Brief Symptom Inventory (BSI), can provide this type of information efficiently and economically.

For some patients, measures of one or more specific psychological disorders or symptom clusters are at least as important, if not more important, than overall symptom or mental health status. Here, if interest is in only one disorder or symptom cluster (e.g., depression), one may choose to measure only that particular set of symptoms using an instrument designed specifically for that purpose (e.g., use of the Back Depression Inventory-II [BDI–II] with depressed patients). For those interested in assessing the outcomes of treatment relative to multiple psychological dimensions, the administration of more than one disorder-specific instrument or a single, multiscale instrument that assesses all or most of the dimensions of interest would be required. Again, instruments such as the SA–45 or the BSI can provide a quick, broad assessment of several symptom domains. Other lengthier, multiscale instruments, such as the MMPI–2 or the PAI, permit a more detailed assessment of multiple disorders or symptom domains using one inventory.

However, there are other reasons for seeking help. Common examples include difficulties in coping with various types of life transitions (e.g., a new job, a recent marriage or divorce, other changes in the work or home environment), an inability to deal with the behavior of others (e.g., spouse, children), or general dissatisfaction with life. Thus, one may find that for some patients, improved functioning on the job, at school, or with family or friends is much more relevant and important than symptom reduction. For other patients, improvement in their quality of life or sense of well-being may be more meaningful.

Thus, there are instances in which changes in psychological distress or disturbance either (a) provide only a partial indication of the degree to which therapeutic intervention has been successful, (b) are not of interest to the patient or a third-party payer, (c) are unrelated to the reason why the patient sought services in the first place, or (d) are otherwise inadequate or unacceptable as measures of improvement in the patient's condition. In these cases, measurement of related variables may be necessary or may even take precedence over the assessment of symptoms. As previously noted, assessment of functionality in life is increasing (Sperry, 1997), and some feel that it is an important component of a "good" outcomes system (Fink, 1997). In many if not most cases, multiple domains are measured. Not only does this allow for the possibility of satisfying multiple needs and interests, the results can also complement each other and permit a better understanding of patients and the care delivery system (Sederer, Dickey, & Eisen, 1997).

What do many of the various stakeholders say are important domains to measure? Berman et al. (1996) indicated that most MBHOs (and likely other organizations) are interested in measuring symptomatology and functioning, as well as either cost or utilization. Participants in the 1999 Santa Fe Summit for the American College of Mental Health Administration were asked to rank the importance of 15 behavioral health indicators from three major areas: access, process, and outcomes ("Outcomes indicators," 1999). Participants included representatives from major accreditation bodies such as NCQA and JCAHO, funding groups, health care organizations, consumers, both the American Psychological Association and American Psychiatric Association, and performance measurement companies. The top-ranked indicator was the rate at which persons served are better, worse, or are unchanged as the result of treatment. The Pallak (1994) survey found that 65% of the respondents reported outcomes studies involving measurement of symptom severity. This was second only to patient satisfaction (71%), which, is this author's opinion, is not a true outcome domain. This same survey also revealed that 58% reported measuring level of functioning, and 49% reported measurement of social functioning. Daniels, Kramer, and Mahesh (1995) found that 50% of those members of the Council of Group Practices surveyed indicated that they used pre- and posttreatment clinical functioning as a quality indicator.

### Considerations for Selecting Outcomes Variables

The specific aspects or dimensions of patient functioning that are selected to be measured as part of the outcomes assessment program will depend on the purpose for which the assessment is being conducted. It is not a simple matter to determine exactly what should be measured. Sometimes the needs or interests of the various stakeholders in the treatment of the patient drive the types of outcomes that are measured.

These interests may vary greatly. For example, Norquist (2002) identified the outcomes interests for the following providers: functioning for patients; clinical status and functioning for providers; clinical indicators, functioning, satisfaction, and expenditures for payers; functioning, workplace variables (e.g., missed days of work), access, utilization, and satisfaction for employers; functioning, expenditures, and public health for policy makers; and all domains for researchers. Campbell (1996) pointed to a study that identified symptom reduction, family relief, and family involvement as being important to consumers, whereas symptom reduction and safety was found to be important to providers. The issue is complicated by a desire to meet the needs of each individual patient, as well as those of the clinician's or the organization's patient population as a whole. Careful consideration of the following questions should greatly facilitate the decision.

*Why Do the Patients Seek Services?*   People pursue treatment for many reasons. The patient's stated reason for seeking therapeutic assistance may be the first clue in determining what is important to measure. Measures selected for use for all patients serviced by MBHOs should reflect the most common reasons reported by the patient population.

*What Does the Patient Hope to Gain From Treatment?*   The patient's stated goals for the treatment that he is about to receive may be a primary consideration in the selection of which outcomes to measure. Organizations again will want to meet the frequently reported goals for the patients they serve.

*What Are the Patient's Criteria for Successful Treatment?*   The patient's goals for treatment may provide only a broad target for the therapeutic intervention. Having the patient identify exactly what would have to happen to consider treatment successful would help further specify the most important constructs and behaviors to measure. As before, organizations will need to determine what criteria their patients generally see as being important criteria for treatment success.

*What Are the Clinician's Criteria for the Successful Completion of the Current Therapeutic Episode?*   What the patient identifies as being important to accomplish during treatment might be unrealistic, reflect a lack of insight into his or her problems, or be inconsistent with what an impartial observer would consider indicative of meaningful improvement. In cases such as these, it would probably be more appropriate for the clinician to determine what constitutes therapeutic success and the associated outcomes variables.

*What Are the Organization's Criteria for the Successful Completion of the Current Therapeutic Episode?*   As with the clinician's criteria for successful completion of treatment, the establishment of one or more measurable criteria for treatment success that are applicable across the organization's patient population would also be desirable.

*What Effects Can One Expect from the Intervention that is Offered During the Therapeutic Episode?*   One may select one or more variables that meet several of the above needs, but they may not be necessarily appropriate for a given patient or patient population. Lyons et al. (1997) gave the example of how one might wish to measure changes in social or role functioning as a result of inpatient treatment. This level of care is intended to stabilize symptoms or manage the risk to self or others, not to improve their marital relationship or ability to function on the job. Thus, assessing functioning at the beginning and end of treatment is fruitless. In another situation, one might wish to use decrease in alcohol or other substance use as an outcomes variable. This is a commonly used variable, but it is not likely to yield any useful information in populations that have a low incidence of such problems or for whom specific substance abuse treatment was not provided.

*Will the Measurement of the Selected Variables Lead to Actionable Information?* An organization could probably identify any number of outcomes variables that would provide information related to the degree to which their patients have benefited from the treatment they received. But one will likely find that only a relative few provide *actionable* information. For example, suppose an organization frequently provides services to health plan members who experience work-related difficulties. Any number of behaviors could contribute to these problems. A detailed assessment of various aspects of these patients' work lives can uncover specific reasons why they are experiencing impairment in on-the-job functioning. Thus, one would routinely want to assess variables such as relationships with peers, relationships with supervisors, productivity, tardiness, and absences with these types of patients. The results will provide clues as to where to focus the intervention efforts and increase the probability of improved work functioning.

*What Are the Criteria for the Successful Completion of the Current Therapeutic Episode by Significant Third Parties?* From a strict therapeutic perspective, this should be given the least amount of consideration. From a more realistic perspective, one cannot overlook the expectations and limitations that one or more third parties have for the treatment that is rendered. The expectations and limitations set by the patient's parents or guardian, significant other, health plan, employer, third-party payer, guidelines of the organization in which the clinician practices, and possibly other external forces may significantly play into the decision about what is considered successful treatment or when to terminate treatment. As Campbell (1996) pointed out:

> Ideally, an outcomes management system considers the range of stakeholders, what they value about the operation of the mental health service system, and what they want to know about it. It is responsive as possible to these concerns, but obviously no one set of outcome indicators covers all situations or satisfies all perspectives. Effective selection of outcomes depends on the careful application of methods for prioritizing multiple perspectives of key stakeholders. (p. 72)

Busch and Sederer (2000) voiced a similar position.

*What, If Any, Are the Outcomes Initiatives Within the Provider Organization?* One cannot ignore any other outcomes or quality improvement programs that have already been initiated by the organization. Regardless of the problems and goals of the individual patient, organization-wide studies of treatment effectiveness may dictate the gathering of specific types of outcomes data from all patients who have received services. Consistency with existing CQI or other outcomes programs will be important for obtaining buy-in from the organization's senior management. As will be discussed later in this chapter, this type of buy-in is critical to the success of any outcomes initiative.

*Are the Outcomes Variables Meaningful or Useful Across the Levels of Care?* Organizations would be well-advised to ensure that the selected measures allow for tracking of desired outcomes domains across the continuum of care. This would allow for a more accurate determination of improvement regardless of whether the patient is seen at only one level of care (e.g., outpatient) or transitions from one level of care to one or more other levels (e.g., inpatient to partial hospitalization to outpatient). For example, the symptom domains assessed by instruments such as the SA–45 or BSI might be better selections as outcomes measures than those domains assessed by the Brief Psychiatric Rating Scale (BPRS) in organizations where there is a relatively high percentage of patients that begin an episode of care through inpatient treatment but later transition to outpatient treatment. Unlike that assessed by the BPRS, the symptomatology measured by both the SA–45 and BSI is much more relevant across the continuum of care and thus lends itself better to tracking a greater percent of patients during an episode of care.

*Do the Outcomes Variables Allow Meaningful Comparisons Across Organizations?* One of the factors that Eisen (2000) identified as being important for enhancing the utility of outcomes data is standardization of the indicators that are measured. Citing the work of Lambert, Ogles and Masters, she indicated that more than 1,430 different outcomes measures were used in 348 outcomes studies published between 1983 and 1988. Obviously, differences in the outcomes variables selected for use by one organization limit their usefulness in determining how it compares to other organizations. As a related issue, Eisen noted that lack of standardization of the operational definitions of those selected measures across organizations poses an additional problem. These issues should not be a major concern for those few organizations that have no need or desire to make industry comparisons. However, for those that anticipate making such comparisons, it will be important to identify the more frequently measured, clearly defined outcomes variables that are employed by either competitors or other organizations that are viewed as leaders in setting standards for the managed care industry. In this regard, participation in performance measurement systems such as the HEDIS and PERMS systems mentioned earlier has clear and significant benefits.

*What Is The Burden of Measuring the Selected Variables?* The task of gathering outcomes data should not become too burdensome in terms of the financial and labor resources that would be required. As a general rule, the more outcomes data one attempts to gather from a given patient or collateral, the less likely he will obtain any data at all. The key is to identify the point where the amount of data that can be obtained from a patient and/or collaterals, and the ease at which it can be gathered, are optimized.

But the issue here not only has to do with the number of variables; there also is the matter of the difficulty one might experience in obtaining data for a single variable. For example, an organization might choose to use data from structured clinical interviews conducted at both the beginning and end of a treatment episode. This type of data might provide excellent, useful outcomes information and meet the needs of several stakeholders. At the same time, the fact that obtaining this data would require a total of two hours of unreimbursed clinical staff time would make it prohibitive. In addition to the cost and availability of labor, a burden might also present itself in other forms, such as the training that would be needed to obtain the desired data, getting patients to complete outcomes at treatment termination or follow-up, or the need to develop customized instrumentation to measure the desired outcomes variable(s) in the organization's patient population. The issue here is one of practicality, given the organization's resources and capabilities.

## HOW TO MEASURE

Once the decision of what to measure has been made, one must then decide how it should be measured. Much of what has just been presented will play into the decision of the "how." In some cases, the "what" will dictate the how. In others, there will be multiple options for the "how" of the measurement.

### Sources of Information

One of the most important considerations related to how outcomes data are obtained is from where or whom this data should come. Certain types of outcomes data will necessitate the use of specific sources of information, whereas other types can be validly obtained from more than one source. In addition, the type of setting and population will also have a bearing on the selection of the best source of data (Berman et al., 1996).

*Patient Self-report.* In many cases, the most important data will be that obtained directly from the patient using self-report instruments. Indeed, self-report measures appear to be the most commonly used sources of outcomes information. As an example, in their review of the 133 outcomes studies reported in *The Journal of Consulting and Clinical Psychology* between January, 1995 and June 2000, Farnsworth, Hess, and Lambert (2001) found that self-report measures were the most frequently used measures in these studies, being used almost seven times more frequently than measures completed by trained therapists and instrumental measures (e.g., heart rate, urine samples). Measures completed by significant others were used even less frequently.

There may be any number of reasons why patient self-report measures are so popular among those clinicians and facilities conducting outcomes assessment. Sederer et al. (1997) indicated that it is more than just the fact that use of these measures reduces the burden on staff. They see information obtained from patients as providing a balance for clinician-reported information, such information possibly being biased by pressures from care delivery systems, issues related to confidentiality, and a need to succeed in a competitive marketplace. Underlying the assertion of the utility or importance of self-report information is the assumption that valid and reliable instrumentation, appropriate to the needs of the patient, is available; the patient can read at the level required by the instrument(s); and the patient is motivated to respond honestly to the questions asked. Barring one or more of these conditions, other options should be considered. Pallak's (1994) survey revealed that 82% of the respondents used patient self-report outcomes data.

Using patient self-report data may be viewed with suspicion by some (Strupp, 1996). These suspicions may be based on the potential problems just mentioned (see Bieber et al., 1999) or others. This author has personally witnessed the rejection of outcomes information that contradicted staff impressions, just because it was based on patient self-report data. The implication was that such data is not valid. Generally, such concerns are not justified. As Strupp (1996) has noted:

> Patients may exaggerate benefits [of treatment] or distort their recollections in other ways, but unless they are considered delusional, there seems to be no reason for questioning their reports. To be sure, one would like to obtain collateral information from therapists, clinical evaluators, significant others, as well as standardized tests, but the information from collateral sources is intrinsically no more valid than the patients' self-reports. None

the less, society is biased in favor of "objective" data and skeptical of "subjective data." (p. 1022)

*Collateral Sources.* Other types of data-gathering tools may be substituted for self-report measures. Rating scales completed by the clinician or other members of the treatment staff may provide information that is as useful as that elicited directly from the patient. Use of observer ratings for outcomes data was reported by 39% of Pallak's (1994) survey respondents. In those cases in which the patient is severely disturbed, unable to give valid and reliable answers (e.g., younger children), unable to read, or is an otherwise inappropriate candidate for a self-report measure, clinical rating scales can serve as a valuable substitute for gathering information about the patient. Related to these clinical rating instruments are parent-completed inventories for child and adolescent patients. These are particularly useful in obtaining information about the behavior of children or adolescents that might not otherwise be known. Information might also be obtained from other patient collaterals, such as siblings, spouses, teachers, coworkers, employers, and (in some cases) the justice system, all of which can be valuable by itself or in combination with other information.

*Administrative Data.* Another potential source of outcomes information is administrative data. In many of the larger organizations, this information can easily be retrieved through the organization's claims and authorization databases, data repositories and warehouses, and other databases that make up the organization's management information system. Data related to the patient's diagnosis, dose and regimen of medication, physical findings, course of treatment, resource utilization, rehospitalization during a specific period of time, treatment costs, and other types of data typically stored in these systems can be useful in evaluating the outcomes of therapeutic intervention. Medical records can also provide important information (e.g., physical findings, course of treatment). In fact, McGlynn (1996) viewed the medical record as being the best source of information about the patient's clinical status. Thirty-nine percent of those responding to Pallak's (1994) survey reported the use of medical record reviews.

*Multiple Sources.* Many would agree that the ideal approach for gathering outcomes data would be to use multiple sources (Berman et al., 1998; Bieber et al., 1999; Lambert & Lambert, 1999; Strupp, 1996). Indeed, outcomes information based on data obtained from patients, collaterals, and administrative sources can provide enhanced insights into the effectiveness of the services offered by organizations. They also may facilitate the identification of root causes of problems within the treatment system. Inherent in this approach, however, are increased costs and the potential for contradictory information and concomitant questions about how to proceed when contradictions occur. As Lambert and Lambert pointed out, "The data generated from these viewpoints are always subject to the limitations inherent in the methodology; none is 'objective' or most authoritative" (p. 116). Berman et al. (1998) have suggested that the potential for this type of problem can be reduced by specifying at the outset which outcomes measure(s) will be given the most consideration. Yet, this tact is not likely to completely eliminate issues that may arise from conflicting data. One therefore must be prepared with other approaches to resolving contradictory information that make sense from the perspective of the organization.

Few would disagree with the contention of Dornelas, Correll, Lothstein, Wilber, and Goethe (1996), that information obtained from several sources is more powerful than information obtained from a single source, and that the combination of qualitative and quantitative information provides a "comprehensive perspective" of the patient. Once again, the issue is one of burden. How realistic is this for the individual clinician or organization? Are resources available to gather and analyze this amount or type of information? It thus becomes a matter of whether the cost involved (financial and staff) justifies the amount and usefulness of the information obtained.

## Who to Measure

Among the many issues related to how one might assess outcomes is the matter of which patients to assess. On the surface, this appears to another no-brainer. One would want include all patients receiving services through the organization to ensure an accurate presentation of the outcomes of those services. In most instances, this is idealistic but not very practical.

*Who to Include.* Including all patient groups receiving services can present a number of problems. First and foremost is determining which outcomes indicators should be followed and which measures to use for the patient population in question. For example, imagine trying to design and implement an outcomes program that includes change in level of symptomatology as an outcomes measure for all patient groups— children, adolescents, adults, and geriatric patients. The "appropriate" types of symptomatology that would be measured and the instrumentation that would be used for this purpose would be different for each of these age populations. Thus, it would be necessary to acquire and train staff in the use of several age-appropriate measures and implementation procedures. This would increase the burden placed on the system and lessen the probability of establishing and maintaining a successful outcomes system.

Depending on the organization or provider setting, similar problems might be encountered as a result of ignoring other potentially complicating or confounding subpopulations based on other demographic or clinical variables (e.g., including all diagnostic groups). This is not to say that an outcomes system should not try to address the needs of all of the types of patients served by the MBHO. Rather, as will be discussed later, trying to measure the outcomes of all services to all patients at the same time will be difficult, and in at least the earlier stages of implementation, it will decrease the chances of establishing and maintaining a successful outcomes assessment system. Accomplishing such a goal would not be impossible, but it would be easier to begin small and measure only one or a few subpopulations on a limited number of outcomes variables. As success is achieved, the system can be expanded to include other subpopulations and or outcomes variables.

*How Many to Include.* Once a decision is made about whom to measure, the next question becomes how many of the targeted patient groups should be assessed during any given measurement cycle. Ideally, one would want to assess every patient (Docherty & Streeter, 1996; McLellan & Durell, 1996), but this becomes increasingly problematic from the standpoints of costs, labor, and logistics as the number of patients served within an organization increases. This is particularly the case when one or more posttreatment follow-up assessments are included in the methodology. The alternative here is to use a sample of each selected group of patients. In fact, using a sample may be preferable, assuming the sample is representative of the target group. It allows for more intensive efforts at obtaining baseline and follow-up data, thus reducing the chances of patient self-selection. Moreover, it provides the same information that would be obtained from all patients in the group under investigation. Berman and Hurt (1996) provided some general guidelines for how many patients should be assessed:

> The number of cases you need to study depends on how you will be using the outcomes data. For provider profiling, one needs at least 20 diagnostically homogeneous patients per clinician to get stable change data. In heterogeneous populations, another order of magnitude is indicated. In facility benchmarking, a random sampling of at least 300 cases per facility is minimum. If quality improvement is the intent, then 12 to 20 cases per predictor variable (or per category) within each setting is a minimum number. If disease management is the goal, 100 percent of the target cases are optimal, unless there is a very large sample. (p. 41)

As a general rule, one should consult with a statistician to determine the minimum acceptable sample size for his or her particular setting and needs.

Berman and Hurt (1996) went on to suggest several target goals for data collection. For instance, within six months of implementation, one should be obtaining data from 90% of the patient population at baseline and, for those still in treatment, 70% at later points in time. For clinician-reported data, one should strive for 100% at baseline and 95% at later points during the episode of care. Completion rates for posttreatment follow-up assessments should be around 50% during the first year of the outcomes system's implementation and in the 50% to 70% range thereafter.

## WHEN TO MEASURE

There are no hard-and-fast rules or widely accepted conventions related to when outcomes should be measured. Some of the issues involved were addressed earlier. Also, Sederer et al. (1997) suggested that clinicians or organizations should take into account some very important considerations about when to conduct outcomes measurement:

> Are you seeking to measure an episode of care? An episode of illness? Short term (< 30 days) or long term? Do you want two, three or more points of measurement, and why? What you measure will also influence when you measure: for example, changes in symptoms can be measured in very short time frames, whereas functioning requires a longer period of intervention; satisfaction must be assessed after a service has been supplied; program evaluation requires an extended period of time for assessment. The cost and convenience of follow-up mail and phone assessment should also be considered relative to face-to-face assessment of the patient during an episode of care. (p. 322)

The common practice is to assess the patient at least at treatment initiation and then again at termination or discharge. Obviously, at the beginning of treatment, the clinician should obtain a baseline measure of whatever variables will be measured at termination of treatment. At minimum, this allows for "outcomes measurement." As has also been discussed, additional assessment of the patient on the variables of interest can take place at other points in time, that is, at other times during treatment and on postdischarge follow-up. The problem with relying solely on this approach is that sometimes the time at which treatment ends is unpredictable (Lyons et al., 1997). Patients may end treatment abruptly with no warning, or treatment may run indefinite periods of time. Either circumstance can make self-report data difficult to obtain. However, there are solutions to this problem.

Measurement can take place at other points in time, that is, during treatment and on postdischarge follow-up. Sperry, Brill, Howard, and Grissom (1996) recommended what they refer to as *concurrent outcomes measurement*. This is similar to what was previously referred to as "outcomes monitoring" in chapter 1. Here, outcomes are measured at various points during the course of the treatment. This has the advantage of not only gathering outcomes information, but also providing feedback to the clinician regarding the effect of the treatment. As Sperry et al. (1996) pointed out, the common prepost treatment assessment methodology provides feedback only after treatment has been completed. This approach provides no information that can be of use for patients while they are undergoing treatment.

This still raises the issue of when to assess outcomes. Should it be done based on the number of sessions that have been completed (e.g., every third session), or at specific points in times from the date of treatment initiation (e.g., every fourth week)? How many times should a patient be asked to complete an outcomes protocol? With regard to the first issue, Berman et al. (1996) argued for the "time-from-initial-contact model" over the "session model." This permits the gathering of meaningful data in organizations that treat patients at multiple levels of care. It eliminates issues relating to equating such things as number of outpatient sessions to number of inpatient or partial hospitalization days, for example, in terms of likely benefit to the patient. The time-from-initial-contact method also allows for meaningful data gathering posttreatment, because there is no session that can be used to gauge the next time of measurement once treatment has been terminated.

Many would argue that postdischarge/posttermination follow-up assessment provides the best or most important indication of the outcomes of therapeutic intervention. Two types of comparisons may be made with follow-up data. The first is a comparison of the patient's status on the variables of interest—either at the time of treatment initiation or at the time of discharge or termination—to that of the patient at the time of follow-up assessment. Either way, this follow-up data will provide an indication of the more lasting effects of the intervention. Typically, the variables of interest for this type of comparison include symptom presence and intensity, feelings of well-being, frequency of substance use, and social or role functioning.

An important question regarding postdischarge/posttermination assessment has to do with how long after discharge follow-up assessment should take place. There are varying thoughts on this matter. As Berman et al. (1996) pointed out, there is no specific or generally accepted time frame for outcomes measurement. Rather, it will depend on the population being measured and the type, modality, and goals of the treatment. Consistent with this line of thinking, McLellan and Durell (1996) suggested that follow-up for inpatients should take place 2 to 4 weeks after discharge, whereas outpatient follow-up should take place at either 3, 6, or 12 months posttermination. In general, this author recommends that postdischarge outcomes assessment probably should take place no sooner than 1 month after treatment has ended, regardless of the patient's last level of care. When feasible, waiting 3 to 6 months to assess the variables of interest is preferred when the patient's last level of care was outpatient treatment.

An equally important issue is how the follow-up assessment is conducted. Typically, a mail-out/mail-back method is used to conduct the follow-up assessment method. The percent of returned assessment forms most often will be relatively low (e.g., 25%) and will probably be lower the further in time the follow-up occurs from the time of treatment termination. From their review of the literature, Smith, Fischer,

Nordquist, Mosley, and Ledbetter (1997) suggested that the minimally acceptable follow-up rate is 80% to 85% (although this author thinks that this is not realistic). Regardless, one should consider a two-step approach—mail-out survey and telephone interview—for gathering follow-up data. Dornelas et al. (1996) recommended trying to obtain the data first by telephone interview, followed by a mail-out to nonresponders. This author's impression, however, is that using the mail-out method first followed by the telephone interview with nonresponders is a more economical means of gathering the desired data.

The second type of posttreatment investigation involves comparing the frequency or severity of some aspect(s) of the patient's life circumstances, behavior, or functioning that occurred during an interval of time prior to treatment, to that which occurred during an equivalent interval of time immediately following termination. This methodology is commonly used in determining the medical cost-offset benefits of treatment and requires a different approach to the timing of follow-up assessments. Assessments being conducted to determine the frequency at which some behavior or event occurs (as may be needed to determine cost-offset benefits) should be administered no sooner than the reference time interval used in the baseline assessment. For example, suppose that the patient reports 10 emergency room visits during the 3-month period prior to treatment. If one wants to know if the patient's emergency room visits have decreased after treatment, the assessment cannot take place any earlier or later than 3 months after treatment termination. Not only can this provide an indication of the degree to which treatment has helped the patient deal with his problems, it also can demonstrate how much medical expenses have been reduced through the patient's decreased use of costly emergency room services.

A final issue related to the "when" of measurement has to do with the number of times one imposes on the patient to complete the outcomes instruments. As Lyons et al. (1997) have astutely observed:

> Measurement at multiple time points is desirable in theory; however, in practice, each additional assessment further burdens respondents, potentially jeopardizes compliance, and complicates data management. Therefore, the coordinator of the outcomes measurement must successfully balance the information needs with the respondent's capacity to complete the assessment accurately and reliably. (p. 41)

One solution they offered is to incorporate the outcomes protocol into the routine assessment activities that normally take place during the course of treatment. This will have the effect of being perceived as the MBHO's standard practice, not as something extra the patient is asked to do. But ultimately, as Dornelas et al. (1996) indicated, "the practitioner [or provider organization] must balance the cost and effort involved in conducting follow-up assessment against the value of having longitudinal data" (p. 239).

Deciding on issues related to the what, how, and when of outcomes assessment sometimes can be difficult. A good rule to follow is to keep the task as simple and free from burden as possible. The reader should always keep in mind the sage advice of Smith, Manderscheid, Flynn, and Steinwachs (1997), who noted that "Outcomes assessment systems that consume too much of the clinician's time or the patient's time are wasteful and unnecessary because the primary focus of the treatment setting should be treatment, not measurement" (p. 1035).

## HOW TO ANALYZE OUTCOMES DATA

An often overlooked consideration, or one that is commonly assigned secondary importance in the up-front planning for an outcomes assessment program, is how to analyze the outcomes data. It is easy to view this as a back-end task that can be dealt with later. The fact is, decisions about how one plans to analyze outcomes data can have a significant impact on many of the considerations discussed earlier. Using an air travel analogy, this author has heard one statistical consultant say many times, "If you want me there for the landing, I need to be there for the takeoff." Not having a decision about how data are going to be analyzed before implementation of the outcomes system can have disastrous consequences later on.

The questions that the gathered data are intended to answer will drive the types of analyses to be performed. These analyses can be nothing more than a simple presentation of mean scores or percentages that are trended over time, or the calculation inferential statistics which examine the significance of changes in the data from one measurement period to the next. It may also involve more sophisticated statistical procedures, such as risk or case-mix adjustment of the data for provider rankings or predictive modeling for identifying at-risk patients. Again, the analyses should be appropriate to the questions that the system is designed to answer. Knowing what types of analyses need to be conducted may have a huge bearing on what data is collected, how it is collected, and when it is collected.

### Comparison to a Standard

Generally, there are two common approaches to analyzing outcomes data. The first is to compare the results to some standard. Falling short of the standard would indicate the need for some form of intervention. In a CQI model, this would be followed by remeasurement after the intervention has had ample time to cause an effect. Meeting or surpassing the chosen standard presents a couple of options. One is to continue with the standard processes of care (i.e., "If it's not broken, don't fix it"). The other option embraces the spirit of CQI by working toward surpassing the current standard. Again, efforts toward improvement are implemented and the results are reevaluated later.

Taking the route of comparing against some standard or set of standards begs the question of which standard to employ. But even before that, one must decide which type of standard best meets the needs of their outcomes system. There are a few options here, each with its own set of advantages and drawbacks.

*Industry Standards and Benchmarks.* The HEDIS, PERMS, and other published data sets can provide valuable information about the success other organizations have achieved on standard performance measures. Use of this information in this way is referred to as *benchmarking*, "an ongoing process of comparing [an] organization's performance on services, practices, and outcomes with some identified standard, such as...competitors' performance" (Christner, 1997, p. 2). Benchmarking allows the MBHO and other stakeholders to see how the organization compares to similar organizations. Use of benchmarks can serve as a powerful marketing tool, particularly when the organization is outperforming its competitors. More important, positive findings can show the organization that it is on track for providing the highest quality of care available. Of course, performing below the industry standard may have negative effects on growing the organization's business; however, it can also identify areas in which improvement is needed.

The downside here is that performance measures on which industry-wide data is available are not always what the organization or its stakeholders feel are most important or relevant to the care of their patients. For example, NCQA's HEDIS measures include the following:

- Mental health utilization—inpatient discharges and average length of stay
- Chemical dependency utilization—inpatient discharges and average length of stay
- Antidepressant medication management

Among the AMBHA's PERMS 2.0 measures are the following:

- 30-, 90-, and 365-day readmission rates for mental health
- 30-, 90-, and 365-day readmission rates for substance abuse
- Availability of psychotherapy, medication management, or both for patients with schizophrenia
- Family visits for children undergoing mental health treatment

Note that for the most part, these data sets (and others like them) actually report performance on structure and process measures, not outcomes measures. However, this does not limit their utility in an outcomes management program. As Aday, Begley, Lairson, Slater, Richard, and Montoya (1999) have pointed out, "structure elements of healthcare influence what is and is not done in the process, in addition to how well it is done. This process in turn influences the outcome . . . that people experience as a result of their encounters with the process" (p. 32).

*Organizational Performance Goals.*  In many organizations, the standard that is used is set by the organization itself. To some degree, it probably will be based on a combination of what the industry standard is and what the organization sees as being realistic given the people it serves, the resources available, expectations from stakeholders, accreditation and regulatory requirements, and whatever other demands it must meet to remain successful and solvent. It is not unusual for organizations to set a performance goal that, based on baseline data, is well within reach of the organization. Once reached and maintained for a reasonable period, the goal is raised and the organization is once again challenged to improve its performance, and so on. This has the effect of rewarding staff with a sense of accomplishment and success, thus reinforcing continued efforts toward quality improvement and moving the organization toward the ultimate goal for the variable in question.

*Normative and Risk-Adjusted Data.*  Population-specific data can serve as yet another standard against which to compare performance. The major difference between using these data and benchmark or industry standards is that these data are more specific to different types of patient populations and the characteristics that distinguish them from other populations. Standardized normative data that typically accompanies published psychological tests is a good example. These data permit a fair comparison of groups of patients with like groups of patients, thus eliminating some of the potential effects of confounding variables. Many of these measures also have nonpatient normative data that also can be a useful (perhaps the most useful) source of comparison information, because they provide a means of tracking patients' progress toward recovery on the variable(s) of interest.

Frequently, appropriate standardized, population-specific comparison data are not available for the outcomes variables that are important to the organization. In these situations, *risk adjustment* procedures are frequently used to allow fair comparisons among different groups of patients. Simply put, risk adjustment generally refers to a statistical process that "corrects results for differences in a population with respect to patient mix, allowing for more valid comparisons across groups" (Bieber et al., 1999, p. 174). Adjustment of outcomes measures based on differences on nontreatment variables that have an effect on outcomes of treatment, has the effect of "leveling the playing field" and thus helps to ensure that any differences that do exist between groups are related to the quality of care they receive. Berman at al. (1996, 1998) have identified several general domains that should be included as variables in risk adjustment procedures. These include patient demographic characteristics (e.g., age, sex), clinical characteristics (e.g., symptom severity at the initiation of treatment, dual diagnosis of mental health and substance abuse disorders), and the psychosocial context of the disorder (e.g., social support, employment). The reporting of risk-adjusted data is rapidly becoming the standard for conveying outcomes data.

### Determination of Amount and Type of Change

The other common approach is to determine if a patient or a group of patients have changed on one or more outcomes variables from one point in time to another as a result of therapeutic intervention. If there has been change, one also wants to know how much. This represents an approach that is probably more in line with the training of behavioral scientists and thus is likely to be much more appealing than making comparisons to some standard.

*Changes in Individual Patients.*   There are two general approaches to the analysis of treatment of individual patient outcomes data. The first is by determining whether changes in patient scores on outcomes measures are *statistically significant*. The other is by establishing whether these changes are *clinically significant*. The issue of clinical significance has received a great deal of attention in psychotherapy research during the past several years. This is at least partially owing to the work of Jacobson and his colleagues (Jacobson, Follette, & Revenstorf, 1984, 1986; Jacobson & Truax, 1991) and others (e.g., Christensen & Mendoza, 1986; Speer, 1992; Wampold & Jenson, 1986). Their work came at a time when researchers began to recognize that traditional statistical comparisons do not reveal a great deal about the efficacy of therapy.

Jacobson and Truax (1991) broadly defined the clinical significance of treatment as "its ability to meet standards of efficacy set by consumers, clinicians, and researchers" (p. 12). Further, they noted that:

> While there is little consensus in the field regarding what these standards should be, various criteria have been suggested: a high percentage of clients improving . . . ; a level of change that is recognizable by peers and significant others . . . ; an elimination of the presenting problem . . . ; normative levels of functioning at the end of therapy . . . ; high end-state functioning at the end of therapy . . . ; or changes that significantly reduce one's risk for various health problems. (p.12)

From their perspective, Jacobson and his colleagues (Jacobson et al., 1984; Jacobson & Truax, 1991) felt that clinically significant change could be conceptualized in one of three ways. Thus, for clinically significant change to have occurred, the measured level of functioning following the therapeutic episode would have to either (a) fall outside the range of the dysfunctional population by at least two standard deviations from the mean of that population in the direction of functionality, (b) fall within two standard deviations of the mean for the normal or functional population, or (c) be closer to the mean of the functional population than to that of the dysfunctional population. Jacobson and Truax viewed the third option (c) as being the least arbitrary, and they provided different recommendations for determining cutoffs for clinically significant change, depending on the availability of normative data.

At the same time, these same investigators noted the importance of considering the change in the measured variables of interest from pre- to posttreatment in addition to the patient's functional status at the end of therapy. To this end, Jacobson et al. (1984) proposed the concomitant use of a reliable change index (RCI) to determine whether change is clinically significant. This index, modified on the recommendation of Christensen and Mendoza (1986), is nothing more than the pretest score minus the posttest score divided by the standard error of the difference of the two scores. But what of those who begin treatment in a functional or "normal" range but make reliable change in the direction of improvement? Following the research of Lambert, Hansen, and Finch (2001), these individuals should be considered improved but not clinically significantly improved. Both those beginning treatment in the functional range and deteriorate into the dysfunctional range, as well as those who begin treatment in the dysfunctional range and deteriorate further would be considered *deteriorators*. The RCI and its use are discussed in more detail in chapter 5 of this volume.

There are other approaches to analyzing individual patient data for clinically significant change. Excellent discussions of the RCI and some of these methods can be found in Saunders, Howard, and Newman (1988), Speer and Greenbaum (1995), Hsu (1996, 1999), Kazdin (1999), and Jacobson, Roberts, Berns, and McGlinchey (1999). Interested readers are encouraged to review these and other articles on the topic before deciding which approach to determining clinically significant change is best suited for their particular outcomes assessment system.

*Changes in Groups of Patients.*   Changes in groups of patients from one point in time to the next have typically been examined through the use of any of a number of tests of statistical differences in mean scores. This is generally quite appropriate and not likely to draw much criticism (assuming the most appropriate test for the data has been employed). Although it may be important to know that a real change in a sample or population has taken place, these types of tests don't provide any indication of the magnitude of that change. For example, one cannot infer that a difference at the 0.001 level is of a greater magnitude than one at the 0.005 level; all that can be said is that the chances that a real difference occurs are much greater when the 0.001 significance level is reached than they are when the significance level is 0.005.

To answer questions related to the magnitude of change, behavioral (and medical) health care researchers are turning more to employing statistics to measure *effect size.* Effect size can be defined as a "standardized measure of change in a group or a difference in changes between two groups" (Kazis, Anderson, & Meenan, 1989). It is typically computed by dividing the difference between the pre- and posttreatment means by the pretreatment standard deviation (of $ES = [m_1 - m_2]/s_1$). Cohen (1988) interpreted ES values of less than 0.1 as indicating a trivial or no effect; 0.1–0.3 as indicating a small effect; 0.3 to 0.5, a moderate effect; and greater than 0.5, a large effect. Note that others advocate for other magnitude cutoffs (for example, see Hopkins, 1997). Regardless, as Kazis et al. (1989) point out, effect sizes provide for a more interpretable measure of change and allow for comparison of differences on different measures within or between outcomes systems.

Another approach would be to analyze the data using both effect size and significance test methods. This is being seen more frequently in the published literature. Doing so would not require significantly more effort beyond that for one or the other method, but it would satisfy the needs of all stakeholders and other interested parties.

### Inclusion of Process Measures

It this author's contention that outcomes is the most important aspect in Donabedian's (1980, 1982, 1985) concept of quality of care. At the same time, the importance of the measurement of process cannot be denied. Knowledge of the processes that accompany outcomes is critical in any endeavor that seeks to improve the quality of care. As Burnam (1996) noted, "Assessment of the types and intensities of specific services received by each client, or the process of care, provides a means to begin to understand the influence of these features of treatment on client outcomes" (p. 15). Knowing associated process variables allows the individual practitioner or organization to determine what works for whom.

Fortunately, data for many of the important process variables are readily and easily available through the provider's claims database or other information systems. Information such as number of outpatient treatment visits, days of stay in an inpatient facility, type and dosage of psychotropic medications, incurred costs, and treatment provider generally can be retrieved from databases or data warehouses that facilities or organizations maintain. On the other hand, there are other types of process information that must be accessed by other means. The type of individual therapy used with patients (e.g., cognitive-behavioral, psychoanalytic) is an example.

### Analysis of Process Data

The importance of gathering and including process data for the analysis of outcomes data was discussed earlier. Using some of the more sophisticated statistical techniques, the combining of these data can yield far more useful information about effectiveness than would be the case when using outcomes data alone, particularly when comparing two or more types of treatment (Burnam, 1996). For instance, one may wish to use both types of data along with other case mix data (e.g., gender, age, diagnosis) to develop statistical models for predicting the likely outcomes of treatment for a given patient. Employing these requires having access to the services of an individual trained in the use of these complex statistical analyses.

## REPORTING OF OUTCOMES DATA

Another often overlooked or neglected aspect of an outcomes system is how the outcomes findings and related data will be reported. Reporting is an important part of any outcomes assessment program. It is the vehicle by which feedback about CQI and other improvement interventions is conveyed and on which judgments about "next steps" are made. It is critical for ensuring that effort toward improving the quality of health care—behavioral or otherwise—is having an effect, and therefore warrants due consideration.

**Intent of the Report**

The first issue to consider in making decisions about outcomes reporting is what the intent of the report is. This should be a relatively easy decision if one has taken the time to define the purpose of the outcomes system and what questions it is supposed to answer. Of course, there may be multiple reasons for initiating the system and multiple questions that need to be answered, and trying to address all questions and matters of interest may be problematic from a reporting standpoint. The amount of available information also may be problematic. Too much information may be burdensome to the reader and detract from the conveyance of what is really important. The issue then becomes one of determining which information is considered primary, which is secondary, and so forth, and how much information can really be showcased and remain meaningful.

**Intended Audience**

Just as important as the intent of the report is who the report will be directed to. Often, these two factors go hand in hand. The stakeholders will most certainly have had say in defining the purpose of the outcomes system, and they will be the primary recipients of the outcomes information. Problems may arise when the needs of more than one stakeholder must be met. One solution to this problem is to develop different reports for the different stakeholders. A good example of this is the development of both a score card and a report card to distribute the outcomes information. The score card would be used to convey information that is most important to the organization's senior management, whereas the report card would be distributed to patients, payers, providers, and other third parties with a vested interest in the organization's quality improvement program.

**How to Report the Data**

How outcomes information is reported depends largely on the intended audience. Different audiences will have different levels of comprehension and different preferences for how they would like to see the information presented. For instance, for organization administrative or other internal uses, tabular reporting of outcomes data may be preferable to reporting via the use of pie charts, histograms, cumulative frequency curves, or other graphic forms of data presentation. Conversely, stakeholders such as patients, payers, and employers may find it easier to interpret the data if they are graphically presented. The use of color and other eye-catching graphics would certainly be the choice in sales presentations or when the data is presented for other marketing purposes.

**When to Report**

The frequency at which outcome data is reported may depend on several variables. The first has to do with the time intervals for which aspects of the selected outcomes variables are considered. For example, the outcomes instrumentation may contain items or entire scales that ask the patient to report how frequently he has been bothered by certain symptoms, engaged in specific behaviors or cognitions, or felt a certain way during a specific time period. With these types of measures, it doesn't make sense to gather, much less report data any more frequently than the interval of time that the patient must consider in responding to the questions. Doing so results in overlapping reporting periods for the measured outcomes variables. If an intervention has been initiated during the period of overlap, the meaning of the results of both periods becomes muddied to the point of uselessness.

Related to this issue is the minimum amount of time one would expect an intervention must have to begin to have an effect on the variable of interest. For example, reporting outcomes data on patients receiving outpatient substance abuse treatment on a weekly basis may not allow enough time to plan and implement an intervention and allow that intervention to have an effect and show results during the next reporting period. Similarly, efforts to bring down 30-day readmission rates for psychiatric inpatients (a frequently reported outcomes measure) would not be served by monthly outcomes reporting. Instead, quarterly or semiannual reporting would allow the organization or clinician enough time to receive and evaluate outcomes data from the previous reporting period, develop and implement a plan of intervention (e.g., ensure the patient has an ambulatory follow-up appointment scheduled to occur within 7 days of the discharge date; see Nelson, Maruish, & Axler, 2000), and then determine the effects of that intervention on the readmission rate for the current reporting period.

One or more stakeholders or other third parties may dictate the reporting cycle. For example, payers may wish to see data on their covered lives on a monthly basis, regardless of the whether this presents any meaningful information. Accreditation organizations such as JCAHO and NCQA may request data on an annual basis, even though more frequent reporting would be much more useful to the organization or its providers. This later situation is less problematic, because more frequent reporting can take place in addition to the required interval of reporting.

Finally, measuring, processing, analyzing, and reporting outcomes all have a cost in terms of the materials, equipment, and manpower that are required for these tasks. Thus, the resources that are available to the organization will limit the frequency of reporting. In some settings, adequate resources may be allocated for quarterly measurement and reporting; in others, the resources may permit only annual measurement and reporting. Other things being equal, the amount of resources that are dedicated to these activities generally is a good indication of the organization's commitment to the outcomes initiative.

### What to Do With the Information

It is important to specify how the outcomes results can or will be used to improve the quality of the organization's services. After all, this is where the rubber meets the road. One needs to have at least some general ideas of what actions should be taken when the need for service-related improvements are indicated. Information related to the clinical and nonclinical aspects of the organization's services is nice to know, but it becomes meaningless and a waste of time, effort, and money if nothing is done with it. This means a willingness to make changes, including changes in treatment, based on findings from the data. Whether this involves the integration of disorder-specific guidelines or something more generally applicable, the challenge may frequently be to get care providers to do things differently from the way they usually do them. The organization should have an idea of what will need to be done (and have a commitment to act on it) before getting started.

## How to Use Outcomes Information

Having outcomes information is one thing; doing something with it is another. One can dedicate a large amount of money and other expensive resources to build an elaborate outcomes assessment system that yields important and useful information. But if this information is not used or not used to its fullest potential, the system may quickly become a white elephant on its way to an untimely death.

Common reasons for developing and implementing an outcomes system within an organization were discussed earlier in this chapter. Any one of these could be a primary, or an important secondary, reason why a particular organization is interested in and therefore seeks to obtain outcomes information. The question here has to do with what must be done with the information that is produced by the outcomes system to fulfill the purpose(s) for which the system was created. Table 7.2 presents examples of ways in which the information can be use to support each of the previously identified common reasons for conducting a program of ongoing outcomes assessment.

TABLE 7.2
Examples of Ways to Use Outcomes Information to Achieve the Purpose of the
Outcomes System

| Reason for Assessing Outcomes | What To Do With Outcomes Information |
| --- | --- |
| Determine outcomes of treatment | • Determine quality of services provided to organization's clientele<br>• Determine what works best for whom |
| Assist in clinical decision-making | • Provide information to clinicians on a timely basis for treatment planning and monitoring |
| Develop guidelines for treatment | • Determine what aspects of care have the most impact on producing positive outcomes |
| Develop predictive models | • Develop algorithms for predicting length of treatment, most appropriate treatment, amount of recovery<br>• Use predictive models for monitoring patients along the projected path of recovery |
| Develop a provider profiling system | • Identify the most effective clinicians and reward their performance<br>• Identify the least effective clinicians and provide remediation<br>• Identify types of patients with whom clinicians are most effective and make referrals accordingly |
| Support CQI efforts | • Identify opportunities for improvement within the organization<br>• Provide feedback about current status of an aspect of care targeted for performance improvement<br>• Provide feedback about the effects of interventions made to improve performance |
| Fulfill regulatory and accreditation requirements | • Use the data to support NCQA/JCAHO quality improvement studies that are required for accreditation or reaccreditation<br>• Use data to fulfill state and federal regulatory requirements |
| Generate score cards | • Use trended data on important performance measures to demonstrate to the organization's upper management the effectiveness of services provided to patients over time |
| Generate report cards | • Compare the organization's data for standard performance measures with those of other organizations |
| Support other marketing efforts | • Combine with financial information to determine cost savings and cost offset of behavioral healthcare services |

The list presented in Table 7.2 is by no means exhaustive. It does help to underscore the need to decide exactly how the resulting information can provide the support for and justify the time, effort, and money needed to maintain the outcomes system. It also should lead one to question whether the amount and type of data that the planned outcomes system would yield would indeed serve the intended purpose(s) of the system. If not, one would need to reconsider and perhaps modify previous decisions related to the who, what, when, and how of the planned measurement activity.

## IMPLEMENTING TEST-BASED OUTCOMES ASSESSMENT SYSTEMS

Developing a useful outcomes assessment system requires careful consideration of many basic but often overlooked issues that are critical to its success. Arriving at the final look and feel of the system can be a long, arduous, and frequently stressful undertaking. If done properly, however, it can yield a great payoff in terms of the information it will yield and the savings from the wasted effort that otherwise would result from poor planning. But deciding on who, what, when and how to measure, as well as how to report and use the resulting information, is only half the battle. The program must be implemented. One must now begin the task of developing the structure and processes for gathering, transmitting, storing, processing, analyzing, and reporting outcomes data and information. Issues related to the implementation of the system into the organization's daily operations warrant at least the same careful consideration that is afforded to the design of the system. Whereas design flaws limit the amount of useful information, flaws and oversights in the implementation plan can cause the system to crash, yielding no useful information. Instead, time, effort, and resources are wasted, and the credibility of the responsible party may be lessened or lost.

Along with addressing these issues, many organizations have yet another major challenge to face: implementation of the outcomes initiative across multiple systems of providers and facilities. Anyone who has been involved in the implementation of even small, ongoing data-gathering efforts knows that this can be a tremendous undertaking. Now consider doing this in a large system on a scale possibly involving tens of thousands of providers from several provider networks scattered throughout the United States. Needless to say, a carefully thought-out plan for implementing an outcomes program across the organization must be developed if the system is to become fully operational and provide useful information.

The remainder of this chapter will focus on the most important issues related to the implementation of outcomes systems within an organization. Attention is given to matters that will bear directly on the success of the implementation process, which in turn will directly bear on the probability that the outcomes assessment system will be successful. Because of this, the approach here will be more directive than that taken in the first section of this chapter.

## EVALUATE THE MBHO'S READINESS TO MOVE FORWARD

Prior to actually beginning to work on a plan to implement an outcomes system, it is important to make sure the organization is ready to proceed with what can be a long, challenging process that will undoubtedly involve a series of obstacles that must be overcome. This is the reality of this type of endeavor—one that cannot be escaped. At the same time, there are many things that can be done to make the implementation of the system proceed on as smooth and steady a course as possible. The first step is to determine how prepared the organization is to proceed in the process. Information obtained at this point can help the organization move through each of the stages of preparation for launching the system, which are discussed later.

**Evaluate the Basic Design of the System**

The first part of this chapter presented many issues related to the basic design of the system. Long before the design completion, the outcomes system designers should have come to the realization that the task is not an easy one. With due consideration of the various issues discussed earlier, the system designers should have overcome the methodological challenges described by Hoffmann, Leckman, Russo, and Knauf (1999), those being "developing measurement strategies that are minimally demanding of the patient and clinician time, and cost as little as possible to implement, yet yield data robust enough to record change following relatively short treatment intervals and to differentiate among patient groups and levels of severity" (p. 211). It is hoped that in initially responding to these challenges, there has not been too much focus on scientific rigor (Speer & Newman, 1996). In the beginning, it is more important to just get started, no matter how simple and limited the system might be.

It is important that at least tentative decisions regarding these few but very important matters have been reached by those leading the effort toward establishing an outcomes system in the organization. Thus, there should be at least a general idea of, and consensus among, those spearheading the outcomes effort on

- What questions will be answered by the outcomes data
- What will be measured (e.g., symptomatology, functionality)
- Who will be measured (e.g., all patients, specific diagnostic groups)
- How it will be measured (e.g., claims data, patient-self-report data, staff ratings)
- When it will be measured (e.g., termination, 6 months posttermination)
- How the data will be analyzed (e.g., comparison against benchmarks, tests of significance)
- How the results of the analyses will be presented to answer the questions being asked (e.g., comparison against a benchmark, case-mix adjustment results)
- How the information will be used (e.g., feedback to staff for CQI projects, development and application of predictive modeling).

Verifying that these issues are indeed resolved to the satisfaction of all stakeholders in outcomes initiative and to others who have been involved up to this point is an important step that should take place before proceeding further. Uncertainty or confusion over any of these matters can have deleterious consequences later on. Thus, it is worthwhile to take the time to take one last look at the decisions related to them.

**Evaluate Organizational Readiness for the System**

Initiating an outcomes assessment program in any behavioral health care setting can be a tremendous undertaking from many perspectives. At the very least, it necessitates change. This, in turn, can (and frequently does) evoke a variety of reactions, ranging from curiosity and doubt, to feelings of anxiety and fear, to subtle or overt oppositional behavior. It therefore becomes important to take stock of the organization as a whole, as well as those aspects that are particularly relevant to the ability to successfully implement an outcomes program, in preparation of actually putting together the nuts and bolts of the system.

Wetzler (1994) has identified five broad factors that a health care organization should consider when assessing itself in preparation of the initiation of an outcomes management system. The first factor to consider is the *institutional environment*. This refers to the size and type of the organization, how its governance is structured, and relevant external factors, such as the penetration of the organization's services into the community it serves. The second factor is the organization's *leadership*. Third, assessment of the organization's *information and analysis capacities* is extremely important as one considers the implementation of a highly data- and information-dependent initiative such as an outcomes assessment and management program. The fourth factor is the *resources* that are or will be available to support the program. The last factor is the current activities that can serve as *leverage* in the implementation and ongoing maintenance of the outcomes program. Wetzler also has identified several aspects within each of these five factors that deserve particular attention. Table 7.3 presents the five factors and each of their associated aspects. Also presented are representative questions that might be asked in assessing each one. Many of the organizational aspects listed in Table 7.3 are considered especially important by this author and will be given due attention in the sections that follow.

### Determine How to Evaluate the Success of the System

As has been previously stated, there are many aspects of an outcomes system that can be neglected in its planning stages. An easily overlooked but extremely important facet of any outcomes program is the method by which the program will be evaluated. In other words, how can the organization tell if the program is successful? Perhaps the issue is even more basic than "how." The idea of conducting an evaluation of the system itself may not even be considered. But unless the organization's leaders are uninformed, it is highly unlikely that the issue will not be raised at some point. It therefore is important from the standpoints of practicality, accountability, and continuous quality improvement that a plan for evaluating the impact of the system on the organization be developed.

The success of an organization's outcomes system can be determined in several different ways. One measure of the success would be its impact on the organization's bottom line. For example, outcomes information might result in savings by assisting in quickly determining the most appropriate level of care for a given patient; identifying the best type of treatment, thus eliminating wasteful, ineffective interventions; or determining the need for additional services beyond those initially authorized. Unfortunate as it might be, the degree to which the outcomes system financially impacts the organization may be what the organization views as the primary measure of the success of the system.

Of course, there are other (and to many, more meaningful) ways to evaluate the success of an outcomes assessment program. Each organization will have at least one, and probably multiple reasons for initiating an outcomes system. Thus, evaluating the program against criteria directly related to the reason(s) for initiating a system of outcomes assessment in the first place is a logical way to proceed in determining the system's success. It speaks directly to providing justification for the system's

TABLE 7.3
Factors to Consider in Evaluating Organizational Readiness to Implement an Outcomes
Assessment Program

| General Factor | Aspects of the General Factor | Representative Question to Ask |
|---|---|---|
| Institutional environment | Commitment to quality | Is a commitment to quality evident throughout the organization? |
| | Appreciation of health care as a science and an art | Is the application of scientific principles evident in the organization? |
| | Willingness to entertain new ideas | Is the organization open to new opportunities and trying new ideas? |
| | Willingness to take risks | Are the organization and its employees willing to take risks? |
| | Level of fear | Does fear of reprisal for mistakes impede learning and seeking alternate solutions? |
| | Appreciation of the consumer's perspective | Does the organization listen to and educate its customers? |
| | Degree to which learning is fostered | Does the organization learn from its staff and its patients? |
| Leadership | One respected person willing to lead | Is there a respected person who is willing to lead the outcomes program? |
| | Organizational goal of outcomes management | Is the organization willing to adopt outcomes management as an organizational goal? |
| | Others willing to participate in the program | Is there other staff willing to participate in the program? |
| | Commitment of senior management | Is senior management 100% behind the outcomes program? |
| Information and analysis capacities | Availability of measurement instruments | Are appropriate outcomes measurement instruments available, or do they have to be developed? |
| | Ability to develop and implement data collection methodology | Can the organization adapt existing procedures to meet the demands of collecting outcomes data? |
| | Availability of statistical expertise | Is a statistical consultant available? |
| | Decision makers comfortable using quantitative analyses | Will clinicians use the information provided by the outcomes system? |
| Resources | Management time | Does the outcomes manager have enough time to manage the system? |
| | Decision makers' time | Do the organization's high-level decision makers have enough time to make well-thought-out decisions about the outcomes program? |
| | Staff time | Does the organization's staff have the time and motivation needed to make the outcomes program a success? |
| | Hardware and software | Are adequate hardware and software available? |
| | Database development and data management | Are adequate database resources available? |
| | Statistical analysis | Is someone dedicated to perform the needed statistical analyses? |

(Continued)

TABLE 7.3
(*Continued*)

| General Factor | Aspects of the General Factor | Representative Question to Ask |
|---|---|---|
| Leverage | Coordination with other quality initiatives | Are there other organization quality initiatives with which outcomes assessment can achieve synergy? |
| | Coordination with other research activities | Are there other organization research activities with which outcomes assessment can achieve synergy? |
| | Sharing of personnel and other resources | Can other organization resources be devoted to the outcomes program on a part-time basis? |
| | Participation in a multiorganizational consortium | Is there an opportunity for the organization to work cooperatively with other organizations on outcomes projects? |

*Note.* General factors and aspects of general factors are from Wetzler (1994).

existence and associated benefits as initially conceptualized. Taking this approach, the criteria selected to judge the success of the program would be specific to each organization. Table 7.4 presents some examples of criteria that might be used to evaluate outcomes systems, developed for each of the common reasons for initiating an outcomes program that were identified earlier. In the end, the set of criteria that is formally adopted may be that which the organization's management team dictates. However, this should not deter those spearheading the outcomes initiative from including additional criteria that would be useful from a CQI perspective.

### Seek Feedback From Key Organization Staff

At this point, those championing the outcomes initiative should be comfortable with the general plan for the proposed system. Now it is beneficial to ask for feedback about the envisioned system from some of the key people in the organization. This might include the medical director, the quality improvement manager, and several clinicians. Ideally, one would have sought input from these people during the project formulation phase, so there should be no major surprises now. But having a final round of input may prevent embarrassing moments when the plan is presented to the organization's decision makers for approval.

## SECURE SUPPORT AND COMMITMENT FOR THE OUTCOMES SYSTEM

Implementation of outcomes systems in any health care delivery system (regardless of its size and complexity) is not an easy task. Once the purpose or goal of the outcomes system is decided on, one of the biggest challenges facing the organization is getting all involved parties (from the organization's leadership to providers and their support staff) "onboard" with the program. This can be quite difficult, and it will probably take a good deal of selling to get the type of commitment necessary to make the program work. All levels of the organization must be convinced that the outcomes system is going to result in changes that will somehow benefit patients and themselves, either directly in their individual work or indirectly through the benefits that will accrue to the organization.

TABLE 7.4

Examples of Criteria for Evaluating Outcomes Assessment Systems

| Reason for Assessing Outcomes | Examples of Relevant Evaluation Criteria |
|---|---|
| Determine outcomes of treatment | • Level of psychological and social role functioning is measured 6 months posttreatment termination.<br>• Amount of symptomatic change from the time of treatment initiation to treatment termination that can be considered statistically significant. |
| Assist in clinical decision-making | • Patient progress reports sent to providers within one day of patient's completion of outcomes instruments.<br>• Clinicians use patient progress reports for treatment authorization and level of care decisions.<br>• Clinicians report that patient progress reports facilitate the clinical decision-making process. |
| Develop guidelines for treatment | • Outcomes-based treatment guidelines are developed for one or more diagnostic groups.<br>• Existing treatment guidelines are evaluated using outcomes information. |
| Develop predictive models | • Statistical model for the prediction of length of stay/episode of care, developed from outcomes data, is found to be accurate 85% of the time.<br>• Clinicians report usefulness of recovery curves in monitoring treatment over time. |
| Develop a provider profiling system | • Generation of annual provider rankings are based on risk-adjusted outcomes data.<br>• Clinician rankings are used to award "preferred provider" status to network clinicians. |
| Support CQI efforts | • Outcomes information is used in root cause analysis of poor patient satisfaction findings.<br>• Outcomes information is used to identify specific areas of clinical care that present opportunities for improvement. |
| Fulfill regulatory and accreditation requirements | • NCQA/JCAHO quality improvement standards are met using outcomes data.<br>• Quality Improvement System for Managed Care (QISMC) Quality Assessment and Performance Improvement program (Domain 1) standards are met. |
| Generate score cards | • Quarterly outcomes score cards are distributed to senior management.<br>• Outcomes score card information is used to determine clinician training needs. |
| Generate report cards | • Organization data is presented with data from other outcomes consortium members on standard measures.<br>• Outcomes report card included in marketing and sales materials is provided to potential customers. |
| Support other marketing efforts | • Increased revenues are attributable to outcomes information.<br>• Outcomes data are included as part of the organization's annual report to shareholders. |

In essence, there needs to be what Sperry and his colleagues have called a "culture of measurement" (Sperry, 1997; Sperry, Grissom, Brill, & Marion, 1997). Creating this culture requires that the clinical and support staff to begin to see measurement as an important tool that can improve the quality of care and significantly contribute to the success of the organization. It also requires management to foster this culture by providing the clinical training, technical support, and whatever else is necessary to clinicians to be receptive and use the outcomes system. As Sperry et al. (1997) noted:

> Until measurement is viewed as important to both professional and organizational suc-
> cess, it will be difficult, if not impossible, to implement an outcomes system that can
> realistically result in substantial improvement in cost effectiveness, increase productivity
> and morale, or engender continuous quality improvement in clinical care. (p. 129)

### Support From the MBHO's Leadership

Perhaps the biggest challenge is "selling" the idea of a system for the measurement and management of treatment outcomes to the organization's leadership. Obtaining the support at this level is consistently identified as a necessary step in the implementation process (Bengen-Seltzer, 1999; Docherty & Dewan, 1995; Kraus & Horan, 1998; Ofstead, Gobran, & Lum, 2000; Smith, Fischer, et al., 1997; Sperry et al., 1997; Wetzler, 1994). The leadership must be convinced that the benefits that will accrue to their organization will far outweigh the cost and other burdens that usually accompany these types of endeavors. They need to be sure that in the long run they are doing the right thing for the organization, themselves, their staff, and, of course, their patients.

*Selling the System.*   What are the key selling points of an outcomes system? These will vary from one organization to another, but there are some general guidelines for identifying those aspects of the system that will help to sell it to the leadership. First, one should be prepared to present a well-thought-out vision of what the system will look like, what it will likely require in terms of initial and ongoing resources, and what the benefits will be for the organization. One should also be able to convey that this vision has been shared with and is supported by key members within the organization.

Second, money will be an issue. Being able to demonstrate cost savings or offset from delivering more effective and efficient services, increased business, or other benefits that will result from the implementation of the system will go a long way in obtaining the leadership's approval. In lieu of this, one should be able to provide cost projections that can be justified by other tangible and intangible benefits that will accrue to the organization from the system.

A third selling point is related to the second. The costs that will be incurred can be tied to the reasons for which the proposed plan for an outcomes program was developed in the first place. For example, if the system will provide information that will meet JCAHO or NCQA requirements for outcomes measurement—requirements necessary for an accreditation status that is required to stay competitive in the marketplace—then this might be used to justify reasonable costs. Similarly, the score cards that can be generated from the outcomes data can provide the organization's management with the opportunity to make more informed decisions about the organization.

Fourth, each organization is likely to have "hot buttons" that can serve as idiosyncratic selling points for the system. The key is to know what those buttons are and tie them into the system.

Selling the proposed outcomes system may not present much of a problem if the organization's leadership initiated the idea for its development (or the exploration thereof) in the first place. Although in this instance one would be "preaching to the choir," it is likely that the proposed system will still be subject to scrutiny. Thus, use of one or more of the earlier selling points may be required.

*Expressed Commitment to the Endeavor.* Being successful in obtaining the leadership's buy-in to the proposed system should involve more than just getting an OK to proceed with its development and implementation. One should also seek the leadership's commitment to the system and all that its implementation entails. A clear demonstration of this commitment is upper management's involvement in the project. As Bengen-Seltzer (1999) indicated:

> Leadership needs to demonstrate its commitment to the new outcomes system or measures in a tangible, proactive way that is hands-on and visible to the staff that will be using the system. It's not enough to make rhetorical statements or just provide fiscal support; leadership needs to be present at regular meetings and be part of the team that develops and refines the system. (p. 7)

The degree of involvement advocated by Bengen-Seltzer might be considered unrealistic in some organizations. However, there are other ways in which management can show its commitment. The first is through the funding that it is willing to budget for the program, both in the present fiscal year and the years that follow. Approval for hiring new employees to meet the staffing needs of the program, budgeting for the necessary computer equipment and software, and joining a consortium for pooling outcomes data can be very important signs of the leadership's commitment. It is also important to communicate this commitment to all levels of the organization. This should occur not only through the usual intraorganizational corporate channels but also through the leadership's acknowledgment of the program's importance to the organization in meetings with middle and lower managers, in public forums, and during other appropriate opportunities.

## Support From the Staff

Commitment from the leadership of the organization is critical to securing commitment from providers and other front-line staff. However, it does not guarantee such commitment at the lower levels of the organization. Efforts must be directed to all levels of staff to ensure that they, too, are committed to having a successful outcomes program.

*Selling the System.* Provider, administrative, and support staff are likely to view the outcomes system as an added burden (Eisen, Leff, & Schaefer, 1999; Kraus & Horan, 1998; Wetzler, 1994). They may also have concerns about the value of the endeavor, patient confidentiality, and use of the results for staff evaluation purposes (Koch, Cairns, & Brunk, 2000). Thus, one should not be surprised by their resistance to the implementation of an outcomes system. Selling of the system should therefore begin by acknowledging their concerns and clearly communicating the purpose of the system and potential benefits that can accrue to the organization and those who are involved in the system's implementation (Bieber et al., 1999). Also, inviting representatives of both the clinical and administrative staffs to become part of the decision-making process will get them involved in the project, promote ownership of the system among them, and help sell the program to their peers.

In addition, several experts have provided suggestions as to how to bring the clinical staff onboard and become supportive of the program. For example, Berman and Hurt (1996) recommended that the system be designed to study processes and not people. That is, providers must know that the information obtained from the system will not be used by the organization to make personnel decisions. Also, ensuring that the system will provide immediate feedback about their patients and thus be useful in clinical decision-making will increase the value of the system in their eyes. (This topic is discussed further in a later section of this chapter.) In addition, Bengen-Seltzer (1999) stressed the importance of making the system and its measures relevant to the clinician's daily practice, including measures of daily functioning as outcomes variables, having benchmark data available for comparison to external providers, and allowing the provider the opportunity to learn more about what works and what doesn't work through the outcomes data. Moreover, Smith, Fischer, et al. (1997) indicated that getting these staff to see that these benefits will help them in their professional development will help in these efforts.

Selling the nonclinical administrative and support staff on how the system may benefit them may be a bit more difficult than selling the clinical staff. Here, the best one may be able to do is to actively seek their input at all points in the development and implementation process, minimize the burden placed on them by the system, and provide incentives or a means of showing appreciation for their efforts. Other organization's clinical care strategies for selling the system to staff are presented in a separate section below.

*Expressed Commitment to the Endeavor.*   Unlike at the upper management and leadership levels, there are only a limited number of things the organization's clinical care and administrative or support staff can do to directly express their commitment to the implementation of an outcomes system. Probably the most important show of commitment would be their involvement in the planning and feedback process for the system, particularly among those staff members who are respected by their peers, open to new ideas, and influential in generating excitement for new projects within the organization.

## FORM AN OUTCOMES ASSESSMENT SYSTEM TEAM

The discussion and recommendations made thus far have not been directed to anyone in particular in the organization. That is, they are intended for anyone who either is directed by the organization's leadership to investigate the possibility of establishing an outcomes assessment system or has taken this initiative on their own, either alone or as part of a task force or work group. The efforts to this point may have been informal and the group (if more than one person) loosely organized. Koch, Cairns, and Brunk (2000) recommended that all staff should be involved in (a) defining the purpose and goals of the system, (b) selecting the domains and indicators that will be measured and reported, (c) selecting the measures for those domains and indicators, (d) developing efficient data collection procedures, and (e) providing opportunities for feedback. However, with the leadership's buy-in and commitment to an outcomes program, it is now important that a formal, empowered committee or team be assembled to the tackle the work that must be accomplished to launch the system and maintain it on an ongoing basis. Formation of such a team should be the first step that follows approval for development of the system.

The question of who or what functional positions should be on the team is relatively straightforward. It should include representatives of each functional unit of the organization that will be impacted be the system. At a minimum, one would expect this to include a representative of the clinicians, administrative staff, receptionists, information system staff, statisticians, leadership, and, ideally, other stakeholders in the outcomes system, such patients, payers, and employers. The team should be large enough to ensure input from all involved parties, but not so large as to be unwieldy and slow to accomplish the work that needs to be done.

Initially, the team should be focused on implementing the system. After the system is up and running, the team's primary task should be shifted to the evaluation of the system's utility, making decisions that will help improve it and ensuring that it meets the needs of the organization. Consequently, the makeup of the team may change from time to time to reflect the team's change in focus. Regardless of the functional makeup, individuals selected to serve on the team should be those who are openly supportive of the system and want to make it work, or at least are open to the idea and are willing to contribute their best efforts to making the program a success.

## ANALYZE THE DAILY WORKFLOW OF THE ORGANIZATION

Needless to say, no single implementation plan is going to be successful across all organizations. The general approach to gathering outcomes data will need to be customized to ensure full integration into each organization's daily workflow. The importance of integrating data gathering into the daily office routine cannot be stressed enough. Overcoming the integration and implementation beast starts with doing a thorough analysis of the organization's day-to-day workflow.

Conducting a workflow analysis in any setting requires a complete and thorough understanding of what goes on in all aspects of the setting in which the outcomes measurement tasks will take place. This includes: knowing how services are requested and how those requests are processed; how referrals are made; what obligations the patient, clinician, and organization have to each other; what is reasonable to expect from each party as far as outcomes-related tasks are concerned; and what are the likely structural and process barriers to successfully incorporating this added work into the organization's routine way of doing things.

The best way to conduct the workflow analysis is through a combination of descriptions of daily processes from the parties involved and through direct observation by someone external to these processes. For example, one should be speaking with intake coordinators, clinicians, care managers, medical records personnel, care providers, clinical directors, and anyone else involved in the provision and management of treatment in the organization. Receptionists and appointment schedulers working at service delivery sites would also be included. Each of these people will have the best perspective on what they do and how they do it. They will also be able to help identify potential barriers to the integration of a test-based outcomes system into the organization's or individual clinician's daily workflow.

In addition to speaking with the staff, it is important for a member of the implementation team who is not actually involved in the daily flow of business to actually observe the process. This has two benefits. First, it allows for a confirmation of what has been reported as being the "standard operating procedures" for the organization. Second, it also affords an opportunity to identify important aspects of the daily workflow that those who are closely involved with it may overlook or consider irrelevant to outcomes management process.

On completion of the workflow analysis, it is always helpful to construct a flow chart of the process into which data gathering and outcomes reporting activities will need to be incorporated. An accurate flowchart will facilitate decisions about how and where to best integrate the required outcomes system activities into the daily flow of business. Thus, having relevant staff verify the accuracy with which the current workflow is portrayed in the chart is critical to avoiding misconceptions about what actually goes on "down in the trenches."

Once there is a clear understanding of what the daily processes are, it is time to develop a plan for integrating the envisioned outcomes system into those processes. This will involve careful thought about what needs to be done, what there is to work with, what additional resources are necessary, and how to put it all together.

## IDENTIFY AND SOLVE BARRIERS TO IMPLEMENTATION

It is through the workflow analysis that one is able to identify most if not all potential barriers to the successful implementation of the system. These barriers can range from the physical facilities themselves, to processes that have been in place for years, to the personnel and their defined roles within the organization. From there, one can begin to develop ways to overcome these barriers. Lyons et al. (1997) have identified three general categories for the types of barriers that can be encountered in implementing an outcomes system. These include ethical considerations, psychological factors, and organizational and operational factors.

### Ethical Considerations

Lyons et al. (1997) equated ethical considerations with "care for the rights of consumers" (p. 129). They break this down to concerns about informed consent, minimization of risk of harm, choice, and confidentiality. These, of course, are the same considerations that must be addressed in any type of psychological research involving human subjects.

*Informed Consent.* Generally, informed consent is required when the gathering and use of outcomes data is done in the context of a specific research project that is not part of the organization's business process. In instances in which the outcomes assessment system is implemented to be part of the organization's service delivery routine, informed consent is probably no more required than it would be if a primary care provider asked for an analysis of a blood sample. It might be useful, however, to include a notice on the organization's standard intake forms that informs patients of the outcomes program, what may be required of them related to this program, and how the data obtained as part of the program might be used. Moreover, Eisen et al. (1999) reported an approach whereby the clinician informs the patient at intake that (a) the outcomes assessment will be used to help identify symptoms and problems, (b) it will serve as a baseline for comparison with data obtained at a later date, and (c) he or she will not be denied services if the assessment is not completed. This information could then be repeated each time that the patient is asked to provide data for the outcomes program.

*Minimization of Any Risk of Harm.* As Lyons et al. (1997) pointed out, the chances of there being any risk of harm from participation in an outcomes program are minimal. Some providers might raise concern about asking questions pertaining to suicide and other psychopathology, but the evidence does not suggest that this should be a matter for concern.

*Choice.* Like risk of harm, the ability to choose to participate or not participate in outcomes data collection is seldom an issue. As Lyons et al. (1997) pointed out, "consumers feel free to answer or to ignore surveys, depending on their wishes" (p. 131). But there may be exceptions, such as when an organization requires the completion of certain paperwork that includes outcomes-related questions, to receive benefits. Lyons et al. (1997) indicated that one way to meet the organization's requirements while still offering patients a choice to participate might be to include a response option on the outcomes measure where patients indicate that they do not wish to respond. This approach would enable patients to meet the requirements of the organization while maintaining their right to choose to participate.

*Confidentiality.*  These issues apply to data that are obtained as part of an outcomes assessment program, particularly as it relates to the storage and reporting of individual patient data. Reporting of outcomes data in aggregate form (e.g., score cards, report cards) is much less of a concern. Regardless, the MBHO can take measures to ensure the confidentiality of outcomes data. For instance, both Lyons et al. (1997) and Kraus and Horan (1998) recommended the use of unique numeric patient identifiers that are not tied to social security numbers, birth dates, or anything else that could be used to identify an individual patient's data. Lyons et al. (1997) also recommended the formation of a committee to oversee the fair information practices identified by Gellman and Frawley (1996).

These and other ethical issues are discussed in detail in chapter 10 of this volume, as well as in Cone (2001) and Maruish (2002). Regardless, it behooves those responsible for the design and implementation of an outcomes system to seek both legal and professional (ethical) counsel about any ethical concerns early in the process.

### Psychological Factors

This set of potential barriers has to do with issues that those who are asked to supply or gather the data may have. This includes both (clinical and nonclinical) staff members and patients.

*Staff Resistance.*  One of the most difficult barriers to pass is that having to do with eliciting the necessary cooperation of the organization's clinical and administrative staff. Lyons et al. (1997), drawing on Rosen's and Weil's (1996) work related to the implementation of computer technology, talked about three types of staff participants in the implementation process. *Eager adopters* are open to the new system and actively welcome its implementation. *Hesitant prove its worthers* are receptive to the idea but put off giving acceptance until the eager adopters demonstrate that it is important or useful to their jobs. They tend to use both support-seeking and problem-solving coping strategies. Thus, placing these type of people in a position where success or benefits can be experienced early, as well as showing them that the outcomes system makes sense, is useful, and can be mastered, will help overcome their lack of confidence in and hesitancies about the system. *Resisters* generally view the initiative as not being worthwhile and will be resistant to attempts to convince them otherwise. Their resistance may be displayed in concerns about confidentiality and the potential negative impact on the therapeutic relationship. According to Lyons et al. (1997), "Resisters tend to use avoidance as their primary coping strategy. Quite likely, the only workable strategy for engaging resisters ... is to have consistent oversight and announce consequences for noncompliance" (p. 136).

Clinicians tend to be extremely busy and already have a number of hoops to jump through to receive reimbursement for their work. As discussed earlier, one way of eliciting the cooperation of clinicians is to make sure that they get something useful for their troubles. Data gathered in support of any outcomes initiative can become most useful to them when they are able to reap some immediate benefit from their efforts. Here, the challenge becomes one of providing information about their patients quickly enough to assist in daily clinical decision-making.

*Patient Resistance.* Patient resistance may stem from any of several sources. Two common reasons for resistance are a lack of understanding of the purpose (and therefore the consequences) of the outcomes program and a failure to see any personal benefit from participation (Lyons et al., 1997). Playing into this are the demands that are being made on the patient's time, particularly if what is being required is the completion of a lengthy outcomes measure on multiple occasions (Eisen et al., 1999). Lyons et al. (1997) suggest that completion of patient self-report measures should be limited to 20 minutes or less. This author's experience, however, suggests that a patient-completed measure should not exceed a completion time of 10 minutes.

In cases of patient resistance, it would be helpful to explain how the information will be used to their benefit. Of course, this approach will be best served if the clinician is convinced of the utility of the data to the individual patient. Berman and Hurt (1996) noted that "if clinicians view the data as clinically valuable, this attitude will be conveyed to the patient" (p. 40).

### Organizational and Operational Factors

Although identified as separate factors, the types of organizational factors referred to by Lyons et al. (1997) are essentially those that were discussed in the preceding sections.

## DEVELOP A SYSTEM FOR MANAGING OUTCOMES DATA

By their nature, outcomes systems are data-driven systems. Thus, the implementation of a system that allows for the necessary gathering, storing, analyzing, and reporting of outcomes data is critical to the success of the system. Knowledge of the organization's daily work flow is important to ensure that the data management system designed for any given organization is efficient, economical, and generally acceptable to the staff members who are involved in the system's daily operations.

### Identify the Instrumentation to Measure the Selected Outcomes Variables

The issue of the selection of what outcomes variables to measure was addressed earlier in this chapter. With these having been determined, one must then decide which instrument(s) can provide the best measure of those variables for the organization. Generally, selection of outcomes instrumentation can be facilitated by the application of the selection criteria presented in chapter 6 of this volume. However, other factors may need to be taken into consideration.

It is possible that some organizations will not be able to find any commercially available or public domain instruments that meet their desired outcomes system requirements. In these cases, there are two options. One is to modify the requirements to be consistent with what is available. This involves some compromise that, in the first year or two of the project, may be quite acceptable. The alternative is for the organization to develop its own instrumentation. This will ensure that the organization will get exactly what it wants. However, such an approach is costly in terms of both development expenses and the delay in implementing the outcomes system that will result from having to await the completion of the instrument development process, especially if one employs the industry standards set by the American Educational Research Association, American Psychological Association, and National Council on Measurement in Education (1999). In these cases, this author recommends going with the first option.

### Identify Processes for Maximizing Patient Participation Rate

Before considering the best means of managing data, thought should first be given to ways in which to obtain the greatest amount of useful data for the outcomes system. Part of this issue was addressed in the previous discussion on overcoming patient barriers. In addition to those recommendations, specific data collection processes can be implemented that can help achieve maximum participation from patients during data collection. Based on Eisen et al.'s (1999) recommendations, this author recommends the following procedures for obtaining baseline measures from patients:

- Have a patient arrive early enough for their first appointment (e.g., 30 minutes early) to complete the initial measurement without running into the time scheduled for the treatment session.
- Inform patients that this and subsequent measurements are part of the provider's or the organization's routine intake procedures and that the obtained information will assist them in providing the highest quality of care. Consider developing a brief script to assist the support staff in enlisting the cooperation of a patient (see Radosevich, McPherson, & Werni, 1994).
- As appropriate to the instrumentation that is selected, patients who cannot complete the outcomes instrumentation unassisted (e.g., because of poor reading ability, visual impairment) should have it administered to them via a structured interview format by a trained clinical or nonclinical staff member.
- Postpone the completion of outcomes measures by severely disturbed patients until they are able to provide valid responses to the instrumentation's questions.
- As appropriate, use incentives (e.g., coffee, pastries) to increase participation.
- Inform patients that the clinician will review the results of the assessment with them.

Eisen et al. (1999) also provided recommendations for maximizing participation in subsequent outcomes assessments. Based on these, the following are recommended for postbaseline measurements taken during treatment, at the time of treatment termination, and posttreatment termination:

- Appoint a support staff member to be responsible for tracking and notifying patients when it is time for the next measurement.
- Coordinate the readministration of the instrument (for outcomes monitoring) to occur with scheduled appointments with the patient's clinician, and inform the clinicians of the schedule for remeasuring their patients.
- Use a combination of mail-out forms and telephone follow-up, along with the opportunity to complete a patient satisfaction survey, to increase responses to posttreatment follow-up measurements.

With experience, the organization will arrive at additional ways to increase the participation of the health plan members that they serve.

## Identify Means of Entering and Transmitting Data

There are several options for entering outcomes data. These include direct online entry via personal computer, Internet, or intranet software by the person providing the information; key entry of respondent data into these same systems by an administrative staff member; scanning of scannable or faxable forms; or interactive voice response (IVR) technology. Selection of the best system for the organization should be based on consideration of cost, the availability of the desired entry format for the instrumentation being used, and compatibility with the organization's business flow. Compatibility with the reporting needs of the organization also must be taken into consideration. Note that in some cases, a particular data entry and reporting system may be found to be optimal from a cost and implementation standpoint; consequently, it may actually dictate the selection of instrumentation to be used for data gathering.

In considering the available technologies, one should keep in mind that clinicians should have access to means of quickly and effortlessly transmitting data and receiving information back (see Smith, Fischer, et al., 1997). The availability of fax in most service delivery offices makes this medium a very practical and inexpensive means of sending and receiving information. The Internet also provides a quick and inexpensive means of transmitting data. However, many practitioners still do not have access to the Internet at their offices, thus posing a significant problem to system-wide implementation. The reader is referred to Maruish (2002) for a discussion of the advantages and limitations of Internet, fax, and IVR technologies.

## Identify a Means of Storing and Retrieving Data

Once transmitted, the data need to be stored for immediate and later use. Databases need to have the capacity to store large amounts of data, permit data entry via the mode selected for use with the outcomes system, and allow easy access to data for both regular, planned analyses and reporting, as well as for special ad hoc reporting and projects.

Radosevich et al. (1994) have identified a set of considerations that should be taken into account in choosing or designing a database. They include the following:

- *Import and export capabilities.* The database should be able to receive input from and send output to other software required for the system (e.g., spreadsheets, statistical packages, report generators).
- *Openness of the database structure.* The ability to modify the database's structure is necessary to handle the inevitable changes that will be required after piloting or initial implementation.
- *Ease in linking from other systems.* The database should be able to import data from any other databases that it may have to interface with (e.g., claims database).
- *Querying capability.* One should be able to view, change, and ask questions of the data, and to use the answers for report generation.
- *Methods for handling missing data.* The database should be able to handle missing data in whatever manner would be appropriate for the system.
- *Exporting capabilities that permit trended data analysis.* Any outcomes system must be able to make comparisons of data obtained at different points in time.

TABLE 7.5
Questions to Consider When Selecting a Data Management Product

---

Issues important to clinicians:

Does the system support the instruments you want to use?

Can your existing staff handle the data management and report generation tasks without much hassle?

Does the system provide meaningful output (reports) in a timely fashion?

Does the system allow the addition of questions or customization?

Can the system support longitudinal patient records so that the clinician can assess change over time?

Will patients find the assessment tools and processes "user friendly?"

Issues important to staff:

Is the technology simple and reliable to use?

Are manuals and adequate technical support readily available?

Is there a training program, or are people expected to learn the system on their own?

How much time does it take to enter data for each patient?

How are errors corrected?

How are reports generated?

What type of assistance will most patients require?

How flexible is the data collection for patients with special needs (e.g., those with vision problems, motor control problems, computer phobia, language or literacy issues, etc.)?

Additional issues important to administration:

Does the vendor have a good track record in this line of business?

Does the system require the user to perform extensive setup or design?

What are the hardware and space requirements needed to run the system?

Will the system be integrated with other programs or used on a network?

Does staff need special training?

Is continuing oversight by an MIS professional required?

Who has control of and ownership of the data?

How much does it really cost to make it work in your practice for the volume of patients needing assessment (including software, hardware, forms, per-patient charges, telephone and fax fees, technical support, training, data analysis, and customization)?

---

*Note.* From Ofstead, Gobran, & Lum (2000, p. 172). Reprinted with permission.

- *Capacity to support a "tickler" system.* The database should have the ability to identify patients requiring follow-up measurement (either during or after the episode of care) at designated points in time and, preferably, to generate letters to these individuals notifying them of the need for reassessment.

In addition, Ofstead et al. (2000) provided an extensive set of questions to consider when selecting a data management system. These are presented in Table 7.5.

## Identify Means of Making Outcomes-Derived Information Useful and Immediately Available for Clinical Decision-Making

The capability of real-time processing of outcomes data collected at intake or during the course of treatment via the Internet, a faxback system, or an in-office PC system makes it possible for the system to support important decisions related to need for treatment. It can also assist in determining the most appropriate level of care for the individual patient. For these reasons, every effort should be made to build into the outcomes assessment system the ability to provide immediate feedback to clinicians (Berman & Hurt, 1996; Lyons et al., 1997). This information will be viewed as being valuable and, as indicated previously, having access to it when it is most beneficial can be a major selling point for clinicians and other staff members who may be involved in the clinical decision-making process (e.g., clinical directors, peer reviewers).

Lambert, Hansen, and Finch (2001) noted that feedback must be both timely and useful to be effective. In planning for the provision of feedback, it therefore is important to elicit from the clinical decision-makers input about the outcomes information they would like to receive and the form in which it should be presented. One way of doing this is to develop several mock reports using various combinations of tables, graphs, and text for conveying the information, and then present the mock-ups to a sample of the clinical decision-makers who will be using these reports. Based on their feedback, a final report can be constructed and programmed for use with the outcomes system. Failure to elicit this type of input may result in the provision of information that will be of little or no value to the intended audience and, consequently, decreased motivation for clinicians to be active participants and supporters of the outcomes system.

## DEVELOP A PLAN TO INTEGRATE THE GATHERING AND PROCESSING OF OUTCOMES DATA INTO THE DAILY WORKFLOW

Armed with the decisions about what the outcomes system is intended to do and how that will be accomplished, along with knowledge of the daily workflow, one must now develop a plan for integrating the proposed outcomes system into the daily business operations of the organization and its clinicians. The trick is to accomplish this task while creating a minimum of disruption and burden for the staff that have to administer the system on an ongoing basis. This is not always an easy task. However, there are a few things that the outcomes team can do to facilitate this.

One may find that it is useful first to examine the outcomes systems of other organizations to find out what has and has not worked in both the gathering of data and the reporting outcomes information (Bieber et al., 1999). Also, it is helpful to list all elements of the data-gathering and reporting process (e.g., determination of which patients to engage, transmission of the data to central processing, faxing the patient report to the provider) and then insert these elements on the organization's current workflow chart. This will result in the development of a revised workflow chart with the outcomes program's processes incorporated into it. As before, one should elicit feedback from all involved parties to determine whether the proposed plan for integrating the outcomes system into the daily workflow is realistic and will actually work.

Figure 7.1 is a workflow chart presented by Bieber et al. (1999) for integrating an outcomes assessment system into a large, multifacility provider of inpatient psychiatric and substance abuse services. Note how the role of each of the key clinical and nonclinical staff members and collaterals in the outcomes data gathering process is detailed as the patient moves through the episode of inpatient care.

Feedback from the staff may reveal that the proposed workflow is unrealistic or not doable for one reason or another. Consequently, changes can be made to help ensure the success of the program. These changes may necessitate modifications pertaining to decisions that were made much earlier in the project planning and development process. These, in turn, may necessitate changes to related procedures. Thus, it is important to approach this part of the process with openness and flexibility, realizing that what was considered a well thought-out plan may require some alteration.

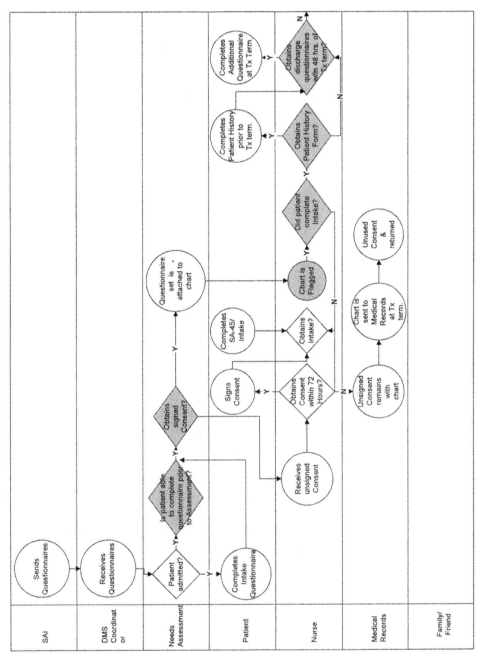

FIG. 7.1. Outcomes assessment workflow for an adult psychiatric inpatient facility. Reprinted with permission.

FIG. 7.1. (Continued)

## PILOT TEST THE SYSTEM

No outcomes system should be fully implemented without first piloting it. In spite of all the thought and revisions that have been put into the system up to this point, one can be sure that even on a small scale, problems will emerge. Identifying problems before rolling out the system throughout the entire organization can ultimately help reduce resistance to the initiative, alleviate unrealistic fears, avoid embarrassment (by the outcomes team), and prevent a lot of wasted time and money. In planning the pilot study, the following are recommended:

- Select only a few clinicians or sites to participate.
- Make sure that both supporters of the outcomes initiative and resisters partici-pate in the project (Bieber et al., 1999; Lyons et al., 1997). Having resistant staff in-volved will ensure that the shortcomings of the implementation plan are quickly revealed.
- Ensure that all aspects of the outcomes system are tested. In multisite organiza-tions, one might even consider having some aspects of the system tested at one site, others at another site, and still others at a third site.
- Allow the pilot to run for as long as it may take to test all aspects of the system. In some cases, only a few weeks of time may be necessary; in other instances, the pilot may need to run for several months. The latter will more likely be the case in large, multisite organization's or with more comprehensive or complicated systems.
- Obtain feedback from all staff—clinical and nonclinical—who participated in the pilot test. Everyone's experience and opinions are important.
- Use of the staff's feedback to fine-tune the system and correct the identified problems. If it was a problem during the pilot, it probably will be a problem during the implementation phase.

## TRAIN STAFF IN THE IMPLEMENTATION PROCESS

An integral part of ramping up for the implementation of a new outcomes system is the training of all organization staff who will be involved in the running of the program on a daily basis. Those who are involved in the gathering, processing, or use of the outcomes data (from the office receptionist to the clinical director) can make or break the system. Thus, training of the involved parties in the implementation of the on-site processes and procedures should be included in the implementation plan. This step should not be an afterthought or be otherwise treated lightly. It is also a step that should be taken only after the "bugs" identified during the pilot phase have been worked out. Bieber et al. (1999) provided some general recommendations with regard to training:

> When conducting training, it is important to identify the learners' current level of knowl-edge and begin teaching from that point forward. Consider what three to five things learners must know to be motivated and able to collect high quality data. Include all em-ployees responsible for providing clinical data, implementing patient surveys, or man-aging medical records. Design training materials so that current staff can use them to train new staff when needed. Depending on the work environment, it might be possible to train in half-day sessions, via video-conferencing, or via telephone conferencing. The

training should be timed so that data collection will begin within a week of the training. It is also important to have a support line in place to answer questions once the actual implementation begins.

Employees will probably resist changes if they feel threatened.... One approach [to countering this reaction] is to identify informal leaders who support the move to outcomes measurement and arrange to have them participate in training sessions. (p. 207)

There are a number of other things that can be done to help maximize the impact of the training. Things like scheduling multiple training sessions at different times to meet different work schedules and developing useful and comprehensive training and reference materials will help increase the chances of meeting the criteria for success for the outcomes system. Lyons et al. (1997) suggested the use of case vignettes to assess the reliability of the data collection procedures. To assist in getting buy-in into the program, Bengen-Seltzer (1999) recommended having the clinical staff train other clinical staff using a "train the trainers" approach. Wetzler (1994) advocated for training senior managers first, the theory being that they can help guide the effort. He also recommended that during training, "outcomes" and their role in the organization be defined, their limitations be identified, and the scope of the system be clarified.

At this point in the process, one would hope that the implementation team has considered all the things that must be done, identified all that can go wrong, and have solutions to all of these problems. This is certainly hoped for, but it probably won't happen. Questions that weren't considered even in passing will be raised. This is good, for it is better for it to happen now than after implementation has begun. If one doesn't know the answer immediately, the response shouldn't be faked nor the question treated lightly. Thank staff members for raising the issue and let them know that it hadn't been considered. Also let them know that the matter will be brought before the outcomes team, and then get back to all of them with the answer.

An important part of the training process is the designation of someone to be the primary overseer of the day-to-day implementation of the outcomes system. This should be someone on-site who is knowledgeable of all aspects of the implementation procedures and in contact with all of the principals of the system's implementation. As suggested by Bieber et al. (1999), it should be someone who can spot-check the adequacy of all aspects of implementation, answer any questions about the system that may arise, and train any new staff who come onboard after the system is implemented. Someone like an office manager or possibly a receptionist (depending on the person's particular capabilities) might be considered, or a full- or part-time position might be created for this purpose. In an organization with multiple sites, it may be wise to appoint an individual at each site to oversee that site's implementation.

## IMPLEMENT THE OUTCOMES SYSTEM

Once the preceding steps have been completed, it's time to start implementing the system. As part of the implementation plan, it's best to begin on a small scale. For example, consider limiting efforts to gathering data on just adult outpatients instead of trying to cover the entire patient population. One may want to focus on measuring just the outcomes of treatment on reduction of symptomatology rather than also looking at increases in social or work functioning. One might also decide that it would be better to wait to be sure that the data gathering and transmission process is working smoothly before adding the clinician feedback piece. As all of the kinks in "Version 1" are worked out, the team may then begin adding one or more other facets of the outcomes system to the process. As these become stable processes, additional pieces can be added until the system is fully operational.

In the beginning, frequent, regular (i.e., weekly) meetings of the outcomes team and the on-site outcomes coordinator(s) are recommended. This will provide an opportunity for the team to find out about any problems that may occur and to provide the on-site coordinator with suggestions for solutions. It is also an opportunity to hear about the successful aspects of the implementation plan. Knowing what works well can provide keys to solving problematic situations. Based on this information, the outcomes team may wish to make changes in one or more of the processes. In some cases, these changes must be made immediately. The team may decide to do relatively minor tweaking or add new components or features at regularly scheduled times (e.g., the first week of each month), or wait until enough of these desired minor changes have been amassed to make the disruption that will accompany the changes worthwhile.

During the initial phase of implementation, it also is important to provide all staff members in the process with some form of positive reinforcement for their efforts. This might come in any number of cost-free or inexpensive forms, such as having the leadership personally visit them or send e-mails conveying congratulations and gratitude for their work, or buying doughnuts and bagels for the nonclinical staff, or allowing an additional casual day during the week. At the very least, all staff should be provided with feedback about how successful they have been in implementing the system. For example, a weekly report of the organization's performance on relevant implementation variables (e.g., how many eligible patients were asked to complete the baseline survey, how many of these patients agreed to participate, how many actually completed the baseline survey, reasons given for declining participation) might be sent to the staff or posted in a common area in the organization's offices.

## EVALUATE THE SYSTEM AGAINST PREVIOUSLY ESTABLISHED CRITERIA AND MODIFY AS NECESSARY

Once it is up and running, it is time to begin evaluating the system against the criteria for success that were established earlier. Here, the outcomes team must determine which criteria are being met as well as those that are not. As for the latter, an analysis of what's been going on with processes, procedures, instrumentation—or whatever—is called for. Identification of the likely source(s) of the problem(s) and modification of the system to overcome these problems follows. Once changes to the system are implemented, the criteria for success are applied again later to determine if the changes suggested by the previous analysis have indeed impacted the program in the expected manner. If they haven't, other solutions will have to be implemented to eliminate the identified problems. These, in turn, are evaluated later in a manner that is consistent with a CQI system for dealing with problems and improving quality and efficiency.

Sometimes, one might find a problem area insurmountable, no matter how many times changes are made. As a result, it might be appropriate to lower or eliminate the success criteria that are not being met, have other criteria take their place, or use both approaches. In addition, one or more aspects of the outcomes system might have to be modified so that the system becomes a more realistic possibility for the organization, given the particular set of circumstances. Facing the reality of the situation should not be viewed as a form of failure or otherwise negatively; at the same time, expending time and money over a problem that just is not going away should not be viewed in a positive light.


## SUMMARY

Increasingly, organizations are responding to demands for the measurement of treatment outcomes being voiced by stakeholders in patients' care. This has been reinforced by other factors that are driving all types of businesses in this new millennium. Organizations are using outcomes information to support clinical and nonclinical aspects of their operations and to answer specific questions related to how to improve the quality of the services they offer.

Designing a system to obtain and report outcomes information in any organization is not a simple task. Those responsible for their organization's outcomes assessment system have a number of issues that should be decided on before detailed plans for actual implementation are made. Questions related to who, what, how, and when to measure, as well as how to analyze and report the data, are all important. Equally important are the questions of if and how the outcomes information can support the intended purpose of the system. Answers to these questions will bear directly on its success. Leaving any of these questions without a well-thought-out answer will have negative if not disastrous effects, possibly to the point of making the system effectively worthless.

Arriving at a good, consensual idea of what an organization's outcomes system should look like, how it should perform, and what questions or needs it should address can be a slow-moving and sometimes painful procedure. However, it is just the first step in a long process that will result in having a useful outcomes system up and running. Champions of the system must then sell it, first to the leadership and then to all other levels of the organization. With the support of the organization in hand, the task of working out the plan for implementing the system should begin. Development of a well-thought-out implementation plan is key to the success of any outcomes system. Unfortunately, this sometimes does not occur, and as a result, the likelihood of having a useful and successful system is jeopardized from the beginning.

First, an outcomes assessment team should be formed to manage the process of developing, implementing, and, later, maintaining the system on an ongoing basis. Then, a thorough analysis of the daily workflow of the organization's service delivery system should be conducted. This will allow for the identification of potential barriers to implementation that must be overcome and may even suggest solutions to these problems. This information will also be useful in arriving at the decisions that must be made related to how to efficiently collect, store, manage, and maintain the confidentiality of outcomes data from patients and clinical staff. With information in hand, a tentative plan for integrating the data gathering and reporting aspects of the program should be developed and passed on to all of those who will be involved in any aspect of the data management process for review. Based on their feedback, the proposed workflow should be revised to take into account any staff-identified barriers that may remain. Next, all aspects of the data gathering and reporting processes should be pilot tested. This will allow for the identification of previously unforeseen barriers to the implementation process and final tweaking of the process.

Training all staff members on the operation of the system in general, along with their particular responsibilities, should then take place. This system can then go "live," starting out on a small scale and gradually increasing the scope of the activities as success is achieved. During the initial phases of the implementation, regular meetings of the outcomes team are recommended, as is provision for reinforcement for and feedback about the fruits of its efforts. As necessary, modifications to the system can be made.

## REFERENCES

Aday, L. A., Begley, C. E., Lairson, D. R., Slater, C. H., Richard, A. J., & Montoya, I. D. (1999). A framework for assessing the effectiveness, efficiency, and equity of behavioral healthcare. *The American Journal of Managed Care, 5*, SP25–SP44.

American Educational Research Association, American Psychological Association, & National Council on Measurement in Education. (1999). *Standards for educational and psychological testing.* Washington, DC: American Educational Research Association.

American Managed Behavioral Healthcare Association. (1995). *Performance measures for managed behavioral healthcare programs.* Washington, DC: AMBHA Quality Improvement and Clinical Services Committee.

American Managed Behavioral Healthcare Association. (1998). *Performance measures for managed behavioral healthcare programs 2.0* (PERMS 2.0). Washington, DC: Author.

American Psychological Association. (1996). *The costs of failing to provide appropriate mental healthcare.* Washington, DC: Author.

Andrews, G. (1995). Best practices for implementing outcomes management: More science, more art, worldwide. *Behavioral Healthcare Tomorrow, 4*, 19–21, 74–75.

Bartlett, J. (1997). Treatment outcomes: The psychiatrist's and healthcare executive's perspectives. *Psychiatric Annals, 27*, 100–103.

Bengen-Seltzer, B. (1999, May). Nine tips for improving staff buy-in on outcomes. *Data: The Brown University Digest of Addiction Theory and Application, 17*(5), 7–9.

Berman, W. H., & Hurt, S. W. (1996). Talking the talk, walking the walk: Implementing an outcomes information system. *Behavioral Healthcare Tomorrow, 5*, 39–43.

Berman, W. H., Hurt, S. W., & Heiss, G. E. (1996). Outcomes assessment in behavioral healthcare. In C. E. Stout, G. A. Theis, & J. Oher (Eds.), *The complete guide to managed behavioral care* (pp. II-D.1–II-D.10). New York: Wiley.

Berman, W. H., Rosen, C. S., Hurt, S. W., & Kolarz, C. M. (1998). Toto, we're not in Kansas anymore: Measuring and using outcomes in behavioral healthcare. *Clinical Psychology: Science and Practice, 5*, 115–133.

Bieber, J., Wroblewski, J. M., & Barber, C. A. (1999). Design and implementation of an outcomes management system within inpatient and outpatient behavioral health settings. In M. E. Maruish (Ed.), *The use of psychological testing for treatment planning and outcomes assessment* (2nd ed.), pp. 171–210. Mahwah, NJ: Lawrence Erlbaum Associates.

Bologna, N. C., Barlow, D. H., Hollon, S. D., Mitchell, J. E., & Huppert, J. D. (1998). Behavioral health treatment redesign in managed care settings. *Clinical Psychology: Science and Practice, 5*, 94–114.

Bologna, N. C., & Feldman, M. J. (1994). Outcomes, clinical models and the redesign of behavioral healthcare. *Behavioral Healthcare Tomorrow, 3*, 31–36.

Bologna, N. C., & Feldman, M. J. (1995). Using outcomes data and clinical process redesign: Improving clinical services. *Behavioral Healthcare Tomorrow, 4*, 59–65.

Burnam, M. A. (1996). Measuring outcomes of care for substance use and mental disorders. In D. M. Steinwachs, L. M. Flynn, G. S. Norquist, & E. A. Skinner (Eds.), *Using client outcomes information to improve mental health and substance abuse treatment* (pp. 3–17). San Francisco: Jossey-Bass.

Busch, A. B., & Sederer, L. I. (2000). Assessing outcomes in psychiatric practice: Guidelines, challenges, and solutions. *Harvard Review of Psychiatry, 8*, 323–327.

Cagney, T., & Woods, D. R. (1994). Why focus on outcomes data? *Behavioral Healthcare Tomorrow, 3*, 65–67.

Campbell, J. (1996). Toward collaborative mental health outcomes systems. In D. M. Steinwachs, L. M. Flynn, G. S. Norquist, & E. A. Skinner (Eds.), *Using client outcomes information to improve mental health and substance abuse treatment* (pp. 69–78). San Francisco: Jossey-Bass.

Christner, A. M. (1997, January). Using baselines and benchmarks can sharpen your outcomes evaluation. *Behavioral Health Outcomes, 2*(1), 1–3.

Christensen, L., & Mendoza, J. L. (1986). A method of assessing change in a single subject: An alteration of the RC index [Letter to the editor]. *Behavior Therapy, 17*, 305–308.

Cohen, J. (1988). *Statistical power analysis for the behavioral sciences* (2nd ed.). Hillsdale, NJ: Lawrence Erlbaum Associates.

Cone, J. D. (2001). *Evaluating outcomes: Empirical tools for effective practice*. Washington, DC: American Psychological Association.

Daniels, A., Kramer, T. L., & Mahesh, N. M. (1995). Quality indicators measured by behavioral group practices. *Behavioral Healthcare Tomorrow, 4*, 55–56.

Depression still undertreated despite efforts to redress. (1997, June). *Behavioral Health Outcomes, 2*, 1–11.

Dickey, B. (2002). Outcome measurement from research to clinical practice. In W. W. IsHak, T. Burt, & L. I. Sederer (Eds.), *Outcome measurement in psychiatry: A critical review* (pp. 15–22). Washington, DC: American Psychiatric Publishing.

Docherty, J. P., & Dewan, N. A. (1995). *National Association of Psychiatric Health Systems guide to outcomes management*. Washington, DC: National Association of Psychiatric Health Systems.

Docherty, J. P., & Streeter, M. J. (1996). Measuring outcomes. In L. I. Sederer & B. Dickey (Eds.), *Outcomes assessment in clinical practice* (pp. 8–18). Baltimore, MD: Williams & Wilkins.

Donabedian, A. (1980). *Explorations in quality assessment and monitoring: The definition of quality and approaches to its assessment* (Vol. 1). Ann Arbor, MI: Health Administration Press.

Donabedian, A. (1982). *Explorations in quality assessment and monitoring: The criteria and standards of quality* (Vol. 2). Ann Arbor, MI: Health Administration Press.

Donabedian, A. (1985). *Explorations in quality assessment and monitoring: The methods and findings in quality assessment: An illustrated analysis* (Vol. 3). Ann Arbor, MI: Health Administration Press.

Dornelas, E. A., Correll, R. E., Lothstein, L., Wilber, C., & Goethe, J. W. (1996). Designing and implementing outcome evaluations: Some guidelines for practitioners. *Psychotherapy, 33*, 237–245.

Eisen, S. V. (2000). Charting for outcomes in behavioral health. *The Psychiatric Clinics of North America, 23*, 347–361.

Eisen, S. V., & Dickey, B. (1996). Mental health outcome assessment: The new agenda. *Psychotherapy, 33*, 181–189.

Eisen, S. V., Leff, H. S., & Schaefer, E. (1999). Implementing outcomes systems: Lessons from a test of the BASIS–32 and the SF–36. *Journal of Behavioral Health Services & Research, 26*, 18–27.

Farnsworth, J. R., Hess, J. Z., & Lambert, M. J. (2001, August). *Frequency of outcomes measures used in psychotherapy*. Poster presented at the annual meeting of the American Psychological Association, San Francisco, CA.

Fink, P. J. (1997). Treatment outcomes: A postscript. *Psychiatric Annals, 27*, 133–143.

Friedman, R., Sobel, D., Myers, P., Caudill, M., & Benson, H. (1995). Behavioral medicine, clinical health psychology, and cost offset. *Health Psychology, 14*, 509–518.

Gellman, R., & Frawley, K. A. (1996). The need to know versus the right to privacy. In T. Trabin (Ed.), *The computerization of behavioral healthcare: How to enhance clinical practice, management, and communications* (pp. 191–212). San Francisco: Jossey-Bass.

Health care costs soared during 2001, federal report says. (2003, January 8). *Minneapolis Star Tribune*, p. A10.

Hoffman, F. L., Leckman, E., Russo, N., & Knauf, L. (1999). In it for the long haul: The integration of outcomes assessment, clinical services, and management decision-making. *Evaluation and Program Planning, 22*, 211–219.

Hopkins, W. G. (1997). *A new view of statistics: A scale of magnitude for effect sizes*. Retrieved October 27, 2002 from: http://www.sportsci.org/resource/stats/efffectmag.html.

Hsu, L. M. (1996). On the identification of clinically significant client changes: Reinterpretation of Jacobson's cut scores. *Journal of Psychopathology and Behavioral Assessment, 18*, 371–385.

Hsu, L. M. (1999). Caveats concerning comparisons of change rates obtained with five models of identifying significant client changes: Comment on Speer and Greenbaum (1995). *Journal of Consulting and Clinical Psychology, 67*, 594–598.

Institute of Medicine: Committee on Quality Assurance and Accreditation Guidelines for Managed Behavioral Health Care. (1997). *Managing managed care: Quality improvement in behavioral health*. Washington, DC: National Academy Press.

Jacobson, N. S., Follette, W. C., & Revenstorf, D. (1984). Psychotherapy outcome research: Methods for reporting variability and evaluating clinical significance. *Behavior Therapy, 15*, 336–352.

Jacobson, N. S., Follette, W. C., & Revenstorf, D. (1986). Toward a standard definition of clinically significant change [Letter to the editor]. *Behavior Therapy, 17*, 309–311.

Jacobson, N. S., Roberts, L. J., Berns, S. B., & McGlinchey, J. B. (1999). Methods for defining and determining the clinical significance of treatment effects: Description, application, and alternatives. *Journal of Consulting and Clinical Psychology, 67*, 300–307.

Jacobson, N. S., & Truax, P. (1991). Clinical significance: A statistical approach defining meaningful change in psychotherapy research. *Journal of Consulting and Clinical Psychology, 59,* 12–19.

Kazdin, A. E. (1999). The meanings and measurement of clinical significance. *Journal of Consulting and Clinical Psychology, 67,* 332–339.

Kazis, L. E., Anderson, J. J., & Meenan, R. F. (1989). Effect sizes for interpreting changes in health status. *Medical Care, 27,* S178–S189.

Koch, R., Cairns, J. M., & Brunk, M. (2000). How to involve staff in developing an outcomes-oriented organization. *Education and Treatment of Children, 23,* 41–47.

Kraus, D. R., & Horan, F. P. (1998). *Outcomes roadblocks: Problems and solutions. One company explains why—and how—to upgrade the practicality of outcomes measurement.* Retrieved October 27, 2002 from: http://www.consultnews.com/Magazines/BHMsept_oct/kraus.html

Lambert, M. J., Hansen, N. B., & Finch, A. E. (2001). Patient-focused research using patient outcome data to enhance treatment effects. *Journal of Consulting and Clinical Psychology, 69,* 159–172.

Lambert, M. J., & Lambert, J. M. (1999). Use of psychological tests for assessing treatment outcome. In M. E. Maruish (Ed.), *The use of psychological testing for treatment planning and outcomes assessment* (2nd ed.), pp. 115–151. Mahwah, NJ: Lawrence Erlbaum Associates.

Lyons, J. S., Howard, K. I., O'Mahoney, M. T., & Lish, J. D. (1997). *The measurement and management of clinical outcomes in mental health.* New York: Wiley.

Manderscheid, R. W., Henderson, M. J., & Brown, D. Y. (n.d.). Status of national accountability efforts at the millennium. In R. W. Manderscheid & M. J. Henderson (Eds.), *Mental health, United States, 2000. Section 2: Decision Support 2000+* (pp. 1–10). Retrieved December 19, 2001, from http://mentalhealth.org/publication/allpubs/sma01-3537/chapter6.asp.

Maruish, M. E. (2002). *Psychological testing in the age of managed behavioral health care.* Mahwah, NJ: Lawrence Erlbaum Associates.

McGlynn, E. A. (1996). Setting the context for measuring patient outcomes. In D. M. Steinwachs, L. M. Flynn, G. S. Norquist, & E. A. Skinner (Eds.), *Using client outcomes information to improve mental health and substance abuse treatment* (pp. 19–32). San Francisco: Jossey-Bass.

McLellan, A. T., & Durell, J. (1996). Outcomes evaluation in psychiatric and substance abuse treatments: Concepts, rationale, and methods. In L. I. Sederer & B. Dickey (Eds.), *Outcomes assessment in clinical practice* (pp. 34–44). Baltimore, MD: Williams & Wilkins.

Mental Health Statistics Improvement Program Task Force. (1996, April). *Consumer-oriented Mental Health Report Card: The final report of the Mental Health Statistics Improvement Program Task Force on a consumer-oriented mental health report card.* Cambridge, MA: Evaluation Center at Human Services Research Institute.

Merrick, E. L., Garnick, D. W., Horgan, C. M., & Hodgkin, D. (2002). Quality measurement and accountability for substance abuse and mental health services in managed care organizations. *Medical Care, 40,* 1238–1248.

Monthly change in average health insurance premiums. (2000, July 17). *Managed Care Week, 10*(25), p. 4.

National Committee for Quality Assurance. (2000). *HEDIS 2001. Technical update #2.* Retrieved October 27, 2002 from: http://www.ncqa.org/pages/programs/HEDIS/hedis2001.htm

Nelson, E. A., Maruish, M. E., & Axler, J. L. (2000). Effects of discharge planning and compliance with outpatient appointments on readmission rates. *Psychiatric Services, 51,* 885–889.

Nelson, E. C. (1996). Using outcomes measurement to improve quality and value. In D. M. Steinwachs, L. M. Flynn, G. S. Norquist, & E. A. Skinner (Eds.), *Using client outcomes information to improve mental health and substance abuse treatment* (pp. 111–124). San Francisco: Jossey-Bass.

Norquist, G. S. (2002). Role of outcome measurement in psychiatry. In W. W. IsHak, T. Burt, & L. I. Sederer (Eds.), *Outcome measurement in psychiatry: A critical review* (pp. 3–13). Washington, DC: American Psychiatric Publishing.

Ofstead, C. L., Gobran, D. S., & Lum, D. L. (2000). Integrating behavioral health assessment with primary care services. In M. E. Maruish (Ed.), *Handbook of psychological testing in primary care settings* (pp. 153–187). Mahwah, NJ: Lawrence Erlbaum Associates.

Ogles, B. M., Lambert, M. J., & Fields, S. A. (2002). *Essentials of outcomes assessment.* New York: Wiley.

Oss, M. E., & Sloves, H. (2000, February). Customer-defined "quality" in behavioral health & social services: Marketing tools to respond to a new "customer-focused" era. *Open Minds,* 4–6.

Outcomes indicators less prevalent atop Summit list. (1999, March 29*). Mental Health Weekly,* pp. 4–5.

Pallak, M. S. (1994). National outcomes management survey: Summary report. *Behavioral Healthcare Tomorrow, 3,* 63–69.

Radosevich, D. M., McPherson, C. A., & Werni, T. L. (1994). The implementation process: A working guide.

In M. Huber (Ed.), *Measuring medicine: An introduction to health status assessment and a framework for application* (pp. 51–73). Washington, DC: Faulkner & Gray.

Rosen, L. D., & Weil, M. M. (1996). Easing the transition from paper to computer-based systems. In T. Trabin (Ed.), *The computerization of behavioral healthcare: How to enhance clinical practice, management, and communications* (pp. 87–107). San Francisco: Jossey-Bass.

Saunders, S. M., Howard, H. I., & Newman, F. L. (1988). Evaluating the clinical significance of treatment effects: Norms and normality. *Behavioral Assessment, 10,* 207–218.

Schlosser, B. (1996). New perspectives on outcomes assessment: The philosophy and application of the subjective health process model. *Psychotherapy, 33,* 284–304.

Sederer, L. I., Dickey, B., & Eisen, S. V. (1997). Assessing outcomes in clinical practice. *Psychiatric Quarterly, 68,* 311–325.

Smith, G. R., Fischer, E. P., Nordquist, C. R., Mosley, C. L., & Ledbetter, N. S. (1997). Implementing outcomes management systems in mental health settings. *Psychiatric Services, 48,* 364–398.

Smith, G. R., Manderscheid, R. W., Flynn, L. M., & Steinwachs, D. M. (1997). Principles for assessment of patient outcomes in mental healthcare. *Psychiatric Services, 48,* 1033–1036.

Speer, D. C. (1992). Clinically significant change: Jacobson and Truax (1991) revisited. *Journal of Consulting and Clinical Psychology, 60,* 402–408.

Speer, D. C., & Greenbaum, P. E. (1995). Five methods for computing significant individual client change and improvement rates: Support for an individual growth curve approach. *Journal of Consulting and Clinical Psychology, 63,* 1044–1048.

Speer, D. C., & Newman, F. L. (1996). Mental health services outcome evaluation. *Clinical Psychology: Science and Practice, 3,* 105–129.

Sperry, L. (1997). Treatment outcomes: An overview. *Psychiatric Annals, 27,* 95–99.

Sperry, L., Brill, P. L., Howard, K. I., & Grissom, G. R. (1996). *Treatment outcomes in psychotherapy and psychiatric interventions.* New York: Brunner/Mazel.

Sperry, L., Grissom, G., Brill, P., & Marion, D. (1997). Changing clinicians practice patterns and managed care culture with outcomes systems. *Psychiatric Annals, 27,* 127–132.

Steinwachs, D. M., Fischer, E. P., & Lehman, A. F. (1996). Outcomes assessment: Information for improving mental healthcare. In D. M. Steinwachs, L. M. Flynn, G. S. Norquist, & E. A. Skinner (Eds.), *Using client outcomes information to improve mental health and substance abuse treatment* (pp. 49–57). San Francisco: Jossey-Bass.

Strupp, H. H. (1996). The tripartite model and the *Consumer Reports* study. *American Psychologist, 51,* 1017–1024.

Strupp, H. H., & Hadley, S. W. (1977). A tripartite model of mental health and treatment outcomes. *American Psychologist, 32,* 187–196.

Surgeon General of the United States. (1999). *Mental health: A report of the surgeon general.* Rockville, MD: U.S. Department of Health and Human Services, Substance Abuse and Mental Health Services Administration.

Wampold, B. E., & Jenson, W. R. (1986). Clinical significance revisited [Letter to the editor]. *Behavior Therapy, 17,* 302–305.

Wetzler, H. P. (1994). Evaluating an organization's readiness for outcomes management. In M. Huber (Ed.), *Measuring medicine: An introduction to health status assessment and a framework for application* (pp. 33–41). Washington, DC: Faulkner & Gray.

# Progress and Outcomes Assessment of Individual Patient Data: Selecting Single-Subject Design and Statistical Procedures

Frederick L. Newman and Stephen E. Wong
*Florida International University*

## HISTORICAL NOTES

One need not apologize for an interest in exploring and making inferences about observations on the individual consumer of psychological services. There has been. a long, rich history of individual subject research in psychology, starting with the psychophysics and sensory psychology studies performed in Europe and the United States during the 1800s (Osgood, 1953; Stevens, 1951). The research methods, mostly relying on extensive within-person replication techniques, were sufficiently rigorous that much of it withstood the tests of replication and generalizability over many individuals (Stevens, 1966). The psychophysics studies were also characterized by their focus on discovering what can be identified as trait characteristics of their subjects, rather than state characteristics.

State characteristics (i.e., characteristics distinguished by the environmental and modifiable character of the individual) became the domain of those interested in the areas of behavior change, (e.g., behavior modification, learning theory, human judgment and decision making, health and clinical psychology, psychopharmacology, and some subsets of physiological psychology). Interest in how behavioral patterns or state characteristics change over time becomes problematic for single-subject methods as practiced by the early psychophysics researchers. Simply stated, replications over time were expected to show change. Three traditions of single-subject clinical research have emerged:

1. The use of clinical case notes over the course of treatment—a procedure used by those who were developing or studying psychodynamic theories, particularly those developing or studying psychoanalytic theories

2. The counting of discrete observable behavioral events over time and under different conditions controlled by the experimenter—procedures employed by behavior therapy and therapeutic process researchers (many of whom would not wish to be identified as belonging to the same category as the behavioral therapy, and vice versa)

3. The scores from a standardized instrument contrasted with established empirical norms, such as those employed by neuropsychologists to understand the current

intellectual or cognitive state of the individual, or by industrial organization researchers working on matching personal characteristics to a job.

## The Use of Clinical Case Notes

Reporting of individual clinical case studies in the form of written narratives taken from the theorist's own clinical notes or those of a close colleague has been an integral part of clinical psychology's and psychiatry's historical development (e.g., as presented in the psychoanalytic and psychodynamic literature). Unfortunately, evidence to support replication has been a subject of some controversy over the scientific credibility of those who have used this approach (e.g., the controversy over whether Freud and Jung reported the evidence in and from their case notes properly). The major difficulty in the early attempts to use clinical case studies as scientific evidence to construct or test theories was the lack of agreement on what methods would be necessary and sufficient to argue for the data's validity. Clinical case notes, in the narrative form, have too many "alternative explanations," including the frailty of human judgment in general (Meehl, 1954; Newman, 1983) and the inherent conflict of interest of having the clinician who is treating the person being both the observer and the synthesizer of the observations into a written narrative.

## Observing Discrete Behaviors Over Time and Manipulating Environmental Conditions

Behavior therapists have been employing single-subject techniques for some time (Craighead, Craighead, Kazdin, & Mahoney, 1994; Hersen & Bellack, 1984; Herson, Michaelson, & Bellack, 1994; Kazdin, 1992). The tradition of those employing behavior therapy techniques is to select a discrete, readily observable behavior that can be tracked reliably over time and is sensitive to the environmental intervention under control of the researcher or clinician. Our review of the behavior therapy literature did not find single-subject studies that employed the types of psychological measures that are the focus of this text. Instead, the investigator selects a marker behavior that is the most suitable indicator of an underlying construct. In the case of phobic, avoidance, or even abusive behaviors, selection of a behavioral marker to track over the course of treatment is quite straightforward. When the type of distress or functioning is more generic (e.g., depression, or interpersonal attachment or commitment), then the selection of one or more marker behaviors may be more problematic. Texts on behavioral therapy techniques (e.g., Craighead et al., 1994) will caution the reader that the selection of the marker behavior or indicator must make sense both theoretically and empirically (for its psychometric qualities).

Manipulating environmental conditions or treatment variables and gauging their effects on individual client outcomes is another important tradition in single-subject designs. One of the main justifications for encouraging the adoption single-subject designs by human service professions was the capability of these designs for evaluating interventions with individual clients (Bailey & Burch, 2002; Bloom, Fischer, & Orme, 2003; Cooper, Heron, & Heward, 1987; Hersen & Barlow, 1984;). This capability would appear to be particularly relevant to the delivery of psychotherapies, wherein even the most potent available interventions are ineffective with 20% to 30% of the clients who apply them correctly and fully. Later in this chapter, we will present an example of a single-subject design demonstrating the framework's ability to identify and refine effective treatment procedures.

### Contrasting Psychological Test Scores for an Individual on a Standardized Instrument With Published Norms

This approach represents the core of the tradition of what is popularly called psychological testing. There are several examples distributed through this text (e.g., the chapters on the MMPI–2, MMPI–A, Conners Rating Scale). A major function of this tradition is to present the results of psychological testing for an individual with those of either a clinical or a nonclinical norm to justify the need for treatment to a third-party payer or an institution (e.g., a hospital or school). This approach is also used to justify continued treatment. Not part of the tradition of psychological testing is to use the results of such tests to indicate when treatment for an individual consumer should stop. Use of psychological testing in follow-up to treatment appears to be confined to treatment outcome studies where results on groups of consumers under one or more treatment conditions are compared.

One conclusion that could be drawn from the traditional uses of single-subject studies is that the use of psychological testing of the sort covered in this text cannot be employed in single-subject research. We are not ready to draw that conclusion for two reasons. First, there is a great need for single-subject studies in developing new treatments (Greenberg & Newman, 1996). Also, there are important applications for the use of tests such as these by the individual clinician (or a clinical team) in tracking the progress of an individual consumer or client, and providing justification for initiating, continuing, shifting treatment strategies to a third-party payer (De Liberty, Newman, & Ward, 2001; Newman & Tejeda, 1996).

## SELECTION AND USE OF PSYCHOLOGICAL TESTS IN SINGLE-PERSON CLINICAL AND RESEARCH APPLICATIONS

Clinicians, supervisors, and mental health administrators, arguably, need to know whether or not the services they provide ameliorate the consumer's symptoms and improve on their capacity to manage their community functioning. Such knowledge should be useful in treatment planning and decision making. For instance, if the intervention yields little or no improvement where such improvement should be expected given what is known in the literature, then the service provider(s) would want to consider a different intervention strategy. If the person is in individual therapy, the clinician might decide that progress could be achieved if the family is brought into the therapy process, or perhaps the frequency of therapeutic contact needs to be modified to be more frequent or changed to another mode, such as group or family therapy. For example, if observed behavior patterns move sufficiently in a negative direction, then more intensive or restrictive treatment (e.g., initiating or increasing the dosage of a medication, the use of day treatment or inpatient treatment) might be justified. However, the charting of the person's functioning might lead the clinician to realize that there has been sufficient symptom reduction and improvement in the management of their day-to-day functioning to warrant a discussion of termination from treatment. Too frequently, however, the clinician has no method for systematically monitoring an individual's progress.

We argue that well-established psychological instruments, such as those reviewed in this book, are ideally suited to monitor the progress of an individual and hence assist service providers in clinical decision making (e.g., when to refer the person to a more or less intensive treatment, when to terminate treatment, when to refer to another type of intervention). The psychological tests discussed in this text are widely used, reliable, and valid measures with established norms. Moreover, most of these tests are easy to administer, score, and interpret. Thus, it appears to be a relatively straightforward procedure to administer and score a few carefully selected instruments repeatedly throughout treatment, plot the scores on a graph, and use this information to assess the individual's progress. What follows are the basic guidelines for designing a procedure to systematically collect and analyze data to assess individual patient progress.

### Selection of Instrumentation

As discussed earlier, the tests and measures reviewed in the current volume can be very useful to individual clinicians because they are widely used and have well-established psychometric properties and norms. But a more important consideration in single-subject research is that the selected test must demonstrate sensitivity to change. In psychotherapeutic work, especially in the early phase of treatment, important changes might be quite subtle. Marked changes in conduct disorder (see examples using the Child Behavioral Checklist (CBCL) by Achenbach or the Child Adolescent Functional Assessment Scale (CAFAS) by Hodges, or when using the Beck Depression Inventory, BDI) are not observable until substance use or abuse is curtailed, the family becomes engaged in the treatment, or both conditions are met (Liddle, Rowe, Dakof, & Lyke, 1998). Moreover, the clinician must make sure that the selected test measures a behavior, attitude, or emotion expected to change as a result of the treatment. For example, in multidimensional family therapy (Liddle & Saba, 1981) of adolescent drug abuse, the clinician targets parenting behaviors. Specifically, the therapists works to change how parents control (i.e., set limits and monitor), nurture (i.e., express love and concern), and grant autonomy to their acting out adolescent. It is important, then, that the clinician measure these specific parenting behaviors rather than overall family closeness, such as is measured by the Family Environment scale (Moos, 1994).

The clinician must be careful to select a measure that is sensitive to the types of changes targeted in the intervention. For example, youth referred for substance abuse treatment frequently have behavioral problems and symptoms that are co-occurring with the drug use. For example, one youth might be particularly aggressive and violent. In this case, one of the first treatment goals would be to reduce the violent and aggressive behaviors. The aggressive behavior scale should be assessed with this particular youth using a measure such as the Child Behavior Checklist (CBCL) or Youth Self Report (YSR, Achenbach, this volume). Another drug-using youth might present with depression and aggression; in this case, the clinician would be wise to measure both aggression and depression. Thus, as in any research, the researcher, or in this case the clinician, must carefully select measures that assess the targets of the intervention (see Newman, Ciarlo, & Rugh, chap. 6, this volume, for a discussion of the guidelines for selecting a measure).

As noted earlier, behaviors or perceptions that are the focus of therapy early in treatment might shift to another domain of behaviors later in treatment. If this is the case, then there are two possible strategies. One strategy is to select a global measure (the Global Assessment of Functioning, GAF, the Externalized Symptom measure on the CBCL, or an overall measure of affect such as the BDI) to track therapeutic progress. Another strategy is to employ two measures tracking different classes of behaviors over time. One would be a global measure (e.g., the GAF or BDI) and the other a measure of the behaviors that are specific focus of that stage of treatment. For example, early in family therapy, the focus might be on reducing blaming behaviors, followed by parent involvement in peer-related activities. In this case, blaming behaviors would be a core measure early in treatment, and then measures of parent involvement with peer interactions might be implemented once blaming behaviors appear to be at a reasonable level. Meanwhile, a global level of the youth's behavior (e.g., the external behavioral measure within the CBCL or aggressive behaviors within the YSR) could be used to track the child over the entire course of treatment.

## Selection of Criterion on Which to Base Clinical Decision-Making

*Targeting Clinical Decisions.* The biggest challenge in what we are proposing is the absence of clear standards for decision making with regard to: (a) admissions, (b) referral to more intense or less intense treatment settings, or (c) termination of treatment. We are entering an era where neither a clinician, a group of clinicians, nor a service agency simply opens the doors of a service and provides treatment for all who enter. Decisions must be made about what the needs are (usually requiring some epidemiological needs assessments estimates) and to what degree these needs are being met by exiting service providers. The epidemiological technology of assessing mental health service needs should provide a profile of the major psychosocial characteristics of those who need a service. These characteristics typically include age, gender, socioeconomic status, major symptoms and diagnostic groups, community functioning level, and level of social supports.

Once a decision is made that there is a group of people who can be served, then a set of measures and instruments need to be selected to support four distinct sets of clinical decisions:

- What are the psychosocial characteristics of those who should be admitted into the service?
- What are the characteristics that indicate the need for referral to a more intensive-restrictive service?
- What are the characteristics that indicate the need for referral to a less intensive-restrictive service?
- What are the characteristics that indicate that services are no longer needed?

To address each of these questions, operational definitions and measures are needed to estimate levels functioning, symptoms, socialization, and overall ability for an individual to manage his or her day-to-day affairs (Newman, Hunter, & Irving, 1987). Moreover, each of the last three questions also raises an issue of (a) the amount (dosage) and type of therapeutic effort and (b) amount of change in symptom distress, functioning, or self-management achieved over time (Barkham et al., 2001; Carter & Newman, 1976; Howard, Kopta, Krause, & Orlinsky, 1986; Howard, Moras, Brill, Martinovich, & Lutz, 1996; Lambert & Hawkins, chap. 5, this volume; Newman & Tejeda, 1996; Newman & Howard, 1986; Newman & Sorensen, 1985; Yates & Newman, 1980).

Figure 8.1 illustrates how an individual consumer may progress relative to the four questions raised above. This example uses technology that is currently available, with one limitation that will be discussed later. The intent of Fig. 8.1 is to show that by employing existing technology, one can describe the impact of two or more interventions in terms of its cost effectiveness in achieving observable criteria.

The example illustrated in Fig. 8.1 offers a graphic analysis in the form of a progress–outcome report for three hypothetical individuals. These three persons have been identified as having similar characteristics at the outset of treatment (i.e., all three

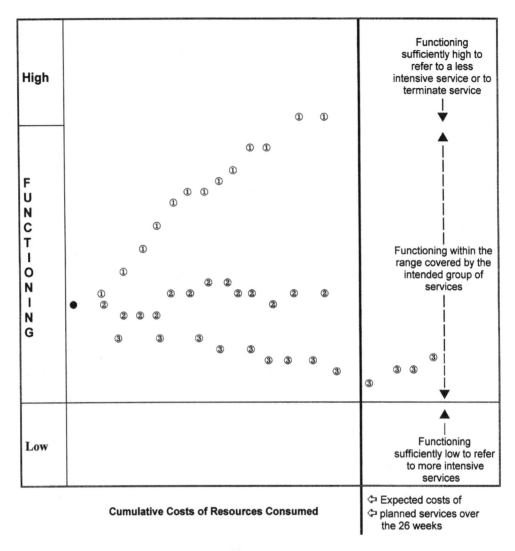

FIG. 8.1. Hypothetical example of an analysis of changes in functioning and costs relative to managed care behavioral criteria for three consumers. Person 1 met the planned objective of improved functioning such that the person was able to move to terminate services within 6 months. Person 2 was able to maintain functioning over the same 6 months but used about the same amount of resources. Person 3 required additional resources to maintain adequate levels of community functioning. The figure is adapted from the paper by Newman and Tejeda (1996). Used with permission from the American Psychological Association.

have similar initial levels of functioning and have service plans for a 26-week period, such that the expected cost of administering the treatment plan is the same). However, two individuals differ with regard to their performance over the course of treatment. Person 1 is expected to improve in overall functioning to a point where she or he can either be referred to a service that is less intensive or may be terminated from services because functioning, self-management, or both is adequate to be independent of formal treatment supports. Person 2 has maintained functioning, or level of self-management, that is within the bounds described as acceptable to community functioning, but only with continued help. Person 3 represents a person whose treatment goals were similar to that of Person 1 and will be discussed later.

The vertical axis of Fig. 8.1 represents a person's overall ability to function in the community. It is understood that this global measure must be supported by a multidimensional view of the persons within each group (Newman, Ciarlo, & Rugh, chap. 6, this volume). The horizontal axis represents the cumulative costs of providing services from the beginning of this episode of treatment. If one were using the dosage of psychotherapy as a guide to amount treatment as recommended by Howard and his colleagues (1986), the horizontal axis would be the cumulative dosage of psychotherapy sessions. The two horizontal dashed lines inside of the box represent the behavioral criteria set a priori, that is, the lower and upper bounds of functioning for which this mental health service is designed to serve. If a consumer behaves at a level below the lower dashed line, then she or he should be referred to a more intensive service. Likewise, if a consumer behaves at a level above the upper dashed line, then either services should discontinued or a referral to a less intensive or expensive service should be considered. Finally, the vertical dashed line inside of the box represents the cumulative costs (or dosage) of the planned services for the 26-week period. In this hypothetical case, all three individuals have treatment plans with the same expected costs (or dosage).

The circled numbers within Fig. 8.1 track the average progress of consumers within each of the groups at successive 2-week intervals. The vertical placement of the circled number represents the group's average level of functioning at that time, and the horizontal placement represents the group's average costs of services up to that point. The sequence of 13 circled numbers represents the progress of a person within 2-week intervals over the 26 weeks of care. For Person 1, with a 6-month objective of improvement above that of the upper dashed line, the objective is met. For Person 2, with the 6-month objective of maintaining functioning within the range represented by the area between two dashed lines, the objective also is met. Person 3 is an example of a client who exceeded the bounds of the intended service–treatment plan after 4 months, 2 months shy of the objective. This person was able to maintain her or his community functioning, but only with the commitment of additional resources. A continuous quality improvement program should focus a post hoc analysis on these consumers to determine if they belong to another cost-homogeneous subgroup or whether the services were provided as intended, and whether modification of current practices are needed.

A major difficulty in attempting to enact these recommendations is that of obtaining a believable database to determine what the appropriate progress–outcome criteria or what the expected social or treatment costs should be. Some have used expert panels to set the first draft of such criteria (e.g., Newman, Griffin, Black, & Page, 1989; Uehara, Smukler, & Newman, 1994). Howard has used baseline data from prior studies, along with measures taken on a nonpatient population. But both strategies have problems. The research literature is largely based on studies where the dosage was fixed within a study, thereby constricting inferences about what type and amount of effort can achieve specific behavioral criteria. Howard's early work on a dosage and phase model of psychotherapy was statistically confounded by combining the results of controlled studies where the number of sessions was fixed, with data from naturalistic studies. Some of the naturalistic data came from persons who had no limit on sessions, whereas others did have limits on the number of sessions imposed by third-party payers. Based on previous experiences, it would appear that the dosage data as reported are probably trustworthy. However, we know of no studies where behavioral criteria were set a priori, nor of studies in which the type and amount of efforts were seen as the dependent variables in estimating the success or failure to achieve these criteria. Yet the logic of managed care and the logic of the National Institute of Mental Health practice guidelines would require that such study results be available to set criteria for using a particular intervention strategy or to set reimbursement standards. This void must be filled by data from well-designed efficacy and cost-effectiveness studies that can provide empirical support for setting behavioral outcome criteria for managed care programs. Without such data, there is faint hope of changing the current practice of setting dosage guidelines independent of behavioral criteria.

*Patient Profiling.* The technique developed by Howard et al. (1996) is sufficiently different from the example given in Fig. 8.1 to warrant a more detailed discussion. Howard et al. (1996) introduced the technique as a new paradigm of "patient-focused research." The paradigm addresses the question of "Is this patient's condition responding to the treatment that is being applied?" (p. 1060). The technique makes use of the progress and outcomes of a large database ($n > 6,500$) of adults who received outpatient psychotherapy and the dose-response curves that were obtained for those in the database. Based on the prior research reported by Howard's group, a predictive model of expected change based on seven intake characteristics can be generated (Lueger, Howard, Martinovich, Lutz, Anderson, & Grissom, 2001; Lutz, Martinovich, & Howard, 1999). The seven intake variables are:

- Level of well-being, a subscale of the Mental Health Index (Howard, Lueger, Mailing, & Martinovich, 1993)
- Level of functioning, a subscale of the Mental Health Index (Howard et al., 1993)
- Symptom Severity, a subscale of the Mental Health Index (Howard et al., 1993)
- Prior psychotherapy (none, 1–3 months, 4–6 months, 6–12 months, more than 12 months)
- Chronicity, "How long have you had this problem?"
- Expectation, "How well do you expect to feel emotionally and psychologically after therapy is completed?"
- Clinician's rating of the Global Assessment of Functioning (Axis V of *DSM–IV*).

Prior to the initial therapy session, the person is asked to complete the Mental Health Index, which includes items covering these six of the seven variables (plus other areas of functioning). The values obtained on these six variables, plus the clinician's rating of the person's Global Assessment of Functioning (GAF), are entered as predictor variables into a growth curve modeling program (e.g., Hierarchical Linear Models, HLM; Raudenbush & Bryk, 2002) to obtain an estimate of the expected dose response curve for that person. Formally, this is called a Level 2 analysis, because the predicted outcome for the individual uses the results of the subset of those people with the database of approximately 6,500 people who have scores on the seven predictor variables similar to those given by the person under study. The HLM program also permits an estimate of what is described as a "failure boundary," based on the growth curve of those persons for whom the expected growth curve was either flat (i.e., a slope of zero) or negative. Once the expected dose response curve for those who showed improvement and the failure boundaries are estimated, then it is just a matter of obtaining and plotting the results of the scores a person obtains on the Mental Health Index after every fourth session. The plot of these data each four sessions

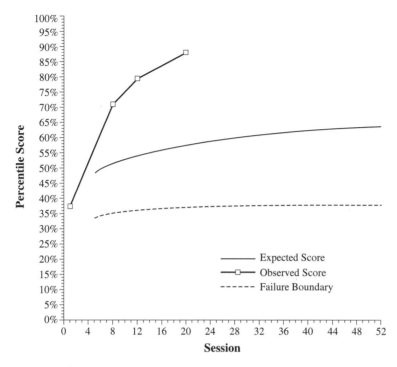

FIG. 8.2. Course of Mental Health Index for a person for whom treatment progress and outcome had a good prognosis and the observed progress and outcome was better than expected (from Howard et al., 1996, p. 1062, by permission from the American Psychological Association).

represents the individual's growth curve, which can be contrasted with the expected growth curve and the "failure boundary" curve. Figures 8.2 and 8.3 provide examples of outcomes relative to the expected and "failure" growth curves for a hypothetical person undergoing psychotherapy treatment.

The patient profiling method, though elegant, would appear to be beyond the resources of most clinicians working in private individual or group practices, small public clinics, or hospital settings without access to a large database from which one could use to estimate the growth curves. Moreover, most professionals currently working in the real world of clinical service delivery were not trained to use the latest statistical packages involving growth curve analysis. There is the possibility that in the future there will be software packages developed that will permit one to enter the normative data on a particular progress measure, and then when the client or the practitioner enters the measures on the individual client's behavior over time, the progress or outcome for that individual client can be identified relative to the norms for either or both a clinical or a nonclinical population. There will be further mention of details on this possibility when later describing Figs. 8.2 and 8.3.

In spite of the limitations mentioned (measures with appropriate norms, standards on which to base clinical decisions, adequate criterion for clinical decision making based on a large sample size), we still propose careful assessment of patient progress on the measures that are available over the course of treatment. Graphing of these measures will then assist in clinical decision making.

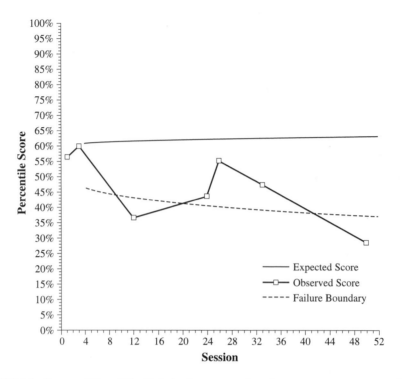

FIG. 8.3. Course of Mental Health Index for a person for whom treatment progress and outcome had a poor prognosis and the observed progress and outcome was even worst than expected (from Howard et al., 1996, p. 1063, by permission from the American Psychological Association).

*Clinical Significance as an Outcome Criteria.* Still another approach is to identify progress or outcome on a standardized measure relative to a criteria of clinical significance (Jacobson & Truax, 1991). This can be done where when the assessment instrument has been administered to both a clinical and a nonclinical group. A clinically significant change in behavior is when a person's score on the psychological test is statistically significant from the pretest average of a clinical group and more like that of the distribution of nonclinical group than the distribution of the clinical group. When there are no norms on a nonclinical group, then the convention recommended by Jacobson and Truax is to say that clinically significant change has occurred if the difference score from pretreatment to posttreatment is significant and statistically equal to or greater than two standard deviations in the direction of improved functioning. Data complied by Howard and his colleagues (1996) recommended that change equal to or greater than 1.8 standard deviations in a positive direction would recommend a score that is more likely to be represented by the nonclinical group than the clinical group prior to treatment. See Lambert and Hawkins (chap. 5, this volume), where there is a detailed descriptive example of employing a graphic analysis of a individual's outcome relative to clinically significant change. All three of these examples (Figs. 8.2 and 8.3 here and Fig. 8.1 in the chapter by Lambert & Hawkins) represent examples of what we believe will be the future of software development. Such software should permit a practitioner to identify the instrument (along with the source of the measure's normative data), then input the data on an individual client, and, finally, the software should produce a graphic of an individual client's progress or outcome

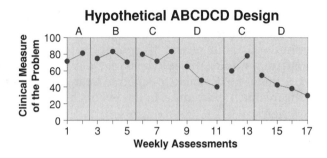

FIG. 8.4. Graph displaying an ABCDCD design with hypothetical data. Design involves a pretreatment baseline condition (A) and three treatment conditions (B, C, and D). Data indicate that the first two treatment conditions are ineffective. The third treatment appears to be effective, and its positive effects are replicated in a fifth treatment phase.

relative to the expected progress or outcomes on that same measure. Software of this type should also be able to tailor the norms to the demographic or clinical profile of a client. Current technology is now capable of achieving these sorts of graphics, but the actual development of such software is probably a few years from being marketable at an affordable price.

### Evaluation of Treatment Variables Using Single-Subject Designs

As mentioned earlier, single-subject designs can permit the manipulation of treatment variables in the search for effective or more effective interventions. Within these formats clinicians use repeated measures, systematically vary treatment conditions, and respond to feedback from incoming data to optimize clinical outcomes. Clinicians can examine the efficacy of certain treatments (e.g., social skills training), treatment components (e.g., therapeutic contracts, peer support groups), or treatment parameters (e.g., frequency of therapy) with a particular client. This application can also compare different treatment procedures (e.g., social skills training vs. cognitive-behavioral therapy) and different parameters of treatment (therapy once a week vs. therapy twice a week).

Although several single-subject designs are available to answer the questions listed above, we will discuss one design to illustrate the general process. The design we will discuss is the ABCDCD design, a variant of the reversal design. This particular design embodies both a trial-and-error process and a replication of treatment effects to determine that the treatment was responsible for the observed change. We will describe the design in the order in which a clinician would implement phases of the design. A graph of an ABCDCD design with hypothetical data is shown in Fig. 8.4.

*A Phase.* Data are collected under pretreatment conditions to obtain a reference point to which performance in the subsequent treatment phase can be compared. (This condition is commonly referred to as a baseline phase.) Data are collected until the clinical measure shows either a stable level or countertherapeutic trend. Either of these two data patterns constitute an acceptable baseline, because either will allow one to detect improvements in a subsequent treatment phase.

*B Phase.* The first treatment procedure is implemented until a new stable level on the clinical measure is observed. In the ABCDCD design, it is assumed that the first treatment applied in the B phase was associated with an unsatisfactory outcome (significantly below the treatment goals established for this client), and so other treatments are tried out in the C and D phases. If the first treatment in the B phase was associated with satisfactory results, it would be unnecessary to introduce additional treatments. Instead, it might be desirable to replicate treatment effects by removing and reintroducing the treatment procedure. In this event, the resulting design would be a simple ABAB design.

*C Phase.* As mentioned earlier, it is assumed here that the first treatment in the B phase was associated with an unsatisfactory outcome. In this situation, a second treatment procedure would be implemented until a stable level of the clinical measure was observed. However, it is also assumed that the second treatment applied in the C phase is associated with an unsatisfactory outcome.

*D Phase.* Use of this design presumes that the first and second treatments (in B and C phases, respectively) were associated with unsatisfactory outcomes. Therefore, a third treatment would be implemented in the fourth phase until a new level of the clinical measure is observed. This time, it is assumed that a satisfactory level on the clinical measure is obtained. At this point, one can proceed to replicate the treatment effects and to demonstrate that the treatment procedures in the D phase caused the observed changes.

*C Phase.* This second C phase serves to demonstrate that the treatment in the first D phase is necessary to produce the observed improvements. In the second C phase, the treatment is reversed or returned to conditions of the earlier phase. If the improvements observed in the first D phase are lost (the level of the clinical measure returns to that observed in the first C phase), one can then infer that treatment procedures in the D phase were necessary to produce those improvements.

*D Phase.* This second D phase provides the opportunity to replicate the improvements observed in the first D phase. If the clinical measure returns to the level recorded in the first D phase, this would confirm that the treatment procedures in the D phase were responsible for the changes observed in this condition and this result was not due to extraneous variables. Therapy would conclude with the client receiving the treatment of the D phase, and follow-up recommendations would encourage the continuation of these conditions, though perhaps with a gradually diminishing dosage.

### Limitations of Single-Subject Design Methodology

Although single-subject designs offer a practical and flexible format for individualizing treatment and producing better treatment outcomes, they are not without their drawbacks. First, the need to collect data until the clinical measure is stable within phases may exceed the client's patience, the time frame for third-party reimbursement, or both. Convincing rationales need to be presented to clients and funding sources for obtaining data to accurately assess problems and ascertain treatment effects.

Second, ethical concerns may be raised about using reversals to evaluate treatment effects. Clients, family members, and clinicians themselves may object to deliberating withdrawing seemingly effective treatments solely for the purpose of proving the effectiveness of those procedures. There are several alternatives for dealing with these objections. Clinicians may choose to forgo reversal designs, retaining the last treatment condition that apparently was effective with their client. The price of this alternative is that the exact cause of the client's improvement is never known and recommendations for future care are highly speculative. Another option is to use a brief reversal phase that is long enough to show a noticeable decline in the clinical measure but not large enough to distress interested parties. Finally, another alternative is to use a single-subject design that does not involve a reversal, such as multiple-baseline design (that staggers treatment across different behaviors, behavior in different settings, or behavior in different participants) or a mixed (Wong & Liberman, 1981; Wong et al., 1993; Wong, Morgan, Crowley, & Baker, 1996) or combined design (Kazdin, 1982).

Third, sophisticated analyses of multiple treatment procedures may not be attainable with this particular design. It is possible that effects of treatments (say, procedures used in the B and C phases) are not apparent in the phases in which they are applied, but carry over into later phases where they interact with and potentiate subsequent treatments (say, procedures used in the D phase). In this situation, effects of subsequent treatments are greater than they would be if used alone, and the observed outcome is the actually the result of multiple-treatment interference. Such interference could also subtract from the apparent effectiveness of treatments, making treatments appear less potent than they would be if they were not preceded by these other interventions. Methods for dealing with multiple-treatment interference include using a different single-subject design, such as the alternating treatments design (Barlow & Hayes, 1979) or a counterbalanced design.

## PRACTICAL CONSIDERATIONS—WHAT DATA TO COLLECT AND WHEN?

There is a diversity in opinion among clinicians about whether to, and/or how often and when (prior to or following a therapy session) to collect client self-report data, clinician data, or both on a standardized instrument. If the reader has gone this far into the current chapter, then it is probably safe to assume that she or he holds some interest in collecting intake and outcome information from the person receiving the treatment.

From our experience, a key issue underlying the question of whether to collect the data using a standardized instrument about the person's status is related to whether the participating clinician feels that collecting such information is useful to therapy. To state the obvious: Those who do not see any reason or use of such information in their treatment strategy do not willingly collect such data, and those who find such information useful to their therapeutic intervention do routinely collect such data. From our personal experience, those who do find such information useful tend to describe their theoretical orientation as behavioral or cognitive-behavioral, although there many exceptions among colleagues within all theoretical orientations. As Beutler (1991) has pointed out, most practicing clinicians make use of a number of different techniques, behaving quite eclectically in their actual practice even when there is a claim that one theoretical orientation guides the core of their treatment strategy. Recent Internet discussion on this topic indicates that the diversity described exists, even among those who say that they have a major professional interest in outcome evaluation.

The recommendations from our own experience and that from the above-referenced discussion were identical. On the basis of this nonscientific review of the issues and the demands for the graphic and statistical analytic methods we have proposed, the following guidelines are offered:

1. Collect data at intake prior to the initial interview to obtain a baseline measure.
2. Select a battery of instruments for the intake assessment, but only select easy-to-complete instruments for progress evaluation:
   a. The selection of the battery of instruments used at intake should be useful for treatment planning and for identifying those intake variables (and circumstances) that would help identify the subset of persons for whom normative data (on either clinical or nonclinical populations, or both) exists. Thus, a key concern in selecting these instruments is whether such normative data are available.
   b. The measure administered during and following treatment must cover the domain(s) that are the foci of treatment. Because the focus of treatment may not be obvious prior to the first clinical interview, the selection and administration will probably follow the intake interview. This requires that the clinician have available a collection of instruments ready for such selection.
3. The person needs to be told in advance that time will be spent before and after the initial interview in performing the tasks required of the instruments.
4. The recommended frequency of administering the instrument should vary in accordance with how the instrument is used and what kind of information the clinician (researcher) is seeking. Howard recommended every fourth session as ideal for estimating change relative to the dose-response curves his group has been studying. Others (e.g., Richard Hunter in Newman, Hunter, & Irwing, 1987) argued for the use of such an instrument at every session that the person is capable to complete such a form. Cognitive behavioral therapists have told us that having the person complete the instrument prior to each session provides information that could guide the direction that therapy might take on that day.

Because it is seldom clear as to when therapy will end, one should not expect that one can easily obtain information from the last session. Thus, a strategy of routinely collecting information on a standardized instrument (e.g., with each session or with every fourth session) is reasonable. With the development of new statistical routines that describe the trajectory of change over time but do not require that there be equal intervals between times of observation, the scheduling of assessment periods can be administered in a way that is tailored more specifically to the treatment strategy.

Suppose a therapist subscribed to the phase model recommended by Howard et al. (1993) and wanted to schedule assessment periods according to what he or she might expect to be critical times for change within specific domains of functioning. For example, one strategy might start with a schedule of such assessments every session for the first 4 weeks during the *remoralization* phase, during the *remediation* (of symptoms) phase, and then once each 8 to 12 weeks during the *rehabilitation* (habit modification) phase. The application of patient profiling recommended by Howard et al. (1996) can readily handle the fitting of these data to the normative data to produce an expected growth curve even though the intervals between data collection occasions do vary.

## TREATMENT INNOVATION

We have focused on how to use psychological tests to track patient progress and inform clinical decision making. The proposed procedures also can facilitate treatment improvement. If the clinician tracks individual patient progress over time in the ways discussed, he or she can use the data collected to compare successful outcomes with unsuccessful outcomes and to identify patterns that might lead to treatment innovations.

Although there is a substantial body of research indicating the benefits of specific psychotherapeutic interventions, few would deny that there is still considerable room for improvement. For example, a review of interventions with children and adolescents revealed that only 5% to 30% of youth participating in such treatments evidence clinically significant change (Kazdin, 1987). The situation with child as well as adult treatment has fueled a movement toward the development of treatment innovations (Beutler & Clarkin, 1990; Onken, Blaine, & Boren, 1993). Kazdin (1994) identified seven steps to developing effective treatments: (1) conceptualization of the dysfunction, (2) research on processes related to the dysfunction, (3) conceptualization of the treatment, (4) specification of the treatment, (5) tests of treatment process, (6) tests of treatment outcome, and (7) tests of the boundary condition and moderators. Repeated administration of one or more of the tests reviewed in the current volume, then, can guide treatment innovation and development.

## CONCLUDING REMARKS—SIMPLE IS BEST

We are somewhat amazed that the technology of single-subject research has not advanced further given its long history in the behavioral sciences. But then, the elegant examples and graphic models provided by the early psychophysics and behavioral researchers set a baseline that has served us well. The key requirements of any research paradigm rest on the care with which the researcher provides adequate operational definitions of exogenous and endogenous variables, along with the care in collecting and presenting the data. These same requirements are particularly important in single-subject research and for the presentation of psychological testing data on a single individual at one point in time and over time. Thus, the traditional presentation of a profile on an individual relative to empirical norms that has been the standard in the reporting of psychological tests is still a worthy tool. The traditional staple of behavior therapists of plotting behaviors over time has been augmented by plotting the results of a psychological test on an individual over time relative to the changes expected in a norm treatment group as recommended by Howard et al. (1996) and shown in Figs. 8.2 and 8.3, or relative to a standard as recommended by Newman and Tejeda (1996), as shown in Fig. 8.1.

The introduction of the logic of "clinically significant change" by Jacobson and Truax (1991) has identified another benchmark for both group and single-subject research that should influence the interpretation of single-subject research and clinical data. The critical question regarding the individual person becomes: Are the changes in behavior as represented by psychological testing over time clinically significant? What is the standard that distinguishes the boundary between clinically significant and a nonsignificant outcome? We would argue that empirical norms as exemplified in Figs. 8.2 and 8.3 in this chapter and Fig. 8.1 in chapter by Lambert and Hawkins in this volume, should be the first choice. At a minimum, an operationally defined standard based on a consensus of experts (Newman, Hunter, & Irwing, 1987; Uehara et al., 1994) could also be considered, but only as a temporary standard while an effort is made to collect normative data to set the standard.

A basic standard set by the traditions of psychophysics and behavior therapy is that of simplicity in the graphic display of the results. The integration of graphics with readily available spread sheets and statistical packages on the PC has made the technology of simple graphic displays available to all of us. We expect to see an expanded use of this technology in both clinical practice and in the clinical research to be common in the near future.

## ACKNOWLEDGMENTS

Thanks are owed to our thoughtful and patient colleagues for their recommendations and comments on the development of the earlier version of the chapter written with Gayle Dakof, Michael Dow, Howard Liddle, and Manuel J. Tejeda.

## REFERENCES

Achenbach, T. M. (This volume). The child behavioral checklist and related instruments.

Bailey, J. S., & Burch, M. R. (2002). *Research methods in applied behavior analysis*. Thousand Oaks, CA: Sage.

Barkham, M., Margison, F., Leach, C., Lucock, M., Mellow-Clark, J., Evans, C., et al. (2001). Service profiling and outcomes benchmarking using the CORE_OM: Toward practice-based evidence in the psychological therapies. *Journal of Consulting and Clinical Psychology, 69*, 184–196.

Barlow, D. H., & Hayes, S. C. (1979). Alternating treatments design: One strategy for comparing the effects of two treatments in a single subject. *Journal of Applied Behavior Analysis, 12*, 199–210.

Beutler, L. E., & Clarkin, J. F. (1990). *Systematic treatment selection: Toward targeted therapeutic interventions*. New York: Brunner/Mazel.

Beutler, L. E. (1991). Have all won and must all have prizes? Revisiting Luborsky et al.'s verdict. *Journal of Consulting and Clinical Psychology, 59*, 226–232.

Bloom, M., Fischer, J., & Orme, J. G. (2003). *Evaluating practice: Guidelines for the accountable professional* (4th ed.). Boston: Allyn & Bacon.

Carter, D. E., & Newman, F. L. (1976). *A client-oriented system of mental health service delivery and program management: A workbook and guide*. Washington, DC: U.S. Department of Health, Education, and Welfare. (DHEW Pub. No. ADM 76-307; Reprinted, 1980, Series FN NO. 4)

Cooper, J. O., Heron, T. E., & Heward, W. L. (1987). *Applied behavior analysis*. Columbus, OH: Merrill.

Craighead, L. W., Craighead, W. E., Kazdin, A. E., & Mahoney, M. J. (1994). *Cognitive and behavioral interventions: An empirical approach to mental health problems*. Boston: Allyn & Bacon.

De Liberty, R. N., Newman, F. L., & Ward, E. (2001). Risk adjustment in the Hoosier assurance plan: Impact on providers. *Journal of Behavioral Health Services & Research, 28*, 301–318.

Greenberg, L., & Newman, F.L. (1996). An approach to psychotherapy process research: Introduction to the special series. *Journal of Consulting and Clinical Psychology, 64*, 435–438.

Hersen, M., & Barlow, D. H. (1984). *Single-case experimental designs: Strategies for studying behavior change*. New York: Elsevier.

Hersen, M., Michaelson, L., & Bellack, A. S. (1984). *Issues in psychotherapy research*. New York: Plenum.

Howard, K. I., Kopta, S. M., Krause, M. S., & Orlinsky, D. E. (1986). The dose-effect relationship in psychotherapy. *American Psychologist, 41* 159–164.

Howard, K. I., Lueger, R. J., Maling, M. S., & Martinovich, Z. (1993). The attrition dilemma: Toward a new strategy for psychotherapy research. *Journal of Consulting and Clinical Psychology, 54*, 106–110.

Howard, K. I., Moras, K., Brill, P. L., Marinovich, Z., & Lutz, W. (1996). Evaluation of psychotherapy: Efficacy, effectiveness, and patient progress. *American Psychologist, 51*, 1059–1064.

Jacobson, N. S., & Truax, P. (1991). Clinical significance: A statistical approach to defining meaningful change in psychotherapy research. *Journal of Consulting and Clinical Psychology, 59*, 12–19.

Kazdin, A. E. (1982). *Single-case research designs: Methods for clinical and applied settings*. New York: Oxford University Press.

Kazdin, A. E. (1987). Comparative outcome studies of psychotherapy: Methodological issues and strategies. *Journal of Consulting and Clinical Psychology, 54*, 95–105.

Kazdin, A. E. (1992). *Research design in clinical psychology*. Needham Heights, MA: Allyn & Bacon.

Kazdin, A. E. (1994). Methodology, design and evaluation in psychotherapy research. In A. E. Bergin & S. L. Garfield (Eds.), *Handbook of psychotherapy and behavior change* (4th ed., pp. 543–594). New York: Wiley.

Liddle, H. A., Rowe, C. L., Dakof, G. A., & Lyke, J. (1998). Translating parenting research into clinical interventions [Special issue: Parenting interventions]. *Clinical Child Psychology and Psychiatry, 3*, 419–443.

Liddle, H. A., & Saba, G. (1981). Systemic chic: Family therapy's new wave. *Journal of Strategic and Systemic Therapies, 1*, 36–69.

Lueger, R. J., Howard, K. I., Martinovich, Z., Lutz, W., Anderson, E. E., & Grissom, G. (2001). Assessing treatment progress of individual patients using expected treatment response models. *Journal of Consulting & Clinical Psychology, 69*, 150–158.

Lutz, W., Martinovich, Z., & Howard, K. (1999). Patient profiling: An application of random coefficient regression models to depicting the response of a patient to outpatient psychotherapy. *Journal of Consulting & Clinical Psychology, 67*, 571–577.

Meehl, P. E. (1954). *Clinical versus statistical prediction.* Minneapolis: University of Minnesota.

Moos, R. H. (1994). Editorial: Treated or untreated, an addiction is not an island unto itself. *Addiction, 89*, 507–509.

Newman, F. L. (1983). Level of functioning scales: Their use in clinical practice. In P. A. Keller & L. G. Ritt (Eds.), *Innovations in clinical practice: A source book.* Sarasota, FL: Professional Resource Exchange.

Newman, F. L., Griffin, B. P., Black, R. W., & Page, S. E. (1989). Linking level of care to level of need: Assessing the need for mental health care for nursing home residents. *American Psychologist, 44*, 1315–1324.

Newman, F. L. & Howard, K. I. (1986). Therapeutic effort, outcome and policy. *American Psychologist, 41*, 181–187.

Newman, F. L. Hunter, R. H., & Irving, D. (1987). Simple measures of progress and outcome in the evaluation of mental health services. *Evaluation and Program Planning, 10*, 209–218.

Newman, F. L., & Sorensen, J. L. (1985). *Integrated clinical and fiscal management in mental health.* Norwood, NJ: Ablex.

Newman, F. L., & Tejeda, M. J. (1996). The need for research designed to support decisions in the delivery of mental health services. *American Psychologist, 51*, 1040–1049.

Onken, L. S., Blaine, J. D., & Boren, J. J. (1993). *Behavioral treatments for drug abuse and dependence.* U.S. Department of Health and Human Services. (NIDA Research Monograph No. 137).

Osgood, C. E., (1953). *Methods and theory in experimental psychology.* New York: Oxford University Press.

Raudenbush, S. W., & Bryk, A. S. (2002). *Hierarchical linear models: Applications and data analysis methods* (2nd ed.). Newbury Park, CA: Sage.

Shadish, W. R., Matt, G. E., Navarro, A. M., Siegle, G., Crits-Christoph, P., Hazelrigg, M. D., et al. (1997). Evidence that therapy works in clinically representative conditions. *Journal of Consulting and Clinical Psychology, 65*, 355–365.

Stevens, S. S. (1951). *Handbook of experimental psychology.* New York: Wiley.

Stevens, S. S. (1966). Metric for the social consensus, *Science, 151*, 530–541.

Uehara, E. S., Smukler, M., & Newman, F. L. (1994). Linking resources use to consumer level of need: Field test of the "LONCA" method. *Journal of Consulting and Clinical Psychology, 62*, 695–709.

Wong, S. E., & Liberman, R. P. (1981). Mixed single-subject designs in clinical research: Variations of the multiple-baseline. *Behavioral Assessment, 3*, 297–306.

Wong, S. E., Martinez-Diaz, J. A., Massel, H. K., Edelstein, B. A., Wiegand, W., Bowen, L., & Liberman, R. P. (1993). Conversational skills training with schizophrenic inpatients: A study of generalization across settings and conversants. *Behavior Therapy, 24*, 285–304.

Wong, S. E., Morgan, C., Crowley, R., & Baker, J. N. (1996). Using a table game to teach social skills to adolescent psychiatric inpatients: Do the skills generalize? *Child and Family Behavior Therapy, 18*, 1–17.

Yates, B. T. (1996). *Analyzing costs, procedures, processes, and outcomes in human services (Applied Social Research Series, Vol. 42).* Thousand Oaks, CA: Sage.

Yates, B. T., & Newman, F. L. (1980). Findings of cost-effectiveness and cost-benefit analyses of psychotherapy. In G. VandenBos (Ed.), *Psychotherapy: From practice to research to policy.* Beverly Hills, CA: Sage.

# Selecting Statistical Procedures for Progress and Outcomes Assessment: The Analysis of Group Data

Frederick L. Newman
*Florida International University*

Manuel J. Tejeda
*Barry University*

The clinical and decision, or administrative, environments in which the procedures are used must drive the correct selection of appropriate statistical procedures in the analysis of psychological test results. This chapter provides recommendations and guidelines for selecting statistical procedures useful in two such environments: (a) screening and treatment planning and (b) progress and outcome assessment. Each environment has unique demands warranting different, though not necessarily, independent statistical approaches.

Concurrently, there must be a common concern regarding a measure's psychometric qualities and its relationship with outcome. For screening and treatment planning, there is greater concern with predicting the effectiveness of outcome and the concomitant costs of resources to be consumed in treatment. For progress and outcome applications, there is the additional requirement of sensitivity to the rate and direction of the change relative to treatment goals. The discussion in this section focuses on issues of analysis that should be addressed and guidelines for evaluating and selecting statistical procedures within each application.

The chapter is organized such that the more commonly used statistical models for the analysis of group data are discussed under a number of different clinical topics (issues or questions), for example, traditional regression or analysis of variance. In each instance, the exact form of the analysis takes on a different format, one that is best suited to the clinical issue under discussion. Moreover, the analysis is usually contrasted with alternative approaches regarding assumptions, interpretations, and practicality. We should note that in each case, the best approach is more dependent on the specific clinical issue under investigation. A major theme throughout the chapter is that the clinical question must drive the selection of the analytic approach bounded by the limits of psychometric and statistical conclusion validity.

## Approach to Presenting the Statistical Material

The logic of the chapter's presentation is to first discuss a specific clinical or mental health service issue and then to recommend one or more statistical procedures that can address the issue. The language of the mathematical expression underlying the statistical procedure serves to bridge the clinical issue with the statistical procedure. The expressions are presented here for three reasons. First, the clinical focus of the discussion is designed to help the reader understand the logical link between the clinical issue and the statistical procedure. Second, the discussion is designed to provide the reader with a sufficient understanding of the statistical logic and vocabulary to read and use a statistical computer package manual and related texts, or to converse with her or his resident statistician. Third, the discussion should help the reader understand where and how the link between the clinical issue and the statistical procedure is strong and where it is weak. References are provided for each technique and computational details, along with examples of how the technique is used in clinical research applications.

Discussion on selecting statistical procedures will follow from two baselines. One is a formal conceptualization of measurement: What does the instrument seek to measure and what are the potential sources of error in the measurement? The second baseline is the clinical or service management question that is being asked of the measure. What follows is a definition of the general model and notation that is used throughout the chapter. We introduce this model and notation for descriptive purposes in this chapter. It is not the only model, nor necessarily the best model, for all situations. It is, however, a model that lends itself to a discussion of treatment planning and outcome assessment in mental health services. The text by Collins and Horn (1991), *The Best Methods for the Analysis of Change*, provides a good review of alternative models.

Suppose that at a specific time (t) we are interested in obtaining a measure $Y_{ijkt}$ that proposes to describe a particular domain of human functioning ($\delta$) on the $i$th individual who belongs to a particular target group ($\beta_k$) and is receiving a specific treatment ($\alpha_j$). In the measurement model, we can describe the influence of the $i$th person belonging to the $k$th target group and being under $j$th treatment at time t, on the observed behavior ($Y_{ijkt}$) of the domain called ($\delta$), as follows:

$$Y_{ijkt} = \alpha\delta_{ijt} + \beta\delta_{ikt} + \alpha\beta\delta_{ijkt} + \varepsilon_{ijkt}.$$

The term $\alpha\beta\delta_{ijkt}$ is the interaction of the $j$th treatment and the $k$th target group that influences the functional domain ($\delta$) for the $i$th subject at the time t, when the measure was taken. As a final note, $Y_{ijkt}$ must contain the characteristic rigor of the traditional operational definition. The measurement of $Y_{ijkt}$ is bound by the same issues regarding accurate and valid measurement as other variables in the equation, such as participant characteristics and treatment assignment.

There are two features of the model offered here that are different from that offered in standard texts. One is that the time that the measure is obtained (t) is included as a subscript in each term, and as such appears to be a constant. Time, of course, is a constant, but $t$ is included here to remind us that all measures, particularly clinical measures of functional status, are time dependent. Such measures reflect states rather than traits (Kazdin, 1986). A more formal statement of the model could have treated time as an additional element of the model, thereby adding complexity to the presentation. Another tactic could have left t out completely. However, the temporal nature of the measure of functional status is important in most clinical service applications. Thus, a simple subscript t is used to indicate the temporal status of the measurement model. The clinical and statistical issues involved in measuring changes in functional status over time (progress and outcome) are discussed in detail later in the chapter, when we focus on the impact of treatment and for whom the treatment works best.

The second feature of the measurement model that differs from the more standard presentation is the addition of the parameter ($\delta$) to represent a particular domain of functioning (behavior). As with the use of the time element in the expression ($\delta$), a specific functional domain is added for emphasis. Each of the elements in the expression (in this case, treatment or target population characteristic) should be seen as interacting with the measure of the individual on a specific functional domain. The inclusion of ($\delta$) is to remind us that the model may not hold if the observation made ($Y_{ijkt}$) does not actually represent the behavioral domain of interest. Prior to treatment, the model reduces to

$$Y_{ikt} = \beta \delta_{ikt} + \varepsilon_{ikt},$$

where the term ($\beta \delta_{ikt}$) is the true value of the domain for the $i$th person belonging to the kth target population at a given time (t).

The last term, $\varepsilon_{ikt}$, is an error term for the $i$th person that combines potential differences (error) because of at least four (potentially interacting) features: (1) item (measure) difficulty ($b_{it}$) at that time, (2) imprecise measurement at that time ($m_{it}$), (3) individual differences introduced by that person (the individual's state) at that time ($d_{it}$), and, (4) unspecified influencing factors ($v_{it}$). The four potentially confounding components of the error term will be discussed later in the chapter. When an additional target population characteristic is considered, the potential for it to interact with each of the other terms will only add to the model's complexity. Because most scoring procedures attempt to derive a composite score for a set of factors, they add sources of variation such as client characteristics, which thus typically compounds error (i.e., combined with $b$, $m$, $d$, and $v$). Because these sources of error are nonsystematic, they cannot simply be subtracted from aggregate scores. The number of sources of variance expand with the addition of just one additional client characteristic ($\Gamma_l$). This would add two fixed interactions with treatment effects ($\alpha\Gamma_{jl}$ and $\alpha\beta\Gamma_{jkl}$) and the potential for up to 15 random interactions with the four confounded components of error (item difficulty $b$, error of measurement $m$, individual differences $d$, and unspecified influence factors $v_{it}$).

Despite what appears to be intractable complexity, there are a number of measures available that have demonstrated sufficient psychometric quality with sufficiently small random error effects and sensitivity to change such that treatment effects can be detected. These instruments may be applied to a fairly wide range of client characteristics. This is consistent with the outcome assessment recommendation of National Institute of Mental Health expert panel (see Newman, Ciarlo, & Rugh, chap. 6, this volume) that an ideal measure should be able to serve a wide range of client groups. The wide applicability of these measures also decreases the costs of providing different measures for each of the client groups and increases the measure's utility (e.g., in planning or evaluating a program of services).

## Measurement and Statistics

Despite advances in methodology and analysis, measurement remains the foundation of statistical inference. The validity of our measures dictates the extent and nature of inferences we can make as a result of our analysis. Thus, measurement issues cannot be underestimated in their importance when considering the presentation of statistical material. The investigator's fluency with measurement issues will impact both the design of studies and the subsequent statistics used in the analysis of their data.

The interaction between design, measurement, and statistics is often overlooked when planning a study. Briefly, consider the impact of an invalid or unavailable measure on design and statistics. Clearly, a study could not be designed if measures were unavailable. Likewise, interpretation of results would be impossible in the presence of an invalid instrument.

In terms of the organization of this chapter, screening is synonymous with measurement, and treatment planning is based on valid measurement. Moreover, progress and outcome analyses as discussed in our subsequent section are impossible without valid and reliable measures. Thus, we present a careful review of the foundations of measurement, as well as new advances in the field of psychometrics, linking these points to our discussion of statistical analysis.

## SCREENING AND TREATMENT PLANNING

### Primary Objectives

There are two. The first is to provide reliable and valid evidence as to the appropriateness of and the client's eligibility for a treatment. If appropriate and eligible, then the second objective is to obtain evidence as to which treatments or services would best help the client progress toward the outcome goals. At a minimum, statistical procedures required to assess reliability and validity must be evaluated in the context of these two objectives.

### Scale Reliability and Consistency of Clinical Communication

Although a scale may have a published history of reliability, it is sometimes useful to determine if the local applications of the scale are reliable and, if not, to identify the factors contributing to reduced reliability. We should note that a number of forms of reliability exist. In the current discussion, we refer to estimates of internal consistency, particularly what is commonly called Cronbach's alpha (Cronbach, 1990). However, other forms of reliability provide valuable information. The coefficient of concordance (sometimes referred to as parallel forms) provides information about how sections of a measure relate to one another and if measurement is consistent over sections measuring the same construct. Similarly, the coefficient of stability (sometimes referred to as test–retest) provides information about change in measurement over time when no intervention has occurred. Such forms of reliability are not discussed in detail here, but nevertheless add to the overall psychometric evaluation of an instrument.

By conducting studies to assess the scale's reliability, in this case alpha, one can investigate the consistency of staff communication about the client. The concern for staff communication emanates from the need for staff to maintain a consistent frame of reference when discussing a client's strengths, problems, treatment goals, and progress. Moreover, if done properly, it will be possible to identify the factors depreciating the reliability of staff communication, and thereby determine the need for staff development and future training.

The general concept of reliability has been described in a number of ways, with each approach providing a slightly different view of the concept of reliability. In one view offered by Cronbach (1990), reliability could be expressed as a proportion where the numerator describes the amount of variability because of a true measurement of individuals functional characteristics ($\beta\delta$). The denominator describes the referent, or baseline variability. The referent is the variability because of the functional characteristics plus the variability because of extraneous factors ($\varepsilon$; e.g., those factors that reduce the consistency with which the instrument is employed). Essentially, the variance that the items have in common is divided by the total variance of the items in the scale. The proportion is expressed as follows:

$$\text{Reliability} = \frac{s^2\beta\delta}{s^2\beta\delta + s_\varepsilon^2}$$

Reliability increases directly with variation because of differences in the functional characteristics in the target population, $s^2\beta\delta$, and decreases with variability because of extraneous factors, $s_\varepsilon^2$:

$$r_{xx} = \frac{\sigma_t^2}{\sigma_x^2}$$

where: $r_{xx}$ is the reliability of measure $x$
$\sigma_t^2$ is the variance of the true scores
$\sigma_x^2$ is the variance of the observed scores, or $\sigma_t^2 + \sigma_\varepsilon^2$.

Hence, an equivalent expression for reliability is:

$$r_{xx} = 1 - \frac{\sigma_x^2 - \sigma_\varepsilon^2}{\sigma_x^2}$$

$$= 1 - \frac{\sigma_\varepsilon^2}{\sigma_x^2}.$$

Reliability increases as the proportion of variability of extraneous factors to variability the functional characteristics, decreases , that is, as $\sigma_\varepsilon^2 - > 0$.

Internal consistency considers the variability among items, $I_p$, used to estimate the functional characteristic, $\delta$. The expected value of a set of unbiased items, $I_p$, equals the expected value of $\delta$ for the $i$th person in the $k$th target group. As the correlation, $r_{I\delta}$, increases, the items are said to have increased internal consistency with each other and with their estimation of $\delta$, and therefore to have increased reliability. This can be seen in following expression:

$$\text{Reliability–internal consistency} = \frac{s^2\beta\delta}{s^2\beta\delta + (1 - r_{I\delta}^2)s_\varepsilon^2}$$

where $(1 - r_{I\delta}^2)$ is the proportion of the total variance that is not described by the relationship between I and $\delta$ across individuals.

Another expression of reliability focuses on item variability:

$$\alpha = \frac{k}{k-1} = 1 - \left[\frac{\Sigma\sigma_i^2}{\Sigma\sigma_i^2 + 2(\Sigma\sigma_{ij})}\right],$$

where: k is the number of items in the measure
$\sigma_i^2$ is the variance of item i
$\sigma_{ij}^2$ is the covariance of items i and j.

Internal consistency reliability can also be expressed as the average r estimate, for example

$$\alpha = \frac{kr_{ij}}{1 + (k-1)r_{ij}}.$$

Earlier in the chapter, *item difficulty* was identified as a potential source of error variance in the basic measurement equation. Item difficulty in the present context could be described as the extent to which the internal consistency of items varies among persons functioning at different levels within the target population at time t, $\beta_{kt}$. Reliability–internal consistency estimates could be used to estimate item difficulty effects. This could be done by obtaining the reliability–internal consistency estimates for persons functioning at the lowest, middle, and highest third of the distribution on a global measure of functioning (e.g., using the current *DSM–IV* Axis V). If the proportions do not differ significantly, then item difficulty, as defined here, is not a significant source of error variance. (It must be noted that in other environments, e.g., educational performance testing and personnel selection, having item difficulty as a significant source of variance is considered to be desirable.)

Procedures for estimating internal reliability are part of most statistical packages (e.g., SPSS, SYSTAT–TESTAT, SAS) as either a stand-alone computer program or part of a factor analysis program.

**Interrater Reliability and Clinical Communication**

The second major concern regarding reliability in the screening and treatment planning processes is interrater reliability. This is particularly relevant where raters are members of a clinical team. If their judgments vary, then treatment goals and treatment actions will differ in ways not necessarily related to client needs. For interrater reliability, the descriptive expression is

$$\text{Interrater reliability} = \frac{s^2\beta\delta}{s^2\beta\delta + s^2_{(rater \times \beta\delta)} + s^2\varepsilon'}.$$

The magnitude of the interaction, $s^2_{(rater \times \beta\delta)}$, decreases as agreement among raters increases. In other words, as the rater differences, $s^2_{(rater \times \beta\delta)}$, approaches 0 and the error term, $s^2\varepsilon'$, approaches 0, interrater reliability approaches 1. Thus, interrater reliability increases as this interaction decreases. Four major features of an instrument are said to increase interrater reliability. The first is to increase the internal consistency of the items, particularly by anchoring the items to objective referents that have the same meaning to all team members. The second is to develop the instrument's instructions so as to minimize the influence of inappropriate differences among raters. Unfortunately, the only means of uncovering "inappropriate" rater behaviors is through the experience of pilot testing the instrument in a variety of situations. Thus, it is also important to look at the testing history of the instrument. The third is training and retraining to correct for initial rater differences and the "drift" in the individual clinician's frame of reference that can occur over time. Fourth and last, it is critical to anchor observation in behaviors as much as possible to reduce inference. The greater the inference required, the greater the likelihood of error being introduced. High inference coding procedures generally produce lower reliability estimates than low-inference coding procedures, because perception varies by individual raters, as well as the intentions of those being rated.

To maximize interrater reliability, training manuals with example cases are critical. As described in Newman and Sorensen (1985), it is possible to fold some of the training and retraining activities into treatment team meetings and case conferences. Discussions of methods of assessing factors that may be influencing interrater reliability are presented in Newman (1983) and Newman and Sorensen (1985). The major computer packages provide programs that permit partitioning the sources of variance (univariate or multivariate) because of differences among raters when multiple-rater data are entered for the same individuals.

**Measurement Model Testing**

Often when a clinician or a researcher is seeking to determine whether a particular psychological assessment instrument will "do the job" of describing the behaviors of a person, the literature will offer the results of studies on one or more tests of the instrument's measurement model, employing structure equation model testing techniques. Such a test of a measurement model typically seeks to affirm that the items within each factor and the factors themselves come together to describe the domains of behaviors that the instrument's developers claim to be covered. In this section, we seek to provide a basis for understanding the statistical/rationale that underlies the application of structural equation modeling to the test of a measurement model.

Measurement modeling testing first requires that the underlying model describing a person's behavior should be described quite explicitly. This is called model specification, and it is done by identifying the factors (constructs) that the instrument is expected to describe, along with the grouping of the instrument's items that are expected to indicate the value (loading) of each factor. For example, for the Child Behavioral Checklist (CBCL), there are two major factors (Internalized and Externalized behaviors) with certain items loading most strongly on the Internalized factor and other items loading most strongly on the Externalized factor.

Consider an example where one wanted to confirm that this two-factor structure was appropriate for a specific target population of adolescents in a southeastern city where the cultures were quite diverse (as it is for the chapter's authors in South Florida). It should be no surprise that the statistical procedure employed here is titled a confirmatory factor analysis, or CFA. In our discussion of CFA, the terms *latent variable*, *construct*, and *factor* are often used interchangeably, with *latent variable* used more often in structural equation modeling.

The formal mathematical statement that represents how well a set of items measures a construct (or latent variable or factor) plus error is

$$\mathbf{x} = \Lambda_x \xi + \delta.$$

Here, $\mathbf{x}$ is a $q$ by 1 vector of indicators of the latent variables (e.g., all externalization and internalization items on the CBCL). $\Lambda_x$ is a $q$ by $n$ matrix of coefficients (loadings) of $\mathbf{x}$ on the latent variables ($\xi$). Finally, $\delta$ is a $q$ by 1 vector of errors in measurement of $\mathbf{x}$. As expressed, the mathematical expression does not yet consider the existence of factors External ($m$) or Internal ($n$), just that of all items plus error.

We can easily expand this equation to include various measures at the measurement level. This is done by increasing the size of the $\Lambda_x$ matrix, that is, adding latent variables ($\xi$) and expanding the vector $\mathbf{x}$.

## Structural Equation Modeling

In the previous discussion of measurement specification, $\mathbf{x} = \Lambda_x\,\xi + \delta$ represents the classical factor analysis model. As such, it describes the systemic relation between the measured indicators (the items) and the latent constructs these are taken to represent. In structural equation modeling, we turn our interest to the specification of the relations between the latent constructs. The expression for the system of linear structural relations is given by (Jöreskog, 1982)

$$B\eta = \Gamma\xi + \zeta,$$

where: $B$ is a $m \times m$ matrix of coefficients (loadings)
$\quad\quad\;\;$ $\Gamma$ is a $m \times n$ matrix of coefficients (loadings)
$\quad\quad\;\;$ $\zeta$ is a $m$ by 1 vector of random disturbance terms,

and the vectors $\eta$ and $\xi$ are not directly observed. Instead, these are observed as

$$\mathbf{y} = \Lambda_y\eta + \varepsilon$$
$$\mathbf{x} = \Lambda_x\xi + \delta,$$

where: $\varepsilon$ and $\delta$ are vectors of measurement errors
$\quad\quad\;\;$ $\Lambda_y$ is a regression matrix ($p \times m$) of $\mathbf{y}$ on $\eta$
$\quad\quad\;\;$ $\Lambda_x$ is a regression matrix ($q \times n$) of $\mathbf{x}$ on $\xi$.

The expression $\mathbf{x} = \Lambda_x\,\xi + \delta$ is familiar from the preceding section on measurement specification. The additional equation $\mathbf{y} = \Lambda_y\,\eta + \varepsilon$ is similar, and taken together these two equations constitute the measurement specification for structural equations as expressed in LISREL (Jöreskog & Sörbom, 1993; Jöreskog, Sörbom, Du Toit, & Du Toit, 1999). The separated measurement models allow for an increased flexibility in the specification of the structural model $B\eta = \Gamma\xi + \zeta$. Notice that the measurement model equations both represent classical factor analysis models, with the differences allowing for dependencies as expressed in the structural model. The latent variables represented by the vector $\eta$ (the endogenous part of the structural model) is conditioned by the vector $\xi$ (the exogenous part of the structural model).

It is also possible to specify higher order relationships among latent factors. Attention has been directed at the high incidence of comorbidity diagnoses of anxiety and mood disorders (Brown & Barlow, 1992) based on the *DSM* nosology. One might posit that latent factors of representing the *DSM* disorders of anxiety (A), depression (D), panic disorder (P), obsessive-compulsive disorder (OC), and social phobia (S) are manifestations of higher order syndromes, positive affect (PA), and negative affect (NA). This seems a reasonable conjecture to account for the comorbidity observed among the *DSM* mood and anxiety diagnoses (A, D, P, OC, S; see Brown, Chorpita, & Barlow, 1998). To handle this type of specification with structural equation modeling, we can specify no $\mathbf{x}$ variables and $B$ as an identity matrix. The resulting equations

$$\eta = \Gamma\xi + \zeta, \quad\quad \mathbf{y} = \Lambda_y\,\eta + \varepsilon$$

reduce to

$$\mathbf{y} = \Lambda_y(\Gamma\xi + \zeta) + \varepsilon,$$

that is, a second order factor analysis model allowing a higher order structure for the anxiety and mood disorders to be tested.

In examining factor structures via measurement modeling, we are interested in assessing how well our a priori structure was reflected in the data. That assessment is termed fit. Two types of fit indexes are distinguished *absolute fit* and *relative fit*. Absolute indexes are functions of the discrepancies between the variance of the specified model and the variance in the sample data. Relative indexes compare a function of the discrepancies from a specified model to a function of discrepancies from the null model (i.e., all variables uncorrelated). A large number of fit indexes have been developed, each of which is designed to reflect the amount by which a model reduces the covariance among items in a set of observed (or item-level) data by describing the results in terms of the factors or constructs instead of describing the results in terms of the individual items. Thus, a fit index of 0.90 suggests that a hypothesized model has reduced covariance by approximately 90%.

In recent years, fit indexes have been developed to allow for model comparisons, assessment of parsimony, as well as covariance reduction. Like structural equation modeling in general, a full discussion of fit indexes is impossible to cover within this chapter. However, Medsker, Williams, and Holahan (1995) recommended the Comparative Fit Index (CFI; Bentler, 1995) as one of the best indicators of fit and should be reported in conjunction with the root mean square error of approximation (RMSEA; Browne & Cudeck, 1993). Based on a review of 41 studies reporting structural equation models, McDonald and Ho (2002) suggested the Goodness of Fit Index (GFI; Jöreskog & Sörbom, 1989), the Comparative Fit Index and the Unbiased Relative Fit Index (CFI, URFI; Bentler, 1990), and the root mean square error of approximation (RMSEA; Browne & Cudeck, 1993) for inclusion in reports of the assessment of model fit.

What does the testing of a structural equation model mean in terms of construct validation? Structural equation modeling provides a method of testing whether various sources of data (cf. self-report and observer) are related to one another, as well as whether various constructs are independent or interrelated. In a nutshell, the structural equation model represents the measures and the interrelationships among the latent constructs represented by the measures employed in any study. A structural equation model supported by a fit index exceeding 0.90 provides evidence that multiple measures, whether by source or method measuring the same construct, are related to one another. Thus, the measures that meet a conservative criteria such as 0.90 provide evidence of construct validity.

## Other Forms of Scale Validation

It is often inexpensive to collect some additional data to estimate the instrument's concurrent and construct validity as a screening instrument. This can be done by first identifying variables that ought to be related to (i.e., predict) the instrument's factor scores (scores derived from the factor analysis). Then a set of multivariate regression or analysis of variance equations are developed to estimate whether relationships that ought to exist do so. Variables often used in such validation analyses for populations of persons with a severe mental illness are: (a) prior psychiatric history (e.g., hospitalizations, number of episodes per year), (b) major diagnosis (e.g., schizophrenic versus nonschizophrenic, with or without a dual diagnosis of substance abuse), (c) employment (or school attendance) history, (4) scores on known measures (e.g., Beck Depression Inventory, SCL–90–R, State–Trait Anxiety Inventory, MMPI–2, current Global Assessment of Functioning), and (e) social support (yes–no, number of contacts per week or month, or number of housing moves over the last 6 or 12 months). In the present context, these variables are referred to as predictor variables, that is, variables that the literature indicates should predict differences in scores on the instrument for persons in the target population.

The selection of the prognostic variables must be tailored specifically to the target population and the types of service screening decisions that need to be made. Once selected, the use of multivariate analysis of variance or regression analysis requires the user to identify these variables in a prediction equation. For the present case, the instrument's factor scores should be listed on the left side of the expression, and the predictor variables are listed as a sum on the right:

$$[Y_1, Y_2, \ldots, Y_p] = \text{Constant} + \text{Sum [Predictor Variables]}.$$

We should note that in the true multivariate case, each of the predictor variables is correlated or regressed on the family of measures $Y_1, Y_2, \ldots, Y_p$ via a statistic called a canonical correlation, that is, a correlation between a set of independent variables and a set of dependent variables. The canonical correlation has an interesting clinical interpretation. First, assuming that the set of dependent measures in the multivariate analysis represents a profile of one or more behavioral domains of clinical interest, then the canonical correlation represents a description of the strength of the relationship of that variable with the clinical profiles represented by the set of dependent measures. That knowledge could lead to setting up hypotheses about how the manipulation or control of that predictor might influence outcome as represented by that set of dependent measures. If the predictor is a potential moderator variable, then the interpretation might be one of trying to determine for whom does an intervention (treatment) work best.

Some sets of predictor variables can be considered as main effects, and some are best considered as a first-order interaction. For example, *DSM–IV* Axis V (Global Assessment of Functioning) at admission is often a significant effect when considered as a first-order interaction with either current social support or prior psychiatric history on multiple factored scales for the seriously mentally ill (Newman, Griffin, Black, & Page, 1989; Newman, Tippett, & Johnson, 1992). Thus, the expression for this example would be

$$[Y_1, Y_2, \ldots, Y_p] = \text{Constant} + \text{Axis V} + \text{Prior Hospitalization}$$

$$+ \text{Axis V}^* \text{Prior Hospitalization}.$$

To do this for a community-based sample, ordinal classes of Axis V scores (1–35, 35–50, 51–65, 65+) and Prior Hospitalization (none last 12 months, once, more than two) were created to produce a sufficient number of participants within each combination (cell) of the interaction. (Newman et al., 1992). For the mixed nursing home and community-based sample, the ordinal classes on Axis V were more detailed at the lower end: 1–25, 26–40, 41–60, 61+ (Newman et al., 1989).

## One Application of Reliable Instruments: Discriminant Analysis

The focus here is on how well the instrument's scoring procedures, often expressed as factor scores, will lead to correctly placing a client into an appropriate service modality or program. The key questions here are: How does one define a correct placement? What is meant by an appropriate service modality or program? There have been two general approaches to answering these questions. One is to contrast the recommendations or predictions made by the instrument with the placement recommendations of an experienced group of clinicians.

Suppose we wish to evaluate a scale with $p$ factors in terms of how likely it will correctly place a person in the appropriate service modality. For a scale that discriminates well, a discriminant score, $D_i$, can be estimated for an individual from the scale's $p$ factor scores, $X_j$ ($j = 1, 2, \ldots, p$), where the value of $D_i$ implies a recommendation of the most appropriate service modality placement. The computation of $D_i$ for the $i$th person is the sum of each of that person's factor scores, $X_{ij}$, weighted by the factor's coefficient, $_j$. Thus

$$D_i = \beta_0 + \beta_1 X_{i1} + \beta_2 X_{i2} + \cdots + \beta_j X_{ij} + \cdots + \beta_p X_{ip}.$$

To determine which service modality group assignment, k, is most appropriate, a Bayesian rule is applied that gives the probability of each group assignment for a given value of $D_i$. In a discriminant analysis, the probability for each group assignment, $G_k$, is computed for each value of $D_i$, and the group with the highest probability, relative to the other possible group assignments, is labeled the appropriate service modality. The specific expression of Baysian's rule for estimating the probability of an assignment to the $G_k$ service modality group for the $i$th person is

$$P(G_k D_i) = \frac{(D_i G_k) \cdot P(G_k)}{\Sigma P(D_i G_k) \cdot P(G_k)}.$$

The second approach to validating the use of the instrument's factor structure (and the discriminant function analysis results) in service modality placement is to estimate the relationships between the test scores, the program of services, and client outcome. If the relationship between service program and outcome is improved by knowing the screening test results, then the instrument can be viewed as beneficial in the screening and treatment planning process. Collecting data for this approach takes considerable time. Thus, the discriminant analysis is best applied first. However, because successful outcome is considered to be the gold standard, the second approach should be planned and conducted as a long-term evaluation of a screening instrument's worth.

### Linking Levels of Need to Care: Cluster Analysis

Another approach can be employed when using a multidimensional instrument to recommend a more complex array of treatments and services, (e.g., services for persons with a serious and persistent mental illness). If an instrument has an internally consistent factor structure, then a cluster analysis technique can be employed to identify a mix of consumers with similar factor scores that are likely to have similar treatment and service resource needs (Newman et al., 1989; Uehara, Smukler, & Newman, 1994).

The approach uses one or more panels of experienced clinicians in a structured group decision process to identify a treatment plan for a person who is described as having a given level of problem severity or functioning within one of the factors. For example, the panel might be given the following description of a person with a moderate level of depression:

Signs of depression—Encompass: insomnia–hypersomnia, low energy–fatigue; decreased productivity, concentration; loss of interest in usual activities and in sex; tearfulness and brooding.

TABLE 9.1
Schemata of the Data Matrix Used in the Cluster Analysis

| | Factor 1 | | | Factor 2 | | | — | Factor 3 | | |
|---|---|---|---|---|---|---|---|---|---|---|
| | Minimal | Moderate | Severe | Minimal | Moderate | Severe | — | Minimal | Moderate | Severe |
| Severe 1 | $xx | $xx | $xx | $xx | $xx | $xx | — | $xx | $xx | $xx |
| Service 2 | $xx | $xx | $xx | $xx | $xx | $xx | — | $xx | $xx | $xx |
| | | | | | | | — | | | |
| | | | | | | | — | | | |
| | | | | | | | — | | | |
| Service 31 | $xx | $xx | $xx | $xx | $xx | $xx | — | $xx | $xx | $xx |

Moderate—The signs are less severe than intense (the previous task considered an intense level of depression) and will often, after a few days or weeks, shift to either periods of normal behavior or moderate manic levels. Because the severity and duration of the signs are less than severe, the person is generally more cooperative with therapeutic efforts but will seldom seek out the assistance himself or herself.

The panel is provided a list of available services and the professional disciplines of those who could provide each service. Using nominal groups procedures, the panel is then asked to indicate which services would be provided for the next 90 days, by whom, how often, and with what duration (e.g., 1 hour per day, week, month or 90 days). In the study by Newman et al. (1989) of nursing home and community care in Utah, 31 services were available. The panels developed an array of services for each of three problem intensities within each of eleven factors: psychotic signs, confusion, depression with suicide ideation, agitated–disruptive behavior, inappropriate social behavior, dangerousness–victimization, personal appearance, community functioning capability, social–interpersonal adaptability, activities of daily living, and medical–physical. This exercise led to 33 treatment-service plans.

The final step in linking level of need to level of care is to cluster together those treatment-service plans that require similar resources (mostly professional personnel) for similar amounts of time. To perform a clustering of similar treatment plans within the total of 33 treatment plans, a common measure of therapeutic effort was developed based on the costs of each unit of service recommended in each of the 33 treatment plans. The employment costs of the professional(s) in a given service was estimated by the usual accounting procedures based on the salaries of who did what, with what resources, how frequently, and for what duration. To complete the cluster analysis, a matrix of service costs for each of the 33 combinations of factor-intensity by service was set. The matrix is shown in Table 9.1.

The statistical cluster analysis that was used here sorts through the columns of the matrix and clustered those columns that have the smallest adjacent cell differences (distances). The various statistical software packages permit the user to employ any one of a number of rules for assessing the distances between the cell entries in adjacent columns. In the Utah study, we employed a Euclidian measure of distance contrasting differences between the costs of the service of adjacent cells in a pair of columns, Distance $(X, Y) = v[(X_i - Y_i)^2]$, where i = 1, 2,..., 31 services. We found that the 33 columns of 31 service-cost cell entries formed six clusters. In other words, there were six patterns (clusters) of services that could be considered together as program modalities to provide coverage for all of the consumers sampled. Stated another way, the services listed under a cluster had similar staffing and scheduling requirements for consumers with a given set of characteristics. Most important, the relationship between the consumers characteristics' and the proposed services could be described by the application of these procedures.

## Closing Thoughts on Evaluating Measures

The well-known influences of initial impressions, when documented by a psychological assessment technique, can be a wonderful asset or an expensive liability. Unless the consumer chooses to terminate treatment, and many do, the initial course of treatment typically persists without major modification for months and often years. Using an assessment technique to screen and to plan treatment is a social commitment by the clinician(s) and those who pay for the service. The strengths, problems, and goals identified with the support of the assessment should guide treatment. We conduct reliability and validity studies on the instrument so that there are hard data to support the decision to influence the life of another person, the client, and to use the clinical and economic resources needed in doing so.

A theme that runs through the first part of this chapter is that there are methods to determine if an instrument is effectively doing the job. Even if there are studies in the published literature that demonstrate the instrument's reliability and validity, it is desirable to perform studies on its local application. An additional theme is that some of these methods can be used as the basis for staff training and development, as well as an empirical basis for utilization and quality assurance review. Thus, the statistical procedures described here can be useful in the internal evaluation of a program's quality, as well as in studies of the instrument's application.

It might be informative to consider a brief example of an internal evaluation study on the consistency of clinical communication in a program serving persons with a severe mental illness. Consistent communication across members of a treatment-service team is considered to be important in supporting this population of consumers. Suppose that it is found that the interrater reliability among members of the service team is low on an instrument that has been demonstrated to be reliable and valid for this population under well-controlled conditions. In this case, one might suspect that members of the service staff have different frames of references when describing a consumer's functioning. If such differences (inconsistencies) exist and go undetected, then the team members will treat the consumer differently based on their different frames of reference. Because consistency is vital to successful outcome in mental health service planning and delivery, inconsistent communication will probably lead to a breakdown in the quality of care.

## PROGRESS AND OUTCOME

The section began with a description of four assumptions about defining treatment progress and outcome goals that need to be addressed prior to selecting a statistical procedure for assessing questions regarding client progress and outcome. The remainder of the chapter focuses on a sequence of six clinical service questions that set the stage for selecting statistical questions. Recommendations for selecting a statistical procedure are given under each of the six questions: (1) Did change occur, by how much, and was it sustained? (2) For whom did it work best? (3) What was the nature of the change? (4) What effort (dose) was expended? (5) Did the state(s) or level(s) of functioning stabilize? (6) What occurred during the process?

## Specifying Treatment-Service Goals

The selection of a statistical approach to describe treatment progress or outcome should depend on the anticipated goal(s) of treatment. There are four assumptions that must be explicit when specifying a treatment goal and selecting a statistical approach. The first is that the consumers (clients, patients) are initially at a clinically unsatisfactory psychological state, level of functioning, or both, and that there is a reasonable probability of change or at least stabilization by a given therapeutic intervention. Second, an agreed on satisfactory psychological state or level of functioning, observably different from the initial state, can be defined for that individual or for that clinical population. Third, it is assumed that a measure, scale, or instrument is available that can reliably and validly describe the status of the person in that target population at any designated time. The fourth assumption is that "ceiling" and "floor" effects do not limit the instrument's score(s) distribution in the specification of satisfactory or unsatisfactory psychological states or levels of functioning.

If each of the assumptions is met, then specifying treatment goals and selecting the statistical approach to estimate the relative effectiveness of client progress or outcome as described in the specific goals can proceed. To support this approach, the remainder of this chapter organizes the discussion of the statistical procedures around the six generic questions regarding the achievement of specific treatment goal(s) for specific therapeutic intervention(s). The six questions and related statistical approaches are ordered from a macro level to a micro level of investigation. This is done to give a context for determining what should be studied and how the data should be analyzed.

A statistical procedure must fit the context of the question being asked. The statistical literature has a rich history of controversy and discussion on which aspects of change should be investigated and how each aspect should be analyzed (Collins & Horn, 1991; Cronbach & Furby, 1970; Francis, Fletcher, Strubing, Davidson, & Thompson, 1991; Lord, 1963; Rogosa, Bryant, & Zimbowski, 1982; Rogosa & Willett, 1983, 1985; Willett, 1988; Willett & Sayer, 1994; Zimmerman & Williams, 1982a, 1982b). Historical controversies can be avoided by carefully articulating the research or evaluation question. The criterion for a well-developed question is that it frames the appropriate unit and level of analysis relevant to the question. To use the following section, the reader should first formulate an initial draft of the question(s) and the unit of analysis. Next, the investigator should check that the four assumptions (previously discussed) have been made explicit, modifying the question(s) if necessary. Then the investigator can match his or her research question(s) to those given below and consider the recommendations offered. Although there is no "perfect" method, the discussion should provide the reader with guidelines for identifying the best method for the situation.

## Question 1: Did Change Occur, By How Much, and Was It Sustained?

Did specific domains of consumer functioning or states change by the end of therapy, by how much, and were the changes sustained over time? This is often considered to be the first question that those developing a therapeutic innovation seek to address: Does the therapy make a difference? There are two general approaches that have been employed when addressing this question. One is to investigate the magnitude of the difference between the pretreatment and the posttreatment scores on the selected measure across participants. The second is to contrast the trends on the status measures taken on participants over time (pre-, during, post-, and following treatment). Each approach has its strengths and limitations, but they both have the potential to provide a gross estimation as to whether the therapeutic intervention makes a difference.

*Difference Scores.*  The difference score, $D_i$ is often considered the most basic unit of analysis, with $D_i = (X_{i1} - X_{i2})$, where $X_{i1}$ and $X_{i2}$ are the observations recorded at Time 1 (usually prior to treatment) and at Time 2 (usually at the end of treatment) for the *i*th person. The mean values of $D_i$ can be contrasted between groups or within a single group against an expected outcome of no difference ($D = 0.0$, or an equal number of positive and negative values of D). There are two issues to be addressed here. One is to decide whether to use $D_i$ as the basic unit of analysis. The second is the research design used to address the question.

There is an extensive and controversial literature on whether to use $D_i$. Discussion has focused on two features of $D_i$: (1) The reliability of the difference score is inversely related to the correlation between the pre- and posttreatment measures and (2) the potential for a correlation between initial (pretreatment) status and the magnitude of the difference score. The potential bias introduced by these two features led Cronbach and Furby (1970) to recommend that the difference score not be used at all. They recommend that researchers instead concentrate on between-group outcome, posttreatment measures. Others have argued for the use of alternatives such as a residualized gain score, where the difference score is adjusted for initial, pretest differences (Webster & Bereiter, 1963).

There is, however, an opposing point of view. Rogosa, Bryant, and Zimowski (1982), Rogosa and Willett (1983, 1985), Willett (1988, 1989), and Zimmerman and Williams (1982a, 1982b) have collectively developed arguments with sufficient empirical support to conclude that difference scores were being damned for the wrong reasons. These authors also provide strong evidence that some of the most popular solutions (e.g., the residual gain score) have worse side effects than the problems they sought to solve.

The potential inverse relationship between the reliability of D and the correlation between pre- and posttreatment scores is not necessarily a problem. The difference score is an unbiased estimator of change (a process), and scores at each of the other times (pre- and post-) are estimators of status (not a process) at those two respective times. When there is low reliability in $D$, it is to be interpreted as no consistent change. But as Zimmerman and Williams (1982a) showed, it is possible for the reliability of the difference score to exceed the reliability of the pretreatment score or the reliability of the posttreatment score. When this occurs, one may still validly conclude that there is reliable change for persons even though there were unreliable measures obtained at Time 1 and Time 2. Although there is a problem of measurement error at each of these times, one can still conclude that there is a consistent change (a reliable process) among the inconsistent measures of status at each time.

The second problem regarding $D_i$ pertains to the correlation between the magnitude of a difference score and the value of the pretreatment score. It is intuitively obvious that a person with a low pretreatment score, indicative of more severe psychological maladjustment, would appear to have a greater probability of obtaining a higher score on the second occasion (posttreatment). Despite this obvious relationship, Rogosa and Willett (1983) have shown that there is a "negative bias" in the estimate of the correlation between the initial score and the difference score. Negative bias must not be misinterpreted as a negative correlation (Francis et al., 1991). Rogosa and Willett (1983) have amply demonstrated that a raw difference score is not the best statistic for estimating the correlation between initial status and change.

A number of texts recommend using a residual gain score to estimate the differences. The residual gain score is calculated by adjusting the difference score by the correlation between initial level and either the posttest score or the difference score. However, we join Rogosa and Willett (1985) and Francis et al. (1991) in recommending that the residual gain score is a poor choice and should be avoided. There are two critical flaws with using the residual gain score. First, when used in the context of clinical practice, it describes a state of affairs that does not exist in reality (adjusting participants to be at the same initial level, which is seldom, if ever, true). Second, it adjusts a measure of change (a process measure) with a status measure (pretreatment scores). The resulting statistic is no longer an unbiased measure of the change process, because it was adjusted by a measure of status, which contains its own unique sources of errors.

Should one use a difference score? The answer is yes, especially in the presence of a valid, reliable instrument, and if the research question is simply stated, "Is there change related to treatment?" Unfortunately, the issues related to a treatment intervention are often more complex. At a minimum, the investigator typically questions the treatment's differential effects with regard to one or more consumer characteristics over the course of treatment. Recently, investigators have become interested in the sustenance of the change after treatment has formally stopped. Some of these concerns can be assessed at the level of the first question: Did change occur, by how much, and did it sustain? In these instances, the issues when addressing these refined questions pertain to design: What groups need to be contrasted? When does one need to sample consumer behaviors? In other instances, the refined question requires going to another level of focus.

*Comparing Trends in Status Measures Over Time.* For those question refinements that can still be articulated as "Did change occur, by how much, and did it sustain?" issues of design and sampling time frames need to be identified. One design issue that can be easily dealt with is whether a Solomon four-group design is required in the evaluation of a therapeutic intervention. The Soloman four-group design attempts to control for or estimate the effects of carryover from pretest to posttest. Half of the participants in the treatment group and half of the participants in the control group are randomly assigned to a "no pretreatment" test condition, and half to both a pre- and a posttreatment test condition.

The carryover effects of testing that are estimated via a Solomon four-group design may not be a factor in most treatment research. Most consumers that enter therapy are not naive as to what their problems are, nor are they naive as to the general purpose of the intervention. This is particularly common in the experience of those working with persons with a severe mental illness or with those who are substance abusers. Moreover, work by Saunders (1991) has clearly shown that the majority of those who have entered psychotherapy and go beyond two sessions had prior experience with at least the intake process for psychotherapy. Given this, serious researchers studying a particular therapy or therapies should, if the opportunity presents itself, run a pilot study with a Solomon four-group design to assure themselves that such carryover effects are not a significant source of variance.

There are two remaining design issues: (1) What groups ought to be sampled? and (2) When does one collect data? The quick answer to the first is to sample those groups that satisfy the question and eliminate alternative explanations. As discussed earlier, it is best to partition consumers by levels of any characteristic that are expected to modify the impact of the treatment. Enough has been written about the difficulty of interpreting single-group results that most researchers will understand the need to develop either a "waiting-list" control or a "treatment as usual" control to contrast with an innovative treatment.

The quick answer to the second question on how often to collect data is: If possible, collect data two or more times during treatment and two or more times after treatment. An optimal minimum is to collect data at four times: pretreatment, halfway through treatment, posttreatment and at least once in follow-up (e.g., 6 months following treatment termination). In this case, the inclusion of a fifth time point, say 1 year following treatment, allows for the testing of the stability of posttreatment effects. Of further concern is how stable is the characteristic being measured? If the behavior fluctuates daily and the assessment is conducted every 3 months, the frequency and intensity of change will be overlooked.

A typical design here would be a mixed between-group repeated-measures design with two between-group variables (treatment variable and an initial consumer characteristic identified as a "moderator" variable, $k$) and one within-group (time) variable of two, three, or four levels. Here, an analysis of variance or multivariate analysis of variance of the linear and quadratic trends can describe between-group differences in the direction and rates of change over time. Between-group contrasts of the linear trends within each group offers a test of whether direction and magnitudes of change vary as a function of groups. Between-group contrasts of the quadratic trends within each group would describe whether there are significant differences among groups in how their initial changes were modified over time. For the analysis of functional status over the three times from pretreatment, midtreatment to immediately posttreatment, the between-group contrast of quadratic trends would describe the course of change over the course of treatment. When considering the changes between pretreatment and follow-up, evidence of regressive or sustenance trends could be tested. The functional form of the trend is dependent on the nature of change. Usually, this can be described by linear, quadratic, or cubic functions and rarely requires higher order terms.

As was true of other forms of univariate and multivariate analysis of variance, the standard statistical packages have programs that can perform these analyses. One problem with these forms of analysis is that they do not tolerate missing data. They discard all participants with data missing at any one point in time. But if the research questions are at the macro level of group trends and effects, these designs will be adequate. From experience, most investigators using these designs are initially satisfied, but then wish to understand some of the differences among participants within the groups. Here, the analysis of variance methods are limited and the more micro-level questions discussed later are found to be more satisfying.

In recent years, random regression models have increasingly dominated the way in which change is described and analyzed. Random regression models defines the set of general statistical models that allow for change to be modeled over time such that individual trajectories are compared to one another, and then groupings of individual participant trajectories by a fixed characteristic (e.g., participants in different treatment groups) are compared for statistical differences in the trajectories among the treatment groups. The more common of random regression models seen in the literature are hierarchical linear models (HLM; Raudenbush, Bryk, Cheong, & Congdon, 2000; Raudenbush & Bryk, 2002). HLM has found success in the outcomes literature because of its ability to model individual and group trajectories and relate these to important clinical questions.

Hierarchical linear models are so named because of the hierarchical structure of data required for analyses. In our present scope of mental health outcome, we can consider one typical hierarchical nesting structure occurring in our studies. Specifically, repeated measures of a symptom are nested within individuals and individuals nested within groups (such as treatment versus no treatment, or innovative treatment versus treatment as usual). We begin our discussion of HLM here in a limited scope by examining the question of whether changed occurred. We return to HLM later using its full application in Question 3: What was the nature of the change?

HLM provides for statistical analyses very similar to a repeated-measures analysis of variance. However, HLM moves beyond analysis of variance (ANOVA)-based models by relieving the necessary restrictions these models place on data. ANOVA-based models require that time points be unvarying when data are collected. Therefore, data collected from participants at 6 months postadmission result in a hard-and-fast rule of a 6-month interval that must be applied throughout the study. However, psychotherapy, as an example, rarely follows a clean delineation of time. Termination from psychotherapy varies and is thus difficult to characterize as simply X months after admission. For the sake of analysis, the involvement of data collected at termination in a series of data collection time points is not immediately possible because of the ANOVA restrictions.

Another situation where HLM provides advantages over ANOVA-based techniques involves missing data. Missing observations have serious impact on ANOVA-based techniques. The result of a single missing observation is the listwise (complete) deletion of the case. Radical loss of power can result when observations are missing at a single time point even if data at subsequent time points are present. Because HLM extrapolates trends based on available observations, missing data does not result in a harsh elimination of observations. Rather, whatever data is available is used in the estimation of the group's change. Thus, data points are recovered in HLM when cases are lost because of any form of attrition and power retained (for a through review of power in HLM, particularly as applied to clinical trials, see Raudenbush & Liu, 2000).

A broader discussion of rates of change is forthcoming the Question 3 below; however, several recommendations and considerations about HLM and ANOVA-based techniques are important to consider at this stage of discussion. First, HLM offers the advantage of allowing for time points that vary across participants. This is only relevant when more that two time points have justifiable differences in terms of time. However, the advantages of HLM over two, and even three, time points is not defensibly superior to ANOVA-based techniques such that they warrant one to conclude that either is better. Beyond the fact that they have served as an historical bedrock, ANOVA-based techniques are rudimentary in describing whether change occurred—the point of Question 1. HLM, too, will describe whether two groups differed significantly from one another over two time points. The advantages of HLM are not immediately apparent until three more time points are included in the analyses. Then, HLM can answer important questions about trajectories and the nature of change that can only be described in a very rudimentary fashion with ANOVA-based techniques.

## Question 2: For Whom Did It Work Best?

What were the characteristics that differentiated those who did achieve a satisfactory state or level from those who did not?

There are two levels of discussion required of the question, "For whom did it work best?" The first is a review of the historical issues and findings of clinical investigations on the interactions between consumer characteristic and treatment. This will conclude with recommendations focusing on how a treatment's theory can be used to identify design variables and classes of consumer variables that may interact with and impact on the outcome of treatment. The second level of discussion focuses on analytic methods that follow from how one develops the design. The study's design, of course, would follow from its theoretical rationale.

When investigating the relationship(s) between initial status and change, the research question should be refined to focus on the consumer characteristic that predicts different rates of change. The refined question considers the characteristic related to initial status as a moderator variable (i.e., that client attribute that alters the effects of the treatment variable). In other words, individuals in one category of a moderator variable experience a different outcome than individuals in other categories of the moderator variable. The logic here focuses on the interaction between the moderator variable and the treatment variable. For the simplest case, the values of $D_{ijk}$ would be predicted by the consumer's initial level on that the characteristic, $\beta_k$, to moderate the potential impact of the treatment, $\alpha_j$, and this influence will be observed as an interaction effect, $\alpha\beta_{jk}$. This conceptualization results in an expression that can then be evaluated by either a regression or analysis of variance using the standard statistical computer packages:

$$D_{ijk} = \text{constant} + \alpha_j + \beta_k + \alpha\beta_{jk} + \varepsilon_{ijk}.$$

There is a strong logical argument for incorporating a well-conceived consumer characteristic as a moderator variable in most therapeutic intervention studies. The field has long claimed that individual therapeutic approaches are not all things to all people. But it is also becoming apparent that we need to refine the next question.

*For Whom Did the Therapy Work More Effectively?* A consumer characteristic moderator variable is just that: a variable that potentially moderates the degree to which the therapeutic intervention will have impact because of a characteristic brought into therapy by the consumer. One could also argue that if the theoretical construct underlying the therapeutic intervention is adequately developed, the moderator variable(s) should be easily identified. It is also possible that the variable might be a "mediating" variable rather than a "moderating" variable. Here a "mediating" variable is one whose refinement, presence, or absence in the design is required for the therapeutic intervention to be observed. Shadish and Sweeney (1991) showed that effect sizes in psychotherapy studies were directly related to moderator variables such as the outcome measure selected, standardization of the therapeutic interventions, and setting in which study is conducted.

By incorporating an appropriate consumer characteristic as a moderator variable in the research design, the investigator will be able to obtain estimates of relationships that can then be employed in a testable structural equation describing how the various variables come together to produce a therapeutic outcome.

*Client–Treatment Interaction.* The client–treatment interaction literature is mixed. Significant interactions of client characteristics and treatment approaches, particularly within the psychotherapy interventions, are typically not found (Garfield, 1986; Shadish & Sweeney, 1991; Shoham-Salomon, 1991). A similar situation exists in educational research regarding student aptitude by instructional technique interactions (Cronbach & Snow, 1977; Snow, 1991). This has fascinated and puzzled investigators for some time, and a number of logical explanations have been offered, often at odds with each other. Smith and Sechrest (1991) have questioned whether such interactions exist. Beutler (1991) argued that there are a number of significant examples with important theoretical impact, albeit few, to recommend continuing development of research techniques that can bring the nature of these interactions to the surface .

Across critics and defenders of investigating the client characteristic by treatment interaction, there appears to be agreement on the issues that need to be addressed if such research is to be done. All agree that better theory development is needed, where the investigator ought to articulate the answers to several questions: Which consumer characteristics will moderate differential outcome and why? Which behavioral progress or outcome measures are sufficiently sensitive to detect the interaction effects? What courses or rates of change are expected among the client-by-treatment groups and why?

The studies that are the exceptions (i.e., those showing significant interactions) had selected dependent measures that were directly related to the theory being tested. The dependent measures were of two types. In one type, the investigators selected measures that described client behaviors closely linked to the theory underlying the intervention (e.g., Shadish & Sweeney, 1991; Shoham-Salomon, Avner, & Neeman, 1989).

The second type of study employed measures of effort as the unit of analysis. Howard, Kopta, Krause, and Orlinsky (1986) showed that persons treated for anxiety had different dose-response curves than those treated for depression. Turner, Foa, and Newman (1983) contrasted the costs of follow-up treatment for persons who had successfully completed a flooding treatment for their obsessive-compulsive behaviors but who had different styles of conceptualizing information. The conceptualization styles contrasted were those that used a one-dimensional cognitive style expected of persons with obsessive-compulsive behaviors, and those with a "normal" three-dimensional cognitive style. Although all participants achieved the experimental criteria of successful outcome in terms of their obsessive-compulsive behaviors (e.g., excessive hand washing) as Beutler (1991) might predict, the amount and costs of follow-up psychotherapy over the next 12 months differed between groups. Ironically, most of the participants with a one-dimensional cognitive style sought out additional psychotherapy care focusing on general anxiety over the next 12 months. Those who exhibited the three-dimensional cognitive style typically avoided follow-up mental health (psychotherapy) care. A 12-month follow-up showed that those who engaged in follow-up psychotherapy had lower levels of general anxiety. These results were interpreted as indicating that cognitive style was a mediating variable whose interaction with therapy should be considered in future research.

Newman, Heverly, Rosen, Kopta, and Bedell (1983) analyzed intake, termination, and service cost data on 949 clients in New Jersey community mental health programs. Clients with a history of unstable employment, a history of aggressive behaviors, and an unwillingness to be in treatment (as perceived by the intake clinician) had statistically higher costs of services during the period from intake to discharge. The authors recommend that in the future, research investigators should consider the interaction of any or all of these variables with treatment in research.

A major problem in testing for interaction effects is the fact that tests of interaction effects under traditional analysis of variance and regression techniques have lower power (Jaccard & Wan, 1995). Through the use of simulation studies, these investigators have provided ample demonstration that detecting interactions and moderator effects typically have low power, even when difficulties because of measurement reliability are minimal. When measurement reliability is a problem, issue of power worsened. But there are some alternative techniques emerging. Jaccard and

Wan (1995) found that structural equation approaches are more powerful in detecting such interactions. Even more exciting are the findings by Willett and Sayer (1994), that structural equation modeling can also be employed to test differences in patterns of change among different subgroups within and between treatment groups. Willett and Sayer end their paper with the strong recommendation that "... we *can* measure 'change'—and we *should*" (p. 379).

Several authors (Bryk & Raudenbush, 1987; Lyons & Howard, 1991; Raudenbush & Bryk, 2002; Willett & Sayer, 1994) have described procedures that can be called on to identify when a source of error variance may be covering the interaction of a moderator and a treatment variable that should be investigated in follow-up research. However, as indicated earlier, one alternative explanation for large error variance is measurement (un)reliability (Lyons & Howard, 1991).

In explaining the lack of significant interaction effects, Beutler (1991) also noted that most consumers who are involved in research are typically motivated to achieve a satisfactory psychological or functioning status. The same could be assumed of the treating clinician. Although the beginning and the end points of the treatment may look similar for consumers with different characteristics, the processes for getting to the end point may be different. Beutler (1991) recommended that investigators consider obtaining more data to describe the progress during treatment. The form of analysis should focus on the course and rate of change during the treatment time frame. If this argument is convincing, then the reader should also consider the analyses discussed under the next question, "What is the rate of change?" In fact, the examples discussed in that section did show rates of change that were related to client characteristics (Francis, Fletcher, Strubing, Davidson, & Thompson, 1991; Willett, Ayoub, & Robinson, 1991). Over the next several sections, we explore the various alternatives to assess the question, For whom?

*Regression or Analysis of Variance of "For Whom?"* A number of authors have argued that it is best to use a traditional approach to describe and test for the nature of an interaction (Cronbach, 1987; Rosnow & Rosenthal, 1989). The expression recommended by Rosnow and Rosenthal (1989) to describe an interaction score, $AB_{jk}$, for the $jk$th cell, influenced jointly by the $j$th treatment level and the $k$th level of client characteristic is

$AB_{jk}$ = (Mean $jk$th cell − Grand Mean) − ($A_{jth}$ Row [Treatment] Mean − Grand Mean)

− ($B_{kth}$ Column [Client Characteristic] Mean − Grand Mean).

An analysis of the interaction's significance is simply that of creating an $F$ test of the proportion:

$$F = \frac{[\Sigma_j \Sigma_k (AB_{jk})^2]/(\text{Degrees of Freedom})}{\Sigma_i \Sigma_j \Sigma_k (Y_{ijk} - AB_{jk})^2/(\text{Degrees of Freedom})}.$$

The numerator represents an estimate of the interaction after adjusting for the main effects of treatment and client characteristics. The denominator is an estimate of the error of prediction that is typical (averaged) across combinations of row and column effects. When the ratio is much larger than 1.00, we can assume that the differences among the cell means, after adjusting for main effects, is greater than differences because of measurement error. Thus, the $F$ ratio provides an estimate of whether treatment effects differ in some systematic way over levels of the client characteristic.

There is one worrisome assumption in the analysis of interaction effects. It is technically identified as the *assumption of independence*. This assumption holds that there is no correlation between error of measurement within the cells and any of the three between-group sources of variance: (a) levels of treatment effect, (b) levels of client characteristic, and (c) combinations of treatment by client characteristic. Why is this considered to be important? First, most tests for a significant interaction effect (e.g., the $F$ test given above) are not valid because both the numerator and the denominator terms are influenced in different ways by the relationships between random error and one or more of the independent variables. When this occurs, the statistical tests of the hypotheses will be either positively or negatively biased, depending on the nature of the relationship. A second issue regarding the independence assumption is that the research question needs to be reconsidered given that the existence of such correlations indicate that the interaction is not one of simple mean differences. If one or more correlations are significant, the mean effects are likely to be confounded with one or more of three sources of random error: interactions with item difficulty, error of measurement, or temporal effects.

Myers and Well (1991) recommended a rough rule of thumb to determine when to be concerned about the existence of heterogeneity of variance, which may be related to such correlations (i.e., hetroscedasticity). They recommend creating a ratio of the largest to the smallest within-cell variance (what is sometimes called the $F$–MAX test), and if the ratio is greater than 4:1 for equal $n$ designs and 2:1 for unequal $n$ designs, then there is reason for concern.

Myers and Well (1991) join Kenny (1979) in recommending a direct analysis of scatter plots and the correlations between individual observations and group means. Specifically, one should consider calculating each of three correlations:

$X_{ijk}$ with $A_j$ treatment groups across levels of $B_k$.

$X_{ijk}$ with $B_k$ client characteristics over levels of $A_j$.

$X_{ijk}$ with all levels of $AB_{jk}$.

If the magnitude of a correlation is equal to or greater than 0.2, then one should look at the covariance structure of the treatment and client characteristics with the measures of change.

Hoyle (R. Hoyle, University of Kentucky, personal communication, November 1993) has pointed out that an additional problem in regression with interaction terms is multicollinearity. Frequently, the interaction term will be correlated 0.90 or more with one of the main effect terms. A strategy recommended by Hoyle and others (e.g., Judd & Kenny, 1981) is to center (i.e., subtract the mean from each participant's score) the two main effect terms before creating the interaction term. If there is multivariate normality, centering reduces the correlation between the variables, and the product term to zero. This can be desirable, because high levels of collinearity between the these terms interfere with the computation of the regression (Jaccard & Wan, 1995).

In summary, the use of analysis of variance or regression models are direct methods of testing for an interaction effect. The scarcity of significant treatment by client characteristic interactions suggests that either our theories relating treatment to client characteristic are fuzzy, or that the measurement technique selected is inappropriate, or that the analysis of variance model (with easily violated assumptions) is inadequate. Another possibility is that Smith and Sechrest (1991) were correct when they asked whether there were any significant sources of interaction variance to detect.

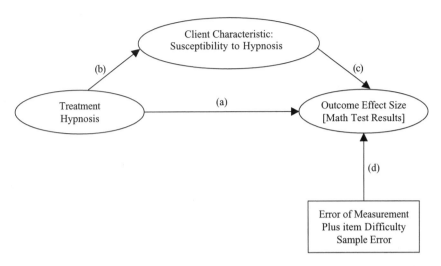

FIG. 9.1. Two paths that could be used to describe relationships between treatment and outcome. A hypothesized example of hypnotherapy focusing on a classroom anxiety and the client characteristic of susceptibility to hypnosis to illustrate the causal model.

*Structural Equations.* Structural equation modeling (*SEM*) represents a method that can describe the magnitude of the relationships among independent variables as antecedent to outcome (i.e., they are either causal to, or mediators of, outcome). Consider the hypothetical example shown in Fig. 9.1, where there are two paths to outcome (effect) from the treatment variable (cause). One path goes directly from the treatment variable to the outcome measure. The strength of this relationship is described by the parameter (a). When estimated, the value of (a) describes the amount of change in outcome that can be predicted by one unit of change in treatment. When treatment is a dichotomous variable (experimental versus control), then the value (a) would be the coefficient that best predicts effect size in a point-biserial regression equation. The coefficient represents the mean difference between groups on the dependent variable. When the treatment variable is ordinal or quantitative (e.g., dosage), then the value of (a) could be the coefficient in a regular regression equation. At this point, one should note that in analysis of variance, and particularly regression, models could be thought of as elementary structural equation models.

The second path to outcome in Fig. 9.1 includes the client characteristic. This route to outcome has two coefficients, (b) and (c). In structural equation analysis, one will often develop a picture of the alternative paths to be considered and then develop and contrast structural equations that predict the relationships for each path. In a formal structural equation analysis, one could contrast the strength of each of the outcome prediction equations developed to represent each of the paths to the outcome variable(s). The critical issue is whether considering the client characteristic enhances the prediction of outcome over the more direct path as described by (a). If the combined relationships of (b) + (c) have greater predictive value of outcome than (a) alone, then the addition of a client characteristic will improve the prediction of outcome for a given treatment level. As outlined by Kenny (1979, p. 44) there are five basic steps in creating a structural model to perform a path analysis:

1. *From theory, draw a set of structural equations that describes relationships among the independent variables (called exogenous variables) and the effect (dependent or endogenous*

*variables).* This step is no different from what has been emphasized throughout this chapter. The prediction of an influential client characteristic must be based on strong theoretical assumptions of how the client characteristic will modify the effects of the treatment on a given set of observable behaviors.

2. *Chose a measurement and design model.* The measures must be directly related to those for whom the treatment is supposed to influence, and the incorporation of these measures into the design model must also be consistent with the theory of the intervention. Here the reader is asked to recall the four assumptions regarding selection of measures for an outcome analysis described at the beginning of the chapter. The design model (true or quasi-experiment) needs to be one that is sufficiently powerful to detect potential differences. Not only does one need to identify groups that will eliminate alternative hypotheses, but also levels of the client characteristics that offer the potential to show differences.

3. *Respecify the structural model to conform to design and measurement specifications.* As is true in any test of a model, the reality of collecting data in the real world takes hold. This step is stated formally to remind the researcher that one can easily commit an error of the third kind: To test a prediction with the wrong statistical model.

4. *Check that there are sufficient numbers of predicted relationships (each called an identification) to test the model.* One of the dangers of using structural modeling is that one can create a model that has more unknowns than one can estimate. The major restriction here is the degrees of freedom in the covariance matrix, where the number of predicted relationships cannot exceed the number of terms identified to covary with each other. It is possible that a study will not produce sufficient information to reach a conclusion about the best model.

5. *Estimate the covariances between the measured variables, and from the covariances, estimate the parameters of the model and test hypotheses.* This is the bottom line where one can decide whether the data support a conclusion that by considering the client characteristic, one enhances the prediction of treatment on outcome.

There are two major limitations of structural modeling. One is that the investigator must be able to develop very specific predictions. The discipline of developing such specific predictions has not been a common practice in clinical research. Thus, its use here will require the researcher to be more explicit in what is being predicted and why. The other is that there must be sufficient data to provide stable estimates of correlations (covariances). This often requires sample sizes in the hundreds rather than those frequently obtained in treatment outcome studies. The reader is referred to the classic texts written on structural modeling (Bentler, 1995; Bollen, 1989; Jöreskog & Sörbom, 1988; Kenny, 1979). Those not familiar with the matrix algebra might find the classic texts by Kenny (1979) or the more recent "how to" test (Byrne, 2001) as the best starting point.

With new advances in technology, structural equation modeling programs such as LISREL, AMOS, and EQS are become increasingly accessible. That accessibility has been translated in increasing ease of use via graphical interfaces that allow for drawings rather than programming code to create models (as in EQS and AMOS). In the history of SEM programs, early versions of LISREL, for example, required the user to learn an arcane programming code consisting of the names of the matrices, numerical values, and few descriptors. Although LISREL continues to read this code, the move toward graphical interfaces is complete, resulting, on the one hand, with

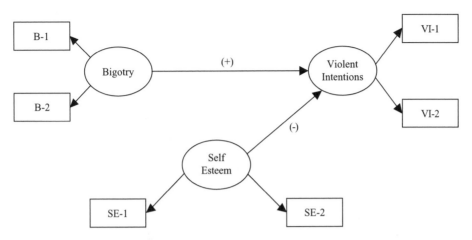

FIG. 9.2. A structural equation model describing the relationship of bigotry and self esteem on violent intentions.

users inexperienced with the mathematics of SEM and, on the other, a broader access and appreciation for the power of the SEM technique.

There is a troubling side to this ease of use. SEM is more than a simple test of parameters generated from covariance matrices resulting in a set of fit indexes. SEM requires that the user develop a theoretical rationale, based on support from the empirical and theoretical literature for the model being tested. Previously, the development of the model required substantial effort on the part of the investigator as computer programming code was generated to represent the predicted relationship. In the present day, that has been replaced by graphical interfaces that allow multiple models to be generated in a single sitting of about an hour. The rapidity at which *SEM* models can be developed places demands on the investigator such that each model developed must be given careful thought, with support from the literature. This is, lamentably, not done as often as it should be (Scandura & Tejeda, 1997).

The latest versions of SEM software permit automatic modification of the model under test such that a reasonable post hoc alternative can be considered. When this happens and the user pursues the model that results from the automatic modification, the confirmatory logic of SEM is lost and the analysis becomes an exploratory analysis rather than confirmatory. It is critical to note that unlike traditional hypothesis testing, SEM provides the opportunity of confirming and falsifying theoretical models. Thus, the construction of models based on automatic modifications obviates the important duty of falsifying existing theories in an effort to improve our understanding of social, psychological, and behavioral processes: the use of automatic modification is simply pure mathematical speculation and solely exploratory.

What degree of attention is warranted by the concerns discussed above? Figure 9.2 provides some results of real data that suggest that the latent variable of bigotry is positively related to the latent variable of violent intentions, and that the latent variable of self-esteem is negatively related to the latent variable of violent intentions. Bigotry, self-esteem, and violent intentions each have two indicators depicted by squares—the convention in SEM. Without entering into detail, the model fit the data quite well, with most fit indexes exceeding 0.95. Figure 9.3 provides the results of automatic modifications that have resulted in fit indexes exceeding 0.99; however, the resulting diagram now includes two new factors and a host of new paths. Whereas Fig. 9.2 provides

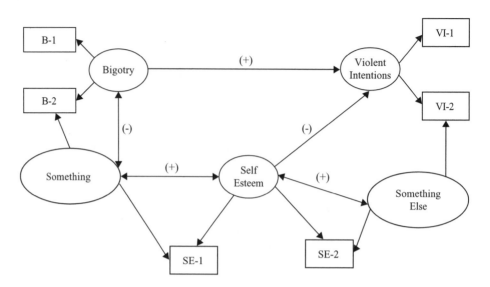

FIG. 9.3. A modified structural equation model recommended by an automatic modification.

an interpretable model, Fig. 9.3 presents a near saturated model of relationships that fails to be parsimonious. Do "Something" and "Something-Else" really add to our understanding of bigotry, self-esteem, and violent intentions? Although this example represents an extreme in the use of automatic modifications, more conservative uses of automatic modification can result in equal gibberish.

Therefore, given that technological changes are inevitable, what recommendations can be made to the use of SEM knowing the concerns just mentioned? First, nothing replaces good theory and careful reflection. The cornerstone of structural equation models must remain careful assertions derived from theory and empirical findings. Second, it is profoundly helpful to construct a graphical representation of any structural equation, including the measurement model. By producing a graphic, hypothesized relationships become very clear. This is exceptionally helpful if the model will be run by another party, such as a statistician. Rival models should be depicted graphically as well. Third, negative findings should result in reflection, as well as publication. Findings that fail to support theory form the basis of the theory's refinement. This refinement should not be driven by mathematics, but rather by careful thought.

## Question 3: What Was the Nature of the Change?

There are several variations on this theme: What was the rate and character of the change? What did or did not change? Are the rates of change consistent within a treatment group? Are the rates of change different among treatment groups? How quickly do individuals or groups of participants achieve a satisfactory level and then stabilize at that level?

The character of the predicted changes is only limited by the constraints of the investigator's questions and the study's design. For most studies, a simple linear change is predicted: What are the rates of change over time? For others, both a linear and a quadratic function are of interest. For example, the investigator could ask whether in addition to potential differences in the rate of change over time, there are differences in how soon the predicted behaviors plateau (i.e., reach an asymptotic level). It is also possible that an investigator will predict three types of change functions over time: first an initial increase, then a plateau, and then a continued increase. This is what is called a *cubic function*. There are two prominent changes in direction. Consider this example: After an initial performance increase because of symptom relief, performance either plateaus or has a slight decline when the client discovers the "tougher problems" (e.g., that they must take some degree of responsibility for managing the factors influencing the problem). Further improvement can only occur when a strategy to deal with the "tougher problems" becomes evident.

As our research question moves from linear to quadratic to cubic predictions, the demands on our study's design increases from at least two waves of data collection (i.e., at two different time points) to three and four waves of data collection. As will be discussed below, most methodologists argue that at least three waves of data collection (pre-, during, and posttreatment) are better than two. But many practitioners might argue that taking repeated measures on a client is intrusive on the clinical process. Another strategy might be to collect pre-, post-, and 6- or 12-month follow-up data. But collecting follow-up data is both costly and often results in more missing data.

There are two general approaches recommended to investigate the nature of change. Each approach has a different emphasis on the character of change and its own assets and liabilities. The traditional approach is a repeated measurement analysis of variance (univariate or multivariate), where between-group linear or curvilinear trends are contrasted among treatment groups (Myers & Well, 1991; O'Brien & Kaiser, 1985). A more recent development is growth curve analysis. This technique can be employed to describe changes in performance (for individuals and for groups) over time as part of an ongoing process (Bryk & Raudenbush, 1987; Francis et al., 1991; Raudenbush & Bryk, 2002; Rogosa & Willett, 1985; Willett, 1989).

The analysis of variance models uses the semantics of, and restricts inferences to, differences among group trends over time, relative to random variances of the trends among participants within the groups. The semantics of growth curve analysis emphasize change as a process. The unit of analysis is the measure of change in the target behaviors over time for each participants. Growth curve analysis can develop hypotheses and describe results in terms of the process of change in individuals' behavior over time, as well as contrast observed change processes among treatment groups.

The starting point for growth curve analysis is to select a growth model (or models) that can be used to estimate the measure of the change process for each individual. Most applications have employed a simple linear or quadratic expression to describe the change process, but almost any mathematical expression can be used to describe the change process (e.g., linear, quadratic, cubic, exponential, Markovian). The major restriction is that there needs to be a theoretical basis for the model.

For the purposes of exposition, discussion will center on predictions of linear change, using an example of treatment of families at risk of maladaptive parenting, child abuse, or neglect (Willett, Ayoub, & Robinson, 1991). These investigators were interested in within-family growth of family functioning (Ayoub & Jacewitz, 1982) over the course of treatment as it related to entry level of family violence or maltreatment. The basic linear model used to describe growth in family functioning (*FF*) for the *i*th family over time, t, in months was

$$FF_{it} = \pi_{0i} + \pi_{1i} + \text{error}_{it}.$$

The term $\pi_{1i}$ is the slope of expression and is the unit of measure of the analysis. When this term is positive, change is in a positive direction, representing increasing levels of family functioning over the months of treatment. The estimation of $_{1i}$ is obtained by using an ordinary least-squares procedure, where the monthly level of family functioning is entered to estimate the slope of the best-fitting straight line. This is easily estimated with any of the standard computer packages (e.g., MINITAB, SAS, SPSS, or SYSTAT). Stable estimates of the slope parameter can be found when measures are taken at three or more different times. Two-point estimations (e.g., pre- and post-treatment) typically do not have sufficient stability. Moreover, as Beutler (1991) has suggested, the course and rate of progress (change) during the time period between the pre- and posttreatment could be where differences because of client characteristics are detected. As we will see, this was the case in the two studies described later.

Once the estimate of the change parameter is obtained ($_{it}$ in this case), it can be entered into its own prediction equation to fit the study design. The study conducted by Willett et al. (1991) focused on describing growth rates as they related to entry levels of family functioning (*FF*), violence or maltreatment (*VM*), and number of distressed parenting problems (*DD*). The between-family linear regression model used to describe the predictive relationship was

$$\pi_{1i} = \beta_0 + \beta_1 FF_i + \beta_2 VM_i + \beta_3 DD_i + \text{error}_i.$$

The investigators found each of these factors to be significant contributors to rates of change in family functioning. For example, the growth rates of families with four or more parenting problems were slower, requiring more treatment to achieve a satisfactory level of family functioning.

Although the example used here focused on a measure of linear change for one treatment intervention, it should be obvious that other measures of change can be estimated as well. For example, Francis et al. (1991) employed a quadratic function predicting the effect of treatment on the level of visual motor impairment ($Y_{it}$) at time t, for head injured children:

$$Y_{it} = \pi_{oi} + a_{it}\pi_{1i} + a_{it}^2\pi_i^2 + \text{error}_{it}.$$

Each participant's slope coefficient, $_{1i}$, and the quadratic coefficient, $\pi_i^2$, is entered into a regression equation with three patient characteristic variables as predictor variables: (a) age at onset of injury, (b) initial severity of injury, and (c) evidence of pupil contraction impairment. Age and initial severity were significant predictors of both the slope and quadratic coefficients. These investigators used an hierarchical linear model (HLM) developed by Bryk and Raudenbush (1987) and a software package for HLM (Raudenbush, Bryk, Cheong, & Congdon, 2000) to test the predictors of the rate coefficients. This software package also provides estimates of the proportions of "true" to "total" variance in rate measures accounted for by the model. In this case, the models developed by Francis et al. (1991) accounted for 79.4% of the variance among the participants' rates of change.

There are several additional advantages of growth curve analysis when contrasted with the traditional trend analysis of variance models. First, the number of repeated measures per subject does not have to be equal, nor does the interval between measures need to be the same. All that is required is a sufficient number of repeated measures to estimate the coefficients of change specified in the prediction model. This is not to say that the investigator does not need to be concerned about how many measures are to be taken or when in the course of treatment the observations are made. Both concerns, along with the structure of the prediction model itself, will influence the precision of the rate measures. If the number and spacing between observations is too haphazard, the precision will deteriorate sufficiently to prevent any significant findings to be detected. However, no data are lost because of minor variations in the number of observations or slight variations in spacing between observations. The HLM computer program does adjust for the degree of precision by considering the number and spacing between observations, when estimating each rate measure and when conducting the test of the prediction equation. Thus, the investigator can inspect the degree to which variation in numbers of observations and spacing has detracted from the estimation of the model's fit to the data.

In summary, each of the two approaches has its uses. The best one is the one that best fits the question raised by the investigator. The investigator, however, ought to experiment with the logic of both forms of analysis (differences in trend versus mean differences in rates). The logic of repeated-measures trend analysis of variance focuses on the average between-group differences in outcome over fixed intervals of time. If measures are taken at more than two intervals, then trend analysis can also test for between-group differences in trends; however, all participants must have an equal number of observations taken at equal intervals. Participants with missing data are discarded from the entire analysis of trends. The growth curve analytical technique changes the focus (and unit) of analysis from the magnitude of a behavioral measure to its direction and rate of change. Growth curve analysis does not require that all participants have the same number of observations or that the spacing between observations be exactly the same, although excessive variation in either will deteriorate the precision and therefore the power to detect significant differences.

### Question 4: What Effort (Dosage) Was Expended?

What was the amount of time or effort expended for a consumer to achieve a "satisfactory" psychological state or level of functioning? Although the issues underlying this question have been proclaimed for some time (Carter & Newman, 1975; Fishman, 1975; Yates, 1980; Yates & Newman, 1980), it was not until the late 1980s that this question began to be recognized as part of a fundamental issue of outcome research (Howard et al., 1986; Newman & Howard, 1986). Recent interest appears to be centered on the economic concern regarding the worth of the investment in mental health care, rather than a scientific concern with how much is enough. The text by Yates (1996) is a wonderful exception. Professor Yates' lead provides a clear description of the steps that are needed for the researcher to understand how to analyze the costs incurred in the therapeutic and material efforts included in the procedures, processes, and outcomes of clinical and human services.

Measures of effort are often easy to develop and are readily available to the researcher if there is a plan to collect the effort data. There are three major classes of effort measures that have served as either predictor or dependent variables in psychotherapy and mental health services research. They are: (a) dosage (i.e., the number of therapeutic events provided over the period of a clinical service episode), (b) the level of treatment restrictiveness (i.e., the use of environmental manipulations to control the person's behavior during the clinical service episode), and (c) the cumulative costs of the resources invested in treatment (i.e., the type of staff, staff time, and material resources consumed during the clinical service episode; Newman & Howard, 1986).

Dosage is the measure most frequently employed when only a single modality is considered (e.g., number of days of inpatient or nursing home treatment). Restrictiveness measures can be developed at a sophisticated or a simple level. Hargreaves and his colleagues (Hargreaves, Gaynor, Ransohoff, & Attkisson, 1984; Ransohoff, Zackary, Gaynor, & Hargreaves, 1982) had panels of clinical experts, employing a magnitude estimation technique, scale the levels of restrictiveness for interventions designed to serve the seriously mentally ill. Newman, Heverly, Rosen, Kopta, and Bedell (1983) used a simpler approach to quantify level of restrictiveness by giving a value of 1 to an outpatient visit, 2 to day treatment, and 3 to inpatient care in the treatment plans proposed by 174 clinicians for a standardized set of 18 cases. To create a dependent measure that combines dosage with restrictiveness of effort, these dosage and restrictiveness scores were cross multiplied. Significant relationships were found between this dependent measure and three predictor variables: (a) levels of functioning at intake, (b) level of social support, and (c) level of cooperativeness at the start of treatment.

A measure of the costs of resources consumed combines the concepts of dosage and restrictiveness, because the costs of staff time and the resources used to exert environmental control during the clinical service episode are summed to calculate the costs. However, the concept of employing costs as an empirical measure of therapeutic effort is still sufficiently new to the field such that there appears to be some misconceptions that inhibit its use in research. Newman and Howard (1986) described the three popular incorrect perceptions.

1. *Confusion of costs with revenues.* Revenues are the monies that come to the service from many different sources (payment of fees charged, grants, gifts, interest on cash in the bank).

2. *Confusion of costs with fees charged.* Fees charged may or may not cover costs of services provided. Profits accrue when fees collected are greater than costs, and deficits accrue when they are less. If all clients have similar diagnoses and problems, if they receive the same type and amount of treatment, and if the fees charged equal the costs of the resources used, then and only then do costs equal fees. However, for mental health programs and for private practice, the costs of the clinical efforts vary across consumers and therapeutic goals.

3. *Confusion of costs and fees in private practice.* This is being recognized as a myth by more and more private practice clinicians. Unfortunately, this myth is being perpetuated by third-party payer reimbursement practices where a single reimbursement rate is being set for a broad spectrum of diagnoses, independent of clients' levels of psychosocial functioning, social circumstances, and therapeutic goals. It is intuitively obvious to most private practice clinicians that not all clients require the same levels of care to achieve a satisfactory psychological or functioning level. It is also obvious that it is more profitable to restrict one's practice to those consumers who can be profitably treated within the limits set by reimbursable fees rather than by the treatment goals achieved. Unprofitable clients might, unfortunately, be referred elsewhere.

There are three statistical approaches that can be usefully applied to measures of effort:

1. *Probit analysis,* focusing on the cumulative proportion of the sample that has achieved a criterion of success (or failure) at each level (dose) of the intervention's events

2. *Log-linear analysis*, using a multidimensional test of independence of two or more variables (each having two or more levels) in predicting two or more classes of outcomes

3. *Univariate and multivariate regression and variance analysis*, focusing on the unique characteristics and limitations of applying these traditional approaches to analyzing effort data.

The shape of the distributions of measures of effort is of some concern. They are typically positively skewed, with as much as 3% to 10% of the participants having effort measures 3 or more standard deviations above the median. The first two approaches are less affected by the precise shape of the distribution of the measure of effort than the last approach. The focus of questions addressed by probit and log-linear analyses is on the relative frequency of observations that fall within given classes or ranges of outcome. The distribution of the measures of effort are more important for univariate and multivariance regression and variance analyses that have the usual assumptions of parametric statistics (e.g., normality, independence between within-group error variance and group assignment).

The difficulty of analyzing extremely skewed distributions is typically dealt with by one of two methods. One is to drop the "outliers," that is, participants with extreme scores (e.g., the top 10% or 20%) from the analysis. Another approach is to transform the values to produce a more normal appearing distribution. The arcsin and the log transformations are two popular transformations. These approaches may have negative consequences of either dropping data that should be considered or transforming the conceptual base to mean something other than it was originally conceptualized to mean. It is the author's experience that investigators will invoke either of these approaches to deal with the statistical issues without considering what the implications are to the clinical aspects.

Although probit and log-linear analyses do not require throwing away data, they use a cumulative probability density function (CDF) transformations of the data (the unit normal distribution , $\Phi$, for the probit and the logistic distribution, $\Lambda$ for the logit) during the analytic process. For the examples we have reviewed, the probit analyses do appear to have preserved the conceptual basis of the studies as they were designed by the investigators.

It also can be argued that both probit and log-linear analyses have their own set of negatives. The principal negative aspect is that relatively large samples are required to assure that observed differences in relative frequencies are stable. With these notes of caution, we now proceed to describe the conceptual basis underlying the applications of each of the three approaches.

*Probit Analysis.*  The basic unit of analysis for a probit analysis is the proportion of participants within a specific group to achieve a satisfactory level of psychological or social functioning after a given dosage of treatment has been provided. Howard et al. (1986, p. 160) described this relationship as "... the amount of treatment [dose] needed to achieve a specific percentage of patient improvement [effect]."

A probit model is created that uses the observed proportions of participants in the $j$th group to achieve a satisfactory outcome at the $i$th dosage level:

$$P_{ij} = A_j + B_j(\log \text{ of dosage} X_{ij}).$$

To estimate the values of $A_j$ and $B_j$ in the model for the $j$th group, the observed values (proportions of participants to achieve a satisfactory criterion at each dosage) are entered into a maximum likelihood procedure. Once estimated for a group, a model is created that generates a function describing the expected relationships between dose and proportions to achieve a satisfactory outcome.

The probit analysis provided in most statistical packages will generate a set of probit values and the estimated standardized proportions of persons expected to achieve a measured satisfactory state or level of functioning for each successive dose level, along with the 95% confidence intervals about each probit value within a given group. Thus, for each group, the analysis provides dosage by success rate functions, along with the envelope of 95% confidence intervals about each function. The extent of nonoverlap between the 95% interval envelopes for two or more groups will describe the statistical significance of between-group differences. Howard et al. (1986) found significantly different dose-effect functions for three diagnostic groups receiving psychotherapy: depression, anxiety, and borderline-psychotic.

There are three major limitations of probit analysis in addressing the question, "How much is enough?" One is that relatively large samples are needed to refine the dosage levels, probably more than 50 participants per treatment group. The second is that only between-group main effects can be tested. However, it is possible to contrast the overlap in the 95% confidence interval across dose levels (or "confidence interval envelop") among any two or more groups. This results in a test of simple effects among groups in a design with two or more between-group variables; therefore, experiment-wise error rates are an important concern and should be controlled (e.g., employing a Bonferroni correction of Type I error rates per comparison). The third limitation is that probit analysis is only applicable to measures of frequency such as the dose–effect relationships. It cannot be applied to measures of intensity such as the restrictiveness or the cumulative cost classes of effort measures. The next two sets of approaches can be used for all three classes of effort measures.

*Log-Linear Analysis of Effort Measures.* The basic unit of measure when applying a log-linear analytic approach is the rank order of the magnitude of the effort measure when considering all participants across all groups. For example, if there are 320 participants in four groups, 80 per group, then the rank-order values on the effort measure can vary from 1 to 320. Once each participant receives his or her rank order score, then any between-group rank order (nonparametric) statistical approach can be applied. Here we will consider the log-linear analysis, because of its ability to consider higher level designs, with at least one treatment and one consumer characteristic variable.

Table 9.2 provides an example of the general form of an analysis that can be considered by log-linear analysis. Consider that we are working with persons who have a serious and persistent mental illness and are entering a community support program. At admission, they are first evaluated for their levels of interpersonal (including communication) skills, along with other characteristics. Half of those who score at a low level of interpersonal skills (Client Group B-1) are randomly assigned to a program that focuses on social and community functioning skills, where the treatment team works out of an office adjacent to a consumer-run drop-in center (Group A-1, B-1). The remaining half of the consumers with low interpersonal skill are assigned to a program whose treatment team interventions focus on symptom control with a case manager who works out of community mental health center (Group A-2, B-1). The same random assignment to Groups A-1 and A-2 are made for those clients scoring at the moderate to high levels of interpersonal skills (i.e., assigned to Groups A-1, B-2 and A-2, B-2, respectively). Thus, in this example, there are two treatment groups

TABLE 9.2

Frequencies of Participants in Each Group for the Successive Quartiles When Ranked by the "Cumulative Costs of the Clinical Service Episode"

| Treatment Group | Client Group | Quartile Ranking of Cumulative Costs of Service Episode | | | |
|---|---|---|---|---|---|
| | | Q-1 Lowest Cost 1st to 25th percentile | Q-2 26th to 50th percentile | Q-3 51st to 75th percentile | Q-4 Highest Cost 76st to 100th percentile |
| A-1, Social rehabilitation treatment team | B-1, low interpersonal skills | $f[111]$ | $f[112]$ | $f[113]$ | $f[114]$ |
| | B-2, moderate to high interpersonal skills | $f[121]$ | $f[122]$ | $f[123]$ | $f[124]$ |
| A-2, symptom control, case manager at CMHC | B-1, low interpersonal skills | $f[211]$ | $f[212]$ | $f[213]$ | $f[214]$ |
| | B-2, moderate to high interpersonal skills | $f[221]$ | $f[222]$ | $f[223]$ | $f[224]$ |
| Sum of columns equals: | | 25% of Total | 25% of Total | 25% of Total | 25% of Total |

*Note:* The cell frequencies are described as $f(ijk)$, for the $i$th quartile, in the $j$th treatment group, and the $k$th level of the client characteristic.

and two levels of a client characteristic (i.e., the moderator variable of entry level of interpersonal skills at low or moderate-high). The client characteristic is expected to interact with the effects of the therapeutic intervention.

The cumulative costs of treatment for each of the 320 consumers can be calculated for the first 6 months of treatment. These include the costs of personnel time and the materials consumed by agency personnel while serving the consumers over her or his first 6 months in the community support program. If cumulative costs of serving these consumers over the 6-month period were independent of either treatment or interpersonal communication skills, then we could expect the 80 participants within each of the four groups to be evenly distributed across the cells of Table 9.2 (i.e., 20 participants per cell). Because the columns represent the four respective quartiles, the columns will always sum to 25% of the sample. Based on the null hypothesis for all effects, there would be 20 consumers in each cell, indicating that the distribution of cumulative service costs are independent of either treatment or client characteristic. The outcome that indicating the most cost-efficient group would be the group-row with the largest observed cell frequencies in the lower quartile cells (Q-1 and Q-2) and the smallest observed cell frequencies in the higher quartile cells (Q-3 and Q-4).

Although the logic here is that of a chi-square test of independence (testing whether row assignments are independent of column outcomes), the multidimensional classification (treatment group–by-client characteristic) nullifies the simple test of independence provided by the ordinary chi-square test. Log-linear analysis can provide a test of a cell frequency's independence of the association with the combinations of column and multiple row classifications that define the cell. As with the classical test of independence (chi-square), observed cell values are contrasted with expected cell values. Given that the cells are embedded in a multivaried classification scheme (three or more classes), the expected cell values need to be adjusted for main and first-order interaction effects.

The mathematical technique employed is to model each cell frequency using a natural log transformation of the observed frequencies. This permits the development of additive rather than exponential models to describe the relationships among classifications. Considering our example, we are interested in testing the independence of each of the two main effects (treatment type and consumer characteristic) and the interaction with quartile ranking of cumulative service costs. We are assessing the likelihood that the magnitude of service costs (level of $Q_i$) is associated with type of treatment ($A_j$), client characteristic ($B_k$), or both. The natural log of the expected cell frequency, $f$, for the $ijk$th cell is

$$f_{ijk} = \ln(f_{ijk}) = +\Omega_{Q-i} + \Omega_{A-j} + \Omega_{B-k} + \Omega_{QA-ij} + \Omega_{QB-ik} + \Omega_{AB-jk} + \Omega_{QAB-ijk}$$

where is the average of all of the natural log frequencies within the table. Each of the omega terms are parameters estimated for each of the marginal effects. Each of the marginal effects is obtained in a fashion similar to a univariate analysis of variance. This can be seen, by example, in computing the parameter for $A_j$, $\Omega_{A-j} = (\mu_j - \mu)$, where $\mu_j$ is the average of the natural log of the cell frequencies contained within $A_j$.

The test statistic for the interaction of costs by treatment (Q by A) would be derived from the ordinary chi-square test for independence

$$0^2 = \sum_i \sum_j \frac{[(\text{Observed } f_{ij}) - (\text{Expected } f_{ij})]^2}{(\text{Expected } f_{ij})},$$

TABLE 9.3
Decisions Possible When Cumulative Costs and Outcome Effectiveness
are Jointly Compared

| | *Cumulative Episode Costs* | | |
| --- | --- | --- | --- |
| *Outcome* | $A < B$ | $A = B$ | $A > B$ |
| A better than B | Choose A | Choose A | No decision |
| A equal to B | Choose A | Choose either | Choose B |
| B better than A | No decision | Choose B | Choose B |

but employing the natural log values, an alternative, and widely used statistic called the likelihood ratio, $L^2$, is computed as

$$L^2 = 2 \sum_i \sum_j f_{ij} \ln \left[ \frac{(\text{Observed } f_{ij})}{(\text{Expected } f_{ij})} \right].$$

Most statistical packages require that the user identify a design describing the interactions of interest and set an hierarchical order to the effects of interest. For our example, the highest order interaction is $Q \times A \times B$, but there are only two other terms of interest: $Q \times A$ and $Q \times B$. As is true of any hierarchal model, if the full (second-order) interaction of $Q \times A \times B$ is significant, then follow-up tests must be contingency tables investigating simple main effects and the interactions. Because the follow-up tests could inflate Type I error, two precautions are recommended. First, plan the follow-up tests in advance, restricting the number of planned comparisons to the degrees of freedom available (three in the example used here). Second, adjust the Type I error level of the follow-up tests to be more conservative using the Bonferroni correction, for example, dividing the Type I error rate used to test the interaction by the number of degrees of freedom: $0.05 \div 3 = 0.017$.

The two major limitations of the log-linear approach are (1) relatively large samples are required to obtain stable results and (2) the analysis leads to conclusions regarding treatment cost efficiency and not cost-effectiveness or benefit. The issue of sample size can sometimes be handled by careful consideration of expected outcomes. As with most chi-square techniques, expected cell frequencies should be greater than or equal to five for the highest order of classification (the ijk*th* cell in the current example). It is possible to establish a model that excludes certain cells from the analysis, provided that the exclusion can be logically defended as to why those cells ought to contain a count approaching zero. This could happen when contrasting a very inexpensive procedure with a very expensive procedure, where the investigator is interested in the middle-level cost values and the interactions with two or more predictor variables. In this case, it is quite possible for the expected cell frequencies for the lowest quartile for the very expensive procedure to have expected values under 5. Most computer packages permit the user to specify the cell structure and the model to be tested. If there is a good rationale for zero frequency cells, then this option should be used in analyzing the data.

The issue that this design only attends to cost efficiency and not cost-effectiveness is best handled by treating this analysis as part of larger analysis, where tests of treatment effectiveness will be considered alongside of the test of treatment costs, as illustrated by Fishman (1975). He used a strategy that considers the results of a treatment effectiveness study along with a cost-efficiency analysis (see Table 9.3).

Fishman recommended a two-dimensional array contrasting the results of the cost study (the columns in the Table 9.3) with the results of the effectiveness study (the rows in Table 9.3). For seven of the nine combinations of dual outcome-cost analyses, an investigator or policy maker would be able to decide on the most cost-effective choice. The issue of the need to consider an outcome (effectiveness) study along with a cost-efficiency study is also to be considered when performing the variance and regression analyses of costs (see the discussion that follows).

*Multivariate and Univariate Regression and Analysis of Variance of Effort Measures.* There are some interesting possibilities when considering regression or variance analysis with cumulative costs, dosage, or restrictiveness measures. One possibility is to use an effort measure alongside progress or outcome measures in a multivariate regression or variance analysis. This would address the research issue of whether the independent (treatment or consumer characteristic) variables produce differences in client outcome profiles alongside of differences in the cumulative costs of serving them. It is obvious that when consumers improve quickly, less long-term effort is needed, and when they are slow to react to treatment and slow to change, more or extended effort is required. Thus, it is defensible to include an effort measure along with the progress or outcome measure in the prediction equation that defines the regression or the variance analysis.

Another possibility is to investigate the covariance structures of effort with consumer characteristics as they relate to outcome in a multiple regression analysis. Here the interaction (covariance) of the level of effort with the level of client characteristic is treated as a predictor variable, and one or more client progress or outcome behavior measures serves as the dependent variable. The specific test is whether the slopes of the regression coefficients on one predictor dimension (e.g., dosage) differ across levels of the other dimension (e.g., initial severity of disorder prior to treatment).

Finally, a major cautionary note regarding positively skewed distributions needs to be restated here. Dropping the data for the outlying top 5% to 20% has been used in many diagnostic-related grouping (DRG) studies and is accepted in some quarters. Others have felt that eliminating data should be avoided and a transformation that will approximate normality should be used instead. Some outliers are so extreme that even accepted transformations (e.g., arcsin, log or natural log) do not sufficiently modify the distribution to be acceptably normal. In these cases, it is often required to drop the drastically extreme cases and do a normalizing transformation as well.

### Question 5: Did the Person's State(s) or Levels of Functioning Stabilize?

Although traditional research and statistical methods are designed to test for differences in behaviors or rates rather than testing for stability, it is possible to evaluate a prediction regarding stabilizing functional behaviors. The key is to carefully develop questions that follow the logic of the treatment goal of stability and to identify and collect the data needed for the corresponding dependent measures. The investigative methods and statistical analysis will follow from well-formulated questions. Below is a presentation of examples of several lines of questions.

*Contrasting Measures of Variations in Behaviors for Specific Periods of Time.* We often ask ourselves, "Did fluctuations per unit of time (day, week, month, year) in psychological state or functioning change (decrease) as a result of the intervention? If so, what was the duration, amount, or rate of this change in variation from an unstable to a stable state within and across groups?" Here, trend or growth curve analysis can be applied, depending on the specification of the dependent measure. Some examples are: Count the number of fluctuations in a target behavior of a given magnitude per unit time; measure the duration of time the person remains within a given range of functioning; or estimate the rate of change from a unstable state to a stable state following a crisis.

*Contrasting Differences in Odds or Probabilities.*   Another example of a question that may be provoked from our results (stated in its formal null form) is, "What are the odds during a given unit of time for no housing or civil crisis to occur for individuals within and across groups?" Here, log-linear analytical approaches could be employed to contrast the outcomes of two or more treatment and/or client groups. As is true of all procedures that analyze relative frequencies or probabilities within and across categories, the definitions of categories or baseline conditions is very important. How does one define a housing or a civil crisis? Two criteria should be reviewed. First, the scheme for categorization identifies individuals as belonging to one and only one group, and to be in one and only one outcome category. Formally, this is the criterion for all events to be mutually exclusive and exhaustive. The second criterion is to assure that assumptions of independence or dependence are logically defensible in terms of the clinical theory.

Still another line of question would follow traditional statistical tests where changes in the magnitude of the behaviors can be contrasted between groups over time: "What is the number of productive employment hours (independent of wages earned) by an individual?" Here, univariate or multivariate analysis of variance or regression analysis can be readily applied. If sample size and precision permits, then structural equation modeling can also be applied. Moreover, the logic of the question could be easily modified to apply growth curve analysis of the rates of change in these magnitude measures.

Thus, for Question 5, the issue is not so much one of what statistics to use, but one of carefully formulating a question (prediction) that can be analyzed. Logical traps that would require acceptance of the null hypothesis to demonstrate the worth of an intervention must be avoided. Predictions of stabilized functioning can be, and should be, tested if they are to be considered as reasonable treatment or service goals. There is a balance required. On the one hand, one does not want to compromise a clinical theory by fashioning a testable question. On the other hand, a good clinical theory ought to be testable. When confronting treatment goals of "stable functioning," most of us have to learn to revise the way we formulate a testable question.

### Question 6: What Occurred During the Process of Treatment?

What characteristics changed during the process of treatment? At what stages in the process did the change occur? How did the changes relate to final outcome characteristics?

*Historical Notes on Process Research and Its Measures.*   To date, most "process" research has been conducted within the content of specific forms of psychotherapy: individual psychotherapy (Orlinsky & Howard, 1986), group psychotherapy (Kaul & Bednar, 1986); and family therapy (Gurman, Kniskern, & Pinsof, 1986). No controlled research has been published outside of the psychotherapy literature. For example, none was found for the treatment team or case management or psychosocial approaches used in treating persons with a serious mental illness.

The focus of the psychotherapy process research has, for the most part, been on the various aspects of the relationship between the therapist and the client or the client's social system (e.g., family). The process measures employed are seldom standardized in the same fashion as the outcome measures discussed (for the most part) in this text. Instead, the process measures focus on the observable behaviors taken from videotapes or transcripts, or from reports by the client or therapist about what occurred during or between the therapeutic interactions.

Although reliability studies are frequently reported on the process measures, the basis for establishing validity of these measures is not clearly understood. Some session report techniques have been extensively studied (e.g., the Orlinsky & Howard "Therapy Session Report," 1975). However, the majority of the techniques reported in the literature were specifically designed for a particular study. Some of the more popular instruments used in recent years are: the Therapy Session Report (Orlinsky & Howard, 1975), Vanderbilt Negative Indicators Scale (Sachs, 1983), Structural Analysis of Social Behavior (Benjamin, Foster, Roberto, & Estroff, 1986), Helping Alliance Scale (Laborsky, Crits-Christoph, Alexander, Margolis, & Cohn, 1983), and Working Alliance Scale (Horwrath & Greenberg, 1988). Others have developed systematic taxonomies for evaluating the content or tone of therapy sessions (Elliot, 1985; Stiles & Shapiro, 1994). Although none have norms that can be applied in the same fashion as those used with traditional psychological testing, each has a record of several published studies showing some degree of significant discriminative validity.

Should process be related to outcome? Orlinsky and Howard (1986) and Silbershatz (1994) have argued strongly that process ought to be related to outcome. Stiles and Shapiro (1994) argued that a true process measure should not be correlated with outcome. It will be left to the reader to decide which side of the argument to take or to join those who still see it as an issue to be empirically settled (Newman, 1994).

Orlinsky and Howard (1986) have offered a fruitful "generic model" that outlines the process-outcome research literature. The review of the literature and refinement of the generic model was updated in 1994 by Orlinsky, Grawe and Parks (1994). The outline presented in the generic model, and the literature cited, is recommended as a good starting point when one seeks to design a study on process-outcome relationships. The *generic model* has five interrelated components describing the therapeutic process:

> (1) The *therapeutic contract* is the purpose, format, terms and limits of the therapeutic enterprise. (2) *Therapeutic interventions* comprises the "business" of helping carried on under the terms of the therapeutic contract. (3) The *therapeutic bond* is an aspect of the relationship that develops between the participants as they perform their respective parts in the therapeutic interventions. (4) *Patient's self-relatedness* refers to the patient's ability to absorb the impact of therapeutic interventions and their therapeutic bond. (5) *Therapeutic realizations*, such as insight, catharsis, discriminative learning, and so on, occur within the session and presumably are productive of changes in the patient's life or personality (Orlinsky et al., 1994).

The areas of process research covered within each of the five areas of process research are well documented in the chapter by Orlinksy et al. (1994). This research literature, for the most part, uses the statistical procedures already covered in this

TABLE 9.4
Interpersonal Interaction-Contingency Matrix (Lower Left 6 × 6 Entries); Intrapersonal
Correlation Matrix for the Client
(Upper triangular array); and Intrapersonal Correlation matrix of the therapist (lower
triangular array).

| | Client Utterances | | | | | | Therapist Utterances | | | |
| | Emotion | | Cognition | | Contract | | Emotion | | Cognition | |
| Variable | 1 (+) | 2 (−) | 3 (+) | 4 (−) | 5 (+) | 6 (−) | 7 (+) | 8 (−) | 9 (+) | 10 (−) |
|---|---|---|---|---|---|---|---|---|---|---|
| Client | | | | | | | | | | |
| 1. + Emotion | — | | | | | | | | | |
| 2. − Emotion | −.39 | — | | | | | | | | |
| 3. + Cognition | .40 | −.17 | — | | | | | | | |
| 4. − Cognition | −.06 | .07 | −.08 | — | | | | | | |
| 5. + Contract | .29 | −.36 | .29 | −.23 | — | | | | | |
| 6. − Contract | −.25 | .41 | −.14 | .18 | −.44 | — | | | | |
| Therapist | | | | | | | | | | |
| 1. + Emotion | .48 | −.23 | −.15 | .12 | −.12 | −.01 | — | | | |
| 2. − Emotion | −.09 | −.01 | .14 | .10 | .02 | .09 | −.30 | — | | |
| 3. + Cognition | −.03 | .17 | −.10 | −.04 | −.34 | −.05 | .19 | −.28 | — | |
| 4. − Cognition | −.10 | .02 | .14 | −.07 | −.07 | −.18 | −.24 | .11 | −.06 | — |
| 5. + Contract | .40 | −.17 | −.20 | −.11 | −.12 | −.22 | .33 | −.44 | .13 | −.28 |
| 6. − Contract | .05 | −.08 | .29 | .10 | −.00 | .07 | −.17 | .46 | −.20 | .12 |

chapter. Thus, no further discussion is needed beyond the recommendation that one can use the generic model to identify one's area of interest in process research and then review the studies they have cited as a guide for designs and statistical models. Having said this, we now turn to one additional approach that was not covered by the literature in the Orlinsky et al. (1994) chapter but nevertheless shows significant promise.

*Interpersonal Interaction Analysis in Therapy.*  Most psychosocial therapies involve the exchange of information and feelings among those involved. The interpersonal interaction process in therapy is not haphazard when done by a professional, but rather is goal directed. Over therapy sessions it should follow a predictable pattern, with understandable variations as a function of the content of the material covered within a therapy session, the stage of the treatment, or both.

The content of a therapy session that is to analyzed is what is said, by whom, and in what context (i.e., within the context of what was said before). During a session, a person (client or therapist) can react to what the other said or to her or his own line of thought from one utterance to another.

Consider a second example as shown in Table 9.4, that was offered by Canfield, Walker, and Brown (1991) as they attempted to describe the interpersonal and the intrapersonal interactions that can take place during a therapy session. The investigators classified all of the words in an utterance by the client and by the therapist according to a whether each word in the utterance represented the degree of positive or negative valance (from +4 to −4) on each of three dimensions: emotional, cognitive, and contract.

Table 9.4 describes the results of this analysis in one therapy session by giving the correlations between pairs of classes of utterances during the verbal interactions between the client and therapist, as well as the correlations of pairs of intrapersonal utterances. The data in Table 9.4 is presented as three correlation matrices. The 36 (6 × 6) entries on the lower left represents the contingent relationships between the client and the therapist. As described by the authors:

> The correlation of .40 between positive emotion and positive cognition in the client's intrapersonal correlation matrix indicates that if a client utterance was rated high in positive emotion, it was likely also to be rated high in positive cognition. Furthermore, the correlation of 0.46 in the therapist's intrapersonal correlation matrix between negative emotion and negative contract indicates that when the therapist utterance was rated high in negative emotion, it was likely to be rated high in contract as well. (Canfield et al., 1991, p. 62).

The major asset of developing the assessment of within-session interactions in this manner is that once the correlation matrix has been developed, then all of the procedures of regression, variance, or path analysis can be applied. Consider some examples: Will the matrices be the same over different stages of the treatment process? Will sessions rated "rough" have a different correlation matrix than "information" sessions? What is the content of sessions that contained a "critical incident" that change the focus of therapy?

It is recommended that the reader focus on the methods rather than on the specific content of the analysis. Other investigators may choose to use different systems for classifying utterances within therapy sessions. The form of the analysis could still be applied to other classification systems. Although the amount of effort to do these forms of analyses is high, it does offer great potential for understanding the basic ingredients of the therapeutic process and their interactions. When, in the not too distant future, the spoken word can be inexpensively digitized onto computer files for analysis, then the applications of these procedures should become as common as outcome studies.

## FINAL COMMENTS

The application of statistical methods to the analysis of data collected to address clinical issues has been traditionally awkward. We are typically taught statistics with examples from the literature. In this chapter, the order was reversed: The clinical issue, along with its theoretical basis and clinical empirical findings, were presented first. Using this base, we then explored the relative merits of various statistical methods that could be applied to data collected to address each clinical issue. The expectation is that if the clinical researcher uses this approach, we may have a better chance of generating studies, with the analysis of the data, that maintain the integrity of the study's clinical issues.

## ACKNOWLEDGMENTS

Thanks are owed to our thoughtful and patient colleagues, Daniel Feaster and Christopher Rice, for their recommendations and comments on drafts of the revised chapter.

## REFERENCES

Ayoub, C., & Jacewitz, J. (1982). Families at risk of poor parenting: A descriptive study of sixty at risk families in a model prevention program. *Child Abuse & Neglect, 6,* 413–422.

Benjamin, L., Foster, S., Roberto, L., & Estroff, S. (1986). Breaking the family code: Analysis of videotapes of family interactions by structural analysis of social behavior (SASB). In L. Greenberg & W. Pinsof (Eds.), *The psychotherapeutic process: A research handbook* (pp. 391–438). New York: Guilford.

Bentler, P. M. (1995). *EQS program manual.* Los Angeles: Multivariate Software.

Beutler, L. E. (1991). Have all won and must all have prizes? Revisiting Luborsky et al.'s verdict. *Journal of Consulting and Clinical Psychology, 59,* 226–232.

Brown, T. A., & Barlow, D. H. (1992). Comrobidity among anxiety disorders: Implications for treatment and *DSM-IV. Journal of Consulting and Clinical Psychology, 60,* 835–844.

Brown, T. A., Chorpita, B. F., & Barlow, D. H. (1998). Structural relationships among dimensions of *DSM–IV* anxiety and mood disorders and dimensions on negative affect, positive affect, and automic arousal. *Journal of Abnormal Psychology, 107,* 179–192.

Browne, M. W., & Cudeck, R. (1993). Alternative ways of assessing model fit. In K. A. Bollen & J. S. Long (Eds.), *Testing structural equation models* (pp. 136–162). Thousand Oaks, CA: Sage.

Bollen, K. A. (1989). *Structural equations with latent variables.* New York: Wiley.

Bryk, A. S., & Raudenbush, S. W. (1987). Application of hierarchical linear models to assessing change. *Psychological Bulletin, 101,* 147–158.

Bryk, A. S., Raudenbush, S. W., Seltzer, M., & Congdon, R. J. (1986). *An introduction to HLM: Computer program and user's guide.* Chicago: University of Chicago Press.

Byrne, B. M. (2001). *Structural equation modeling with AMOS.* Mahwah, NJ: Lawrence Erlbaum Associates.

Canfield, M. L., Walker W. R., & Brown, L. G. (1991). Contingency interaction analysis in psychotherapy. *Journal of Consulting and Clinical Psychology, 59,* 58–66.

Carter, D. E., & Newman, F. L. (1975). *A client-oriented system of mental health service delivery and program management: A workbook and guide* (Series FN No. 4, DHHS No. 80-307). Rockville, MD: Mental Health Service System Reports.

Collins, L. M., & Horn, J. L. (Eds.). (1991). *Best methods of the analysis of change: Recent advances, unanswered questions, future directions.* Washington, DC: American Psychology Association.

Cronbach, L. J. (1987). Statistical tests for moderator variables: Flaws in analyses recently proposed. *Psychological Bulletin, 102,* 414–417.

Cronbach. L. J. (1990). *Essentials of psychological testing* (5th ed.). New York: Harper & Row.

Cronbach, L. J., & Furby, L. (1970). How we should measure "change"—or should we? *Psychological Bulletin, 74,* 68–80.

Cronbach, L. J., & Snow, R. E. (1977). *Aptitudes and instructional methods: A handbook for research on interactions.* New York: Irvington.

Der, G., & Everitt, B. S. (2002). *A handbook of statistical analysis using SAS.* (2nd ed.). New York: Chapman & Hall.

Elliot, R. (1985). Helpful and non-helpful events in brief counseling interviews: An empirical taxonomy. *Journal of Consulting and Clinical Psychology, 32,* 307–321.

Fishman, D. B. (1975). Development of a generic cost-effectiveness methodology for evaluating patient services of a community mental health center. In J. Zusman & C. R. Wurster (Eds.), *Evaluation in alcohol, drug abuse, and mental health service programs* (pp. 139–159). Lexington, MA: Heath.

Francis, D. J., Fletcher, J. M., Strubing, K. K., Davidson, K. C., & Thompson, N. M. (1991). Analysis of change: Modeling individual growth. *Journal of Consulting and Clinical Psychology, 59,* 27–37.

Garfield, S. L. (1986). Research on client variables in psychotherapy. In S. L. Garfield & A. E. Bergin (Eds.), *Handbook of psychotherapy and behavior change* (pp. 503–543). New York: Wiley.

Gurman, A. S., Kniskern, D. P., & Pinsof, W. M. (1986). Research on marital and family therapies. In S. L. Garfield & A. E. Bergin (Eds.), *Handbook of psychotherapy and behavior change* (pp. 525–564). New York: Wiley.

Hargreaves, W. A., Gaynor, J., Ransohoff, R., & Attkisson, C. C. (1984). Restrictiveness of care among the severely mentally disabled. *Hospital and Community Psychiatry, 35,* 706–709.

Howard, K. I., Kopta, S. M., Krause, M. S., & Orlinsky, D. E. (1986). The dose–effect relationship in psychotherapy. *American Psychologist, 41,* 159–164.

Horwrath, A. O., & Greenberg, L. (1986). The development of the Working Alliance Inventory. In L. Greenberg & W. M. Pinsof (Eds.), *The psychotherapeutic process* (pp. 529–556). New York: Guilford.

Jaccard, J., & Wan, C. K. (1995). *LISREL approaches to interaction effects in multiple regression.* Thousand Oaks, CA: Sage.

Jöreskog, K. G. (1982). The LISREL approach to causal model building in the social sciences. In K. G. Jöreskog & H. Wold (Eds.), *Systems under indirect observation, Part I* (pp. 81–99). Amsterdam: North Holland.

Jöreskog, K. G., & Sörbom, D. (1988). *LISREL VII.* Chicago: SPSS.

Jöreskog, K. G., & Sörbom, D. (1989). *LISREL 7: A guide to the program and applications* (2nd ed.). Chicago: SPSS.

Jöreskog, K. G., & Sörbom, D. (1993). *LISREL 8: Structural equation modeling with simple command language.* Chicago: Scientific Software.

Jöreskog, K. G., Sörbom, D., Du Toit, S., & Du Toit, M. (1999). *LISREL 8: New statistical features.* Chicago: Scientific Software International.

Judd, C. M., & Kenny, D. A. (1981). *Estimating the effect of social interventions.* New York: Cambridge University Press.

Kaul, T. J., & Bednar, R. L. (1986). Research on group and related therapies. In S. L. Garfield & A. E. Bergin (Eds.), *Handbook of psychotherapy and behavior change* (pp. 671–714). New York: Wiley.

Kazdin, A. E. (1986). The evaluation of psychotherapy: Research design and methodology. In S. L. Garfield & A. E. Bergin (Eds.), *Handbook of psychotherapy and behavior change* (pp. 23–68). New York: Wiley.

Kenny, D. A. (1979). *Correlation and causation.* New York: Wiley.

Laborsky, L., Crits-Christoph, P., Alexander, L., Margolis, M., & Cohn, M. (1983). Two helping alliance methods for predicting outcomes of psychotherapy: A counting signs versus a global rating method. *Journal of Nervous and Mental Diseases, 171,* 480–492.

Lord, F. M. (1963). Elementary models for measuring change. In C. W. Harris (Ed.), *Problems in measuring change* (pp. 21–38). Madison: University of Wisconsin Press.

Lyons, J. S., & Howard, K. I. (1991). Main effects analysis in clinical research: Statistical guidelines for disaggregating treatment groups. *Journal of Consulting & Clinical Psychology, 59,* 745–748.

Medsker, G. J, Williams, L. J., & Holahan, P. J. (1995). A review of current practices for evaluating causal models in organizational behavior and human resources management research. *Journal of Management, 20,* 439–464.

McDonald, R. P., & Ho, M. R. (2002). Principles and practice in reporting structural equation analysis. *Psychological Methods, 7,* 64–82.

Myers, J. L., & Well, A. D. (1991). *Research design and statistical analysis.* New York: HarperCollins.

Newman, F. L. (1983). Therapists' evaluations of psychotherapy. In M. Lambert, E. Christensen, & R. De Julio (Eds.), *The assessment of psychotherapy outcome* (pp. 497–534). New York: Wiley.

Newman, F. L. (1994). When is observing non-significance enough? (Introduction to special feature). *Journal of Consulting and Clinical Psychology, 62,* 941.

Newman, F. L., Griffin, B. P., Black, R. W., & Page, S. E. (1989). Linking level of care to level of need: Assessing the need for mental health care for nursing home residents. *American Psychologist, 44,* 1315–1324.

Newman, F. L., Heverly, M. A., Rosen, M., Kopta, S. M., & Bedell, R. (1983). Influences on internal evaluation data dependability: Clinicians as a source of variance. In A. J. Love (Ed.), *Developing effective internal evaluation: New directions for program evaluation* (No. 20, pp. 61–69). San Francisco: Jossey-Bass.

Newman, F. L., & Howard, K. I. (1986). Therapeutic effort, treatment outcome, and national health policy. *Journal of Consulting and Clinical Psychology, 41,* 181–187.

Newman, F. L., & Sorensen, J. E. (1985). *Integrated clinical and fiscal management in mental health: A guidebook.* Norwood, NJ: Ablex.

Newman, F. L., Tippet, M. T., & Johnson, D. A. (1992, June). *A screening instrument for consumer placement in a level of CSP: Psychometric properties.* Paper presented at the National Institute of Mental Health National Conference on Mental Health Statistics, Washington, DC.

O'Brien, R. G., & Kaiser, M. K. (1985). MANOVA method for analyzing repeated-measures designs. *Psychological Bulletin, 97,* 316–333.

Orlinsky, D. E., Grawe, K., & Parks, B. K. (1994). Process and outcome in psychotherapy—Noch einmal. In A. E. Bergin & S. L. Garfield (Eds.), *Handbook of psychotherapy and behavior change* (4th ed., pp. 270–376). New York: Wiley.

Orlinsky, D. E., & Howard, K. I. (1975). *Varieties of psychotherapeutic experience.* New York: Teachers College Press.

Orlinsky, D. E., & Howard, K. I. (1986). Process and outcome in psychotherapy. In S. L. Garfield & A. E. Bergin (Eds.), *Handbook of psychotherapy and behavior change* (3rd ed., pp. 311–381). New York: Wiley.

Ransohoff, P., Zackary, R. A., Gaynor, J. A., & Hargreaves, W. A. (1982). Measuring the restrictiveness of psychiatric care. *Hospital and Community Psychiatry, 33,* 361–366.

Raudenbush, S. W., & Bryk, A. S. (2002). *Hierarchical linear models: Applications and data analysis methods* (2nd edition). Newbury Park, CA: Sage.

Raudenbush, W. W., Bryk, A. S., Cheong, Y., & Congdon, R. T. (2000). *HLM 5: Heirarchical linear and nonlinear modeling.* Chicago: Scientific Software International.

Raudenbush, S. W., & Liu, X. (2000). Statistical power and optimal design for multisite randomized trials. *Psychological Methods, 5*, 199–213.

Rogosa, D. R., Bryant, D., & Zimowski, M. (1982). A growth curve approach to the measurement of change. *Psychological Bulletin, 90*, 726–748.

Rogosa, D. R., & Willett, J. B. (1983). Demonstrating the reliability of the difference score in the measurement of change. *Journal of Educational Measurement, 20*, 335–343.

Rogosa, D. R., & Willett, J. B. (1985). Understanding correlates of change by modeling individual differences in growth. *Psychometrika, 50*, 65–72.

Rosnow, R. L., & Rosenthal, R. (1989). Definition and interpretation of interaction effects. *Psychological Bulletin, 105*, 143–146.

Sachs, J. S. (1983). Negative factors in brief psychotherapy: An empirical assessment. *Journal of Consulting and Clinical Psychology, 51*, 557–564.

Saunders, S. M. (1991). *The process of seeking psychotherapy: Routes, difficulty and social support*. Unpublished doctoral dissertation, Northwestern University, Psychology Department.

Scandura, T. A., & Tejeda, M . J. (1997). *Models as fiction in structural equation modeling*. Paper presented at the annual meeting of the Academy of Management, Boston, MA.

Shadish, W. R., & Sweeney, R. B. (1991). Mediators and moderators in meta-analysis: There's a reason we don't let dodo birds tell us which psychotherapies should have prizes. *Journal of Consulting and Clinical Psychology, 59*, 883–893.

Shoham-Soloman, V. (1991). Introduction to special section on client–therapy interaction research. *Journal of Consulting and Clinical Psychology, 59*, 203–204.

Shoham-Soloman, V., Avner, R., & Neeman, R. (1989). Your are changed if you do and changed if you don't: Mechanisms underlying paradoxical interventions. *Journal of Consulting and Clinical Psychology, 57*, 590–598.

Silbershatz, G. (1994). Spurious or uncorrelated? Comments on Stiles and Shapiro. *Journal of Consulting and Clinical Psychology, 62*, 949–951.

Smith, B., & Sechrest, L. (1991). Treatment of aptitude × treatment interactions. *Journal of Consulting and Clinical Psychology, 59*, 233–244.

Snow, R. E. (1991). Aptitude–treatment interaction as a framework for research on individual differences in psychotherapy. *Journal of Consulting and Clinical Psychology, 59*, 205–216.

Stiles, W. B., & Shapiro, D. A. (1994). Disabuse of the drug metaphor: Psychotherapy process–outcome correlations. *Journal of Consulting and Clinical Psychology, 62*, 942–948.

Turner, R. M., Newman, F. L., & Foa, R. (1983). Relating obsessive-compulsive emotional structure to the cost and outcome of long term behavior therapy. *Journal of Clinical Psychology, 39*, 933–938.

Uehara, E., Smukler, M., & Newman, F. L. (1994). Linking resource use to consumer level of need in a local mental health system: Field test of the "LONCA" case mix method. *Journal of Consulting and Clinical Psychology, 62*, 695–709.

Webster, H., & Bereiter, C. (1963). The reliability of changes measured by mental test scores. In C. W. Harris (Ed.), *Problems in measuring change* (pp. 39–59). Madison, WI: University of Wisconsin Press.

Willett, J. B. (1988). Questions and answers in the measurement of change. In E. Z. Rothkopf (Ed.), *Review of research in education* (Vol. 15). Washington, DC: American Educational Research Association.

Willett, J. B. (1989). Some results on reliability for the longitudinal measurement of change: Implications for the design of studies of individual growth. *Educational and Psychological Measurement, 49*, 587–602.

Willett, J. B., Ayoub, C. C., & Robinson, D. (1991). Using growth modeling to examine systematic differences in growth: An example of change in the functioning of families at risk of maladaptive parenting, child abuse, or neglect. *Journal of Consulting and Clinical Psychology, 59*, 38–47.

Willett, J. B., & Sayer, A. G. (1994). Using covariance structure analysis to detect correlates and predictors of individual change over time. *Psychological Bulletin, 116*, 363–381.

Yates, B. T. (1980). *Improving effectiveness and reducing costs in mental health*. Springfield, IL: Thomas.

Yates, B. T. (1996). *Analyzing costs, procedures, processes, and outcomes in human services*. Thousand Oaks, CA: Sage.

Yates, B. T., & Newman, F. L. (1980). Findings of costeffectiveness and cost–benefit analyses of psychotherapy. In G. VandenBos (Ed.), *Psychotherapy: From practice to research to policy* (pp. 163–185.) Beverly Hills, CA: Sage.

Zimmerman, D. W., & Williams, R. H. (1982a). Gain scores in research can be highly reliable. *Journal of Educational Measurement, 19*, 149–154.

Zimmerman, D. W., & Williams, R. H. (1982b). The relative error magnitude in three measures of change. *Psychometrika, 47*, 141–147.

# 10

## Ethics Concerns in Outcomes Assessment

John D. Cone and Constance J. Dalenberg
*Alliant International University*

### INTRODUCTION

This chapter is about evaluating the outcomes of work with clients. More specifically, it is about the ethics of evaluating those outcomes, a relatively unexplored area in psychology. The Ethical Principles of Psychologists and Code of Conduct of the American Psychological Association (APA Code, American Psychological Association, 2002) covers the delivery of services and the conduct of research. If one accepts that *ethical* service delivery includes evaluation of its effects (cf. Bloom, Fischer, & Orme, 2003), it is reasonable to expect the APA Code to include guidelines for conducting such evaluations. In reality, the code is noticeably silent on this matter, not directly addressing professional behavior unique to outcomes evaluation. It does provide suggestions regarding some of the activities comprised in such evaluation, however, those coming both from guidelines dealing with service delivery and those having to do with research. We will argue later, however, that the ethical delivery of services as defined by the APA Code does indeed necessitate evaluation.

For an adequate treatment of the relatively unexplored topic of outcomes evaluation ethics, we draw on contributions from three major sources: (1) the practice of psychology, (2) the conduct of behavioral research, and (3) the conduct of outcomes evaluation. We start by reviewing the definitions of terms basic to our discussion. This is followed by distinguishing outcomes evaluation from research. Then major ethical concepts relevant to both outcomes evaluation and research are discussed, including voluntariness and informed consent, confidentiality, anonymity, and deception. Ethical concepts specific to outcomes evaluation are then covered, including the important issue of whether practitioners are obliged to evaluate the services they provide. Final sections treat the assurance of anonymity and confidentiality in outcomes evaluations, how to respond ethically to critics of one's findings, preventing ethical conflicts, and dealing with those that escape prevention.

### Defining Ethics

By ethics we mean a collection of moral principles or statements about right or wrong ways of behaving. In this chapter, we refer to right and wrong ways of evaluating outcomes. A number of theoretical bases might be considered for our discussion, including hedonism, utilitarianism, perfectionism, or deontology (cf. Lloyd & Hansen, 2003). Without getting into the details and arguments for and against each, however, suffice it to say we ground the present treatment squarely in utilitarianism, or "consequential ethics." From this perspective, "right" or ethical ways of evaluating outcomes are those likely to lead to the greatest benefits for society in general. Deciding or predicting societal benefits can be tricky, especially in outcomes evaluation, because of the relatively uncharted state of its ethics. Nonetheless, some help results from drawing on analogous circumstances in research and practice in psychology. For example, evaluating outcomes often involves the use of standardized assessment instruments. To the extent the ethical practice of assessment is codified and similarly based in utilitarianism, we can apply the analogy. Absent such precedents, we will have to use a "golden rule" logic and guess. That is, we will imagine what we would like to happen if we were the client and use that standard as a basis for determining the ethical course.

### Defining Outcomes Evaluation

It is useful to distinguish among related ways of referring to outcomes assessment. Terms such as treatment research, treatment evaluation, practice evaluation, effectiveness research, and efficacy studies are often encountered in the literature. By outcome, we mean the behavior of someone after a service has been provided, behavior that is assumed to be different as a result of that service. The source of outcomes is found in the goals for which a person seeks the service in the first place. In this regard, we borrow from Rosen and Procter (1981) in distinguishing two principle types of goals: ultimate and instrumental. Ultimate goals encompass what the client wants to be different as a result of the service. Such goals are client determined (e.g., "I want to feel less anxious," "I want to have a steady job"). Instrumental goals encompass what the provider believes must change to reach the client's ultimate goal(s). These provider-determined goals are theory driven and involve variables relevant to the provider's formal or informal understanding of the client's problem. Examples would be relaxing in the face of fearful stimuli as instrumental to managing anxiety or participating in an increased number of social activities as a means of reducing depression.

Evaluating outcomes can be broadly viewed as the activities involved in identifying goals, selecting measures to represent variables implied in the goals, arranging both the administration of the measures and the application of treatments so as to allow clear answers to evaluation questions (i.e., coming up with a design), administering the measures, scoring them, interpreting the scores for the client, using the scores and other client data to establish the impact of a service, and communicating the results of findings to others. Administering and scoring assessment instruments after a service or treatment documents the behavior of a client at that point in time. Whether that behavior is different than before the service and, if so, whether the service can be viewed as causing the difference are matters of evaluation design. Each type of design involves its own implications concerning ethics. For example, using time series methodology might require delays in services to permit baseline data collection. This can raise ethical questions. Using between-case methodology that might require placing clients into treated (experimental) or untreated (control) groups can raise ethical questions as well (Kazdin, 1998).

## Distinguishing Outcomes Evaluation From Research

Examining the impact of services via outcomes evaluation sounds a lot like conducting research. Indeed, it is research in the dictionary sense meaning studious inquiry or examination (Neilson, Knott, & Carhart, 1950). It is not scientific research, however, in which the aim is to discover generalizable new facts or information about phenomena so as to understand them better. It is research in this latter, scientific sense that the federal government has established formal mechanisms for reviewing (e.g., institutional review boards, IRBs). Studious inquiry or fact gathering for purposes of a more practical nature (e.g., evaluating outcomes, administrative decision making, demonstrating research in classrooms) are typically not considered the purview of IRBs (Sieber, 1992).

Hayes, Barlow, and Nelson-Gray (1999) referred to *treatment research* and *treatment evaluation*, distinguishing between them on the basis of the ultimate intent of the investigator. If the overarching concern is advancing scientific knowledge, treatment research is involved. If the overarching concern is improving client functioning, treatment evaluation is involved. From their perspective, treatment research is subject to human participants review; treatment evaluation is not. Efficacy studies in which novel interventions are examined in tightly controlled randomized clinical trials are clearly treatment research, as are effectiveness studies occurring under more natural, less tightly controlled conditions (Seligman, 1995). Both types of research seek new information and explore its generalizability, thus falling under the purview of IRBs.

A broader enterprise, *practice evaluation*, was not specifically dealt with by Sieber (1992) or in the Hayes et al. (1999) formulation. There are many activities making up practice evaluation that do not involve the effectiveness of treatments. Evaluation questions can arise that are examined in relational designs involving no direct influence on clients' behavior. For example, studying the relationship between distances traveled to the practice's office and satisfaction with services, or determining whether net profits are higher if credit cards are accepted for payment both relate to overall practice effectiveness. A liberal view of what does and does not require IRB approval might contend that practice evaluation activities such as these are mainly data gathering for administrative decision-making. Thus, following Sieber, they would escape IRB oversight.

A more conservative view could attempt to accommodate practice evaluation into the Hayes et al. (1999) formulation. For example, though unlikely, a service provider could undertake evaluation principally for the purpose of improving her or his practice. Decisions during the course of treatment (e.g., type of design, length of baseline) might be controlled primarily by whether they will advance the goal of learning about the practice's effectiveness. That is, the welfare of the client would be a secondary consideration in making these decisions. When practice evaluation goals take precedence over client welfare, the client is obviously at some risk and protections seem warranted. In such situations, it would be prudent for the provider to submit her or his plans to some review body for oversight. Persons practicing in large agencies can rely on the agency's IRB. Independent practitioners do not have such an obvious resource. They might apply to the ethics committee of their local professional organization for review and guidance. Absent such a committee, they could seek input from several peers. At the very least, issues of voluntariness, informed consent, anonymity, confidentiality, right to withdraw without prejudice, and minimization of harm should be addressed with potential clients, as should debriefing them after the evaluation is completed. These concepts are discussed in the next section.

**Major Concepts in Discussions of Ethics in Research and Outcomes
Evaluation Voluntariness and Informed Consent**

The concept of informed consent entered American case law in the mid-1950s and did
not immediately achieve wide currency, even in the most obvious medical circumstances (Simon & Sadoff, 1992). It is fair to state that the concept is now an accepted part
of the standard of care, and yet the majority of psychotherapists do not utilize written
informed consent except in the areas of fee arrangements and limits of confidentiality
(Handelsman, Kemper, Kesson-Graig, McLain, & Johnsrud, 1986; Stein, 1995). Some
evidence exists that documentation of oral informed consent also is poor (Schachter,
1998). The APA Code is still a bit vague on the subject, requiring informed consent
but failing to specify the range of topics necessary and the form (written or oral) that
the consent should take. In the Standard of Care Guidelines for the California Victims
Compensation Board, it is suggested that the potential evaluator document the following, either in the form of a written consent form or a written series of questions
given to the client to prompt inquiries:

1. Education and training of the evaluator
2. License or registration status of evaluator
3. Availability in emergency and alternative call numbers
4. Complete financial policy
5. Agreed-on purpose of evaluation
6. Description of the evaluation process
7. Alternatives to the chosen process and the reason for the choices made
8. Benefits and risks to the client who participates in the evaluation
9. Suggestions for what the client might do if he or she feels uncomfortable with
   the process or fears harm
10. Description of the record to be kept
11. Names of all supervisors or consultants who will see the material
12. Relationship of the evaluation to therapy, if any
13. Duration of evaluation
14. Specific skills training or training in diagnostic assessment possessed by the
    evaluator that is relevant to the client's problem.

Wilkinson (2001) adds that the ethical researcher/clinician should disclose sponsor-
ship of the study, because the nature of the sponsor may lead to different probability
of agreement by the client. Handelsman and Galvin (1988) provided an example of
such a question-and-answer format for informed consent.

   To the extent that written consent forms are used, most surveys reveal that they are
presented at a reading level far above that of the typical client. A review of informed
consent forms submitted to three IRBs revealed an average reading level of 2nd year
of college (Goldstein, Frasier, & Curtis, 1996). Hochhauser (1999) argued that in the
medical setting, the average consent form is five to six grade levels above the reading level of the average patient. Further, one study (Parikh, Parker, & Nurss, 1996)
found that most low-literacy clients do not report their difficulty with the forms. More
positively, if reading levels are adjusted, stable schizophrenics or those with schizoaf-
fective disorder are able to understand consent forms as well as healthy controls

(Pinals, Malhotra, Breier, & Pickar, 1998). It is worrisome, however, that researchers find higher percentages of minorities and those with less education in studies with passive consent (i.e., consent is assumed unless written withdrawal is received) than those with active consent (Dent, Galaif, & Sussman, 1993). Legally and morally, a signature on a piece of paper is not the equivalent of true informed consent.

Levine and Stagno (2001) expressed concern that the practice of informed consent may itself create ethical problems. If the evaluation takes place in the context of psychotherapy, the authors fear that the client will be potentially harmed by concerns about exploitation or retaliation should she or he refuse.

To the present authors, the deciding factor should be the research on clients' typical reactions to the varying scenarios. That is, do we have any evidence that the informed consent procedure helps or harms clients? Levine and Stagno (2001) presented some case examples of clients who became extremely agitated regarding the informed consent questions, although they did appear to value the process. In Braaten's and Handelsman's (1997) survey of former clients, most of the categories of informed consent information were rated as "very important;" the authors provided a brief set of guidelines for the preferred timing of informed consent disclosures. Sullivan, Martin, and Handelsman (1993), in a vignette study, also showed that professionally managed informed consent procedures have a positive impact on the client's first impression of the therapist or evaluator. Most contemporary informed consent researchers state that there is little research substantiating the negative effects of informed consent (cf. Braaten & Handelsman, 1997).

**Privacy, Confidentiality, and Anonymity**

Privacy and confidentiality violations are among the most frequently adjudicated problems that come before professional ethics committees (APA, 1988; Koocher & Keith-Spiegel, 1998). Confidentiality is often presented as one of the cornerstones of the profession of psychotherapy; in fact, some have argued that psychotherapy cannot occur effectively without it (Epstein, Steingarten, Weinstein, & Nashel, 1977). The concept of confidentiality grew out of the right to privacy granted by the Fourth, Fifth and Fifteenth Amendments to the U.S. Constitution. An extended discussion of confidentiality in psychotherapy is beyond the scope of this chapter; however, confidentiality of test and outcome data present special complexities. For instance, the duty to protect test security as well as individual client data (see later discussion of the Health Insurance Portability and Accountability Act, HIPAA) may require added layers of protection for outcome data. In addition, the client may not be fully aware during the informed consent process of the meaning of a release of test data, complicating these issues.

For instance, it is quite common in a general evaluation (e.g., worker's compensation, personal injury, custody) for the client to be given the Minnesota Multiphasic Personality Inventory (MMPI) or the Millon Clinical Multiaxial Inventory (MCMI). As the client signs the informed consent, she or he is likely to have in mind the disclosure of the therapist's diagnosis of depression, anxiety, or posttraumatic stress. Embedded in the individual answers to the questions, however, are many individual item responses that the client may find especially personal and irrelevant to the current evaluation question. Examples are questions regarding the client's feeling about his or her mother, the nature of his or her sexual practices, or the existence of an incest history. Thus, it may be necessary to consider the likelihood of public access to test data in choosing these instruments. For specific evaluation questions, the broader based and more intrusive instruments may be unnecessary. Further, to the extent that the data are to be used in a manner that does not directly benefit the client (e.g., in treatment research or program evaluations), the evaluator should address confidentiality issues again in the debriefing process.

For individuals requesting data about the client in legal or research settings, the professional should carefully consider the use to which the data will be put. Researchers and therapists have a duty to protect against misuse of their data to the extent that this is possible. The 2002 guidelines for disclosure of data (Standard 8.14, Sharing Research Data for Verification) are quite clear in stating that the individual holding client records should guard against disclosure of any confidential data and against the release of disguised data for purposes outside the original informed consent of the client. Those seeking access to the outcome data should be doing so only to "verify the substantive claims through reanalysis." Those receiving a professional request for the release of data should ask for a letter of clarification as to the potential use of the data. If a version of the data that does not violate confidentiality can be created, the evaluator should require a clear statement of all intended uses of the data before release.

Confidentiality issues should be more prominent in the minds of researchers and clinicians who are dealing with vulnerable populations or who are studying topics that are contentious or that involve socially taboo information. Instances of break-ins to researcher or therapist offices to locate data on a celebrity, a government official, or a spouse involved in a custody battle are no longer rare. Many commentators have questioned the behavior of well-known therapists who have disclosed personal information about famous clients (typically with a relative's permission) after their deaths. Recent examples are disclosures by a psychotherapist who briefly treated Nicole Simpson, murdered wife of O. J. Simpson (cf. Koocher & Keith-Spiegel, 1998) and the release of therapy tapes of the deceased Pulitzer Prize–winning poet Anne Sexton by her analyst (cf. Burke, 1995; Rosenbaum, 1994). Researchers and clinicians in this situation may consider keeping demographic and outcome data in separate files with a link known only to the involved professionals.

### Deception

The issue of deception is most commonly associated with research rather than clinical evaluation. Ethical standards related to deception are contained in the APA Code section devoted to research and publication, and warn the psychologist not to use deceit unless the study's value warrants it and "effective nondeceptive procedures are not feasible" (Standard 8.07, Deception in Research). Standard 8.07 states that the psychologist should debrief the participant and explain any deception as soon as it is feasible.

Implicit in our concerns for test security, however, is the understanding that we are not fully disclosing to our clients the ways our outcome measures work. Some tests, such as the TOMM (Test of Memory Malingering: Rees, Tombaugh, & Gansler, 1998) or the VSV (Victoria Symptom Validity Test: Doss, Chelung, & Naugle, 1999) are entirely based on deception; clients are misled about the purpose of the test within the test instructions. Evaluation texts, however, are more likely to warn of the ethical problem of failure to use some tests of malingering, almost all of which involve deceit.

Further attention in the literature must be given to the effect of disclosing the existence of validity scales (without revealing their nature) to those who take outcome measures. This is often termed coaching in the literature and regarded as a form of undermining the test. Some research indicates that the individual informed of the existence of validity scales will be a more successful malingerer, if that is the goal (Bury & Bagby, 2002). However, such studies are typically conducted in forensic settings or with populations of individuals told to lie. It is unclear whether they would apply to the more widespread evaluation tasks. In the latter case, when exaggeration or minimizing is more likely to be a result of shame or social desirability bias, disclosure or full debriefing are less problematic.

A more liberal view in this area would hold that the client must be informed of the nature and purpose of the evaluation but need not be informed of the mechanism in which the goals of the evaluation are achieved. The surgeon who receives informed consent for an appendectomy is not required to demonstrate or detail the mechanics of the operation itself. Nonetheless, once the client does learn of the existence of malingering tests within a battery, some offense may be taken. In these instances, the process of debriefing might include explaining to the client why the scales might aid in supporting a valid assessment.

## ETHICS CONCEPTS IMPORTANT IN ASSESSING TREATMENT OUTCOMES

### The Ethical Obligation to Document Outcomes

Earlier, it was suggested that the practice of psychology carries a built-in requirement to evaluate whether that practice is making a difference. This is also true of other disciplines. For example, the National Association of Social Workers' Code of Ethics makes the evaluation of interventions mandatory (Bloom et al., 2003). The Association for Advancement of Behavior Therapy (AABT) includes evaluation among the necessary components of ethical practice (AABT, 1977). Such a requirement of service providers is analogous to the automobile mechanic test-driving a car after repairing its brakes. She or he does this to make sure the intervention was effective. After all, letting the car owner drive away with failing brakes could have very serious consequences. If the postrepair test drive reveals the brakes still have problems, the mechanic goes back to work, continuing until the problems are resolved. In the event that the required repairs are beyond the mechanic's capabilities, she or he communicates this to the customer and makes appropriate recommendations, including referrals to others to effect the repair.

It seems the ethical practice of psychology demands at least the same level of postintervention checking expected of automobile mechanics and many other service providers. If so, why is there no principle or standard specific to outcomes evaluation in the APA Code? The closest the code comes to requiring the examination of service impact is Standard 2.04 (Bases for Scientific and Professional Judgments), in which psychologists' work is said to be *"based upon* established scientific and professional knowledge of the discipline" (APA, 2002, p. 1064, emphasis added). This is a rather broad and imprecise exhortation for psychologists to act responsibly. Unfortunately, it is even less precise than the 1992 version of the code, in which psychologists were exhorted to *"rely on* scientifically and professionally derived knowledge when making scientific or professional judgments . . . " (APA, 1992, p. 1600, emphasis added). The new version of the "basis" standard appears to define ethical practice merely as engaging in the application of psychology. This is because the discipline *is* the sum of its scientific and professional knowledge.

The previous version of the standard appeared to require scientific or professional bases for specific judgments, not merely that psychologists' work be based in the general discipline. Greater precision seems necessary if the public is to be protected adequately. What does "based on established scientific and professional knowledge" mean, for example? Is the psychologist expected to use this knowledge in ethical ways? This might seem like a fine point, but it is conceivable that a psychological therapist could arrange a very satisfactory design of a treatment's impact from a scientific perspective and end up using the information from the inquiry in questionable ways. Imagine data from a particular intervention indicating that treatment benefits have yet to reveal themselves. However, the client thinks she or he has made great gains, is very appreciative, and calls to say she or he will no longer be coming for treatment. Is the ethical therapist obligated to make this known to the patient, perhaps even letting the patient know she or he is terminating AMA (against medical advice)? Or, imagine a client in treatment who thinks that treatment is effective in spite of data that convince the psychologist that an alternative approach is needed. The client resists suggestions to try an alternative, insisting on continuing the ineffective approach. Would the ethical therapist refuse to continue or participate in the existing treatment?

As a recent example, children with autism and gastrointestinal symptoms have been anecdotally described as benefiting from intravenous administration of the hormone secretin. In addition to reductions in GI symptoms, language skills are reported to improve. However, Lightdale and colleagues showed no significant increases in language in a single-blinded study testing language before and after secretin infusion (Lightdale et al., 2001). Nor were there changes in the children's problem behaviors. Nonetheless, 70% of the parents of participating children reported from moderate to high levels of change in language and behavior. More significantly, when asked whether their child might benefit from another infusion of secretin, 85% said yes. Would the clinician be on firm ethical grounds if she or he provided additional treatment with secretin?

Though Standard 2.04 does not appear to offer clear ethical guidance in this situation, Standard 10.10 (Terminating Therapy) does. It requires that "psychologists terminate therapy when it becomes reasonably clear that the client/patient no longer needs the service, is not likely to benefit, or is being harmed by continued service (APA, 2002, p. 1073). Thus, on the "not likely to benefit" basis alone, psychologists would be prevented from recommending that a physician administer more secretin.

Termination decisions in the context of psychological therapy rely on data of multiple types. These range from informal, qualitative impressions of the client or therapist to formal, quantitative accounts of progress using measures meeting specific scientific requirements. Outcomes evaluators are likely to prefer the latter. Indeed, ethical practice appears to require their use, given their relatively lower probability of bias and unreliability. Standards 2.05 and 10.10 are again relevant. Making termination decisions exclusively on the basis of impressionistic data runs afoul of the requirement that practice be "based on established scientific and professional knowledge" (APA, 2002, p. 1064). Complying with such a requirement protects us against fooling ourselves. "Nothing is so easy to deceive as one's self; for what we wish, that we readily believe" (Demosthenes, cited in Bloom et al., 2003, p. 676).

Joint consideration of both Standards 2.05 and 10.10 provides support for the view that ethical practice requires its evaluation. Moreover, together they suggest how that evaluation should occur. In other words, decisions to terminate services are based on data about progress (i.e., sufficient to no longer need, not likely to benefit, being harmed). These data must be other than mere impressions, because psychologists are required to base their actions on scientific knowledge.

If an ethical therapist must terminate the client if treatment harms or lacks effectiveness, it follows that the therapist must ethically take measures to become aware that harm or ineffectiveness are occurring. Therapist discomfort with evaluation and the slow but widening split between research scientists and practitioners (cf. Dawes, 1996) may lead some to resist the introduction of such evaluative components. Therapist discomfort may be communicated to clients, who may have their own reasons for wishing not to spend the added time (and money) that evaluation may require. But if ethical therapy demands that the therapist know his or her effectiveness, as Principle 10.10 (Termination of Psychotherapy) seems to require, and if practitioners came to believe that this should be so, then patients may come to expect or demand evaluation as part of treatment and to see lack of evaluation as a sign of incompetence. Would the typical diabetic patient accept treatment from a physician who regards monitoring of insulin levels to be irrelevant?

The response most often given to the authors from those least comfortable with evaluation in therapy is that the evaluation instruments themselves may lack application to a specific clinical case. What instruments measure the progress made by a client who came to therapy to "better understand myself," to "help me get over my resentment of my stepchildren," or to "help me make a decision to stay with or leave my spouse?" Patient problems do not always come in easily definable categories, and the most pressing problem may change from week to week. Continuing with the medical analogy, however, the imperfection of the tests for measuring certain mental or bodily changes (predicting probability of cancer reoccurrence under varying conditions, for example) does not free the physician from the responsibility to do his or her best to evaluate the client's ongoing disease or health status. Instruments such as Service Satisfaction Scale, the Treatment Perception Questionnaire, and other recently proposed instruments measure general client satisfaction and would allow client and therapist to keep an eye on the rate of progress and to evaluate the need for change (cf. Boechler, Neufeld, & McKim, 2002; Marsden et al., 2000).

**Evaluation-Specific Ethics Guidelines**

Whereas the APA Code does not specifically address the ethics of outcomes evaluations, several individuals and professional organizations concerned with evaluation have developed guidelines that are relevant. The principles of the American Evaluation Association (AEA, 1994) are presented in Table 10.1 Additional recommendations are available in Bloom et al. (2003). Their recommendations are specific to the types of outcomes evaluation normally associated with the provision of psychological therapy. Bloom et al. (2003) recommend getting the clients' informed consent to the evaluative aspects of their treatment at the outset, minimizing the intrusiveness of evaluation and balancing the costs and benefits of evaluation. They also recommend conferring with clients about the means by which progress will be measured.

Considering these recommendations makes it clear that we as practitioners are in the early phases of systematic efforts to evaluate our effectiveness. Attention is still directed to the evaluative aspect of our work as though it is unique, something tacked on to the more basic treatment itself. We are still self-conscious about evaluation and seek consent for it as though there were a choice to be made. That is, we inform the client and seek consent specifically for evaluation even though we have already done this for the treatment itself. This separate process will not be necessary when

TABLE 10.1
AEA's Guiding Principles for Evaluators

---

A. *Systematic Inquiry*: Evaluators conduct systematic, data-based inquiries about whatever is being evaluated.

B. *Competence*: Evaluators provide competent performance to stakeholders.

C. *Integrity/Honesty*: Evaluators ensure the honesty and integrity of the entire evaluation process.

D. *Respect for People*: Evaluators respect the security, dignity, and self-worth of the respondents, program participants, clients, and other stakeholders with whom they interact.

E. *Responsibilities for General and Public Welfare:* Evaluators articulate and take into account the diversity of interests and values that may be related to the general and public welfare.

---

*Note:* Adapted from American Evaluation Association (1994).

continuous measurement of our effectiveness is accepted as a natural part of the service offered. When it is, we will include it in the description of our approach and obtain consent for its use along with and inseparable from consent for the overall treatment.

With respect to outcomes evaluation there are several ethical concerns of particular relevance that merit closer attention. These have to do with evaluator competence, assessment, evaluation design, agency or sponsor involvement, data ownership, and requirements to debrief clients whose data are used in outcomes evaluations. We treat each of these in the next sections.

## Competence

The AEA (see Table 10.1) guidelines include a competency requirement. This refers to the ethical necessity for evaluations to be undertaken by persons with the skills and other resources appropriate for completing the task effectively. While the APA Code is not specific to outcomes evaluation, it, too, includes standards related to competence (Standards 2.01–2.06). Standard 2.01 (Boundaries of Competence) is the most generally relevant: "Psychologists provide services, teach, and conduct research with populations and in areas only within the boundaries of their competence, based on their education, training, supervised experience, consultation, study, or professional experience" (APA, 2002, p. 1063). The AEA elaborates their recommendations, noting that evaluators "decline to conduct evaluations that fall substantially outside" the limits of their training and competence. When it is not feasible to decline, it is incumbent on ethical evaluators to inform those seeking the evaluation of any significant limitations that can result. Moreover, the evaluator is advised to pursue the necessary competence either directly or through the involvement of others who have the expertise already. With respect to this last point, the AEA recommends that "evaluators continually seek to maintain and improve their competencies," a suggestion consistent with the general APA code requirement for continued competency development (Standard 2.03, Maintaining Competence).

Skills specific to outcomes evaluation are beginning to be identified and recommended in discussions of ethical concerns. Pratt, Berman, and Hurt (1998) addressed the competencies needed for effective outcomes evaluation in managed care settings, with particular emphasis on research skills. Maruish (2002) recently called attention to testing competencies needed in such settings, noting that specific training on the types of instruments (e.g., briefer, more focused measures) likely to be used is desirable (see Clement, 1999; Hawkins, Mathews, & Hamdan, 1999). In addition, he noted the importance of training in basic measurement science (psychometrics) and instrument construction if "one's involvement in an outcomes assessment program includes the development of outcomes instruments" (Maruish, 2002, p. 289). Finally, he recommended competence in business-related concepts such as continuous quality improvement (see Juran, Seder, & Gryna, 1962) and information management (see Smith, Fischer, Nordquist, Mosley, & Ledbetter, 1997).

Though Bloom et al. (2003) do not mention competence specifically in their recommendations, their entire book is about the skills required for effectively using within-case (single-subject) methodology to evaluate work with individual clients. They recommend that graduate programs include course work and field experience to teach this approach. More generally, graduate programs must address the competence of their students to provide services in the most ethical manner. From our point of view, this means educating them to evaluate the services they are ultimately to provide.

## Assessment-Related Concepts

The APA Code of Ethics' (APA, 2002) includes 11 standards specific to assessment. These cover (1) bases for assessments, (2) use of assessments, (3) informed consent, (4) release of test data, (5) test construction, (6) interpreting assessment results, (7) assessment by unqualified persons, (8) obsolete tests and outdated test results, (9) test scoring and interpretation services, (10) explaining assessment results, and (11) maintaining test security. A more elaborate treatment of ethical assessment is provided in the collaborative *Standards for Educational and Psychological Testing*, published jointly by the American Educational Research Association, American Psychological Association, and the National Council on Measurement in Education (AERA, APA, NCME, 1999). Other treatments are also available, including *Responsibilities of Users of Standardized Tests* (American Counseling Association, 1989) and *Principles for the Validation and Use of Personnel Selection Procedures* (Society for Industrial and Organizational Psychology, 1987). Although none of these documents addresses the ethics of assessment specifically related to outcomes evaluation, it is evident that most of the assessment-related recommendations apply to assessment in outcomes or program evaluation contexts, albeit with some modifications. Others have addressed this issue as well (cf. Pratt, Berman, & Hurt, 1998).

In assessing the outcomes of their own work or that of others, psychologists select and use instruments and procedures appropriate to their evaluation question(s). In the case of individual practitioners, assessment methodology should address both the ultimate and instrumental outcomes previously mentioned. The different nature of these outcomes requires different methods be used. For example, helping a client accomplish the ultimate goal of managing anxiety so that it no longer interferes with daily functioning can be assessed via the administration of a standardized, psychometrically sound instrument tapping anxiety. This can be administered before and at the end of treatment, and perhaps at specific points (e.g., midway) during intervention. Demonstrating change associated with treatment and the clinical significance of this change typically focuses on the accomplishment of ultimate goals. Measures appropriate for assessing ultimate goals, namely, clinical change criteria, are norm-referenced devices standardized on large numbers of persons and refined to achieve acceptable levels of reliability and validity. Showing a client has moved from being closer to the mean of a clinical sample to that of a nonclinical sample and that the amount of this movement is reliable suffices to establish the clinical significance of the change (Hsu, 1999; Jacobson & Truax, 1991; Speer, 1992). Obviously, the norms must be available to make this determination.

Instrumental goals are more often monitored on a continuous basis throughout treatment. For this purpose, measures sensitive to small changes are needed, and they must be specific to the variables the practitioner or program theorizes are relevant to accomplishing the ultimate goals of the client. Thus, measures of instrumental goals are likely to be more locally developed, client-specific procedures.

Whether selecting and using psychometrically sound, norm-referenced instruments to assess ultimate goal attainment or constructing, using, and showing the soundness of methods to assess instrumental goals, ethical practice requires outcomes evaluators to choose (APA Code, Standard 9.02, Use of Assessments) or construct (Standard 9.05, Interpreting Assessment Results) appropriate measures, and to be competent to do so (AEA Principle 2). In addition, evaluators obtain the informed consent of clients before monitoring their progress (APA Code, Standard 9.03, Informed Consent in Assessments). Bloom et al. (2003) also recommended discussing with clients the evaluative aspects of their treatment. They encourage this to occur at the outset and suggest that the client be allowed to have input and be given a chance to agree with the plan. They seem to stop short of giving the client evaluative veto power, however. In their sixth statement, they suggest using alternative procedures if the client appears to be uncomfortable with the selected ones, but they do not recommend halting evaluation altogether. Consistent with our view that ethical treatment is evaluated treatment, clients would be encouraged to comment on the overall service plan, including evaluative components, and efforts would be made to make whatever changes are in keeping with applying the treatment faithfully and evaluating it effectively. If agreement on a suitable approach cannot be reached, the ethical course would be to refer the client to other providers.

Note that the APA Code allows for circumstances in which informed consent for assessments, evaluations, or diagnostic services is not required. Standard 9.03, "Informed Consent in Assessments," lists these as (1) legally or legislatively mandated assessments, (2) cases in which consent is implied (as when testing occurs as a routine part of an educational program or some institutional or organizational activity, and (3) testing to determine the capacity to make decisions. This standard appears to support an argument that informed consent for outcomes evaluations may not be necessary when those evaluations occur as a "routine part" of ethically delivered psychological therapy.

Another assessment-related ethical concern in outcomes measurement involves the selection of appropriate methods and instruments. APA Code Standard 9.02, "Use of Assessments," provides for psychologists to use methods that are appropriate for the evaluative purpose, including being adequately reliable and valid, and tailored to the individual(s) being assessed. Further, psychologists do not use obsolete tests and outdated test results (Standard 9.08, Obsolete Tests and Outdated Test Results). Bloom et al. (2003) encouraged evaluators to use unobtrusive measures if possible, and, as mentioned, avoid procedures associated with client discomfort.

It happens that the recommendation to use unobtrusive measures is consistent with the use of procedures likely to yield the most direct, highest quality information (Cone, 2001). Unfortunately, evaluators face an ethical dilemma when implementing such suggestions because of the inverse relationship between obtrusiveness and privacy rights. That is, the least obtrusive measurement occurs without the client's awareness. One of us (JC) once consulted in an experimental school that employed video cameras in each classroom, wired to monitors in the principal's office. Teachers could see the camera in the room but did not know when it was operating. Assertiveness researchers have telephoned clients after treatment posing as members of the same college class and making a series of successively more unreasonable requests (McFall & Lillisand, 1971). Researchers have hidden in men's public bathrooms to time speed of urination as a function of whether another man was in the room, ostensibly studying the relationship between personal space and arousal (Middlemist, Knowles, & Matter, 1976).

To varying degrees, the data obtained in these examples are free of the reactivity normally associated with knowing one is being assessed. That is, the teachers, college students, and men in bathrooms are unlikely to have altered their behavior as a result of knowing that assessment was occurring. Several APA Code standards bear on these examples. For the videotaping of teachers, Standard 4.03 (Recording) admonishes psychologists to obtain permission from persons or their legal guardians before recording their voices or images. Standard 3.10, (Informed Consent) speaks to obtaining informed consent of persons to be assessed. At the same time, Standard 8.03, (Informed Consent for Recording Voices and Images in Research) requires informed consent "unless (1) the research consists solely of naturalistic observations in public places, and it is not anticipated that the recording will be used in a manner that could cause personal identification or harm..." (APA, 2002, p. 1069). Institutional review boards typically require their permission and oversight before observing public behavior. Their approval is likely to be readily forthcoming in situations where the observees are not personally identifiable, the data will not place them at risk for civil or criminal prosecution, and the behavior observed does not involve sensitive content (e.g., drug use, illegal acts, sexual activity, or alcohol use; Adler & Adler, 1994).

Informing clients of assessment procedures includes telling them what behavior is being assessed, by whom, and under what conditions (Barrios, 1993). The reactive impact of such knowledge is immediately obvious. It can be mitigated, however. In the teacher videotaping example, the teachers were told they might be observed via the cameras at any time. Because cameras are present continually, it is likely that the teachers adapt to them and that their behavior is minimally affected. Family interaction has been audiotaped unobtrusively by telling the family that a tape recorder in a closet would be activated at random times (Jacob, Tennenbaum, Seilhamer, Bargiel, & Sharon, 1994). Clients might be told at the outset of treatment that aspects of their behavior during sessions will be noted for effectiveness monitoring purposes. They would not necessarily know what behavior or when, but would be asked to agree to this form of direct observation. Participants in large-scale health programs (e.g., managed care organizations) or educational programs give implicit permission to have aspects (e.g., services used, class attendance, grades achieved) of their behavior recorded routinely. True, the reactive effects of knowing about the data collection might compromise information quality. It is more plausible that the participants adapt or habituate to being "observed," however, and the reactive effects diminish over time. The ethical use of high-quality direct observational assessment can be relatively easily accomplished in this way, obviating reliance on indirect, self-report measures.

This addresses the dilemma posed by the inverse relationship between assessment obtrusiveness and client privacy. It is noteworthy that self-report measures asking about a client's sex life, medical condition(s), psychological symptoms, religious beliefs, and so on are often accused of invading privacy. Such instruments might be viewed as highly intrusive, and newer personality inventories have eliminated such items to minimize complaints. The Trauma Symptom Inventory (Briere, Elliott, Harris, & Cotman, 1995), for instance, is published in two forms, the TSI and the TSI–A, the latter removing questions about sexual practices.

It is interesting that when test takers are asked how well they enjoyed reading and responding to various objective personality inventories, those with "intrusive" items are judged more favorably (Fiske, 1969). One possibility is that such items are more obvious in terms of their social desirability implications, making it easier to respond to them (Cone, 1971). It may be that obtrusive assessment procedures are, paradoxically, less privacy invading because of their transparency. That is, test takers can determine more easily how to create a certain impression. It can be argued that there is greater loss of privacy when this form of "countercontrol" is minimized.

Additional assessment-related ethical concerns of relevance to outcomes measurement include interpreting and explaining test results. APA Code Standards 9.06 (Interpreting Assessment Results) and 9.10 (Explaining Assessment Results) are relevant. The first requires psychologists to take into account factors (e.g., test factors, test-taking abilities, characteristics of the test taker) that might affect the accuracy of the psychologist's interpretation. The second requires the psychologist to take reasonable steps to ensure the person tested gets an explanation of the results. In situations where the nature of the relationship between the psychologist and such persons precludes making results available, it is incumbent on the psychologist to inform them of this restriction ahead of time.

The interpretation and explanation standards of the APA Code have obvious relevance in outcomes evaluations, especially where treatment evaluation is the issue. When programs or entire services are being evaluated, the psychologist has parallel interpretation and explanation responsibilities. He or she interprets the findings of the evaluation in a written report to relevant stakeholders, including any qualifications necessitated by factors such as methodological limitations, personal predispositions, or other constraints imposed by the evaluation process. Similarly, explanations of the findings should be included in the report. A draft of the evaluation report could be given to program administrators for their comments and input. Ultimate responsibility for the contents of any outcomes evaluation reports rests with the evaluator, of course (Joint Committee on Standards for Educational Evaluation, 1994).

Related to interpretation and explanation requirements are issues involving the release of test data and the maintenance of test security. In recent court decisions, the rights of test takers to review test material have been expanded. For example, the New York Truth in Testing Law requires testing companies to make copies of actual test items available to students requesting them, including the student's answers and the correct ones (Kaplan & Saccuzzo, 2001). In addition, recent legislation at the federal level (the HIPAA) requires health care providers to release some types of health-related information to clients if they request it. These legislative initiatives have necessitated changes in the 1992 APA Code dealing specifically with psychologists' ethical responsibilities. On the one hand, they are expected to release test data to clients or their representatives if requested. On the other hand, they are expected to protect the security of test materials. Standards 9.04 and 9.11 of the new code address these issues. Standard 9.04 (Release of Test Data) provides for psychologists to convey test data to clients or other persons, provided the appropriate release of information forms are on hand. Further, Standard 9.04 defines what constitutes test data as

> raw and scaled scores, client/patient responses to test questions or stimuli, and psychologists' notes and recordings concerning client/patient statements and behavior during an examination. Those portions of test materials that include client/patient responses are included in the definition of *test data*. (APA, 2002, p. 1071)

Standard 9.11 (Maintaining Test Security) requires psychologists to protect the security and integrity of "test materials and other assessment techniques." It defines *materials* to include "manuals, instruments, protocols, and test questions or stimuli and does not include test data as defined in Standard 9.04" (APA, 2002, p. 1072). Thus, the code clarifies the ethical strictures the psychologist is under. Whether a court would view the distinction between test data and test materials as legally conforming is another question. It is likely that a judge presiding under the New York Truth in Testing Law would view test items as disclosable and require their presentation by psychologists, if requested by a client. Disclosure of test items may or may not be expected by courts in other jurisdictions.

Psychologists using formal assessment instruments are placed in a difficult situation by these legislative changes. This is as true for the outcomes evaluator as for the psychologist using tests for diagnostic or forensic purposes. Imagine a psychologist routinely contracted to provide developmental assessments for a community agency serving preschool-aged children with disabilities. Children are enrolled in agency programs if they show substantial disabilities in one or more of the major developmental areas (e.g., cognitive, language, motor, social, adaptive/self-help). Services are allocated on the basis of individual child needs and are available without charge to the family. After the child has been with the agency for a period of time, the assessing psychologist finds substantial improvement. It appears the child no longer needs the type of service being provided, and the psychologist recommends appropriate changes. The parents take issue with the changes recommended and request a hearing on the matter. Their advocate asks for copies of all of the psychologist's testing data and, specifically, the complete protocols showing the test items themselves and the child's scores on them.

If the psychologist complies, she or he may escape legal consequences (assuming the psychologist is in a truth-in-testing jurisdiction). At the same time, she or he runs afoul of the ethical requirement (Standard 9.11) to maintain test security. The psychologist will call on his or her own ethical strictures in deciding. If that position is based in utilitarianism, the decision might be to withhold the items. This derives from concluding that the greatest good for the greatest number results from protecting the integrity of the test. To permit free and open access to test content will alter the validity of the tests the psychologist uses, making them less useful for children generally. As a result, test publishing companies will have to revise and publish new tests at a rate that appropriate standardization efforts cannot sustain. The result will likely be more expensive tests, tests with lower overall quality, or both (Kaplan & Saccuzzo, 2001). Of course, the basis for the psychologist's decision might be other than utilitarianism, leading to a different conclusion about disclosure.

The second author (CD) handles this issue forensically by providing a separate sheet for client answers that does not contain test items. This would constitute the "test data" that can be disclosed in most legal situations without concern for compromise of test security. "Test materials" then can be handled with greater care, sent only to other professionals as mandated in Section 9.11.

### Design-Related Concerns

The choice of evaluation design is dictated by the question one asks. If it does not dictate the design, at least the question should be most influential in making this choice. What makes outcomes evaluation interesting from the standpoint of ethics is that the evaluation question is not the only factor influencing choice of design, however. Two additional variables must be considered: experimental control and statistical power.

*Experimental Control.*    To answer outcomes questions unequivocally, evaluation designs must be of high quality. This generally means the evaluator has exercised sufficient care to permit ruling out alternative explanations of major findings. Setting up a study so that outcomes can be unambiguously attributed to the treatment requires holding variables other than the treatment constant. Achieving experimental control in outcomes evaluations is largely the result of: (a) limiting access to treatment, (b) maintaining internal validity, and (c) fostering external validity. Incidentally, though we treat them independently here, these activities overlap a good deal.

Access to treatment must be limited carefully so that comparisons can be made between conditions in which the treatment is present and those in which it is absent. The simplest design accomplishing this, at least on a conceptual level, is the classic two-group, experimental vs. control, with random assignment of participants to groups. The ethical challenge when potentially beneficial therapies are being evaluated is justifying the placement of persons into conditions anticipated to have no or minimal positive impact. How can we deny access to the independent variable to persons in need of help? We can choose a design involving time series methodology, but the ethical challenge is mitigated only somewhat, as the person(s) participating must still be denied access to treatment for a period of time (baseline).

There is extensive literature on the use of control conditions in outcomes research (cf., Bersoff & Bersoff, 1999; Bloom et al., 2003; Kazdin, 1998; Kendall, Flannery-Schroeder, & Ford, 1999; Speer, 1992). Speer (1992) pointed to the classic true experimental design as not likely to be feasible in most service settings. Bersoff and Bersoff (1999) suggested that control groups are "sometimes contraindicated" (p. 46) in treatment studies. Kazdin (1998) noted that the design one chooses can vary with the nature of the participant. When community volunteers are used, it is less problematic to deny treatment than if participants are drawn from persons specifically seeking treatment for some problem.

The greatest concern with the use of untreated control participants is the complete denial of treatment. Designs involving delayed treatment can mitigate this concern. One such design uses a wait-list control condition in which, rather than denying participants access to treatment, their access is merely delayed. They are placed on a waiting list and exposed to treatment at a later time, usually a period equivalent to the time taken to deliver services to experimental (or treated) participants. Wait list participants might be assessed before and after being on the list so that their status can be compared with that of the participants treated immediately. An ethical difficulty with the approach involves asking people to delay having their problems addressed. This can mean several months, in the best of circumstances, and many more in typical ones. A number of problems with wait-list designs from a scientific perspective include the high likelihood of attrition generally, and differential attrition specifically. Persons in need of treatment are unlikely to wait, seeking services somewhere else during the interim. This could lead to a loss of power as too few people remain in the wait-list group for adequate comparisons with the treated group. In addition, persons most likely to go AWOL might be those in the greatest crisis, resulting in loss of equivalence between treated and wait-list participants.

In time series methodology, the delayed access equivalent to the wait-list control includes procedures involving baseline conditions that precede treatment. For example, a multiple baseline arrangement begins by obtaining data from participants for varied periods of time before intervening (Hayes et al., 1999). The first behavior to stabilize in baseline can be treated while the others continue to be monitored. Then the next behavior to stabilize can be treated, and so on. Note that various multiple baseline designs exist. Some variations include observing multiple behaviors in one person, the same behavior in multiple people, or the same behavior in one person in multiple settings. When the design involves withholding all treatment to a client until baseline data are available, it is tantamount to a wait-list control approach. As with wait-list control groups, time series designs of the AB, ABA, ABAB, or multiple baseline varieties (cf. Gaynor, Baird, & Nelson-Gray, 1999) carry some risk of attrition. If the client is in considerable discomfort, she or he is likely to be reluctant to wait until comparison data are available from a period of no (i.e., delayed) treatment. Premature termination would jeopardize the outcomes evaluation and, if often enough, the therapist's livelihood. Moreover, it is conceivable there are differences between persons willing to tolerate a baseline condition and those who are not, thus posing the possibility of differential attrition in time series methodology as well.

Limiting access, either completely or on a delayed basis, is no less of a problem when large social or educational programs are evaluated. Imagine the ethical difficulties posed by randomly assigning customers of a managed health care organization to those receiving certain medications (e.g., CerebreX, Viagra) as part of their plan, and others not, to study the effects of such medications on long-term physical and behavioral health. Or, imagine randomly assigning zip codes in a city to those receiving extended school-day social programs and those who do not. Parents in the untreated control neighborhoods are likely to voice strong opposition to their children being denied access to the program. Using a multiple baseline across zip codes design promises eventual access on a delayed basis. This alternative is likely to mollify some critics, but certainly not all of them.

Another alternative that avoids random assignment to treated and untreated groups is the regression discontinuity design (RDD), originally discussed by Thistlethwaite and Campbell (1960). With it, persons are assigned to groups depending on their score relative to some cutoff. Thus, the experimental group will be those scoring above or below the cutoff, depending on the purpose of the particular study. In the social program example previously described, children scoring below a cutoff score on a measure of social functioning get assigned to participate, thus comprising the experimental group. Such a design offers a balance between evaluative, ethical, and social concerns in that it avoids random assignment of all potential children and provides services on the basis of need. The use of such designs comes with reductions in statistical power, however, potentially increasing the time and expense of evaluative efforts (Goldberger, 1972; Trochim & Cappelleri, 1992). Further, imagine that the program is found to be extremely effective in terms of lowered school dropout and antisocial behavior. Cutoff-based designs deny treatment to all those scoring above (or below in some cases) a certain score. This results in more children being denied the program than might have occurred if a completely randomized trial were used.

Ethical issues concerning access to treatment arise early in planning and executing outcomes evaluations. Design-related ethical quandaries do not end with resolution of access issues, however. Once the evaluation begins, it is critical to maintain control to protect whatever internal validity has been provided by procedures for assigning participants to treatment. Threats to internal validity are well-known (cf. Shadish, Cook, & Campbell, 2002), and they apply to both between- and within-case (time series) designs. Random assignment is an effective way to minimize many of these threats in between-case, multigroup designs. For within-case studies, however, more care is needed to protect against these threats. For example, natural occurrences in the lives of participants (history effects) can cloud the attribution of benefits solely to a treatment. Exercising tight controls over these is ethically, as well as practically, challenging. Do you want to tell participants to avoid any potentially beneficial extratherapeutic variable during the evaluation so you can minimize the impact of such extraneous or confounding events? Suppose, for example, you are evaluating a treatment for depression. Would you want to suggest that participants avoid changes in their lifestyles (e.g., becoming more physically active, spending more time with friends), because these might confound the treatment you are evaluating?

Diffusion or contamination also pose threats to the internal validity of between-case designs. Imagine you are exploring the effectiveness of a community program for stress reduction in unemployed single mothers. Participants in the treatment group learn certain meditative tactics that they then share with friends, some of whom just happen to be in the control group. Such between-group communication (diffusion of treatment) threatens the internal validity of the evaluation. How strenuously do you want to work to prevent this? Even if it were possible, would you want to deny the stress-lowering benefits to mothers in the untreated group? Or, suppose you paid mothers to attend the stress reduction classes and did not pay mothers in the control group. If word gets out about this inequality, unpaid mothers might resent it and experience more stress as a result. This resentful demoralization, a threat known as compensatory behavior, can affect the dependent variable such that clear interpretations of treatment effects are more difficult (Neuman, 1997).

There are also design-related ethical issues having to do with external validity. As an example, imagine you are evaluating the outcomes of a community safety reaction program, part of which involves teaching how to respond in emergency situations where criminal behavior is imminent or already in progress. After the last class you stage a rape scene near the parking lot and observe the reaction of program participants. Most respond appropriately, either running with others to assist directly or to obtain the assistance of a nearby security guard. Some of the participants do not respond appropriately, however. After the staged rape, you approach and inform all participants of the evaluative nature of the event and thank them again for attending the safety classes. What are the ethical implications of such an assessment procedure? What might be the long-range impact on a person who failed to respond appropriately? Optimum authenticity would result from assessing the reactions of participants unprepared for and completely surprised by the staged scene. Thus, the generalizability of the study's results (and its external validity) can be determined more fully. However, recall that the APA Code (Standard 9.03) requires psychologists to "obtain informed consent for assessments, evaluations, or diagnostic services" (APA, 2002, p. 1071). Unfortunately, fully informing participants in this example can jeopardize the external validity of the evaluation. It is very likely that knowing there is to be a pretend "emergency" after the class will sensitize at least some people to respond differently than they would without the warning. Moreover, even if (or possibly, especially if) previously warned, persons responding inappropriately still have that reaction to carry with them in the future.

Finally, there are design-related ethical questions connected with the statistical power arranged for the design. At the outset, evaluators must assess their own tolerance for Type I and Type II errors. Both forms will be present in even the best of studies. If the evaluator wants to be sure to find an effect, a large number of participants will be included. This enhances statistical power and minimizes Type II errors (i.e., failing to find an effect when there is one). At the same time, it increases the probability of Type I errors (i.e., concluding an effect when there really is not one). Imagine you are evaluating a costly new medical procedure for a managed health care organization (MHCO). Including a large number of participants will increase the likelihood of showing the procedure is effective. Including too few runs the risk of inadequate statistical power and increased likelihood of a Type II error. Which type of mistake would you be most comfortable making: (a) showing the procedure works when it really does not or when its effects are small, thereby moving the MHCO to spend money wastefully, or (b) showing the procedure does not work when it really does, thereby contributing to the MHCO's failure to adopt a procedure that might provide important health benefits to its members? You will have to call on your own sense of ethics in deciding which type of risk is more acceptable, offering an ineffective or marginally effective procedure at considerable expense to the MHCO, or failing to offer an effective procedure that will benefit the health of participants. Incidentally, this is a dilemma faced every day in our system of justice, where there is a decided bias in favor of Type II errors. We are much more comfortable judging a guilty person to be innocent (Type II error) than finding an innocent person guilty (Type I error).

Added complications occur in individual practice when treatments are conceived as a series of $n = 1$ designs. Again, critics of evaluation as we present it here might point to the unique needs and characteristics of each patient and the need to tailor treatment to meet individual needs. This undermines the capacity to control confounds and to generalize beyond the client, but it does not render evaluation irrelevant. For instance, even if practicalities dictate against the ABA design, value placed on evaluation would suggest the AB design. Here, the client would cooperate in assessing the true baseline of the relevant behaviors or cognitions. It is well-known that observation itself may have some effect on behavior (Lam, Cole, Shapiro, & Bambara, 1994; Shabini, Wilder, & Flood, 2001); it is interesting, however, that at least part of this effect may be because of the client receiving accurate evaluative information (e.g., that panic attacks are of a greater or lesser frequency in Setting X than in Setting Y).

### Agency-Sponsored Evaluations of Treatment and Program Outcomes

As the examples above suggest, personal morals, professional ethics, and the interests of one's employer may sometimes be out of synch with each other. Most evaluators, like it or not, are beholden to someone who is likely to have an interest in the outcomes of their work. Many are employees of agencies with an interest in assessing their effectiveness. Many receive grant support from state or federal agencies (e.g., National Institute of Mental Health, U.S. Department of Education). Even the typical "independent" practitioner is apt to see clients whose bills are paid by a third party, whether an insurance company, MHCO, or the client's employer (as in employee assistance programs, EAPs). Any of these "sponsors" is very likely to influence the conduct of outcomes evaluations, either directly or indirectly.

Sponsor influence can extend to all aspects of an evaluative effort, including the choice of dependent variables and measures of these, choice of design, participants, and matters related to disseminating the study's findings. On a large scale, of course, governments can determine what will be funded and the questions to be asked. Evaluators will be motivated to propose projects in those areas most likely to receive financial support. Moreover, they will be likely to address the specific questions of most interest to the sponsor (aka, funding agency) (e.g., "How can we treat__?" rather than "What are its origins?" or "How can we prevent__?"). An evaluator might have a personal interest in whether a treatment works with a particular type of person (e.g., outpatient behavioral health clinic client complaining of depression). If federal funds are earmarked for treatment of persons incarcerated in state and federal correctional facilities for alcohol and drug-related offenses, however, the opportunistic evaluator might refocus on these persons instead.

A program evaluator in a large social agency might be asked to determine whether a certain novel early intervention approach for children with autism is making a difference. The evaluator proposes randomly assigning children to this approach or the community standard. The agency does not support random assignment, however, saying families have a right to choose the intervention approach most suitable to their child. The evaluator reluctantly selects a quasi-experimental design instead. The data are collected, analyzed, and presented to the directors of the agency. Concurrently, the evaluator prepares to disseminate the findings to the professional community via conference presentations and peer-reviewed journals. Within the limits of the design used, the outcomes show the statistical superiority of the novel approach. They do not show the clinical superiority of the approach, however. Moreover, because the novel intervention is three times more costly than the community standard, the agency is unenthusiastic about encouraging families to choose it for their child. The agency's directors recommend that the evaluator emphasize the clinical equivalence of the improvements of the two approaches, downplaying their statistical differences. Further, the agency's public relations firm prepares press releases completely omitting any reference to statistically significant differences favoring the novel approach.

There are a number of ethical implications implied in this fictitious example of sponsor influence over the conduct of outcomes evaluations. And, it would be easy to introduce others. They illustrate the ethical minefields evaluators traverse when undertaking sponsored evaluations. Given their inevitability, it is wise for the evaluator to have frank discussions with agency staff before committing to a particular outcomes study (Joint Committee on Standards for Educational Evaluation, 1994). The concerns to address involve essentially the degree of control the evaluator will have over the entire process, from phrasing the question(s) to selecting the design, collecting, analyzing, and eventually disseminating the results. Be sure to include discussion of how and when the agency might communicate results to the general public. After talking with sponsors about these matters, the evaluator must assess her or his comfort with the ethical implications to be confronted. If ethical concerns exceed the evaluator's personal threshold and cannot be resolved, she or he will have to withhold participation.

**Data Ownership and Data Management Concerns**

As with the collection of information about persons in any endeavor, questions can arise as to ownership of data. The recently enacted federal HIPAA, mentioned earlier, is relevant in that it deals with the handling of protected health information (PHI), or information that is individually identifiable and relates to a health condition of a patient. It includes demographic information, information about past, present, and future physical or behavioral health conditions, the services provided, and how payment occurred. The HIPAA makes it clear that patients have a right to access their records and that psychologists and other health care providers must release at least certain types of information if their clients ask for it. It also directs providers to inform clients about their rights and how the agency will use information about them. The HIPAA is very similar to legislation requiring that financial and certain other public companies disclose the type of information collected about customers, how that information is shared within the company and between it and others, and the customer's right to opt out of certain uses of their information. Opt out clauses generally involve ways information will be shared, not other uses of that information.

Note that there is a generally accepted distinction between records themselves and the information contained in those records. It is clear that the records belong to the service provider or agency. The HIPAA directs providers to release information, but not that they give up the physical records containing the information. Nor does it prohibit internal uses of the information, such as for quality assurance purposes, including outcomes evaluations. Thus, an evaluator would appear bound to release PHI if asked by the client, but could still use that information as data in evaluative activities. There is no mandated provision that the client be permitted to have her or his data omitted from use in this way.

Thus, it would appear that the issue of information ownership is not completely settled. Neuman (1997) called attention to the masses of information collected on each of us daily, noting that it is used in innumerable ways about which we know nothing. Further, the data are frequently sold to others without our knowledge and used in still further ways of which we are uninformed. Some of this data "sharing" is now covered in legislation such as that previously mentioned. The vast majority is not, however, and this permits the continued sale of information about us without any requirement that we be allowed to share in the proceeds. As Neuman suggested (1997), personal information can be regarded much as intellectual property in which we have a continued interest after the initial transaction releasing that information to others. In this regard, such "private property" is different from physical property that typically holds no further relevance for us once we sell it to others. The ethical outcomes evaluator would do well to consider data ownership issues at the outset and share as much as is reasonable about how data will be used with potential participants as part of an informed consent process.

In human service agencies, it can occur that data collected for outcomes evaluations have clinical, or practical, implications as well. What are the evaluator's responsibilities if asked by others in an agency for information of this sort? For example, imagine you are evaluating the effectiveness of an educational program and you observe teacher–pupil interactions directly. Knowing you are doing this, school administrators ask you for information as to how effective you think a particular teacher is with students in your study. What is your obligation to provide this information? Presumably, the teacher you are observing has an agreement with the school permitting such observations. It would be well for the evaluator to inquire of this, however, before making the observations. Moreover, it would be important to ask whether the school and teacher's agreement covers all uses of any information collected. It might be simpler to anticipate such situations and deal with them in the original discussion of the nature of the evaluation and the types and uses that can be made of any data to be collected.

Finally, managing the data after they are collected presents some ethical challenges. How long should one keep them? In what form? With access by whom? With respect to the first question, program evaluation standards (e.g., AEA, 1994; Joint Committee on Standards for Educational Evaluation, 1994) are silent. Some extrapolation from the APA Code suggests clinical records are kept for a period of time consistent with law (Standard 6.01, Documentation of Professional and Scientific Work and Maintenance of Records). The form data are kept in is controlled primarily by the requirement for confidentiality (APA Code, Standard 6.02, Maintenance, Dissemination, and Disposal of Confidential Records of Professional and Scientific Work). Good practice involves coding each person's information and then removing names from the data, leaving only the identifier code. A cross-referenced list of codes and names is kept separately from the data, accessible only to the evaluator. Access to evaluation data is carefully controlled and generally limited to the evaluator unless prior agreement has established that specific other persons have access rights as well.

### Providing Feedback to Clients Whose Data Are Used

If a client's information is used in an outcomes evaluation, is the evaluator obligated to inform the client of the results of the study? The APA Code requires debriefing research participants, to wit, "Psychologists provide a prompt opportunity for participants to obtain appropriate information about the nature, results, and conclusions of the research . . ." (Standard 8.08, Debriefing, APA, 2002, p. 1070). To the extent outcomes evaluations are distinct from research, as argued earlier, debriefing may or may not be expected. In the routine collection of data to monitor treatment effects, it would seem there are both ethical and clinical rationales for informing the client. Standard 9.04, Release of Test Data (APA, 2002) requires that "psychologists provide test data to the client/patient" (p. 1071), and it includes in the definition of data, "psychologists' notes and recordings concerning client/patient statements and behavior during an examination" (p. 1071). Although clearly directed at psychological assessment, the language seems applicable to data obtained in the ongoing monitoring of treatment effectiveness as well. Finally, Standard 10.10, Terminating Therapy (APA, 2002) requires that psychologists terminate when clients no longer need the service, are not benefiting, or are actually being harmed by continuing. Sharing objective, progress monitoring data continuously with clients during treatment would seem an important means of minimizing surprise and contentiousness when the therapist concludes termination is in order.

In their Client Bill of Rights covering psychological therapy, Bloom et al. (2003) state that "Clients have the right . . . to be a part of and informed about the *evaluation* of their own situations, so that they may profit from and make decisions based on these data" (p. 680). Thus, it would seem prudent, ethically responsible, and clinically beneficial to share evaluative information with individual clients in therapeutic relationships. What of outcomes evaluations involving programs?

Standard P6 of *The Program Evaluation Standards* (Joint Committee on Standards for Educational Evaluation, 1994) states, "The formal parties to an evaluation should ensure that the full set of evaluation findings along with pertinent limitations are [*sic*] made accessible to the persons affected by the evaluation, and any others with expressed legal rights to receive the results" (p. 109). In their discussion of this standard, the Joint Committee noted that persons who may be affected by the results of an evaluation will be disadvantaged if they cannot have sufficient access to findings and the details of the study on which they are based. For example, if outcomes suggest the program should be discontinued, stakeholders with an interest in its continuing, including participants contributing data to the outcomes, will want access to information that would help develop a counterargument. In such cases, it does not appear incumbent on the evaluator to make available individually identifiable information. An exception would be the unusual circumstance in which one person's data were the primary basis for some major administrative action related to the program's operation or continued viability. For example, if a client had a psychotic break or a child were substantially traumatized by some aspect of a program, there might be changes resulting therefrom. If so, the client or client's legal representatives would be permitted access to relevant data.

This is similar to situations that can arise in research contexts when an experimenter becomes aware of some "clinically relevant" information concerning a participant. Bersoff and Bersoff (1999) beseeched researchers not to collect information they are not prepared to handle. Some clinically sensitive data (e.g., about depression, anxiety, sexuality) can be anticipated to have the potential for negative participant reaction, and ethical behavior requires anticipating this and preparing effective ways of handling it. In research with children, the Society for Research in Child Development's (SRCD) ethics code requires that investigators discuss with parents information coming to their attention that the child's well-being might be jeopardized in some way. Further, the SRCD's ethical code requires the researcher to involve experts that can arrange assistance necessary to minimize difficulties for the child.

Again, while the Bersoff and Bersoff (1999) and SRCD recommendations apply specifically to research activities, they appear relevant to program evaluations as well. An evaluator who becomes aware that a participant's welfare is jeopardized during participation in a program has an obligation to act to minimize potential harm. This would apply whether the harm is a direct result of the program or merely associated with participation in it. Imagine a situation in which you were employed to evaluate an early intervention program. In the course of aggregating data on a particular program over several months, you observe that a child is getting progressively worse. What is your notice obligation? Are you morally bound to react in some way? Applying the SRCD code to the evaluative context suggests it is in the child's best interest for you to act. At the very least, discussing the decline with program administrators would seem appropriate. They might not be aware of it or of the extent of the decline.

### Using Program Evaluation Data for Clinical Purposes

The preceding discussion is related to concerns that arise when data obtained specifically to evaluate a program are converted to some other use. Imagine a situation in which information is collected specifically for program evaluative purposes. Using the early childhood intervention example previously described, imagine that developmental profiles are procured every 90 days to examine overall program effectiveness. The instruments used are specific to the evaluation and not routinely employed by the program in its own assessment activities. The parents of one of the children in the program file a complaint, stating their child is not making adequate progress. Program administrators ask for your data on the child to document growth more thoroughly. Is there any ethical difficulty in providing it? On its face, this seems like a relatively uncontroversial request that can be responded to positively, assuming the planned use of the data is consistent with published information concerning reliability and validity of the instruments in question. It also assumes you have an agreement about such uses with the persons who hired you to conduct the evaluation and that participants have given their consent.

Now let's make this a bit more complicated. Suppose your data support the parents' contention that the child is not making adequate progress. You make it available to the program's administrators as requested. After seeing it, they decide not to use it and instruct you not to mention it to the parents. What are your ethical responsibilities in this situation? Recall Standard P6 of *The Program Evaluation Standards*, requiring that a "full set of evaluation findings along with pertinent limitations are made accessible to the persons affected by the evaluation" (Joint Committee on Standards for Educational Evaluation, 1994, p. 109). The guidelines for this principle emphasize that "both the evaluator and the client bear responsibility for meeting this standard" (p. 110). Further, they note the evaluator's responsibility to "Encourage clients to provide all affected persons with information that is appropriate, timely, in appropriate linguistic form, and that helps them to be enlightened contributors, consumers, critics and observers" (p. 110).

The Joint Committee also lists common errors evaluators make with respect to disclosing findings, including failing to be adequately involved in information release. In this regard, they warn against allowing the client to release information selectively. Ethical evaluators discuss disclosure of findings with clients in detail before entering into contractual agreements. They include clauses in their contracts specifically related to these matters. With respect to our early intervention example, such a clause should cover the release of information pertaining to individual participants, as well as to aggregated data. Thus, the program administrators would be expected to share any data obtained from the evaluator with the child's parents, regardless of whether it placed the program in a favorable light. One can imagine this obligation extending to other contexts as well. For example, an MHCO could not selectively present data showing treatment effectiveness while withholding data showing patients not improving or getting worse. If a client withholds findings from intended users or misrepresents them, "in violation of the formal agreement [between client and evaluator], the evaluator must inform the client and subsequently take steps as necessary to inform the user" (Joint Committee on Standards for Educational Evaluation, 1994, p. 54).

## ETHICAL CONCERNS IN COMMUNICATING TREATMENT OUTCOMES

### Assuring Anonymity, Protecting Confidentiality

As argued earlier, protection of confidentiality is one of the most consensually agreed-on markers of an ethical evaluation. Issues in the communication of evaluation to insurance companies, client, family, and involved others have already been covered. In the last decade, however, a new layer of complexity has been added to the discussion of confidentiality in case reports.

The APA Code clearly states that the responsible psychologist protects the confidentiality of the client (Standard 4.01, Maintaining Confidentiality). In publication, this has traditionally been translated as the duty to disguise case material, although the manner and depth of disguise is a matter of some debate (Gabbard & Williams, 2001; Goldberg, 1997; Renik, 1994). The debate centers on the potential conflict between the duty of the clinical scientist to present data honestly and the duty to protect client confidentiality. For instance, when the therapist changes the career of the presented client from doctor to engineer to protect the doctor's privacy, does the therapist author render the case study less useful to others (and less honest)? Perhaps. Many clinical scientists solve this dilemma by completely deleting individual descriptive data. Unfortunately, this prevents others from noticing possible connections between individual difference variables and outcome variables.

A relatively new area for discussion concerns whether the duty to protect client confidentiality is a shared professional duty as opposed to (or as well as) an individual professional duty. Do psychologists have a duty to the field and to society to refrain from behavior that compromises confidentiality of their colleagues? We would argue that this duty does exist, following from the explicit recommendation to "encourage ethical behavior by . . . colleagues" (APA Code Preamble) and to refrain from behavior that would fail to "respect the dignity and worth of all people, and the rights of individuals to privacy, confidentiality and self-determination."

This issue was brought to the attention of psychologists recently when a researcher sought to support an alternative theoretical understanding of a published case study. To do so, she attempted to discover the identity of the client to obtain personally relevant data pertinent to the alternative explanation. The client's consent was not obtained. A series of publications divulging the client's personal data ensued. This action was viewed as ethically appropriate by the researcher, because of her belief that the original case study material was inaccurate, incomplete, or inadequately interpreted, and therefore could be harmful to the public. Following this argument, a behavioral psychologist could defend the decision to hire private investigators (as was done in the above case) to find the patient of an analytic therapist who had published an outcome study. No matter how deep the disguise, it is likely that a skilled investigator could track car license numbers or photograph clients entering a therapist's office and "out" the clients. Thus, no therapist could give reasonable assurance of privacy and confidentiality to any client or set of clients if she or he anticipated publishing their case histories. The potentially negative impact on the dissemination of knowledge in contentious areas is obvious.

The second author, and others known to her, also has had the experience of authors seeking to receive copies of taped client treatments, considering these tapes the "data" of a published case study, available to other authors after publication. The APA Ethics Code precludes disclosure of "data" when client confidentiality cannot be preserved, as it cannot be so here. However, more explicit standards are likely to be needed as more requests such as these accumulate within forensic and other potentially controversial cases.

## Responding Responsibly to "Irresponsible" Critics

At several points previously outlined, we dealt with sharing information from outcome evaluations. As we have seen, when a program or individual client's evaluation is completed and results are disseminated, there are likely to be those who disagree with them. Others may not take issue with the results, but challenge the appropriateness of the study in the first place. Still others might express concern with certain aspects of the methodology, design, or analysis. When such criticism is formalized, as in published reactions in professional journals, it is a straightforward matter to respond to the issues being raised. Generally, journal editors monitor criticisms and rebuttals, making sure both are responsible and appropriate. Public programs that disseminate data on their effectiveness often do so less formally, however, making use of in-house technical reports, newsletters, and the popular media. This puts information in the hands of a wider variety of people and opens the door to less formalized critiques than are customary in academic circles. Persons unhappy with some aspect of the evaluation (usually its outcomes) may express this in numerous ways, including personal attacks, picketing the evaluator's presentations, calling the head of the agency and demanding a public accounting of funds expended for the evaluation, and taking out newspaper advertisements criticizing the study and its principals. As just mentioned, they might demand copies of the data so they can check the accuracy of the original analyses, run their own analyses, or take both approaches.

Responding appropriately to criticism involves taking steps to anticipate (and prevent or minimize) it in the first place. When an evaluation involves public programs, it is a good idea to include the public in discussions at the planning stage. These can identify concerns and take steps to mitigate them. They can also empower the persons most likely to be affected to provide suggestions that increase the perceived fairness of the evaluation to them. Forming an advisory committee that includes prominent members of affected groups can be an effective means of getting organized input at the outset and over the course of an evaluation study. Indeed, this group can even help deal with "irresponsible" critics as they arise.

Requests for copies of original data are difficult, especially when publicly funded programs are being evaluated. The APA Code (Standard 8.14, Sharing Research Data for Verification) discusses data sharing where research is concerned, noting that "psychologists do not withhold the data on which their conclusions are based from other competent professionals who seek to verify the substantive claims through reanalysis and who intend to use such data only for that purpose" (APA, 2002, p. 1071).

The code obliges such sharing after the data are published, however, and only when the participants' confidentiality can be protected and legal rights concerning proprietary data do not preclude releasing them. The American Evaluation Association and the Joint Committee on Standards for Educational Evaluation both emphasize open access to evaluative information, especially when public programs are at issue. They do not restrict access to specific purposes as implied in the APA Code (e.g., to independent verification). For example, the AEA recommends that evaluators give relevant stakeholders access to evaluative information, and it recommends that evaluators make efforts to distribute that information to stakeholders, assuming sufficient resources to permit it (AEA, 1994). Nor do these organizations restrict access to certain times (e.g., after publication). Nonetheless, the APA's restriction of access to research data until after they are published is sensibly applied to outcomes evaluations as well. In cases where publication is not planned, access should be permitted after a final report has been prepared and made available to the client for review.

Timeliness is important. The Joint Committee recommends establishing realistic time lines for making reports available to intended users and sticking to them. Standard U6, Report Timeliness and Dissemination, addresses timeliness, noting that "significant interim findings and evaluation reports should be disseminated to intended users, so that they can be used in a timely fashion" (Joint Committee on Standards for Educational Evaluation, 1994, p. 53). Common errors mentioned by the Joint Committee in this regard include (a) releasing findings too soon, before they are checked for errors and corrected, (b) delaying release inappropriately, and (c) failing to estimate time lines adequately. Avoiding these errors and delivering results to the client and other users in a timely manner can help reduce suspicion about the evaluation and remove a legitimate basis for criticism.

## AVOIDING AND DEALING WITH ETHICS CONFLICTS

The APA Ethics Code places considerable stress on the collegial resolution of ethics conflicts. It is a violation of the code to file a complaint against a colleague for frivolous reasons, that is, "with reckless disregard for or willful ignorance of facts that would disprove the allegation" (Standard 1.07, Improper Complaints). Informal resolutions of ethical violations by colleagues are encouraged when feasible. Whether or not such informal resolutions are likely to occur, the aggrieved professional is well advised to consult with colleagues about the allegedly unethical conduct. If theoretical orientation or other professionally relevant dimensions distinguish the accused and aggrieved professional, the wronged professional should attempt to select a consultant who is likely to give a fair evaluation to the alternative point of view.

Outcome evaluation is a prime arena for these conflicts between professionals. Therapists may show an almost religious adherence to their own therapeutic orientations and may be quite zealous in their criticism of competing orientations or instruments. The current controversy over use of the Rorschach (cf. Gacono, Evans, & Viglione, 2002) and the battle over the appropriate manner of interviewing child witnesses during abuse evaluations (cf. Eisen, Quas, & Goodman, 2002) are two examples, with critics moving rather quickly to demeaning language that is unlikely to advance the debate (e.g., "child abuse hysteria"). It is not only more ethical (respecting others' points of view, respecting diversity) but also more effective to attempt to reformulate the problem in a way that does not belittle one side of an argument. This process may help to isolate the important dimensions that lead to the varying positions and may lead to more constructive dialogue.

As referenced earlier, the process of informed consent and structured agreement also may aid in the prevention of ethical conflicts. Koocher and Keith-Spiegel (1998) championed the positive effect of imposing structure in dealing with volatile or difficult associates. Clear agreements about the nature, use, interpretation, and ownership of evaluative data are useful in such situations.

## SUMMARY AND RECOMMENDATIONS

The foregoing covers a lot of material concerning the ethics of outcomes assessment. The principal points we want readers to consider are the following:

1. The APA Code states that an ethical psychologist will terminate or change services for a client for whom initial services are ineffective. This recommendation cannot be followed without periodic service evaluation. Thus, we recommend that all professionals institute some form of effectiveness or outcome evaluation if they are involved in practice.

2. Evaluating outcomes should involve identifying goals, selecting reliable and valid measures to represent variables implied in these goals, and arranging treatment and evaluation processes to maximize clarity of answers to the evaluation questions.

3. Care should be taken in choice of instruments for measurements. These should be appropriate to both ultimate and instrumental goals. Moreover, they should ensure that undue invasion of privacy (and collection of unnecessary private data) is minimized and guarantee a valid assessment. Obsolete instruments and shotgun demographic questionnaires containing sensitive questions should be avoided.

4. Professional evaluators should be aware that human beings are prone to bias. To protect their clients and their science, they should rest at least part of the evaluation on objective assessment with established methods or established norms.

5. As we continue to recognize the importance of evaluation of outcomes as a part of ethical treatment, we should realize the need for further continuing education training. The competent professional must have adequate skills in psychometrics and in outcome evaluation.

6. High-quality designs are necessary to evaluate outcomes. For many, the development of these designs might require expert consultation, particularly in program or practice evaluation. Within-case, wait-list control, and regression discontinuity designs may be ethically acceptable alternatives to no-treatment control groups.

7. In cases of outcome evaluation for the single client, within-case designs should be considered. The baseline period can be used to determine treatments likely to be effective when implemented after stable data are available.

8. Informed consent should be undertaken as a part of the treatment process, involving clients as much as is feasible in the identification of goals, choice of reliable and valid assessments, and preferred method of feedback between client and evaluator. The evaluator should focus on informed consent as an ethical duty, not likely to be met by a simple signature to a complex jargon-laden document.

9. If practice or outcome evaluation is taking place in large part or in whole for reasons that do not involve the welfare of the specific clients being evaluated, evaluators should seek consultation with colleagues, and preferably should involve a local or agency IRB.

10. Special care should be taken to guard the confidentiality of the clients' data. The informed consent discussion should include full disclosure of what type of information will be generated and what choices the client will have as to its dissemination. If the client does not need the information, the evaluative data should be kept in a manner that precludes a link between client identification and test answers.

11. Confidentiality of client outcome data is the responsibility of the individual psychologist, and of the field. Psychologists should not take actions that jeopardize the confidentiality of clients voluntarily participating in research or outcome evaluation.

12. The timing of release of information, both to clients and to the public, is an important issue that deserves close attention. Realistic time lines for dissemination of information should be developed, with time built in for double-checking of potentially upsetting or controversial findings.

13. Client feedback should be clear and helpful, taking into account personal factors regarding both client and evaluator that could negatively impact the accuracy of the evaluation. The nature of this feedback, and particularly any restrictions thereon, should be part of the informed consent.

14. The above discussion should include the rights of the researcher or evaluator to share the data with other researchers or agencies. Evaluators should not forward data without clarification as to the use that is planned for the data by the receiving professional.

15. Even in the best of circumstances, ethical professionals should expect occasionally to be challenged by colleagues within and outside the field. Discussions with involved stakeholder groups in the planning stages of the design help to minimize criticism later. Involving trusted colleagues at various points in the evaluation process, particularly colleagues whose opinions or theoretical orientation differ from yours, can also be a good preventive maneuver.

16. Above all, data collected in ongoing efforts to evaluate work with clients, whether one person or many, should be used to inform decisions related to that work. These decisions include what intervention to use, whether it is being effective, when to terminate, and when to give up and refer the client to someone else.

## REFERENCES

Adler, P. A., & Adler, P. (1994). Observational techniques. In N. K. Denzin & Y. S. Lincoln (Eds.), *Handbook of qualitative research* (pp. 377–392). Thousand Oaks, CA: Sage.

American Counseling Association. (1989). *Responsibilities of users of standardized tests*. Alexandria, VA: Author.

American Educational Research Association, American Psychological & Association, & National Council on Measurement in Education. (1999). *Standards for educational and psychological testing*. Washington, DC: Author.

American Evaluation Association. (1994). Guiding principles for evaluators. *New Directions for Evaluation, 66*, 19–26.

American Psychological Association. (2002). Ethical principles of psychologists and code of conduct. *American Psychologist, 57*, 1060–1073.

American Psychological Association Ethics Committee. (1988). Trends in ethics cases, common pitfalls, and published resources. *American Psychologist, 43*, 564–572.

Association for the Advancement of Behavior Therapy. (1977). Ethical issues for human services. *Behavior Therapy, 8*, 763–764.

Barrios, B. A. (1993). Direct observation. In T. H. Ollendick & M. Hersen (Eds.), *Handbook of child and adolescent assessment* (pp. 140–164). Boston: Allyn & Bacon.

Bersoff, D. M., & Bersoff, D. N. (1999). Ethical perspectives in clinical research. In P. C. Kendall, J. N. Butcher, & G. N. Holmbeck (Eds.), *Handbook of research methods in clinical psychology* (2nd ed., pp. 31–53). New York: Wiley.

Bloom, M., Fischer, J., & Orme, J. G. (2003). *Evaluating practice: Guidelines for the accountable professional* (4th ed.). Boston: Allyn & Bacon.

Boechler, V., Neufeld, A., & McKim, R. (2002). Evaluation of client satisfaction in a community mental health center: Selection of a tool. *Canadian Journal of Program Evaluation, 17*, 97–117.

Braaten, E., & Handelsman, M. (1997). Client preferences for informed consent information. *Ethics and Behavior, 7*, 311–328.

Briere, J., Elliott, D., Harris, K., & Cotman, A. (1995). Trauma Symptom Inventory: Psychometrics and association with childhood and adult victimization in clinical samples. *Journal of Interpersonal Violence, 10*, 387–401.

Burke, C. (1995). Until death do us part: An exploration into confidentiality following the death of a client. *Professional Psychology: Research and Practice, 26*, 278–280.

Bury, A., & Bagby, R. (2002). The detection of feigned uncoached and coached posttraumatic stress disorder with the MMPI-2 in a sample of workplace accident victims. *Psychological Assessment, 14*, 472–484.

Clement, P. W. (1999). *Outcomes and incomes*. New York: Guilford.

Cone, J. D. (1971). Social desirability scale values and ease of responding to personality statements. *Proceedings of the 79th Annual Convention of the American Psychological Association*, 119–120.

Cone, J. D. (2001). *Evaluating outcomes: Empirical tools for effective practice*. Washington, DC: American Psychological Association.

Dawes, R. (1996). *House of cards: Psychology and psychotherapy built on myth*. New York: Simon & Schuster.

Dent, C., Galaif, J., & Susman, S. (1993). Demographic, psychosocial, and behavioral differences in samples of actively and passively consented adolescents. *Addictive Behaviors, 18*, 51–56.

Doss, R., Chelung, G., & Naugle, R. (1999). Victoria Symptom Validity Test: Compensation-seeking vs. non-compensation-seeking patients in a general clinical setting. *Journal of Forensic Neuropsychology, 1*, 5–20.

Eisen, M., Quas, J., & Goodman, G. (2002). *Memory and suggestibility in the forensic interview*. New York: Lawrence Erlbaum Associates.

Epstein, G., Steingarten, J., Weinstein, H., & Nashel, H. (1977). Panel report: Impact of law on the practice of psychotherapy. *Journal of Psychiatry and Law, 5*, 7–40.

Fiske, D. W. (1969, September). *Subject reactions to inventory format and content*. Paper presented at the meeting of the American Psychological Association, Washington, DC.

Gabbard, G., & Williams, P. (2001). Preserving confidentiality in the writing of case reports. *International Journal of Psychoanalysis, 82*, 1067–1068.

Gacono, C., Evans, F., & Viglione, D. (2002). The Rorschach in forensic practice. *Journal of Forensic Psychology Practice, 2*, 33–54.

Gaynor, S. T., Baird, S. C., & Nelson-Gray, R. O. (1999). Application of time series (single-subject) designs in clinical psychology. In P. C. Kendall, J. N. Butcher, & G. N. Holmbeck (Eds.), *Handbook of research methods in clinical psychology* (2nd ed., pp. 297–329). New York: Wiley.

Goldberg, A. (1997). Writing case histories. *International Journal of Psychoanalysis, 78*, 435–438.

Goldberger, A. S. (1972). *Selection bias in evaluating treatment effects: Some formal illustrations* (Unpublished discussion paper 123-172). Madison: University of Wisconsin, Institute for Research on Poverty.

Goldstein, A., Frasier, P., & Curtis, P. (1996). Consent form readability in university-sponsored research. *Journal of Family Practice, 42*, 606–611.

Handelsman, M., & Galvin, M. (1988). Facilitating informed consent for outpatient psychotherapy: A suggested written format. *Professional Psychology: Research and Practice, 19*, 223–225.

Handelsman, M., Kemper, M., Kesson-Graig, P., McLain, J., & Johnsrud, C. (1986). Use, content, and readability of written informed consent forms for treatment. *Professional Psychology: Research and Practice, 17*, 514–518.

Hawkins, R. P., Mathews, J. R., & Hamdan, L. (1999). *Measuring behavioral health outcomes: A practical guide.* New York: Kluwer Academic/Plenum.

Hayes, S. C., Barlow, D. H., & Nelson-Gray, R. O. (1999). *The scientist practitioner: Research and accountability in the age of managed care* (2nd ed.) Boston: Allyn & Bacon.

Hochhauser, M. (1999). Informed consent and patient's rights documents: A right, a rite, or a rewrite? *Ethics and Behavior, 9*, 1–20.

Hsu, L. M. (1999). Caveats concerning comparisons of change rates obtained with five methods of identifying significant client changes: Comment on Speer and Greenbaum (1995). *Journal of Consulting and Clinical Psychology, 67*, 594–598.

Jacob, T., Tennenbaum, D., Seilhamer, R. A., Bargiel, K., & Sharon, T. (1994). Reactivity effects during naturalistic observation of distressed and nondistressed families. *Journal of Family Psychology, 8*, 354–363.

Jacobson, N. S., & Truax, P. (1991). Clinical significance: A statistical approach to defining meaningful change in psychotherapy research. *Journal of Consulting and Clinical Psychology, 59*, 12–19.

Joint Committee on Standards for Educational Evaluation. (1994). *The program evaluation standards: How to assess evaluations of educational programs.* Thousand Oaks, CA: Sage.

Juran, J. M., Seder, L. A., & Gryna, F. M. (1962). *Quality control handbook.* New York: McGraw-Hill.

Kaplan, R. M., & Saccuzzo, D. P. (2001). *Psychological testing: Principles, applications, and issues* (5th ed.). Pacific Grove, CA: Brooks/Cole.

Kazdin, A. E. (1998). *Research design in clinical psychology* (3rd ed.). Boston: Allyn & Bacon.

Kendall, P. C., Flannery-Schroeder, E. C., & Ford, J. (1999). Therapy outcome research methods. In P. C. Kendall, J. N. Butcher, & G. N. Holmbeck (Eds.), *Handbook of research methods in clinical psychology* (2nd ed., pp. 330–363). New York: Wiley.

Koocher, G. P., & Keith-Spiegel, P. (Eds.). (1998). *Ethics in psychology: Professional standards and cases* (2nd ed.). New York: Oxford University Press.

Lam, A., & Cole, C., Shapiro, E., & Bambara, L. (1994). Relative effects of self-monitoring on-task behavior, academic accuracy, and disruptive behavior. *School Psychology Review, 23*, 44–58.

Levine, S., & Stagno, S. (2001). Informed consent for case reports: The ethical dilemma of right to privacy versus pedagogical freedom. *Journal of Psychotherapy Practice and Research, 10*, 193–201.

Lightdale, J. R., Hayer, C., Duer, A., Lind-White, C., Jenkins, S., Siegel, B., et al. (2001). Effects of intravenous secretin on language and behavior of children with autism and gastrointestinal symptoms: A single-blinded, open-label pilot study. *Pediatrics, 108*(5), 1199–1200.

Lloyd, A., & Hansen, J. (2003). Philosophical foundations of professional ethics. In W. T. O'Donohue & K. E. Ferguson (Eds.), *Handbook of ethics for psychologists.* Thousand Oaks, CA: Sage.

Marsden, J., Stewart, D., Gossop, M., Rolfe, A., Bacchus, L., Griffiths, P., et al. (2000). Assessing client satisfaction with treatment for substance use problems and the development of the Treatment Perception Questionnaire (TPQ). *Addiction Research, 8*, 455–470.

Maruish, M. E. (2002). *Psychological testing in the age of managed behavioral health care.* Mahwah, NJ: Lawrence Erlbaum Associates.

McFall, R. M., & Lillisand, D. B. (1971). Behavior rehearsal with modeling and coaching in assertive training. *Journal of Abnormal Psychology, 77*, 295–303.

Middlemist, D., Knowles, E. S., & Matter, C. F. (1976). Personal space invasions in the lavatory: Suggestive evidence for arousal. *Journal of Personality and Social Psychology, 33*, 541–546.

Neilson, W. A., Knott, T. A., & Carhart, P. W. (Eds.). (1950). *Webster's new international dictionary of the English language* (2nd ed.). Springfield, MA: G. & C. Merriam.

Neuman, W. L. (1997). *Social research methods: Qualitative and quantitative approaches* (3rd ed.). Boston: Allyn & Bacon.

Parikh, N., Parker, R., & Nurss, J. (1995). Shame and health literacy: The unspoken connection. *Patient Education and Counseling, 27*, 33–39.

Pinals, D., Malhotra, A., Breier, A., & Pickar, D. (1998). Informed consent in schizophrenia research. *Psychiatric Services, 49*, 244.

Pratt, S., Berman, W. H., & Hurt, S. W. (1998). Ethics and outcomes in managed behavioral health care: "Trust me, I'm a psychologist." In R. F. Small & L. R. Barnhill (Eds.), *Practicing in the new mental health marketplace: Ethical, legal, and moral issues* (pp. 121–137). Washington, DC: American Psychological Association.

Rees, L., Tombaugh, T., & Gansler, D. (1998). Five validation experiments of the Test of Memory Malingering (TOMM). *Psychological Assessment, 10,* 10–20.

Renik, O. (1994). Publication of clinical facts. *International Journal of Psychoanalysis, 75,* 1245–1250.

Rosen, A., & Proctor, E. K. (1981). Distinctions between treatment outcomes and their implications for treatment evaluation. *Journal of Consulting and Clinical Psychology, 49,* 418–425.

Rosenbaum, M. (1994). The travails of Martin Orne: On privacy, public disclosure, and confidentiality in psychotherapy. *Journal of Contemporary Psychotherapy, 24,* 159–167.

Schachter, D. (1998). Psychiatrists' documentation of informed consent. *Canadian Journal of Psychiatry, 43,* 1012–1017.

Seligman, M. E. P. (1995). The effectiveness of psychotherapy: The *Consumer Reports* study. *American Psychologist, 50,* 965–974.

Shabini, D., Wilder, D., & Flood, W. (2001). Reducing stereotypic behavior through discrimination training, differential reinforcement of other behavior, and self-monitoring. *Behavioral Interventions, 16,* 279–286.

Shadish, W. R., Cook, T. D., & Campbell, D. T. (2002). *Experimental and quasi-experimental designs for generalized causal inference.* Boston: Houghton Mifflin.

Sieber, J. E. (1992). *Planning ethically responsible research.* Thousand Oaks, CA: Sage.

Simon, R., & Sadoff, R. (1992). *Psychiatric malpractice: Cases and comments for clinicians.* New York: American Psychiatric Press.

Smith G. R., Jr, Fischer, E.P., Nordquist, C.R., Mosley, C. L., & Ledbetter, N. S. (1997). Implementing outcomes management systems in mental health settings. *Psychiatric Services, 48,* 364–368.

Society for Industrial and Organizational Psychology. (1987). *Principles for the validation and use of personnel selection procedures.* (3rd ed.). College Park, MD: Author.

Speer, D. C. (1992). Clinically significant change: Jacobson and Truax (1991) revisited. *Journal of Consulting and Clinical Psychology, 60,* 402–408.

Stein, E. (1995). *The effect of ethical and legal presentations upon therapists' attitudes and projected practices of informed consent in clinical treatment.* Unpublished doctoral dissertation, California School of Professional Psychology, San Diego.

Sullivan, T., Martin, W., & Handelsman, M. (1993). Practical benefits of an informed consent procedure: An empirical investigation. *Professional Psychology: Research and Practice, 24,* 160–163.

Thistlethwaite, D. L., & Campbell, D. T. (1960). Regression-discontinuity analysis: An alternative to the ex post facto experiment. *Journal of Educational Psychology, 51,* 309–317.

Trochim, W., & Cappelleri, J, (1992). Cutoff assignment strategies for enhancing randomized clinical trials. *Controlled Clinical Trials, 13,* 190–212.

Wilkinson, T. (2001). Research, informed consent, and the limits of disclosure. *Bioethics, 15,* 341–363.

# 11

# Future Directions in the Use of Psychological Assessment for Treatment Planning and Outcomes Assessment: Predictions and Recommendations

John S. Lyons, Jena Helgerson, and Kya Fawley
*Northwestern University*

In initiating a reform of how psychological testing was provided in the Illinois Department of Children and Family Services (DCFS), Denise Kane, the inspector general of the DCFS, got everyone's attention by referring to the existing psychological testing practice as "another form of abuse of the children." Although extreme, her point was that the children were repeatedly tested regardless of their needs and regardless of whether psychological testing could actually answer any questions that were pertinent to the children's service needs. The reform that the DCFS undertook involved two simple steps. First was the creation of a decision tree for case workers that required (1) an identifiable problem and (2) no psychological testing in the past 12 months. Second, the case workers would then take the problem to a consulting psychologist, and this consultant would identify whether psychological testing could address the identified issue. This simple reform resulted in a nearly immediate decline of more than 80% in the use of psychological testing within the DCFS.

This story is illustrative of the primary challenges faced by practitioners of psychological testing in our current environment. Clearly, psychological testing was being overused and misused in the child welfare system. At the service system level, planners complained that too much money was spent on assessment relative to treatment. However, this reform did not eliminate testing. In fact, a large number of children were still seen as benefiting from a formal psychological assessment. Thus, the question becomes: How can psychological testing best serve the marketplace of behavioral health care services?

There is little doubt that assessment in its broadest definition is a critical aspect of both treatment planning and outcome monitoring. It is impossible to imagine moving forward with treating a person and his or her problems if you have not yet identified and conceptualized them (Korchin & Schuldberg, 1981; Moreland, Fowler, & Honaker, 1992). The questions are: What should be the focus of the assessment? Who does the assessment and how? What approaches to testing are most reliable, valid, and cost-effective? When can the assessment be routine, and when is a specialty assessment required? These are the questions that must be answered fully and consistently to ensure psychological testing's future in the behavioral health care field. To begin to understand how we might address these questions, it is useful to understand the current climate of the behavioral health care marketplace.

## TRENDS IN MENTAL HEALTH CARE

Since the publication of the previous version of this book, much has changed in the health care system generally and the behavioral health care system specifically. The penetration of managed behavioral health care in its initial incarnations appears to have met something close to a saturation point. In many places, much of the private sector mental health service system is managed through carved-out managed care entities. However, the trend now is to have fewer and fewer, larger and larger carved-out firms. There are currently only three national firms, and one is in bankruptcy. Further, the trend is to carve behavioral health care back into the general health care. Initially, behavioral health was carved out because it was believed that significant specialty knowledge was required to manage these services. Now it is possible to bring these services back under the umbrella of a larger health maintenance organization or preferred provider organization, as this specialty knowledge has become increasingly available.

It could be argued that the movement toward outcome measurement and management has been supplanted somewhat by the movement toward the identification and implementation of evidence-based practices as a policy priority. However, the successful implementation of evidence-based practices is not simply the insertion of interventions that have worked in clinical trials into the service delivery system. Therefore, whether this movement is real or whether it will become simply one more example of practitioners merely changing the names by which they refer to their practice approaches will be dependent on our ability to effectively implement outcomes measurement to ensure the field effectiveness of practice approaches that work in randomized clinical trials (RCTs). It also will depend on our ability to design and implement techniques for monitoring the fidelity to which treatments in the field match the philosophy and technique of the treatments established as efficacious through RCTs.

## TRENDS IN NATIONAL PROGRAMS

There are several national attempts to create standard approaches to outcomes management. The Joint Commission on the Accreditation of Healthcare Organizations (JCAHO) has its ORYX project, which identifies outcome measures for use by agencies that seek JCAHCO accreditation (Joint Commission on Accreditation of Healthcare Organizations, 2003). The design of this system is that JCAHO requires entities to submit proposed outcome measures and then determines whether they are acceptable. Measures are divided into core and noncore measures depending on their centrality to the goals of the treatment. ORYX has 10 key attributes that it seeks for the outcome measures that it endorses:

- Targeted improvement in the health of populations
- Precise definition and specification
- Validity
- Ability to be interpreted
- Risk adjustment or stratification
- Data collection that is assessed
- Usefulness in the accreditation process
- Being under provider control
- Public availability

The Substance Abuse and Mental Health Services Administration (SAMHSA) sponsors the Mental Health Statistics Improvement Program (MHSIP). The program is intended to help states design and use more effective mental health information systems. The MHSPI provides uniform statistical information about mental health services from its participating members.

SAMHSA also requires the use of the Government Performance and Results Act (GPRA) measure for all contracted projects. The GPRA is an interview-based assessment that includes the measurement of primary social, mental health, and substance use outcomes (Substance Abuse and Mental Health Services Administration, 2001).

Finally, SAMHSA also has a significant national evaluation effort in more than 50 children's system of care sites around the country. The Comprehensive Community Mental Health Services for Children and Their Families Program, started in 1993, provides grants to communities to improve their existing systems of care to better assist children with severe emotional disturbance and their families. This program was implemented by the Center for Mental Health Services (CMHS) within the Substance Abuse and Mental Health Services Administration (SAMHSA). This program also annually reports to Congress with an evaluation of the program. The national evaluation investigates which families are participating in the programs and the outcomes of these participants. The evaluation was designed during the first year of funding and was implemented nationally during the second year. Individual site evaluators were trained and then were responsible for further training their individual site staff. The outcomes assessed are evaluations at intake, 6 months, 1 year, and annually throughout a child's involvement with the program. Also, information on exiting the program and reasons for the termination are collected. Outcome data assessing the child's clinical and social functioning are measured using the Child and Adolescent Functional Assessment Scale (CAFAS), the Child Behavior Checklist (CBCL), and the Youth Self-Report (YSR), all of which are discussed in the second volume of this work. The child's educational performance was assessed with school attendance and grade performance. Also, contact with law enforcement, living arrangements, and child and family satisfaction were assessed. There was much variability across sites as to the amount of data collected and the detail of the information collected and reported, so broad conclusions, according to the CMHS, should be made cautiously with these limitations in mind. Overall, the program evaluators conclude that scores on the CAFAS, CBCL, and the YSR improved over time, and five factors may have led to these outcomes. The five factors include: range of services, continuity of services, intensity level of services, home-based services, and case management and case coordination (Substance Abuse and Mental Health Services Administration, 2001).

Although advocates of each of these national efforts to organize and systematize outcomes would be more enthusiastic, it is fair to say that these programs have met with mixed success at best. The ORYX system requires vendors who are marketing outcomes to pay for the process of endorsing their outcome measure. This has the effect of increasing the costs of outcomes. Since outcome measurement and management is generally an unfunded mandate, making it more expensive is simply a further burden on providers. Second, the ORYX rules allow for some unusual choices. For example, a psychiatric hospital could use the rate of skin rashes as its primary outcome measure. Third, there are a large number of behavioral health entities that do not seek JCAHO accreditation and thus would be unlikely to participate in ORYX. In all likelihood, psychiatric hospitals would be the service type in which this system could make significant "market penetration."

The MHSIP project has suffered from a lack of broad participation on the parts of states. Less than one third of states actively participate in this initiative. The consumer-focus report card has languished in the planning stages for years. The process of moving forward in a collaborative manner across multiple and complex bureaucracies over multiple changes in administration, at both the state and federal level, is glacial.

The GPRA has been widely implemented, because it is required as a part of receiving funding from SAMHSA. That it will be adopted outside of a SAMHSA-funded demonstration project is quite unlikely, because it requires a detailed interview with service recipients, and the information is not designed to be supportive of service planning or other service delivery operations.

Finally, the SAMHA system of care evaluation is far too intensive for widespread applicability. The full evaluation is so burdensome that it seldom is fully implemented even in funded sites. The assessments take nearly 3 hours per family for each time point. Maintaining compliance with this degree of assessment is nearly impossible. Conceivably, it may be that data from this evaluation could be used to support a scaled down version of the assessment approach. However, a number of the assessments included in the evaluation are proprietary, so the authors would have to accept the loss of their tools (and income) for this to occur. Such work seems unlikely under these circumstances.

It is difficult to imagine that any national effort at establishing uniform approaches will be successful. Top-down efforts at outcomes management generally fail unless funding for services is directly tied to the effort. Since the United States has a complex, multiple payor system, it would be difficult to get all payers to agree on an approach. In addition, there are many outcomes management entrepreneurs who would fight any attempts to choose only one approach. A consensus conference convened at Vanderbilt University on psychotherapy outcomes comes to mind in this regard. When all the leaders of psychotherapy outcome research were convened, they could not develop a consensus on the measurements to use. They could only agree on the constructs that should be measured: symptoms, subjective well-being, and functioning (Frank et al., 1992).

## TRENDS IN STATE AND LOCAL PROGRAMS

There has been greater, albeit still limited, success in implementing outcomes strategies at the state and local levels. Many states and counties have successfully implemented standard outcomes measures, and some have even moved to performance contracting based on very simple outcomes. Because the primary barriers to the use of standard outcomes approaches are primarily in the implementation, it should not be surprising that it is easier to overcome these barriers in more confined areas.

An elaborate example of this process can be found in New Jersey's Partnership for Children. In the Partnership, four assessment tools have been designed, and three have experienced initial implementation. The Crisis Assessment Tool was easily implemented in new mobile response and stabilization programs as the tool was imbedded in the program plan. The Needs Assessment, which is a referral and eligibility tool, has been implemented statewide, with more than 600 possible referral sources, including child welfare case workers, probation officers, and community mental health providers trained in its reliable use. However, reliability issues remain in some areas. The Strengths and Needs Assessment, a service planning tool for residential treatment or community wraparound, was the third to be implemented. This tool was easily implemented with residential providers but faced some resistance from community wraparound providers, as it was required after these organizations had already established procedures for working with children and families. These issues have only recently been addressed directly with care managers. The final assessment, the Family Assessment, is in the design phase with family advocates and parent representatives.

It may be that state-level strategies hold the greatest potential for successful implementation of outcomes approaches. These strategies have the advantages of clear relationships with purse strings and the ability to manage implementation at a level closer to the direct service provider.

## TRENDS IN LEGISLATION

### Health Insurance Portability and Accountability Act

In August 1996, the Health Insurance Portability and Accountability Act (HIPAA) was passed into law. This act has three main purposes. First, it was established to guarantee insurance portability. This means that if an individual changes insurance coverage from one plan to another, there will be continuous coverage during the transition period. Also, this ensures that no individual changing insurance plans will be denied a new plan because of a preexisting condition. The second purpose of the act was to increase protection against fraud in the insurance industry. The third aspect of the HIPAA is administration simplification, and a subpart of this section is the Privacy Rule. The Privacy Rule is the aspect of the HIPAA that is relevant to outcomes management projects and researchers. This rule involves new requirements for researchers who wish to obtain and use health information. The objectives of the rule are threefold. First is to limit the use and disclosure of protected health information. Second is to allow the use of health information only to the minimum number of individuals necessary to complete the research. Finally, the rule gives patients the right to receive information about the rule and about how their private health information will be used and by whom. The HIPAA applies to studies using any information from a medical record or other identifiable health information that relates to past, present, or future physical or mental health conditions, treatment, or payment for care. This health information is referred to as protected health information (PHI). Although these rules do not necessarily apply to outcomes management projects in which the outcomes data is used only for purposes of health care operations, if any individual later want to share these data more broadly through professional publication, the new HIPAA privacy rules apply (Northwestern University Office for the Protection of Research Subjects, 2003; Department of Health and Human Services Office for Civil Rights, 2002).

The Privacy Rule in general requires written authorization in addition to consent from an individual before his or her PHI can be shared orally, via paper, or electronically for research purposes. Not all research studies qualify under the HIPAA, and thus not all research studies need to follow the guidelines established by the Privacy Rule. Also, some studies that fall under the HIPAA rule may qualify as an exception to the authorization rule or a waiver of the authorization may be granted by the individual institutions' institutional review board (IRB). Some institutions may vary as to which studies they feel fall under the rule and which they feel qualify for exemptions. In general, those studies that do not require participant authorization under the

HIPAA are studies that have finished enrolling participants or have been completed before April 14, 2003, those studies in which all health-related information will be obtained directly from the participants, or those studies in which no individual health information will be collected.

Studies exempt from the HIPAA authorization policy are those in which information is deidentified according to HIPAA guidelines; is a part of a Limited Data Set; is used solely for preparing for research and no identifying information will be obtained; is research involving descendant's information; or is research involving educational records or student health records. The HIPAA describes a limited data set as a set of data in which certain personal identifiers are removed and those individuals who will be using the data have signed a data use agreement.

Studies that may receive a waiver of authorization from the IRB must satisfy three main criteria. First, the sharing of information involves no more than a minimal risk to the individuals' privacy. This is accomplished by researchers developing a plan to protect against inappropriate use of the information, destroying the identifiers as soon as possible, and providing written assurance that the information will not be shared with any other party. Second, the research requires the waiver of authorization to be conducted. Finally, the research requires PHI.

If a research project requires HIPAA compliance, a separate authorization form must be completed by each participant, in addition to a general consent to participate in research. In research using psychotherapy notes or information relating to HIV, mental health, genetic testing, or drug or alcohol abuse, a specific type of authorization form should be created by the principle investigator. Guidelines and form templates are available at HIPAA Web sites and may vary between institutions.

The goal of the HIPAA privacy rule is to ensure the privacy of PHI and to inform individuals of their rights. The rule is not designed to hinder research involving health information. Some believe that the new guidelines will increase participation in research, because individuals will be more confident that their private health information is being protected. However, some providers and covered entities with protected health information might experience increased administrative burden from the HIPAA guidelines and thus may become less willing to share health information (Department of Health and Human Services Office for Civil Rights, 2002; Northwestern University Office for the Protection of Research Subjects, 2003).

## Mental Health Parity

The 1996 Mental Health Parity Act (MHPA) requires employers providing group health insurance to more than 50 employees to offer equal lifetime and annual monetary limits on mental health, and medical and surgical, benefits. Although the act is intended to improve access to mental health treatment by eliminating disparities between mental health and medical coverage, it has several loopholes (APA, 2002; Hennesy & Goldman, 2001; Zuvekas, Regier, Rae, Rupp, & Narrow, 2002).

For example, the MHPA, which is set to terminate on December 31, 2003, does not require employers to provide any mental health benefits. Nor does it prohibit them from setting higher costs for copayments and deductibles, or setting higher limits on the number of inpatient and outpatient visits allowed. Further, the law fails to specify which mental illness must be covered in the plans, and it does not mandate parity for substance abuse treatment.

Despite its deficiencies, the passage of the MHPA set a precedent for state legislators. Approximately 37 states now have parity laws, many of which are more comprehensive than the federal statute (Newman, 2002). However, although some states require coverage for all diagnoses listed in the *DSM-IV*, others limit coverage to severe mental illnesses (Harrison, 2002). In addition, state parity laws do not apply to millions of Americans with self-insured employer health plans, because of an exemption specified in the Employee Retirement Income Security Act (ERISA).

A study by the U.S. General Accounting Office and additional research on the effects of mental health parity indicated that the legislation has failed to substantially eliminate inequalities between mental health and medical benefits, because employers have been able to restrict their mental health coverage through the loopholes in the law (Harrison, 2002; Sturm & Pacula, 1999). To address this issue, in March 2001 Senators Peter Domenici and Paul Wellstone created the Mental Health Equitable Treatment Act (MHETA), which prohibits differences in copays, deductibles, and limits on the amount of visits. Although this bill failed to pass, in April 2002, President Bush expressed his support for a new mental health parity bill. In February 2003, the Paul Wellstone Mental Health Equitable Treatment Act was presented to Congress. If it is passed, this bill will not only outlaw inequalities in fees and number of visits, it will also require plans with mental health benefits to cover all illnesses listed in the *DSM–IV*. However, like the MHPA, the Wellstone MHETA will not require employers to provide mental health benefits, nor will it require parity in substance abuse treatment (Zuvekas et al., 2002).

The implications of parity legislation for psychological testing are not yet clear. However, it is possible that parity could improve the chances of third party reimbursement for assessment services if these visits are comparable to medical diagnostic visits, procedures, or both. To the degree that outcomes measurement remains an unfunded mandate, it will continue to be implemented inconsistently.

## TRENDS IN MEASUREMENT

Over the past decade, we have developed a different approach to measurement for use in clinical settings. The majority of outcomes assessments have been derived from psychometric approaches, using either classical test theory or item response theory. While these approaches have served the research field well, they have some limitations for application in service delivery settings. Among these limitations is the requirement of multiple items to create a scale, the de-emphasis of face validity relative to item performance, and the requirement of relatively complex scoring approaches that create numbers requiring norms to attempt to intuit clear meaning from results.

In the field of medicine, an approach called clinimetrics has been used in place of psychometrics for the development of outcome assessments (Feinstein, 1986). Apgar (1966) is generally credited with publishing the first clinimetric measure for the assessment of the health status of newborn babies. Clinimetric tools are quite common in medicine (e.g., Gates, 2000; Stone, Salonen, Lax, Payne, Lapp, & Inman, 2001). According to Feinstein (1986) there are six principles of clinimetrics that distinguish it from psychometric approaches:

1. Selection of items are based on clinical rather than statistical criteria.
2. Factors need not be weighted.
3. Scoring is simple and readily interpretable.

4. Variables are selected to be heterogeneous rather than homogeneous.
5. The measure must be easy for clinicians to use.
6. Face validity is required, and subjective states are not measured because of limited sources of observation.

We have evolved the clinimetric approach into a strategy we call communications-based measurement (Lyons, Weiner, & Lyons, 2003). The concept of this approach is that the primary role of measurement in service delivery is communication. Feedback is central to quality improvement (Koike, Unutzer, & Wells, 2002). This requires the integration of measurement into the information feedback process (Lichtman & Appleman, 1995).

Communication theory is a broad and diverse field. However, there are several threads throughout this domain that have supported the development of our approach to measurement. First is the theory of communicative action. This strategy is a consensus-based approach that relies on mutual definitions of how to reach a goal (Habermas & Seidman, 1989). Second, White (2001) posits that all innovations in science are fundamentally communication processes. Thus, the dissemination of innovations such as evidence-based practices can be thought of as communication processes as well. Similarly, providing the evidence for the effectiveness of a program is a communication process. Finally, the advances in organizational theory and change emphasize the importance of effective communication in these processes (Harris, 2002).

Communication-based measurement builds on both psychometric and clinimetric traditions and adds the following criteria:

- Representatives of all partners in the service delivery system of care should participate in the development and uses of the measure.
- The goal of item selection is to include single items that represent each of the key constructs, identified by consensus, that inform good decision making and service planning in the service delivery operation.
- The levels of each item should be directly translatable into action steps for treatment planning.

One of the most commonly used action levels within communication tools is the following model that is used for the assessment of needs:

0    Indicates no evidence of need, no need for any action
1    Indicates a need for watchful waiting prevention
2    Indicates a need for action—some intervention is required
3    Indicates a need for immediate or intensive action—the need is at a dangerous or disabling level.

For each tool, anchored definitions are created, but they are designed to map into these action levels, and trainees are instructed to use these levels as "trumps" if the specifics of the individual do not clearly match any of the levels in the anchored definitions.

There are currently a number of communication-based tools in fairly widespread use in the United States and Canada, including Child and Adolescent Needs and Strengths (Lyons, Weiner, & Lyons, 2003; Anderson, Lyons, Giles, Price, & Estes, 2003), the Adult Needs and Strengths Assessment (Lyons, 2002), Intermed (Huyse, Lyons,

Stiefel, Slaets, de Jonge, & Latour, 2001), and two newly created tools: the Arthritis Comprehensive Treatment Assessment (ACTA) and the Entrepreneurial League System Assessment (ELSA).

Through a series of studies (Lyons, Weiner, & Lyons, 2003; Huyse et al., 2001), we have demonstrated that this measurement approach results in easy-to-use, reliable, and valid tools that are appealing to clinicians while still allowing the three primary applications of decision support, quality improvement, and outcomes monitoring.

## IMPLICATIONS

Whether the glass is half full or half empty depends on your perspective. The days in which psychological testing is a major, distinct component of the behavioral health care system in which solo providers develop large and lucrative testing practices may be over. However, the role of information in the behavioral health care system has likely never been more important. It is in this area that a renaissance of psychological assessment is possible. However, the conditions for this rejuvenation are dramatically different. The following issues must be addressed:

1. Specialty psychological assessments must be designed that have direct implications for treatment planning and outcome monitoring. The criteria for a specialty assessment would be that a notable level of specialty knowledge and skills are required by the assessor to complete the assessment. Areas such as trauma assessment, cognitive functioning, sexual aggression and deviance, fire setting, and substance abuse may represent important areas of specialization in assessment. The development of professional credentialing in specialty assessment would be a desirable strategy.

2. Any temptation to suggest or imply that everyone needs a full assessment must be tempered. Branching models of assessment that lead to a specialty assessment when indicated represent the best hope for the cost-effective use of psychological testing. Allowing lower levels of behavioral health professionals to participate fully in the lower levels of assessment would further the utility and distinctness of the specialty assessments. For example, in the New Jersey Partnership for Children, a branching system has been set up that establishes an overall assessment for use as a primary outcome and then specialty assessments in the areas of substance use, trauma, developmental disabilities, sexual aggression, sexuality, and fire setting. All providers in the system will be trained in the overall assessment, and no special reimbursement will be provided for its completion beyond the normal rate for an outpatient visit. Appropriate assessors will be identified and separate rates established for the specialty assessments.

3. Broadening our approach to measurement to allow the inclusion of clinimetric and communication-based strategies may facilitate the rapid use of assessment information for the consumers of assessment results. These approaches are generally more acceptable to clinicians, and thus some barriers to widespread implementation are reduced.

In sum, no treatment system can operate without assessment. Also, it is increasingly obvious that accountability in behavioral health care requires the monitoring of outcomes. These two factors ensure the ongoing role of assessment in the behavioral health care system. What is less clear is precisely what the nature of assessment will be.

Likely, assessment methods will change with emerging technologies. The method will determine who will be able to complete the assessments, depending on the technical skills required. So, while an ongoing role for psychological assessment in outcomes is clear, how that role is fulfilled is wide open, providing many opportunities for innovation and creative solutions.

## REFERENCES

Anderson, R. L., Lyons, J. S., Giles, D. M., Price, J. A., & Estes, G. (2003). Examining the Reliability of the Child and Adolescent Needs and Strengths–Mental Health (CANS–MH) Scale from two perspectives: A comparison of clinician and researcher ratings. *Journal of Child and Family Studies.*

American Psychological Association. (March 2002). *Parity loopholes should be closed for all mental illnesses.* Retrieved April 15, 2003 from http://www.apa.org/practice/parity2001.html

Anonymous. (2003, March 3). Comprehensive mental health parity legislation formally introduced. *Mental Health Weekly*, 1–3.

Apgar, V. (1966). The newborn (Apgar) scoring system. Reflections and advice. *Pediatric Clinics of North America, 13,* 645–650.

Department of Health and Human Services Office for Civil Rights. (2002, December 3). *OCR HIPAA Privacy.* Retrieved February 20, 2003, from http://www.hhs.gov/ocr/hipaa/

Feinstein, A. R. (1986). Multi-item "instruments" vs. Virginia Apgar's principles of clinimetrics. *Archives of Internal Medicine, 159,* 125–128.

Frank, J. D., Luborsky, L., Wallerstein, R. S., Howard, K. I., Orlinsky, D. E., Bergin A. E., et al. (1992). Historical developments in research centers. In D. K. Freedheim & H. J. Freudenberger (Eds.), *History of psychotherapy: A century of change* (pp. 391–449). Washington, DC: American Psychological Association.

Gates, G. A. (2000). Clinimetrics of Meniere's disease. *Laryngoscope, 110,* 8–11.

Habermas, J., & Seidman, S. (Eds.). (1989). *Juergen Habermas on society and politics: A reader.* Frankfurt, Germany: University of Frankfurt Press.

Harris, T. E. (2002). *Applied organizational communication: Principles and pragmatics for future practice.* Mahwah, NJ: Lawrence Erlbaum Associates.

Harrison, B. (2002). Mental health parity. *Harvard Journal on Legislation, 39*(1), 255–279.

Hennesy, K., & Goldman, H. (2001). Full parity: Steps toward treatment equity for mental and addictive disorders. *Health Affairs, 20*(4), 58–68.

Huyse, F. J., Lyons, J. S., Stiefel, F., Slaets, J., de Jonge, P., & Latour, C. (2001). Operationalizing the biopsychosocial model. The INTERMED. *Psychosomatics, 42,* 1–9.

Joint Commission on Accreditation of Healthcare Organizations. (2003). *Performance measurement.* Retrieved May 5, 2003 from http://www.jcaho.org

Koike, A. K., Unutzer, J., & Wells, K. B. (2002). Improving the care for depression in patients with comorbid medical illness. *American Journal of Psychiatry, 158,* 1738–1745.

Korchin, S., & Schuldberg, D. (1981). The future of clinical assessment. *American Psychologist, 36,* 1147–1158.

Lichtman, D. M., & Appleman, K. A. (1995). Measures of effectiveness: A methodology of integrating planning, measurement, and continuous improvement. *Military Medicine, 160,* 189–193.

Lyons, J. S. (2002). *Adult needs and strengths assessment* [Manual]. Winnetka, IL: Buddin Praed Foundation. Retrieved from www.buddinpraed.org

Lyons, J. S., Weiner, D. A., & Lyons, M. B. (2003). *Outcomes measurement as communication: The Child and Adolescent Needs and Strengths.* Winnetka, IL: Buddin Praed Foundation. Retrieved from www.buddinpraed.org

Moreland, K. L., Fowler, R. D., & Honaker, L. M. (1992). Future directions in the use of psychological assessment for treatment planning and outcome assessment: Predictions and recommendations. In M. E. Maruish (Ed.), *The use of psychological testing for treatment planning and outcome assessment,* pp. 581–602.

Newman, R. (2002). Professional point: One step (and 3 votes) away from parity. *Monitor on Psychology, 33*(3), pp. 581–602.

Northwestern University Office for the Protection of Research Subjects. (2003, March, 19). *Northwestern University HIPAA policy.* Retrieved March 20, 2003, from http://www.northwestern.edu/research/OPRS/irb/hipaa

Stone, M., Salonen, D., Lax, M., Payne, U., Lapp, V., & Inman, R. (2001). Clinical and imaging correlates of response to treatment with infliximab in patients with anklylosing spondylitis. *Journal of Rheumatology, 28,* 1605–1614.

Sturm, R., & Pacula, R. (1999). State mental health parity laws: Cause or consequence of differences in use? *Health Affairs, 18*(5), 182–192.

Substance Abuse and Mental Health Services Administration. (2001). *Programs in brief.* Retrieved May 5, 2003, from http://www.samhsa.gov/programs/programs.html

White, W. J. (2001). A communication model of conceptual innovation in science. *Communication Theory, 11*, 290–314.

Zuvekas, S., Regier, D., Rae, D., Rupp, A., & Narrow, W. (2002). The impacts of mental health parity and managed care in one large employer group. *Health Affairs, 21*(3), 148–159.

# Author Index

Note: **I** denotes Volume 1, **II** denotes Volume 2, **III** denotes Volume 3. Numbers in *italics* indicate the page where the complete reference is given.

## A

Aalberg, V., **II**-487, *503*
Aaronson, A. L., **III**-463, *471*
Aaronson, N., **I**-28, *62*, **II**-495, *503*, **III**-697, 699, 711, 714, 717, 718
Aaronson, S. T., **III**-28, *40*
Aasland, O. G., **I**-86, 87, 88, *106*
Abara, J., **I**-94, *104*
Abashian, S. W., **III**-20, *40*
Abbasi, Q. A., **III**-173, *181*
Abbott, B. V., **III**-603, 614, *620, 622*
Abdalla, M. I., **III**-698, 713, *715*
Abdel-Khalek, A. M., **II**-13, *29*
Abdoh, A., **III**-702, *716*
Abe, J. S., **III**-197, *230*
Abel, K. M., **III**-166, *180*
Abeles, R. P., **III**-*787*
Abell, W., **III**-331, *361*
Abeloff, M., **III**-22, 31, *32, 33, 34*
Abetz, L., **II**-357, *369*, 443, 444, 445, 449, 450, 451, 452, 453, 454, 455, 456, *457, 458*, 482, 483, 485, 487, 493, 498, *507*
Abou-Saleh, M., **III**-386, *397*
Abraham, I., **III**-381, *395*
Abraham, P. P., **III**-567, *585*
Abrams, R. C., **III**-364, *375*
Abramson, L. Y., **II**-8, *36*, **III**-759, *787*
Abu-Saad, H. H., **II**-481, *503*
Achenbach, T. M., **I**-276, *288* **II**-100, 109, *118*, 143, *176*, 179, 180, 181, 183, 184, 186, 187, 189, 190, 192, 193, 194, 195, 196, 199, 200, 201, 204, 206, 207, *211*, *212, 213*, 247, 254, *270*, 284, *301*, 311, 329, 349, *352*, 357, *368*, 412, 421, 431, *438*, 492, *503*, **III**-115, 116, 117, 121, 122, 124, 130, 131, 132, 133, 134, 135, 140, 143, 144, 146, 149, *150, 151, 152*
Ackerman, A., **III**-381, *396*
Ackerman, S. J., **III**-543, *548*, 558, *585*
Acklin, M. W., **III**-556, *585, 586*
Acquadro, C., **III**-711, *714*
Adachi, N., **III**-158, *180*
Adams, C. D., **II**-348, 349, *352*
Adams, H. P., **III**-713, *716*

Adams, L., **II**-392, *400*
Adams, W. L., **I**-*97*
Aday, L. A., **I**-239, *269*, **II**-481, *507*
Addington, D., **III**-169, *180*
Addington, J., **III**-169, *180*
Addis, I. B., **III**-162, *182*
Addis, M. E., **III**-79, 92, *110*
Adelman, H. S., **II**-487, *503*
Adelmann, P. K., **III**-851, *863*
Aderibigbe, Y. A., **III**-157, *183*
Adessky, R. S., **III**-779, *796*
Adey, M., **III**-297, *311*, 379, 381, 395, 397
Adler, A. B., **I**-119, *142*
Adler, C. M., **III**-162, *186*
Adler, G., **III**-161, *180*
Adler, P., **I**-347, *362*
Adrian, C., **II**-8, *32*
Advances in Outcomes Measurement, **I**-11, *57*
Ae Lee, M., **III**-14, *32*
Ager, J. W., **I**-*107*
Agnew, R. M., **III**-29, *32*
Agostini, C., **III**-818, 819, 824, 825, 830, *834*
Agrawal, S., **I**-202, *214*
Agren, H., **III**-163, *189*
Aguiar, P., **I**-130, *143*
Agustin, C., **III**-334, *361*
Ahadi, S. A., **III**-680, 685, *691*
Ahava, G. W., **III**-319, 320, 324, *325*
Ahmed, T., **III**-191, *230*
Ahmedzai, S., **II**-495, *503*
Ahnberg, J. L., **III**-314, 316, *325*
Ahrens, A. H., **III**-758, *787*
Aiduk, R., **III**-171, *180*, 451, *471*
Aikman, G. G., **III**-607, *622*
Ainsworth, M. D., **I**-129, *137*, **III**-556, *586*
Aitken, M. E., **II**-451, *456*
Akanuma, N., **III**-158, *180*
Akeson, W. H., **III**-464, *476*
Akiskal, H. S., **II**-1, *33*, **III**-303, *308*
Al Zubaidi, A., **III**-400, *417*
Alamir, S., **III**-175, *188*
Alaranta, H. T., **III**-*37*
Albanese, A. L., **I**-125, *139*

Carbonari, J. P., **I**-123, *143*
Carbone, E. G., **III**-466, *472*
Card-Higginson, P., **III**-305, *309*
Cardin, D., **I**-90, *108*
Carek, D. J., **II**-8, *36*
Carey, K. B., **III**-18, *33*
Carey, M., **II**-1, 8, 9, 19, *30*, *31*, *36*, 44, *62*, 68, *78*, 141, *177*, *318*, **III**-18, *33*
Carhart, P. W., **I**-337, *364*
Carlbring, P., **III**-779, *788*
Carleton, B. C., **II**-481, *507*
Carline, J. D., **I**-86, *108*
Carlson, G., **II**-1, 2, 8, *29*, *32*, *36*, 306, *330*
Carlson, J. G., **I**-119, *139*
Carlson, M. J., **III**-818, *833*, 844, *863*
Carlson, R., **II**-85, *121*
Carlson, S., **II**-410, *440*
Carlston, D., **II**-285, *302*
Carmody, T., **III**-170, *181*
Carnelius, J., **III**-5, *39*
Caron, C., **II**-141, *176*
Carpay, H. A., **II**-481, *504*
Carpenter, D., **I**-198, 208, 212, 213, **II**-22, *34*, 137, *139*, 206, 207, *213*, 259, *273*, 291, 292, *303*, 365, *369*, 394, *403*, 408, 427, 428, *440*, 452, *458*, **III**-67, *78*, 97, *112*, 146, 147, *152*, 227, *233*, 305, *309*, 321, 322, *325*, 350, 351, *361*, 373, *376*, 392, *396*, 440, *445*, 496, *508*, 536, 537, *550*, 584, *586*, 663, 664, 665, *675*, 686, 690, *691*, 780, *794*
Carpenter, J. T., **III**-22, *37*
Carpenter, L., **I**-90, *99*, **III**-17, *33*, 328, 345, 347, *359*, *362*
Carpenter, W. T., Jr., **III**-164, *184*
Carpinella, S., **II**-472, *475*
Carr, K. F., **III**-*37*
Carr, S. J., **III**-30, *35*
Carrington, P., **III**-10, 29, *33*
Carroll, B. J., **III**-327, *359*
Carroll, I. G., **III**-818, 819, 826, 829, *833*
Carson, M., **III**-303, *309*
Carter, A. S., **II**-196, *212*
Carter, C., **I**-156, *168*
Carter, D. E., **I**-277, *288*, 319, *331*
Carter, M. M., **II**-52, *60*
Carter, S. P., **II**-350, *353*
Carter, W. B., **III**-713, *715*
Cartwright, D. S., **I**-178, *192*
Carver, C., **III**-*40*
Carver, C. M., **III**-607, *623*
Carver, J. R., **I**-50, *62*
Casas, C., **II**-487, *506*
Casat, C., **II**-203, *213*
Cascardi, M., **III**-163, *181*
Casey, R. J., **II**-238, *271*
Cashel, M. L., **I**-10, *58*, **III**-518, *548*
Caspar, F., **I**-113, 122, *139*
Caspi, A., **III**-134, *151*, *152*
Cass, A. R., **I**-*108*
Cassady, S., **III**-164, *183*
Cassano, G. B., **III**-156, 167, *181*, *182*, 303, *308*
Cassel, J. C., **III**-694, *715*
Castaneda, A., **II**-63, 65, *78*
Castellanos, F. X., **II**-341, *354*

Castine, M. R., **III**-167, *181*
Castro, C. M., **II**-487, 494, *510*
Catalano, R., **I**-126, *144*, 175, *195*, **II**-376, 391, 392, *400*, *401*
Cates, J. A., **III**-619, *620*
Cathebras, P., **III**-237, *289*
Cattell, J. M., **III**-625, *638*
Cattell, R. B., **I**-134, *139*, **III**-9, *36*, 425, *444*, 678, 679, *690*
Caudill, M., **I**-4, *60*, 226, *270*
Cavan, R. S., **III**-721, *745*
Cavanaugh, D., **III**-22, *38*
Cavuto, S., **II**-484, *509*
Cella, D. F., **II**-479, 481, 495, 497, *504*, **III**-23, *40*
Censits, D. M., **III**-162, *187*
Center for Disease Control, **I**-*99*
Center for Drug Evaluation and Research (CDER), **III**-*639*
Center for Mental Health Services, **III**-85, 105, *110*
Center for Substance Abuse Treatment, **II**-385, 386, *400*
Centers for Disease Control, **III**-294, *308*
Centers for Medicare and Medicaid Services, **I**-1, *58*
Centor, R. M., **I**-*98*
Cepeda-Benito, A., **III**-612, 613, *621*
Chaffin, M., **III**-465, *472*
Chakos, M., **III**-177, *181*
Chakrabhand, M. L. S., **III**-172, *181*
Chalk, M., **III**-839, *863*
Chall, J. S., **II**-11, *30*, **III**-84, *110*
Challinor, J. M., **II**-350, *353*
Chamberlain, J., **II**-425, *439*
Chamberlin, J., **III**-269, 284, *287*, *288*
Chambers, L. W., **II**-499, *504*
Chambless, D., **III**-400, 401, 402, 406, 408, 409, 410, 412, *417*, *418*, 533, *548*
Chambliss, C. H., **III**-753, 772, 773, *788*
Chambon, O., **III**-172, *181*
Chan, A. W., **I**-*99*
Chan, C., **III**-556, *585*
Chan, D. W., **II**-13, *30*, **III**-156, 158, *181*
Chan, J., **I**-197, *212*
Chan, R. C., **III**-743, *745*
Chang, G., **I**-86, *99*
Chang, P. N., **II**-481, *504*
Chang, S. S., **III**-400, *417*
Chang, S. Y., **II**-371, 389, 392, 394, *404*
Chanpattana, W., **III**-172, *181*
Chao, D. V. K., **III**-244, *288*, *289*
Chapman, J., **III**-22, *36*, 156, *187*
Chapman, L., **III**-541, 542, *550*
Charbonneau, Y., **I**-116, *143*
Charney, D. S., **III**-162, 177, *180*, *189*, 347, *361*
Chartier, G. M., **II**-13, *30*
Chastagner, P., **II**-454, *459*
Chelune, G., **II**-350, *353*
Chelung, G., **I**-340, *363*
Chemtob, C. M., **I**-119, *139*
Chen, J. Y., **II**-358, *368*
Chen, M. K., **III**-744, *745*
Chen, M. M., **III**-694, *716*
Chen, R., **III**-175, *189*
Chen, Y-W., **II**-203, *213*

## Q

## R

# Subject Index

Note: **I** denotes Volume 1, **II** denotes Volume 2, **III** denotes Volume 3. Numbers in *italics* indicate the page where the complete reference is given.

## A

A phase, **I**-283
a:p ratio, **III**-576, 580
AABT, *see* Association for Advancement of Behavior Therapy
AAI, *see* Adult Attachment Interview
AAIS, *see* Adolescent Alcohol Involvement Scale
AB design, **I**-353
ABA design, **I**-353, **III**-800
ABAB designs, **II**-206
Abbreviated multidimensional measures, **I**-22, *see also* Multidimensional measures
A-B-C-D paradigm, **II**-91
ABCDCD design, **I**-283
ABCL, *see* Adult Behavior Checklist
Absolute index, **I**-299
Abstinence outcomes, **I**-162, 163, 164–165
Abstraction, **III**-486
Academic habits (AH), **II**-163, 164
Academic retention, **III**-778–779
Academic settings, **I**-84–86
Academic underachievement, **II**-77–78
Acceptability, **III**-262
Access, **I**-49
Access scale, **III**-813, 826, 827
Accountability, **I**-206, 217, **III**-101, 102
Accreditation, **I**-217, **III**-850
Accuracy, **II**-11, 103, **III**-670
    rate, **II**-316, **III**-257
Achenbach System of Empirically Based Assessment (ASEBA)
    ages 1.5 to 18 years
        cross-cultural applications, **II**-195–197
        interpretive strategy, **II**-197–198
        multi-informant assessment, **II**-188–191
        normative, psychometric, and validity data, **II**-191–195
        outcomes assessment, **II**-204–210
        profiles for scoring forms, **II**-181–188
        treatment monitoring, **II**-202–204
        treatment planning, **II**-198–202
    case study, **III**-146–149

cross-cultural applications, **III**-131–135
forms for ages 18 to 59/60 and 90+, **III**-117–118
historical overview, **III**-115–117
interpretive strategy, **III**-135–138
multi-informant assessment, **III**-124–130
normative, psychometric, and validity data, **III**-130–131
outcomes research, **III**-144–146
profiles for scoring forms, **III**-118–124, 125, 126
treatment planning, **III**-138–141
treatment monitoring, **III**-141–144
Achromatic color, **III**-574
ACK scale, **II**-99, 111
ACL, *see* Anxiety Checklist
Acting out, **II**-75–77
Action, stages of change, **I**-149
Action-oriented paradigm, **I**-154
Active participation, **I**-19
Activities of daily living (ADLs), **I**-33
Actuarial functions, **III**-523
Actuarial norms, **III**-634
Actuarial validity, **III**-608
Acute Recall Form, **III**-696–697, *see also* SF-36
Acute stage, Hamilton Depression Inventory, **III**-348
Adaptations, **III**-486
Adaptive functioning, **II**-208
Adaptive functioning scales **II**-186, 188, **III**-124, 125, 126
Adaptive inflexibility, **III**-495
Adaptive skills, **II**-333
Addiction Severity Index (ASI), **III**-104, 642, 646, 647, 655
Addictions, **I**-154, *see also* Individual entries
ADHD, *see* Attention deficit/hyperactivity disorder
Adherence, treatment, **III**-304
ADIS, *see* Anxiety Disorders Interview Schedule
ADIS-C, *see* Anxiety Disorders Interview Schedule for Children
Adjusted goodness-of-fit (AGIF), **II**-219, 312
Adjustment
    Adult Personality Inventory, **III**-682